The Laws of Alfred

Alfred the Great's *domboc* ("book of laws") is the longest and most ambitious legal text of the Anglo-Saxon period. Alfred places his own laws, dealing with everything from sanctuary to feuding to the theft of bees, between a lengthy translation of legal passages from the Bible and the legislation of the West-Saxon king Ine (r.688–726), which rival his own in length and scope. This book is the first critical edition of the *domboc* published in over a century, as well as a new translation. Five introductory chapters offer fresh insights into the laws of Alfred and Ine, considering their backgrounds, their relationship to early medieval legal culture, their manuscript evidence, and their reception in later centuries. Rather than a haphazard accumulation of ordinances, the *domboc* is shown to issue from deep reflection on the nature of law itself, whose effects would permanently alter the development of early English legislation.

Stefan Jurasinski is Professor of English at SUNY Brockport. He is the author of *The Old English Penitentials and Anglo-Saxon Law* and, with R. D. Fulk, *The Old English Canons of Theodore*. With Andrew Rabin, he edited *Languages of the Law in Early Medieval England: Essays in Memory of Lisi Oliver*.

Lisi Oliver, author of *The Beginnings of English Law* and *The Body Legal and Barbarian Law,* was Houston Alumni Professor of English and Distinguished Research Master at Louisiana State University. With Andrew Rabin and Stefan Jurasinski, she edited *English Law Before Magna Carta.*

T0370656

See the Studies in Legal History series website at
http://studiesinlegal history.org/

Studies in Legal History

EDITORS

Sarah Barringer Gordon, University of Pennsylvania
Holly Brewer, University of Maryland, College Park
Michael Lobban, London School of Economics and Political Science
Reuel Schiller, University of California, Hastings College of the Law

Other books in the series:

The Laws of Alfred

The Domboc *and the Making of Anglo-Saxon Law*

STEFAN JURASINSKI
State University of New York, Brockport

†LISI OLIVER
Louisiana State University

CAMBRIDGE
UNIVERSITY PRESS

Shaftesbury Road, Cambridge CB2 8EA, United Kingdom

One Liberty Plaza, 20th Floor, New York, NY 10006, USA

477 Williamstown Road, Port Melbourne, VIC 3207, Australia

314–321, 3rd Floor, Plot 3, Splendor Forum, Jasola District Centre, New Delhi – 110025, India

103 Penang Road, #05–06/07, Visioncrest Commercial, Singapore 238467

Cambridge University Press is part of Cambridge University Press & Assessment, a department of the University of Cambridge.

We share the University's mission to contribute to society through the pursuit of education, learning and research at the highest international levels of excellence.

www.cambridge.org
Information on this title: www.cambridge.org/9781108744379

DOI: 10.1017/9781108881708

First published 2021
First paperback edition 2023

A catalogue record for this publication is available from the British Library

ISBN   978-1-108-84090-3   Hardback
ISBN   978-1-108-74437-9   Paperback

Cambridge University Press & Assessment has no responsibility for the persistence or accuracy of URLs for external or third-party internet websites referred to in this publication and does not guarantee that any content on such websites is, or will remain, accurate or appropriate.

et nunc reges intelligite
erudimini qui iudicatis terram

Psalm 2:10

Ongytað nu, kyningas, and leorniað ge domeras þe ofer
eorðan demað.

King Alfred's Old English Prose Translation of the First Fifty
Psalms, ed. Patrick P. O'Neill (Cambridge, MA: Medieval
Academy of America, 2001): 101.

Observe how parts with parts unite
In one harmonious rule of right;
See countless wheels distinctly tend
By various laws to one great end;
While mighty Alfred's piercing soul
Pervades, and regulates the whole.

William Blackstone, "A Lawyer's Farewell to His Muse," in *A
Collection of Poems in Six Volumes by Several Hands*, ed.
Robert Dodsley (London: J. Hughs, 1758), 227.

Contents

Figures

Tables

Preface

William the Conqueror's coronation in Westminster Abbey on Christmas Day of 1066 placed in his care the only European polity excepting Ireland to have been for some time governed (at least in aspiration) by laws written in its native tongue.[1] The development of this tradition had unfolded over nearly five centuries. It survived even the accession of the Danish king Cnut in 1016, whose two-book compilation of ecclesiastical and secular ordinances, written by an English bishop, repurposed in its second half ("II Cnut") much of what had come before.[2] Though his dealings with the English people and their institutions would prove, of course, anything but gentle, those who supplanted the Anglo-Saxon aristocracy in the wake of William's victory at Hastings were keen to understand and preserve the legal learning of those they had vanquished. To the care of Anglo-Norman scribes and translators we owe much of what may be known about law in England before the Conquest. There is every reason to think that they grasped its importance and, in some respects, inaugurated the scholarly study of its remains.[3]

The origins of this tradition of vernacular lawmaking, unparalleled anywhere else in Europe in its duration and depth, may be traced ultimately to the Kentish kingdom of the seventh century. Yet its halting experiments in legal prose, now surviving only in a manuscript prepared nearly a century after the Conquest, did not form the greater part of the foundations on which later Anglo-Saxon

---

[1] On the coronation, see Douglas 1964: 206–207.
[2] Richards 2010: 147.
[3] See especially Chapter 4, 132–144.

monarchs would build. These would instead be established by King Alfred ("Alfred the Great") in a text to which he devoted the last years of his life. Here Alfred assembled in one compilation the judgments ("domas") of his own era along with those issued by the West-Saxon king Ine toward the end of the seventh century. To these, Alfred attached a lengthy translation into English of biblical materials – the earliest extant as we have no trace of Bede's rendering of the Fourth Gospel – and a short historical account of English law tracing its origins to conciliar legislation.[4]

The significance of Alfred's *domboc* to later developments in English law has until the last few decades been overlooked by historians. For the most part, attention has been drawn instead to the twelfth century, a period rightly credited with establishing as the preserve of the kings' justices matters previously deemed civil wrongs.[5] Yet the *domboc* held the seeds of these developments. As the present volume will show, much in the formation of English common law might have proved impracticable (and perhaps inconceivable) without Alfred's having earlier dissolved somewhat a firm association between law and notions of unwritten custom – a problem over which Kentish kings seem to have fretted ineffectually, and which had assumed a new importance during the reign of Charlemagne and his successors.[6] Alfred's orientation of legislative practice toward Carolingian models lent form and an intellectual superstructure to such efforts.

To an extent not yet appreciated by commentators, the *domboc* also effected (and doubtless sought) a pronounced shift in the way subsequent kings would regard the practice of lawmaking. Alfred's "revolution" was, to be sure, a conservative one. None of the ideas animating it was new. In seventh-century Kent as well, the impetus to make law a matter of writing as much as custom had been felt from across the Channel, and all such aspirations recalled (knowingly or not) the rather guarded view of custom as a source of norms earlier articulated in Justinian's *Digest*.[7] But while the emulation of

---

[4] According to the younger Cuthbert's "Epistola de obitu Bedae" (ed. and trans. Colgrave and Mynors 1969: 82–83), Bede had spent his final months at work on "the gospel of St. John, which he was turning into our mother tongue to the great profit of the Church (*in nostram linguam ad utilitatem ecclesiae Dei*)." On the identity of Cuthbert, see Whitelock 1976: 33.

[5] See Chapter 1, 8.

[6] See Chapter 2, 55–56.

[7] The matter is considered at §1.3.32 (ed. Watson 1985: I, 13–14). See also the discussion in Rio (2011: 5).

Continental modes of lawmaking had been earlier cultivated in seventh-century Kent, the kingdom's submission to the ultimately doomed Mercian empire halted any subsequent developments along these lines. Only in Wessex, first at the close of the seventh century, and again at the very end of the ninth, would the possibilities of the Kentish experiment be realized. And these involved less the mimicry of Frankish examples than a daring synthesis of native resources with Frankish-derived reflection on the nature of law itself.

That this should have happened in Wessex rather than elsewhere was not inevitable. Though the inclination of many historians is to deny Alfred some of the credit given him by earlier generations for the achievements of his reign, it is hard to ascribe the success of the *domboc* to any cause other than Alfred's forceful and somewhat fixated personality.[8] Prior to Alfred's accession, Wessex had not been one of the more promising kingdoms of the "Heptarchy."[9] Where Bede mentions it at all in his *Historia Ecclesiastica*, it is rarely to say anything favorable, Wessex having come late to the developments that brought Kent (and then Bede's Northumbria) into close contact with the wider West European world.[10]

Given his other pursuits, a lawbook distinguished from its predecessors in emphasizing the renewal of learning is what might be expected of Alfred. In overseeing the preparation of the *domboc*, Alfred also achieved the practical end of bringing honor to his West-Saxon ancestor Ine, a king all but ignored by Bede. But the efforts of one great king and his counselors, however strenuous, cannot alone explain the depths of legal culture evidenced by the *domboc*. Alfred's achievement presupposes a reservoir of West-Saxon learning to which the thin documentary evidence of this period does not attest. If we believe Alfred, what learning (inevitably clerical) had built up in Wessex in the intervening centuries was all but decimated prior to his accession. His cryptic remarks about the backgrounds and purpose of the *domboc* provoke a range of questions. What textual resources beyond the handful mentioned by Alfred might have been available to the king and his circle, and what use did they make of them? Did Alfred's ambitions for the *domboc* extend to reforming

---

[8] On the debate over Alfred's authorship of the works attributed to him, see Chapter 1, 31–32.

[9] The term is an Elizabethan coinage with foundations in pre-modern sources: "The idea that the early Anglo-Saxon kingdoms were seven in number derived ultimately from Bede but crystallized in twelfth-century histories, notably Henry of Huntingdon's" (Goffart 1997: 55).

[10] See Chapter 1, 17–18.

rather than modestly recording (as prior kings claimed to have done) the legal norms and practices of his day? What did written legislation mean to people who seem to have had little use for it prior to the issuance of the *domboc*?

The following five chapters deal with these and related questions. Though the *domboc* has, over the centuries, attracted a fair amount of learned commentary, many of these questions remain inadequately addressed or have not really been dealt with at all. It is hoped that considering these matters anew will scrape away some old accretions to shed light on matters long thought settled. Chapter 1 offers a sense of the circumstances under which written legislation was adopted and refined in the centuries preceding Alfred's reign. Its later sections consider the relation of the *domboc* to the educational reforms on which much of his fame rests. Particular attention is given to how Wessex came to benefit from the earlier achievements of Kent, a kingdom that had pioneered the use of vernacular legislation in the century prior to Ine's accession.

Chapter 2 addresses the derivation of both Ine's and Alfred's laws. It begins by considering anew the relationship between Ine's and Wihtred's codes (and their relative chronology) before turning to questions suggested by Alfred's curious adaptation of Mosaic law in the *domboc*, a feature of the text we think has never been adequately understood. This chapter offers new arguments about the role of "Irish" sources in structuring the Prologue and a fresh perspective on Alfred's claim, toward the Prologue's conclusion, that he derived some of his laws from prior "synods."

Chapter 3 concerns provisions of the *domboc* long assumed to constitute legislative innovations. Here doubt is cast on the view, accepted for more than a century, that Ine's laws are the first to acknowledge use of the ordeal. Reconsideration of the relevant clauses in light of others (as well as the tenth-century Fonthill Letter) suggests instead that the chronology of the ordeal in England ought to be rewritten. The chapter also traces to their roots in ecclesiastical legislation – as has not been done before – the admonitions about oaths and their gravity with which Alfred's portion of the *domboc* famously begins. That these provisions are not (as Wormald supposed) the echoes of an "oath of loyalty" imposed by Alfred on his subjects becomes clear when they are viewed in light of early pastoral writings on the oath and its spiritual hazards. Here the *domboc* probably exhibits influence, heretofore unappreciated, from Alfred's clerical advisors, whose learning had been sought by the king to make up for what had been lost before his reign.

Remaining chapters consider the intermediaries through which we encounter the *domboc* in the present day and their capacity to obscure its contents. Chapter 4 examines its manuscript transmission, its reception in the post-Conquest period, and its rediscovery by the Elizabethan antiquarians who were the first to circulate the text in print. A particular concern is the twelfth-century reception of the *domboc,* which receives a substantial reassessment. Chapter 5 considers how the *domboc* was employed and imagined after Alfred's lifetime. Early sections move from the reigns of Alfred's successors into the waning centuries of the Anglo-Saxon period. The chapter proceeds thence to trace the reception of the *domboc* into the later Middle Ages and the age of print. Here we show how the editing of the *domboc* had just begun to shed some of the baggage of William Lambarde's 1568 *editio princeps* when what remains its standard edition was published as part of Felix Liebermann's *Gesetze der Angelsachsen* (1903–1916). While Liebermann's is indeed a brilliant performance, its achievement is somewhat vitiated by excessive trust of Lambarde's work and by the creeping fog of German Romanticism, a movement then at the height of its influence.

The book concludes with a critical edition and translation of the *domboc.* Here innumerable smaller questions suggested by particular clauses are dealt with in the edition's interpretative commentary, which brings to bear on these texts the century of scholarship since Liebermann's work. This section in particular was undertaken in the hope of making the *domboc,* whose importance to the early history of English law was maintained from the outset of its reception into the nineteenth century, once again fully accessible to an Anglophone readership.

Readers should note that the numeration of chapters in *Alfred* and *Ine* differs in our edition from those employed by Liebermann; these he had adopted from the earlier editions of Schmid (1832; revised 1858) and Thorpe (1840). The rationale for the revised numeration is set forth in the headnotes accompanying the editions of Alfred's and Ine's laws (the numeration of clauses in the Prologue remains unchanged). It is understood that assigning new numbers to these chapters is an unattractive expedient given their long use. But unhappiness with the standard numeration has been expressed with increasing urgency by editors and commentators from Liebermann's lifetime into the present. Liebermann himself left Schmid's chapter divisions intact only out of resignation: doing otherwise, he felt, would be detrimental to scholarship on the laws. Nonetheless, he compiled a short list of chapters he would have rather seen renumbered.[11] By far the most substantial scholarly treatment of the twentieth century – Richard Dammery's doctoral dissertation of 1990 – likewise criticizes Schmid's "misleading numeration" and laments that subsequent editions by Attenborough and Whitelock, in not departing from it, "perpetuat[ed] the problem."[12] While Dammery's edition retains Schmid's numeration, it simultaneously offers new chapter numbers as suggested "alternative[s]."[13] Wormald seems to insist on a more decisive approach than Dammery's for any future editors of Old English legislation: "[Liebermann's] numbering of royal codes followed Schmid's, even where he knew this to be wrong"; "Few things better betray the enslavement of early English legal studies to traditional practice than continuing use of numeration for Æthelstan's laws that everyone at least since 1858 has known to be wrong."[14] Our remarks in the headnotes to Alfred's and Ine's laws should lay out adequately how the standard numeration does no less violence to these texts than it does to Æthelstan's (and others'). Nor is the matter of Schmid's chapter numbers merely some arcane problem of textual editing alone. In a notable essay by Thomas Charles-Edwards, much depends upon the insight that *Ine* §§63–66 (Liebermann's numeration) constitute not disconnected clauses (as is suggested by the standard chapter numbers) but a logical unit, with "64–6, all subordinate to 63, deal[ing] in turn with decreasing areas of land, twenty hides, ten hides, three hides."[15] Examples of similar arguments published in the years since Liebermann's edition could doubtless be multiplied. So that there are no impediments to comparing our text with prior editions, we nonetheless supply (in square brackets, e.g., *Alfred* 20 [L18]) each renumbered clause with the number assigned in Liebermann's *Gesetze*. But to avoid crowding the page unnecessarily with cross-references,

---

[11] "Otherwise I would have had, for example, *Alfred* §5.5, 9.2, 18.1 and 40.2 begin new chapters" ("[S]onst hätt ich z.B. mit Af 5,5. 9,2. 18,1. 40,2. ein neues Kapitel begonnen") (Liebermann 1903–1916: III, 40).

[12] Dammery 1990: I, 186 and n. 16.

[13] Dammery 1990: II, ix: "[A]n editor of this material must have considerable reservations about perpetuating a practice so misleading, despite its now conventional use. Alternative clause numbers have therefore been provided with this text, in angled brackets, at the right-hand side of the page."

[14] Wormald 1999a: 22 and 291 n. 129, respectively.

[15] Charles-Edwards 1976: 185. The points that follow these in Charles-Edwards's essay are no less damaging to the view that the standard numeration even of clauses subsequent to these is anything but a hindrance to their appropriate interpretation.

citations of clauses in the *domboc* in the introductory chapters that follow (and in the commentary on the edited texts) employ our revised numeration rather than Liebermann's. Oliver's 2002 edition of the Kentish laws, now recognized as superseding Liebermann's, also revised the standard numeration. Accordingly, citations of the Kentish laws in the present study follow Oliver's numeration, but do so with the old numbers also given in square brackets (as described above) for those without access to Oliver's edition.

Acknowledgments

This book considers the emergence of written legislation in Wessex from the seventh through the ninth centuries. It concludes with the first scholarly edition of the *domboc* ("book of judgments") issued during the reign of Alfred the Great (d.899) to appear in print since Felix Liebermann's *Gesetze der Angelsachsen* (1903–16). Along with the laws of Alfred, the present volume contains those issued by the seventh-century West-Saxon king Ine (r.688–726). Appended by Alfred to his own and appearing in no manuscript apart from Alfred's laws, Ine's legislation appears to have been regarded as intrinsic to the *domboc* in spite of (or perhaps because of) its age. While some of its clauses are superseded in Alfred's, others were likely seen as applicable to ninth-century problems. Subsequent legislation of the pre-Conquest period repurposed or alluded to the legislation of both kings with seeming indifference to their periods of origin. What mattered was less their association with one king or another than their appearance within "the *domboc*," which remained for the duration of the Anglo-Saxon period the only legislative text of its kind.

Work on the present book commenced in 2006, when Professor Oliver and I first agreed to prepare it in collaboration. Its progress accelerated during a year-long period of leave made possible by an American Council of Learned Societies Collaborative Research Fellowship awarded for the 2014–15 academic year. The painful events that followed immediately after the completion of the fellowship need not be rehearsed here, but some account of how these circumstances altered the trajectory of the project may be thought desirable by some readers, not least because responsibility should not be imputed to Oliver for work she did not have the opportunity to see. At the time of her death, Professor Oliver had established the texts of Alfred's and Ine's laws (and their rubrics) from comparison with the principal manuscript (Cambridge, Corpus Christi College 173) and we had completed the bulk of the commentary that now accompanies the editions; the text of the Prologue and its commentary was also complete. Four of the present five chapters, to which Oliver contributed the basis of a discussion of Ine's reign, existed in a very undeveloped state; at the time, these materials were conceived of as sections appearing within a lengthy Introduction (as is conventional in scholarly editions published by the Early English Text Society or the Selden Society) rather than stand-alone chapters.

Toward the conclusion of our shared work on this project, it became evident to both of us, given the many new insights unearthed by sustained examination of these texts, that the book was going to be something more than a conventional scholarly edition and should probably be recast as a monograph. Beginning in 2016, I began the process of collating the principal manuscript with all other witnesses and cataloguing variant readings for the scholarly apparatus. All of the chapters were also drastically rewritten at this time. In their final form they bear little resemblance to what had been prepared during the fellowship; nonetheless, I feel that they bring to fulfillment conclusions on which Oliver and I had agreed at various stages of the project's development even as they depend in many cases upon new insights that emerged after 2015. Chapter 3 was prepared in this period, and though Oliver did not see it in any form, it confirms her doubts about Liebermann's discovery of the ordeal in *Ine* (set forth in her own words in the commentary for *Ine* chapters §§38 [Liebermann §37] and 66 [Liebermann §62]) with textual evidence she did not have the opportunity to consider and arguments she did not formulate. While the other chapters do not diverge from Oliver's views as I understood them, I have refrained from using "we" and "our" in attributing the conclusions argued for therein since they represent for the most part work she was unable to comment on. In the editions, however, I have left such language in place as these represent less ambiguously our shared views.

Naturally, a work that has been in progress for almost fifteen years will leave its authors indebted to many people. For their letters in support of our application, much gratitude is offered to Paul Hyams and James Q. Whitman. Matthew Goldfeder of the American Council of Learned Societies (ACLS) offered valuable guidance over the course of the fellowship year. Robin K. Collor and Ann Whitmer, both of Louisiana State University, were of tremendous help in sorting out the practical aspects of the fellowship.

For their many kindnesses during our visit to the Parker Library in March of 2015, particular thanks are due to Steven Archer and Elizabeth Dumas. Zoe Stansell of the British Library answered several questions about a particularly mysterious sixteenth-century manuscript. Katherine Barclay and Pru Kemball of the Winchester Excavations Committee offered tremendous help under difficult circumstances concerning knowledge of Alfred's coinage. Andrew Rabin, Nicole Marafioti, and Wallace Johnson read early drafts of the book and offered many helpful suggestions. The readers commissioned by Cambridge University Press expertly tracked down errors and infelicities, and Michael Lobban's commentary, offered during multiple readings of the typescript, resulted in improvements too numerous to count (as well as a solution to the unanticipated difficulties of assigning the book a title). Enough good things cannot be said about the patient and careful work of Rachel Blaifeder and Ruth Boyes in helping to prepare the manuscript for delivery to the press, and Sarah Turner brought an astounding meticulousness to the task of editing the final text.

Some last-minute insights into Isidore of Seville were provided by Bruce Brasington. Advice less formally offered but nonetheless valuable was furnished at various stages by David Pelteret, Bruce O'Brien, Robert Dennis Fulk, Alice Rio, Abigail Firey, Rory Naismith, Paul Brand, Tom McSweeney, Charles Insley, Robert Berkhofer, and Susannah Brietz Monta. Our work also owes a great deal to the generosity of Mary Richards.

Some sections of this book have appeared elsewhere. Portions of Chapter 2 appear in Stefan Jurasinski, "Royal Law in Wessex and Kent at the Close of the Seventh Century", in Stefan Jurasinski and Andrew Rabin, eds., *Languages of the Law in Early Medieval England: Essays in Memory of Lisi Oliver* (Leuven: Peeters), 25–44. Some material from Chapter 3 appears in Stefan Jurasinski, "The Emergence of the Ordeal in Anglo-Saxon England", *The Mediæval Journal* (forthcoming). Translations from ancient and modern languages are our own unless otherwise indicated; where others' translations have been employed, these works are cited immediately after the primary text.

Part I
Backgrounds

I

The Emergence of Written Law in Early England

The *Domboc*, Before and After: An Overview

When Alfred the Great (r.871–899) issued toward the end of his reign the compilation of laws his successors would call *seo domboc* or "the book of judgment[s]," the practice of writing legislation in English was already around three centuries old.[1] Yet its being the most ancient of the Old English prose genres did not make the place of written law as an instrument of governance more secure prior to Alfred's accession than it had been generations before. Its adoption in England began with a lengthy assemblage of decrees authorized by the Kentish king Æthelberht (d.616), an event prompted in some fashion by the arrival of missionaries in Canterbury.[2] The reigns of Hloðhere and Eadric (*c*.679–685) and Wihtred (690–725) would likewise see the appearance of laws, also in English.[3] That these compilations disturb an otherwise near-total silence of documentary

---

[1] On the difficulties of dating Alfred's *domboc*, see Keynes and Lapidge 1983: 304; Frantzen 1986: 11 and n. 1; Richards 2014b: 282. William of Malmesbury held Alfred's laws to have been composed "amid the braying of trumpets and the roar of battle" (*inter stridores lituorum, inter fremitus armorum*); Mynors, Thomson, and Winterbottom 1998: I, 188–189 (ii.121). The view is rightly dismissed by Turk (1893: 50–51).

[2] On the background of Æthelberht's laws, see 12–15 of the present chapter.

[3] On the dating of these texts, see Oliver 2002: 120 and 148; Hough 2015 offers a contrasting view on the provenance of Æthelberht's laws.

evidence for this period gives them the appearance of inaugurating some new epoch in the legal history of Britain. But to the extent that these texts reveal the intentions of the kings under whose names they circulated, there is little to warrant such a conclusion. At no point in this first unfolding of English legislation do we see any attempt to explain why an otherwise obscure tongue was here favored over Latin, the preferred language of lawmaking on the Continent. The concerns of the laws are invariably parochial and their prefatory material modest about the kind of sway legislation might be expected to have over the affairs of subject populations.[4] The impression given by the last such compilation before Kent was absorbed into the kingdom of Mercia is that the employment of writing, rather than widening the scope of royal authority over law-making, had instead made legislative activity the sphere of bishops, with the king reduced almost to a spectator.[5]

As the Kentish laws do not suggest a kingdom even dimly aware of what these texts would mean to later generations, it was possible only in retrospect to see in them a foreshadowing of what Anglo-Saxon England would achieve in later centuries.[6] (Alfred, as we will see, was probably the first to suggest as much.) Purely local circumstances were likely determinative in shaping these first works of English legislation. The presence within its borders of Britain's most powerful archiepiscopal see, and not any particular investment in the vernacular as such (or sense of its possibilities), may well have been the foremost stimulus for the production of written law in Kent.[7]

---

[4] "We have spoken of Æthelberht's 'laws', but it is desirable to make it clear that these laws are not legislation in a wide sense. They do not enounce general principles or new principles, such as might have followed Æthelberht's conversion to Christianity, nor do they provide a code for every justiciable cause in the kingdom" (Richardson and Sayles 1966: 5).

[5] See Chapter 2, 51–52. The Kentish king Eorconberht (r.640–664) also issued laws according to Bede (*Historia ecclesiastica* [henceforth *HE*] iii.8), but their language goes unremarked in his account; they do not survive into the present. Liebermann (1903–1916: I, 9) includes Bede's paraphrase in his edition.

[6] See, e.g., Wormald 2005. While later legislators did make use of Kentish materials, it cannot be safely assumed that those who prepared these texts in the seventh century appreciated the full significance of what they were doing (which does not detract from its importance).

[7] The laws of Wihtred are concerned almost exclusively with ecclesiastical matters. On the possibility that Archbishop Theodore of Tarsus "may have deliberately encouraged the use of written English," see Brooks 1984: 95–96.

Use of the vernacular probably began as a concession to the already recondite legal vocabulary of Old English. A similar compromise between ecclesiastical learning and the practical realities of litigation is suggested by the "Malberg glosses" of the *Lex Salica* – words in the Frankish vernacular essential to the conduct of law and thus supplied where needed (and occasionally gathering themselves into fragments of near-prose) throughout an otherwise Latin text.[8] We see something comparable in the laws of Æthelberht, where the meaning of clauses frequently depends on compound nouns (e.g., *cearwund* "grievously wounded, bedridden," *þurhðirel* "pierced through") enclosed within a simple "if *x* happens, then pay *y*" syntactic frame.[9] It is probably no coincidence that a separate category of poetic compounds underlay the structure of Old English verse before it adapted itself to writing in later centuries and shed these vestiges of oral composition in favor of a more discursive style.[10] In the earliest phases of both English law and verse, to learn the tradition involved committing its characteristic terms to memory.

During the reign of Ine, Wessex appears to have become the first neighboring polity to follow the Kentish example. But aside from Alfred's assertion that his *domboc* relied in part upon materials issued by Offa of Mercia (r.757–796), we have no evidence that any other early king before Alfred issued laws in his own name.[11] If we take Alfred at his word that Offa's laws were in some sense available to him, the period between the *domboc* and the last royal code to precede it may well encompass a nearly century-long void. A more skeptical response – warranted given the faint evidence for Offa's legislative activity – suggests an even wider chasm separating Alfred's laws from Ine's. Most of what we know about lawmaking in Offa's kingdom comes not from any legislation attributed to him but from a report by papal legates on the condition of Mercia. The

---

[8] On the "Malberg glosses," see Schmidt-Wiegand 1989 (who notes that these are not limited to single words or phrases but sometimes preserve vernacular legal formulae as well); also Oliver 2011: 18.

[9] One clause characteristic of this tendency is *Æthelberht* §68: *Gif wælt[-]wund weorðeþ*, III *scillingum forgelde(n)*, ("If a 'welt-wound' occurs, let him pay three shillings"). Oliver 2002: 76–77.

[10] See Fulk 1992: 254.

[11] That Alfred's remarks are the only evidence for Offa's legislation is made clear in Wormald 1999a: 106.

circumstances of its later transmission may, in Patrick Wormald's view, have lent it the appearance of royal law; indeed, Wormald was so taken with this conjecture that he considered the legates' report to be what Alfred had in mind when he claimed knowledge of Offa's laws.[12] Given the general scarcity of evidence for this period, the "Legatine Capitulary" is indeed a valuable witness to the state of Mercia in the eighth century, and the present edition takes note of it where necessary. But few of its statements seem to have any clear bearing on clauses of the *domboc*. The odds are therefore good that, while Alfred may have heard of laws attributed to Offa, he had in mind as concrete precedents to his own legislative undertaking primarily the laws of Ine and those earlier issued in Kent.

That the decades between Offa's reign and Alfred's involved such a lengthy silence, not only in law but in other forms of writing as well, of course had much to do with the arrival of the Vikings. The raid on Lindisfarne in 793, just as the reign of Offa neared its end, presaged decades of humiliation and loss for kingdoms whose learning had once been the envy of Western Europe. Alongside the achievements of Bede, Alcuin, and Boniface and the heyday of the Kentish church (a favorite subject of the former's *Historia*), royal legislation in English issued during the seventh century probably took on new associations during Alfred's lifetime. In a text likely composed before the *domboc*, Alfred refers to books written in England prior to the onset of Danish raiding as "tracks" to be followed.[13] It may not be ruled out that the laws of Kent figured in his

---

[12] Wormald 1999a: 107: "Since the proceedings in southern England are said to have been 'read out both in Latin and in the vernacular (*theotisce*),' it is not impossible that the English version was preserved with a more or less continuous gloss, so accentuating its resemblance to the codes of seventh-century kings." For a full exposition of the possible (but unlikely) relationship between this text and the *domboc*, see our headnote to the edition of Alfred's laws in the present volume.

[13] Alfred's Preface to the *Pastoral Care* (see also, in this chapter, 32–33) begins by imagining the clergy of his and prior generations looking back on the age of Bede and Alcuin and exclaiming, upon seeing Latin books they were unable to read, "In this we can still see their tracks, but we cannot follow them, and therefore we have lost both the wealth and the wisdom, because we would not incline our hearts after their example" (*Her mon mæg giet gesion hiora swæð, ac we him ne cunnon æfterspyrigan, forðæm we habbað nu ægðer forlæten ge þone welan ge þone wisdom, forðamþe we noldon to ðæm spore mid ure mode onlutan*); Sweet 1871: I, 4–5; cf. also Schreiber 2002: 193. Throughout the present study, *Regula pastoralis* designates Gregory's work and *Pastoral Care* the translation by Alfred and his circle.

imagination among such texts. To any king of this era with the time and wherewithal to reflect on more than survival, the early kingdom of Kent would have served as much as Northumbria as a paradigmatic example of what might be achieved through wise governance. Only the most fortunate could dream of establishing such conditions among their own people.

The final collapse of these rival powers afforded Alfred just such an opportunity to restore what they had lost, and there is every reason to think that the *domboc* was as much affected by his ambitions for the education of his people as other texts of this period. With respect to its most basic aims alone, legislation could remain in these new circumstances what it had been in Kent: as did earlier compilations, the *domboc* collects in one place, presumably for future reference, solutions to disputes earlier resolved by the king and his judges.[14] (It may not be ruled out that some of the judgments enumerated therein were issued during the reigns of prior West-Saxon kings.) But Alfredian additions to this core structure effectively establish law alongside historical writing and translation from Latin as the fields in which Alfred's house of Cerdic would win fame in (relative) peace as it earlier had in war.[15] The result was something much more complex than the mere "propaganda" or narrow assertion of royal "power" that some earlier commentators have seen in the *domboc*.[16] As will be shown throughout the present volume, Alfred and his circle sought to alter both the relationship between writing and legal practice and the meaning of "law" itself for contemporaries and successors. They did so in part by answering the doubts and hesitations with which earlier kings had presented their laws to populations unaccustomed to writing and suspicious of norms lacking a clear basis in oral tradition. In its unapologetic treatment of laws *as texts* and its deliberate arrangement of them into a historical framework, the *domboc* is a major (and largely

---

[14] According to Lambert (2017: 265), "Alfred's law code [...] is filled with what look very like royal judgements issued to resolve legal quandaries, which could well have come to the king's attention as appeals."

[15] On the origins of the West-Saxon kingdom with Cerdic and Cynric, see the *Anglo-Saxon Chronicle* s.a. 495 and 519 (Plummer and Earle 1892: 14 and 16; Bately 1986: 19–20).

[16] See, in the present chapter, 31–32; also Chapter 3, 79–80.

unrecognized) step along the path from law as we find it in the early
Kentish materials to the fully "bureaucratic" institution realized in
England during the reign of Henry II (r.1154–1189), the foundations
of which, as has long been acknowledged, lay deep in the pre-Conquest past.[17] It is the first English legislative statement to present law
as primarily something to be learned from books and to suggest that
it may not be adequately grasped without some depth of historical
knowledge. And there is every reason to think that the kings who
succeeded Alfred not only made further use of the *domboc* but
accepted its premises. Though records of litigation from the Anglo-Saxon period offer no citations of royal law – a circumstance that
has long suggested the inefficacy of the latter – the reception of the
domboc indicates that Alfred succeeded to a modest extent in making his ordinances binding on his successors. Quotations of its contents and assertions of its authority persist from the earlier tenth
century until the end of the Anglo-Saxon period.[18] No legislating
king seems to have felt free to disregard it in formulating his own
laws. Thus much commentary of the past two centuries, emphasizing
as it has the basis of the *domboc* in orally transmitted custom, has
proceeded from a sense of its significance somewhat at odds with
what is known of how it was used in the generation immediately following Alfred's death. And this, in turn, has implications (to be
explored in subsequent chapters) for the much-disputed question of
whether legislation of this period was in any sense efficacious or
even useful.[19]

Alfred's aspirations for the text necessitated many departures
from convention. While some prior legislation in English had begun
by naming the bishops and magnates consulted and the circumstances to which the provisions respond, the *domboc* commences
with the extraordinary "Mosaic Prologue" (henceforth *MP*), a loose

---

[17] A point often made, the classic demonstration being Maitland 1897. An essential
later exposition of such ideas is Campbell 2000 (particularly its first chapter, "The
Late Anglo-Saxon State: A Maximum View"). See also Wormald 1998.

[18] Its influence on subsequent legislation is considered in Chapter 5.

[19] On the apparent indifference of Anglo-Saxon litigation to royal law, see Wormald
1999a: 148 and 264. Yet Wormald occasionally urges a more qualified view, as in
Wormald 1997b: 348 ("[T]here are ample indicators that cases were run roughly
as laid down by royal authority"). See also Chapter 3, 78–81.

and at times remarkably unfaithful translation of the laws of Moses (as given in Exod. 20–23) and the Apostolic "Council of Jerusalem" (Acts 15: 22–29).[20] Another short chronology of royal legislation in England – effectively, a second prologue – precedes Alfred's own laws (*MP* §49.7–8). Here he traces English legislation to a series of unnamed synods before offering assurances that his own ordinances will diverge little from the prior compilations of Ine, Æthelberht, and Offa. The compilation concludes with the laws of Ine, which are nowhere attested independent of the *domboc*. In effect, at least half of the *domboc* – more, if we include in our calculation the laws of Ine – constitutes a sustained meditation on the nature and history of written law in England.[21] While deference to earlier legislation was customary in royal lawbooks of the early Middle Ages, no prior or subsequent king went to such lengths to represent his laws as the mere ripening of tradition.

Whether Alfred employed or even had access to the books of laws claimed in the "second" prologue as the basis of his own is uncertain. While there may be traces of Æthelberht's code toward the conclusion of Alfred's, the only prior English legislation that indisputably survives in the *domboc* is Ine's.[22] What Alfred's laws themselves owe to written and unwritten traditions is a complex question, to be explored from different angles throughout this book. No such inquiries will be possible, however, without first establishing the broader historical background that underlay the West-Saxon achievement in lawmaking. Accordingly, the present chapter narrates the steps by which Wessex emerged from inauspicious beginnings to become, by the late ninth century, the center of English political life

---

[20] Cf. the short prefaces attached to the laws of Hloðhere and Eadric, Wihtred, and Ine. Of the three, the first is the most self-conscious rhetorical performance. The convention seems to have undergone developments of which Alfred was probably mindful (see Chapter 2, 57–59). On biblical introductions in other works of Germanic legislation that may shed light on Alfred's, see Chapter 2, 64–66.

[21] King Alfred's will (Harmer 1914: 15–19) bears comparison with the *domboc* given the substantial historical prologue (again, nearly as long as the will itself) preceding its provisions, an unusual feature of such documents at this time.

[22] For evidence that Alfred or members of his circle had at least read the laws of Æthelberht, see Oliver 2015. Knowledge of at least the preface to the laws of Hloðhere and Eadric is suggested by evidence discussed in Chapter 2, 57–59.

and custodian of earlier kingdoms' achievements. Particular attention will be given to the development of written law and its movement from an uncertain to a major feature of governance. Intertwined with its emergence in England is the somewhat anomalous use of the vernacular for such purposes, a feature of these texts on which the following pages will shed some new light as well.

None of these subjects may be considered apart from the rapidly changing situation of the West-Saxon church and its institutions, which enjoyed sudden prosperity during the reign of Ine and renewal through Alfred's efforts. Conventionally, the church is referred to in historiography as introducing literacy to the English kingdoms who welcomed it. But such generalizations risk concealing the particulars of what it offered to early English polities as they struggled with neighboring kingdoms, their own sometimes-restive nobility, and (ultimately) the Vikings.

Here it helps to have a clear sense of what "the church" was to those who encountered it. The notion of Christianity as a "religion of the book" may not be invoked to explain its role in encouraging literacy (as is sometimes done) without distorting some crucial realities of the earlier Middle Ages. In all likelihood, Christianity would have struck laity and clergy alike as a religion of *books*. This was the case in part because manuscripts containing the entirety of the Bible were exceedingly rare. While an oath sworn on the Gospels was a potent way of visualizing the litigant's putting his or her salvation at risk, we may not doubt that the custom arose in part because these were the portions of the Bible likeliest to be on hand in a church.[23]

It is the content of these books, however, that points us to what may have stimulated the kinds of reflections culminating in the *domboc*. Anyone attentive to the readings during Mass would have been struck by their fundamentally legal concerns, a quality by no means diminished in the pages of the New Testament.[24] (We have seen that

---

[23] See, e.g., Marsden 2004: 72.

[24] See L'Huillier 1997: "All attempts to identify a precise moment to indicate a turning point in the transformation of the primitive Church from a purely charismatic movement to a structured institution fall short under rigorous examination" (119). According to Hough (2018), it cannot be ruled out that the laws of the Old Testament played some role in shaping even the earliest Kentish laws.

Acts 15 is reworked in the opening passages of the *domboc*; reference to the event described therein as a "council" had been the norm as early as the lifetime of St. Jerome, which may itself have suggested its relevance to the historical narrative sketched in the Prologue.[25]) Though a system of canon law as later generations would know it did not emerge until the twelfth century, churchmen nonetheless came to early Kent and Northumbria bearing with them an already formidable and subtle tradition of written law at times reliant upon the language of the Bible.[26] It would be a mistake to suppose that these texts did not shape in some fashion Ine's and Alfred's reflections on the forms that secular legislation might assume, particularly when the latter makes so clear his fascination with them at the outset of the *domboc*. Accordingly, the fortunes of the church play a prominent role in the narrative that follows – probably more than was typical in commentary of the nineteenth and even twentieth century, which laid at times excessive emphasis on Alfred's debts to ancestral Germanic traditions.[27] That the importance of specifically clerical learning in the formation of the *domboc* should have been so little emphasized is surprising given the role of sustained reflection on passages of Scripture in Alfred's own piety (as described by Asser).[28] Though Alfred's collection of these passages into a personal "enchiridion" or *handboc* is now lost, the king's involvement in a partial translation of the Psalter adds credibility to Asser's account.[29] As Alfred is shown in Asser's biography earnestly seeking the assistance of clerical advisors in his own devotional life as well as more public endeavors (such as the translation of the *Regula pastoralis*), it

---

[25] Plumer 2003: 107 n. 85; see also Chapter 2, 59–60.

[26] Regarding the close dependence upon Scripture in some canonical materials antedating the reign of Alfred and coeval with Ine's, see, e.g., Flechner 2009: 25, where it is noted that the A-recension of the *Collectio canonum hibernensis* gives "approximately five hundred citations from the bible"; "[t]wo-thirds of the biblical citations were derived from the Old Testament."

[27] See Chapter 5, 168–172.

[28] For Asser's account of the formation of the *handboc*, see Stevenson 1959: 73–74 (§88–89).

[29] William of Malmesbury gives a brief account of the "enchiridion" in his *Gesta Regum Anglorum* (Mynors, Thomson, and Winterbottom 1998: I, 192 [ii.123]). According to Toswell (2014: 69–70), "Alfred styled his personal behavior on the daily round of the Office that a monk would live." Pratt (2007: 243) notes parallel developments in the life of Charles the Bald.

seems probable that their help was also sought as the king set about assembling the *domboc* and that we should expect to find in it traces of their influence.

Beginnings

It will be impossible to give a proper account of the *domboc* without first considering the laws from which it purports to derive. Even if Alfred's use of them remains a matter of debate, there is no doubt that they formed in some fashion a part of the intellectual background of his achievement. As was the case with most other polities of its time, Wessex, prior to its first encounters with the Roman church, was governed by an oral legal tradition whose claims to authority did not cease with the arrival of writing. While some residue of this tradition may well survive in the *domboc*, tracing its influence is not as easy as scholars once assumed. It is true that this body of unwritten law must have had features in common with what was observed at this time in other parts of western and central Europe. The shared legal vocabulary of the Germanic-speaking peoples, giving us words such as *murder* (a term whose Old English cognate is strangely absent from the *domboc* where we would most expect it) and alliterative tautologies such as *to have and to hold*, is the strongest evidence in favor of such a tradition.[30] These and other terms attest to beliefs that survived independent of writing and had spread themselves by the late ninth century from Iceland to the Italian Peninsula.[31] That scholars of the nineteenth century became giddy at the possibilities such terms afforded for reconstructing vanished institutions should not dissuade us from accepting that there was such a thing as "Germanic" law.[32] But this body of norms

---

[30] On *murder* and the seeming omission of the concept in an instance of concealed homicide, see *Ine* §35 and n. On *to have and to hold*, see *Beowulf* l. 658 (Fulk, Bjork, and Niles 2008: 24), viewed by Day (1999: 314) as referring to the transfer of Hrothgar's "power of possession and protection over both the persons of his household and its physical space."

[31] Tiersma 1999: 10–15.

[32] Legal historians have grown reluctant to credit the capacity of oral traditions to preserve bodies of knowledge over vast expanses of time and distance. But as Fulk (1992: 34) noted, such assumptions are fundamental to the study of Germanic verse: "That poets should have striven to be as conservative as possible is to be

probably lacked the uniformity assumed by even more sober scholars of this period and should not be invoked incautiously.[33] Nor was it wholly untouched by the influence of Roman law.

Amid the decline of the Roman state, Visigothic kings, preeminently Alaric II (d.507), sought to organize the remains of its legal tradition for use in territories stretching from the Iberian Peninsula to cities well north of the Pyrenees.[34] It was Alaric who commissioned the *Lex Romana Visigothorum* (also known as the *Breviary of Alaric*), a text that would be the principal point of access to Roman law for most literate persons in western Europe until the rediscovery of Justinian's *Digest* in the twelfth century.[35] Though it sheds little light on their characteristic legal behaviors when compared with subsequent texts, the story of lawmaking among the Germanic peoples is conventionally understood to begin with the *Breviary*, given its broad influence.[36] Not long thereafter, kings in Francia would issue a range of laws in Latin ostensibly less indebted to Roman tradition. These compilations, as we have seen, occasionally record elements of Germanic custom and legal vocabulary.[37]

Access to the *Breviary* has seemed at least possible in England in the years after the mission organized by Gregory the Great to the people of Kent, which sought to acquaint its inhabitants with Catholic (as opposed to Arian or British) Christianity and establish

---

expected of a culture as saturated as this with veneration for old things and a firm belief in the degeneracy of the present age in comparison to the past. Other evidence for scops' conservatism is their ability to transmit old Germanic lore orally from one generation to another with surprising accuracy: the parallels between *Beowulf* and *Grettis Saga*, between the Hæthcyn/Herebeald story and the Baldr myth, and between the Scyld Scefing story and the Bergelmir myth, are truly remarkable examples of this sort."

[33] See Chapter 5.

[34] On the afterlife of Roman law in the earlier Middle Ages, see Wieacker 1944: 195–284 at 199–206. The standard edition of the *Lex Romana Visigothorum* remains Zeumer 1902; for its origins and subsequent recensions, see Zeumer 1902: xii–xiv.

[35] Roman law saw no sustained revival until the twelfth century, on which see Wieacker 1944: 207–228; Breen 1944–5: 244–287; Brasington 2016: 32–61.

[36] The legislation of Alaric's father Euric, though of less consequence for the whole of Europe, should also not be overlooked: Levy called his code, which shows greater evidence of Germanic legal practice, "the best legislative work of the fifth century" (1942: 28).

[37] See Ebel and Thielmann 2003: 117; Oliver 2011: 8–25.

an archiepiscopal see under Roman authority.[38] But any such knowledge is unlikely to have circulated prior to the establishment by Theodore and Hadrian of a famed cathedral school in Canterbury.[39] Nor do the earliest laws in English, issued not long after the baptism of the Kentish king Æthelberht in 597, evince awareness of Roman law in spite of Bede's somewhat cryptic assertion that they were composed *iuxta exempla Romanorum*.[40] Given the marriage of Æthelberht to the Frankish princess Bertha, the vigorous trade between Kent and West Francia, and the accompaniment of Augustine (provost of Gregory's mission to Kent, subsequently the first Archbishop of Canterbury) by Frankish translators, we would expect the prevailing influence over his lawmaking activities to be the Frankish compilations mentioned earlier, which may account in some way for Bede's seeming assumption of external sources.[41]

Arguable traces of Frankish legislation have indeed led many scholars to conclude that, as Wormald put it, "Bede's 'Romans' may

---

[38] See Cook 1924 and Winkler 1992. Though soundly defeated, Arianism remained a matter of concern in western Europe at least as late as the middle of the eighth century: see Krutzler 2011: 59–61.

[39] See *HE* iv.2 (Colgrave and Mynors 1969: 333–337); Cook 1924: 105 and *passim*; Brooks 1984: 94–95; Bischoff and Lapidge 1994: 147 (where it is implied that the Roman law curriculum of the cathedral school was not limited to the *Breviary*).

[40] Bede's description indicates at least some acquaintance with the text of Æthelberht's laws: "Among other benefits which he conferred on the race under his care, he established with the advice of his counsellors a code of laws after the Roman manner (*iuxta exempla Romanorum*). These are written in English and are still kept and observed by the people. Among these he set down first of all what restitution must be made by anyone who steals anything belonging to the church or the bishop or any other clergy; these laws were designed to give protection to those whose coming and whose teaching he had welcomed." *HE* ii.5 (Colgrave and Mynors 1969: 150–151). The editors' rendering of the problem phrase ("after the Roman manner") departs from the strict sense of the Latin; as Wallace-Hadrill (1988: 60) points out, "By *exempla* he [Bede] could have understood that exemplars of continental law had been brought to Canterbury by the missionaries or by Bertha's Frankish following; not for slavish copying but as models of codification proper to a Christian king."

[41] Among Augustine's entourage were "interpreters from the Frankish race"; see *HE* i.25 (Colgrave and Mynors 1969: 73). The editors point out (n. 4) that "[t]hese would speak some form of the Franconian dialect, possibly not unlike the Kentish dialect of Old English." On the trade between Kent and West Francia in Æthelberht's time, see Gautier 2006.

actually have been Franks."[42] But in recent decades, closer attention to the laws themselves has yielded more compelling conclusions about their provenance. Though preserved uniquely in a manuscript of the twelfth century, the laws of Æthelberht have been shown to retain a number of lexical, morphological, and syntactic archaisms.[43] For this and other reasons, the text may preserve some features of oral composition and elements of native practice, leaving hypothetical Frankish *exempla* with a more limited role to play in the preparation of this text than some have assumed.[44] However warranted in light of the circumstances that brought written law to sixth-century Kent, Oliver's work shows that speculation about Frankish sources may distract from the more important questions raised by this text about matters such as marriage and the social hierarchy, for which it furnishes some of our most important (if often ambiguous) evidence.

Whatever their backgrounds, Æthelberht's laws are certain to have initiated the first sustained attempts by any Germanic-speaking people to record laws in their own language. By the time the kingdom of Wessex assumed more-or-less settled boundaries toward the close of the seventh century, it was positioned to benefit from established traditions of written royal legislation and even explore new possibilities for its use.

---

[42] See Wormald, 1999a: 97; also 98–98, in which are tabulated the structural similarities between Æthelberht's laws and those issued on the Continent in this period. Oliver (2002: 35) instead understands *iuxta exempla Romanorum* to refer merely to the writing of legislation, a view endorsed in some publications by Wormald as well.

[43] See Oliver 2002: 25–34. All Kentish royal legislation of the seventh century is found only in this witness, the *Textus Roffensis* (on which see Chapter 4, 136–142). One remarkable survival of an oral manumission formula in the laws of Wihtred (§7), its archaism demonstrated by retention of the disyllabic conjunction *ænde* (cf. Old High German *enti*) and other terms, is explored in Oliver 1998.

[44] Oliver holds that the laws of Æthelberht "stand boldly at the watershed between orality and literacy in the Anglo-Saxon legal tradition," being "the first Germanic laws to be recorded in the vernacular" (Oliver 2002: 36). Evidence for the fundamentally oral derivation of Æthelberht's laws comes chiefly from the organization of subject matter (36–41), which would in Oliver's view have facilitated memorization; in contrast, as Oliver shows, earlier written legal compilations, including those as archaic as the laws of Hammurabi, show no such patterns of distribution.

The First Christian Kings of Wessex

Deliberately or not, Alfred's laws conceal somewhat just how unlikely was the ascendancy of the West-Saxon kingdom in the late ninth century. Inclusion of Ine's laws as a presumably historical appendix rather than those of Ine's Kentish contemporaries may reflect the same West-Saxon triumphalism that has been seen in the *Anglo-Saxon Chronicle*, another product of the Alfredian era.[45] If they were not still all in effect – unlikely, given that they sometimes contradict Alfred's – Ine's laws as deployed in the *domboc* seem meant, among other things, to furnish evidence of a tradition of written law in Wessex durable enough to rival Kent's.[46] (West-Saxon insecurity over the achievements of Kent has, as we will see, a long history.) In minimizing the achievements of other early kingdoms, the *domboc* thus shares some qualities of the *Chronicle*.[47] But the point should not be pressed too far. Alfred was careful to flatter those who needed flattering, or at least not to give needless offense. Such motives go some lengths to explain the deference (however specious) to Kent and Mercia in the *domboc*'s Prologue.

In comparison to Kent, which presumably benefited from its proximity to Frankish centers of learning, the early history of Wessex offers few portents of the role it would later assume in the governance of later Anglo-Saxon England. When its internal politics

[45] The classic argument in favor of this view of the *Chronicle*'s origins, contested in later years (Meaney 1986: 193–194) but still hard to gainsay, is Plummer and Earle 1899: civ–cxiv. It is significant that Alfred names only the laws of Æthelberht in the short remarks that introduce his laws, omitting to mention the laws of Hloðhere and Eadric and of Wihtred even though the *domboc* offers direct evidence that these compilations, rather than Æthelbert's, were in some fashion sources of influence (see Chapter 2, 57–59).

[46] On Alfred's several contradictions of Ine's laws, which argue for the latter's authenticity, see Wormald 1999a: 278; also Lambert 2017: 105. Such circumstances throw into confusion Alfred's statement that he ordered Ine's laws to be held "in another way," which may be a tactful way of acknowledging their (partial) abrogation; see also n. 144. As will be seen subsequently, the rubricator of Alfred's laws, whose work was undertaken at an early stage of their transmission, regarded the laws of Ine and Alfred as a continuous whole.

[47] See, e.g., McKitterick 2004: "[The *Anglo-Saxon Chronicle*'s] narrative strikes the reader as a strong and very particular vision of history from the vantage of late ninth-century Wessex. It has a triumphalist agenda and a very clear political and ideological message about the pre-eminence of the kings of Wessex to communicate" (280).

first emerge in the historical record – one restricted almost entirely to Bede's *Historia ecclesiastica* – it appears very much in subordination to Northumbria. The baptism of King Cynegisl "together with all his people" (*cum sua gente*) in 635, for whom Oswald of Northumbria stood sponsor, was probably meant above all to deepen "an alliance between the two kingdoms in the face of a common enemy, the pagan Penda of Mercia, which was later confirmed by the marriage of Oswald to Cynegisl's daughter."[48] Birinus, who was shortly to become the first West-Saxon bishop, had, according to Bede, found those under the rule of Cynegisl "completely heathen" (*paganissimos*) prior to the king's baptism.[49] And Birinus's mission seems not to have had quite the effect of Augustine's, which saw Kent within a century of Æthelberht's baptism become (along with Northumbria) a major center of ecclesiastical learning.[50] Instead, the royal household of the West-Saxons would revert to paganism under the rule of Cynegisl's son Cenwealh, who upon his accession "refused to receive the faith and the mysteries of the heavenly kingdom and not long afterwards lost his earthly kingdom also," if only for a while.[51]

That Cenwealh ultimately changed his mind was probably owing to the same pressures that had first brought his father to the baptismal font. An attack by Penda, the Mercian king against whom Cynegisl had sought an alliance with Oswald of Northumbria, forced Cenwealh to seek refuge at the East Anglian court where he found himself newly receptive to the faith, "for the king with whom he lived in exile was a good man and blessed with a good and saintly family."[52] Though Cenwealh would in time be restored to the throne, his inattention to ecclesiastical affairs deprived the West-Saxon people of a bishop for a long while (*tempore non pauco*), leaving the church in Wessex on no sound footing when compared with its

---

[48] *HE* III.7.vii (Colgrave and Mynors 1969: 232–233); Yorke 1995: 171.

[49] *HE* III.7.vii (Colgrave and Mynors 1969: 232–233).

[50] Of course, the structures established by Augustine had to overcome the major obstacles posed by the reign of Æthelberht's son Eadbald, who refused entry into the church for some years after his accession.

[51] *qui et fidem ac sacramenta regni caelestis suscipere rennuit, et non multo post etiam regni terrestris potentiam perdidit. HE* III.7.vii (Colgrave and Mynors 1969: 232–233).

[52] *HE* III.7.vii (Colgrave and Mynors 1969: 235).

neighbor and rival to the east.[53] The opening sections of Ine's laws suggest that these were mistakes the king was anxious not to repeat, though it cannot be known to what extent Ine was mindful of Cenwealh's troubles as these clauses took shape.

The outline of early West-Saxon regnal history just given, which relies entirely on Bede's account in the absence of other evidence, ought to be received with some qualifications. In particular, Bede's description of the circumstances Birinus is likely to have encountered among the *Gewisse* (as they were then known) has come into doubt. The view that the West-Saxons were almost wholly unaffected by Christianity prior to his mission has found particular disfavor.[54] Indeed, it has been suggested that the rapid conversion from paganism envisaged by Bede disguises a likelier absorption of churches theretofore belonging to the British aristocracy.[55] The influence of the Irish church as well over this region is suggested by the correspondence of Aldhelm, who served as abbot of Malmesbury from 675 onward and, along with Boniface, was one of the two most celebrated ecclesiastics to emerge from early Wessex.[56] All of this renders less probable Bede's view that Cynegisl was unacquainted with Christianity prior to the arrival of Birinus.

Whatever character it may have assumed, the British presence in Wessex remains significant for the texts considered in this volume and further illustrates the peculiar position of the *Gewisse* with respect to other early kingdoms. References to the Welsh or *wealhas* (as the Anglo-Saxons called them) are nowhere as numerous in royal legislation as they are in Ine's laws, and they surely made up a large portion of those subject to the house of Cerdic, whose arrival in England commenced (according to the *Chronicle*) with warfare against them.[57] Given Alfred's eagerness to secure as a royal counselor the Welsh churchman Asser, too much should not be made of their occasionally servile aspect in Ine's legislation.[58] In

---

[53] Cenwealh established Winchester as an episcopal see, a venture that began poorly according to Bede (*HE* III.7; Colgrave and Mynors 1968: 234–235).

[54] Yorke 1995: 177.

[55] Yorke 1995: 177. On the vitality of the British church in western England see Chadwick *et al.* 1958; Bassett 1992; Pryce 1992.

[56] Yorke 1995: 162, 181.

[57] See *Ine* §§23, 32, 33, 47.1, 58, and 75.

[58] See *Asser's Life* (Stevenson 1959: 63–66 [§79]); Keynes and Lapidge 1983: 93–96.

context, Alfred's relationship with Asser, priest of St. David's and subsequently Bishop of Sherborne, seems part of a long tradition of close relations between the West-Saxon elite and what remained of the British aristocracy; relations that perhaps owe something to the mixed Celtic–Germanic ancestry of the Kingdom of Wessex itself.[59]

Though the ecclesiastical history of early Wessex is more complex, and perhaps richer, than the standard histories suggest, it must be admitted that stable governance was conspicuously lacking prior to the accession of Ine in 689. West-Saxon kings' reasons for cultivating the faith seem to have developed little beyond the pragmatism that was likely manifest in Cynegisl's alliance with Oswald. The clearest case in point is Ine's immediate predecessor Cædwalla (c.659–689), whose name, "an anglicized form of the British Cadwallon," perhaps "points to a British strain in his ancestry."[60] In spite of being an eager benefactor of the church, Cædwalla waited to be baptized until he had abdicated and was a pilgrim to Rome on the verge of death.[61] The manner of his baptism suggests an attempt to extract the maximum advantage from the sacrament after having led what Stenton called "a life of incessant violence."[62] One may see in it something of the rather utilitarian understanding of baptism evidenced elsewhere in this period that the church was at pains to

---

[59] John 1996: 6. According to Orme (2007: 9), Alfred's appointment of Asser as Bishop of Sherborne "had the merit of placing the Cornish under a trusted royal servant, while providing for their special needs with a bishop whose language and religious traditions were similar to their own."

[60] Stenton 1947: 68; also Colgrave and Mynors (1969: 380): "His name is clearly British and points to some connection by blood with the British race."

[61] Constantine and Theodosius had also waited to be baptized until they were near death. On the practice of delayed or "clinical" baptism in late antiquity, see Gaddis 2005: 63. The Northumbrian king Edwin (c.585–633) offers only a superficial parallel, as Bede (ii.9–14) narrates in some detail his training as a catechumen and the king's own reflective and cautious nature. Stenton (1947: 69–70) attributes Cædwalla's delayed baptism to "the simple reverence in which he held the Christian mysteries" but adds in a note that Cædwalla's baptism "is an illustration of the custom which in the seventh century still allowed an individual, unbaptized in infancy, to decide the circumstances of his formal admission into the church" (70 n. 1). Yet some continuity with late antique ideas seems more plausible here.

[62] Stenton 1947: 70. The classic account of early royal abdications is Stancliffe 1983.

correct.[63] The penitential of Theodore, for example, establishes a three-year fast for those who seek baptism in order to expunge a particular impurity while remaining silent on the subject of "clinical" baptism.[64] In a clause concerning priests who fail to baptize the sick (§5 [L6]), the laws of Wihtred may furnish more direct evidence that some laymen were continuing to deliberately postpone baptism. But any official acceptance of "clinical" baptism in Kent seems improbable around the time of Cædwalla's death given its status as the preeminent center of ecclesiastical life. According to Lynch, infant baptism was established in the English kingdoms at least by the 670s, years in which the "missionary phase of Christianity was coming to a close," and one would expect the requirement to have been observed more in Kent than elsewhere.[65] The prompt baptism of newborn infants is a norm forcefully articulated at the outset of Ine's laws (§2).

While Cædwalla's generation was probably the last for which an adult catechumenate remained a practical reality, the gestures accompanying his baptism would continue to shape expectations during Ine's reign. Abdication, typically followed by adoption of monastic life, was commonplace in seventh-century England; Centwine, who held the throne of Cerdic prior to Cædwalla, seems to have concluded his reign in this fashion, though the evidence is scant and ambiguous.[66] Cædwalla was thus likely following convention, though entry into Rome was probably his own spectacular addition to this practice.[67] His arrival in the city seems to have had the intended effect. Sixteen lines of Latin verse composed by Crispus, Archbishop of Milan, which were subsequently inscribed on

---

[63] See, for example, Augustine, *De civitate Dei,* wherein it is argued (XIII.7) that "[T]hose who have been baptized when they could not postpone their death and have departed from this life with all their sins wiped out (*baptizati sunt deletisque omnibus peccatis ex hac uita emigrarunt*), have won less merit than those who could have deferred their death but did not, because they chose to end their life by confessing Christ, rather than by denying him to arrive at his baptism (*quia maluerunt Christum confitendo finire uitam quam eum negando ad eius baptismum peruenire*)"; Bettenson 1984: 516; Dombart and Kalb 1955: 390.

[64] *Poenitentiale Theodori* I, x, ii (Finsterwalder 1929: 303).

[65] Lynch 1998: 70–71.

[66] See Stancliffe 1983: 154–155.

[67] He seems to have been the first English king to reach Rome: see Stancliffe 1983: 156.

Cædwalla's tomb, commemorate the event. Colgrave and Mynors relate that "[t]he sepulchral stone on which [the poem] was carved was discovered in the sixteenth century by the builders of the present St. Peter's, though it now seems to have disappeared again."[68] The verses survive, however, in Bede's account, whose own narrative of Cædwalla's baptism presents it as the mere extension into the spiritual realm of the ambitions that had consumed the king in life.[69]

That Cædwalla spent his last days in Rome in the company of Pope Sergius probably forged a durable link between the house of Cerdic and the apostolic see to be exploited in later years by Ine, Æthelwulf, and Alfred. Domestically, Cædwalla's reign was a success in very narrow terms, expanding somewhat the territory over which the kingdom of the *Gewisse* held permanent control and leading it out from under the shadow of Mercian and Northumbrian power. (Efforts to subjugate Kent, however, yielded little, with the burning of Cædwalla's brother Mul in a Kentish insurrection bringing a temporary end to West-Saxon rule.)[70] The victories of Cædwalla's reign, modest though they were, may also have occasioned the first attempts to conceive in stricter terms of Wessex as a political entity. If the epitaph given in Bede's *Historia* may be trusted, it may be significant that Cædwalla is here styled "rex Saxonum" and that use of the term *Gewisse* dies out after his reign.[71] As will be seen subsequently, political self-definition would remain a preoccupation during the reigns of Ine and Alfred, with the latter in particular building (perhaps unconsciously) upon Cædwalla's efforts in formulating his own more enduring solution.

---

[68] Colgrave and Mynors 1969: 470–471 n. 1.

[69] "He was anxious to gain the special privilege of being washed in the fountain of baptism within the threshold of the apostles; for he had learned that by the way of baptism alone can the human race attain entrance to the heavenly life; at the same time he hoped that, soon after his baptism, he might be loosed from the bonds of the flesh and pass, cleansed as he was, to eternal joy" ([H]oc sibi gloriae singularis *desiderans adipisci, ut ad limina beatorum apostolorum fonte baptismatis ablueretur, in quo solo didicerat generi humano patere uitae caelestis introitum; simul etiam sperans quia, mox baptizatus, carne solutus ad aeterna gaudia iam mundus transiret*). Bede, *HE* v.vii (Colgrave and Mynors 1969: 470–471).

[70] Stenton 1947: 69. The event and its background are recounted in the *Anglo-Saxon Chronicle* in its entries for the years 686 and 687 (Plummer and Earle 1892: 38–39; Bately 1986: 32).

[71] Bede, *HE* v.7 (Colgrave and Mynors 1969: 472–473); Yorke 2004: 2.

The Reign of Ine

Ine King of the West-Saxons, the conqueror, the lawgiver, the pilgrim to the threshold of the Apostles, stands out as one of the most famous names in the early history of the English people.[72]

Edward A. Freeman voices here (in characteristically high decibels) the favorable view of Ine's reign that has long been a stable feature of historiography. It owes much to West-Saxon tradition. Bede says remarkably little about Ine.[73] Much of what we know must be pieced together from scattered bits of evidence such as charters and genealogies as well as a handful of references in the *Anglo-Saxon Chronicle*. That many of the conclusions drawn by Freeman from these materials nearly a century and a half ago remain undisputed shows how little historians have to work with.[74] What follows is an outline of those facts about which there is general agreement.

At the time of Ine's accession in 688, Wessex was ruled by various sub-kings under the governance of one overking.[75] Ine was not the descendant of any of the kings who immediately preceded him, nor did he leave the throne to his own offspring.[76] Probably he "came in by that mixture of election and hereditary right" which characterized some early medieval patterns of succession.[77] His father, Cenred, was likely a sub-king of Wessex from whose territory Ine was called to the head kingship. Cenred (if the identification is correct) is named in S1164 as having granted estates to an otherwise unknown abbot

---

[72] See Freeman 1872: 1.

[73] Bede mentions Ine's accession after Cædwalla's abdication (v.7; 1969: 473) and alludes to the former's continuation of his predecessor's harsh rule over Sussex (IV.15; Colgrave and Mynors 1969: 381). Stancliffe (1983: 154) notes that Bede was "poorly informed about Wessex."

[74] Freeman's work (1872 and 1874) remains the fullest statement on Ine's reign, though it should be read alongside Wormald 2004b.

[75] The arrangement was arrived at after the death of King Cenwealh in 672: "[S]ub-kings took upon themselves the government of the kingdom, dividing it up and ruling for about ten years" (*acceperunt subreguli regnum gentis, et diuisum inter se tenuerunt annis circiter x*); *HE* iv.12 (Colgrave and Mynors 1969: 368–369); see also Keynes 1993: 2–3. For charter evidence, see Edwards 1988: 13, also S1165.

[76] The future line of Wessex eventually descended from Ine's brother Ingeld, who was Alfred's direct ancestor.

[77] Freeman 1872: 9.

Bectun in the early 670s, indicating, according to Edwards, that "he was a minor ruler around 670."[78] In S45 he attested a charter as *Rex Westsaxonum*; Ine also attests the charter but without any title. Edwards plausibly suggests that Cenred was recognized as *subregulus* of the western (as opposed to eastern) Saxon territories, and that, as "a mature man with a grown up son, [he] adopted the expedient of making his son king in the first place. During his own lifetime this probably made little difference, he and Ine working together and ruling jointly, but on his death it meant that Ine simply continued as king."[79] Use of such a practice would explain the absence of Cenred's name among the kings of Wessex in either Bede's *Historia* or the *Anglo-Saxon Chronicle*.

That Ine names his father as one of his closest counselors in the preface to his laws may indicate that some provisions date from a period of joint rule. But should Cenred have retired to a monastery in his old age, as did a number of his contemporaries, we should not assume that this would have made him unavailable to Ine as a source of counsel, for abbots are named among the *Christi famulos* at a council convened by Ine.[80] Freeman supposed that Ine was suggested specifically by his predecessor Cædwalla.[81] The nomination by a head-king would in any event have carried great weight with the *witan* who would have to approve the succession.

Not long before Ine's accession, the West Saxons ceased their expansion to the north and north-west, perhaps losing some of the latter to Mercia, and shifted focus to the west. Ine himself continued to push the boundaries of the kingdom westward, bringing under his rule territory containing Welsh subjects, though some of these gains

---

[78] See discussion in Edwards 1988: 229–234; citation from 235. Numbers for charters are those given in "The Electronic Sawyer."

[79] Edwards 1988: 297–299, citation at 298.

[80] Haddan and Stubbs, 1871: 295–6; see also Chapter 2, 47. Ine's sisters, Cwenburh and Cuthburh, would be venerated as saints. The latter married Ealdfrith, king of the Northumbrians; she eventually retired to become abbess at Wimbourne, where "her head, enclosed in silver, was the great object of local reverence down to the time of Henry the Eighth" (Freeman 1872: 15).

[81] Freeman 1872: 16.

may have been reversed by the 720s.[82] In any case, the distinction between the Anglo-Saxons and the *wealhas,* so prominent a feature of Ine's laws, appears, as Freeman notes, to have lost some of its significance by the time of Alfred's.[83] Measures dealing with the Britons show Ine in the view of one commentator to be "striking a skillful balance": though they "were clearly given an inferior rank," the "official legal status" nonetheless granted Celtic subjects "in the form of a wergeld and the right to give a public oath" attests to a restraint uncharacteristic of Cædwalla: "[F]requent warfare on every one of his borders could have forced Ine to keep from antagonizing a numerically significant portion of his population."[84]

Ine's reign, though one of the longest of the early kings of Wessex, thus had no prospect of being the most peaceful. The early years, at least, saw mostly successes for the king, chief of which was the establishment of Taunton as a border-fortress between the West Saxons and the Britons. (The subsequent demolition of Taunton by Ine's queen Æthelburh in 722 "suggest[s] a domestic crisis" in the closing years of his reign.)[85] While Ine's position with respect to rival kings remained nearly as precarious as Cædwalla's, the former effected a reconciliation with Kent that no doubt proved fruitful for both kingdoms. According to the *Anglo-Saxon Chronicle,* the people of Kent settled with Ine in the year 694 for the burning of Mul; the payment was likely the equivalent of a king's wergild.[86] To view this event as sealing the triumph of Wessex over Kent has become customary.[87] But it cannot have been lost on Ine that settling this inherited dispute would put him in close touch with England's preeminent

---

[82] Wormald 2004b: 2. On the conditions of the Welsh under West-Saxon rule, see Collingwood and Myres 1937: 447.

[83] "A comparison of the laws of Ine with those of Ælfred shows that, in the West-Saxon kingdom at large, the distinction between Englishman and Briton, which was in full force in the days of Ine, had been quite forgotten before the days of Alfred" (Freeman 1872: 11). Such omissions in later laws may be why Freeman assigns Ine's "special value as the one authentic picture of the relations between English and Briton within the English dominion" (1872: 3).

[84] Alexander 1995: 37.

[85] Kirby 1991: 131. The event is described in the *Anglo-Saxon Chronicle* s.a. 722, narrated alongside a major battle with the kingdom of Sussex (Plummer and Earle 1892: 42–43; Bately 1986: 34). See also Wormald 2004b: 2.

[86] See *Mircna Laga* §2 (Liebermann 1903–1916: I, 462–463); also Oliver (in press).

[87] See Charles-Edwards 1997: 175; Yorke 1999: 251.

see. Archbishop Theodore had similarly reconciled the kings of Northumbria and Mercia (*HE* iv.21), and so it is possible that the peace negotiated between Wessex and Kent was the handiwork of Theodore's successor Berhtwald, perhaps owing something to earlier efforts by Theodore.

The laws issued in Wihtred's name date approximately to the settlement just described. Language shared by his laws and those issued by Ine suggests amicable relations between the courts of Kent and Wessex and, perhaps, an exchange of ideas unusual among kings of this period.[88] But a reference in Wihtred's prologue to Berhtwald as "Archbishop of Britain" (*Bretone heahbiscop*) may give some sense of the attitude of the Kentish elite toward Wessex.[89] It is not the language one might expect of a kingdom brought to heel, being almost certainly based upon Theodore's prior reference to himself (in the preamble to the Council of Hatfied [679]) as "by the grace of God archbishop of the island of Britain and of the city of Canterbury" (*gratia Dei archiepiscopo Brittaniae insulae et ciuitatis Doruuernis*).[90]

Such an impression is borne out by what little we know of the position of Wessex with respect to Kent. Willibald's description in his *Vita Bonifatii* of a council convoked by Ine 710x716 seems particularly revealing. Here we are told that the assembled bishops and other clergy sent legates to Berhtwald informing him of their proceedings, so fearful were they that the archbishop would ascribe their having met in his absence to "presumption" or "temerity" (*ne eorum præsumptioni aut temeritati adscriberetur, si quid sine tanti pontificis agerent consilio*).[91] If Ine and his bishops trembled at the possibility of offending Berhtwald in the second decade of the

---

[88] Liebermann 1903–1916: III, 23–24; Hough 2014a: 9. Liebermann asserts that Wihtred had access to a text of Ine's laws perhaps more archaic than Alfred's exemplar. He notes as well that the former's use of Ine's laws is the earliest-known case in which a lawgiving English king borrowed from the legislation of a neighboring kingdom (III: 24). The evidence to this effect seems rather thin; see Chapter 2, 44–51.

[89] Oliver 2002: 152–153.

[90] *HE* IV.17 (Colgrave and Mynors 1969: 384–385); see also Keynes 1993, where such language is held to reflect a period in which the archbishop's "aspirations soared" (3).

[91] Haddan and Stubbs 1871: 295 (§4). A slightly different reading of the passage is given in Levison's edition (1905: 13–14).

eighth century, one may imagine how much authority the prelate enjoyed beyond Kent immediately after succeeding Theodore of Tarsus.

At the time of Ine's accession, only fifty-four years had passed since Christianity was first preached to the West Saxons by Birinus in 634 (notwithstanding the prior efforts of British clergy). Yet amid incessant fighting, Ine made more substantial efforts than any of his forebears to place the church in Wessex on firm foundations and make full use of its resources. The first West-Saxon synods, or at least, as Stenton says, "the first [...] of which there is definite evidence," were convoked during his reign and perhaps reflect the interest in ecclesiastical affairs that is also manifest at the outset of his laws (§§1–5).[92] The new bishopric of the West Saxons was placed in Dorchester, where King Cynegisl had been baptized in 635. In the meager details of his biography, as in the opening chapters of his laws, we see a king anxious to make up for lost ground by protecting and, where possible, strengthening ecclesiastical institutions. "[Ine's] acts, then, his laws, his foundations, his pilgrimage, must all be looked on as tinged with something of the zeal of recent conversion."[93] So said Freeman. Yet we have seen that the desire to catch up with rivals to the east furnishes a likelier motivation than pious "zeal," Ine's conversion (he was likely baptized as an infant) being in any case hardly "recent." Nor should we attach too much importance to the pilgrimage with which he concluded his reign, a conventional gesture of the time as has already been noted.[94] Whatever his motives, however, Ine's reign did see sustained efforts to shore up the West-Saxon church, whose derelictions were probably brought into relief by the achievements of Kent:

- Under Bishop Hædde, the seat of the West Saxon see was moved from Dorchester to the royal city of Winchester; Hædde brought with him the relics of Saint Birinus.[95]

---

[92] Stenton 1947: 71; also Cubitt 1995: 29 and 47.
[93] Freeman 1872: 4.
[94] Stancliffe 1983.
[95] *HE* iii.7 (Colgrave and Mynors 1968: 232–233).

- After Hædde's death in 705 – but still during Ine's reign – the diocese would be divided; Ine named Aldhelm bishop of the new see of Sherborne.[96]
- Ine seems likely to have played some role in establishing – more likely, re-establishing – the minster at Glastonbury. Like Winchester, it would become a major site for royal burials by the tenth century.[97]
- Foundation of the church at Wells that would later become a bishopric under Edward the Elder may be tentatively dated to Ine's reign.[98]

A charter of Ine from 704 (S245) grants "freedom from all secular obligations to the churches and monasteries of his kingdom."[99] Although its authenticity has been questioned, even a forgery might reflect in some fashion the king's reputation for ardent piety.[100]

Ine vanishes from the historical record after his departure for Rome. Thanks to their preservation by Alfred, he leaves behind what Freeman considered the foundational text of English legislation:

The Laws of Ine, the earliest monument of West-Saxon jurisprudence, are the laws which, as Wessex grew into England, we may look on as the beginning of the Laws of England, as the ground-work of the last law which has received the assent of the sovereign who wears the crown of Ine. As such, they are among the most precious monuments of our early history.[101]

Though Freeman's works are now more often read as artifacts of Victorian historiography, his judgment of Ine's achievement has

---

[96] See Abrams 1991: 117 n. 88 for discussion of the date of Aldhelm's accession as Bishop of Sherborne; also Yorke 1995: 178.

[97] Freeman, 1874: 2; Marafioti 2014: 65 and n. 57. But see Wormald 2004b.

[98] Establishment of the church began as a modest undertaking. Rodwell (1982: 56) maintained that the site in question had seen earlier use as a Roman mausoleum; "[t]he mausoleum was destroyed, in the middle to late-Saxon period, to make way for the construction of a near-square mortuary chapel [...] Dating evidence for the early cemetery includes fragments of colored window and vessel glass (possibly Merovingian), and early eighth-century Frisian *sceatta* and a radio-carbon date from a skeleton of 730±70." But cf. Blair 2005: 32 n. 93.

[99] See Edwards 1988: 107ff. for discussion of this charter.

[100] If authentic, the charter attests to his practical sense as well: "[I]n early Christian England, as in Ireland, minsters functioned as prototowns, focuses of settlement and economic activity sufficient to sustain increasingly permanent market sites" (Wormald 2004b: 3).

[101] Freeman 1872: 46.

proved lasting. Stenton concluded that Ine "was a statesman with ideas beyond the grasp of any of his predecessors," his lawbook "stand[ing] for a new conception of kingship, destined in time to replace the simple motives which had satisfied the men of an earlier age."[102] There is probably no reason to dissent from these views, though it seems fair to wonder if the laws of Ine would enjoy such a reputation were they not so closely associated with Alfred's. Nor is the "new conception of kingship" they are held to manifest as obvious a feature of Ine's laws as Stenton maintains. Like much legislation of its time, this text seems more plausibly understood as an assemblage of judgments issued perhaps over decades in response to varied disputes.[103] But Ine may appropriately be credited with "set[ting] the style of West-Saxon kingship before the days of its greatness" and thereby establishing patterns of royal behavior on which Alfred would draw amid more severe crises some two centuries later.[104]

Ine's most far-reaching achievement, like Æthelberht's nearly a century before, was to have assembled laws in writing for a kingdom that theretofore had seen no use in employing the written medium for such purposes. His doing so brought to Wessex a tool of governance on which Kent had until then held the monopoly. That the laws of Ine were longer than anything attempted in Kent is probably no indifferent detail either. Clauses shared with the much briefer laws of Wihtred suggest that laws were written at this time at least in part to be broadcast beyond the kingdoms in which they originated, their reproduction being perhaps seen as evidence of prosperity and stability. That legislation at this point might take on an "international" aspect may help explain why Ine's laws are the first documents in the vernacular to make reference to the English as a people (§§24, 47.1, 58, 75). In doing so, Ine's laws favor the vernacular form of the term (*Angli*) used at roughly the same time by Bede and Boniface to refer to the post-conversion English, their usage reflecting Bede's "concept

---

[102] Stenton 1947: 70–71. See also Richardson and Sayles 1966: "The legislator is coming to understand his task better. Ine's legislation strikes one as more mature, less experimental in some ways, than the surviving body of Kentish law."

[103] See Chapter 2, 51–52.

[104] Wormald 2004b: 4. Of particular interest is the way in which Ine asserts royal authority over lawmaking (in contrast to Wihtred) in his Preface: see Chapter 2, 52.

of a people who were 'Saxons' when pagan, but English from the moment of their reception of the Gregorian mission."[105] Bede's purpose was, in part, to hint that the evangelization of England had effectively brought about at least the possibility of a new political entity in which the bonds of Christian fraternity would supersede older ethnic divisions and rivalries.[106] The language of Ine's laws perhaps shows such a development unfolding some decades before the completion of Bede's *Historia,* though the extent to which his laws reflect the intellectual atmosphere of his time is difficult to know.

The Ninth Century: Ascendancy and Near-Collapse

We have seen that, prior to the second quarter of the eighth century, a succession of West-Saxon kings had exhausted themselves in largely fruitless attempts to expand their empire eastward. That Alfred would at least not count this among his worries is owing in part to the expansion of Mercian hegemony under Offa, who managed to do what Cædwalla and Ine could not upon effecting the subjugation of Sussex and Kent.[107] The Battle of Ellendun in 825, which saw the defeat of Offa's successor Beornwulf by Ecgberht, King of Wessex (r.802–839), put these territories under West-Saxon control.[108] A subsequent alliance between Mercia and Wessex is evidenced by a shared coinage that persisted into the reign of Alfred.[109] Though his reign is not well documented, it is undoubtedly under Ecgberht, grandfather of Alfred and (arguably) descendant of Ine's brother Ingeld, that the West-Saxon kingdom began to realize its seventh-century ambitions. Ecgberht was also able to establish Frankish connections that would be drawn upon by his descendants,

---

[105] Brooks 2003: 36; see also Wormald 1994: 13.
[106] Brooks 2003: 36: "His [Bede's] purpose [in once employing the term *gens Anglorum sive Saxonum*] was to prepare the reader for the fact that the pagan people that in Book I he had hitherto called 'Saxons' were to be termed 'English' (*Angli*) and to be regarded as one people from the moment of the arrival of the Gregorian mission."
[107] Stenton 1947: 206–209.
[108] The event is narrated under the year 823 in the A and E versions of the *Anglo-Saxon Chronicle* (Plummer and Earle 1892: 60–61; on the erroneous date, see Plummer and Earle , 1899: 70–71; also Bately 1986: 41).
[109] Keynes and Lapidge 1983: 12, 37.

having spent a period of exile in Charlemagne's court in Aachen before becoming king of Wessex.[110]

That the territorial rivalries of the seventh century should begin to abate in the first half of the ninth was fortunate given the troubles to come. The fate of King Edmund of East Anglia, martyred in 869 at the hands of Ívarr the Boneless, shows how helpless Anglo-Saxon kings sometimes were to confront Viking aggression.[111] Alfred's father Æthelwulf (839–858) enjoyed better luck, defeating a large invasion at *Aclea* in 851.[112] But his victory also coincides, according to the *Chronicle*, with the first wintering of the Danes in England. Four years later, Æthelwulf granted a tenth of his land to the church for the good of his soul and undertook that same year a pilgrimage to Rome, acquiring along the way a daughter of Charles the Bald as a wife. He returned from Francia to a kingdom left in disarray by the rebellion of his son Æthelbald, a subject "about which the Chronicle is curiously silent."[113] Upon Æthelwulf's death two years later, Wessex was a divided kingdom, with Æthelbald ruling Wessex and Æthelberht the people of Kent, Essex, and Sussex.

FIGURE I Rings given by Alfred's father Æthelwulf (right) and sister Æthelswith (left), probably as tokens of fidelity to the royal household. Photograph © Trustees of the British Museum.

---

[110] Yorke 1995: 94.
[111] The king's martyrdom is memorialized in Ælfric's "Passion of St. Edmund," Skeat 1890–1900: II, 314–335.
[112] *Anglo-Saxon Chronicle* (MS A), s.a.
[113] Smith 1935 [repr. 1966: 21 and n.]. The rebellion, as Smith notes, is discussed only in Asser's biography of Alfred.

In the *Anglo-Saxon Chronicle*, the years between Æthelwulf's demise and the accession of Alfred are a bleak litany of catastrophes wrought by the Vikings that the now bicephalous kingdom of Wessex sought ineffectually to contain. The first seven years of Alfred's reign likewise saw unrelenting crises occasioned by the arrival of Viking armies. Having already seized Northumbria, they began to control much of Mercia as well, even taking what was then the Mercian city of London.[114] Viking dominance of Mercia allowed their forces to move deep into Wessex and ultimately render Alfred a fugitive. It was at Athelney (to become later in Alfred's reign the site of one of two monasteries established by the king) that Alfred seems to have hit his lowest point; accounts of his experiences there bear likely signs of imaginative embellishment.[115] Shortly thereafter, in 878, he assembled forces to confront the Vikings at Edington (*Eþan dune*). His victory marks one of the most dramatic turning points in the history of English relations with the Vikings, and the treaty subsequently established with the Danish king Guthrum is Alfred's earliest known work of written legislation.[116] Less than a decade later, in 886, Alfred took London from the Vikings, a victory of such magnitude that it caused "all the English people that were not under subjection to the Danes" to submit to his rule.[117] In sentiment, if not in actuality, Alfred had become the first king of all the English-speaking peoples.

The aftermath of these triumphs occasioned a sudden profusion of documentary evidence, much of it in the vernacular, and much of it, as R. H. C. Davis pointed out, probably "originat[ing] with Alfred himself or his immediate entourage."[118] As we have seen, this evidence includes sources as fundamental to our knowledge of the pre-Conquest period as the *Anglo-Saxon Chronicle*.[119] Given the descent of these materials from the royal court, commentators have urged

---

[114] Keynes and Lapidge 1983: 20.

[115] Yorke 1995: 111.

[116] The event is the subject of a long entry for the year 878 (Plummer and Earle 1892: 75–77; Bately 1986: 50–51).

[117] Plummer and Earle 1892: 80 (MS A): *Þy ilcan geare gesette Ælfred cyning Lunden burg, ⁊ him all Angel cyn to cirde, þæt buton Deniscra monna hæftniede was.* Also Bately 1986: 53.

[118] Davis 1971: 169 [repr. 1991: 33].

[119] Yorke 1995: 104.

caution in making use of them: in J. M. Wallace-Hadrill's judgment, "We hold that Alfred was a great and glorious king in part because he tells us he was."[120] Such suspicions did not always accompany the reception of these texts. Like Cædmon, Alfred was once assumed a more prolific author than seems possible now, being credited with translations and original prose works whose composition required an advanced knowledge of Latin as well as considerable literary skill. The mood of scholarship is, at present, such that few will risk being too precise about the nature of his involvement in any of the texts attributed to him.[121] For some time, it has been customary to refer instead to an Alfredian "revival" of learning traceable in some fashion to one of the few texts now securely attributed to the king. That this text – the Preface to the Alfredian *Pastoral Care* – has enjoyed such success into the present, sharing with Wulfstan's *Sermo Lupi ad Anglos* a place in the textbooks from which generations of students have learned Old English, shows just how successful were Alfred's efforts to establish the terms on which he would be judged by history. Here Alfred laments the degradation of English learning prior to his reign, claiming, among other things, that he was not aware upon his accession of a single person south of the Thames able to understand the liturgy or translate from Latin into English.[122]

---

[120] Wallace-Hadrill 1950: 216–217. Pratt (2007: 2) notes that Wallace-Hadrill used more qualified language in a subsequent reissue of this essay.

[121] On this question, see especially Godden 2007: "[T]here have to be reservations about the proposition that Alfred had the time or the linguistic and intellectual skills required for such ambitious tasks of translation, adaptation, and expansion, an Alfred who spent much of his life in desperate warfare against invaders, who claimed that knowledge of Latin was non-existent in his kingdom when he became king at the age of 22, who did not learn Latin himself until he was 39 [...] and who apparently crammed his translation programme into the last six years or less of his life, of which the first three were dominated by extensive warfare against Viking armies" (2). But cf. Discenza 2005: 1 n. 1 and Chapter 4, who supports forcefully Alfred's role as author of texts now attributed to him; also Bately 2009, which asks penetrating methodological questions about some studies that argue against the integrity of the Alfredian corpus. Mediating this dispute is well beyond the ambit of the present volume. Subsequent references, explicit and implicit, to Alfred as the "author" of the *domboc* and other texts, should be understood as a matter of expediency, implying nothing about the author's sense of his own role in their composition.

[122] "There were so few of them that I cannot remember a single one south of the Thames when I came to the throne" (*Swæ feawa hiora wæron ðæt ic furðum anne*

Studies by Lapidge and Brooks show this judgment to be not far from the mark, though others urge a more qualified view.[123]

Whether the Preface may be used as a source of broader historical knowledge is a matter for separate consideration. Though replete with the sorts of details about life in ninth-century Wessex eagerly seized on given their scarcity for this period, its observations about the state of learning seem meant above all to lay the groundwork for the programme of education devised by Alfred, which would have as many free-born men as were willing receive instruction from clergy on how to read in their own language.[124] Such measures were intended ostensibly to ensure that the Latin works that had accumulated in Northumbrian monasteries during the seventh and eighth centuries had some audience among the elite members of late-ninth-century English society, even if not in their original language.[125] It should not be overlooked, however, that concerns extraneous to the situation of ninth-century Wessex may also have contributed to Alfred's ambitions. An attempt by the Frankish king Chilperic I (r.561–584) to add characters to the Latin alphabet, "presumably to facilitate the writing of Germanic words," suggests that cultivation of the vernacular had been a goal long sought by kings in western Europe.[126] According to Gregory of Tours, Chilperic "sent instructions to all the cities in his kingdom, saying that these letters should be taught to boys in school, and that books using the old characters should have them erased with pumice-stone and the new ones written in."[127] Though the significance of the reforms sought by

---

ánlepne ne mæg geðencean besuðan Temese ða ða ic to rice feng); Sweet 1871: I, 3; Schreiber 2002: 191.

[123] See Lapidge 1996: 409–454; Brooks 1984: 164–174 at 171–172: "By the 870s it is clear that the decline of learning in the Canterbury community had produced a crisis. [...] The truth, as far as the metropolitan see is concerned, of Alfred's assertion that he could remember no-one at his accession (871) who could comprehend their services or even translate a letter from Latin is witnessed by a number of Canterbury charters." For an attempted refinement of these views, see Snook 2015: 38–41.

[124] Sweet 1871: I, 6.

[125] On the state of literacy in Alfredian England, see Morrish 1986; Thijs 2005.

[126] Murdoch 1983: 9.

[127] Krusch and Levison 1937–1951: 254 (V.44): "Et misit epistulas in universis civitatibus regni sui, ut sic pueri docerentur ac libri antiquitus scripti, planati pomice, rescriberentur"; Thorpe 1974: 312. Thorpe observes (n. 94) that "[n]one of the

Chilperic, which in any event came to nothing, has long been a matter of debate, it seems reasonable to agree with one commentator that the changes sought were intended to make Latin orthography more accommodating to composition in the Germanic vernaculars of Francia.[128] The letters in question, misunderstood by Gregory of Tours, may well have been drawn from the Runic alphabet. According to Nicholas Brooks, their introduction may even have been "intended for schoolbooks written in the language of the Franks but in the letters of the Roman alphabet."[129]

Though the reforms sought by Chilperic may have fallen flat, the durability of the thinking behind them is perhaps attested by the broader use of the vernacular for official purposes evident in the Carolingian era.[130] The most celebrated examples of such developments are the *Strasbourg Oaths* establishing a treaty between Charles the Bald and Louis the German in 842.[131] But the partial survival of an Old High German version of the *Lex Salica Carolina* dating to the early ninth century is probably no less revealing of wider tendencies at work in these years.[132] That the expansion of vernacular writing owed something to direct pressure from Aachen has seemed inevitable to a number of commentators. But we possess no Carolingian directives to this effect as clear as is Alfred's for his bishops.[133] Instead, Einhard's observations are the fullest witnesses to Charlemagne's interest in such undertakings. In his *Vita* we are told that Charlemagne commanded to be written down the *barbara et antiquissima carmina* that memorialized the deeds and wars of great kings, and it was presumably in connection with such aims that Charlemagne even began a grammar of his own tongue (*inchoavit et grammaticam patrii sermonis*).[134] No such text survives, but

poems of King Chilperic has survived," but the commentary of Krusch and Levison's edition (254 n. 1) indicates otherwise.

[128] Sanders 1972: 83: "wollte er das lateinische Alphabet auch für die Schreibung des Fränkischen gefügiger machen."

[129] Brooks 2015: 127.

[130] Karl Ubl (2014: 10) discerns continuities between Chilperic's activities and Charlemagne's.

[131] For discussion of the Old High German portion, see Murdoch 1983: 18–19.

[132] Sonderegger 1964: 114.

[133] See Mühlpfordt 1956: 296; McKitterick 2008: 318.

[134] Waitz 1911: 33 (Chapter 29); *barbara* is taken by the editor (n. 4) to be a synonym for "Germanic." On the "grammar" and its disputed meaning, see Green 1994: 45.

Einhard's account of Charles's preoccupations appears trustworthy, given Chilperic's earlier dilettantism.

Nor was an interest in the renewal of legal learning isolated to the Germanic kingdoms. A striking parallel to the career of Alfred is evident in the reign of one near-contemporary monarch, the Byzantine emperor Leo VI (r.886–912), who likewise found the time amid various crises and humiliations to "sponsor[] the *Basilica*, the greatest legislative achievement since Justinian I, and other works on law, protocol, and strategy that won him the epithet of the Wise."[135] The ambitions of the *Basilica*, whose contents stretched back to the reign of Justinian, are perhaps paralleled by the early ninth-century collection of Carolingian capitularies by Ansegisus and analogous compilations of older legislative materials dating to this period.[136] In 895, four years before the death of Alfred, the little town of Trebur became the site of "one of the most important assemblies of the Carolingian age."[137] The text that resulted, itself laden with biblical allusions, offers an heretofore unrecognized analogue to a peculiar clause of Alfred's laws (§15). Even if they were not available to Alfred and his circle, all of the texts just mentioned suggest the atmosphere of legislative monumentalism in which the *domboc* took shape.

Evidence in the Preface of a different crisis – the decline of monasticism itself in the years leading up to Alfred's accession – is less disputed. The problem is considered as well by Asser, though he admits uncertainty as to its causes (*nescio quare*) while describing a plurality of likely culprits, not the least of them foreign invasions (*alienigenarum infestationibus*).[138] But however much Alfred's concerns seem to anticipate those of the mid-tenth-century monastic reform movement, it now seems doubtful that Alfred had much interest in a revival of monasticism as an end in itself.[139] His establishment of a nunnery at Shaftesbury and a monastery at Athelney, though they appear to reflect the first such efforts in a century, conform to a pattern held to by earlier kings in which monastic houses

---

[135] Treadgold 1997: 470.
[136] For an overview, see McKitterick 2008: 264–266.
[137] Carroll 2001: 9.
[138] Stevenson 1959: 81 (cap. 93).
[139] Yorke 1995: 203.

were set up primarily to serve the interests of the royal household.[140] It would seem instead that the main significance of the Preface to the history of kingship in Wessex lies elsewhere. That Alfred begins the letter with a lengthy allusion to the Northumbrian golden age, when York Minster furnished the court of Charles the Great with one of its leading theologians, suggests the associations with which he hoped his audience would view his own efforts to assemble a cohort of eminent Frankish and Mercian clergy. As did Æthelberht centuries before (and on a more modest scale), Alfred drew on practices inaugurated in West Francia to establish himself as a king of international importance, perhaps even consciously modeling himself on Charlemagne.[141] Even Alfred's self-designation as *Angulsaxonum rex* in late charters may represent a further self-conscious adoption of terms long used on the Continent (and earlier hinted at by Bede), though this resolution of long-standing terminological uncertainties probably had as much to do with religious as "national" aspirations given the manner in which this phrase unites two terms previously used to designate not distinct political entities but rather the Christian and pagan populations of England.[142]

Such hinting at the significance of his reign, risible if indulged in by one of Alfred's predecessors of the seventh or eighth century,

[140] This is, at any rate, the conclusion of Yorke (1995: 203). But see Blair 2005: 347: "His principal religious foundations, for monks at Athelney and for nuns at Shaftesbury, were both monastic in a strict sense, and it was evidently the official stance of his court that the 'true' monastic life, as practised on the Continent and formerly in England, was more virtuous than that lived in contemporary English minsters. [...] Such views in Alfred's circle, doubtless genuinely felt, began a broadening of horizons that was to culminate in monastic reform under Eadgar." Cf. also Dumville 1992: 193.

[141] This seems to be one of the points made in Godden 2007, who likens the Preface to Charlemagne's *Epistula de litteris colendis* (authored by Alcuin); the latter is "a personal letter to individual churchmen complaining about the low standards of Latinity among the clergy, urging their participation in reform, and proposing the establishment of schools" (4).

[142] For a catalogue of such usages in Alfredian documents and discussion of their pre-history, see Brooks 2003: 47. One of several notable usages on the Continent pre-dating Alfred's reign is found in Willibald's *Vita Bonifatii,* where it is said regarding the city of London, *usque hodie antiquo Anglorum Saxonumque vocabulo appellatur Lundenwich* (Levison 1905: 16 [§4]).

reveals the relatively secure position from which Alfred was able to envisage the reorganization of his sub-kingdoms and undertake the improvement of clerical and lay learning.[143] That the *domboc* bears so little resemblance to other legislation probably owes something to Alfred's unusual good fortune. His circumstances by the close of his reign resembled those of no prior English sovereign. The absorption of Mercia and Kent into a new West-Saxon overkingdom left in Alfred's hands the renewal of ecclesiastical institutions and of learning itself, both of which had prospered in England as in few other parts of western Europe until the close of the eighth century. It is not hard to imagine how such events might call for new approaches to the promulgation of royal law in what may have been the first such compilation since the reign of Offa (or Ine).

Yet the frames within which Alfred encloses his laws impede, perhaps deliberately, any efforts to read the *domboc* as the product of these historical circumstances. That it is in some way a response to Alfred's triumph over the Danes seems inevitable. But the latter are hardly mentioned in the *domboc,* being notably absent from the corpus of Alfredian prose as a whole with the exception of the *Anglo-Saxon Chronicle* and a few other documents. If its purpose were to administer a West-Saxon empire now encompassing the kingdoms of Kent and Mercia, it is difficult to see why so much of the *domboc* consists of materials not obviously applicable to their circumstances. The seeming deference to Mercia and Kent in its "second" Prologue was perhaps meant to ease the shock to their respective aristocracies as both kingdoms found themselves first overrun by Scandinavian armies and then, upon being rid of them, subject to the house of Cerdic.

While the *domboc* may close with the laws of Ine under the assumption that they were still in some respect binding on his

---

[143] And in the view of some scholars, texts appearing immediately after Alfred's reign, such as the Fonthill Letter, point to the success of his educational reform: "King Alfred's school may not have produced an Ælfric – that was to be the privilege of that other great English school almost a century later – but it certainly could provide responsive minds with a firm grounding in pragmatic literacy, if not more. The 'Fonthill Letter' attests to its efficacy in that respect" (Gretsch 1994: 98).

contemporaries, as remarks in his Prologue seem to suggest, their inclusion also allows Alfred's triumph over the Vikings (and consequent sway over most English-speaking territory) to be viewed as the fulfillment of long-cultivated West-Saxon ambitions: an impression perhaps adventitiously deepened by Ine's earlier use of the word *Englisc* when referring to those of his subjects who shared his language and his obedience to Rome in matters of doctrine.[144] As with

FIGURE 2 A silver penny of Alfred excavated at Winchester (CG 306, WCM C.4159; Blunt and Dolley 2012: 612 [no. 4]). Its legend (✠AELFREDREXSA✠, "Alfred Rex Sa[xonum]") seems to exhibit the same search for an appropriate name for his people also evidenced in Alfredian charters and other documents. (Courtesy of the Winchester Excavations Committee.)

[144] Alfred's claim that he "requested [the laws of prior kings] to be held in another respect" (*on oðre wisan bebead to healdanne*) should be weighed against the clauses of Alfred's laws that contradict or otherwise diverge from Ine's, on which see Wormald 1999a: 279. Wormald's suggested paraphrase is worth quoting in full: "I made a collection of 'synod-books,' and selected some for inclusion while rejecting what neither I nor my counsellors liked. But when I found precedents set in the reigns of Ine, Offa or Æthelberht, I allowed myself to be influenced by those with the most potential and left the others alone" (1999: 279–280). There is ground for being a little less confident than Wormald about the meaning of "synod-books" in this portion of the *domboc* (a matter to be taken up subsequently) but otherwise little here to dispute. Charles-Edwards (2013: 429) notes that Ine's British subjects "had remained faithful to the traditional Easter date followed by the Britons, the Irish and the Picts even though the West Saxon Church had long followed Roman practice."

most Alfredian texts, it may be assumed here that rhetorical purposes were at least as important as practical concerns in determining the shape the *domboc* would assume.

Properly understood, Alfred's *domboc* may be seen as a text that begins and ends, much like the famous Preface, with retrospection. The preoccupation of the *domboc*'s Prologue in particular with historical questions was rightly identified by Liebermann as one of its chief peculiarities when compared with other legislation of the period. The Prologue perhaps reflects the thoughts of a people whose political and religious institutions had very nearly escaped annihilation by the Danes and would now have to be rebuilt in ways that shunned the errors of the past.[145] Of particular concern was the neglect of instruction in literacy (a great worry to Charlemagne's court as well, as evidenced by texts such as the celebrated *De litteris colendis*). That English institutions at least seemed as if they were being reconstituted almost *ex nihilo* may explain the monumental and encyclopedic character of the *domboc*. Such circumstances, which also left Alfred with a freer hand than any prior king in crafting legislation, may account as well for the many apparent innovations of his laws, which will see further discussion in later sections.

What has just been said about the *domboc* is of course at odds with its self-presentation. While departing from convention, the *domboc* simultaneously works harder than any other legislation of its time to give the impression that nothing had changed. In place of the narrative furnished by his own and his contemporaries' experience – of a disaster narrowly averted, perhaps through divine intervention – the *domboc* posits instead the largely uninterrupted development of a legal order whose stewardship Providence has now assigned to Wessex. In narrating the divine origins and subsequent development of written law, the *domboc* leaps as easily from Sinai to the apostolic era as it does from seventh-century

---

[145] To describe the condition of Wessex upon Alfred's accession in such dire terms is probably not an overstatement: see, e.g., Wormald 1994.

England to Alfred's own lifetime.[146] That such continuities might be possible was doubtless a source of consolation amid the crises of the ninth century. Peeling away such rhetorical embellishment from the substance of Alfred's *domboc* will be among the tasks of the following chapter.

---

[146] "That a layman sought to construct a bridge between the world of Moses and that of the Church, that a lawgiver even attempted to shed light on the legal situation of his time in a historical manner, is remarkable for the ninth century" (*Dass ein Laie den Gegensatz zwischen Mosaismus und Kirche zu überbrücken, das ein Gesetzgeber historisch den Rechtszustand zu erklären auch nur versuchte, ist furs 9. Jh. bemerkenswert*). Liebermann 1903–1916: III, 35.

2

Legal Erudition in Seventh- and Ninth-century Wessex

Essential to Alfred's restoration of Latin and vernacular literacy within his newly expanded kingdom was the recruitment of clerical advisors from abroad – a lamentable necessity the king acknowledges in the Preface to his *Pastoral Care*.[1] Though the texts they brought with them can only be speculated about, we can be sure that monks such as Grimbald of St. Bertin and "John the Old Saxon" came bearing books and that their learning was made available to the king as he assembled the *domboc* much as it had been for his efforts with Gregory's *Regula pastoralis*.[2] While Alfred's enlistment of such figures was indeed a response to the crises of the earlier ninth century, it ought also be seen as an attempt to conform to expectations of governance in place at least by the late seventh century. Given his claims to have relied in some sense on the "instruction and teaching" of the bishops of London and Winchester, Ine had himself drawn upon native traditions of clerical learning in formulating his laws – or at least some of them – as

---

[1] Toward the outset of the Preface, Alfred observes "how foreigners came to this land in search of wisdom and instruction, and how we should now have to get them from abroad if we were to have them" (*hu man utanbordes wisdom 7 lare hieder on lond sohte, 7 hu we hie nu sceoldon ute begietan gif we hie habban sceoldon*); Sweet 1871: 1, 3; Schreiber 2002: 191.

[2] Both Grimbald (d.901) and "John the Old Saxon" – the epithet derives from Asser's biography (§94) – outlived Alfred, the latter significantly. For a possible example of the learning brought to Alfred's court by John, see Lapidge 1981: 72–83.

is sure to have been the case for his contemporary Wihtred (in spite of the illiteracy he acknowledges elsewhere).[3] Indeed, Ine's laws show how rapidly written legislation had developed in the decades since Hloðhere and Eadric's ordinances, wherein it was presented as the mere vessel of an oral tradition on which it depended for its claims to authority. The likelihood that neighboring kings were consulting and even borrowing from one another's legislation – one implication of clauses shared by Ine's laws and Wihtred's, to be considered (among other subjects) in the present chapter – seems an outcome of heightened expectations for legal prose in elite circles, implying as it does that royal enactments might float free of the customs that occasioned them (or on which they depended for their binding force) and enter the atmosphere of intellectual cross-pollination.

We are, then, justified in assuming that Alfred's and Ine's laws owe as much to a range of textual antecedents – some specifically legislative, some not – as they do to "custom," an infinitely malleable substance in the hands of prior commentators that has probably been given more weight than necessary. Identifying the texts after which Ine and Alfred modeled their laws has proved, however, a source of particular frustration for editors and commentators.[4] In the case of Ine's laws, their emergence from one of the murkiest periods of English history makes reconstructing likely influences more a matter of conjecture than one might prefer. Even concrete instances of textual influence such as clauses shared by Ine's and Wihtred's laws raise as many questions as they resolve. Though these likely attest to exchanges of some sort between the royal

---

[3] On the increasing "bookishness" of law by Wihtred's lifetime (and evident in his laws), see Liebermann, 1903–1916: III, 23–24; Wormald 1999a: 102–103; Oliver 2002: 165–166. Wihtred's grant of immunity to Kentish secular and religious establishments (S21; Brooks and Kelly 2013: I, 294–303 [no. 7]) closes with a subscription "incorporat[ing] a reference to his illiteracy" (302) found in other charters witnessed by him (*propria manu signum sancte crucis pro ignorantia litterarum expressi*; Brooks and Kelly 2013: I, 298). The hints of Latinate phrasing in Ine's laws detected by Ivarsen (in press) should perhaps be seen as traces of the counsel offered by his bishops.

[4] Liebermann (1903–1916: III, 64) saw no trace of clerical learning anywhere beyond the first few clauses of Ine's laws. But in light particularly of Wormald's remarks (to be discussed later), Liebermann's view seems rather extreme.

households of Wessex and Kent, their usefulness in establishing a relative chronology for these texts has, as we will see, probably been overstated.

Alfred's *MP* and laws confront us with a different set of problems. Ostensibly we seem on safer ground here given the king's insistence that, in preparing the *domboc,* he relied on prior English legislation and dared not make many additions of his own. But we have seen that this assertion amounts to one of the conventional gestures of legislating kings in the early medieval West, most of whom emphasized the basis of their laws in traditions written and unwritten.[5] Alfred's use of this *topos* appears hard to reconcile with the seeming absence of any such indebtedness, though we cannot know with certainty in what form the earlier laws of Kent, Wessex, and (perhaps) Mercia were available to him.[6]

Much of what follows will attempt to disentangle these and other elements of legislative convention from the kinds of debts suggested by analysis of the *domboc.* Our discussion begins with Ine's laws, giving particular attention to their relations with Wihtred's. We move thence to *MP*, whose backgrounds remain one of the more controverted features of the *domboc.* Different but no less complicated questions suggested by the "second prologue," in which Alfred derives legislation in English from unnamed "synods," take up the remainder of the chapter. In the editions, readers will find more detailed discussions of possible sources of influence on particular clauses of Alfred's and Ine's laws.

Wessex and Kent: The Laws of Ine

Though it is by far the longest work of legislation in English to survive from the seventh century, Ine's code offers few clues as to when or how it first took shape. Alongside the authorities named as supplying Ine with "advice and instruction" somehow touching on its preparation, the king mentions Earconwald, Bishop of London. Earconwald's death, customarily dated 693x694, furnishes for most commentators the only secure *terminus ad*

---

[5] See Wormald 1977: 113.
[6] This matter is discussed later in the present chapter (69–76).

quem.[7] In contrast, the laws of Wihtred establish the date and setting of their promulgation in remarkable detail. We are told that they result from an assembly of bishops taking place during "the fifth winter [year] of his reign, in the ninth indiction, sixth day of Rugern, in that place which is called Berghamstead."[8] According to Bede, Wihtred "died on 23 April" in the year 725, leaving to his sons "the kingdom which he had governed for thirty-four and a half years."[9] His accession may thus be assigned to the year 690, and the fifth year of his reign, when assumed to proceed from this year, "tallies with the date established by that of the indiction," according to Oliver.[10] The result would seem to be that, should Wihtred share any contents with Ine, the former, being a year or so later, must be the borrower.

Liebermann's edition appears to have been the first in which such an argument was put forth.[11] It has not met with universal assent. In his edition of 1922, whose commentary otherwise depends closely on Liebermann's, Frederick Levi Attenborough retreats from such claims toward a more qualified description of their relationship, acknowledging "communication between the two courts" but refusing to speculate about the direction of borrowing.[12] Stenton's remark that commonalities between Ine's laws and Wihtred's show the latter to have been "legislating in the same spirit at the same time" signals further backpedaling, as does, in our own era, Carole Hough's assertion that materials shared by the two compilations show "a degree

---

[7] The king also names as acting in this capacity "Cenred my father and Hædde my bishop." On the career of Earconwald, see Bede, *HE* IV.6 (Colgrave and Mynors 1969: 355 n. 3).

[8] Oliver 2002: 153. *Rugern* means "rye-harvest"; see Oliver 2002: 165

[9] *HE* v.23; Colgrave and Mynors 1969: 556–567.

[10] Oliver 2002: 165. Establishing what is meant here by "the ninth indiction," a standard form of reckoning time in documents of this period, is a matter of some complexity. See also Liebermann 1903–1916: III, 24.

[11] Liebermann 1903–1916: III, 23–24. An earlier and somewhat fuller version of the arguments presented in this section is given in Jurasinski 2019.

[12] Attenborough 1922: 3; also Attenborough 1922: 34: "It has been observed that cap. 20 of Ine's laws is practically identical with cap. 28 of Wihtred's laws, which date from 695. This may be regarded as pointing to communication between the governing authorities of the two kingdoms, such as would naturally follow the restoration of friendly relations in 694."

of co-operation between the kingdoms of Wessex and of Kent."[13] Oliver is similarly guarded in her assessment of Liebermann's thesis. A clause repeated nearly verbatim in both texts (*Ine* §20; *Wihtred* §23 [L28]) that had seemed to Liebermann irrefutable evidence of influence from Ine may instead "stem from a common original."[14]

Reservations expressed in the works just mentioned seem warranted. Prefatory remarks in each compilation may indeed place the codes of Wihtred and Ine about a year apart. Whether the laws themselves should be so dated is another question. Some of the hazards of assuming lines of transmission as clear as those envisaged by Liebermann are suggested by Wormald's observations regarding the disorder of Ine's laws, which in his view exceeded that of any legislation issued in Old English before or after: "Granted that the organization of early medieval *leges* can be baffling, it beggars belief that logical arrangement can have been so constantly defied as here."[15] One sees in Ine's laws "not just a recurrent topic but near-identical wording."[16] Such anomalies point to a severe disjunction between the code's preface and the realities surrounding its composition: "It is hard to see how Ine's laws could appear in the order that they do, were the code in any way pre-planned. [...] The most plausible conclusion is that Ine's so-called code was not a code at all but a series of enactments added to an original core over years or decades."[17] The most fruitful analogues to the peculiarities of Ine's laws may be

---

[13] Stenton 1947: 71n2; Hough 2014a: 2–25 at 9. D. P. Kirby (1991: 125) is likewise cautious: "The laws of Ine and Wihtred contain one clause in common concerning the need for a stranger to shout or blow his horn if straying off the trackway if he did not wish to be mistaken for a thief. This clause and the adoption in Wihtred's laws of the West Saxon term *gesið* for noble in place of the *eorlcund* of the laws of Aethelberht, Hlothhere and Eadric perhaps strengthen a possibility that some degree of collaboration attended the drawing up of these codes." Mary Richards's language (2014b: 303) seems to allow for the possibility of Wihtred's influence upon Ine; nonetheless, she affirms (given the assumed dates of the two codes) that *Wihtred* §23 [L28] is derived from *Ine*.

[14] Oliver 2002: 179.

[15] Wormald 1999b: 190.

[16] Wormald 1999b: 188. The repetitive chapters are (in Liebermann's numeration) "16 and 35, 28 and 35, 28 and 36, or 18 and 37."

[17] Wormald 1999a: 105; also Lambert 2017: 68, which suggests on the basis of Wormald's observations that "laws issued by later kings – perhaps even earlier ones – [may] have been falsely attributed to Ine here."

found not in other English legislation but in Latin laws issued on the Continent:

[I]t is well-known that *Lex Burgundionum* consists of a basic collection assembled by Gundobad, or more probably Sigismund, which was then supplemented by what it is not too much to call novella, one amounting to a mini-code in its own right. Here, the distinct origin of the later laws in the series is demonstrated by their explicit terms of reference and/or dating. Yet *Lex Burgundionum* appears in nearly all manuscripts as a continuous sequence of numbered chapters.[18]

Much the same phenomenon is witnessed according to Wormald in recensions of the *Lex Salica,* where subsequent capitularies "are numbered in some manuscripts as if they were further chapters of the 'sixty-five title' text," leading to repetitions not unlike those found in Ine. Comparanda such as these suggest that the text presented in the *domboc* as the code of Ine "is in fact a series of statutes, each designed to deal with newly obtruding concerns." Wormald's conclusion bears great significance for attempts to fix a date on Ine's laws: "[N]one of them after the first [set] need be Ine's."[19]

Other aspects of Ine's laws not considered by Wormald likewise suggest a text much less stable than typically thought. One implicit assumption of Liebermann's thesis is that Ine's preface functions in much the same way as Wihtred's, naming authorities consulted and assemblies held in order to fix the date at which the text was issued. But the language of Ine's preface seems notably ambiguous when compared to Wihtred's. It is true that, like Wihtred, Ine attributes some of his laws to an ecclesiastical assembly, in this case a "great convocation of the servants of God" (7 *éac micelre gesomnunge Godes ðeowa,* literally "and also a great assembly of God's servants") of unknown date. The "also" (*eac*) perhaps signals that the deliberations of this assembly should be distinguished from advice given by his most intimate counselors mentioned at the outset of the preface. The character of the assembly may be guessed at. Attenborough held that *Godes ðeowa[s]* "denotes the whole of the clergy both secular and regular," noting the elaboration on this term

18 Wormald 1999b: 190.
19 Wormald 1999b: 191.

in v *Æthelred* §4, where "*Godes þeowas* are defined as *biscopas and abbudas, munecas and mynecena, preostas and nunnan.*"[20] But a more apt parallel was originally suggested (if not pursued to its logical conclusion) by Liebermann. §4 of Willibald's *Vita Bonifatii* describes a synod convoked by Ine on the occasion of a rebellion. The assembly, organized by the bishops (*a primatibus æcclesiarum*), includes the abbots of Nursling, Tisbury, and Glastonbury, who exercise a leading role.[21] Such evidence seems to weigh in favor of interpreting the assembled "servants of God" referred to in Ine's laws as abbots, some of whom may well have been erstwhile members of the nobility.[22] The language of *Ine* §1 ("First we command that God's servants [*Godes ðeowas*] hold their proper rule according to law") does not contradict such a view even though the provisions immediately following deal with matters of pastoral care. As Nicholas Brooks noted, "the distinction between monks living the regular life and a body of clerks who lived under communal discipline had not always been apparent" as late as the ninth century; where secular clergy "adopted the common life, their establishment [was] frequently termed an *abatia* or *monasterium,* and the inmates *fratres* or even *monachi.*"[23]

The foregoing suggests that Ine refers in his preface to two distinct sources of counsel: that of his bishops and father, whose advice was given as needed and over an indefinite period of time, and that offered by an assembly of regular and secular clergy perhaps like the one described in Willibald's *Vita Bonifatii.* Nor does Ine's preface echo Wihtred's in holding the assembly to be the exclusive source of the laws. Its purpose was merely to offer counsel to Ine, who assumes for himself an essential part in determining the content of the laws: *Ic Ine [...] wæs smeagende be ðære hælo urra sawla 7 be*

---

[20] Attenborough 1922: 183 n. 3.

[21] Liebermann 1903–1916: II, 432 (4a); Haddan and Stubbs 1871: 295–296. Attendance by abbots and even high-ranking members of the laity was a feature of many synods convoked in this period: see Keynes 1993: 25–27; Cubitt 1995: 44–47 (on lay attendance).

[22] To tonsure a rival king and compel him to seek exile in a monastery was in Ine's day a typical way of forcing an opponent into retirement: see Stancliffe 1983: 155 n. 7. Some form of the practice is possibly alluded to in *Alfred* §36.4, and one may imagine that the same procedure might be applied to elite figures other than kings.

[23] Brooks 1984: 188.

ðam staþole ures rices, lit. "I, Ine [...] was thinking about the
health of our souls and about the security of our kingdom." As much
as the distribution of provisions, the preface points to a code of com-
posite and perhaps disparate origins.

Whether more material may have entered Ine's laws once promulgated under the circumstances alluded to in the preface – a possibility all but conceded by Wormald – seems the crucial question. The
first several clauses, perhaps amounting to Wormald's "original core"
of provisions, seem like what might emerge from an assembly of
"God's servants" like the one described in the *Vita Bonifatii.* Issued
in the first-person plural (*We beodað* ...), they are a series of injunc-
tions on matters of manifest concern to clerics, requiring that infants
be promptly baptized, Sunday labor shunned, church dues paid, and
sanctuary honored. They bear the closest resemblance to the principal parts of Wihtred's laws, where a focus on ecclesiastical matters
predominates.

But the code soon (by §6) drifts more or less permanently into
subjects not likely of much interest to churchmen. What bishop or
abbot would have weighed in on the fine to be paid by the owner of
pigs intruding on another's pasture, or on the thickness of bacon
paid as rent?[24] Questions dealt with in these clauses might very well
have risen to the attention of Ine and his ealdormen during their
exercise of appellate jurisdiction, and resulting decisions may have
been added to the text(s) of Ine's code over the course of his long
reign. The ensuing repetitions attest to the many years over which
this process must have unfolded.

For the purposes of establishing some relative chronology
between the laws of Ine and Wihtred, it is significant that the same
impression of episcopal edicts trailing apparently extraneous secular
laws is suggested even by the latter, whose "heavily ecclesiastical
code finishes with a set of clauses on the killing or capture of thieves
with no obvious rationale in this setting save as textual borrowings
from Ine."[25] Liebermann likewise conceded that the concluding section of Wihtred's laws seems "a mere appendage" (*ein blosses*

---

[24] *Ine* §§51–52.
[25] Wormald 1999a: 102. Wormald surely misspoke here, as only one of the clauses in
    question (§23 [L28]) is an alleged borrowing from Ine.

Anhängsel), its "xenophobic attitude" (*fremdenfeindliche Sinn*) being at odds with the sensibility of the church, which sought friendly dealings among the minor kingdoms of England.[26] The likelihood seems great that the codes of both Ine and Wihtred as we now have them result from secular judgments fastening themselves over time to the texts of synodal decrees.

For Wormald, the circumstances just described cast no doubts on Liebermann's relative chronology: "[T]he fact that at least one of [Ine's] laws was echoed by Wihtred confirms that his code (or part of it) dates to the first years of his reign."[27] But does the instability of these texts, both of which show signs of growth beyond the circumstances described in their prefaces, permit such a conclusion? Given the evidence for a text that accumulated over the decades of Ine's reign, are we obliged to see the death of Earconwald as the point beyond which nothing can have been added to Ine's "code"? To persist in assuming, as did Liebermann and (with qualifications) Wormald, that Ine's laws appeared just in time to supply material to Wihtred's ignores the evidence, acknowledged by both, that the extant versions of these texts reflect further development as documents of secular law, more vigorous in the case of Ine, beyond their stated origins.

Such possibilities cast in a different light the matter of the "echoed" clauses raised by Wormald (*Ine* §20/*Wihtred* §23 [L28], *Wihtred* §§8–8.2 [L9–11]/*Ine* §§3–3.2, *Ine* §12/*Wihtred* §20 [L25]). Fuller discussion of these will be found in the commentary of the present edition. Suffice it to say now that, with the exception of *Ine* §20/*Wihtred* §23 [L28], the echoes seem faint indeed and give little confidence about which text was the borrower. (How *Ine* §12 and *Wihtred* §20 [L25] entered this list is unclear, as they seem at odds with one another and show no similarities in phrasing.) As for the first of these – the well-known clause treating as a thief any traveler through a forest who "neither shouts nor blows a horn" – even this, as Oliver sensed, does not seem an unambiguous case of borrowing from Ine. It is true, as Liebermann and Wormald both note, that *Wihtred* §23 [L28], the last clause of the code, seems inharmonious

---

[26] Liebermann 1903–1916: III, 30 n. on *Wihtred* §23 [L28].
[27] Wormald 1999a: 103.

with what came before. But this appears no less true of the impact of this clause in Ine's code, where neighboring provisions seem to spread from it like ripples from a drop of water. At §16, Ine had established that "He who kills a thief may declare on oath, that he killed him because he was [found] guilty [in the act]; this does not apply to his associates." After *Ine* §20 (=*Wihtred* §23 [L28]), which permits the presumptive thief to be slain or held for ransom, the condition laid down in §16 must be stated again (§20.1); the clause immediately following lays down what is to be done if the slayer of the alleged thief should have concealed this act. The repetitions and qualifications that surround it may indicate that the clause did not sit comfortably in Ine's laws either. Certainly it seems an unlikely part of its putative "original core." *Ine* §20/*Wihtred* §23 [L28] also seems to contradict *Ine* §28 – as it does *Wihtred* §21 [L26] – both of which reserve to the king alone the power to fix the punishment of a captured thief. Given its discordance with the prevailing emphases of both Ine's and Wihtred's laws, its derivation from some source common to both, the possibility suggested by Oliver, seems more probable than its transmission from Ine to Wihtred. The hypothetical source need not have been clerical, as Liebermann supposed (only to dismiss the possibility).[28]

If the foregoing observations result in a more ambiguous picture of how the laws of Ine and Wihtred took shape than is found in other editions, the effect is probably salutary. The shadowy history

---

[28] Liebermann 1903–1916: III, 30 n. on *Wihtred* §28 [according to Liebermann's numeration]. Aside from these "borrowed" clauses, the evidence most often adduced to imply that Ine's laws exerted some sort of influence upon Wihtred is the latter's use of *gesiðcund* ("noble"), a West-Saxon word commonly attested in the *domboc*, in place of *eorlcund* (the equivalent used in prior Kentish laws): See Attenborough, 1922: 180 n. 5.1 ("The word *gesiðcund*, which is used in the laws of Ine and Alfred, now takes the place of the antiquated word *eorlcund*, which is used in the earlier codes"); also Oliver 2002: 155 n.a and 168. It is nowhere implied outright that use of the term indicates textual influence, nor does any such implication seem warranted, as this term may (as the most guarded assessments imply) merely appear in Wihtred's laws as a loanword. It should be noted that the career of Earconwald may shed some light on the similarities of Ine's and Wihtred's laws. As Kelly notes, "it seems very likely indeed that he had a family connection with the royal dynasty of the people of Kent. His name is ultimately Frankish, and it shares a first element with the names of several members of the Kentish dynasty, which was connected by marriage with the Merovingian royal house" (2015: 3). Earconwald was made Bishop of London by Theodore of Tarsus (4).

of England in the seventh century affords many opportunities for learning with Keats how to be "capable of being in uncertainties," and the relationship between Ine's and Wihtred's laws seems one instance in particular in which too much has been made of the little we know.[29] Particularly where Wessex is concerned, the scarcity of primary sources for this period permits little certainty about events of the late seventh century. Evidence discussed in the previous chapter of Ine's probably deferential relationship with Kent and its bishops, who were more powerful in Ine's time than in Alfred's, should at least caution against assuming that all apparent commonalities in Wihtred's and Ine's laws must issue from Wessex.

Ine and Alfred

The foregoing at least establishes with some certainty that, as early as the seventh century, vernacular laws were being read and refined even outside the kingdoms for whose benefit they were devised. We also see, though more pronouncedly in Wihtred's laws than in Ine's, that clerical learning was fundamental to royal legislation from the outset of its development. Their treatment by Alfred shows that Ine's laws were, by the late ninth century, part of the legal erudition of Wessex (and perhaps elsewhere). How long they enjoyed this status is impossible to say.

The extent to which Ine's laws functioned as sources for Alfred's is likewise unknowable in any absolute sense. We have already seen that Alfred cannot have left their provisions in place in spite of his assertions to the contrary.[30] It is more likely that Ine's laws influenced Alfred's in less tangible ways. Some appear to have furnished inspiration along with clauses of Exodus translated in the Prologue whose contents are revisited in the code proper.[31] The perhaps unprecedented extent to which royal clout is asserted in Ine's laws – their most conspicuous legacy for Alfred's – becomes clear when their preface is contrasted with Wihtred's code. Only in the latter's presumably inauthentic rubric are the laws attributed

[29] Gittings 2002: 41–42.
[30] See Chapter 1, 16.
[31] See, for example, *Ine* §44 (on burning a tree), *Alfred* §14.

directly to the king. The preface itself attributes composition of Wihtred's laws to "the great men" (*ða eadigan*) assembled at *Berghamstyde*.[32] Neither Ine nor Alfred was so self-effacing. As did Ine, Alfred fixes the promulgation of his laws to no particular place or time and assigns himself the leading role in their preparation. While the provisions of his laws may have found their way to the court through channels little affected by the exercise of royal authority, Ine appears to have been the first to assert forthrightly that assembling these judgments in writing was a matter over which the king had the final say.

As for the "advice and instruction" supplied by Cenred, Hædde, and Earconwald, might the counsel alluded to here be the sort offered Alfred by his circle of clerics? Perhaps, though some qualifications are probably in order. While Alfred similarly acknowledges their assistance in preparing the *domboc,* his clerics are presented as occupying a role less central than Ine's, nor does Alfred mention what must have been their crucial efforts in preparing the Prologue given its dealings with Scripture. In the event that Wihtred's laws represent anything like "the norm" for the late seventh century – a reasonable assumption given the centrality of Kent to the ecclesiastical organization of the English kingdoms – synods might in this period have furnished some of the raw materials for royal legislation. Alfred's may well have extended the drift away from this convention evident in the preface to Ine's code in having his own laws issue from no particular assembly at all.[33] Yet Alfred was probably mindful of Wihtred's example (among others) in asserting that legislative activity in England owed something to early "synods."

We thus may credit Ine with memorializing in writing, and perhaps establishing, a number of strategies that would prove fundamental to the Alfredian contents of the *domboc.* The royal persona encountered in the preface to Ine's laws – that of a king humbly taking counsel from secular and ecclesiastical elites before offering legislation *on his own* – may well have been newly devised. The sheer length and scope of Ine's laws, seventy-eight chapters covering

---

[32] Oliver 2002: 152.
[33] The Laws of Hloðhere and Eadric, issued no later than 686 (see Oliver 2002: 120), acknowledge no debt to clerical learning or instruction.

every conceivable contingency, made it a potent witness to the authority of written law in a period in which it doubtless struggled to compete with orally transmitted norms. Finally, the shared concerns of Wihtred's and Ine's laws suggest that royal legislation had come to be more than a record of *domas,* perhaps attaining the status of a prose genre whose effects went beyond the merely hortative.[34] That we associate such developments with Alfred shows how thoroughly he absorbed the lessons afforded by Ine's unusually long reign.

Backgrounds and Motivations: The Laws of Alfred

Compared with the last decades of the seventh century, the late ninth offers a relative wealth of textual evidence. This abundance creates its own problems. Before delving into them, some brief account of the likely purposes underlying Alfred's laws will be necessary. As Alfred himself stresses, his was by no means the first collection of laws to be issued under the authority of an English-speaking king and his *witan.*[35] Yet in spite of Alfred's insistence on the conservatism and restraint of his own undertaking, his *domboc* has no parallel among either prior English compositions or Frankish laws after which these may have been patterned, and the likelihood seems very great that it displays the same sort of inventiveness characteristic of other Alfredian texts.[36] In particular, its lengthy Prologue, which rivals the code proper in length, has long proved an enigma.

Most commentators date the text to the last years of Alfred's reign, primarily because it is difficult to imagine the king busied with such a project while still fending off Danish armies.[37] Beyond what is found in the text itself, we have no direct account of the circumstances behind Alfred's preparation of the *domboc.* But remarks in

---

[34] Wallace-Hadrill (1962: 116) noted that the *Lex Salica* attained early in its transmission the status of a "literary as well as a legal text" and held (116 n. 3) this generalization "appli[cable] to all the barbarian laws."

[35] See the last clause of the Prologue (edited here at the outset of the code proper).

[36] On Frankish inspiration, see Frantzen 1983: 125. O'Neill (2001: 74–76) notes a number of parallels, both in phrasing and in methods of translation, between the *domboc*'s Prologue and the Alfredian Prose Psalms.

[37] See Frantzen 1986: 11 n. 1, and the bibliography given there.

Asser's biography of the king may come close to fulfilling this function, in the process shedding some light on the Prologue in particular. Here we learn of Alfred's keen interest in the conduct of law, a feature of the biography to some extent corroborated by the Fonthill Letter, which recalls Alfred's role in adjudicating a case of theft.[38] According to Asser,

[Alfred] would carefully look into nearly all the judgments which were passed in his absence anywhere in the realm, to see whether they were just or unjust; and if he could identify any corruption in those judgments, he would ask the judges concerned politely, as is his wont, either in person or through one of his trusted men, why they had passed so unfair a sentence – whether through ignorance or because of some other malpractice (that is to say, either for love or fear of the one party or for hatred of the other, or even for the sake of a bribe).[39]

This section seems to have particular relevance to *MP* §§40–49 given their concern with judging and judicial malpractice. (Concern with correcting judicial abuses had been a recurrent theme in Carolingian writing, manifest particularly in the work of Theodulf of Orléans.)[40] Ealdormen and reeves may well have been among the intended addressees of the *domboc,* a conjecture supported by the opening statement in Edward the Elder's first collection of laws, which

---

[38] On the Fonthill Letter (S1445), see Brooks 2009; Brooks and Kelly 2013: II, 852–862 (no. 104); also Chapter 3, 98–101. Wormald (1999a: 118–125) also argues for the importance of Asser's account of Alfred's involvements with judges, though there are significant differences between his analysis and the one offered in the present volume. Briefly, Wormald sees Alfred as here urging the pursuit of wisdom on his judges and not simply literacy. But Alfred's concern for the latter seems more deserving of emphasis for reasons that will become evident later in this chapter. Certainly Wormald's arguments here against points made by the editor of Asser's *Life,* W. H. Stevenson, who had claimed that in these passages Asser showed ignorance of English law, seem necessary and wholly convincing.

[39] *Nam omnia pene totius suae regionis iudicia, quae in absentia sua fiebant, sagaciter investigabat, qualia fierent, iusta aut etiam iniusta, aut uero si aliquam in illis iudiciis iniquitatem intelligere posset, leniter utens suatim illos ipsos iudices, aut per se ipsum aut per alios suos fideles quoslibet interrogabat, quare tam nequiter iudicassent, utrum per ignorantiam aut propter aliam quamlibet malevolentiam, id est utrum pro aliquorum amore vel timore aut aliorum odio aut etiam pro alicuius pecuniae cupiditate.* Stevenson 1959: 93 (§ 106); Keynes and Lapidge 1983: 109.

[40] For an overview of Theodulf's treatment of judicial malpractice, see Geary 2008: 83–86.

assumes their familiarity with Alfred's legislation.[41] Likewise revealing is the rebuke of judicial ignorance attributed to Alfred by Asser
in the text that follows. Alfred is "astonished" at the "arrogance" of
his judges, who through both divine and royal authority "enjoyed
the status of wise men, yet have neglected the study and application
of wisdom."[42] Shaken by his criticism, the judges "applied themselves
in an amazing way to learning how to read, preferring rather to
learn this unfamiliar discipline (no matter how laboriously) than to
relinquish their offices of power."[43]

Some have asserted that, in having his *domboc* begin with a
selection of Mosaic laws, Alfred sought to acquaint his judges with
a model work of legislation, or even to endow his own laws with
some patina of divine authority.[44] But the pains taken by the
authors of the *domboc* to make the Torah fit for a Christian audience perhaps point to a broader emphasis on written law itself as
the preeminent tool in matters of adjudication. The currency of
such views is amply witnessed by Einhard's remark that
Charlemagne, upon assuming the imperial title, ordered all subject
nations that made use of unwritten laws to put these laws in writing.[45] The preeminence of written law as a tool of instruction for
judges is also made clear in Charlemagne's *Admonitio generalis*
(789), where diligent study of "law composed by wise men for the

---

[41] See 1 *Edward* (Prol.), Liebermann 1903–1916: I, 138; Keynes and Lapidge 1983:
275 n. 256.

[42] *Nimium admiror vestram hanc insolentiam, eo quod, Dei dono et meo, sapientium
ministerium et gradus usurpastis, sapientiae autem studium et operam neglexistis.*
Stevenson 1959: 93 (§ 106); Keynes and Lapidge 1983: 110.

[43] *praepositi ac ministri literatoriae arti studerent, malentes insuetam disciplinam
quam laboriose discere, quam potestatem ministeria dimittere.* Stevenson 1959: 94
(§ 106); Keynes and Lapidge 1983: 110.

[44] See Wormald 1999a: 425; for the latter interpretation, see Withers 1999: 59;
Wormald 2004: 13 ("To set West Saxon laws in the tradition inaugurated by God
through Moses implied that they were just as inspired, as binding, as God's laws");
also Snook 2015: 51.

[45] *Omnium tamen nationum, quae sub eius dominatu erant, iura quae scripta non
erant describere ac litteris mandari fecit.* Waitz 1911: 33 (Chapter 29). Wallace-
Hadrill (1962: 117) characterizes the reign of Charlemagne as a period in which
"traditional law was wearing thin and men wished to consult something written
before giving judgement."

people" (*lex a sapientibus populo conposita*) is the first obligation of those so occupied.[46] Indeed, the ends Alfred had in mind for the Prologue are amply suggested by Charlemagne's "General Capitulary" for the *dominici missi*. Issued in 802, this text promulgated a presumably new requirement "[t]hat judges shall judge justly in accordance with the written law, and not according to their own will" (*Ut iudices secundum scriptam legem iuste iudicent, non secundum arbitrium suum*).[47] That some in Wessex may have resented such impositions is conceivable, particularly given what Asser relates about Alfred's uncomfortable relations with his judges. Tracing these perhaps unwelcome "innovations" (in reality just a return to the Roman model) to the laws of Exodus likely afforded ready means of silencing such complaints.[48] Moreover, the invocation of Mosaic law with which Alfred's laws begin would have kindled associations with Josiah, already a "model of Carolingian kingship" who undertook a drastic reform of his kingdom in accordance with the words of a rediscovered scroll containing the Law.[49] Josiah's reforms (2 Kings 22–23) pointedly assert the supremacy of writing in matters of law.

That the text chosen for this purpose was an extract of the laws delivered at Sinai also has much to do with the role of Moses himself in the biblical narrative. The chapters leading up to those translated in the Prologue pertain to what has already been identified as a major impetus for the preparation of the *domboc*; they are concerned primarily with the role of judges in resolving the disputes of the newly liberated Israelites. Exodus 18 relates that Moses, at the urging of his father-in-law Jethro, abandoned his role as sole judge and established instead layers of appellate jurisdiction so that he would be obliged to deal only with the most difficult cases. While a

---

[46] Mordek, Zechiel-Eckes, and Glatthaar 2013: 212 (Chapter 62). The passage is discussed as well in Pratt (2007: 163), where it is taken to show the importance attached to "comital wisdom" rather than the written word itself. According to Wormald (2004: 13), "The main aim [of the *domboc*] was to show the West Saxons as a people of written law, like others made vehicles of civilization by God."

[47] Boretius 1883: 96 (§26); Munro 1900: 23.

[48] On the Roman view of customary law (as given in Justinian's *Digest*), see Preface, xiv.

[49] Contreni 1995: 107.

literary tradition in which the Anglo-Saxons were likened to biblical Israel on the basis of a shared history of migration perhaps played some role in making the laws of Moses the centerpiece of the Prologue, a likelier source of inspiration may have been the catastrophes that befell the English in the early years of Alfred's reign, which necessitated, as Alfred seems to suggest in his Preface to the *Pastoral Care,* a remaking of the social order not wholly unlike that undergone by the Hebrews of Exodus after being delivered from Egyptian captivity.[50]

The Prologue: Aims

The concern of the Prologue to establish the written medium as the basis of a stable legal order is anticipated by prefatory material in some of the earliest English legislation. While Alfred's was the first legislative prologue to adduce a lengthy selection of Mosaic law, we have seen that the legislative prologue itself was by the time Alfred prepared this text a well-established feature of royal lawmaking. The earliest of these in English, whose alliteration and rhythm point to deliberate rhetorical strategies that underlay their composition, occurs in the laws attributed to Hloðhere and Eadric. In this text, and in the preface to Wihtred's laws, we encounter a trio of legal terms (*æ/þeaw* "custom," *dom* "royal decree," and *eacan* "extend") found also in Alfred's.[51] The first two are particularly deserving of attention. As Wormald notes, it is not until Alfred's laws that we see *æ(w)* used in legislation to mean anything other than "unwritten custom"; *domas*, however, are from the earliest phases of written Old English associated with royal enactments.[52] That *æ(w)* has such a

---

[50] The point made here should be distinguished from the view (widely assumed) that literate persons in Anglo-Saxon England were in the habit of conceiving of their nation as a "chosen people" as biblical Israel had been. The thinness of evidence for this proposition is exposed in Molyneaux 2014; Heydemann (2020: 95) shows that such a notion was fundamentally alien to Christian thought from late antiquity through the Middle Ages.

[51] For a full discussion of how these early prologues dealt with questions of unwritten law, see Jurasinski 2015a.

[52] Wormald 1999a: 95 n. 330.

meaning in the Old English *Pastoral Care* as well suggests an Alfredian initiative of long standing.[53]

In all three texts, these terms structure the way in which kings envisage the relationship of their own legislation to custom and tradition. The earliest of the laws in question assert that Hloðhere and Eadric "extended the customary laws that their ancestors earlier wrought with these [written] judgments" (*ecton þa ǽ þa þe heora aldoras ær geworhton ðyssum domum*). Perhaps sensing that some under their rule will not welcome the substitution of royal legislation for custom, Hloðhere and Eadric attempt here to disguise the profound differences between the two forms of lawmaking by claiming to have merely "extended" ancient observances through writing.[54] Wihtred goes further, attributing his legislation (*domas*) to the great men of the kingdom (*ða eadigan*) who, in setting laws to writing, extended only the *just* customs of the people of Kent (*Cantwara rihtum þeawum æcton*). Evident here is a prerogative more forthrightly asserted to distinguish between sound and defective customs and to perpetuate the former through writing – one echoed toward the conclusion of Ine's preface, where *æ* and *domas* likewise see emphasis.

Though they are dispersed in the Prologue, *æ/þeaw, dom,* and the carefully chosen verb *eacan* further develop the themes just outlined in earlier Kentish and West-Saxon legislation.[55] (That Ine's laws omit the crucial *eacan* in their short preface suggests that Alfred's Prologue is here mindful of Kentish tradition in particular.) When Alfred refers to apostles sent to Antioch and Syria *Cristes æ to læranne* ("to teach Christ's law"), the term must, given the context, mean "(individual) decree" rather than "custom," making the ordinances designated by the term indistinguishable formally from the *domas* given to Moses at Sinai. (Alfred had already explored

---

[53] Sweet 1871: 28 (also Schreiber 2002: 217–219), where *æ* and *bebodu* are used interchangeably.

[54] On the changes wrought by the introduction of written law in Iceland, which probably furnish an appropriate analogy for the situation in early Anglo-Saxon England, see Miller 1991.

[55] The verb bears associations with duplication and human reproduction; *eacnan* meant "to become pregnant."

such possibilities in his partial rendering of the Psalms.)[56] As reimagined by Alfred, Christ makes use of the same device employed by early legislating kings in claiming not to abolish the laws of the Torah, but rather *mid eallum godum to ecanne,* "to extend them with all good (?laws)."[57] Old English *eacan,* here in the inflected infinitive, is no accurate translation of the Vulgate's *adimplere,* "fulfill."

Allusion has already been made to the "cynical" interpretation of Alfred's Prologue so often encountered in commentary of the past few decades, where it is assumed that Alfred makes use of the Bible for no other reason than to pilfer some of its authority.[58] The foregoing suggests that attributing such motives to Alfred is misguided – not to mention anachronistic given clerics' insistence that the Torah was a mere foreshadowing of the New Law.[59] Nonetheless, one may see in the Prologue's description of Christ's ministry how the language of politics and theology might become intermingled. The Old English terms just referred to have Christ adopt the same language whereby seventh-century kings smuggled new practices into observance while claiming to do no more than replicate ancient customs. Unconsciously, perhaps, Christ is here made to adopt the idiom and

---

[56] Cf. Ps. 1:2 (*sed in lege Domini voluntas eius, et in lege eius meditabitur die ac nocte*), given the following rendering by Alfred (O'Neill 2001: 100): *[A]c his willa byð on Godes æ, and ymb his æ he byð smeagende dæges and nihtes.*

[57] Interpretation of this passage hinges on how we understand *godum,* a dative plural adjective that may be understood here either as a substantive or as having its antecedent in the likewise plural *bebodu* "commandments, laws." According to Turk (1893: 31), the latter was to be preferred: "[T]hese Mosaic Laws are not abrogated by Christ under the new dispensation, for He desired but to augment them with all good (laws)." Liebermann rejected this quite sensible interpretation, perhaps because it conflicted with Schmid's; see Liebermann 1903–1916: III, 48 n. 6. The interpretation argued for by Turk is harmonious with Carolingian views on the Sermon on the Mount (manifest in legislation as much as commentaries), which presuppose that Christ did indeed emend the covenantal law: see Heydemann 2020: 118.

[58] For examples, see n. 42 of the present chapter.

[59] In his *Versus de patribus regibus sanctis Euboricensis ecclesiae,* Alcuin praises a beloved teacher (Ælberht of York) who "fathomed the depths of the rough and ancient law" (*rudis et veteris legis patefecit abyssum*) in the course of "revealing the great mysteries of holy Scripture" (*maxima Scripturae pandens mysteria sacrae*); the editor notes that the referent is plainly "the Old Testament" (Godman 1982: 114–115).

conventions of Saxon lawmaking, much as he does those of the *comitatus* in the *Dream of the Rood* and other heroic verse of the period.

Yet it seems more likely that theological rather than political concerns occasioned this disquieting translation. The rhetoric of seventh-century legislation perhaps offered a pleasing way to pass over the interpretative difficulties long posed by Matthew 5:17. The Council of Jerusalem (described in Acts 15) had itself been a response to these challenges, and its mode of dealing with them – written decrees that resolved prior uncertainties – seems to have captured Alfred's imagination. Where Alfred meddles here with the sacred page, he does so in order to have it privilege unambiguously the written over the unwritten. As narrated in the Prologue, the apostolic mission to the gentile churches of Antioch and Syria does not succeed until their concerns are voiced in an *ærendgewrit*. The term very likely meant something along the lines of "royal writ" and was used (in the "Metrical Preface") to describe the Alfredian translation of Gregory's *Pastoral Care*, which had been delivered to Alfred's bishops with a royal letter.[60] In any case, nothing like this assertion may be found in the biblical source (Acts 15: 22–33), where there is no prior failed attempt to communicate orally the outcome of the Council of Jerusalem to the Gentile churches.[61]

In any case, it is safe to say that the goals of the early Kentish laws are brought to fulfillment in Alfred's. While prior Kentish kings had sought in their legislation only to minimize the prestige of oral traditions of law that may have competed with their own efforts, Alfred's Prologue presents the written medium as the vehicle of law. Reminding his judges and other readers of the divine origins of written law perhaps allowed Alfred to disentangle himself from the constraints faced by his predecessors and make the

---

[60] Harmer 1952: 11; See Dobbie 1942; for discussion, Pratt 2007: 122.
[61] It is significant that "[a]llusion to [Acts 15] as a precedent or as a model for conciliar action first arose in the fourth century" (Hess 2002: 5). Alfred and his circle were probably aware of this tradition as they made this (crucially *written*) "synod" the intermediary between the Mosaic law and the ecclesiastical legislation leading to Alfred's.

conduct of law even more a matter of textual knowledge than it had been before.

The Prologue: Sources

It is regrettable that so much prior commentary, particularly in the earlier twentieth century, held the Prologue to have "no bearing" on questions of early English law and assumed that the laws of the *domboc* may safely be considered apart from it.[62] What permitted commentators of the past century to sidestep the question of the Prologue's role in the *domboc* was the habit of attributing its divergences from the biblical text to dependence on some unnamed Latin source it was assumed to have submissively reproduced. Until the late 1990s, the standard assumption was that the Prologue translates from an Irish compilation known as the *Liber ex lege Moysi*.[63] Thinking on the matter did not begin to shift until Patrick Wormald suggested in 1999 that the model Alfred followed was instead (or, perhaps, in addition) the late-antique curiosity known as the *Collatio legum Mosaicarum et Romanarum*. This vestige of the period in which Christianity was winning acceptance by the Roman state puts Mosaic ordinances from Exodus and Leviticus alongside the judgments of Roman jurists; its purpose was to show the agreement of the two legal traditions.[64] Given use of the *Collatio* by Archbishop Hincmar of Rheims (806–882) during the trial of Theutberga, it is certain to have circulated in West Francia during Alfred's lifetime and likely to have thereby become available to Alfred and his circle.[65] Along with it, Wormald holds, came the influence of Hincmar's ideas. To Wormald, "Hincmar and Alfred had the

---

[62] Such reasoning underlay Attenborough's decision to omit the Prologue from his edition: see Attenborough 1922: 35.

[63] See Fournier 1909.

[64] For the text of the *Collatio*, see Frakes 2011. Wormald's arguments in favor of the *Collatio* as a source (1999: 419–425) are, it should be said, devoted less to establishing use of the *Collatio* than the influence on Alfred of Frankish thought concerning the applicability of biblical ordinances to daily affairs.

[65] On Hincmar's use of the *Collatio* to defend the Frankish Queen Theutberga from remarkably lurid charges of incest made by her husband Lothar II, see Frakes 2011: 35–46 (where likely use of the *Collatio* outside of the work of Hincmar is considered as well).

same conception of the structure of human legal history. Both saw Mosaic law as basic. [...] Alfred's code demonstrably met the archbishop's criterion that man's law should so far as possible resemble God's."[66] Discernible in Wormald's remarks is the notion (earlier mentioned) that the laws of Moses were meant in the Prologue to serve as an example to be followed, an ideal work of legislation.

However close the parallel between the Prologue and *Collatio* may seem, evidence of influence is largely circumstantial. The lone textual parallel adduced by Wormald concerns the handling of clauses in Exodus on the slaying of a thief. It may be best to allow Wormald to speak for himself in defense of his hypothesis:[67]

[T]he most intriguing problem is Alfred's inclusion of references [in his translation of Exodus 22:2] to night-time and self-defence in the clause about burglary, which are not in the Vulgate at all. They could be spontaneous glosses by Alfred, deduced from the context and from West-Saxon practice. It happens, however, that both are found in the afore-mentioned *Collatio*. Its clause on theft began with the Twelve Tables on nocturnal thieves killed when daring to defend themselves. 'Know, jurisconsults', it continued, 'that Moses decreed this first', and the Exodus verse then followed, with 'nocte' inserted.

Wormald's thesis has been examined critically in a pair of articles by Carella aimed at restoring the consensus of the early twentieth century while adding some new emphases.[68] These studies argue, each from different vantage points, that Alfred's principal debt was not to the *Collatio* but rather to Irish compilations of biblical law, chiefly the *Liber ex lege Moysi* (a possibility never rejected outright by Wormald, as Carella concedes).[69] In particular, Wormald and Carella differ in how they regard the point at which the Prologue shifts to translating portions of the New Testament, which begins with the curious rendering of Matthew 5:17 referred to earlier. This quotation

---

[66] Wormald 1999a: 425.
[67] Wormald 1999a: 419–420. The Vulgate text only implies that the events in question take place at night.
[68] Carella 2005 and 2011.
[69] Carella 2005: 93 (where it is rightly noted that Wormald saw the *Liber* as one of several influences upon Alfred's thinking). The suggestion had earlier been made in Fournier 1909, and this article remains the most widely cited argument in favor of this view. The standard edition of the *Liber* is now Meeder 2009.

is followed by a more or less faithful translation of the Council of Jerusalem narrated in Acts 15 (though not of the circumstances behind it). Alfred moves thence to the "synods" held throughout Christendom to which he traces the payment of compensation for offenses; among those he perhaps had in mind, as we have seen, were Ine's laws, which give the appearance of originating in synodal legislation. These unnamed synods, Alfred implies, underlie his own book of judgments.

To Carella, this narrative signifies "that Alfred viewed Anglo-Saxon native law as tantamount to Christian law – specifically, as the product of a tradition beginning with Moses and later modified by conciliar proceedings."[70] That the Council of Jerusalem is also mentioned in the letter of Archbishop Fulk of Rheims to Alfred has, as Carella notes, seemed reason enough to attribute the conclusion of the Prologue to Frankish influence. Here, Fulk offers a patronizing reminder to Alfred that his people were once positioned not unlike the early Gentile Christian communities.[71] The difficulty, according to Carella, is that closer and wholly unrecognized parallels are at hand in the texts that accompany the *Liber ex lege Moysi,* an acknowledged likely source of the Prologue, in its four extant textual witnesses (not one of which, Carella concedes, can have been available to Alfred and his circle).[72] Chief of these is the *Collectio canonum hibernensis,* an assemblage of canons whose "compilers make no overt attempt to recommend what punishment is most appropriate [...] beyond citing biblical and patristic examples of these punishments."[73] As Roy Flechner has observed, extensive use by the compilers of the *Hibernensis* of biblical examples was an "innovation [...] challeng[ing] the monopoly of the traditional

---

[70] Carella 2011: 5.

[71] Carella 2011: 10–11.

[72] "Though none of the surviving manuscripts could have been the one Alfred used, the one available to him may have contained a group of texts similar to the surviving four; and since we know he used the *Liber ex lege Moysi* for the introduction to his law code, he may have been aware of the manuscript's other contents as well" (Carella 2011: 18). But do we *know* that Alfred used the *Liber ex lege Moysi?*

[73] Carella 2011: 21.

sources of canon law."[74] This text, along with the *Excerpta de legis Romanorum et Francorum,* a collection of purely secular prescriptions for compensation that is another fellow-traveler of the *Liber,* Carella holds to have helped crystallize Alfred's reflections on law in his own day:[75]

Alfred may well have understood the *Excerpta* as the final element in this core group of texts reflecting the historical development of Christian legislation: while the Decalogue remained the basic statement of the law, it could be modified by New Testament provisions, clarified and illuminated by the church fathers, and expanded by ecumenical and provincial synods that inform and shape secular (or, in this case, quasi-secular) legislation.

There is little to dispute in the passage just quoted.[76] But to accept the dichotomy implied particularly in the work of Carella of either Frankish *or* Irish influence may come with some risks. Three of the four extant textual witnesses to the *Liber ex lege Moysi* were prepared in Brittany; the fourth was copied in Tours.[77] Thus even if the texts consulted by Alfred and his circle were in some sense ultimately of Irish descent, the direction of influence was still from across the Channel – which is what we would expect given Alfred's ties to Continental centers of learning.[78] That the Prologue may reflect multiple influences is suggested in particular by its retention of readings found in various strands of biblical transmission. Some are characteristic of the *Liber* (as seems quite likely in *MP* §24), while others are closer to the Old Latin version employed by the author of the *Collatio* (as *MP* §25). At least one rendering seems both consistent with the Vulgate and inconsistent with the version employed in the *Liber.*[79] In the final analysis, assuming a strict division between Frankish and Irish influence faces the difficulty that Carolingian theology in the years leading up to Alfred's accession assumed a varied character as clerics

---

[74] Flechner 2009: 25. On the reliance of the *Collectio canonum hibernensis* on the Old Testament, see Chapter 1, 11.

[75] Carella 2011: 25.

[76] Frakes (2011: 50 n. 58) offers tentative support to Carella's view over Wormald's.

[77] See Meeder 2009: 183.

[78] The possible role of Breton exiles in disseminating these texts should not be discounted either. See Yorke 1995: 209; Dumville 1992: 156–159.

[79] For example, *eácniende wif* (MP §18) has a closer parallel in the Vulgate's *mulierem prægnantem* than the *Liber*'s version of the clause: *Si rixati fuerint uiri et percuserit quis mulierem et abortum fecerit.*

from Ireland and elsewhere established themselves in Frankish monasteries and in Charlemagne's court, leaving in their wake a pastoral literature that may not always fit the mold of one particular tradition.

In any case, whether the Prologue drew inspiration from the *Collectio* or the *Liber*, it must be conceded that the curious renderings of Mosaic ordinances found in the *domboc* are convincingly traceable to neither of these texts, which for the most part amount to faithful copies of the Vulgate or, in the case of the *Collectio,* the Old Latin versions of the Bible.[80] At best, these texts show the extent to which Old Testament law remained a preoccupation in Ireland and in Francia at the time in which Alfred's laws were prepared.[81] Indeed, the example of Mosaic law had proved irresistible to secular lawmakers long before Alfred's accession.[82] Yet even if we expand the range of comparanda to others vaguely alluded to in Liebermann's edition, Alfred's treatment of Exodus still appears *sui generis*. None does to Exodus what we find in the *domboc*. Perhaps the nearest parallel is one so far hardly considered in prior commentary. The preface to the *Lex Baiwariorum (c.745)* commences with a brief history of written law (drawn almost entirely from Book Five of Isidore of Seville's *Etymologiae*) tracing its production from Moses through various Greek and Roman legislators and concluding with a short treatise on the relationship between law and custom.[83] (Isidore's phrasing perhaps shaped Alfred's thinking as to the

---

[80] Meeder (2009: 178) notes a handful of instances in which the *Liber* does not precisely follow the Vulgate. Most amount to little more than substitutions of single words or reordering of verses and thus do not approach the freedom of Alfred's version.

[81] Carella makes this very point: "The enormous importance of the Old Testament in Irish jurisprudence hardly needs to be re-emphasized here. [...] What has become clear is that, for the early Irish church, Old Testament law was basic, not only as a precursor to Christian law, but also as the foundation for law in Ireland before the conversion." Carella 2005: 116.

[82] Upon his return to Arles in 506, Caesarius intervened against a popular decision to stone his rival Licinianus. According to William E. Klingshirn (1994: 96), "It is significant that this was not the Roman but the biblical punishment for false witness" – a punishment Caesarius ultimately "intervened to prevent [...] pardon[ing] his betrayer, who had earlier been identified with Judas."

[83] The relevant part of the *Lex Baiwariorum* is von Schwind 1926: 197–203; see also the discussion in Murdoch 1998: 217. A chronology of earlier Germanic compilations is given in Oliver 2011: 17. The parallel is also noted briefly in Pratt 2007: 223.

significance of Mosaic law.)[84] Yet the Mosaic laws themselves are not given.[85] We wonder if it perhaps makes more sense to consider the *Liber* and *Collectio* – undoubtedly the two texts having the most plausible claims to some linkage with the *domboc* – as possible *influences* rather than sources.

The more pressing questions concern the sweeping changes Alfred makes to the text of Exodus in whatever form(s) it was available.[86] These features of the Prologue receive strangely little discussion in the few published works to consider this portion of Alfred's laws closely. In most commentary on the Prologue, one may even detect a tendency to minimize the extent of Alfred's departures from his source. The reluctance of some scholars to comment on this aspect of the Prologue may result from the impression that no contemporaneous text affords any real basis for comparison. But the *Admonitio generalis*, whose relationship to the *domboc* has often been assumed but rarely discussed in any detail, illumines even this aspect of the text more than prior commentators have indicated. Though the direct adaptation of Exodus characteristic of the *domboc* is absent here, the thinking that underlay these adaptations seems amply attested. The theology implicit in a number of the *Admonitio*'s provisions, where norms given *in lege* are carefully juxtaposed with those given *in evangelio*, has also practical implications for the exercise of spiritual and secular authority: if Christ is the fulfillment of the law of Moses, then the latter may not be properly understood without

---

[84] "*Moyses gentis Hebraicae primus omnium divinas leges sacris litteris explicavit.*" Lindsay 1911: I, 181 (V, i). Isidore's emphasis is not quite captured by the now-standard translation: "Moses of the Hebrew people was the first of all to explain the divine laws, in the Sacred Scriptures" (Barney *et al.* 2006: 117). What Isidore means here is suggested by his more general view that "Law gets its name from reading, because law is written" ([L]*ex a legendo vocata, quia scripta est*) (Lindsay 1911: 91 [II, x]). The section of Isidore's *Etymologiae* concerned with law sometimes circulated independently in the ninth century: see Tardif 1895: 662.

[85] That the origins of the *Lex* are traced in the Preface to Theuderich's oversight of an initial compilation (von Schwind 1926: 202), which subsequently discards laws deemed useless, does seem to anticipate the role assumed by Alfred toward the conclusion of his Prologue.

[86] Marsden (1995: 402) concludes that "none of the translation, where it is close enough to its source for analysis to be possible, provides any useful information about the exemplar. [...] Little can be said about the exemplar used in Wessex in the late ninth century for the Exodus extracts, except that it seems to have contained a fairly good Vulgate text with few surprises."

the former.[87] The *domboc*'s adaptations of Exodus seem a laconic enactment of the same interpretative principle. The procedure it follows bears some resemblance to that of the *Rule* of St. Benedict (4.1–9), wherein the Decalogue is rewritten in accordance with the New Testament.[88] Theodulph of Orléans would quote the *Rule*'s adapted Decalogue in his first *Capitula*, a text that would be twice translated into Old English (though well after Alfred's lifetime).[89]

The safest conclusion is that the laws of Exodus are invoked not as models – for models would not be altered so drastically – but because they establish the divine origin of written law, whose claims to authority Alfred, like his Kentish forebears, was at pains to establish. Mosaic laws also underlay the only substantial tradition of written law extant in Alfred's day, i.e., the laws of the church, whose remedies for wrongdoing, as will be discussed later, influenced Alfred's provisions to an extent not found in the laws of any prior English king, and whose place among the sources of the *domboc* is, as we will see, very likely acknowledged in the Prologue. Alfred's thinking on the matter is perhaps suggested by one Irish jurist's "choos[ing] in his own written lawbook to characterize the ecclesiastical legal tradition (but not his own) as *recht litre*, 'written law'", a decision reflecting at least to some extent (according to Robin Chapman Stacey) "the impact of the Scriptures and other early Christian writings on a hitherto exclusively oral culture."[90] It is perhaps because Alfred and his circle were in the habit of seeing Mosaic law in this context, as the foundation of ecclesiastical law, that we find the legal clauses of Exodus so thoroughly sanitized and adapted to the ethical teaching of the church. What was done to the laws of Moses in Alfred's Prologue is, in fact, not very different from what was sometimes done to them when they served as the raw materials of vernacular canon law, as is evident in the remarkable similarity between a provision of the *Scriftboc* on "sick-maintenance" and Alfred's translation of the biblical original.[91]

---

[87] See especially caps. 63 (on oaths and perjury) and 65–66 (on homicide and hatred): Mordek, Zechiel-Eckes, and Glatthaar 2013: 214 and 218, respectively.

[88] Fry 1980: 180–183.

[89] Brommer 1984: 117 (§21); Sauer 1977: 326.

[90] See Stacey 2007: 1, also (for further discussion) 179–180.

[91] See Jurasinski 2014b.

TABLE I Sick-Maintenance Clauses

Exodus 21:18–19 (Vulgate): Si rixati fuerint viri et percusserit alter proximum suum lapide vel pugno, et ille mortuus non fuerit sed iacuerit in lectulo, si surrexerit et ambulaverit foris super baculum suum, innocens erit qui percussit; ita tamen ut operas eius et inpensas in medicos restitutat.	*Penitential of Cummean* (Bieler 1975: 120–21): Qui per rixam ictu debilem <u>uel</u> <u>deformem</u> hominem reddit, inpensa in medicos curat <u>et</u> <u>maculae pretium</u> et opus eius donec sanetur restituat et dimidium anni peniteat. Si uero non habeat unde restituat haec, i. annum peniteat.	*MP* §16: Gif hwa slea hys ðone nehstan mid stane oððe mid fyste, 7 he þeah utgongan mæge bi stæfe, begite him læce 7 **wyrce his weorc** þa hwile þe he self ne mæge.	*Scriftboc* (Spindler 1934: 186): Swa hwylc man se ðe in gecynde oðerne gedo wánhalne oððe hine womwlite on gewyrce, forgylde him þone womwlite, and **his weorc wyrce** oð þæt seo wund hal sy, and þæt læcefeoh ðam læce gylde, and fæste twa æfestena oððe þreo; gyf he nyte hu he hit gylde, fæste XII monað.
"If men quarrel, and the one strike his neighbor with a stone or with his fist, and he die not, but keepeth his bed; if he rise again, and walk abroad upon his staff, he that struck him shall be quit, yet so that he make restitution for his work, and for his expenses upon the physicians."	"He who by a blow in a quarrel renders a man incapacitated <u>or maimed</u> shall meet [the injured man's] medical expenses and shall make good <u>the damages for</u> <u>the deformity</u> and shall [compensate for lost] work until he is healed and do penance for half a year. If he has not the wherewithal to make restitution for these things, he shall do penance for one year."	"If someone should strike his neighbor with a stone or with a fist, and the latter may nonetheless walk about with a staff, let [the attacker] obtain a physician for him and **perform his work** while he is unable."	"Whoever renders a man injured in his genitals or inflicts *womwlite* upon him, let him compensate his victim for the *womwlite,* and **let him perform his victim's work** until the wound has healed, and let him make payment to the physician, and let him fast for two or three of the ordained fasting periods; if he does not know how he might make compensation for the injury, let him fast for twelve months."

One may see here a process of adaptation to the norms of the newly evangelized frontiers of Europe. Cummean adds to Exodus a concern with injuries to one's appearance and a requirement of compensation for these, a common feature of early laws such as Æthelberht's. Later texts incorporate thinking more characteristic of pastoral writings. Alfred's version of Exodus 21:18–19 omits, along with the Latin and vernacular penitentials also derived from it, the biblical source's *innocens erit qui percussit*, a statement incompatible with the view that violence issues from a spiritually disordered state. Alfred also recommends along with the *Scriftboc*, a text seen by some as datable to the Alfredian period, that the pugilist humble himself more than is required in either Exodus or Cummean; he is to do his victim's work himself, a measure perhaps intended to cure the spiritual ills that brought on his violent act.[92] As will be seen in the edition and its commentary, examples of this sort may be multiplied. In spite of what Liebermann and others have suggested, alterations of Mosaic law are most often meant to bring them into conformity with the juristic traditions of the church rather than "Germanic" or West-Saxon custom as scholars have understood it. Above all, the Prologue effects the same attenuation of unwritten law as a source of authority that resounds through English legislative prologues from the earliest period, and more decisively than prior lawgiving kings had thought possible.

The Laws

While Alfred offers no clues on the sources underlying his Prologue, he shows no such reticence about the backgrounds of his laws. Yet these passages also require cautious reading. The most overt acknowledgment of sources occurs in a section just prior to the first chapter of his code, in which he claims to have made use of prior legislation by Æthelberht, Offa and his "kinsman" Ine. We have seen, however, that this section is preceded by another in the Prologue locating the origins of Alfred's laws in prior "synods." Liebermann doubted that the term *synod* was of much significance: "*Synod* is here identical with *witena gemot*. [...] Pre-Christian

---

[92] On the possibly Alfredian date of the *Scriftboc*, see Cubitt 2006: 53.

assemblies are here only ignored, not disavowed."[93] Catherine
Cubitt has offered some support to this view, noting that the term
synodus, being a loan from Greek used originally to refer to "a gathering of bishops of one area (later the whole empire)" and later to "a
church council," could designate assemblies of a much more varied
character in England, including those convoked under royal authority. In her brief remarks on the passage (which, as she notes, features
probably the earliest usage of the English loan *seonoð*) Cubitt
appears to suggest that Alfred's employment of the term shares in
the general pattern of English usage, where *synodus* sometimes designated the sorts of assemblies more often labeled *concilia* during
the Carolingian period; in the Prologue, it "denote[s] English councils at which lawcodes were promulgated."[94] Though Liebermann
was perhaps mistaken in implying that every assembly of the *witena
gemot* was a synod, the mixed character of assemblies labeled synods in England makes his observations, according to Cubitt, essentially sound.

The view just described is not, however, the only one now in circulation. Others have argued this passage should be understood as a
riposte to condescending remarks by Fulk of Rheims, successor of
Hincmar and correspondent of Alfred, about the foundering clerical
culture of England.[95] Here, Fulk refers to the "councils frequently
summoned not only from neighboring cities and provinces but also
from lands across the sea; hence synodal decrees were frequently
issued; hence holy canons were established and consecrated by the
Holy Spirit."[96] Fulk goes on to tell Alfred that "the beneficial and

---

[93] "Synode ist hier identisch mit Witenagemot. [...] Vorchristliche Staatsver-
sammlungen sind hier nur ignoriert, nicht geleugnet." Liebermann 1903–1916: III,
49; also Liebermann 1913: 12–13 ("A very frequent name for the national assembly is Latin *synodus,* two sounds of which the Anglo-Saxon changed but slightly
for his loanword. [...] Even Alfred did not discern between the ecclesiastical council, common to Christian countries, and the secular national assembly legislating
English criminal law").

[94] Cubitt 1995: 5 n. 11.

[95] Keynes and Lapidge 1983: 305 n. 3; 331 n. 4.

[96] *Hinc sunt concilia non solum ex vicinis civitatibus vel provinciis, sed etiam ex
transmarinis regionibus totiens contracta, hinc synodalia decreta sepius edita, hinc
sacri canones Sancto Spiritu conditi et consecrati* [...]; Whitelock, Brett, and
Brooke 1981: 9; trans. Keynes and Lapidge 1983: 184.

religious observation and ever-cherished transmission of them was
either not fully observed among your peoples, or else has largely
fallen into disuse."[97] Though these assertions may well underlie in
some fashion Alfred's "synods," there are some important differences
between Alfred's discussion of prior ecclesiastical legislation and
Fulk's that are as yet unremarked. Whereas Fulk refers here to
ancient canonical legislation whose authority is recognized univer-
sally, Alfred refers to specifically English "synods." Moreover, Fulk
seems to have in mind canons of a disciplinary nature. Just prior to
the remarks earlier quoted, Fulk asserts that the church, in issuing
these canons, "never ceased to seek the benefit of the sons whom it
begets daily for Christ, and to further their progress, whether in private or in public, through the flaming fire of the Holy Spirit."[98] That
the canons in question concern "private" and "public" admonition
seems an allusion to the so-called "Carolingian dichotomy" that was
the norm on the Continent at this time (though not in England), a
requirement of private penance and reconciliation for minor infrac-
tions and public penance for great crimes.[99]

Fulk's letter thus may point us in a different direction from what
is suggested by Liebermann and Cubitt, while Alfred's concern with
English ecclesiastical legislation may narrow down the range of
sources to which this passage seemingly refers. Indeed, the concern
of the synods with ecclesiastical discipline may explain an aspect of
this portion of the Prologue for which no solution has been offered:
namely, why Alfred simultaneously claims influence from these
unnamed early English "synods" while disparaging them for offering

---

[97] *aut non pleniter innotuit, aut ex maxima iam parte refriguit*; Whitelock, Brett, and
Brooke 1981: 9; Keynes and Lapidge 1983: 184.

[98] *nunquam cessavit utilitatem filiorum, quos cotidie Christo parturit, exquirere,
eorumque profectum sive privatim sive publice, igne Sancti Spiritus inflammata*;
Whitelock, Brett, and Brooke 1981: 9; Keynes and Lapidge 1983: 184.

[99] "The dichotomy supposedly emerged during the councils convened in 813, where
reform-minded bishops tried to promote the revival of public penance according to
the *canones* [...] Their efforts were only partly successful, for what emerged was
an awkward compromise between the repeatable, and therefore highly successful
private penance, and its much harsher canonical counterpart." See De Jong 1997:
864, whose qualifications to these views should be noted.

"in one place one judgment and in one place another."[100] As a
descriptor of the disorder inherent in Ine's laws, this statement
works reasonably well; and it is probably significant that Ine's laws
also claim to originate in a clerical assembly, one perhaps made up
of abbots. Rectifying the uncertainties of older observances is
undoubtedly a concern in Alfred's laws (see, e.g., *Alfred* §11.1). But
one may also hear in this statement some faint echo of the letter of
Ebbo of Rheims to Halitgar of Cambrai (d.831). Here Halitgar is
urged to prepare a handbook of pastoral canons to replace the
multitude of contradictory sources then circulating in Francia.[101]
(Halitgar's text, issued decades prior to Alfred's accession and copied
at St. Augustine's, Canterbury in the immediate aftermath of Alfred's
death, would collect the sorts of canons to which Fulk seemingly
alludes.)[102] In the letter, Ebbo says that "the judgments regarding
penitents in our priests' handbooks are so confused and also so
diverse and in such disagreement among themselves and supported
with no authority" (*ita confusa sunt judicia paenitentum in presbit-
erorum nostrorum opusculis, atque ita diversa et inter se discrepan-
tia et nullius auctoritate suffulta*).[103] The reference here is to Latin
compilations of canons, most of which circulated under the names of
eminent English clergy of the seventh and eighth centuries even
though some of their contents may ultimately have been of Irish
descent. Many churchmen of the ninth century thought these compilations were authored by Theodore, Bede, and Ecgbert; their association with the English church and its early history probably
contributed to the prestige enjoyed by these texts in the years before
Alfred's reign.[104] If the ecclesiastical legislation attributed to these

---

[100] *Hie ða on monegum senoðum monegra menniscra misdæda bote gesetton, 7 on
monega senoðbéc hie writ[on], hwær anne dom hwær oþerne* ("Then they established remedies for many of men's misdeeds in many synods, and they wrote in
many synod-books, in one place one judgment and in one place another.")
Liebermann 1903–1916: I, 46–47 (*hier ein Gesetz, dort ein anderes*).

[101] Ebbo's letter forms part of the preface to Halitgar's penitential.

[102] On the circulation of Halitgar's penitential in Canterbury, see Rusche 2002.

[103] Dümmler 1899: 617. The translation given owes something to Somerville and
Brasington 1998: 76.

[104] See Frantzen 1983: 122. Doubts about the provenance of these texts, which formed
the basis of their condemnation by the bishops of Chalons in 813 (on which see
Frantzen 1983: 97–98), seem not to have taken hold among English ecclesiastics,
perhaps because they were the beneficiaries of these erroneous traditions.

figures is the referent in this portion of Alfred's Prologue – and it is difficult to imagine what else he had in mind – it is surely significant that he refers to these texts with the same mix of regard and reserve found in Ebbo's letter.[105]

That Halitgar's collection was known either to Alfred or, more probably, to members of his circle, cannot be ruled out. Direct influence from penitentials or ecclesiastical legislation seems very likely in various clauses of Alfred's laws (see *MP* §§11, 12, 13, 16, 17, 30; Laws §42). The most compelling examples of possible influence show Alfred using the language of late-antique councils (namely, the councils of Ankara and Elvira) whose provisions circulated within Halitgar's collection.[106] Given the nature of influence discernible in the *domboc*, we should consider the possibility that Alfred and his circle had access to collections of conciliar legislation – perhaps Halitgar's or similar compilations. Whether they also made use of the earlier *libri poenitentiales* has been disputed on the ground that they are unlikely to have circulated in England at this time.[107] Given the general lack of documentary evidence surrounding Alfred's reign and the destruction of monastic life that seems to have preceded it, such doubts are not easily dispelled. Nonetheless, it remains possible (as has been suggested) that knowledge of Frankish penitentials was brought by the clerics recruited by Alfred even if such materials cannot be assumed to have survived in England.[108]

What is of particular importance about this portion of the Prologue is the absence of any transition between these "synods" in which English royal legislation is alleged to originate and the written vernacular laws of his own day. Alfred says flatly that the laws introduced by the Prologue are derived at least in part from these discordant "synod-books": "Ic ða Ælfred cyning þas togædere gegaderode," "I, then, Alfred the king, gathered these together." The

---

[105] Though typically seen as repudiating these texts, it is significant that Halitgar actually attempts their recuperation; though excluded from the body of his penitential, they are included in Book 6, a compilation Halitgar claimed to have discovered in an unknown Roman library.

[106] The direct influence of Frankish penitentials, including a clause from the fourth-century Council of Elvira excerpted in the ninth-century reformist penitential of Halitgar, is argued for in Jurasinski 2010: 39–42.

[107] See Hough 2000.

[108] See Frantzen 1983: 50; Lapidge 2006: 171.

significance of this passage is disputed, with Wormald holding that the referent here is the Legatine Capitulary: "A 'senoðboc' from 'the time of King Offa' is extant. It is the report by the papal legates."[109] Pratt's view is rather different, emphasizing the rhetorical effects of Alfred's claim to have derived elements of secular law from episcopal assemblies:[110]

Drawn from multiple "synod-books", the *Domboc* now offered law from a single source, in partially imagined appropriation. All Hincmarian distinction between divine and secular law was now radically blurred by the synodal origin of merciful compensation. The effect was to place native law, and Alfred's judgments, directly at the head of God's own legal continuum.

Both views are difficult to dispute given probably unresolvable uncertainties surrounding the *domboc*'s sources. Yet both present undeniable problems as well. Wormald proceeds from an assumption that Alfred had in mind a single source even though his language points to a multiplicity (*þas*, "these") of gathered influences. Pratt resists this view, but seems to suggest that the "synod-books" in question are wholly fictive. Yet we have seen that Wihtred's laws constituted a "synod" in all but name and that Ine's are presented as issuing from just the sort of clerical assembly described by Cubitt. If we take Alfred's language for granted – something Pratt (2007: 221) is reluctant to do – and bear in mind the kinds of specifically English sources of ecclesiastical law likely to have been familiar to Alfred and his contemporaries, some of which prescribed the sorts of money-compensations Alfred refers to here, we perhaps gain some sense of what "these" laws are.[111] While "synods" may refer to the sorts of assemblies referred to by Liebermann and Cubitt, it seems just as likely, given the content of Alfred's *domboc*, that the term alludes as well to the conciliar legislation then circulating on the Continent, whose authority was held superior to Irish canons of uncertain descent. Codes such as those of Ine and Wihtred perhaps mingled in

---

[109] Wormald 1999a: 106.
[110] Pratt 2007: 228.
[111] "The referent of 'þas' ('these') has become a distraction: whether it looks forward in the same sentence, or back (to 'synod-books') there is no difficulty in accepting cognizance of extra-English law. The question is primarily grammatical, the latter involving an awkward change of object." It has already been seen that penitential literature prescribed compensations for acts of violence; see *supra*, 68–69.

the imagination with other prescriptive texts attributed to famed English clergy of the Northumbrian golden age to produce Alfred's "synods."

The more explicit acknowledgment of Alfred's sources mentioned earlier poses no fewer problems of interpretation. Most commentators have agreed in thinking that Alfred's claim merely to have reworked the laws of earlier English kings should not be taken seriously.[112] To be sure, evidence for Alfred's *awareness* of these laws, as has been shown above, is indeed available. His schedule of tariffs for injuries certainly resembles that of Æthelbert in form and style and probably drew inspiration from it.[113] But direct borrowing did not occur on the scale Alfred implied. And while the debt to Offa's laws is impossible to know, given their disappearance from the written record, it may be supposed that any prior Mercian legislation, should it have circulated in ninth-century Wessex, was treated much as the other laws from which Alfred claimed his own were descended. Indeed, it is doubtful that Alfred established such an ambitious framework for his own laws merely to repeat what others had said before, though it was surely useful for his intended audience to think that this was what he had done.[114]

For a sense of the textual influences upon Alfred's laws, therefore, Alfred's own remarks seem to lead us down many blind alleys. While he emphasized his reliance on native English resources, most commentators have detected instead the influence of Carolingian materials. This is hardly surprising. Though work on the *domboc* took place at some remove from Aachen and other centers of Carolingian culture, Francia continued, as it had in Æthelberht's day, to furnish models for the ritual aspects of Anglo-Saxon governance. Moreover, a likely stimulus to the preparation of the *domboc*, as was earlier noted, was Alfred's correspondence with Archbishop Fulk of

---

[112] See Hough 1997: 2; Wormald 1999a: 279; Pratt 2007: 218–219.

[113] See Oliver 2011: 162.

[114] Wormald (2004: 13) suggested that the prior kings mentioned at the outset of Alfred's laws were chosen primarily for their historical significance: "Æthelberht was the first baptized English king, Offa had welcomed the legates of Pope Gregory's successor in 786 [...], while Ine died a pilgrim in Rome and supposedly founded its 'Saxon School'. The passage thus subtly evoked the main turning-points in English relations with God and with Rome. It was another mark of the emerging status of the Angelcynn as 'the chosen'."

Rheims, from whom Alfred obtained some of the clerical advisors named in the latter's Preface to his translation of Gregory the Great's *Cura pastoralis*. Thus we may be sure that, as he sought to rebuild English institutions, Alfred had one eye on his immediate surroundings and the other fixed on developments across the Channel.

Even less certainty surrounds other possible sources of influence. Whether any traces of Roman law may be found in the *domboc* seems doubtful: one seeming allusion to the *Theodosian Code* probably reflects the survival of one of its provisions into the writings of Hincmar of Rheims.[115] Presumptive instances of "noxal liability" conform not in the least to the form of this institution as it was known in antiquity, which has not stopped generations of scholars from invoking this term; indeed, they seem on closer inspection to be further borrowings from biblical ordinances whose presence suggests that the thinking underlying the Prologue and the code proper may not be as distinct as some editors would have it.[116] Although Alfred's are the most erudite of the royal laws to have circulated in Anglo-Saxon England, there is hardly a trace of the classical learning evident in his other translations. Upon close inspection, they seem in large part to be the opposite of what he maintains they are. Many of the *domboc*'s provisions seem almost wholly original, and their acceptance by subsequent kings attests in part to careful management of expectations in the Prologue, the most sophisticated affixed to any legislation of the Anglo-Saxon period.

Conclusion

The foregoing has shown some of the ways an increased legislative self-assurance manifested itself early in the laws of Ine and underwent further development in Alfred's portion of the *domboc*. Written law may have begun in Kent as an attempt to mimic the style of Frankish governance. But by the reign of Ine its use had ceased to be merely experimental. The ambition inherent in Ine's laws is evident not only in its seventy-eight chapters, many of them highly intricate,

---

[115] Wormald 1999a: 282–283; see also Chapter 3, 105 and note on *Alfred* §33.
[116] Jurasinski 2014a. The clauses in question are §§15, 27, 28, and 37 (the last of these being the well-known provision concerning a spear carried over one's shoulder).

but also in its brazen management of ecclesiastical affairs and acute dealings with the finest points of agriculture and estate management. Though his purpose was not to issue a "code" in anything like the modern sense, Ine's laws would certainly have struck contemporaries as one of the most exhaustive compilations of judgments, a tremendous resource for reeves, bishops, and anyone else invested with jural authority. The impression would only have deepened should Ine's laws have grown (as Wormald suspected) over the course of his reign, and perhaps beyond it.

Ine's and Alfred's laws also exhibit the intellectual resources upon which legislation was coming to rely. It is probably in the light of such resources that we should see the Prologue, intended perhaps as a *tour de force* of erudition meant to make his laws the definitive collection for succeeding generations. The gambit nearly worked, as is shown by allusions to the *domboc* in later legislation. It is quite possible, however, that the Prologue (over which Alfred and his circle seem to have labored greatly) is the one element of the *domboc* that was not received enthusiastically in later centuries.

As the concern of this book so far has been to sketch the circumstances in which Ine's and Alfred's laws took shape, the introductory portions of these texts have received the greater share of attention, as these disclose (sometimes misleadingly) the process by which these texts were assembled. Consideration of the laws themselves has been put off deliberately, since what we make of them is determined in large part by what we expect of them as products of particular times and places. The following chapter, devoted particularly to laws appearing in the *domboc* whose apparent aim was to reform prior practice, will show that the significance of these laws has been in many cases misapprehended. Prior commentators' reluctance to credit early West-Saxon governance with the sophistication and learning for which the present chapter has argued has played no small role in disguising the import of these ordinances.

3

Reshaping Tradition: Oaths, Ordeals, and the "Innovations" of the *Domboc*

The laws of Anglo-Saxon England have been objects of scholarly attention much longer than the other vernacular texts for which it is rightly celebrated. While *Beowulf* and the major poems of the Exeter Book were not edited until the first decades of the nineteenth century, it has been nearly half a millennium since the appearance of Lambarde's *Archaionomia* and other works wherein royal legislation first saw print.[1] Yet study of these materials, as will be seen in Chapter 5, has been characterized from the beginning by frequent interruptions and long periods of stagnancy. Accordingly, many aspects of how Anglo-Saxon law worked in practice that were once taken for granted have emerged only in the past few decades as areas of deep uncertainty.

Perhaps nothing better demonstrates the state of scholarly opinion than lack of agreement on such matters as whether the legislation of this period gave expression to anything other than the wishful thinking of kings and their counselors. Though the point originates with J. M. Wallace-Hadrill, it is now associated primarily with the work of Patrick Wormald. In Wormald's view, the laws issued by pre-Conquest English kings, being unmentioned in contemporaneous records of litigation, may have amounted in some cases to little more than demonstrative gestures "inspired by ideological or

---

[1] On the Exeter Book, see Roberts 1979: 16–17. The *editio princeps* of *Beowulf* was edited by Grímur Jónsson Thorkelin in 1815 (see Fulk *et al.*, 2008: xxii).

symbolic considerations."[2] Their importance resided less in their provisions than in their being written down, which allowed kings to
depict themselves "as heirs to the Roman emperors, as counterparts
to the Children of Israel, or as bound together in respect for the traditions of the tribal past."[3] What written legislation did not do, at
least in its earliest phases, was tamper with the substance of law,
which remained at this time the product of oral tradition.

Wormald made this point in a range of publications, each time
with new emphases and qualifications.[4] From the outset, Wormald
made clear that he did not intend for his views to be applied dog-
matically.[5] Moreover, the thesis just described may be read as com-
peting with a quite different interpretation of Anglo-Saxon legal
history for which he argued toward the end of his career. In one
posthumous publication, for example, Wormald held that "royal legislation throughout the reigns of his [Alfred's] successors makes clear
that kings fully intended to achieve a rigorous and ruthless control
of their subjects' behaviour," a development anticipated by "royal
charters from Alfred's time reveal[ing] a quite remarkably high proportion of forfeitures for what can only be called (and indeed was
called) 'crime.'"[6] Whether it is fair to characterize these and similar
claims as contradicting those previously described is difficult to say:
Wormald's works overflow with insights, often very brilliant ones, in
a manner that makes them resistant to paraphrase.

In spite of his own apparent reservations, Wormald's arguments
for the essentially "ideological" nature of earlier royal legislation
were received favorably in their immediate aftermath and served as

---

[2] Wormald 1977 [repr. 1999b]: 38. Wormald acknowledges that these ideas derived
ultimately from the work of J. M. Wallace-Hadrill, especially such remarks as the
following (Wallace-Hadrill 1962: 181): "[T]he mere fact of his [Clovis's] law-giving
makes him more of a king. It puts him on a level with men like Alaric II, and it
even recalls to his Romans, little though they benefit from the *Lex Salica*, the legislative activity proper to the emperor himself." See also Wallace-Hadrill 1962: 129–
130.

[3] Wormald, 1977 [repr. 1999b]: 38.

[4] Wormald 1999a: 264 and 284. But Wormald seems to allow that Æthelstan's laws
on Sunday trading show a relationship between legislation and practical realities
(1999a: 291 and n. 130). Cf. also Wormald 1986: "Legislation was never actually
quoted in the cases we know of, but their proceedings corresponded closely with
official directions" (163).

[5] Wormald 1977 [repr. 1999b]: 39.

[6] Wormald 2009: 194.

the basis of much subsequent commentary. The eagerness with which they were adopted may owe something to the prevailing skepticism found in academic writing of the late twentieth and early twenty-first century toward most claims to authority. For decades, scholars delighted in reducing such discourses to mere "truth-effects" and "propaganda." Wormald himself, it should be noted, was unsympathetic to such arguments when applied to texts of the earlier Middle Ages and sometimes disparaged them.[7]

Only in the past several years does one sense a substantial retreat from Wormald's view that legislation was largely symbolic royal posturing – one perhaps anticipated by his own statements in the latter part of his career. More than was the case decades ago, commentators are willing to consider the possibility that royal legislation was at least intended to shape the practice of litigation, whether it did so effectually or not.[8] What the contents of the *domboc* may offer to such inquiries – a question that has seen little sustained discussion even amid the present reappraisal of Wormald's views – is suggested in the present chapter.[9] Given allusions in the laws of Alfred's successors as well as the relative abundance of manuscripts in which it survives, it is safe to say that the *domboc* was never the ideal vehicle for Wormald's thesis (if an argument expressed in such varied and even contradictory ways should be so termed). Earlier chapters have given reasons for thinking the *domboc* a testament to the possibilities both Ine and Alfred saw in the written medium as an instrument of statecraft, as well as a decisive turning away from prior kings' legislative

---

[7] Wormald 1977 [repr. 1999b]: 38: "I use the word image rather than propaganda, because propaganda implies an audience, and we can neither know nor imagine enough about the circulation of our texts to talk confidently about their audience; whereas an image can be sufficient unto itself, and whoever else they were trying to impress I see barbarian kings as concerned primarily to impress themselves." Wormald refers elsewhere (2004a: 3) to the "view taken by more student essays than [he] could count – and many more than [he] ha[d] enjoyed – that Alfredian sources are 'biased,' if not 'propaganda.'"

[8] See, e.g., Pratt 2007: 217; Roach 2013; Taylor 2016; Lambert 2017. Though Taylor's book focuses on developments in Scotland, it offers useful analogies for dealing with problems posed by most early medieval legislation and offers a forceful defense of its utility and evidentiary worth for historians (see especially Chapter 3).

[9] The notable exception is Lambert 2017, though the focus of this chapter is on portions of Ine's and Alfred's laws not discussed at comparable length by Lambert (or with similar priorities in mind).

timidity. It is surprising, then, to note how often in Wormald's studies the *domboc* serves less as peripheral than central evidence for the
fundamentally "ideological" nature of much pre-Conquest legislation. Wormald was referring specifically to the *domboc* when he
wrote, "*Legislation,* commitment of law to writing, showed what the
law was, whether in custom or as the result of royal adjudication or
decree. It was not, at this stage [i.e., the late ninth century], necessarily the same thing as *making law*."[10] It is an odd thing to say about
the most ambitious work of legal prose to appear before the
Conquest, a number of whose clauses (e.g., *Alfred* §§11.1, 14, 35,
41) evince an expectation of practical consequences. Much the same
intentions are evident even in Ine's laws, which occasionally place
under royal supervision matters that might theretofore have been
dealt with privately (§§6.4, 55).

The clauses of Alfred's and Ine's laws to be considered in the present chapter suggest that early West-Saxon kings and their *witan*
apprehended more than Wormald suggests the utility of writing as
an instrument for establishing legal norms and consciously used it to
reshape traditional ideas and practices. Even Wormald was compelled to concede some instances (as will be seen toward the close of
this chapter) in which Alfred must have done more than passively
record what was long recognized in practice. The pages that follow
expand the list of clauses that ought to be so classified and suggest a
fuller picture of what legislative activity meant to earlier English
kings even as they show Ine's and Alfred's perspectives on ordeals
and oaths to be quite different from what has long been assumed.

Iudicium Dei

We may begin by considering a form of proof whose presence in the
domboc is not as disputed as it perhaps should have been. Of all that
appears unique to Ine's laws – and, perhaps, "innovative," though
the term is potentially deceptive in the absence of prior legislative
evidence – the most significant clauses concern the ordeal. Ine's code
is conventionally seen as the first to offer evidence of this institution
in England as well as one of the earliest witnesses to its use in

---

[10] Wormald 1999a: 284.

western Europe.[11] Its retention of such an ancient practice was one
way in which Ine's "code" fulfilled earlier historians' expectations by
seeming to act as the record of customs long observed rather than as
evidence of royal initiative.[12]

The habit of assigning the ordeal to Ine goes back no further,
however, than Liebermann's edition. Its presence in the text, assumed
by just about every commentator over the past century, is owing
entirely to an emendation suggested by the great editor on the basis
of shared variants found in three manuscripts of the *domboc*, none
of which was prepared before the second half of the eleventh century. The earliest attestation of the variant – *ceac*, "kettle, cauldron,"
for *ceap*, "bargain, purchase" – is found in **G**'s rubric for Ine §66.
(Explanations of these manuscript *sigla* are given in Chapter 4.)
While it does retain Alfred's Prologue, **G**'s text of Ine's and Alfred's
laws is no longer extant, so it cannot be known with certainty
whether this was anything more than an error. But other renderings
of early West-Saxon legal vocabulary in **G** suggest that confidence in
the scribe's grasp of his exemplar(s) is not always well placed. In his
hands, Ine's *ðeowwealh*, "Welsh slave" (*Rubr.* CXVI) becomes
þeofwealh, "thieving Welshman?"; *werfæhðe* "illicit feuding to be
recompensed by payment of *wer*" becomes nonsensical *werfæhte*.
Composed perhaps just after the Conquest, **G** is the first witness to
evince a sweeping modernization of the *domboc*'s orthography into
Late West Saxon, one that seems not to have occurred even as late as
the outset of the eleventh century, when **Ot** was prepared.[13]
Wormald detected in one variant Wulfstanian influence, which may
show its debt to an exemplar prepared during the bishop's lifetime.[14]
A number of its variants are shared with **H**, and so it is conceivable

---

[11] Specifically, Ine's laws are viewed as furnishing evidence of the hot-water ordeal, in
which the proband reached into boiling water to retrieve a ring or stone. The hand
would be bandaged and subsequently examined: if visibly infected, the proband
lost his or her claim.

[12] See, e.g., Pollock and Maitland 1898: I, 26–27: "The very slight and inconspicuous
part which procedure takes in the written Anglo-Saxon laws is enough to show
that they are mere superstructures on a much larger base of custom. All they do is
to regulate and amend in details now this branch of customary law, now another."

[13] On the dating of **G** (more properly, section "A" of **G**), see Wormald 1999a: 224 n. 241.

[14] Wormald 1999a: 226 n. 252. The clause in question is §43 of Alfred's Prologue; see
apparatus.

that clauses of Ine's laws giving *ceac* instead of **E**'s *ceap* derive from **G** if they do not come to **H** directly from **B** (a possibility that may not be ruled out given observations to be made in Chapter 4).

Liebermann's arguments in favor of emendation on the basis of the latest manuscripts are most fully developed in a remarkable essay of 1896 entitled "Kesselfang bei den Westsachsen im siebenten Jahrhundert." Of all Liebermann's shorter publications, it is the most widely cited, the argument presented therein being considered by Wormald "a masterly piece of textual and philological research."[15] The brilliance of Liebermann's solution to the problems posed by the divergent witnesses to these clauses of Ine's laws is not in question. Yet its not having undergone critical examination in over a century furnishes reason enough to give Liebermann's solution a second look.

The particulars of Liebermann's argument are best understood when situated among the prevailing ideas of his time concerning the ordeal. In Liebermann's day, the conventional wisdom on its origins was that set forth by Heinrich Brunner, whose *Deutsche Rechtsgeschichte* (1887) figures prominently in Liebermann's argument. "Having developed from Indo-European foundations," Brunner maintained, "the practice of the ordeal was once an institution common to the Germanic peoples. [...] The differences [with respect to the forms it assumed] are to be understood for the most part from the attitude adopted by the Church toward ordeals among the distinct Germanic groups after their conversion."[16] In arguing for the ultimately Indo-European origin of the ordeal, Brunner doubtless had in mind the views of (among others) Henry Charles Lea, whose *Superstition and Force* Brunner praised as "a painstaking work."[17] In Lea's study, we likewise see the hot-water ordeal characterized as one of the "pagan usages of the ancient Aryans [...] adopted and

---

[15] Wormald 2014: 75.

[16] "Auf arischer Grundlage erwachsen, waren die Gottesurteile einst eine gemeingermanische Institution. [...] [D]ie Verschiedenheiten erklären sich zum großen Teile aus der Haltung, welche die christliche Kirche zu den Ordalien bei den einzelnen Stämman nach deren Bekehrung einnahm." Brunner 1887–1892, II: 400–401; see also Bartlett 1986: 7 n. 5.

[17] "[...] eine sorgfältige Arbeit." Brunner 1887–1892, II: 399 (headnote); the author is referred to as "Henry Lee."

rendered orthodox by the Church."[18] Ultimately, these views would find their way into the opening pages of Pollock and Maitland's *History of English Law*. Here it is held that, in both early and late Anglo-Saxon England, "[a]n accused person who failed in his oath, by not having the proper number of oath-helpers prepared to swear, or who was already disqualified from clearing himself by the oath, had to go to one of the forms of the ordeal."[19] The presence of this practice as early as the seventh century was, it is maintained, "until lately concealed from our view by the misreading of one letter in the text"; Liebermann's "Kesselfang bei den Westsachsen" had just been published and is here cited in support of this newly revised chronology of developments.[20]

Arguments for the basis of the ordeal in ancient custom did not survive reevaluation in the twentieth century. To Robert Bartlett, who remains the institution's preeminent historian, the "trials of fire and water [...] were not of pan-Germanic origin" and therefore not necessarily to be expected in Ine's laws by virtue of its Germanic ancestry alone. Rather, "the tap-root of the ordeal was [...] Frankish," a judgment sufficiently proved by the circumstance that, "apart from the specific case of Ireland, all early non-Frankish occurrences of the ordeal can be plausibly attributed to Frankish influence."[21] Bartlett's doubts about the old consensus are, perhaps, reflected in his noting that "the existence of the ordeal [in Ine's laws] here hangs on a palaeographical thread – Liebermann's emendation of *ceape* (market) to *ceace* (cauldron)."[22] This is a rather less fulsome endorsement of the proposal than Pollock's had been. James Campbell's judgment (made decades later) is even more cautious: "[I]t is not quite certain that the references [in Ine's laws] really are to the ordeal for they depend on an emendation."[23]

---

[18] Lea 1892: 278. Lea's study, a tremendously learned assemblage of materials, remains as valuable as Brunner said it was, though its utopianism and evolutionist model of history mark it as a product of its time. An earlier edition had appeared in 1878.

[19] Pollock and Maitland 1898, I: 39.

[20] Pollock and Maitland 1898, I: 39. For a later articulation of similar views, see Green 1999: 62–63. Liebermann's argument for the ordeal in Ine was based ultimately on assumptions about the practice as the common inheritance of Germanic-speaking peoples (Liebermann 1896: 835).

[21] Bartlett 1986: 6–7.

[22] Bartlett 1986: 7.

[23] Campbell 2001: 14. See also Campbell 2003: 17–18.

Bartlett goes on to assert that "there do seem to be grounds here for seeing an isolated occurrence of the cauldron ordeal in early Anglo-Saxon law."[24] But the evidence adduced amounts solely to an assertion made in Eadmer of Canterbury's *Vita Bregwini* where the reference is to Kentish and not West-Saxon tradition. Here Eadmer (d.1125) lists among the achievements of St. Cuthbert, Archbishop of Canterbury from 740–760, his establishment in close proximity to the cathedral of a church dedicated to St. John the Baptist. Though intended foremost as a baptistery, the church was also, according to Eadmer, meant to provide a venue for what he calls "examinationes iudiciorum."[25]

There are multiple ways of looking at this passage. The tradition that Cuthbert intended for his church to be used for ordeals may be, as Nicholas Brooks seems to suggest, a later accretion: "Post-conquest writers at Canterbury may have assumed that the roles that the church had fulfilled in the late-Saxon period represented accurately the intention of its builder."[26] Brooks will vouch only for its use as a baptistery (a safe enough conclusion given its dedication) while offering tentative support to Eadmer's assertion that the church was to serve as a site of burial for archbishops. We may, however, go a bit further than Brooks. Might the tradition mentioned by Eadmer concerning the *examinationes* even post-date the Conquest? By the twelfth century, the ordeal had been augmented in England to include methods theretofore unknown (though used elsewhere in western Europe) such as trial by combat, which suggests, perhaps, a surge in enthusiasm for such rites.[27] Eadmer would presumably have had no reason to doubt that the practices of his contemporaries might have been observed by an eighth-century Archbishop of Canterbury.

The foregoing of course begs the question of whether *examinationes iudiciorum* refers unambiguously to ordeals. Uncertainties over the meaning of this phrase led one commentator to render this phrase "judicial functions" while allowing that Eadmer had in mind

---

[24] Bartlett 1986: 7 and n. 6.
[25] Scholz 1966: 139–140 (§3); on the context of Cuthbert's establishment of the church, see Gittos 2013: 75–76.
[26] Brooks 1984: 51.
[27] See Bartlett 1986: 104.

"presumably the ordeal and the like."[28] The phrase is rather rare and suggests vagueness on Eadmer's part. As used in the *Liber de virtutibus Sancti Hilarii* of Venantius Fortunatus, *examinatio iudicii* may well refer to something like the ordeal, though only in that it concerns the resolution of a dispute by miraculous means. A reference in the same passage to St. Hilary as an *incorruptibilis arbiter* seems to point to his (postmortem) exercise of a different aspect of the judicial office; his intercession is to be sought by parties in dispute because it may lead to a fair outcome.[29] Uncertainties over the meaning of *examinatio iudicii* in this text may attest to the faint boundaries between the ordeal and other ways in which the miraculous might intervene in human affairs.

Eadmer's assertion that these *examinationes* were directed "at the punishment of wrongs" (*ad correctionem sceleratorum*) suggests still more problems.[30] This is not the typical way of describing ordeals, though it is not necessarily inappropriate to them. Strictly speaking, the ordeal was not always regarded as a form of *punishment* (though the distinction was probably lost on those who lowered their arms into boiling water). Rather, by offering means of appealing to the supreme *iudex*, it opened up the way for an innocent party to *avoid* punishment once all other options had been exhausted. Some ninth-century liturgies for the ordeal refer to the history of Susannah and the Elders, one of two sections of the Prophecy of Daniel that appear only in the Septuagint, and the narrative seems to have been conventionally associated with this institution at least within the Frankish world.[31] About to be executed for a false accusation of adultery, Susannah is spared when "the Lord raised up the

---

[28] Franklin 1992: 178.

[29] *O quam incorruptibilis arbiter claret! Castior est iste in examinatione iudicii quam in electione florum illa quae ceram casta producit.* The dispute is over wax: one merchant wishes to offer it to the relics of St. Hilary, while another attempts secretly to withhold it; the wax thereupon divides itself, to the shame of the impious merchant. The miracle has some of the properties of the ordeal. Yet St. Hilary is also acting as arbiter, effecting a fair distribution of the wax rather than simply punishing the one miserly merchant. See Krusch, 1885: 10; also Jones 2009: 192.

[30] On bishops as judges, see Brasington 2016: 4–20 and *passim*.

[31] Firey 2009: 47–49. See also the text edited by Liebermann (1903–1916: I, 406) as *Iudicia Dei II […] et sicut tres pueros supradictos de camino ignis ardentis liberasti et Susannam de falso crimine eripuisti, sic manum innocentis, omnipotens Deus, ab omni lesionis insanie saluare dignare.*

holy spirit of a young boy, whose name was Daniel" (13:45). The
boy takes charge of the blundering investigation, with the result that
Susannah's accusers are put to death, having been "convicted [...]
of false witness by their own mouth" (13:61). Though the narrative
does not imply that anything like the ordeal was used to demonstrate their guilt – a fact seized on by Archbishop Agobard of Lyons,
one of its ninth-century opponents – the point seems to have been
that a defendant as devout and virtuous as Susannah might hope for
divine aid if falsely accused.[32] The solace litigants would have found
in the prospect of the ordeal may be hard for us to fathom, but there
can be no doubt that it offered genuine hope to those whose positions were as desperate as Susannah's.

Questions so far raised about whether the ordeal is attested in
English sources prior to the tenth century should not be taken as
implying that this and similar practices were necessarily unheard of
in England.[33] Even in the absence of explicit evidence for it, we can
be reasonably sure that litigants knew about the ordeal and perhaps
tried their hands at it from time to time.[34] What is at issue is whether
(and at what time) the English kingdoms came to assimilate this
practice into their own legal processes to the point that it ceased to

[32] Firey 2009: 49.
[33] Alfred's laws evince no real interest in the ordeal. Of the 130 or so chapters that
make up the Alfredian portion of the *domboc,* the sole possible trace of the ordeal
amounts to no more than a single word in the biblical Prologue (§28) of doubtful
significance. Alfred's *geladige hine selfne* ("let him clear himself") while used in
later legislation in reference to the ordeal (cf. II *Æthelstan* §14.1), seems in this
instance an adequate shorthand rendering of the Vulgate's *iurabit* ("he will
swear"), particularly given that what follows in the latter reads very much like an
oath formula. Within the same clause of the Prologue, an oath is explicitly required
(*swerige he þonne*) for an accused thief lacking witnesses to his innocence – a situation not altogether different from that of the defendant earlier urged to "clear himself" to show that he did not steal property lent to him.
[34] Though even this point ought not be pressed too far. If trial by battle furnishes a
valid analogy, it is significant that Anglo-Saxon England remained untouched by
the practice until after the Norman Conquest, a circumstance that has long puzzled
commentators greatly invested in the notion of a shared Germanic legal inheritance: see Bartlett 1986: 104. The characteristically Germanic prohibition on concealed homicide, attested from Francia to Iceland, also seems to have played no
role in the formulation of Ine's laws (see §§20.2 and 35). Nottarp (1956: 111) was
surely mistaken in seeing Coifi's destruction of the idols he had made and violation
of other rules observed by pagan priests as an ordeal; the priest simply acts upon
his knowledge of the falsity of his prior beliefs (*HE* I.ii.13).

be the private concern of those making use of it. At a minimum, this could not be accomplished before votive liturgies were prepared and rationales for its (ultimately uncertain) place in ecclesiastical practice devised.[35] The earliest evidence we possess for such developments in England is the manuscript known as Durham Cathedral Library A. iv. 19, portions of which appeared in Liebermann's *Gesetze* in the section entitled *Iudicia Dei*. Liebermann did not attempt to date the text, instead vacillating between a prior suggestion by Henry Sweet that allowed for its being prepared during Alfred's lifetime and another by Walter W. Skeat that forbade it.[36] But Sweet's proposal would find little favor in the years after Liebermann's death. By 1927, Thompson and Lindelöf maintained the following in their edition of the manuscript: "[T]here do not seem to be any arguments of weight which induce us to assume a higher antiquity than the tenth century for the Latin text of the main portion of our MS."[37] Recent commentators are no less firm in assigning the most archaic substrate of this manuscript a date no earlier than the tenth century.[38] Thompson and Lindelöf's judgment regarding the provenance of the manuscript likewise suggests that its liturgies for the ordeal tell us little about English conditions: "It contains no sign that it was compiled in the North of England, or in England at all."[39] In their view, Durham Cathedral Library A. iv. 19 seems a thoroughgoing product of the "Gallican" church given its repeated commemoration of St. Martin and omission of distinctly English festivals: it may well derive, in their view, from "an original compiled for us in the famous

---

[35] Clerical objections to the ordeal would culminate in its rejection by the Fourth Lateran Council (1215). On the background of this development, see McAuley 2006.

[36] Liebermann 1903–1916: I, 401: "um 875 [Sweet *Oldest English Texts* 175] oder 925 [Skeat *Transact. Philolog. Soc.* 1877/9 App. 51*] in oder nahe Kent geschrieben [...]."

[37] Thompson and Lindelöf 1927: xlix.

[38] See, e.g., Jolly 2013: 180: "The base from which Durham Cathedral A.IV.19 was constructed is a collectar thought to be from southern England and dated to the early tenth century, written by a single scribe labeled 'O'." Cf. Corrêa 1992: "The actual writing of the Durham Collectar cannot be dated more specifically than between the years 890 x 930" (80–81).

[39] Thompson and Lindelöf 1927: xiii. Corrêa's much later examination (1992) holds the work of scribe O to be "unmistakably Anglo-Saxon" (80) but concedes that the materials he copied, including the liturgies for the ordeal, "owe nothing to Anglo-Saxon England" (82).

church of St. Martin at Tours."[40] That rituals for the ordeal should figure in this text is in keeping with Bartlett's conclusion (referred to earlier) that the "tap-root" of the ordeal, at least as a formal element of litigation, was Frankish. While copying and subsequent glossing of this manuscript attest to avid interest in the ordeal in post-Alfredian England, its date and provenance suggest, along with other evidence to be explored subsequently, that the practice was an import and not a survival from prior eras of English royal legislation.

That the earliest English liturgical witness to the ordeal must be later than Liebermann assumed is not the only obstacle to finding traces of this institution in the laws of Ine and Alfred. The rather hazy distinction between oaths and ordeals is itself a formidable problem.[41] At the most fundamental level, both the oath and the ordeal involve the same process of calling God to witness to the truth of an assertion, with the implication that the person doing so mendaciously should expect divine retribution sooner or later.[42] In the greater part of its manifestations, the ordeal seems meant to hurry the perjuror along to the consequences of his sacrilege, a point made eloquently by John Niles:

> While it is true that the ordeal was reserved for special cases where a defence by oath alone was insufficient, one should not therefore conclude that it was a separate procedure that had nothing to do with the oath. On the contrary, the *raison d'être* of the ordeal was that it was a means of assaying the validity of the oath by direct appeal to God as supreme witness, whose judgments were not prone to error. The ordeal was an extension of the oath by material means, not an alternative to it.[43]

Niles's points are well borne out by the liturgical evidence. Rites for the ordeal typically oblige the proband to first, after a period of fasting, attend Mass and receive the Host under a solemn warning by the celebrant: "May this body and blood of our lord Jesus Christ be to you for proof on this day" (*Corpus hoc et sanguis domini nostri Iesu Christi sit uobis ad probationem hodie*).[44] It may be assumed

---

[40] Thompson and Lindelöf 1927: xiv.
[41] On the essential likeness of the oath and the ordeal, see Hyams 1981: 92; also Lea 1892: 371–374.
[42] See McAuley 2006: 485.
[43] Niles 2009: 36.
[44] Liebermann 1903–1916: I, 402.

that failure at the ordeal will be a consequence, not of his original offense, but of unworthy reception of the Eucharist.

One likely witness to the emergence of the ordeal as an official remedy is to be found in the laws of Alfred's son Edward the Elder (1 *Edward* §3). It is worth being particularly attentive to the language used: "We have further declared, with regard to men who have been accused of perjury: if the charge has been proved, if the oath on their behalf has collapsed, or has been overborne by more strongly supported testimony, never again shall they have the privilege of clearing themselves by the oath (*hy siððan aðwyrðe næran*), but only by the ordeal."[45] This provision is phrased as one of a series of declarations (*eac we cwædon*) – presumably *additions* to existing law as envisaged in the *domboc*. As will be seen later (Chapter 5, 150–151), the legislation of Æthelstan and subsequent kings, when making either overt or implicit use of the *domboc*, occasionally replaces remedies earlier prescribed with the ordeal. There is reason to assume, therefore, that this provision announces the formal bifurcation of oath and ordeal in matters of litigation, and that "never again," while presumably referring to the situation of the defendant, may also revoke a privilege exercised by disputants as late as Alfred's reign.[46] It is perhaps no coincidence that our oldest liturgical prescriptions for the ordeal date to this time and were copied in a part of England subject to West-Saxon rule.

The legislation just quoted of course does not preclude the possibility that what we have in the earlier ordinances of Ine is some halting acknowledgment of the ordeal subsequently clarified by Edward. Such an assumption, however, runs into the difficulties posed by *Wihtred* §18 and §18.1 [L23]. In spite of their ambiguities, they make clear the alternatives for a litigant unable to summon a supporter in the oath: he was either to compensate the plaintiff for the offense or allow himself (or his underling?) to be flogged (*oþþe gelde, oþþe selle to swinganne*).[47] One finds a similar principle at work in *Ine* §§14.1 and 18. In the first, no provision is made for the defendant unable to find oath helpers, whose only option is to pay

---

[45] Attenborough 1922: 116–117.
[46] Cf. Campbell 2001: 14: "It is with this solitary sentence [1 *Edward* §3] that the continuous history of the ordeal in England begins." See also Campbell 2003: 18.
[47] Oliver 2002: 160.

what compensation is demanded. The "churl" of §18 who has often faced prior accusations of wrongdoing may not even attempt the oath if caught in malfeasance; he makes amends by losing a hand or a foot. That the ordeal was not made available in such instances (as it would be in post-Alfredian legislation) perhaps gives some sense of the tradition against which Edward legislated. The clauses just mentioned suggest that the ordeal emerged into English law as a way to grant defendants an additional layer of protection.

In any case, we may see in the case of Pollock and Maitland's *History* how prior assumptions about the antiquity of the ordeal among the Germanic-speaking peoples ensured a receptive audience for Liebermann's "Kesselfang bei den Westsachsen." With the work of Brunner having established both its basis in pre-Christian superstition and its fundamental role within Germanic civil procedure, commentators were induced to assume that the ordeal must have been an acknowledged element of Anglo-Saxon practice from the beginning in spite of all evidence to the contrary. Where the ordeal was absent from written evidence, it seemed only reasonable to expect it – particularly in a work of legislation as archaic as Ine's.

Liebermann's Emendation: *Ceape* or *Ceace?*

We may now move to the clauses in Ine alleged to give evidence for the ordeal. Everything, as we have seen, hinges on the word *ceap,* the ancestor of Modern English "cheap."[48] What is now an adjective was in the Anglo-Saxon period both a noun and a legal *terminus technicus* of occasionally uncertain meaning, which may explain its capacity to be misunderstood by later scribes. While by no means isolated to legislation of the seventh century, its semantic field in this period seems notably less restricted than in later legislation, where it denotes primarily "purchased item" or "item for sale," as in IV *Edgar* §7 and II *Æthelstan* §24.1. In the case of Æthelberht's laws, we see repetition of the word in ways that reflect an assumed knowledge of more varied shades of meaning, as in the following instance, where

---

[48] The quality of the original Old English vowel survives somewhat in the family (once occupational) name *Chapman,* which was unaffected by the Great Vowel Shift.

the situation involves not the purchase of goods but a transfer of guardianship: "If someone buys a maiden [for the purposes of marriage] with a [bride-]price (*ceapi*), let the bargain be [valid] (*geceapod sy*), if there is no deception."[49] Public bargaining itself seems likewise to be the referent in the laws of Hloþhere and Eadric, wherein a litigant is permitted in a dispute over property to "declare at the altar [...] that he bought that property (*feoh*) without secrecy by his public purchase (*undeornunga his cuþan ceape*) in the town."[50]

Given their chronological proximity to Ine, the passages just quoted are probably more disposed to tell us something about the meaning of the term as we find it in Ine than are examples from tenth- and eleventh-century legislation. While its use in the Kentish laws does not exclude the meaning "price" and "marketplace" that would predominate in later legislation, it seems as well to have sometimes meant "bargain" or "negotiation." Given Ine's concern with fraud in the context of buying and selling (§§25, 77), this may well be the meaning in this clause, the first of two in which the scribes of **B** and **H** give *ceace* in place of *ceape*:

TABLE 2 First instance of *ceace* for *ceape* in the laws of Ine

38 [L37] Se cirlisca mon se ðe oft betygen wære ðiefðe, ⁊ þonne æt siðestan synnigne gefó in ceape [ceace BH] oððe elles æt openre scylde: slea him mon hond óf oððe fót.	38 [L37] A man of the rank of *ceorl*, who has often been accused of theft, and finally, then, is openly caught either with the goods or in the unlawful act: let his hand or foot be struck off.

There seems no compelling reason to adopt the late emendations over what appears in **E**. *Ine* §38 essentially repeats what was earlier said in §18, where a "churl" often accused of misdeeds and finally caught in the act is handed over for bodily punishments, the implication being that he has no option of making an oath (a privilege granted to certain defendants in §§16 and 17). Given that this is the

---

[49] *Gif man mægþ gebigeð ceapi, geceapod sy gif hit unfacne is.* Oliver 2002: 78–79 (§76 [L77]).
[50] Oliver 2002: 132–133 (§11.2 [L16.2]).

case, "synnigne gefó in ceape" here seems unlikely to refer to some
subsequent judicial process (a possibility expressly forbidden in §18).
Instead, *ceap* likely refers to stolen goods discovered in one's possession (as in §61), or to the accused person being proved to have
engaged in fraudulent bargaining or the sale of stolen items, a common enough concern in Ine's laws. In the latter case, the circumstances referred to by *in ceape* would be those of *Ine* §§25–25.1,
which mandate that all transactions be conducted in the presence of
witnesses and that a merchant (*ciepmon*), if alleged to be in possession of stolen property (*Gif ðiefefioh mon at ciepan befo* [...]), satisfy his accuser(s) of his legitimate possession by assembling
oath-helpers whose combined worth equals the penalty for theft
(*wite*). Failure either to summon exculpatory witnesses or, subsequently, oath-helpers, would then be what is meant here by being
caught "in ceape."

We may now move to the greater difficulties of the later chapter:

TABLE 3 Second instance of *ceace* for *ceape* in the laws of Ine

66 [L62] Þon*ne* mon bið tyhtlan betygen, ⁊ hine mon bedrifeð to ceape [ceace BH], nah þon*ne* self nane wiht to gesellanne beforan ceape [ceace BH]: Þon*ne* gæð oðer mon seleð his ceap fore, swa he þon*ne* geþingian mæge, on ða rædenne, þe he him ga to honda, oððæt he his ceap him geinnian mæge. Þon*ne* betyhð hine mon eft oþre siðe ⁊ bedrifð to ceape [ceace BH]: Gif hine forð nele forstandan se ðe him ær ceap fore sealde, ⁊ he hine þon*ne* forfehð, þolige þon*ne* his ceapes se ðe he him ær fore sealde.	66 [L62] When someone is accused of an offense, and he is required to compensate in goods and he does not have property to give for such compensation: if another man goes and gives his property for him – in whichever way he may settle [with the accuser] – [let it be] on the condition that [the accused] goes into his hands [in servitude] until he can restore to him [the value of] his property. If he is later accused a second time and required to compensate in goods: if the person who earlier gave the property for him does not wish again to stand up for him, and [the second accuser] captures him, then the man who earlier stood surety for him forfeits his property.

Here the difficulty involves also the meaning of the verb *bedrifan*
(and *fordrifan* in the later rubric). According to the Toronto

Dictionary of Old English, the meaning of both is in some cases identical with the simplex *drifan* "to force to move, drive" (II.A).[51] Liebermann assumes that the idiom used here – *bedrif*[*an*] *to ceace* in **B** and **H** – is to be understood as identical with Latin phrases in Frankish legislation ("ad aeneum prouocare, admallare") indicating a summons to the ordeal.[52] It is not hard to imagine why someone would need to be "driven" or otherwise compelled to the ordeal of hot water, indicated here (in the latest witnesses) through synecdoche by the noun *ceac.*

Uncharacteristically, Liebermann concludes his essay with something of a victory lap: "Thus do legal history, philology, manuscript study and necessity itself propose, against all analyses offered thus far, that the riddle of Ine 37 and 62 be resolved with a single key."[53] Whether Liebermann's proposal lives up to such an exuberant peroration seems doubtful: its problems are real and by no means confined to one area of inquiry. Wormald notes that *ceac* in other Old English prose designates "jug" (a cumbersome instrument for the hot-water ordeal to say the least) rather than "cauldron."[54] And the situation is perhaps a bit worse for Liebermann's emendation than Wormald allows, for the Toronto *Dictionary of Old English* assigns something approaching the meaning "cauldron" (s.v. *ceac,* sense c) *only to the emended clauses of Ine's laws.*[55] In its dozen other attestations, *ceac* designates objects far less frightful than a cauldron and certainly not suited for use in the ordeal: "bowl, basin, waterjar, laver"; "a. specifically used for washing: a basin or laver"; "b. specifically used for drinking: a bowl or cup." The etymon of the Old English term is Latin *caucus,* a rare noun but not unknown in England in Ine's time: Bede refers to the "bronze drinking cups" set up by King Edwin of Northumbria "for the refreshment of travelers"

---

[51] See *fordrifan* sense 5 "of necessity: to compel, force (someone *acc.* to an action)"; also *bedrifan* senses 1, 3. 3a.

[52] Liebermann 1896: 831.

[53] "Gegen alle bisherigen Erklärungen sprechen also Rechtsgeschichte, Sprachwissenschaft, Handschriftenkritik und die Nothwendigkeit, die Räthsel von Ine 37 und 62 mit einem Schlüssel zu lösen" (Liebermann 1896: 835).

[54] Wormald 2014: 75 n. 193.

[55] The definition given is "c. specifically used for an ordeal; hence the ordeal itself (in legal texts)."

as *aereos caucos.*[56] Liebermann himself conceded that the term *ceac* is used nowhere else to refer to the ordeal, and one wonders whether the Toronto *Dictionary* ought to retain this meaning on the basis of Liebermann's proposal alone.

Legal history itself, even as understood in Liebermann's day, suggests further difficulties. If the "system" of Germanic litigation is any guide for what is happening here, the sequence of events is not quite right. As understood by Liebermann, *Ine* §66 has an individual accused and then brought forcibly to the ordeal, whereupon his accuser learns that he has no money or other resources with which to evade the ritual (*to gesellanne beforan ceape*). Leaving aside the fact that the preposition *beforan* appears only twice to have meant something like "in place of" (and even these instances seem doubtful), the ordeal is conventionally prescribed in other legislation for cases in which a plaintiff has no one to vouch for him (1 *Edward* §3; 11 *Cnut* §22.1) and thus has no hope of assembling the number of supporters necessary for an oath.[57] Though earlier Frankish laws permitted a defendant to buy his way out of the ordeal, he was still obliged to find oath-helpers once he had done so.[58] Such circumstances cannot be at issue in this clause, which deals instead with the question of what should happen when someone intercedes on behalf of an accused man, positions himself to claim his property or the fruits of his labor in return for this advocacy, and then, when new accusations are leveled at the same man, must fend off claims by

---

[56] *HE* 11.16, Colgrave and Mynors 1969: 192–193.

[57] The first of the two instances cited by the Toronto *Dictionary* (s.v. *beforan*) for such a meaning (B.6.b, "in preference to, above, before [someone/something]") is *Ine* §66, presumably understood by the editors in accordance with Liebermann's interpretation. The second is a translation of Deuteronomy 5:7 ("Thou shalt have none other gods before me" [Authorized Version]) that may or may not have such a meaning: the editors suggest that its presence or absence here depends upon whether the translator understood himself in using the phrase *beforan me* to be rendering the Old Latin version of this passage (*præter me*) rather than the Vulgate (*in conspectu meo*).

[58] Drew 1991: 116–117. Earlier she notes that "This ability to buy out of the ordeal seems to have been limited to the Franks and Anglo-Saxons" (35). Drew does not mention Ine's laws (or any Anglo-Saxon legislation) in connection with this, but it may be assumed that she had in mind *Ine* §66.

other litigants on the assets of his charge.[59] Given its status within the economy of justice, one would not typically be rescued from the ordeal: it became one's sole remaining option *specifically because* one had run out of powerful friends.

Just what the plaintiff is being driven toward, perhaps with threats or intimidation, may be suggested by co-occurrences of *drifan* (without a prefix) and the noun *ceap* in later Old English texts. (These go unmentioned in Liebermann's study.) Though they are not direct parallels to the language of Ine's laws, they ought not be ignored either.[60] To these instances of *ceap drifan* the Toronto *Dictionary* assigns the meaning "transact business." The *Oxford English Dictionary,* treating the same phrase in Old English (and noting its being an ancestor of the phrase "drive a hard bargain") perhaps brings us closer to the connotations of *bedrifan* in this chapter of Ine's laws: "To carry on vigorously, 'push,' prosecute, conduct, practise, exercise (a custom, trade, etc.); to carry through or out, to effect; to bring to a settlement, conclude (a bargain)" (IV.19.a).[61] That *ceap* might hold such a meaning in Ine's day is plainly established by §76, where it is stipulated that a free person is not obliged to make a monetary settlement on behalf of a slave unless he wishes to bargain (*ofaceapian*) for the latter a way out of anticipated reprisals.

The clauses of Ine's laws just considered suggest that there was little to distinguish dispensing justice from the sordid business of

---

[59] Lambert (2017: 258) refers (though not with this passage in mind) to "lords [who] had the power to rescue men who faced ruin because they lacked sufficient oath-helpers, and could exact a high price for their assistance." This seems the implied situation in *Ine* §66.

[60] A notable example occurs in an Old English version of the *Rule* of St. Benedict §57, Schröer 1885: 94–95, where those who sell objects made in the minster (ða, ðe ðone ceap drifað) are admonished that there be no hint of fraud in the course of the transaction (nan ðing facenlices on ðam ceape ne don). The translator relies on an Old English idiom as nothing close to his language is found in the Latin: "Si quid vero ex operibus artificum venumdandum est, videant ipsi per quorum manus transigenda sint ne aliquam fraudem praesumant" ("Whenever products of these artisans are sold, those responsible for the sale must not dare to practice any fraud"); Fry 1981: 264–265. The passage just quoted is among several examples given (which encompass a vast chronological range) in the Toronto *Dictionary of Old English* for sense 1 of *ceap*: "1 purchase or sale, bargain, business transaction; ceap drifan 'transact business.'"

[61] Simpson and Weiner 2017.

buying and selling, a feature of early medieval procedure long acknowledged.[62] Determining the worth of injuries and rights over people probably involved, in this era, a lot of unceremonious haggling for which the slippery word *ceap* seems perfectly suitable. As we have seen, *ceap* is used by Æthelberht's laws in reference to engagement and marriage, and the context here is not dissimilar as it concerns the acquisition of authority over another person, *ga to handa* being here a legal metaphor referring to such a transfer of power (cf. *Alfred* §44.1).[63] Early legal prose used *ceap* to describe arrangements as disparate as purchasing wares and acquiring wives and dependent laborers because most matters were settled by negotiation. If we assume this meaning, which is warranted by evidence contemporary with Ine's laws, we see that the clause (as given in **E**) lays down a sensible rule. If a defendant should lack the wherewithal to satisfy the plaintiff and a third party then intervene on his behalf, making the payment in his place, the defendant's troubles are not quite over. Until he has in some fashion rendered duties equivalent to the amount of the *ceap* or paid its worth outright, the defendant is to live in subjection to his benefactor (*ga to handa*).[64] And should this same defendant again be accused of a subsequent offense and, failing or refusing to compensate, be captured by his accuser – presumably for servitude or some other form of bound labor – his benefactor is to have no means of recovering the money spent rescuing the miscreant in the first place.

As given in the earliest witness, the clause seems a deft solution to two interlocking problems. It at once hinders the troublemakers who rely on well-placed connections to evade the penalties of their misdeeds (about whom more will be said shortly) and the wealthy opportunists who enable them. The latter are given added reasons for limiting their generosity only to those who are assuredly

---

[62] Referring to the practice of wergild and other forms of compensation, Lea notes that "This system introduced into legal proceedings a commercial spirit which seems strangely at variance with the savage heroism commonly attributed to our barbarian ancestors" (Lea 1892: 17). See also Lambert 2017: 37–38.

[63] Jurasinski 2010: 144.

[64] Lambert (2017: 98 n. 117) discerns in another clause (*Ine* §55) a concern with "helping an offender to evade or disregard assembly judgements, thereby avoiding paying what he owes."

innocent and unlikely to offend again.[65] Its sense seems more than adequately established by *Ine* §50, wherein someone newly reduced to penal slavery (*witeðeow niwan geðeowad*) is accused of having committed a theft before he entered this condition (*ær geðiefed ær hine mon geðeowode*). The accuser is permitted to flog him once in a manner commensurate with his *ceape* (*be his ceape*), a phrase that may mean "in accordance with the stolen property" or, alternatively, "as much as is agreed to by the accuser and the slave's owner" (approximately the sense of *ceape* in *Ine* §66). The word *ceap* is not emended to *ceac* in this instance by **G**'s rubric, **B** or **H**. In the final analysis, *Ine* §§38 and 66 seem far too specific to be (as Liebermann and others held) reiterations of ancient custom. Both deal instead with particular circumstances that had risen to the attention of Ine's justices and perhaps Ine himself; they are put in writing not as symbolic displays of royal authority but to offer guidance to disputants and arbitrators.

Bargaining and Advocacy

We are not without legislative evidence outside of Ine's laws suggesting that the earliest witness to §66 should be favored over copies of the post-Conquest era. The laws of Alfred offer several instances in which defendants are forced by their accusers to engage in bargaining over compensation amounts (§§2, 44). The situation envisaged in *Ine* §66 is also not far removed from that of the recidivist thief Helmstan, whose crimes are narrated by Ealdorman Ordlaf in the Fonthill Letter, a valuable if ambiguous witness to the legal situation of Alfredian Wessex.

Helmstan first requests Ordlaf's intercession after being accused of stealing "a belt belonging to a certain Æthelred."[66] The accusation has placed Helmstan at the mercy of his powerful neighbors. Having heard of his troubles, one rival magnate, Æthelhelm Higa, is seeking "along with other claimants" (*mid oðran onspecandan*) to wrest Helmstan's lands from him, presumably by leveling new charges.[67]

---

[65] Similar efforts towards weakening the bonds between offenders and their sureties may be evident in *Ine* §41.

[66] Keynes 1992: 64.

[67] Keynes 1992: 64.

Here we see an offender "driven" to "bargaining." Though no great crime, Helmstan's theft renders him vulnerable to litigation, presumably because he is unable to summon the requisite *consacramentales* as easily as someone whose reputation is intact. His is the very situation, as Simon Keynes notes, for which litigants in later years would be obliged to face the ordeal, and it may tell us something about the legal environment of early Wessex that resort to the practice is at no point suggested as a possibility in the Fonthill Letter.[68] We have already seen that the language of 1 *Edward* §3 suggests the revocation of a privilege enjoyed by litigants perhaps as late as the reign of Alfred. The Fonthill Letter seems to witness to a period before 1 *Edward* §3 had taken full effect. Wormald takes omission of the ordeal as evidence that "written law was apparently irrelevant, though Alfred's imposing *domboc* (incorporating Ine's laws) must have been issued only a few years before the episode."[69] Taken as we find it in the earliest witness, however, *Ine* §66 seems reasonably harmonious with the situation just described. In any case, the variant witnesses containing *ceac* in place of *ceap* would not be prepared for at least a century or more, and there is nothing beyond conjecture to establish their presence in a witness coeval with the Fonthill Letter.

Upon finding himself in such straits, Helmstan implores Ordlaf to act as his advocate before King Alfred. Helmstan does this not necessarily out of loyalty or personal affection. Ordlaf was Helmstan's godfather, and spiritual kinship conferred great privileges on those in Ordlaf's position: the final chapters of Ine's laws entitle the godfather of a plaintiff or decedent to compensation "equal to the amount paid to the dead man's lord."[70] Along with these privileges presumably came an expectation that one might act on behalf of one's godson in the course of litigation.

Ordlaf's advocacy wins Helmstan something of a reprieve. Alfred affirms that the theft ought not suffice to hand the victory to Æthelhelm Higa and appoints to decide the case a body of arbitrators named in the letter. Helmstan produces his charter to the land and supports it with an oath. But in return for his advocacy with the

---

[68] Keynes 1992: 65.
[69] Wormald 1999a: 148.
[70] Attenborough 1922: 61.

king, Helmstan is obliged to confer this charter on Ordlaf, who allows Helmstan to retain the property described therein in usufruct "as long as he lived, if he would keep himself out of disgrace" (*ða hwile ðe he lifde, gif he < ... > hine wolde butan bysmore geheal-dan*).[71] Here we have the offender's compensation for another's hav-ing brought him out of a hard bargaining he was sure to lose, in this instance by interceding to have the dispute transferred to a friendlier venue. To Keynes, Ordlaf's deal with Helmstan has the scent of "brib-ery and corruption" and suggests on the basis of this and other evi-dence that "behind every oath-swearing lurked every kind of intrigue and abuse."[72] It is surely significant that Ine, if we understand §66 as a reference to bargaining rather than the ordeal, seems to have recog-nized how advocacy often amounted to an unsavory business that advantaged the well-connected. His legislation restrains both male-factors and those positioned to profit from their misdeeds while tac-itly acknowledging that such practices may never be rooted out.

In the end, Helmstan shows himself constitutionally unable to meet the terms of his agreement with Ordlaf. One year or two later, he steals "the untended oxen at Fonthill" and is "completely ruined" (*forwearð*), forfeiting both his lands at Tisbury (which had remained his possession) and his usufructuary rights to the five hides at Fontill.[73] Some sense of the impossible situation in which Helmstan now found himself is suggested by *Ine* §47, which stipulates that an accusation of having stolen cattle may be refuted only by an oath of sixty hides – so long as the accused person is "oath-worthy" (*gif he aðwyrðe bið*).

Again, there is no hint of the ordeal as an option for Helmstan. Instead, Edward the Elder declares him an outlaw (*flyman*) and claims his lands at Tisbury. Ordlaf retains outright the property at Fonthill. Yet his pointed question to the king's reeve who arrives to claim the land for the royal demesne ("I then asked him why he did so") suggests to Keynes that Ordlaf "considered that the punishment was too severe for the crime."[74] We might add that some of Ordlaf's displeasure may come from his finding himself in the position of the

[71] Keynes 1992: 77.
[72] Keynes 1992: 75.
[73] Keynes 1992: 83–85.
[74] Keynes 1992: 83.

offender's advocate in *Ine* §66. Ordlaf had certainly prospered from Helmstan's friendship, and so the arrival of the reeve was bad news for both men.

Ordlaf's final mention of Helmstan shows that options still remained, even in a desperate situation:

> Then he sought your father's [Alfred's] body, and brought a seal to me, and I was with you at Chippenham. Then I gave the seal to you, and you removed his outlawry and gave him the estate to which he still has withdrawn.[75]

What ought to be made of Helmstan's gesture is difficult to know. Simon Keynes has suggested that Helmstan's intent in seeking the king's body was to swear an oath, perhaps about something the king had said or done on his behalf, the seal serving as proof.[76] Alternatively, it is possible that Alfred's tomb was already a site of pilgrimage, lending penitential overtones to Helmstan's journey there.[77] In any case, Helmstan's gambit works. Relying once again on Ordlaf's advocacy, Helmstan gives him a "seal" (*insigle*) perhaps witnessing to an oath or penitential act undertaken at Alfred's grave. The faintness of the boundary between oaths and ordeals earlier noted may be perceptible here; perhaps the latter had not yet fully detached from the former as a matter of practice.

Once transferred to King Edward by Ordlaf, the seal wins Helmstan release from his sentence of outlawry and a small estate to which he withdraws.[78] Alfred thus confers on Helmstan, this time by obscure and perhaps spiritual means, the same mercy he had shown him in life. Remarkably, there are few traces in this text – one of our few detailed records of litigation – of the "system" of Germanic procedure (as outlined by Brunner and Pollock) that formed the basis of Liebermann's conclusion regarding *Ine* §66. Instead, the will of the king stands at the center of the disputing process, and what happens over the course of Helmstan's criminal career is in fact quite close to what the early (unemended) legislation of Wessex would have us expect.

[75] *Đa gesahte he ðines fæder lic 7 brohte insigle to me, 7 ic wæs æt Cippanhomme mit te. Đa ageaf ic ðæt insigle ðe. 7 ðu him forgeafe his eard 7 ða are ðe he get on gebogen hæfð.* Keynes 1992: 88.

[76] Keynes 1992: 88.

[77] Marafioti 2015.

[78] Keynes 1992: 88.

Oaths and Vows

If Ine's laws have long been positioned as the earliest witness to the ordeal, Alfred's statements on oaths have enjoyed a comparable status in historical accounts of how formal proof took shape in early English law, being most often invoked as evidence for the solemnity with which the oath was regarded at this time.[79] The most significant addition to this body of commentary is Wormald's view that Alfred's concern with the oath indicates his having introduced (presumably for the first time) a "general oath of loyalty," as had Charlemagne.[80] The presumptive introduction of such an oath was an important element of Wormald's broader reassessment of the pre-Conquest legal order. Older scholarship had held that elements of English common law such as "felony" and "crime," both of which presuppose a vigorous state, emerged only during the reign of Henry II. But Wormald maintained that the ground for such developments had already been prepared "from the late ninth century onwards" by "an oath taken by all free men at the age of twelve, the effect of which was to make serious crime of any sort into a species of treason (or, as French-speakers came to call it, felony): the thief, quite simply was as much the king's enemy as a traitor."[81] On the basis of this assumption, Wormald held that introductory clauses of the *domboc* must "hold the key to early English law and order." (Liebermann had earlier viewed this section as forming *der Kern des Werkes*.)[82]

While a full assessment of Wormald's views concerning the origins of the loyalty oath is beyond the scope of this study, it should be noted that, in this instance, broader polemical aims may be at work here. While he recognized that the clauses of Alfred's laws concerning oaths constitute "legislation in the sense that they seem to establish new legal principles," the absence of direct evidence for an "oath of loyalty" forced Wormald to conclude that the clauses in question must be *allusive* in nature, acknowledging reforms already enacted by other means. Since there is much about their contents (as we will

---

[79] See, e.g., Keynes and Lapidge 1983: 306 n. 6.
[80] Wormald 1999a: 283; 2009: 194.
[81] Wormald 2009: 194.
[82] Liebermann 1903–1916, III: 33 (§21). His reference is to this concern as manifest specifically in Alfred's laws.

see shortly) that suggests an attempt not to heighten but mitigate, in accordance with clerical learning, the stringency of obligations assumed under vows and oaths, these clauses cannot have been themselves the instruments by which an oath of loyalty became embedded in judicial practice.[83]

Wormald's hypothesis also depends on some rather hoary views of the nature of proof itself in this period. As we will see, one commonplace assumption that may be found in studies from the later nineteenth century into the present is that the mainstays of proof in litigation, the oath and the ordeal, were inflexible elements of custom whose workings must have remained roughly the same in both the early and late Anglo-Saxon period. No commentator on earlier English law has considered the development of these practices over time – presumably because they are understood not to have a history. It is easy to imagine a ninth-century king wanting to channel this reservoir of devout feeling toward himself.

But to speak complacently of "the oath" as some changeless aggregate of practices risks ignoring both the varied nature of our written evidence and the circumstances under which it was composed. As we have seen, laws were put in writing (and, in many instances, devised) by bishops and other ecclesiastics from the outset of their development. In the case of the means of proof just referred to, this point assumes particular importance. Elite clergy were trained in a tradition that did not always look with a friendly eye on either the oath or its sibling, the ordeal, and often sought to minimize the spiritual hazards of each.[84] Moreover, presupposing some immutable "system" by which civil litigation proceeded among the Germanic-speaking peoples has, as will be shown in the following pages, tempted commentators to see things in the written evidence that probably aren't there and to assume that written laws refer to this system even when their language suggests otherwise.

Let us turn, then, to the language of the clauses in question, and consider them apart from any speculations about the descent of institutions. Having shown his laws, he tells us, to all of his councilors

---

[83] This point Wormald seems to have tacitly recognized (1999a: 282).

[84] On resistance to the oath and ordeal among bishops and clergy, see Brasington 2016: 26, 46, 59–60.

and won their unanimous assent, Alfred begins their enumeration by urging what this body felt "most needful" (*þæt mæst ðearf ís*): that each man prudently keep his oath and his vow (*þæt æghwelc mon his að 7 his wed wærlice healde*). That Alfred's aim in having his laws begin this way was to emphasize the peculiar sanctity of such gestures seems obvious enough; indeed, this is often all that is said about these provisions. But the pairing of "oath" with "vow" suggests a concern, little remarked in published commentary, not so much with "the oath" as with the consequences of varied kinds of solemn declarations. Subclauses that follow confirm such purposes. The first (§1.1) concedes that, for anyone finding himself bound by a promise or oath (the text does not say which) either to betray his lord or give aid to any illicit undertaking, it is better to be false (*áleogan* is the etymon of Modern English "lie") than to fulfill the obligation. Subsequent provisions (§1.2–4) offer remedies to those failing to fulfill even *legitimate* obligations. Those so offending are to be placed "in the prison on an estate of the king for forty nights" (*feowertig nihta on carcerne on cyninges tune*) where they shall make amends "according to what the bishop prescribes" (*scrife*). The specifically penitential nature of the imprisonment here prescribed has been emphasized by Daniel Thomas.[85] To his observations we may add that, if prior West Frankish practice is any guide, it might be said that these provisions are rather lenient. In the first *Capitula* of Theodulf of Orléans (§26), a layman confessing perjury is to be assigned the same period of penance as an adulterer or a homicide; refusing to confess in a case of manifest guilt is punished with excommunication.[86] A penance of forty days, in contrast, is assigned by the *Pœnitentiale Theodori* for clerical drunkenness (I.i.3) and the offense of desiring fornication without opportunity (I.i.10).

The presence of such offenders on a royal estate also, perhaps significantly, ensures their protection from those they have wronged. Their kin are permitted to provide them with food, while offenders without relatives who might so assist them may expect the king's

---

[85] Thomas 2014: 104–105.

[86] Sauer 1978: 340–341 (with post-Alfredian Old English translation); Brommer 1984: 123; McCracken and Cabaniss 1957: 391. The *Capitula* notes, so as to emphasize the magnitude of the offense, that perjury is *in lege et prophetis sive evangelio prohibitum*.

reeve to act in their stead. So long as they attempt no escape during
these forty days, offenders are understood to have fulfilled their obligations. Fleeing prior to the completion of this term of days is punished with excommunication, or, if others have stood surety,
compensation of the same as well as a further remedy to be determined by a confessor (*swa him his scrift scrife*) for having broken yet
another agreement (*wedbryce*). Subsequent clauses mandating compensation for violating either the sanctuaries of royal minsters or the
"king's security" (*cyninges borg*) indicate that, whatever may be the
modern connotations of imprisonment, the royal "prison" reserved
for those in breach of solemn agreements is above all a place of refuge from violent reprisals.

   As we have seen, Wormald classed these opening ordinances on
oaths and pledges among a relative handful of Alfredian laws that
"establish new legal principles."[87] Their aim, as in later legislation to
this effect, was in his view to assert that keeping one's word was
"one of the duties owed by the Christian citizen, along with regular
resort to the sacraments and avoidance of all imaginable vices."[88]
Into this category Wormald also places a clause punishing a person
guilty of *folcleasung* ("slander") with "no lighter settlement than
that one should cut out his tongue" (§33) and a prescription of
remedies for those in breach of a "pledge sworn by God" (*godborg*)
(§34), as well as a handful of attempts to regularize penalties for
theft and other offenses. While Wormald regarded these as heteroge-
neous in nature, the clause on *folcleasung* perhaps being derived ultimately from the *Theodosian Code,* he was in no doubt that §1 gives
evidence of broader purposes. Turning to "a 901 charter record[ing]
the forfeiture of Ealdorman Wulfhere" for having deserted the king
contrary to the terms of a prior oath, Wormald asserts that the
agreement in question "sounds very much like an oath of loyalty";
thus "it is a fair deduction that the *að* of the laws was one too."[89]
There is no doubt that such a general oath was in place by the reign
of Edward the Elder, who refers (II *Edward* §5) to an "oath and
agreement [...] taken by the whole nation" (*ðe eal ðeod geseald*

[87] Wormald 1999a: 282.
[88] Wormald 2014: 121; also Green 1999: 62–63.
[89] Wormald 2014: 119; also Wormald 1999a: 148, 284.

hæfð). Edward's clause is one of several that allude to the *domboc*.
But it may not for this reason be assumed that Edward's understanding of *að and wedd* is the same as that underlying *Alfred* §1. At the
outset of the present chapter, we observed that Edward's provisions,
however much they brandish the *domboc* as the foundation of
sound judgments, were not guided by any scruples about modifying
its provisions.

Wormald is perhaps right in seeing the preoccupations of §1 as
characteristically Alfredian. As he observes, the collocation *að and
wed* may be found as well in the Old English *Orosius* and (with
some regularity) in the *Anglo-Saxon Chronicle,* both of which are
traceable to the revival of learning in late ninth-century Wessex.[90]
Other commentators have not gone quite as far as Wormald, however, in their assumptions about how §1 is to be understood.
Typically, the clause is paraphrased to indicate Alfred's concern for
oaths and pledges as solemn obligations "on which order in Anglo-
Saxon society depended."[91] Even this view, however, seems difficult
to maintain given what we have just seen. In effect, the provisions of
§1 vitiate somewhat the binding nature of promissory oaths and
vows. Instead of adding to the force of such obligations, Alfred here
offers assurances that vows undertaken foolishly may be abandoned
as well as protections for those who have failed to fulfill lawful
vows; the latter are in effect placed under the care of the church. If
Alfred's principal intent was to assert the inviolability of oaths and
pledges, he had a strange way of making his point. These clauses
seem meant above all to ensure that such matters be dealt with by
clerical and not worldly means of justice.

How may these provisions be reconciled with the opening exhortation? In making sense of *Alfred* §1, we ought to consider more
closely a word whose significance to the ordinance has been rather
mistakenly overlooked. Wormald translates the opening sentence as
follows: "First we teach, as is most necessary, that each man carefully (*wærlice*) keep his oath and pledge."[92] To gloss *wærlice* as
"carefully," which assumes a concern with *fulfilling* obligations

---

[90] Wormald 2014: 119.
[91] Keynes and Lapidge 1983: 306 n. 6
[92] Wormald 2014: 112.

established through solemn agreements, certainly bears the sanction of tradition. *Quadripartitus* rendered the term *multa* [...] *observantia;* Lambarde gave *diligenter* (*Archaionomia,* fol. 27); Schmid *wahrhaft* ("truly, faithfully"); Liebermann *sorgfältig* ("carefully"). Yet Thorpe gives "warily," and Liebermann himself, in his commentary, suggests the meaning is perhaps closer to *bedacht* ("prudently"). This latter meaning seems preferable, in part because the clause immediately following this one insists that one is *not* obliged to fulfill all such agreements, and in part because of how Alfred (or his amanuensis) uses this term in the Old English *Pastoral Care*:[93]

xv. *How the teacher must be discreet in his silence and useful in his words.*

Let the teacher be moderate and discreet and useful in his words, lest he keep unsaid what is useful to speak, or speak what ought to be kept silent. For as unguarded and careless speaking (*unwærlicu & giemeleaslicu spræc*) leads men astray (*menn dweleð*), so the excessive silence of the teacher leads into error those whom he might teach if he were willing to speak.

There are further reasons to think that "unguarded and careless speaking," and mitigating the effects thereof, might be the principal concern of this and other sections deemed by Wormald to be Alfredian innovations. A sequence of clauses in the *Pœnitentiale Theodori* sound very much like what we see in *Alfred* §1. Here we are told (I.xiv.5–7) that if a man or woman has vowed virginity and is subsequently married, he or she "shall not set aside the marriage but shall do penance for three years" (*non dimittat illud sed peniteat III annos*).[94] A woman "tak[ing] a vow [of virginity] without the consent of her husband [...] can be released, and she shall do penance according to the decision of a priest" (*dimitti potest et peniteat iudicio sacerdotis*).[95] The principle underlying these clauses is stated bluntly: "Foolish vows and those incapable of being performed are to be set aside" (*Vota stulta et inportabilia frangenda sunt*).[96] Elsewhere (I.viii.6), after establishing periods of penance for false oaths sworn on sacred objects or "on the hand of a bishop or of a presbyter," the *Pœnitentiale* asserts that "If anyone swears on the

93 Sweet 1871: 88.
94 Finsterwalder 1929: 307.
95 Finsterwalder 1929: 307.
96 McNeill and Gamer 1938: 196; Finsterwalder 1929: 307.

hand of a layman, among the Greeks there is no offense" (*Qui autem in manu hominis iurat, apud Grecos nihil est*), an allowance for pastoral leniency.[97] Significantly, the remedy is left in these clauses (as in Alfred's laws) to the *iudicio sacerdotis,* the "judgment of the confessor." The Theodorean clauses also hint at the overall sense of *Alfred* §1. While both compilations assert the gravity of solemn agreements, both also provide means of evading their consequences when these are foolish, impractical, or immoral, Alfred's *unryhtum* having a potentially broader meaning than "unlawful," the standard gloss.[98]

Alfred's opening clauses on oaths and vows also bear some resemblance to Ælfric's later treatment of the subject in his sermon on the Decollation of St. John the Baptist. Here Ælfric uses the same adverb (*wærlice*) found at the outset of Alfred's laws in a sense probably identical to what we find in the *Pastoral Care:* "Yet if we anywhere heedlessly swear, and the oath compel us to a worse deed, then it will be more advisable for us to avoid the greater guilt, and atone to God for the oath" (*Þeah-hwæðere gif we hwær unwærlice swerion, and se að ús geneadige to wyrsan dæde, þonne bið us rædlicor þæt we ðone maran gylt forbugon, and ðone að wið God gebétan*).[99] Though it is possible that the passage reflects some awareness of the *domboc,* it seems likelier that both the *domboc* and Ælfric are drawing from the same stream of patristic teaching on the hazards inherent in oaths, one manifestation of which is furnished by the *Poenitentiale Theodori.*[100] That the passage occurs in Ælfric's sermon shortly after a discussion of Christ's "swear not at all" (cf. Matthew 5: 34–37) suggests that what is at issue for the abbot (and, perhaps, for Alfred) is not so much establishing ways out of one's obligations as admonishing auditors to see caution with their speech as a requirement of their baptism.

---

[97] McNeill and Gamer 1938: 228.

[98] See Bosworth-Toller, 1898, s.v. *riht.*

[99] Thorpe 1844: 482–483.

[100] Bede's sermon on the Decollation of St. John the Baptist, which likewise asserts that some oaths ought not be fulfilled (and was a likely source for Ælfric's, on which see Förster 1894: 23), may derive in part from Origen's commentary on Matthew, though no Latin translation of the latter text survives. See Bonner 1973: 75.

The necessity of watching one's tongue resounds through passages of Scripture that were probably familiar to Alfred and his circle (cf. Ecclesiasticus 20: 5–9; James 3:5–8). One prominent example that seems particularly appropriate to Alfred's concerns in the *domboc* is Sirach 23:7–11, which bears in the Vulgate the subheading "Discipline of the Tongue" (*DOCTRINA ORIS*). The text warns in particular against habitual oaths (23:9; 23:11) and addresses the matter of whether oaths made casually are still binding: "The one who swears many oaths is full of iniquity, and the scourge will not leave his house. If he swears in error, his sin remains on him, and if he disregards it, he sins doubly; if he swears a false oath, he will not be justified, for his house will be filled with calamities."[101] If the theme is only suggested by *Alfred* §1, its presence seems certain in other clauses identified by Wormald as devised by Alfred and his circle. The *folcleasung* clause in particular seems an appropriate punishment for someone who has used his tongue to harm others. In the following century, the commandment against murder (*non occides*) was glossed by Ælfric as a condemnation of those who, through false accusations, condemned others to death: "He is guilty of manslaying who kills someone, and who condemns another to death through slander (*forsegð*)."[102] Ælfric's exegesis of Scripture is elsewhere scrupulous in its dependence on earlier commentary, and it may be assumed that this remains the case with his interpretation of *non occides*.[103]

The clause concerning *Godborg* is of particular interest in this regard. It would be a mistake to presume that we have any firm knowledge of what is meant by the term, a compound unattested elsewhere that may be broken down to the constituents "God" and "surety." The standard view is that this term is to be explained as a survival of the pre-Christian era, in which security for an agreement was established through "invocation by one or both parties of

---

[101] Coogan 2001.

[102] Godden 1979: 119.

[103] Godden finds no patristic source for Ælfric's addition of "death by false accusation" (Godden 2000: 459). But the abbot's cautious reliance on established authorities throughout his corpus of writings and his horror of novelties (see Green 1989: 63) suggests that this cannot have been his own addition to the text and therefore owes something either to patristic teaching or to the exegetical traditions of the church in England.

supernatural powers as guarantors of the engagement," the "ancient practice" being "subsequently Christianized."[104] The gesture as described in Irish and Welsh materials left D. A. Binchy in "little doubt that the Welsh *briduw* and the Anglo-Saxon *Godborg* are similar vestigial survivals."[105] Wormald accepted Binchy's views without qualification.[106] One wonders, however, whether some refinements are in order. In this clause (§34), which follows immediately after the provision on *folcleasung*, we are told what is to happen should one wish to make an accusation of having been falsely promised something by means of a *Godborg*. The accuser is to make his assertatory oath in four churches. The person so accused, however, must make his oath in twelve churches. If we take for granted that *Godborg* was a form of asseveration invoking one's baptism or salvation as a pledge (*borg*), we can see that *Alfred* §34 is perhaps a response to casuistry on the part of the person making the specious promise. One imagines that the accused may, once confronted with his failure to fulfill the promised obligation, have retreated to a claim that he had not made an oath *per se*, as no clergy had been present and no sacred objects touched. In the later Middle Ages, such stratagems led ecclesiastical courts to enforce "contractual obligations [...] backed up by oaths or genuine, full-blooded promises equivalent to oaths," among which were promises made by one's body or one's faith.[107] Alfred's remedy establishes, as did these courts in later centuries, that any invocation of the divine will for assurance in an agreement is *tantamount* to an oath. As with his opening clauses on adherence to one's *að and wed*, he places these disputants under the care of the church by obliging them to swear formal oaths, this time overseen by clergy. His ordinance offers a major disincentive for casual invocations of sacred matters in the course of transactions. It also echoes the remonstrances of early homilists whose works were avidly read in Anglo-Saxon England, such as that of Caesarius of Arles (d.543):

Accustom yourself not only to avoid perjury but to avoid the oath as well, for it is written: "The one who swears many oaths is full of iniquity, and the

---

[104] Binchy 1972: 362.
[105] Binchy 1972: 363.
[106] Wormald 1999a: 283.
[107] Ibbetson 1999: 136.

scourge will not leave his house"; and the Lord: "Do not swear at all," he said, "let your speech be 'yes, yes', 'no, no'."[108]

Caesarius's concern, it should be noted, is with habitual swearing (*nec iurare consuescite*), which inevitably leads to violation of the Decalogue's stricture against casual invocation of God's witness: *Non adsumes nomen Domini Dei tui in vanum* (Exod. 20:6). The offense remedied is the one for which the revelers of *The Pardoner's Tale* are punished – an oath uttered carelessly that nonetheless binds the speaker to the promised act and its consequences.

Conclusion: "Making Law"

Wormald's overall assessment of the *domboc* was mentioned toward the outset of this chapter. The legislation contained within it, he says, does not show kings "making law"; rather, it "showed what the law [already] was," whether by custom or by "royal decree." The foregoing has suggested some qualifications to this view. What we see in these clauses are attempts to exploit the new possibilities of writing by infusing elements of traditional law – the "bargaining" (*ceap*) over wrongs and remedies, the solemnity of one's *að and wed* – with norms derived either from accumulated judicial experience (as in Ine) or ecclesiastical learning (in the case of Alfred).[109] The provisions thus enact in miniature what many works of royal legislation do as a whole. They begin with insistence that the laws change none of the old ways of doing things, whether by leaving the traditional language unchanged (Ine) or commencing with an exhortation that appears to affirm existing custom (Alfred). But by offering specifics about the implementation of these practices that might formerly have resided with the judges and litigants themselves, the laws of Alfred and Ine alter the content of the law by setting it within the mold of elite expectations.

In that they presuppose a division between what is written and what was customary, Wormald's remarks disclose a larger problem

---

[108] *Non solum periurare, sed nec iurare consuescite, quia scriptura dicit:* "*Vir multum iurans implebitur iniquitate, et non discendit de domo illius plaga*" [Sir. 23:12] *Et Dominus:* "*Nolite, inquid, iurare omnino; sit autem sermo vester: est est, non non*" [Matth. 5:37]. Delage 1971: 436 (14§3).

[109] Wormald 1977 [repr. 1999b]: 8.

with how we conceive of law in early Wessex. As we have seen, Wormald's work was preceded by a long historiographical tradition that sought to separate the unwritten (and therefore older and more "authentic") from the written, even to the extent of superimposing the former on the latter. In making such assumptions – which were never confronted "head on" by Wormald and occasionally even resorted to – do we not ignore shifting notions of what the word "law" was coming to mean? It is hard to imagine that, by the end of the Alfredian period, the concept was any longer wholly divorced from what was written. The *domboc* itself cannot avoid seeming like one long exercise in uniting what had been in prior centuries disparate notions of customary law (*æ*) and royal (written) decrees (*domas*). Given the uses to which the *domboc* was put in these later centuries, not only by kings descended from Alfred but also Wulfstan and Ælfric, it is perhaps time that the text be seen in light of the Alfredian achievement in general, rather than abstracted from it as some last survival of the *leges barbarorum*. The *domboc* was not simply the grandest exercise in royal self-advertisement that England had yet seen. It was a careful attempt to make law a matter of books, learning, and royal initiative, and to demonstrate, perhaps in order to justify this definitive break from prior practice, the long history of such ideas within the kingdom of Wessex.

4

The Transmission of the *Domboc:* Old English Manuscripts and Other Early Witnesses

The best evidence that the *domboc* was felt by contemporaries and later generations to be a work of exceptional importance is the atypically large number of witnesses in which it survives. The past century of research has shown the perils of arranging them into a *stemma* as did Liebermann in his edition. "All in all," Wormald wrote, "it is impossible to say how many branches there are to the textual tree of Alfred's lawbook; though one may perhaps think in terms of up to half a dozen."[1] The present chapter describes the extant Old English witnesses in which Alfred's *domboc* appears, briefly considering as well post-Conquest witnesses such as *Quadripartitus* and *Leges Henrici Primi* in which Alfred's text was translated or otherwise adapted for use by antiquarians of the Anglo-Norman era.[2] These manuscripts may be arranged chronologically as follows:[3]

[1] Wormald 1999a: 266. Other comments are no less discouraging: "Liebermann's stemmatic analysis of these textual witnesses was so vitiated by misconceptions about manuscript origins, major lost codices and so on that it would be pointless to reproduce here; while any attempted substitute would fall foul of a plethora of irresolvable uncertainties" (265). It will be shown in the pages that follow just what Wormald meant by this.

[2] Turk (1893: 19–24) maintained that **Ot** and **Bu** derive perhaps immediately from **E**; he suggested such a possibility for **G** as well. **B** and **H** he held to derive from some common (lost) witness given a number of shared variants (on which see Chapter 3, 82–83; also, in the present chapter, 134–140). But the stemma given in his edition (24) seems at odds with these remarks.

[3] The dates given are those assigned in Ker 1957 and, where his conclusions differ, Wormald 1999a.

TABLE 4 Surviving Old English manuscripts of the *domboc*

E	CCCC 173 (s. x^{med}).
Ot	BL Cotton Otho B.xi (1001x1012 [Wormald 1999a: 173]).
Bu	BL Burney MS 277 (s. xi²).
G	BL Cotton Nero A.i ff. 3-57 (s. xi^{med} [Ker]; "on or just after the 1066 watershed" [Wormald 1999a: 228]).
B	CCCC 383 (s. xi/xii).
H	Medway Archive and Local Studies Centre, Strood, England MS DRc/R1: *Textus Roffensis* (1123-1124 [Wormald 1999a: 245]).

Upon examining more closely the state in which these materials survive, one cannot fail to be struck by the toll exacted on manuscripts of the *domboc* by various misfortunes. Efforts by Alfred and his successors to make the text available in a number of witnesses – perhaps more than are now known – were no match for the historical and linguistic amnesia that set in by the later Middle Ages or the catastrophes that befell many Anglo-Saxon manuscripts from the sixteenth to the eighteenth century. One witness, surviving in a single leaf (**Bu**), had been "used as a wrapper in or before s. xiii, to judge from the scribbles."[4] Others underwent careless and probably destructive rebinding in the aftermath of the Henrician Reformation. The greatest disaster awaited what was probably one of the most important witnesses to have remained thus far intact (**Ot**), which was "largely destroyed" by the 1731 fire at Ashburnham House, surviving now only in a few "charred fragments."[5]

Calamity has so much accompanied Alfred's laws that they may be found complete only in two manuscripts. Each appeared at opposite ends of the *domboc*'s early medieval transmission and was thus prepared with very different purposes in mind. In Cambridge, Corpus Christi College 173, assigned the *siglum* E in Liebermann's *Gesetze der Angelsachsen*, the *domboc* appears in a hand dated by Ker to the middle of the tenth century, making this the only witness traceable to a period in which events of Alfred's reign were still in living memory.[6]

---

[4] Ker 1957: 172. Ultimately **Bu** came into the possession of the Rev. Charles Burney (whence the abbreviation), being subsequently acquired by the British Library in 1818 after Burney's death.

[5] Grant 1974: 112; Dammery 1990: 39.

[6] Liebermann 1903-1916: I, xxiv. The manuscript is no. 39 in Ker 1957. The laws of Alfred and Ine, occupying ff. 33-52v, are written according to Ker "in a hand ... of s. x med. which is intermediate in character between hands (2) and (3) of the

As it was bequeathed by Queen Elizabeth's Archbishop of Canterbury, Matthew Parker, to the library of Corpus Christi College, Cambridge, it is sometimes labeled the "Parker Manuscript." This codex – really a collection of "booklets" prepared at various times, as Malcolm Parkes noted – is devoted above all to historical materials, and in the judgment of Wormald it is more as an historical monument than a binding work of legislation that Alfred's *domboc* is here preserved.[7] The earliest of these "booklets" (fols. 1–25, "a booklet of s. ix ex. extended in s. x in.") commences with the West-Saxon royal genealogy (fol. 1r) and proceeds thence (fols. 1v-25v) to "the earliest surviving copy of the compilation known as the *Anglo-Saxon Chronicle*."[8] In spite of its archaism, the "booklet" containing the *Anglo-Saxon Chronicle* probably did not stand too close to the archetype, though it does, according to Parkes, "reflect the nature and sometimes even the format of the various exemplars from which it was copied."[9]

The ultimate origins of E are disputed. That a pairing of the laws with the *Anglo-Saxon Chronicle* is owing to Alfredian influence was asserted by Geffrei Gaimar in his *Estorie des Engles* (1136x37), who says of the king:[10]

> Il fist escrivre un livre engleis
> des aventures e des leis
> e dé batailles de la terre
> e des reis k'i firent la guere,
> e maint livre fist il escrivre
> u li bon clerc vont sovent lire.

[He had a book written in English of the events that took place, the laws that were enacted, the battles fought in the country, and which kings waged war, and he had a large number of books written which good scholars frequently consult.]

chronicle" (59). For a facsimile edition, see Flower and Smith 1941. Turk (1893: 19) held that E "gives altogether the most correct text of the code, copied conscientiously at a time when Æ[lfred's] laws were still of vital importance from an Ælfredian MS. in his capital city."

7 "Even the most hard-headed scholar can hardly deny that the laws were consciously associated with the Chronicle half a century after their composition" (Wormald 1999a: 167). Parkes suggested as a parallel Paris, BN lat. 10758, a manuscript "compiled at Rheims in the ninth century ... contain[ing] a combination of historical and legislative texts" (Parkes 1976: 167).

8 Parkes 1976: 149–150. The description of the manuscript given here is greatly informed by Parkes's.

9 Parkes 1976: 149.

10 Short 2009: 188–189 (ll. 3449–3454).

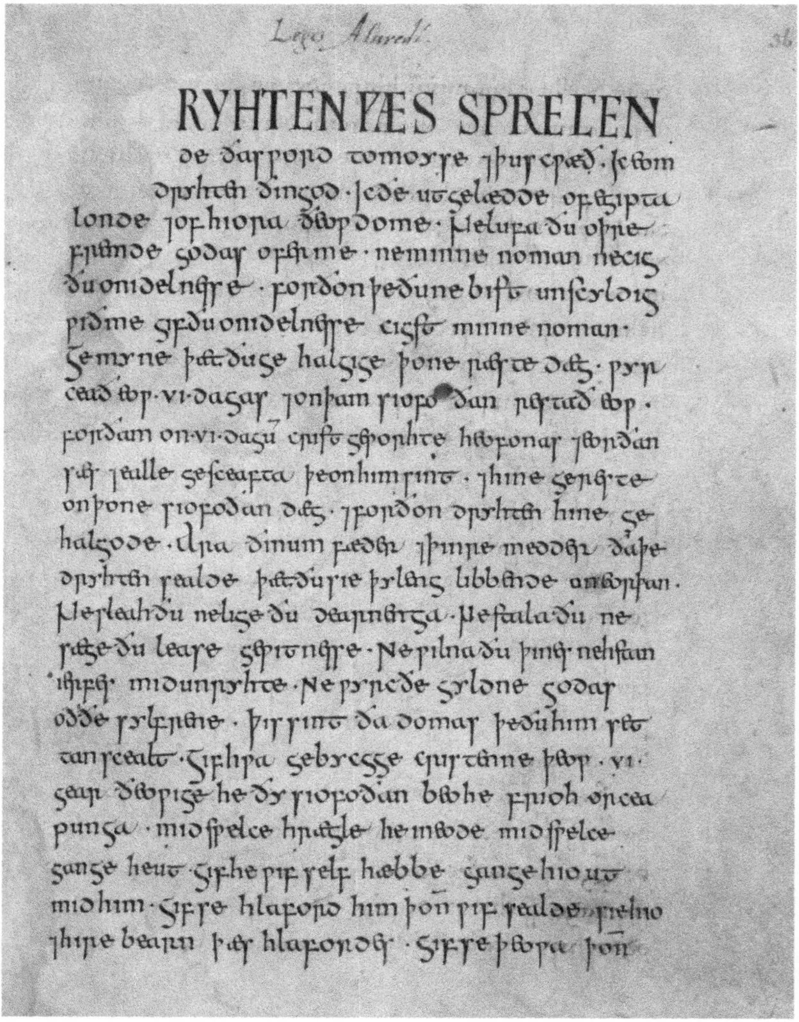
Leges Aluredi. 36

RYHTEN ÞÆS SPRECEN
de ðas word to moyse 7 þus cwæð. Ic eom
dryhten ðin god. Ic ðe utgelædde of egipta
londe 7 of hiora ðeowdome. Ne lufa ðu oþre
fremde godas ofer me. Ne minne noman ne cig
ðu on idelnesse. forðon þe ðu ne bist unscyldig
wið me gif ðu on idelnesse cigst minne noman.
Gemyne þæt ðu gehalgige þone ræstedæg. Wyr
ceað eow .vi. dagas 7 on þam siofoðan restað eow.
forðam on .vi. dagum crist geworhte heofonas 7 eorðan
sæs 7 ealle gesceafta þe on him sint. 7 hine gereste
on þone siofoðan dæg. 7 forðon dryhten hine ge
halgode. Ara ðinum fæder 7 þinre medder ða þe
dryhten sealde þæt ðu sie þy leng libbende on eorþan.
Ne sleah ðu. Ne lige ðu dearnenga. Ne stala ðu. Ne
sæge ðu lease gewitnesse. Ne wilna ðu þines nehstan
ierfes mid unryhte. Ne wyrc ðe gyldne godas
oððe sylfrene. Þis sint ða domas þe ðu him set
tan scealt. Gif hwa gebycge cristenne þeow. vi.
gear ðeowige he. ðy siofoðan beo he frioh orcea
punga. Mid swelce hrægle he ineode mid swelce
gange he ut. Gif he wif self hæbbe gange hio ut
mid him. Gif se hlaford him þonne wif sealde sie hio
7 hire bearn þæs hlafordes. Gif se þeowa þonne

FIGURE 3 Cambridge, Corpus Christi College, MS 173, fol. 36r. Note the space left blank for a large initial at the beginning of the *MP*, also a feature of **G**. (Photograph courtesy of the Master and Fellows of Corpus Christi College, Cambridge.)

The attribution to Alfred seems doubtful, but the lines at least allow for the possibility that Gaimar was acquainted with a manuscript such as E; perhaps, as Plummer wrote, even a now-lost antecedent.[11] In particular, Gaimar's description of the *livre englais* as consisting both of laws (*leis*) and accounts of kings making war (*reis k'i firent la guere*) seems an adequate summary of its contents. To Parkes, manuscript E amounts to

a record of the achievements of the West Saxon royal house in war – down to the last campaign of Edward the Elder, and in peace – down to the legislation of Alfred. It is as though the compiler had in mind Alfred's high regard for the kings before him as expressed in the letter which accompanied the exemplars of the *Cura Pastoralis* – how they heeded both God and his messengers, how they prospered both in martial prowess and in knowledge, how they extended their native territory outwards and maintained their peace, their morality and their authority within the realm.[12]

Though housed in the library of Christ Church Canterbury by the late eleventh century, a Winchester provenance has long been assumed, the basis of which, as A. H. Smith notes, is the belief of some medieval writers active long after Alfred's reign – Gaimar included, who claimed to derive some of the episodes of his text from *l'estorie de Wincestre* – that Winchester was in some sense the "capital" of Wessex during Alfred's reign.[13] Though this view has been repudiated, the Winchester provenance of E has fared better in commentary over the past few decades.[14] Moreover, what is known of royal activity in Winchester around the time of Alfred's death accords well with the contents of E. Grimbald of St. Bertin's, perhaps the leading member of the circle of clerics assembled by Alfred, was established by the king as abbot of a small monastic community within the city.[15] The first years of the tenth century, during which work on E is sure to have commenced, saw the construction there of the New Minster "around a nucleus consisting of the site of

---

[11] See Smith 1935, summarizing Plummer and Earle 1899, who felt that "Gaimar represents an earlier stage than E in the development of the E tradition" (ii, lx).
[12] Parkes 1976: 167.
[13] Plummer and Earle 1899: II, lx; Short 2009: 350 (l. 6467); see also Wormald 1999a: 141. Winchester seems unlikely to have enjoyed this status during Alfred's reign; see Smith 1935: 8.
[14] See Wormald 1999a: 167–171.
[15] Grierson 1940: 533.

Grimbald's *monasteriolum* with its church and stone dormitory."[16]
Though it may not have been meant at first to serve as a royal mausoleum, the New Minster had certainly assumed this function by the
middle of the tenth century, containing by this point the remains of
Alfred (translated from the Old Minster), his wife, and his sons.[17]
The same concerns with memorializing the achievement of Alfred
seem to extend to E, whose copy of the *domboc* dates to this time.

We have seen that the laws of Edward the Elder and Æthelstan
assert that copies of the *domboc* were available for consultation by
judges. The features of early West Saxon orthography found in E's
domboc suggest its indebtedness to texts (since lost) prepared in the
last years of the ninth century. E's *domboc* regularly gives:

1   *o* before nasal consonants (*hond, mon, lond*) where late West-
    Saxon manuscripts give *a*;
2   *sellan, geselle, self* in place of late West-Saxon *syllan, gesylle, sylf*;
3   <io> for late West-Saxon <eo> in *hio, sio, frioh*; and
4   spellings in <ie> (*ierfes* for late West-Saxon *yrfes, fierst* for later
    fyrst), reflecting a practice that appeared "during the latter half of
    the ninth century ... reach[ing] its highest point towards the end
    of the century."[18]

These forms are of particular interest given that they are regularly
(but not uniformly) replaced in late manuscripts of the *domboc,* an
indication that they were felt to be archaic from the eleventh century
onward. They survive as well in **Ot,** and their occasional retention in
B and **H** (more pronouncedly in the latter) suggests their debt to
exemplar(s) not unlike **Ot** – or perhaps, in the case of **H,** to **E** itself.
E's *domboc* also retains words that must have seemed outworn or
obscure to later scribes, such as *mennen* "female slave" (e.g.,
þeowmennen [MP §21]). **G** gives instead *þeowne* and **H** *þeowene*

---

[16] Biddle 1976: 314.
[17] Biddle 1976: 314.
[18] Sweet 1871: xxix, whose judgment is largely confirmed in Campbell 1959: 126–
    128 (§§299–301); see also Schreiber 2002: 89. The digraph represented a range of
    sounds at this time. The resemblance between the orthography of E's *domboc* and
    the Alfredian *Pastoral Care* and *Orosius* is asserted by Liebermann (1903–1916:
    III, 32 [§16]). On *o* before nasals, a feature found "especially in the Pastoral Care,"
    see Fulk 1992: 295. On early West Saxon *sel-*, see Campbell 1959: 134 (§325). On
    <io> for <eo> see Campbell 1959: §293–296; also Gretsch 1994: 65.

"female slave"; both reflect a tendency toward the "modernization" of the *domboc*'s vocabulary also manifest in **B**.[19]

Though **E**'s *domboc* exhibits strong traces of a ninth-century exemplar, it should be noted that the pervasiveness of these early West-Saxon forms in this witness does not quite approach that of other Alfredian texts. The earliest witness to the *Pastoral Care*, for example – Bodleian, Hatton 20 – has *mildhiortnes* in place of **E**'s *mildheortness* (*MP* §49); though the word is frequently used throughout the *domboc*, ðiow (also characteristic of some ninth-century manuscripts) is wholly absent from **E**, which gives instead ðeow without exception.[20] That the form *ciorl* (also appearing in Bodleian, Hatton 20) so often appears in **H** where **E** has instead *ceorl* (<*ciorl*> never occurs in **E**'s *domboc*) suggests that among **H**'s exemplars was a text older than **E** or retaining a substantial number of relict forms (though a calculated orthographic archaism on the part of the scribe, as will be shown later, cannot be ruled out).[21]

Other spellings typical of Bodleian, Hatton 20 and other Alfredian manuscripts – <oe> to represent /o/ under front mutation, omission of initial <h> (also, deceptively, a feature of later manuscripts, particularly those composed after the Conquest) – are found nowhere in **E**'s *domboc*.[22] The process of phasing out archaisms thus had already begun when the scribe of **E** set to work. Indeed, it had during Alfred's lifetime, as **E**'s version of Ine suggests a regularization of the text that likely took place during the late ninth century. According to Liebermann, "No grapheme, no inflection, no word occurs in our text of Ine that would have been entirely antiquated and impossible to use around the year 890."[23] On this basis Liebermann concludes

---

[19] In *MP* §12, however, *mennenu* (**E**) is retained in **G**, though replaced by **H** (accurately) with *þeowwifman*. On the Anglian and thus archaic status of *mennen*, see Wenisch 1979: 303.

[20] On these forms in the *Pastoral Care*, see Campbell 1959: §296.

[21] See Sweet 1871: 99. For instances of *ciorl-* in **H**, see Rubr. LXXXIIII, *Alfred* §§ 29, 40 (2x), *Ine* §§ 18, 38, 39, 41, 43, 61, 64. **E** overwhelmingly gives *ceorl-* and, occasionally, *cierl-*.

[22] On <oe>, see Campbell 1959: §203 (where the form is categorized as Mercian given its occurrence in the Vespasian Psalter); on omission of word-initial *h*, see Sweet 1871: xxxi.

[23] See Liebermann 1903–1916: iii, 63 [§3]: "Keine Lautdarstellung, keine Flexion, kein Wort kommt in unserem Ine-Text vor, das für 890 gänzlich veraltet und unmöglich wäre."

that Alfred, being no antiquarian (*Altertümler*) but a lawgiving king, felt few reservations about modernizing the text in a sweeping fashion. Yet there were limits placed upon Alfred's undertaking. Ine's laws in E retain a number of rare terms and *hapax legomena* (noted in the edition). Syntactic features also found in the Kentish laws of the seventh century, such as frequent use of the instrumental without prepositions and of an implied subject where one is explicit in later legislation, are likewise residual from a pre-Alfredian text of Ine. On the basis of such forms, Liebermann concluded that "Ine sounds, on the whole, more archaic than the nearly contemporary [laws of] Wihtred."[24]

Though the text of the *domboc* as we have it in E is at some remove from whatever was promulgated by Alfred (as was Alfred's text of Ine from the original), there can be no doubt that it affords the best possible view of the *domboc* as it is likely to have been known to Alfred and his contemporaries. In addition to being the earliest extant witness by far to Alfred's laws, it is the witness wherein we find the greatest abundance of undoubtedly Alfredian orthographic features and (in Wormald's view) the one most closely tied by content and circumstance to the activities of the royal court.[25] E therefore serves as the base manuscript of our edition. Other surviving witnesses do not begin to approach it in authority, nor are they likely to retain variants from witnesses older than E.

The two witnesses closest in date to E, these being BL Cotton Otho B.xi (Liebermann's **Ot**) and BL Burney MS 277 (**Bu**), are damaged almost beyond use, though the latter is sufficiently legible in portions of what remains to suggest something of its provenance.[26] From a transcript by Laurence Nowell (to be discussed later) and a description of the manuscript authored by Humfrey Wanley in 1705, some details of **Ot** may, with considerable caution, be reconstructed.[27] In structure and conception **Ot** resembled somewhat the

---

[24] "Im ganzen klingt Ine archaischer als der fast gleichzeitige Wihtræd." Liebermann 1903–1916: iii, 64 [§3].

[25] See Wormald 1999a: 172.

[26] **Ot** is no. 180 in Ker 1957, where it is dated "s. x med.-xii" and assigned a Winchester provenance (234).

[27] See Richards 2014b: 285; Ker 1957: 230–234 (no. 180).

organization of **E** and appears to have been in part derived from it; this seems particularly likely of its version of the *domboc*. As had been the case with **E**, the manuscript commenced with historical materials (in this case, portions of an Old English version of Bede's *Historia ecclesiastica* composed in the middle of the tenth century, "[t]he West-Saxon genealogy to Alfred," a copy [likewise partial] of the Parker *Chronicle*, and "a list of popes to Damasus and of archbishops of Canterbury and bishops of Rochester, Essex, Sussex, Wessex, and Sherborne, with later additions"); legal materials, however, were limited to II *Æthelstan* and the *domboc*, which concluded here with *Ymb Æwbricas,* a treatise on adultery.[28] Though the version of the Burghal Hidage that followed the *domboc* in **Ot** seems to bear some connection to what came before, the texts with which the manuscript concluded (the poem *Seasons for Fasting* and "a collection of medical recipes, many known from the Leechbook") seem extraneous; according to Richards, it is at least possible that these last three items "share a regulatory aspect that could have interested a compiler when he broadened the scope of the collection taken from CCCC 173."[29]

The Winchester provenance of **Ot** makes it potentially traceable to the activities of the West-Saxon royal court, a circumstance that perhaps explains its relatively conservative orthography. In at least two instances, it offers suggestions of an orthography even *more* conservative than **E** (e.g., *Ine* §68), though its scribe was not above making occasional errors (*Alfred* §44.2, 46). The state in which it survives permits little more in the way of observations; much of it is simply impossible to read by any means.[30]

---

[28] Ker 1957: 231; Richards 2014a: 3. The treatise is translated and discussed in Wormald 1999a: 372–373, who contends that the scribe of **Ot** was possibly "concern[ed] to make it part of the *domboc*" given "Nowell's failure to mark a break between it and what had gone before (or Wanley's to notice it at all)."

[29] Richards 2014a: 4 and 12.

[30] Those examining the manuscript will want to know that the surviving leaves are mounted in the following order: f. 49v gives rubrics I–XXVI, f. 49r rubrics XXVII–LIII, f. 50v *Alfred* §§41–44.3, f. 50r *Alfred* §§44.4–56, f. 52v *Ine* §§ 67.3–72, f. 52r *Ine* §§74.1–76, f. 53r *Ine* §§77–78.2, f. 53v *Ine* §§72–74. An indispensable aid is Dammery 1990: 40, where similar guidance is given (but in accordance with Liebermann's clause numbers).

The Nowell Transcripts: An Excursus

It has been said that some knowledge of the orthography of Ot is potentially supplied by a partial transcript of its contents prepared by Laurence Nowell omitting the West-Saxon genealogy and the list of popes and bishops.[31] Before considering such a possibility, a word should be said here about Nowell's transcription work in general, which played a great role in reviving the study of Old English – more than was routinely acknowledged prior to the 1920s. In 1923, Kenneth Sisam noticed certain anomalies in two works of legislation attributed to King Æthelstan in Lambarde's *Archaionomia* (1568). These variants had earlier led Liebermann to suppose that, here and elsewhere, Lambarde had access to manuscripts now lost. For this reason, Liebermann (as did Thorpe, Schmid, and Turk before him) noted scrupulously in his critical apparatus variants from the *Archaionomia* (given the siglum "Ld") in all texts of the *Gesetze* that were earlier printed by Lambarde. Liebermann's *stemma* likewise included the *Archaionomia* under the same assumption.

Sisam's conclusion, arrived at after a close examination of the discrepancies in question, held devastating implications for Liebermann's textual criticism: "Lambard's ancient manuscript is a ghost, despite the pedigree Liebermann has prepared for it: and Lambard's texts of *I Athelstan* and the *Ordinance* are translations of the *Quadripartitus* into Elizabethan Anglo-Saxon."[32] Sisam went on to trace these anomalies to the fourteenth-century manuscript of *Quadripartitus* likely used by Nowell, who prepared the transcription of these texts employed by Lambarde as the latter acknowledges himself.[33] Sisam saw his claims supported in work by Robin Flower, who showed (in Sisam's description) "that when Nowell transcribed the Old English version of Bede's History from MS. Otho B.xi into B.M. MS. Addit. 43703, he added pseudo-Anglo-Saxon renderings of

---

[31] See Ker 1957: 230–231. On Nowell's transcript of 1562, now BL Add. 43703, see Grant 1996, Richards 2014a, and Richards 2014b: 285. The matter of Nowell's transcripts is of immense complexity, as is made clear in Wormald 1997a: 165. In assessing Nowell's contribution to *Archaionomia*, one must contend not only with Nowell's transcript of Ot, but a range of other copies and editions in his hand that may or may not owe something to this manuscript.

[32] Sisam 1923–1925: 234.

[33] Sisam 1923–1925: 235; cf. Lambarde 1568: aiii.

sentences that are in the Latin original but not in any other manuscript of the English version."[34] In all likelihood, Lambarde believed himself to be printing authentic transcriptions of the texts in question and cannot have known the extent to which Nowell's exuberance compromised the witnesses used.[35]

Sisam revisited the subject in 1925 in order to refute objections raised by Liebermann. In the course of doing so, he found evidence that Lambarde's texts of *Norðleoda laga, Mircna laga,* and *Að* were "also modern."[36] Other transcripts uncovered by Flower would reveal the full debt of Lambarde to Nowell's tainted work. One such text, Canterbury Cathedral Lit. MS E.2, is in Wormald's description "essentially a transcript of Harley 55(B) [...] featur[ing] all the linguistic solecisms which characterize *Archaionomia* texts, and which are thereby shown to be products of Nowell's pen rather than lost textual traditions."[37] Here as well, Nowell "smother[ed] the Harley text with interlinear or marginal emendations drawn from variants in Nero A.i(A) and Corpus 383, from translations of *Quadripartitus,* or from his own fertile mind."[38] Though the existence in the second half of the sixteenth century of lost witnesses employed by Lambarde may not be wholly ruled out, even the most generous analysis must conclude that the evidence for them is rather faint.[39] Meanwhile, subsequent investigation has revealed still more translations from *Quadripartitus* masquerading as authentic Old English, some extending even into Nowell's transcripts of materials from the *domboc.*[40]

The likelihood that Nowell's transcripts contain his own renderings from *Quadripartitus* must haunt any reader who searches these texts for evidence of lost manuscripts. Even where Nowell acted only in the role of copyist, however, his texts could not avoid laying yet more traps for subsequent editors. Before preparing the transcripts of **Ot** in 1562, Nowell had studied Old English for at most a year.[41] While his

[34] Sisam 1923–1925: 237.
[35] Sisam 1923–1925: 236.
[36] Sisam 1923–1925: 247.
[37] Wormald 1999a: 261.
[38] Wormald 1999a: 261.
[39] This is the conclusion of Wormald 1997a: 175–177.
[40] Dammery 1990: 162
[41] Richards 2014a: 15–17.

script displays what seems a revealing mimicry of his exemplar, his unsure grasp of the language leads to a number of errors and omissions. The judgment of Raymond J. S. Grant is particularly damning: "[I]t is clear that Nowell's transcript of the Bede is of no use to the student of spellings, phonology or inflections and no dialect indications can be drawn from it. [...] It can safely be assumed that Nowell brought a similar attitude to bear on the other texts he copied."[42]

These problems, along with the likelihood that Nowell's version of the *domboc* in BL Add. 43703 was corrected against other Old English witnesses or *Quadripartitus,* suffice to show the hazards of assuming it to furnish anything like a reliable picture of **Ot**.[43] One source of variants in this transcript seems likely to have been **G** (to be discussed later).[44] Other variants correspond to no known witnesses. Sourceless variants in another Nowell transcript identified as such by Carl Berkhout in 1990 (BL, Henry Davis Collection, M30) prompted Dammery to conclude that anomalies in this text "almost certainly provide evidence of at least one lost manuscript, which existed in the sixteenth century."[45] But another transcript unknown to Dammery suggests a more mundane explanation for variants unexampled elsewhere. This text is in private hands, with only photographs being owned by the British Library. The manuscript is designated RP 9865: "Manuscript on vellum of the laws of King Ine (promulgated between 688 and 694), in facing Anglo-Saxon and Tudor English, written in the formal hand of Laurence Nowell, with autograph additions by his friend, colleague, and executor William Lambarde."[46] Its date of "*c.*1565" places it some years after BL Add. 43703 but prior to the publication of *Archaionomia.*

Any sense of what the medieval exemplar of this transcript might have been is wholly obscured by the peculiarities of Nowell's approach already described.[47] Nowell's manner of dealing with his Old English exemplars here may be illustrated by the following table:

---

[42] Grant 1974: 124. See also Grant 1996: 28.
[43] Richards 2014a: 16; Dammery 1990: 84.
[44] Dammery 1990: 88.
[45] Dammery 1990: 103. The identification was made at a conference in Manchester described by Dammery (1990: 102).
[46] Zoe Stansell, p.c.
[47] While at work on the present edition, Oliver prepared a transcript of RP 9865 which is here quoted.

TABLE 5 Nowell's version of *Ine* §22 in RP 9865

Nowell (RP 9865)	E (fol. 48b)	Bu (fol. 42v)	B (fol. 25r)	H (fol. 26v)
Be elþeodiges monnes slyht . Gif mon elþeodne ofslea: se cy: ning ah twædne dæl þæs weres. þriddan dæl sunu oþþe magas; Gif he þonne mægleas sie: healf cyning healf se sið; Gif hit þō: ne abbod sie oðð abboddesse: dæ:len len on þa ylcan wisan wið þone cyning.	[lxvii be elðeodies monnes slege fol. 34r] Gif mon elðeodigne ófslea secyning ah twædne dæl weres þriddandæl sunu oððe mægas. Gif he ðonne mægleas sie healf kyninge healf sege sið. Gif hit ðonne abbod sie oððe abbodesse dælen onþa ilcan wisan wið þone kyning.	lxvii Gif mon elþeodigne ofslea se kining ancwæd ne dæl weres driddan dæl sunu oððe mæges	BE ælðeodiges mannes slæge. Gif mon ælþeodigne mon of slea. se cyng ahtwegen dælas þæs weres . ðriddan dæl sunu oððe magas gyf he ðonne mæg leas sy half cyning . half segesið. Gif hit ðonne abbud sy oððe abbudisse dælon onða ilcan wisan . wið ðonne cyning.	[Lxvii Be ælþeodiges mannes slæge fol.10r] Gif man ælðeodigne ofslea se cyning ah twegen dæl^as þæs weres . ðriddan dæl sunu oþþe magas. gif he ðonne mægle^as sy . healf cyninge . healf sege sið. Gif hit ðonne abbud sy . oððe abbudisse . dælon onða ilcan wisan wið ðone cyning.

Much about the behavior of this transcript is familiar from Nowell's other work. We have forms unattested in all extant witnesses: *slyht* (in the rubric) for *slege/slæge*; *elþeodne* for *elþeodigne/ælþeodigne*; nonsensical *sið* for *gesið*. We have also a mixture of early West-Saxon forms with those typical of later witnesses, which we would not expect of **Ot**: While retention of <o> in *mon, monnes* may have been characteristic of his exemplar, this seems unlikely for Nowell's *magas* for *mægas* or *ylcan* for *ilcan*, these being the preferred forms in **G** and all subsequent witnesses. Alongside these we have forms almost certain to derive from **E** (though with scrambled spelling) as they are found in no other witness, such as *abbod* for *abbud* and *dælen* for *dælon*. For these variants a range of causes is discernible and few of these require access to lost witnesses. Nowell's *elþeodne* seems a case of eye-skip, *ylcan* evidence of an indifference to the finer points of orthography perhaps motivated by Elizabethan spelling habits.[48] But his use of *sið* in place of *gesið* (it occurs in his text as *se sið*) seems perfectly explicable given the treatment of this word in both **E** and **H** (in Old English manuscripts, the *ge-* prefix often detaches itself from the words it modifies).

To isolate the source of a particularly striking variant in the Nowell transcripts is, more often than not, to find oneself in an inescapable maze. In the case of Nowell's *se sið*, for example, the source would seem to be **E** rather than **H**, particularly given the view, argued for by Dammery, that Nowell "probably did not know that manuscript [i.e., **H**], and Lambarde did not see it until after the publication of the *Archaionomia* in 1568."[49] But Dammery makes this point in order to explain away variants in other Nowell transcripts that "resemble **H**," the presence of which, given his prior conclusion, renders "the sources with which Nowell collated his transcript [...] a mystery."[50] Other variants suggest a similar problem. Nowell's *dæl þæs weres*, including a genitive demonstrative absent in **E** and **Bu**, seems in some sense derived from **B**. But it is only in **H** that we find Nowell's *dæl*, subsequently corrected by the scribe to *dælas* in order to bring the text into conformity with **B**.[51]

Where does this leave the Nowell transcripts as evidence for the transmission of the *domboc*? It is true that Sisam's was not the last word, and weighing the question of lost witnesses properly obliges one to consider as well the qualified defenses of Liebermann by Roland Torkar, Richard Dammery, and Patrick Wormald. Yet the results of these inquiries were less encouraging than might be hoped. After sorting through all the available evidence (excluding the

---

[48] Dammery notes that in "Elizabethan practice ... 'i' and 'y' were used almost interchangeably" (Dammery 1990: 92) and holds this to account for some variants in Nowell's BL Add. 43703.

[49] Dammery 1990: 157.

[50] Dammery 1990: 157.

[51] Close comparison of RP 9865 with the 1568 *Archaionomia* shows this particular Nowell transcript to have had no effect upon Lambarde's edition in spite of his awareness of it. Occasionally it exhibits evidence of rushed preparation, e.g., where Lambarde gives *gefæstenode* 7 *getrymed*, RP 9865 gives the nonsensical *gefæstrymed*; prefixes and inflectional endings are also frequently omitted.

transcript described here), Wormald observed "half a dozen" readings in BL Add. 43703 (here described as "Nw1" [the transcript] and "Nw2" [corrections to the former made by Nowell]) unattested in other witnesses that "would make one think that Nowell had consulted *Textus Roffensis*."[52] Yet the crucial point for Wormald remains that Lambarde had no access to H prior to 1568 ("*Archaionomia* shows no signs of *Roffensis* features, until Lambarde began to note them by hand in his own copies"); accordingly, we are obliged in his view to assume that these features "must come from another vernacular manuscript: one that no longer survives."[53] It is hard to see how such a conclusion does not beg the question of whether Nowell was acquainted with H, which, as we have seen, Dammery is not willing to rule out.[54] When one considers the "Ld" variants that echo readings from H – for example, *Alfred* §1.2, which supplies a subordinate clause absent in E but attested in H and in *Archaionomia* as well as Liebermann's "So" (another Nowell transcript) – there seem few reasons not to see in them the hand of someone as inattentive to the orthography of his sources as Nowell apparently was.

One's confidence in the possibility of a lost medieval source is by no means strengthened by Wormald's concession that Nw1/2, while undoubtedly contributing to Lambarde's text in some fashion, were among a range of sources employed by Lambarde, the full scope of which remains unknown. Indeed, Wormald's qualifications seem to open up the possibility that the worth of Nw1/2 rests in their being at best *witnesses to the witnesses* used by Lambarde, the latter being not medieval but prepared by Nowell. Wormald's general assessment of Lambarde's resources seems to furnish uncertain ground at best for the supposition that one may hope to find in *Archaionomia* traces of an early witness no longer extant:

As with II and V Æthelstan, there are many indications that Nw1/2, Nw3 and Nw4 contributed to *Archaionomia*, in so far as its idiosyncrasies (errors included) often recur there, can even be seen in the process of germination. But there are also major features of Lambarde's text which they do not rehearse. This is often a matter of his debt to Corpus 383, whose effect on the transcripts remains, by comparison, scant. Sometimes, it is rather that

---

[52] Wormald 1997a: 176.
[53] Wormald 1997a: 176.
[54] See *supra* n. 50.

trends that are manifest in the transcripts, like use of *Quadripartitus,* are intensified in Lambarde. Sometimes too, Lambarde and the transcripts both have readings that occur neither in each other nor elsewhere, but which look like a product of the same spirit of cavalier enterprise.[55]

We have seen that much rests, in the arguments put forth by Dammery and Wormald, on the impossibility of Lambarde's having been acquainted with *Textus Roffensis* until after the appearance of *Archaionomia* in 1568. For both, the argument in favor of a lost medieval manuscript essentially boils down to this: If Lambarde did not know the text until 1568, Nowell cannot have known about it either, for he surely would not have kept Lambarde in the dark about its existence. Thus *Textus Roffensis* variants, or traces of them, attest to some lost witness: "If it did not come from Corpus, and cannot have come from *Roffensis,* it may be another relic of a lost source."[56] Notably, the point was made with greater caution by Dammery ("Nowell probably did not know the manuscript") than it would be later by Wormald: "That he [Nowell] would have withheld knowledge of a collection like Rochester's from Lambarde while exploiting it to annotate his own transcripts beggars belief."[57] Close inspection of the evidence suggests Dammery's language is somewhat closer to the mark.[58] Wormald's table implies that one variant disclosing a lost witness related in some fashion to *Textus Roffensis* is "[geclips]/geclefs" in Nw1/2 (see *MP* §41; Lambarde gives *gecleps*), which comes close to *geclebs* in *Textus Roffensis* (**G** and **E** give instead *geclæsp* and *geclysp,* respectively).[59] Were this a variant sug-

---

[55] Wormald 1997a: 165–174.

[56] Wormald 1997a: 177.

[57] Wormald 1997a: 176.

[58] Dammery in fact comes very close to conceding Nowell's awareness of **H** prior to 1568 elsewhere in his study. While allowing that it is "highly probable" Nowell did not know of the text at this time, he goes on to say the following: "It is, nevertheless, curious that some of the interpolations in Nowell's transcripts (Nw1–Nw4) appear closer to **H** than to any other extant manuscript. Moreover, reference is made in an eighteenth-century list of 'Collectanea of Lawrence Nowell and William Lambarde' to passages 'ex textu Roffensi' in a 'Rhapsodia; containing various short Excerpta, written by Lambarde in 1568.' On the face of it, this could indicate that Lambarde became acquainted with the *Textus* before 1573, but one must also admit the possibility that this 'Rhapsodia' was a commonplace book, begun in 1568 and continued for some years" (Dammery 1990: 79–80).

[59] Wormald 1997a: 167. That the evidentiary weight assigned this variant was not trivial is evident from its being mentioned again in Wormald 1999a: 262 n. 384.

gesting some alternate reading that might plausibly have embedded itself within a line of transmission unattested in all other manuscripts, the argument might be more persuasive. But the term arrived at by the *Textus Roffensis* scribe seems merely a garbling (unattested elsewhere) of a word he probably did not understand. What are the odds that another manuscript would contain the same error?

Yet more difficulties emerge from the variant that is effectively the centerpiece of Wormald's argument.[60] Only in *Textus Roffensis* does Alfred §26 conclude with "⁊ fo to þam wite." This variant does not occur in *Archaionomia*. Instead it is found in one of the Nowell transcripts – Liebermann's "So" – which unlike Nowell's transcript of Ot (BL Addit. 43703) is "undated," being "[no] earlier than 1562" and "[no] later than 1567 (since it was related to Nw1 [BL Addit. 43703] which was written in 1562, and Nowell left England permanently in 1567)."[61] The likely date of the transcript suggests that Nowell did have some knowledge of H prior to the appearance of *Archaionomia*. The possibility that Lambarde ignored this variant is suggested by the fact that this transcript was undoubtedly in his possession and perhaps used as one of the base texts for *Archaionomia*.[62] Could it have arisen by Nowell translating from *Quadripartitus,* which has "et reddat witam preposito"?[63] Wormald doubts this on the ground that "these words" do not "recur elsewhere in the Anglo-Saxon legislative corpus, enabling Nowell to guess successfully what underlay *Quadripartitus*."[64] But in a footnote, Wormald refers readers to I *Æthelred* §1.9a and II *Cnut* §30.9, where something very close to this idiom is indeed found ("fo se cyning to þam were" in both).[65] Wormald holds nonetheless that "[t]his time at least, Nowell must have had inside information."[66] It is not too much to say that this lone variant is the nail on which the possibility of a lost manuscript hangs for Wormald.[67]

---

[60] See Wormald 1999a: 262 n. 384.
[61] On Liebermann's "So," see Chapter 5, 165. The quoted text is from Dammery 1990: 98.
[62] Dammery 1990: 97.
[63] Liebermann 1903–1916: I, 63.
[64] Wormald 1997a: 176–177.
[65] Wormald 1997a: 177 n. 84.
[66] Wormald 1997a: 177.
[67] Wormald 1999a: 262 n. 384, where the variant in question is held "above all" to prove the likelihood of a lost manuscript alongside three single-word variants and one two-word phrase.

In spite of the ambiguities just enumerated, Wormald maintains at the close of his essay that "*Archaionomia* variants should in principle be restored to the textual apparatus."[68] Dammery had already gone a step further by including in his apparatus variants from all of the known Nowell transcripts in addition to those of the medieval manuscripts – a tremendous feat of editorial patience. But one wonders whether such efforts are merited given Wormald's conclusion that "post-Sisam orthodoxy is very largely right," though "Liebermann was not entirely wrong." Though Wormald's essay was an attempt to recuperate Liebermann's stemma, all that is left of it is the following conjecture: "[I]t is more likely than not that he [Nowell] saw one manuscript that has since disappeared."[69] Does the evidence warrant even this attenuated restatement of Liebermann's view? Did Wormald retreat yet more from this position some years later, when he asserted that *Archaionomia* depended on a manuscript that "may be lost, but then again may be not" and warned that "any attempted substitute [for Liebermann's stemma] would fall foul of a plethora of irresolvable uncertainties"?[70]

Given that even the most ardent defender of Liebermann's hypothesized lost witness seems to withdraw from what is itself a highly qualified argument in its favor, and given that even this argument was offered with so many concessions as barely to make claims on one's assent, there seems no more prudent course than to heed Sisam's warning. As their perceived value as evidence for the transmission of the *domboc* has plummeted since Liebermann's lifetime, our edition does not regularly take note of variants from sixteenth-century versions. It may be *possible,* as Torkar maintained, that Elizabethan antiquaries had access to manuscripts unknown to us now, and that a word here or there might allow us to perceive their influence; in a similar way, perhaps, it is possible at the right time of year to spot Jupiter between the clouds of a hailstorm.[71] In the end, however, the hypothesis of lost manuscripts, now whittled down to perhaps a single lost witness suggested by variants known to occur in *Textus Roffensis*, rests on more certainty than seems appropriate about what

[68] Wormald 1997a: 178.
[69] Wormald 1997a: 177.
[70] Wormald 1999a: 260 and 265, respectively. (See also n. 1 of the present chapter.)
[71] Torkar 1981: 110.

resources were available and unavailable to Lambarde and Nowell. The views of Ker (which are, admittedly, offered on the basis of Sisam's discoveries) probably afford the safest ground: "[T]he manuscripts used for *Archaionomia* are not, as Liebermann thought, numerous and now largely missing, but few and extant" (li). Or, to put it more generously, it is a matter of "irresolvable uncertainties."

Remaining Old English Witnesses

We may now turn to the other unfortunate specimen of the *domboc,* Liebermann's **Bu**; a somewhat later text, it is dated by Ker as "s. xi²."[72] Its history has already been described; in its present state, it offers no more than a glimpse of a possibly Kentish copy of §§1–22 of Ine's laws.[73] "The two pages containing the central portion of the text are stained and partly illegible from exposure."[74] So said Ker. But the condition of this witness may be more accurately set forth by observing the vastly different condition of 42r and 42v, the latter being quite readable. It is on this page that chapters of Ine's laws came to be surrounded by exercises in penmanship at some point during the thirteenth century.

In its orthography, **Bu** stands close to E but not as close as **Ot.** Even with its substantial admixture of Kentish spellings, **Bu** retains most of the forms characteristic of early West Saxon and virtually none of the deliberate modernizations widespread in subsequent manuscripts. The handful of instances in which its readings agree with **H** against all other manuscripts (Ine §§3, 5, 8, 13, 20.2) may offer some suggestion of its use later in the Anglo-Saxon period. But the evidence is too faint to permit more than speculation, as most of its commonalities with **H** involve no more than minor points of orthography.

---

[72] See Ker 1957: 171–172 (no. 136). Dammery (1990: 51) dates the text to the post-Conquest period on palaeographical grounds, though with little elaboration.

[73] A Kentish provenance was suggested by Liebermann (I: xx), who offers as evidence a few words representative of the dialect; Ker offers no further comment. The Kentish derivation of the text seems, however, adequately demonstrated by the several instances in which it exhibits <e> for West-Saxon <y>, as in *Ine* §§3 (E *wyrce,* Bu *werce*), 5.1 (E *forwyrce,* Bu *forwerce*), 16 (E *gecyðan,* Bu *geceþan*), 17 (E *gedyrneð,* Bu *gederneð*; E *ofspyreð,* Bu *ofspereð*), 21 (E *angyldes,* Bu *angeldes*). (Some of these are noted by Liebermann.)

[74] Ker 1957: 171.

Three vernacular witnesses remain, the earliest of which was prepared either just before or just after the Conquest. All seem to reflect the changing circumstances under which the *domboc* was being read. Sure signs of renewed interest in Alfred's laws *as legislation* are evident in British Library, Cotton Nero A.i (Liebermann's **G**), fols. 45ʳ–48ʳ 51ʳ–57ᵛ, where material from the *domboc* appears only in the first ("A") section of this two-part manuscript (Ker no. 163).[75] (The two halves of **G** were bound together by 1580 according to Ker and seem to have little if any inherent connection.)[76] Section "A," the only portion of this manuscript with which we are concerned, commences with the laws of Cnut and Edgar before we arrive at the *domboc,* whose Prologue is the only portion reproduced. Wormald detected meddling by Wulfstan in its version of *MP* §43, and it is certain that Alfred's language was substantially modernized – apparently to the consternation of John Joscelyn, whose annotations emend the text in accordance with **E** and supply the missing final sections of the Prologue from this witness as well.[77] As the priority of Cnut's laws seems to indicate, this manuscript may witness to the reexamination of the *domboc* (and adaptation of its contents) evident in legislation authored by Wulfstan, though its pre-Conquest exemplar does not survive.

The production of what Wormald has called "legal encyclopedias," phenomena of which **G** appears the earliest manifestation, undoubtedly accelerated after the Norman Conquest.[78] Oddly, it was at this time that the *domboc* acquired some of the major witnesses now extant, both of which are to some extent compromised by the kinds of dialectal modernization already evident in **G**. The earliest clear example of the "compilatory tradition" that emerged fully during the reign of Henry I is Cambridge, Corpus Christi College 383, to which Liebermann gave the *siglum* **B**.[79] That this manuscript was prepared at St. Paul's, London, is not disputed. The language of **B** has been

---

[75] Dated by Ker as "s. xi med." For a facsimile edition, see Loyn 1971.

[76] Ker 1957: 215. Wormald (1999a: 198) doubts that the two parts were linked in any fashion prior to this date.

[77] See Ker 1957: 215 (art. 7); Wormald 1999a: 226.

[78] Wormald 1999a: 224–225.

[79] The phrase is Wormald's: for a discussion of the manuscript, see Wormald 1999a: 228–236. Much of what follows is indebted to Wormald's analysis of the manuscripts. The manuscript is no. 65 in Ker 1957, where it is dated "s. xi/xii."

described either as lapsing into a kind of incipient Middle English or as the handiwork of someone who did not well understand spoken or written English.[80] Certainly it gives evidence of the same modernization of scribal dialects as is found in **G**; *mon* regularly becomes *man*, *sie* becomes *sy*, *gesellan* becomes *gesyllan*, *ierfe* becomes *yrfe*. The handful of exceptions (cf. Ine §§68–69) suggest that not all of these modernizations were present in **B**'s exemplar. Whether its omission of the Prologue means that its scribe shared the same concerns as the author of *Quadripartitus* about the soundness of Alfred's undertaking is uncertain, as **B** probably contained more material than is evident from its present state, though not much more.[81]

Though some commentators have lately cast doubt upon the twelfth-century date this witness has traditionally been assigned, its ties to the "antiquarian" work undertaken at this time are nonetheless securely established by its extensive post-Conquest marginalia.[82] Most of these jottings attempt to correct readings in **B** and rely either on other manuscripts or the scribes' own (at times faulty) judgment.[83] The manuscript is also alone in placing rubrics above many of the clauses; most paraphrase those occurring in **E**, where they precede the body of the text.[84]

That Ine's laws in both **B** and **H** conclude with "Be Blaserum" ("Concerning Arsonists") and other short treatises suggested to Liebermann a shared exemplar.[85] But Wormald offered grave and likely justified cautions about the probative value of the "Be Blaserum" addition and others where **H** is concerned, noting that "the ink of these pieces is darker and the lettering larger than in the immediately preceding text of Ine (f. 31v)."[86] Their place in the manuscript is perhaps best explained by what they offered the clergy who made use of *Textus Roffensis,* many of whom likely found

---

[80] See Wormald 1999a: 234; also Liebermann's observations on the orthography of texts edited from **B**, most of which occur in volume III of his edition.

[81] Wormald 1999a: 231.

[82] A substantial challenge to the standard twelfth-century date is Powell 2010. The marginalia have attracted little discussion: see Ker 1957: 111, where it is noted that annotations assigned a sixteenth-century date by Liebermann should, except for one, be assumed to date to the twelfth century; also Wormald 1999a: 234 and n. 285.

[83] See Jurasinski 2015b.

[84] See the discussion in the headnote to the edition.

[85] See, e.g., Liebermann 1903–1916: III, 82 (n. 3 for cap. 76.3).

[86] Wormald 1999a: 249; also Hough 2001: 61.

themselves overseeing the ordeals whose procedures are outlined in these texts.[87] As there is every reason for the scribe of **H** to have sought them out, we need not assume that these texts appear in *Textus Roffensis* by virtue of mechanical copying alone.

Yet there is no disputing that versions of the *domboc* in **B** and **H** display a profound affinity. Aside from the innumerable instances of shared orthography noted in the apparatus, similar or identical phrases extant only in **B** and **H** offer *possible* evidence for Liebermann's thesis that both derive from a common source ("hq" in Liebermann's stemma).[88] The occasional substitution of *ceac* for *ceap* discussed in Chapter 3 should be grouped among these, and its occurrence in **G** suggests that this hypothetical late witness employed in **B** and **H** (not exclusively, in all likelihood) is at least coeval with **G**. Liebermann's "hq" thus may not be entirely dismissed, though its commonalities with **G** place it firmly at the later end of the date assumed by Liebermann (should it have existed at all).[89]

There is reason to be very cautious, however, about attributing with too much confidence all shared **B** and **H** variants to some shared exemplar such as Liebermann's "hq." One such variant potentially revealing how these readings found their way into **H** occurs in a clause dealing with violation of the Sunday repose. The penalties assigned a freeman for this offense are given in **B** and **H** as follows (with bold text indicating variants exclusive to these two witnesses):

Ine §3.2: If, however, a freeman works on that day without his lord's command, let him lose his freedom **or pay sixty shillings; and a priest will be liable for twice the amount.**

The variant likely proceeds from a scribe's assumption at some earlier point in the *domboc*'s transmission that the first several provisions of Ine's laws must pertain to the conduct of the "servants of God" (*Godes þeowas*) mentioned at the outset of the text. As was

---

[87] Karn (2015: 61) holds that "*Textus Roffensis* was meant for use by those priests of the church of Rochester who attended local courts in Kent, both as representatives of their church and as functionaries of the court in performing ordeal rituals."

[88] The most conspicuous evidence may be found in B and H's handling of the following clauses: *Alfred* §§ 15, 21.1, 21.2, 23, *25, 36.2, 38.2, 40.2, 41.1, 64.1; *Ine* §§ 11, 20.1, 23, 29, 31, 37, 43.1, 52, 54, 56, 78.1, 78.2.

[89] Liebermann assumes that "hq" ("hbq" in his *Stammbaum*, as it is held to explain also variants in *Quadripartitus*) appeared at some point between 920 and 1080 (Liebermann 1903–1916: III, 32).

earlier established, the term was understood to encompass regular as well as secular clergy. It also adds leniency to the clause by permitting a freeman who violates the Sunday repose to buy his way out of penal slavery. Though it is difficult to know at what point this variant entered the transmission of Ine's laws, it likely postdates **Bu**, where this addition is absent. Given that the scribe of **B** was given to supinely (and often uncomprehendingly) copying what he saw or thought he saw, it seems improbable that this addition reflects his private judgment. As for its appearance in **H**, it is quite likely that the scribe added it to the margin of his text after consultation of **B** (a practice of the scribe to be discussed in more detail subsequently). Such an impression seems adequately borne out by the manuscripts themselves. Particularly noteworthy is the addition in the right margin, just above the added material about priests, of another **B** variant (*oððe hydgyld*) absent in **E** (**Bu** is completely illegible here).

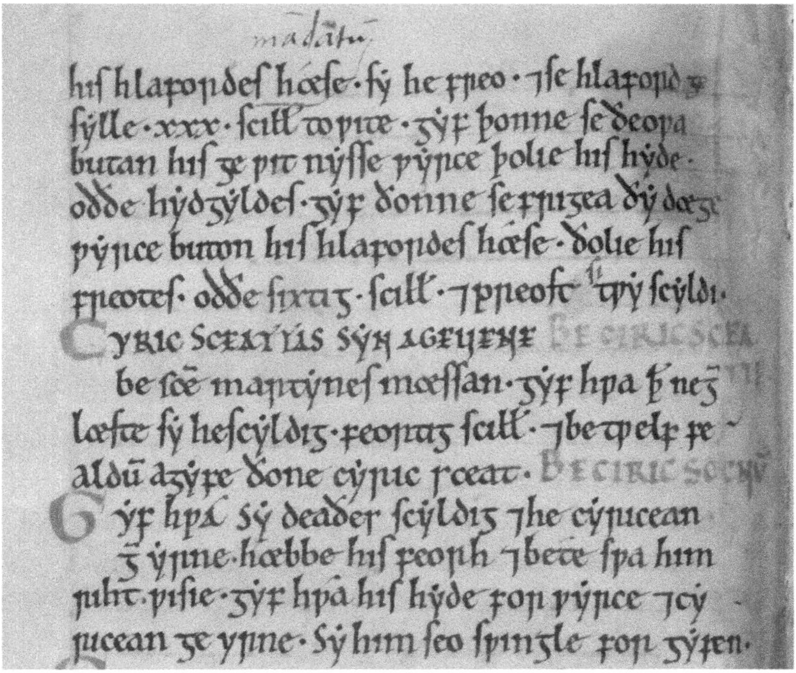

FIGURE 4 Cambridge, Corpus Christi College, MS 383 fol. 23v. Ker no. 65, "s. xi/xii." (Photograph courtesy of the Master and Fellows of Corpus Christi College, Cambridge.)

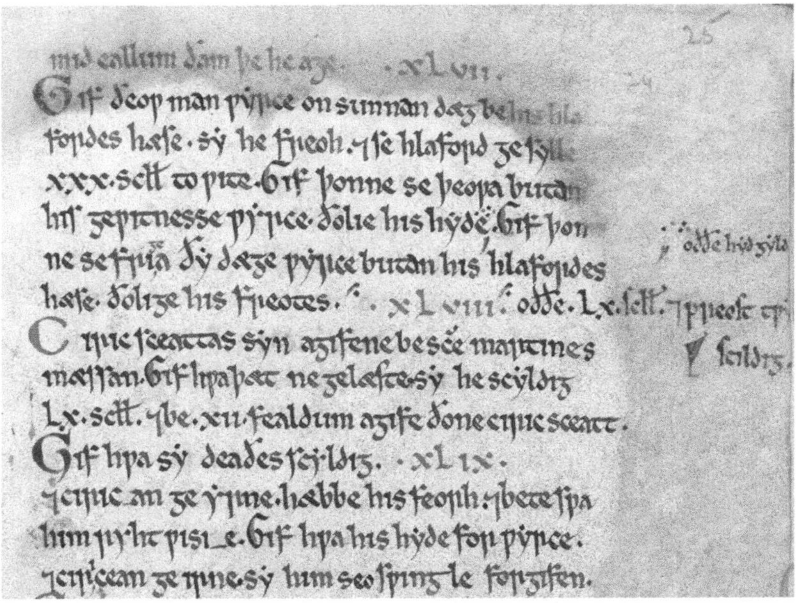

FIGURE 5 Medway Archive and Local Studies Centre, Strood, England: MS
DRc/R1 (*Textus Roffensis*), fol. 25r. (Photograph courtesy of Rochester
Cathedral.)

We may now turn our attention fully to the jewel of the "compilatory
tradition," *Textus Roffensis* (Liebermann's **H**; Ker no. 373), which
alone among witnesses that postdate **E** contains the *domboc* in full
and is arguably, given several instances in which it supplies words
and brief passages lacking in **E**, an even more complete witness to the
text than the earliest manuscript.[90] *Textus Roffensis* was prepared at
Rochester Cathedral, "almost certainly in the time of Bishop Ernulf
(1115–1124)," and contains uniquely the laws of Æthelberht, the
joint legislation of Hloðhere and Eadric, and the code of Wihtred; the
laws of Alfred and Ine are copied at fols. 9–31.[91] While some evi-
dences of Early Middle English surface in the language of this scribe
as well, the copyist of **H** seems to have read texts of pre-Conquest
legislation with insight; some of his modernizations are astute glosses

---

[90] See e.g. *Alfred* §§1.2, 32.
[91] Ker 1957: 443. The manuscript is now housed at the Medway Archive and Local
Studies Centre, Strood, England (MS DRc/R1).

of words that had not likely been in use for some time.[92] His efforts perhaps anticipate the work of scribes such as the "Tremulous Hand" of Worcester, who likewise sought to rescue Old English vernacular learning from oblivion by supplying the then-current equivalents of old words.[93]

The seriousness and care with which the scribe pursued these ends has perhaps not been appreciated to the fullest extent. Earlier it was said that Liebermann hypothesized a shared exemplar for H and B labeled "hq." But we also saw, as in the clause on Sunday observance, that not everything in "hq" (should it have existed) found its way into H during the first round of copying. In fact, many of the variants suggestive of "hq" were added to H later, almost certainly by the same scribe.[94] This poses a serious problem for the "hq" hypothesis. An abundance of evidence suggests that one of the H scribe's exemplars both in the copying *and* correcting phases of his work was not "hq" but B itself, a possibility countenanced neither by Liebermann's remarks nor Wormald's strident assertion that H's use of B was confined to the later corrections: "These amendments, *not* his original readings, bring the Alfred–Ine text into line with that of Corpus."[95] For example, B uniformly substitutes for Ine's verb *oðsacan* "to deny an accusation" the semantically all-but-identical verb *ætsacan,* presumably because the former had fallen into disuse (see *Ine* §§ 42, 47, 47.1, 48, 57).[96] H gives instead *oðsacan* in all instances – with a single exception (*Ine* § 42), which suggests a lapse in his otherwise comprehensive restoration of the older form. H's occasional lack of confidence in B is evident as well in the many instances in the main body of his text in which he leaves a space for

---

[92] See 118–19; also *Ine* §§ 61, 78.1–2.

[93] On the "Tremulous Hand," see Franzen 1991.

[94] On the identity of the main scribe and the corrector (Liebermann's "Hcor"), which seems never to have been in doubt, see Ker 1957: 444 ("Numerous linguistic alterations on ff. 1–37v are probably in the main hand").

[95] "However, a common descent (*Stammverwandtschaft*) is illuminated by the numerous errors (*zahlreiche Fehler*) that H and Hcor share with B. They require the assumption of a lost manuscript 'hb'; also the corrector of H (Hcor) must have used 'hb'" (Liebermann 1903–1916: III, 31); Wormald 1999a: 249.

[96] B does the same with other verbs containing the oð-prefix: see *Alfred* §§ 30.3, 49.1; *Ine* § 36 (3x).

a letter blank, the gap being indicated invariably by a low horizontal line. The space typically seems left in order to accommodate a letter missing in a word as it appears in B's orthography but present in E.[97] At *Ine* §74, where B had written *losie*, H wrote *losi_e*; at *Ine* §43, where B gave *gemæne* and E *gemænne,* H wrote *gemæ_ne*; at *Ine* §50, where B gave *swingelan* and E *swingellan,* H wrote *swinge_lan*; at *Alfred* §5.2 (also 5.4 and 7), where B gave *ciricean* and E *cirican,* H wrote *ciric_an*; at *Alfred* §17, where B gave *gebrede* and E *gebregde,* H wrote *gebre_de*. In one clause (*Ine* §78.1–2), H twice reproduces a word-length gap in B. Both H and B (a different hand

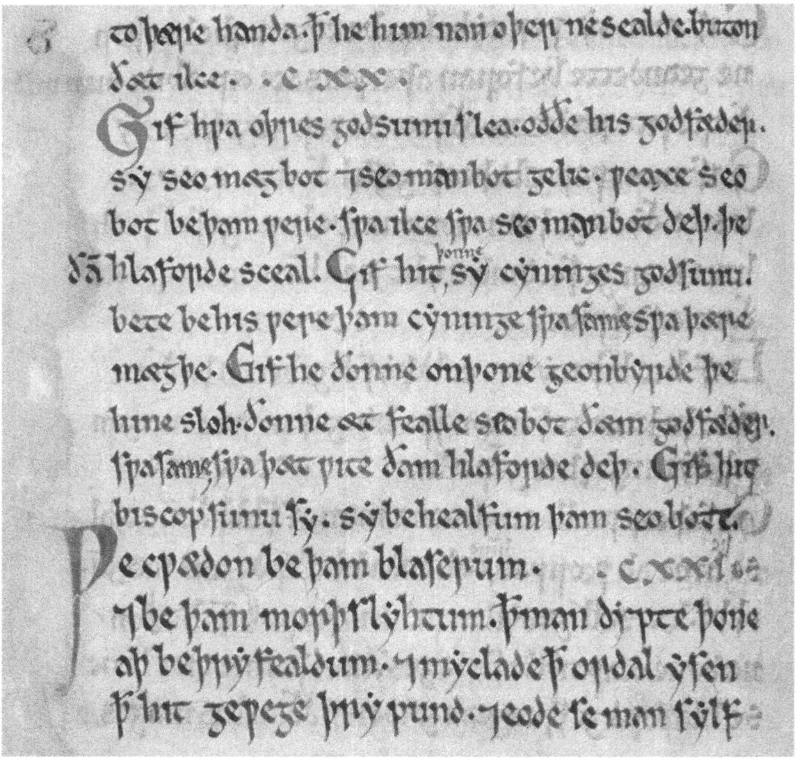

FIGURE 6 Medway Archive and Local Studies Centre, Strood, England: MS DRc/R1 (*Textus Roffensis*), fol. 31v. (Photograph: courtesy of Rochester Cathedral.)

---

[97] The scribe follows this procedure elsewhere in the manuscript (Oliver 2002: 21).

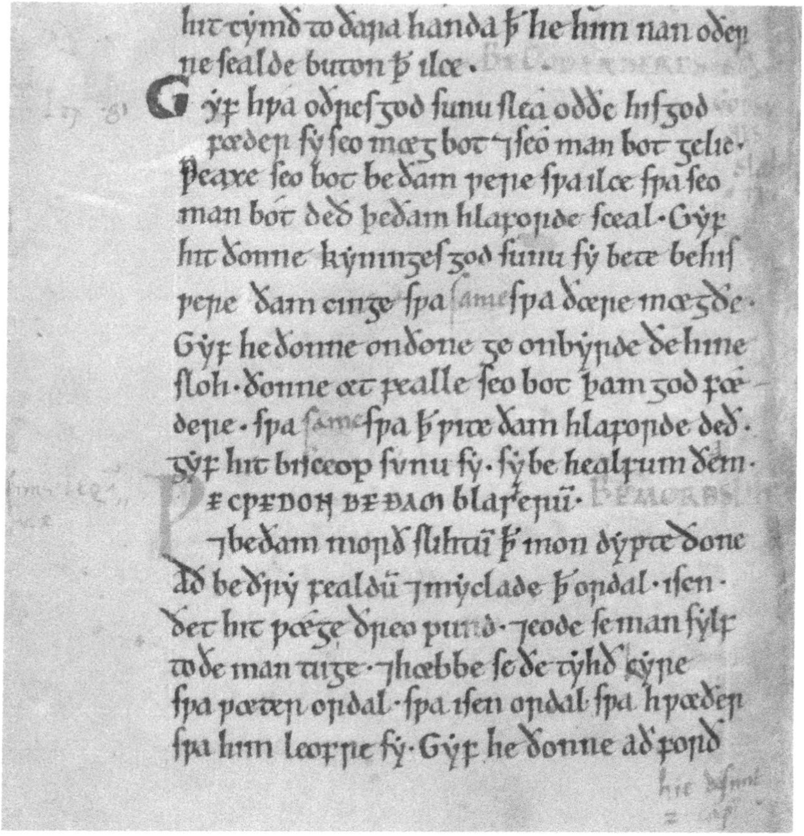

FIGURE 7 Cambridge, Corpus Christi College, MS 383, fol. 30v. (Photograph courtesy of the Master and Fellows of Corpus Christi College, Cambridge.)

in **B**) subsequently fill these gaps with the word *same* in place of Ine's apparently archaic *ilce*, the gap in **H** being discernible by the word being written in a more cramped script than the surrounding text.

H's adherence to this procedure obliges us to realize the depth and complexity of his work. To posit his use of "hq" or the like to explain what separates his text and that of **B** from all the other witnesses is to assume, against all evidence to the contrary, that he saw his task as that of a copyist alone. This has not been the prevailing view among commentators for some decades.[98] What is evident from consideration of the manuscript undertaken in the present study is instead a careful collation of whatever witness(es) he had – *as he wrote the text* – with what he found in **B**. (The examples just given show that he did not always trust what he saw there.) *Textus Roffensis* is not only the most complete witness we possess of pre-Conquest law; it is also, in the case of the *domboc* at least, the first to take the form of something like a critical edition.

Though the result may adventitiously resemble modern editorial procedures, the assumptions under which the scribe worked should not be likened to those of the present era. These assumptions are disclosed by the portion of **H** that is not always given due attention by modern legal historians: namely, the cartulary which commences: "Here begin the privileges granted to the church of Saint Andrew of Rochester from the time of king Æthelbert, who, having received the Christian faith from Saint Augustine, caused this church to be built."[99] What follows is an arsenal of royal diplomas beginning, as does the section on laws, with the activities of Æthelberht – in this case, a charter having no credibility in the view of present-day commentators.[100]

Though they were composed at different times (by the same scribe), there is little doubt that the portion of **H** devoted to charters and the one devoted to laws were "productions meant to accompany one another."[101] The full implications of their relationship extend well beyond shared content. We have seen so far that the *Textus Roffensis* scribe was eager to have his texts retain the appearance of archaic orthography. At the same time, however, he went to greater lengths than any of his contemporaries to substitute for archaic words and phrases synonyms known to his contemporaries. It has gone largely

---

[98] See, for example, Hough 2001: 67; Richards 2015: 25. There has been general agreement that the scribe of **H** used multiple sources for the *domboc*, though their nature and identity have seemed less certain.

[99] *Incipiunt priuilegia aecclesię sancti andreae hrofensis concessa a tempore ęthilberhti regis. qui fide [Christ]iana a beato augustino suscepta. eandem ecclesiam construi fecit* (DRc/R1 f.119 r).

[100] The authenticity of charters immediately subsequent to this one has seemed less doubtful: see Richards 1988: 54. Richards 1988 remains the most important and eloquent discussion of *Textus Roffensis*.

[101] Richards 1988: 44.

unremarked in published commentary that this approach is charac-
teristic of cartularies composed in the twelfth century and later.[102]
The procedure employed by the *Textus* scribe in fact bears an unno-
ticed resemblance to that of his contemporary, the scribe of BL
Additional 15350, the *Codex Wintoniensis* or cartulary of the Old
Minster in Winchester, whose work likely dates to the middle of the
twelfth century. As in **H**, the scribe responsible for the *Codex
Wintoniensis* has his text retain forms long gone even in the late
West Saxon period – all evidence, according to Kathryn Lowe, for
his "orthographic conservatism," with "later features" sometimes
"replaced with earlier forms."[103] The procedure is particularly conspicuous in the will of Wulfgar (S1533), which dates to the first half
of the tenth century and exists in an early, probably original, witness
in addition to what appears in the *Codex Wintoniensis*.[104] In this
earlier version (London, British Library, Cotton Charters viii. 16), we
see the somewhat regular retention of long and short <ie> typical of
Early West Saxon in the words such as *hiere, ieldran, hierede*, and
gehieraþ (which is broken up into three constituents by the scribe:
<ge hie raþ>) alongside other spellings characteristic of this scribal
dialect.[105] The twelfth-century *Codex Wintoniensis* not only retains
the early West Saxon <ie> digraph, abandoned not long after the
middle of the tenth century, but goes a bit further than the likely
exemplar, adding the digraph for good measure in the conjunction
gif, as well as a non-etymological *h* before the *r* in *riht*. This is
hypercorrection, an archaism that is more properly called pseudo-
archaism. The scribe of **H** likewise occasionally exceeds even **E** in
adherence to archaic spelling. We can see this in his handling of a
rubric (XII) concerning the molestation of a "churlish woman": neither **E** nor any other witness gives the *<ie>* digraph, but **H** does.[106]

---

[102] The culmination of tendencies long at work in English cartularies throughout the
Middle Ages is the *Liber Abbatiae*, a fifteenth-century compilation giving Old
English, Middle English, and Latin versions of charters granting privileges to Hyde
Abbey.

[103] Lowe 1993: 10.

[104] See discussion in Lowe 1993: 9; an image of the manuscript is given at Lowe
1993: 5.

[105] An edition of Wulfgar's will is given in Robertson 1956: 52–53 (no. 26).

[106] *Be cirliscre fæmnan onfenge* (E); *Be cierliscre fæmnan onfænge* (H).

What can we conclude from all of this? There can be no question that the laws of Æthelberht (and those that followed) were meant as the overture to the *Textus* scribe's spectacular assembly of charters. The intended effect was perhaps something like what was achieved decades later by the artist of the Guthlac roll, who adorns his text with a cloud of royal witnesses summoned from the remote past (and holding aloft their charters) to testify to their relationship with Crowland Abbey.[107] In the case of the *Textus Roffensis,* the royal laws are meant to prove, perhaps implicitly, that Rochester Cathedral Priory (first, as St. Andrew's Priory) had in fact enjoyed such a privileged status from the moment the Catholic faith established itself in Kent. From the work of one of the scribe's contemporaries, we can see that in retaining with such care the orthographical and syntactic archaisms of his exemplars, the *Textus* scribe was following a method practiced by others working to safeguard the privileges of their foundations – work that probably took on new urgency in the aftermath of the Conquest and amid growing concerns about forgery throughout western Europe.[108] In such an environment, what was old acquired a new value as evidence of a relationship between these establishments and the royal household, and the preservation of it came to be attended, perhaps for the first time in centuries, with copying methods sensitive (as the scribes of **G** and **B** were not) to the importance of forms authentic to earlier texts. Knowing this was the case gives us some sense of why *Textus Roffensis,* even though it is the latest witness to the *domboc,* gives the appearance at times of greater archaism than **E**. That it preserves with such care the orthography of its exemplars is owing not to the idiosyncrasies of the scribe but to techniques employed by many monastic foundations in the twelfth century.

---

[107] Harley Roll Y 6 (1175–1215), f. 19r.
[108] The (occasionally pseudo-)archaism of some post-Conquest charters extended even to the use of "imitation Anglo-Saxon letter forms in Latin text" (Lucas 200: 155); see also Crick 2016. On the ways in which concerns about forgery led the papal chancery to devise new methods of authentication throughout the twelfth century, see Berkhofer 2016. On the threats that probably occasioned *Textus Roffensis,* see Richards 1988: 43.

The "Compilatory Tradition": Reading and Reshaping the *Domboc*

The post-Conquest witnesses thus constitute, in essence, the first attempts at subjecting the *domboc* to acts of editorial emendation and excision. Choices made by these scribes have held far-reaching consequences for the reception of the *domboc* into the present era. Already in the post-Conquest era, the Prologue to Alfred's laws began to suffer at the hands of scholars impatient with its idiosyncrasies. While the *domboc* survives in six Old English witnesses – more than any other example of Old English legislation – the Prologue may be found in only three of these: **E, G** (where it has lost its concluding section, here supplied by Joscelyn), and **H**, where the text undergoes a fair amount of modernization. Not all omissions reveal much about the reception of the Prologue after Alfred's reign. It has already been noted that its absence from **B** seems a consequence of the vagaries of transmission. Upon being rebound at some point prior to its acquisition by Archbishop Parker and his circle, the portion of the manuscript likely containing the Prologue was lost.[109] A more definite if still uncertain set of aims may, however, be imputed to the author of *Quadripartitus*, who in preparing his translation of the *domboc* substituted without explanation the text of the Vulgate for the Old English.

The treatment of the Prologue in *Quadripartitus* would determine the way in which the *domboc* would be edited centuries later. The consequences are most plainly apparent in the version of the Prologue appearing in Lambarde's *Archaionomia*, whose text, as we have seen, relied upon transcripts that included material translated from *Quadripartitus*. The effect was to disguise just how significantly Alfred's Prologue often departs from the text of Exodus. For example, Lambarde's text occasionally supplies language missing from all of the extant vernacular manuscripts, as in his version of MP §8: *Ne sæcʒe þu leas gewitnesse wiþ ðinum nehstan = Falsum testimonium contra vicinos ne dicito.*[110] Liebermann gave these variants in the apparatus of his edition, yet it is safe to say that they reveal nothing about the pre-modern reception of the *domboc*.

---

[109] This, at least, is the conjecture in Wormald 1999a: 230–231.
[110] Lambarde 1568: 19v. The Latin is not that of the Vulgate but Lambarde's own rendering of Alfred's text (as he received it from Nowell).

In spite of improved editorial methods, most twentieth-century commentary on Alfred's laws has belittled or ignored the Prologue.[111] The decision of Frederick Levi Attenborough to omit the Prologue from his edition of Alfred's laws in 1922 due to its "having no bearing on Anglo-Saxon law" (35) excluded it from the most widely consulted edition to date. (His description of its contents, as has already been seen, errs in saying that the closing portion of the Prologue narrates "the growth of church law, as laid down by ecclesiastical councils, both ecumenical and English" [34]; the relevant chapter [*MP* §49.7] considers instead the origins of royal legislation, implying no distinction between secular and ecclesiastical law.) Such have been the consequences of decisions made by this first generation of editors, who were as impatient as their successors centuries later to ignore perceived irrelevancies in order to get at the substance of Anglo-Saxon law. The ends to which their efforts were directed are perhaps most plainly evident in *Leges Henrici Primi,* a twelfth-century legal treatise prepared by the author of *Quadripartitus.* Here the contents of the *domboc* appear dismembered alongside clauses from the laws of Cnut (and other Anglo-Saxon kings), the *Lex Ribuaria,* Latin and Old English penitentials, and bits of patristic and canonical writings. The result was a strange *catena* purporting to represent the laws of Henry I (r.1100–1135).[112]

* * *

Had all known witnesses survived unscathed, a sense of loss would still surround the *domboc.* We have one contemporaneous witness to Alfred's translation of the *Regula pastoralis;* in the absence of the Ashburnham House fire of 1731, we would possess two.[113] Yet our earliest witness to the *domboc,* appearing decades after Alfred's

---

[111] Outright contempt for the Prologue, along with the conviction that the laws ought to be considered apart from it, may be traced to the latter part of the eighteenth century; see Chapter 5, 167–168.

[112] Downer 1972.

[113] This is Bodleian, Hatton 20 (4113), Ker no. 324, where it is dated "890–7" and identified as one of the copies of the text "[s]ent to Worcester by order of King Alfred" (384–386). BL, Cotton Tiberius B. xi, assigned the same date in Ker 1957 (where it is no. 257, discussed 257–259), was almost wholly destroyed in the fire of 1731.

death, already gives evidence of the forces that would shape the reception of the text in the following centuries. Remarks in subsequent legislation by Alfred's son and grandson offer ambiguous indications that the *domboc* still enjoyed the force of living law within the West-Saxon kingdom.[114] But the organization of E suggests that even as the king's agents were being instructed to acquaint themselves with its provisions, the *domboc* was beginning its transformation into an historical artifact.

That the reception of the *domboc* should have followed such a course is perhaps an unintended consequence of the way in which it took shape. The *domboc* is a book of laws only in part. Much of it is taken up with Alfred's own brooding on the early history of England and of his own kingdom, a feature of the text evident both in its Prologue and in its inclusion of the laws of Ine, which occupy nearly as much space as Alfred's. No subsequent English king would offer as legislation something of such uncertain utility. Evidence that his efforts were nonetheless valued by later readers in Anglo-Saxon England, particularly during the "second Viking age" of the tenth and eleventh centuries, will be explored in the following chapter. It is in the records of this period, it will be shown, that one finds evidence of the *domboc* being used alongside non-legislative works that appeared during Alfred's reign by those obliged once again to rebuild English institutions and learning.

[114] See Chapter 5, 148–150.

5

Reception, Editorial History, and Interpretative Legacies

The year 1901, which saw the passing of Queen Victoria on 22 January, also marked (by some historians' reckoning) the millenary of the death of King Alfred.[1] The coincidence was not lost on those attending the lectures, festivities, and processions long planned to commemorate the latter; few more elaborate than that held in Alfred's "capital" Winchester to accompany the unveiling of a seventeen-foot-tall statue of the king.[2] For a few years, Anglo-Saxon England was a popular concern in a way it has never been since. As he had centuries prior, Alfred emerged as its most important figure, allowing a nation then at the peak of its sway over world affairs to imagine its greatness foreshadowed in the remote past.[3]

Though the anniversary of Alfred's death dotted the English landscape with this and similar monuments, its traces in the scholarly literature are surprisingly scarce. Of all the books timed to coincide with the event, Charles Plummer's *Life and Times of Alfred the*

---

[1] As Keynes (1999: 226) notes, Alfred's death was at this time wrongly understood as occurring in 901 (the date given in the *Anglo-Saxon Chronicle*), though not by all: see, e.g., Plummer 1902: 12; also Plummer and Earle 1899: 112–114.

[2] The essential account of the millenary commemoration remains the compilation prepared by Alfred Bowker, then Mayor of Winchester (see Bowker 1902; Keynes 1999: 349–350; Wormald 2004: 2). Plummer (1902: 21) related the displeasure of a learned friend at the "impertinence of Winchester to attempt to monopolise the millenary celebration."

[3] See especially Keynes 1999: 349–350.

Great (1902) is perhaps the only one still consulted.[4] Plummer's study owes some of its enduring appeal to how little it has in common with other books on Alfred published around this time. For various reasons, Alfred had proved in the years leading up to Plummer's work a powerful magnet for error and wishful thinking (not unlike Magna Carta). While narrating such accumulated fantasies ("Alfred did not 'invent the shires'"), Plummer was moved to quote a letter of his friend C. S. Taylor: "[It] is surely a mistake to make Alfred, as some folks seem to do, into a kind of ninth-century incarnation of a combined School Board and County Council" (6). To meet the sudden demand for works of scholarship on Alfred was, more often than not, an exercise in disappointing one's audience.

The favorable reputation long enjoyed by Alfred, rising occasionally to sustained fits of "Alfredomania" such as the one just described, is indeed, as Plummer and (in our own time) Simon Keynes have noted, a distinctly modern phenomenon.[5] But its roots lie deep in the Middle Ages.[6] The purpose of this final chapter is not to rehearse the development of Alfred as the subject of popular legend, a subject dealt with at greater length elsewhere, but rather to consider the reception of the *domboc* specifically – a process indeed shaped by the larger "cult of Alfred," but distinct from it as well.[7] We begin by considering the reception of the *domboc* from the decades after Alfred's death to the middle of the thirteenth century. Beyond this point, even the faintest echoes of the *domboc*'s reputation, discernible in some vernacular writing of earlier decades, seem not to survive. The chapter concludes with some observations on the rediscovery of Alfred's laws in the early modern period and on later developments that culminated in Liebermann's great edition. As we have seen in prior chapters (particularly Chapter 3), some prevailing views of the *domboc* (and Ine's laws in particular) remain the

---

[4] Wormald (2004a: 3) called Plummer's study "the best book on the king for almost a century."

[5] Keynes 1999.

[6] The point is emphasized by both Plummer (1902: 7–9) and Keynes (1999: 227–237).

[7] Liebermann's edition includes a similar discussion to which the present chapter is inevitably indebted. See Liebermann 1903–1916: III, 39 ("Der Nachruhm Ælfreds").

product of ideas that took shape in the nineteenth century and underwent little scrutiny afterwards.

Alfred's Successors and the *Domboc*

It has already been noted that the *domboc* is one of the few works of royal legislation whose authority is asserted in subsequent royal laws. In fact, its conventional label – *domboc* – owes its circulation more to later texts than to Alfred's laws themselves, whose only use of the term may not be self-referential (*MP* §49.6). Evidence that the *domboc* continued to be consulted comes first from the legislation of Alfred's son, Edward the Elder. It is not without some difficulties. At the outset of his laws, Edward appears to insist that all judgments conform to what is found in the *domboc*: "Edward the king bids all his reeves, that you make judgments as rightly as you can and as it stands in the judgment-book" (*Eadwerd cyning byt ðam gerefum eallum, ðæt ge deman swa rihte domas swa ge rihtoste cunnon, ꞇ hit on ðære dombec stande*).[8] Attenborough's translation of the last clause, "in accordance with the written laws," suggests his own doubts about whether *dombec* here refers specifically to Alfred's leg-islation, in contradistinction to Liebermann's earlier pronouncement ("The reference is to Alfred–Ine").[9] But the language of II Edward §5 is sufficiently free of ambiguity to show what the king earlier had in mind. Here Edward prescribes that those who violate the general oath (see Chapter 3, 105–106) ought to make amends "as the *domboc* teaches" (*swa dómboc tæce*); those harboring offenders (§5.2) are likewise to compensate "as the *domboc* says" (*swa seo domboc sæcge*). The usage of one of Æthelstan's subsequent ordinances (II *Æthelstan* 5) suggests continued official employment of Alfred's compilation: "And we declared regarding breaking into a church: if he [the accused] is shown guilty in the threefold ordeal, let him amend for it as the *domboc* says" (*ꞇ we cwædon be ciricbryce: gif he ful wære on ðam þryfealdan ordale, bete be þam þe sio dómboc segce*). The implied referent seems to be Alfred §7, though no

---

[8] Liebermann ed. 1903–1916: I, 138; Wormald 1999a: 286–290; Richards 2014b: 297.

[9] "Gemeint ist A[l]f[red]–Ine." Liebermann 1903–1916: III, 93 (n. 5).

reference to the ordeal is made here – a significant omission, given what was observed in Chapter 3.

If these are indeed allusions to Alfred's *domboc* – a possibility hard to dismiss, given that such references occur only in the immediate decades after Alfred's death, and in laws issued by Alfred's descendants – they attest, along with the extensive copying of Alfred's laws, to the impact this text was perceived to have had on the conduct of litigation. That the legislation of both kings insists so stridently on the conformity of judgments to *written* laws shows the extent to which aims announced in the Prologue to Alfred's laws appear to have been realized. Determining the relevant norm is no longer a matter of assembling witnesses to unwritten customs (*ǽ*), as it had been for the earliest Kentish kings. As we have seen, however, adoption of this view did not oblige kings to refrain from adding to or otherwise altering the *domboc*'s provisions.

It is thus fair to say that the *domboc* succeeded in its underlying aim, expressed most forcefully in the Prologue, of establishing written legislation as foundational to the governance of Wessex; something attempted by the seventh-century kings of Kent but not seriously pursued by any English kingdom in the years prior to Alfred's accession. The model of statecraft inaugurated by Alfred would survive even the crises of Æthelred II's reign, which saw the renewal of Viking activities and ultimately the overthrow of the West-Saxon dynasty. Most legislation written at this time was the handiwork of Archbishop Wulfstan, Æthelred's preeminent counselor, who would retain this station under Cnut. Wulfstan's concerns in the laws drafted for Cnut, first in 1018 and subsequently in 1020, seem at first quite different from Alfred's. By this point, Wulfstan's laws admonish as much as they lay down rules; their aim, scarcely separable from those evident in homilies written just before this period, is the restoration of morality and piety, whose waning, as was maintained in the *Sermo Lupi ad Anglos*, had brought the Danes back to England as instruments of divine wrath.[10]

Yet Alfred's laws continued to form the basis of some Wulfstanian ordinances. (It is just possible, as we will see, that at roughly the same time the enthusiasm of Ælfric of Eynsham for Alfredian prose

---

[10] See, e.g., Rabin 2015: 14–15.

was extending to the *domboc*.) As was the case in the laws of Edward the Elder and Æthelstan, Wulfstan's employment of material from the *domboc* shows Alfred's laws being not only used but *adapted* to the circumstances of late Anglo-Saxon England.[11]

TABLE 6 Rewriting the *domboc* in Wulfstanian legislation

Alfred §§4–4.1: Gif hwa ymb cyninges feorh sierwe, ðurh hine oððe ðurh wreccena feormunge oððe his manna, sie he his feores scyldig ⁊ ealles þæs ðe he age. [4.1] Gif he hine selfne triowan wille, do þæt be cyninges wergelde.	v *Æthelred* §30 (Liebermann 1903–1916: I, 244): ⁊ gyf hwa ymb cyninges feorh syrwe, sy he his feores scyldig; ⁊ gif he ladian wille, do þæt be ðæs cynges wergylde oððe mid þryfealdan ordale on Engla lage.
"If someone plots against the king's life, either by his own actions, or by the harboring of one who has been banished or of his men, let him be liable for his life and all that he owns. If he wishes to exculpate himself, let him do so by [an oath in the amount of] the king's wergild."	"And if someone plots against the king's life, let him be liable for his life; and if he wishes to clear himself, let him do so [with an oath] equal to the king's wergild or, according to English law, with the threefold ordeal."
Alfred §§3, 4.2: [3] Gif hwa cyninges borg abrece, gebete þone tyht swa him ryht wisie, ⁊ þæs borges bryce, mid v pundum mærra pæninga. Ærcebiscepes borges bryce oððe his mundbyrd gebete mid ðrim pundum. Oðres biscepes oððe ealdormonnes borges bryce oððe mundbyrd gebete mid twam pundum. [4.2] Swa we éac settað be eallum hadum, ge ceorle ge eorle: se ðe ymb his hlafordes fiorh sierwe, sie he wið ðone his feores scyldig ⁊ ealles ðæs ðe he age, oððe be his hlafordes were hine getriowe.	II *Cnut* §§57–59 (ed. Liebermann 1903–1916: I, 349–50): [57] *Gif hwa ymb ciningc oððe hlaford syrwe, si he his feores scyldig ⁊ ealles þæs ðe he age, butan he ga to þryfealdan ordale* [cf. v *Æthelred* §30]. [58] Gif hwa cyninges borh abrece, gebete þæt mid v pundan. [58.1] [G]if hwa arcebisceopes borh oððe æþelingces abrece, gebete þæt mid þrim pundan. [58.2] Gif hwa leodbisceopes oððe ealdormannes borh abrece, gebete þæt mid II pundan. [59] Gif hwa on ciningces hirede gefeohte, þolige þæs lifes, butan se cingc him gearian wille.

[11] Traces of Alfredian influence are also apparent in the early Wulfstanian legal treatise *Grið*, on which see Rabin 2015: 76–81.

"If someone breaches the king's security, let him compensate for that conduct [for which the security had been offered] as law indicates, and for the breach of that security with 5 pounds of greater pennies. Let him compensate breaching an archbishop's security or violation of his *mund* with three pounds. Let him compensate breaching the security of a bishop [of other rank] or an ealdorman, or the violation of [their] *mund* with two pounds. Thus we also establish for all ranks, either *ceorl* or *eorl*: he who plots against his lord's life, let him be liable for his life and all that he owns, or exculpate himself by [an oath in the amount of] his lord's wergild."	"If someone breaches the king's security, let him compensate with five pounds. If someone breaches the security of an archbishop or an atheling, let him compensate with three pounds. If someone breaches the security of a suffragan bishop or an ealdorman, let him compensate with two pounds. If someone should fight against [a member of] the king's household, let him lose his life, unless the king wishes to show him mercy."

Though the "homiletic" element in Wulfstan's legal writing has long been emphasized, his use of Alfred allows us to see the work of a careful legislator. Deference to the Danelaw as a distinct political entity (*on Engla lage*) was a perceived necessity in Wulfstan's time, as was use of the ordeal: completion of the threefold ordeal in the example just given substitutes for Alfred's requirement of an oath by the king's wergild.[12] As was shown in Chapter 3, Alfred's laws exhibit no knowledge of the ordeal, nor should its presence in ninth-century Wessex be assumed on the basis of an ambiguous variant in late manuscripts of Ine's laws.

Evident as well in the legislation for Cnut just quoted is a consistent effort to make the Alfredian source more specific and concise. The eagerness with which Alfred's laws were copied even late in the Anglo-Saxon period – most of the extant witnesses date from the eleventh century or later – testifies to continuing interest in his laws, even if their worth, as is suggested both by the organization of Corpus 173 and by the manner in which they were adapted for use, was increasingly historical in nature.[13]

[12] Bartlett (1986: 11–14) views the ordeal of hot water as a largely Carolingian contrivance not seeing "routine" use until "later Anglo-Saxon England." See also Chapter 3, 84.

[13] Liebermann 1903–1916: III, 39 sec. 36.

The *Domboc* as Literary Artifact

Alfred's reputation in the period before the Norman Conquest was as much secured by the translations attributed to him as by his ambitious legislation. To Ælfric of Eynsham in particular, these texts proved valuable resources. Probably the most important author of prose works to have lived during the Anglo-Saxon period, Ælfric was responsible for, among other achievements, one of the earliest sustained attempts (next to Alfred's) to translate portions of the Bible into English.[14] As Alfred was the first to have pursued such an undertaking, albeit on a modest scale when compared with those who prepared the *Old English Heptateuch*, it seems likely enough that Ælfric would at least have consulted the *MP* if a witness were available to him.[15] Yet the question has yet to receive much consideration by commentators even amid the wealth of scholarship that now surrounds the abbot's work.

The evidence, it must be admitted, is quite cryptic. Much about how we understand the possible influence of the prologue hinges on what we make of remarks in the Preface to Ælfric's *Catholic Homilies*. Ælfric here describes his own reluctance to undertake writing in the vernacular, a task made nonetheless essential by the "great foolishness in many English books, which unlearned people in their simplicity took for great wisdom" (*mycel gedwyld on manegum engliscum bocum. ðe ungelærede men ðurh heora bilewitnysse to micclum wisdome tealdon*).[16] Authentic learning, he laments, is available to those who either know Latin or have access to the Alfredian translations:[17]

7 me ofhreow þæt hí ne cuðon ne næfdon ða godspellícan lare on heora gewritum. buton ðam mannum anum ðe þæt leden cuðon. 7 buton þam

---

[14] As Marsden (1995: 401) notes, the *MP* is "[t]he earliest surviving example of continuous biblical prose translation in Old English."

[15] The *Old English Heptateuch* was only in part the work of Ælfric; according to Marsden (2000: 41), "Ælfric's contribution apparently amounted only to the first half of Genesis, the second half of Numbers, and the abbreviated version of Joshua. The origin of the rest of the translation – the second half of Genesis, Exodus, Leviticus, the first half of Numbers, and Deuteronomy – remains obscure."

[16] Clemoes 1997: 174; Godden 2009: 139.

[17] Clemoes 1997: 174; Godden 2009: 139.

bocum ðe ælfred cyning snoterlice awende of ledene on englisc. ða synd to hæbbene.

"[A]nd I was sorry that they did not know or possess the Gospel teaching in their writings, apart from those people who knew Latin and apart from the books which King Alfred wisely translated from Latin to English, those which are to be had."

Malcolm Godden has considered this passage exhaustively, noting that "none of the texts traditionally associated with Alfred seem particularly relevant to the context of Ælfric's preface."[18] He goes on to observe that "[i]f we interpret *godspellican* loosely as 'biblical', the psalm translation might just claim to fit"; other candidates might be the *Pastoral Care*, "so packed with biblical quotation and exegesis that it would count as 'gospel teaching' too"; or the biblically derived portions of the Old English *Soliloquies*, a possibility remote in Godden's view, given that "this is highly heterodox material."[19] Whether Ælfric had in mind the *MP* is a possibility not taken up by Godden's study or any other. While the point is not to be argued for too strenuously, it seems worth noting that the Prologue is the only Alfredian text that is a straightforward translation of materials from the Old and New Testaments. Its derivation from Alfred would have been well known in Ælfric's lifetime.

There are, moreover, some similarities in phrasing shared by Alfred's version of the Decalogue and Ælfric's in his sermon for Mid-Lent Sunday.[20] For example, in their rendering of the commandment concerning Sabbath observance, both Alfred and Ælfric omit the enumeration of those who are to abstain from labor. Ælfric adds in his exegetical remarks the Augustinian view that the Sabbath rest is to be understood spiritually, perhaps as a caution to those whose understanding of the third commandment was insufficiently attuned to its typological significance: "Another day of rest is approaching us: that is eternal life, in which there will be one day without any night, in which we will rest eternally if we now

---

[18] Godden 2009: 141.
[19] Godden 2009: 142.
[20] Many are noted in Liebermann's interpretive commentary, but without further discussion; the observations made here and in the commentary of the edition expand upon his.

abandon servile works, that is to say, sins" (*Oðer restendæg is us toweard. þæt is ece líf. on ðam bið an dæg buton ælcere nihte. on þam we ús gerestað ecelice. gif we nu ðeowtlicera weorca. þæt sind synna geswicað*).[21] In addition, both Alfred and Ælfric omit *contra proximum tuum* in rendering the commandment on bearing false witness; in their version of the following commandment, the list of things not to be coveted (*Non concupisces ... uxorem eius, non servum, non ancillam, non bovem, non asinum, nec omnia quae illius sunt*) becomes a prohibition on coveting one's neighbor's "possessions" (*þine nehstan ierfes* [Alfred]; *oðres mannes æhta* [Ælfric]).[22] Both also manifest a concern that readers of Genesis not understand Christ to have been in any sense created by God the Father, Alfred by attributing the creation to Christ himself, and Ælfric by sticking closely to the language of the Nicene Creed.[23] Beyond these parallels, there is not much to work with, though the usage of the *Old English Heptateuch*, a text not authored entirely by Ælfric but in which he may have had some role, offers at least one intriguing parallel to a peculiarity of Alfred's text. As in the Prologue, references to taking a slave to the "gods" give way to a description of a manumission ritual to be performed before a temple. The phrasing is remarkably close and just might attest to some awareness of Alfred's earlier efforts.

---

[21] Godden 1979: 118–119. Augustine's thoughts are given in his commentary on the Gospel of St. John (Migne 1845: col. 1404): "In a spiritual manner the Christian keeps the Sabbath, abstaining from servile work. What does it mean, therefore: *from servile work?* From sin. And whence may we prove this? Ask the Lord: *Each who sins is a slave to sin* (John 8:34). Therefore the observance of the Sabbath in a spiritual sense is urged on us" (*Spiritualiter observat sabbatum christianus, abstinens se ab opera servili. Quid est enim ab opere servili? A peccato. Et unde probamus? Dominum interroga:* Omnis qui facit peccatum, servus est peccati (Joan. VIII, 34). *Ergo et nobis præcipitur spiritualiter observatio sabbati*). The passage is indebted ultimately to Hebrews 3–4. For discussion of this passage and its relation to legislation on the observance of Sunday, see Haines 2010: 4.

[22] Godden 1979: 119. Omissions in both texts probably indicate the shared influence of Augustine; see Chapter 7, 229–231. It may not be ruled out, however, that Alfred's version, being the first known rendering of the Decalogue into Old English, may have determined somewhat the form of Ælfric's treatment.

[23] Godden 1979: 117: "þurh ðone sind ealle ðing geworhte" (= *per quem omnia facta sunt*).

TABLE 7 Shared translation practice in the *Mosaic Prologue* and the Old English *Heptateuch*.

Alfred, MP §11: Gif se þeowa þonne cweðe: "Nelle ic from minum hlaforde ne from minum wife ne from minum bearne ne from minum ierfe," brenge hine þonne his hlaford to ðære dura þæs temples 7 þurhþyrlige his eare mid æle, to tacne þæt he sie æfre siððan þeow.	*Old English Heptateuch* (Marsden 2008: 116): Gif se wiel cwið, "Me ys min hlaford leof, and min wif and mine winclo: nelle ic gan ut, ne beon frig," bringe his hlaford hine **to þæs haligdomes dura** and þyrlie his eare mid mid anum æle and be he his þeow a world.
"If, however, the slave should say: 'I will not [depart] from my lord nor from my wife nor from my child nor from my possessions,' then his lord shall bring him to the door of the temple and pierce through his ear with an awl, as a token that he shall be thenceforth and forever a slave."	"If the slave says, 'My lord is dear to me, and my wife and my children: I do not wish to go out, nor to be free,' let the lord bring him to the door of the sanctuary and pierce his ear with an awl and let him be his slave forever."

It is difficult to say whether these correspondences reflect consultation of Alfred's Prologue or the shared influence of some exegetical tradition. The latter may not be ruled out, given the debt of both Alfred's and Ælfric's treatment of the Decalogue to Augustinian teaching, with precedent for recasting the Decalogue established by the *Rule* of St. Benedict and the works of Carolingian ecclesiastical legislation that repeated this portion of the *Rule*.[24] In this instance, however, what is perhaps more likely is that Ælfric's homily and the *Old English Heptateuch* attest to continuities in translation practice of which the Prologue to Alfred's *domboc* may furnish some of the earliest evidence.[25]

---

[24] See Chapter 2, 66–67.
[25] Alternatively, the similarities may be owing to the tendency of some manuscripts of the Vulgate to compensate for the ambiguities of this passage (Exod. 21:6). In the *Liber ex lege Moysi*, "offeret eum dominus diis" ("let the master offer him to the gods") becomes "offeret eum dominus domino" ("let the master offer him to the Lord"); the version of the *Liber* appearing in Cambridge, Corpus Christi College 279 also gives "ad hostium tabernaculi" in place of "ad ostium" (see Meeder 2009: 193), a variant just a bit closer to the Heptateuch's *þæs haligdomes dura* than the Prologue's *dura þæs temples* but similar to both. Use of the *Liber* in either the Prologue or Heptateuch is uncertain, however, as neither text gives any trace of the *Liber*'s solution to "offeret eum dominus diis" ("offeret eum dominus

The texts just considered at least allow for the possibility that the Prologue may have been read as a translation of Scripture as well as a legislative work by the close of the tenth century. We have seen that the legal import of the *domboc* was somewhat overshadowed by its perceived historical worth by the time manuscript **E** was composed, and it is conceivable that the text continued to defy categorization and thus be used for whichever purposes seemed apposite. At the very least, the *domboc*'s Prologue ought to be considered alongside Alfredian influences upon later Old English prose that seem beyond argument, the most familiar example of which is the theory of the "three orders" of society. This idea, surfacing for perhaps for the first time during "the reign of Charles the Bald (843–877) in the work of two abbots of Auxerre, namely Haymo (d. 866) and his successor Heiric (d. 877x83)" before emerging again in the Alfredian *Boëthius* and subsequently in the work of Ælfric, shows how lasting were the contributions of Alfred's era to political thought in the later Anglo-Saxon period.[26]

After the Conquest

For some time after the Battle of Hastings and the subsequent accession of Duke William of Normandy, one may perceive in historical writings uncertainties over whether Cnut's or Alfred's laws should be more prized as representatives of English law. Both had to compete with a third alternative: the mythical laws of Edward the Confessor, known to us only through an Anglo-Norman forgery.[27] In time, Edward the Confessor's "laws" would overshadow both, retaining their reputation well into the Early Modern period.[28] Remarks from this period and later nonetheless suggest fitful encounters with the text of Alfred's laws. A continuation of Alfred's biography composed by a monk of St. Neots in the first decades of the twelfth century refers to Alfred having ordered to be written "just laws between the

---

domino") or even of the original reading: both texts simply omit the troublesome language altogether.

[26] Powell 1994: 106. It should be said that Powell doubts whether such ideas came directly to Alfred through his Frankish counselors.

[27] O'Brien 1999.

[28] See Greenberg 2001, 2010.

powerful and the meek and much else of use both for clerics and lay-men" (*iusta iudicia inter potentes et inpotentes et alia multa utilia tam cleri quam plebe*). In Liebermann's view, *iudicia* here translates *domas.*[29]

We have seen that Geffrei Gaimar, whose work dates to a slightly later period, seems also to have had some direct acquaintance with the *domboc*, perhaps as it appears in Corpus 173.[30] Yet Gaimar's *Estorie* also shows signs of the same shift discernible in other sources of this period toward the idealization of Cnut as an alternative to Alfred. The reasons lay at least in part in the circumstances of Cnut's accession, which held more favorable implications for the Anglo-Norman elite.[31] Alfred's reputation as legislator would be buoyed, however, by Geoffrey of Monmouth's ludicrous assertion that his laws were translated in part from a British source: namely, laws in a Celtic vernacular issued by "Marcia," wife of the king Guizelinus:[32]

Erat ei nobilis uxor Marcia nomine omnibus artibus erudite; que inter plurima proprio ingenio reperta legem quam Britones Marcianam appellant adineuit. Hanc rex Aluredus inter cetera transtulit et Saxonica lingua Merchenelaga uocauit.

He [Guizelinus] had a noble wife named Marcia, learned in all subjects; who, among other things obtained by her wisdom, issued a law that the Britons call the Marcian [law]. King Alfred translated this law among others and called it in the Saxon tongue the *Merchenelaga*.

Geoffrey's account perhaps evinces some faint awareness of the debt to prior Mercian legislation acknowledged in Alfred's Prologue – a suggestion of eyes having scanned the page uncomprehendingly – but not much else.[33] Claims to this effect were repeated in Laȝamon's

---

[29] Stevenson 1959: 143; Liebermann 1903–1916: III, 39 sec. 37 ("[D]iese *iudicia*, d. i. *domas* 'Gesetze', können nur Af-Ine meinen"). Cf. also the translation in *Quadripartitus* of Ine's prologue, where *iudicia* renders *domas* (Liebermann 1903–1916: I, 89).

[30] See Chapter 4, 115–116.

[31] Short 2009: xliii.

[32] Wright 1988: 41 (III.47).

[33] Liebermann 1903–1916: III, 39.

Brut, a reworking into Early Middle English of an Old French translation of the *Historia* by Wace.[34]

From this point, assertions about Alfred's legislative activities
enter the realm of pure fiction. The so-called *Proverbs of Alfred*,
originating in the twelfth century and quoted in other Early Middle
English texts, present the king as a Solomonic figure, dispensing wisdom on such matters as the hazards of excessive drinking and the
proper choice of a wife.[35] That the "proverbs" are delivered at a
meeting of the king's *witan* perhaps ties them in some way to the
reputation of the *domboc*. At the poem's outset, the king is depicted
as sitting with

> fele Biscopes.
> and feole. bok-ílered.
> Eorles prute.
> knyhtes egleche.
> þar wes þe eorl Alurich.
> of þare lawe swiþe wis.
> And ek Ealured
> englene hurde.
> Englene durlyng:
> on engle londe he wes kyng.

> many bishops and many learned in books, proud earls and fear-
> some knights. There was the earl Ælfric, very wise in matters of
> law, and also Alfred, the shepherd of the English people and their
> darling; he was the king of England.[36]

The rubric with which this text is introduced in Bodleian, Jesus
College Library 29, *Incipiunt documenta Regis Aluredi*, gives some
sense of how the facts of Alfred's reign were being displaced by

---

[34] Liebermann 1903–1916: III, 39.

[35] The *Proverbs* exist in four manuscripts, the earliest of which (Cotton Galba A XIX
[C]), dates "to the early thirteenth century" (Arngart 1955: II, 16); the text itself
likely was composed toward the middle of the twelfth century (II, 55–56), a date
made fairly certain by quotations of the *Proverbs* in the *Owl and the Nightingale*
and (possibly) Layamon's *Brut*.

[36] Arngart 1955: II, 136. The "Alurich" here referred to is impossible to identify.
Andrew Rabin (p.c.) has suggested that the name might reflect a distant recollec-
tion of Archbishop Ælfric of Canterbury.

fabrications.[37] It has been suggested that the *Proverbs* may owe something to knowledge of pre-Conquest royal legislation, though the author discovers in the *Proverbs* traces not of the *domboc* but of Cnut's laws.[38] What residues even of this text may be said to survive in the *Proverbs* appear faint at best, and the significance attributed to them seems uncertain.

No work of late-medieval Alfredian apocrypha compares in sheer audacity to the legal treatise composed no later than 1290 and known as the *Mirror of Justices*. The text, whose author claims access to "old rolls of the time of King Alfred" (*vieus roulles del tens le Roi Alfred*), was taken as a genuine witness to pre-Conquest conditions until well into the modern era.[39] Among other inventions, the *Mirror* narrates Alfred's sentence of death on forty-four corrupt judges and even gives their names and those of their victims.[40] Most derive from place-names ("Watling"), hagiography ("Cuthbert," "Dunston"), and vernacular romances such as *King Horn* ("Athelbrus," "Berild").[41] However irresponsible, the *Mirror* at least witnesses to how inaccessible knowledge of pre-Conquest England had become even to learned persons in thirteenth-century England. It also speaks to a renewed longing to appropriate its remains. The atmosphere in which it took shape is perhaps suggested by the reign of Henry III, who undertook the restoration of Westminster Abbey as an act of devotion to his chosen patron saint, Edward the Confessor.[42] The *Mirror*'s focus on Alfred's difficult relationship with his judges also shows some debt to texts contemporary with his

---

[37] Arngart 1955: II, 71. The manuscript "cannot be earlier than 1276, nor is it likely to be of much later date" (II, 37).

[38] Yeager 2014: 115–118.

[39] Whittaker 1895: x; 54–55.

[40] "It is an abuse that justices and their officers who slay folk by false judgments are not destroyed like other homicides. And King Alfred in one year had forty-four judges hanged as homicides for their false judgments" (*Abusion est qe justices e lur ministres qi occient la gent par faus jugement ne sunt destruz al foer dautres homicides. Que fist le Roi Alfred prendre xliiij. justices en un an taunt cum homicides pur lur faus jugemenz*); Whittaker 1895: 166–167.

[41] Jurasinski 2006. The list of executed justices and their victims is given in Whittaker 1895: 166–170.

[42] Lewis 1995: 144. According to Tim William Machan (2003: 52), Henry III "cultivated more than an affection for the Anglo-Saxon past," even naming his sons after Anglo-Saxon monarchs.

reign, though there is only the faintest relationship between what is narrated in Asser's biography and what we find here.

By the onset of the fourteenth century, it is perhaps fair to say that the near-total ignorance surrounding Alfred's laws that would prevail until they were reexamined by Elizabethan antiquaries had already set in. Having been displaced by the laws of Cnut in the immediate aftermath of the Conquest, and subsequently by a Norman forgery, Alfred's *domboc* ceased to be read outside of its translation in *Quadripartitus* (in as much as it was read at all). Even in the vernacular literature that had once celebrated his achievements, events of his reign would be eclipsed by those attributed (spuriously) to his grandson Æthelstan.[43] Yet some texts of this period show awareness of Alfred's *domboc,* if only of its existence. Writing at the close of the thirteenth century, Robert of Gloucester was probably reciting the received wisdom of his day when he said of Alfred, "Lawes he made riȝtuolore . & strengere þan er were."[44] The details may have been wrong, but the weight of tradition, dimly evident in sources as early as the *Proverbs of Alfred,* favored the view that Alfred's laws were among the greatest achievements of his reign. Well into the later Middle Ages, some traces of the *domboc*'s fame are still apparent, even if knowledge of its contents was virtually non-existent.

The *Domboc* in Print: 1568–1916

Not until the era of the Reformation would the *domboc* be recovered in any meaningful sense, its improved fortunes owing to a combination of circumstances prior generations could not have envisaged. The dissolution of England's religious orders, overseen by Henry VIII's minister Thomas Cromwell, put into private hands manuscripts until then kept in monastic libraries.[45] Many of these were of great antiquity and gave evidence of an English church

---

[43] Hibbard 1921; Treharne 1999.

[44] Wright 1887: 393 (l. 5391).

[45] The extent of their disuse on the eve of the Reformation is sometimes exaggerated: see Cameron 1974, who concludes that "the ability to read [Old English] never died out completely in England" (226). On the Dissolution, see Dickens 1959: 124–140.

appearing to make more use of the vernacular than it would in the later Middle Ages. This feature of the Old English corpus, along with Ælfric's adherence to a Eucharistic theology indebted in some fashion to Ratramnus of Corbie's *De corpore et sanguine domini* – a work seized on by opponents of Rome in the early decades of the Reformation – made Anglo-Saxon materials of keen interest to a generation of English clerics trained in the wake of Thomas Cranmer's flirtations with Geneva.[46]

While some details of its recovery have already been reviewed, more remains to be said about how bringing the *domboc* to light at a time of such violent divisions shaped its reception in later centuries. Those who rescued this and other texts from near-oblivion were, of course, anything but disinterested in their use of them; it might well be said that the dissemination of premodern texts had never been pursued with as much calculation as it was in the seventeenth century. In works such as the Latin "Praefatio" of the *Hêliand* (first published by Luther's troublesome disciple Matthias Flacius Illyricus in 1562) and the sermons of Ælfric, German and English reformers alike saw evidence that the near-exclusive use of Latin in the liturgy, along with reluctance to undertake vernacular translations of the Bible, made Rome, and not the "evangelical" faction (as it was then called), the purveyor of novelties injurious to the church.[47] The motivations underlying the work of Parker and his

---

[46] See Leinbaugh 1982, whose appraisal of these first attempts to edit Ælfric is thorough if harsh. His account should be weighed against others': e.g., (in the same volume) Murphy 1982: 3. One minor problem with Leinbaugh's account is its labeling Parker's sacramental theology "Anglican." According to Chapman (2012: 151), "It is not implausible to suggest that Anglicanism began in the year 1660." Chapman views the English Church in the years of Cranmer and Parker as scarcely differing from others of the "Magisterial Reformation" in matters of doctrine and worship, though inclining more toward Geneva than Wittenberg. In any case, there is little doubt that Ælfric was influenced by the Eucharistic doctrine of Ratramnus of Corbie, adherence to which was ultimately the cause of the troubles faced by Berengar of Tours: see McCracken and Cabaniss 1957: 112. On the rediscovery of Ratramnus during the Reformation, see Bakhuizen van den Brink 1954: 62–65.

[47] See Behagel 1882 [rev. 1984: xxiv]; also Andersson 1974, where it is observed that M. Flacius Illyricus once corresponded with Matthew Parker (278). It should be noted that objections to offering the Mass in the vernacular had principally to do with a suspicion that the Reformers overestimated the rewards of such a change. See, e.g., Thomas More's *Confutation of Tyndale's Answer*: "And surely yf all the seruyce were in englyshe: yet wold yt not therby be much more vnderstanden, whyche was all the mater that saynt Paule spake" (Schuster *et al.* 1973: 162).

circle are now held to have compromised their impartiality – a rare commodity in any period, to be sure. But one cannot but be impressed by the industry with which this first generation of Anglo-Saxonists tackled the enormous task of editing and translating texts that few had been able to read for well over 300 years.

Though the *domboc* would seem to have little direct bearing on theological questions then in dispute, its *editio princeps* could not avoid being colored by passions surrounding the Reformation. In the sole interpretative note to accompany Alfred's laws in the *Archaionomia*, Lambarde admonishes his reader not to attribute the omission of Exodus 20: 4–6 in Alfred's version of the Decalogue to either the author's or the scribes' carelessness (*aut nostra aut librariorum incuria*).[48] The culprit, we are told, was rather the Second Nicene Council of 794 (*recte* 787), which approved the adoration of images (*simulachrorum confirmavit adorationem*) and thereby gave license to meddling with the sacred page. Lambarde goes on to note the same omission in versions of the Decalogue occurring in all other Anglo-Saxon texts of which he was aware (*Neque vero [quod sciam] in ullo usquam Saxonice conscripto exemplari reperitur*). Problems with Lambarde's understanding of the omission, some aspects of which survived into Liebermann's *Gesetze*, are addressed in the notes to the edition.[49] For now, it should be observed that the

---

[48] Lambarde 1568: fol. 18v. The omitted passage of Scripture is as follows (Coogan 2001: 111): "You shall not make for yourself an idol, whether in the form of anything that is in heaven above, or that is on the earth beneath, or that is in the water under the earth. You shall not bow down to them or worship them; for I the LORD your God am a jealous god, punishing children for the iniquity of parents, to the third and the fourth generation of those who reject me, but showing steadfast love to the thousandth generation of those who love me and keep my commandments." It is easy to see why a passage of this length would be omitted given that the Decalogue was a text to be memorized. In any case, the sense of the missing text (as understood by Augustine) is supplied in *MP* §10, from Exodus 20:23; see also Turk 1893: 34.

[49] See note for *MP* §1. A curious trace of Lambarde's thinking may be found in Liebermann's note holding that, in omitting the prohibition on images, Alfred "followed not his own whim (*Willkür*), but the Catholicism of his day (*damaligen Katholismus*) and its veneration of images (*Bildverehrung*), the prohibition of which, said one later English canonist, lasted only until Christ's Incarnation" (III: 43a). Liebermann's summary of the *damaligen Katholismus*, drawn, as it turns out, from a remark by a fifteenth-century canonist (!) quoted in Maitland 1898: 12 n. 1, effectively begs the question of what Catholic belief amounted to in the ninth century. (The "incarnational" argument adduced by this canonist [William Lyndwood] – i.e., the incarnation of the Word effectively abrogated the prohibition on images,

peculiar form assumed by the Decalogue in pre-Conquest texts probably has less to do with the influence of II Nicaea than with Augustinian teaching; it certainly (as later commentators would suggest) cannot be explained by Alfred's having caught a lifelong case of Popery during his boyhood in Rome.[50]

At all events, Lambarde's assertions furnish another instance in which the influence of other members of his circle is apparent. Underlying Lambarde's sentiments are observations in Matthew Parker's *Testimonie of Antiquitie* (1566), where Alfred's *MP*, or at least its Decalogue, would appear in print for the first time (see Figure 8). Here Parker observes that the omission is found:

> in all copyes of Alfredes lawes written in the Saxon tounge: and not onely in them, but in many other bookes, as hath beene seene eyther Saxon, or Lattyne intreating of the commaundementes, which were written before the Conquest, and since the second Nicene councell, wherein was decreed the worshipping of images. See what followed of taking away from the worde of God contrarye to the express commaundement of the same upon the ungodly decree of that councell. When this thing was espied by them that translated these lawes into the Lattyne tounge sone after the Conquest, these words were restored agayne by the translatours to their due place, as by the Lattyne bookes of the lawes it is to be seene.[51]

Christ being himself the image of the invisible God [Colossians 1:15] – was, as Noble observes [2009: 114], unknown to, or at least unremarked by, Bede.) As the prevailing influence upon Alfred would have been from the Frankish church, whose reservations about the pious use of images ran deep (see Fichtenau 1957: 69–70; Noble 2009), Liebermann's is a regrettable reading of the clause, explicable only as an effect of editorial habits traceable to the *Archaionomia* that were subsequently filtered through editions such as Wilkins's. Lambarde and Parker were, in any case, right to note how scrupulously the omission of this clause is maintained in pre-Conquest texts. It is absent even in the Old English *Heptateuch* (Marsden 2008: 115). The response of Charlemagne's theologians was well known to Parker, as is clear from the concluding remarks concerning the Alfredian Decalogue in his *Testimonie*.

[50] The latter was argued by Wilkins in his edition of 1721: "Ælfredus a patre Æthelvulpho Romam delegatus [. . .] Ecclesiæ Romanæ doctrinam de ommitendo præcepto Decalogi de imaginibus addicit" (28 n. c). That the ordering of the Decalogue is in fact owing to Augustine's thinking is shown in Kleist 2002; see also Chapter 7, notes on *MP* §§ 1, 6, 8, and 9, where Augustinian influence is apparent.

[51] Parker 1566: f. 86v–87r. It is probably relevant to the concerns of Parker and his contemporaries that, in the 1559 *Book of Common Prayer*, the Decalogue had

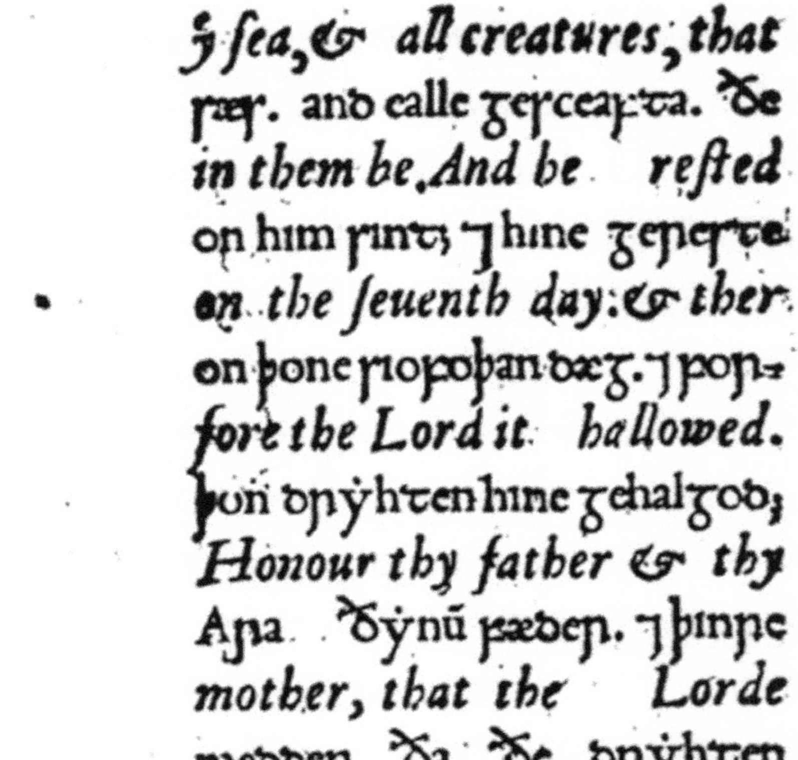

ȝ *sea, & all creatures, that*
rex. anð ealle ȝeyceaƿꞇa. Ꝺe
in them be. And he   reſted
on him ƿinꞇ; ꞇ hine ȝeƿeyꞇe
on the ſeuenth day: & ther
on þone yoƿoþan ðæȝ. ꞇ ƿoy-
fore the Lord it   hallowed.
þon ðyȝhꞇen hine ȝehalȝoð;
Honour thy father & thy
Aƿa ðynū ƿæðeƿ. ꞇ þinƿe
mother, that the   Lorde
meððeƿ ða Ꝺe ðyȝhꞇen
gaue thee, ỷ thou be longe
yealoe Ꝺe. þ Ꝺu ƿie ðylenȝe
lyuing in ỷ earth. Ne kill
libbenðe on eoyþan; Ne yleah
That is,   *thou. Ne *liȝ he ỷ priuelye.*
commit no Ꝺu ; Ne*liȝe þu ꞇeaƿnenȝa;
adultery.   *Ne*

FIGURE 8 Parker's *Testimonie of Antiquitie*, fol. 85v.; the first printing of
material from the *domboc*. (Public domain image.)

Parker seems not to have realized that manuscripts of *Quadripartitus* (the "Lattyne bookes of the lawes") give the text of the Vulgate without exception rather than approximating Alfred's version. Pious horror seems mistakenly attributed to its translator, who in all likelihood followed the Hieronymean text in order to give himself a respite from tangling with the difficulties of the Old English.

As was observed in Chapter 4, Lambarde's edition of the Prologue is greatly undermined by the fact that Laurence Nowell enjoyed such a challenge. Both its version and that occurring in another Nowell transcript (mistakenly attributed by Liebermann to William Somner (1606–1669), and listed among the variants in the *Gesetze*'s apparatus) occasionally follow the Vulgate rather than Alfred's text – presumably, the version given in *Quadripartitus*.[52] Thus would begin the lamentably durable practice of assuming that Alfred's aim in preparing the Prologue was to reproduce rather than adapt the text of Exodus. Over the centuries, this view of Alfred's translation practices would transform itself into the supposition that divergences from the Vulgate in his Prologue must be attributable to his following a source since lost.[53] Scholarship on other Alfredian texts over the course of the twentieth century has since given us a sense of Alfred's

been substituted in the Communion rite for the appointed psalm and the *Kyrie* of the 1549 text and was simultaneously the preferred substitute for pre-Reformation images and rood-screens in parish churches (Cummings 2011: 728). Preston (2012: 86) notes that the author of the *Testimonie* may well have been John Joscelyn, another member of Parker's circle. Though Preston's chapter on the sixteenth-century reception of Alfred's laws is impressively learned, its claims are somewhat vitiated by a misplaced (and probably anachronistic) emphasis on "nationalism" as a motive for the work of Parker and his cohort. Their motivations were assuredly more religious than political in any modern sense.

[52] The transcript is question is Canterbury, Christ Church Cathedral Library, MS Literary B.2. "Felix Liebermann thought that this transcript of Alfred-Ine was the work of Somner himself (hence the siglum *So*). He was, however, mistaken; it was undoubtedly made by Laurence Nowell, probably with reference to his other transcript (Nw1 with Nw2). It was not annotated by William Lambarde, nor does it bear any signs of use by a printer; but it is clearly a working copy, and … presumably came from the library of William Lambarde" (Dammery 1990: 96–97).

[53] See Liebermann 1912: 22: "[I]n translating the Decalogue he seems to have followed a separate version. Some slight divergences from the Exodus Vulgate may indeed be explained by contamination with the parallel passage in Deuteronomy, but in other places Alfred omits just the same lines which are wanting in other Decalogues as well. He therefore must have used some text besides the Vulgate, which, however, seems now not to be known."

freedom as a translator – one that has only begun to inform study of the *domboc*.[54]

Though its shortcomings were greater than would be understood for centuries, Lambarde's *Archaionomia* did the important service of undermining some historical myths concerning the origins of English common law. The effects were not instantaneous. In the late sixteenth century, Sir Edward Coke traced the formation of English law back to an amalgam of medieval legends (Trojan exiles led by Brutus, the "Laws of Edward the Confessor") while exhibiting some genuine knowledge of the *domboc* and other texts edited by Lambarde.[55] But the latter would soon come to displace the former as scholars in England and on the Continent persevered in the work initiated by Lambarde and Nowell.[56] Along with these efforts would arise a new myth: that Alfred had established trial by jury (and much else besides).[57] William Blackstone's *Commentaries* repeat such claims, perhaps with a note of reluctance. But his description of the concluding portions of the *domboc*'s Prologue, however misguided, suggests at least some direct knowledge of its contents: "[A]lfred also, like another Theodosius, collected the various customs that he had found dispersed in the kingdom, and reduced and digested them into one uniform system of code of laws, in his *dom-bec,* or *liber judicialis.*"[58]

Blackstone's errors in describing the *domboc* are those of his time. They reflect the same eagerness to make English law equal in dignity to the Roman-derived civilian tradition that runs through legal

---

54 See, e.g., Wittig 1983 (which argued against the earlier view that divergent translations in Alfred's *Boethius* depended upon a Latin commentary no longer extant); also Discenza 2005.

55 Smith 2014: 125. Coke's knowledge of Anglo-Saxon law was of considerable depth and he would, on occasion, argue from the evidence of pre-Conquest legislation: see, e.g., *La neufme part des reports del Sr. Edw. Coke chivalier*, Sheppard 2003: 292–294.

56 Excerpts from the Kentish laws would be published (in Latin translation) by Johann de Laet in 1640 and Sir Henry Spelman in 1664. See the invaluable annotated bibliography in Oliver 2002: 251–256.

57 Wormald (1999a: 7 n. 21) observes that the evidence for the earliest purveyors of this legend was not drawn from the *domboc* but from III Æthelred 3.1, the prologue to the Laws of Edward the Confessor, and Alfred and Guthrum §3.

58 Blackstone 1769 [repr. 1979: 404] (vol. IV); Wormald 1999a: 5. On the reception by contemporaries of Blackstone's views regarding the *domboc*, particularly with respect to the origins of the jury, see Stanley 2000: 117–122.

historiography in England perhaps from its inception. Among Blackstone's purposes in authoring the *Commentaries* was establishing English common law as an object worthy of formal study in an academic setting.[59] Doing so inevitably involved imputing to earlier English legal materials a sophistication and pedigree comparable to Roman law, the study of which had occasioned the rise of universities in the twelfth century. And so it is that Alfred becomes a second Theodosius and his *domboc* a "code" in the strict sense of the word.

The latter decades of the eighteenth century perhaps represent the apogee of Alfred's reputation as a legislator. These were also the last years in which flipping through the *domboc* – if only in Latin translation – was seen as a necessary (if peripheral) element of legal learning.[60] By the close of this period, Anglo-Saxon law was beginning to acquire new and less favorable associations, particularly as half-understood fragments of this tradition came to be brandished by polemicists of the "Enlightenment" as evidence of "barbarism" and "superstition."[61] From his perusal of the *domboc*'s Prologue as given in Wilkins's edition, Gibbon concluded that "even the wise Alfred adopted, as an indispensable duty, the extreme rigour of the Mosaic institutions," subject as he was to the "intolerant spirit" of his age.[62] It seems unlikely that Gibbon recognized the distinction between the

---

[59] See the Introduction by Stanley N. Katz to Blackstone 1765 [repr. 1979]: iv–v. The origins of the Commentaries lie in "his enormously popular undergraduate lectures on English law," delivered after Blackstone was elected a fellow of All Souls College, Oxford; he was later "named the initial incumbent of the Vinerian chair, the first chair ever to be established for English law" (iv).

[60] Blackstone and his generation consulted the *domboc* from David Wilkins's *Leges Anglo-Saxonicae Ecclesiasticæ & Civiles* (1721: 14–46), a text that advanced little beyond the prior work of Lambarde and incorporates a fair amount of the latter's interpretative observations.

[61] Mary Wollstonecraft may have been thinking of pre- or immediately post-Conquest institutions, and perhaps of legislation, when, in her response to his *Reflections on the Revolution in France* (1790), she mocked Edmund Burke's veneration of an English constitution "settled in the dark days of ignorance, when the minds of men were shackled by the grossest prejudices and most immoral superstition. [...] Were the rights of men understood when the law authorized or tolerated murder?" (Wollstonecraft 1790: 18–19). Here and elsewhere in this section of the book, Wollstonecraft seems to refer to the allowances for vendetta typical of legislation of this time as well as the practice of wergild payment (though not by name). On the hostility toward medieval art and architecture that followed the French Revolution, see, e.g., Idzerda 1954.

[62] Gibbon 1781: 552 (III, cap. 37).

Prologue and the laws proper – an error not made by David Houard in his *Traités sur les coutumes Anglo-Normandes* (1776). Here, however, the Prologue is dismissed (to lasting effect) as extraneous to the whole, a mere "hors d'œvre que quelque dévot Copiste a composé, pour sanctifier son travail."[63] Though in America the "Saxons" (and Alfred in particular) continued to be invoked as political heroes, their ascendancy depended largely upon mythmaking and, when sources were consulted at all, solipsistic readings of the past aided by the doubtful conclusions of late eighteenth-century historians.[64] Thomas Jefferson's enthusiasm for Alfred's laws was contingent upon his belief, derived from Houard, that the biblical Prologue was a fraudulent "Monkish fabrication."[65] The remaining portions of the *domboc*, along with other examples of Old English legislation, left Jefferson in no doubt that law as it had developed among the "Saxon Kings" was somehow wholly untouched by influence of religion.[66]

Though the *domboc* would some decades later find superior editors and benefit from the increasing sophistication of textual criticism, the purposes for which it was consulted for much of the nineteenth century in time grew utterly distinct from those prevailing before. Romanticism, particularly its German manifestations, established the academic study of Old English as we know it today. The results for the *domboc* were somewhat mixed. Rather than search the text for the origins of English legal practices surviving into the present (the jury trial, the shire court), scholars of this period tended

---

[63] Houard 1776: 87.

[64] For a summary of reflections on "Saxon" antiquities before and after the American revolution, see Colbourn 1965.

[65] Washington 1854: 317 (Letter to Thomas Cooper, 1814).

[66] The whole of Jefferson's letter constitutes a remarkably detailed diatribe against the biblical prologue ("the falsification of the laws of Alfred") animated by his hostility toward established religion: "[N]one of these [the laws edited by Lambarde and Wilkins] adopt Christianity as part of the common law. If, therefore, from the settlement of the Saxons to the introduction of Christianity among them, that system of religion could not be part of the common law, because they were not yet Christians, and if, having their laws from that period to the close of the common law, we are able to find among them no such act of adoption, we may safely affirm (though contradicted by all the judges and writers on earth) that Christianity neither is, nor ever was a part of the common law" (315). See also the discussion in Colbourn 1965: 170–171.

to regard Alfred's laws and those of other pre-Conquest kings as manifestations of a legal tradition attested elsewhere in western Europe during the period in which the *domboc* was composed.

In itself, this was not an inherently harmful development, and work in this vein persists into the present. But problems arose as the emphasis shifted from tracing the lineal descent of particular provisions to finding analogues in other legislative texts. Soon the latter were sought in just about any legal tradition that might be labeled "Germanic," a word increasingly bearing almost mystical connotations. As Wormald and others have noted, the aim of Jakob Grimm in particular (whose *Deutsche Rechtsalterthümer* effectively established the study of "Germanic law" along the lines described above) differed little from work undertaken in his *Deutsche Grammatik*.[67] In the same way that Grimm reasoned in the *Deutsche Grammatik* backward from modern Germanic dialects to a single prehistoric tongue, the goal of much legal-historical scholarship was to abstract from the scattered and disparate observances of the Germanic-speaking peoples some sense of the laws and practices that obtained among them before these were vitiated by external influences from Roman law or the Roman church.[68] Along with this came the Romantic fetish for spontaneity over deliberation, "primitive" over high culture, which heightened the appeal of legal materials prior generations had dismissed as mere specimens of "barbarism."

One may see the outcomes of these views in the two major editions of the nineteenth century, Rheinhold Schmid's *Die Gesetze der Angelsachsen* (1832; substantially rev. 1858) and Benjamin Thorpe's *Ancient Laws and Institutes of England* (1840). Both editors drank deep of the philological methods just described, with varying results.[69] Of the two editions, Schmid's, though soon overshadowed by Thorpe's, would prove the more lasting achievement. Though the

---

[67] Wormald 1999a: 11–12.
[68] The development was not initially welcomed in England: Sir Henry Maine disparaged "that pride of nationality which has led German writers to exaggerate the completeness of the social fabric which their forefathers had built up before the appearance of the Roman world" (Maine 1884: 287).
[69] On Thorpe's career, which began with study under Grimm's rival Rasmus Rask and a close friendship with Grimm's student, John Mitchell Kemble, see Pulsiano 1998: 75–77. The Introduction to Schmid's edition justifies the study of Anglo-Saxon law with the standard appeals to "das Verständnis des nationalen Rechtslebens" and

edition is compromised by Schmid's excessive emendations, the remarkable *antiquarisches Glossar* with which it concludes was the first and, until Liebermann's *Gesetze*, only work of its kind: a comprehensive and minutely detailed synthesis of Anglo-Saxon law in encyclopedic form.[70] Schmid's method doubtless owed much to Grimm's *Deutsche Rechtsalterthümer*, the first of the great German legal encyclopedias. Yet his *Glossar* seems to have avoided the failings of Grimm and his admirers. More than a century and a half after its publication, Schmid's unsung *magnum opus*, whose final form might have reflected more ambition had work not been cut short by rumors of Thorpe's impending edition, still repays careful reading.[71]

While Schmid's work reflects the exacting philological study then establishing itself in German universities, Thorpe's edition seems undermined by some of the least prepossessing tendencies of the Germanist school. The analogues resorted to in order to elucidate obscure passages cannot avoid seeming far-flung even to the most dyed-in-the-wool Germanist. References to Swedish and Danish laws of the twelfth and thirteenth centuries, and Frisian laws of the fourteenth, sometimes outnumber discussions of texts likely to have been known to Alfred and his circle. One senses that Thorpe's studies with Rasmus Rask left him with something to prove. In contrast, every page of Schmid's commentary shows evidence of a deep immersion in English materials uncommon for this period.[72] Thorpe was also less willing than one might have hoped to consider the meanings of obscure terms in Old English, often leaving them untranslated. The shortcomings of the edition were doubtless owing to the tremendous pressures under which it was prepared; in the years prior to its

---

"die Ergründung des germanischen Alterthums" (1858: xv). Yet one sees remarkably little of this in the text itself.

[70] The densely printed *antiquarisches Glossar* takes up the final 160 pages of Schmid's *Gesetze* as it appeared in 1858. On Schmid's aggressive approach to emendation, which characterized much of the work of his generation, see Oliver 2002: 252.

[71] The work was originally assigned to Richard Price, who died in 1833 before he could complete the project. Schmid laments his abandonment of decades-long plans for a second volume in the preface to the 1858 edition (x–xii).

[72] This curious feature of Thorpe's edition may, however, owe something to Wilkins's, whose commentary methodically plods through the laws of other Germanic territories in search of analogues; a method unusual for its time (Oliver 2002: 252). The approach was also endorsed by Schmid (1858: xv).

appearance in 1840, Thorpe was obliged to plead for regular employment.[73]

The Germanism manifest in both editions implies a rationale for studying the *domboc* wholly different from what we find in Blackstone less than a century prior. Ultimately, Anglo-Saxon materials came to be prized for the evidence they supposedly furnished of a legal order wholly *unlike* that of Imperial Rome: one driven by the imperatives of pagan superstition and a sacralized passion for vengeance.[74] Perhaps the most regrettable consequence of these developments is the tendency of some studies that appeared after the editions of Schmid and Thorpe to atomize the *domboc*, discussing only those parts that seemed to bear some relation to the preoccupations of the moment.[75] While it is true that notions of literary unity were probably unknown to those who prepared texts in Alfred's time, it is also fair to say that, in preparing the *domboc* – particularly its Prologue, which displays many characteristically Alfredian traits – Alfred strove for a deliberate gathering of persuasive force in a way that prior legislating monarchs had not. But in much scholarship of the Germanist school, what might be called the "writerliness" of the *domboc* is lost as its provisions dissolve in the stew of "Germanic" laws alongside provisions from the *Lex Ribuaria* and the *Sachsenspiegel*.[76]

The survival of Liebermann's edition beyond this rather peculiar phase of Anglo-Saxon scholarship has in part to do with the unusual situation of its author. Liebermann absorbed the conclusions and methods of the *Rechtsschule* along with everyone else of his generation, and his work did its part in perpetuating some of its most unfortunate qualities. But he also sought for much of his career the

---

[73] Pulsiano 1998: 83.

[74] See, e.g., Jurasinski 2014a. It should be said that neither Schmid's nor Thorpe's edition played much of a role in the formation of this consensus.

[75] A superb edition appearing between Schmid's and Liebermann's that has been unfortunately overshadowed by the latter is Turk 1893. Milton Haight Turk was Professor of English at Hobart College in Geneva, New York, and his edition is remarkable for its focus on editing the text according to conventional philological methods then being applied to literary texts. Its discussion of the manuscripts and presentation of the text is of continuing importance and should not be overlooked by readers.

[76] See esp. Brunner 1890.

acceptance of the English scholarly establishment, which, in spite of
the work done by Kemble and Thorpe, had never fully embraced
German methods and occasionally viewed them with disdain.[77] His
early work on post-Conquest legal texts and other materials that
had never fallen under the gaze of the *historische Rechtsschule*
exposed him to methods not practiced by his German contemporaries.[78] He also was a formidable expert on manuscripts, editing them
with greater care than any of his predecessors.[79] In fairness to
Thorpe, it should be said that Liebermann enjoyed the inestimable
advantage of never having had to worry in the least about money.[80]

Among the many improvements to the standard text made by
Liebermann's edition was the restoration, at the expense of chronological ordering, of Ine's laws to the close of the *domboc* (their position in
Thorpe's edition, but not Schmid's), as well as a densely learned commentary synthesizing just about all that had been said in print on the
significance of particular clauses. There was thus much in the *Gesetze*
for Liebermann's English contemporaries to celebrate. Yet the *Gesetze*
could not avoid representing the ultimate victory of German over
English scholarship, leading Frederic William Maitland to lament, in a
review of the edition, "We have lost the Anglo-Saxon laws."[81]

Conclusions

In some other period, the appearance of an edition such as
Liebermann's might have occasioned a renaissance for the study of
Anglo-Saxon law. But in the years following its publication, a range
of circumstances conspired to ensure that this edition would become
less a gallery than a tomb for the texts edited therein. Two world

---

[77] See, e.g., Ackerman 1982. The remarks of Plummer (1902: 8–9) are particularly
revealing of attitudes at this time: "It is one of the great characteristics of English
learning that it has never been the monopoly of a professorial caste, as in Germany
[...] To this fact it owes many of its best qualities – its sanity and common sense,
its freedom from fads and far-fetched fancies, its freshness and contact with reality
– qualities in which German learning, in spite of its extraordinary depth and solid-
ity, is sometimes conspicuously wanting."

[78] Liebermann's talents as a biographer and church historian are noted in Hazeltine
1938: 17.

[79] On the accuracy of Liebermann's transcriptions, see Wormald 1999a: 22.

[80] On the wealth of the Liebermann family, see Rabin 2010.

[81] Quoted in Wormald 1998: 9.

wars would interrupt work on Anglo-Saxon law and most other academic pursuits. Passions surrounding the first regrettably did not leave Liebermann's edition untouched. The defense of Germany's cause with which Liebermann introduced volume II of the *Gesetze* did lasting damage to his reputation in England.[82] By the late 1940s, few academics in England or North America were drawn to the German-language scholarship that had invigorated the study of Old English in the previous century even though the racialism with which it came to be associated had been commonplace in Europe and North America prior to the war.[83] Though it once occupied the center of the curriculum, the decline and ultimate collapse of compulsory Old English for doctoral students at British and American universities further shrank the audience for Anglo-Saxon prose and verse.[84]

If institutional support is the sole index of its health, Old English as an academic discipline remains in an unenviable position. Yet the study of Anglo-Saxon, and of Anglo-Saxon law in particular, has long shown a capacity for cactus-like survival amid bleak conditions. First emerging in the aftermath of the Marian reprisals against Protestants, it persisted through generations of institutional neglect. Not until 1878, for example, did the University of Cambridge have a chair of Anglo-Saxon; the position came about not due to internal momentum but through a donation by Joseph Bosworth, who then held a chair established by Richard Rawlinson at Oxford in 1750.[85] The study of legal materials attained unparalleled heights of refinement in the unlikely person of Liebermann, who held no academic position and whose relationship to elite specialists in Germany and England was always uncertain.

Patrick Wormald's *Making of English Law* (1999) was an event comparable in significance to the appearance of Liebermann's *Gesetze*. In sifting the best of Liebermann's insights from those that

---

[82] For a discussion and translation of the text, see Wormald 1999a: 20–21.

[83] It is seldom appreciated that the foundations of such attitudes lay in the fashionable Social Darwinism and eugenicism of the time, whose traces may occasionally be found in discussions of pre-Conquest England meant for more general audiences (e.g. Halleck 1900: 12–14).

[84] See Parker 1967: 346–350.

[85] Momma 2013: 80 and 94.

were the product of his period (or his own human fallibility), Wormald partially returned the study of Anglo-Saxon law to the Anglophone world.[86] That there remains much more to be said about the *domboc* after the centuries of heroic labors just described might seem hard to believe. But as we have seen, Alfred's coyness about the ultimate aims of the *domboc* rendered it for subsequent generations a canvas in which historians and polemicists could see the most varied suppositions confirmed. If one may discern in the efforts of these editors and commentators the unfolding of anything like "improvement" in our knowledge of the text, it has happened, more often than not, in spite of their conscious purposes.

---

[86] And only partially. It is fair to say that much of what has been published on Anglo-Saxon law in the years since Wormald's *magnum opus* takes no notice of Liebermann's commentary – a dangerous development, as the *Gesetze* represents (particularly in its second volume) by far the fullest statement on pre-Conquest institutions yet published. To ignore Liebermann's carefully devised encyclopedia of Anglo-Saxon law is to risk reinventing the wheel.

Part II
Editions
(Rubrics, Alfred's Prologue, Alfred, Ine)

Editorial Procedure

Our reasons for using Cambridge, Corpus Christi College 173 (**E**) as the base manuscript of our edition are established in Chapter 4. Given the state in which witnesses to Alfred's laws survive, the choice (we hope) requires little further justification. Only in our edition of the rubrics has it seemed necessary to include the readings of another manuscript (**B**) alongside those of **E**, as the former exceed in length what might reasonably be included in the apparatus.

Emendations have been kept to a minimum. In the few cases where it is probable that an authentic reading survives in another manuscript and not in **E**, or where a lacuna in **E** is potentially resolved by another witness, text from this manuscript is supplied and enclosed within square brackets. Word divisions not present in the manuscript are silently introduced. The punctuation of Modern English replaces that employed by the scribe. But in keeping with the practice initiated by Turk's and Liebermann's editions, abbreviated text is italicized (though not in the apparatus). Colored or shaded initials are indicated by bold type. Our edition also gives the Tironian note 7 where it appears in the manuscript. To do otherwise would be improper given the ambiguity of this symbol, which may denote both "and" and "or." The difference, as will be seen, has real interpretative implications for a number of clauses.

Scribal corrections added to the text after it was first written are enclosed by \ / and, when written above the line, given in superscript; letters, morphemes or words added by a hand other than that of the main scribe are italicized and placed in small type. An exception has been made for Joscelyn's additions to **G**, which date to the second half of the sixteenth century. As these merely correct the text in accordance with the orthography of **E**, they are excluded from the apparatus.

The apparatus notes all orthographic variants with some exceptions. Where the divergence amounts to use of *þ* in place of *ð* (and vice versa), or the presence or absence of an accent over a vowel, it is not catalogued. Variations between syllabic *i* and *y* are also not noted, as the distinction seems not to have mattered even to the scribe of **E**. Otherwise, the apparatus is meant to capture as much as possible features present in the different witnesses of the *domboc*. Later additions to other witnesses are enclosed within \ / as in the main text; but for practical reasons, these are not rendered in superscript when given above the line. In preparing the apparatus, it has seemed expedient sometimes to leave as they appear in the manuscripts even erroneous divisions of words and morphemes rather than bring them into conformity with the main text. This principle is observed especially when one manuscript's treatment of a word or phrase seems suggestive of its transmission in subsequent witnesses. Empty square brackets, employed with some frequency for **Ot**, indicate illegible or otherwise lost segments of words and phrases. The low horizontal line filling some spaces in words in **H** appears here exactly as it does in the manuscript.

Though variants from **Bu** and **Ot** are given in the apparatus, its guidance on the contents of these manuscripts should be used with caution. It should not, for example, be assumed that when variants of a form present in **E** are not listed for **Bu** and **Ot** that these witnesses necessarily agree with **E**. Our examination *in situ* and through other means of these witnesses found **Ot** to be rather less legible than it was to Liebermann a century ago, though digital imaging of **Bu** allowed for some variants over which Liebermann was in doubt to be transcribed with certainty in our apparatus. Liebermann's transcription of **Ot** in his *Gesetze* thus remains indispensible, and we are not certain that the perhaps worsened condition of the manuscript would allow for any improvements on it.[1] Variants are listed from

---

[1] Indeed, Liebermann's transcription of **Ot** is so much better than what the fragments would seem to allow in their present state as to have invited a little suspicion: see Grant 1996: 32.

these fragments as much as they may be ascertained and primarily for their possible worth in tracing the transmission of the *domboc*.

The text is presented on facing pages. Notes on the left concern textual matters not dealt with in the apparatus, and notes on the right pertain to interpretative questions. Where other works of legislation are mentioned, chapter numbers rather than page numbers are given. For the most part (i.e., excluding instances where the views of prior editors receive close scrutiny), page numbers are also omitted where reference is made to remarks in the major prior editions of Anglo-Saxon legislation (i.e., those of Schmid, Thorpe, Turk, Liebermann, Attenborough, Robertson, and Whitelock [*EHD*]). It should be assumed (unless otherwise indicated) that the cited remarks correspond to the chapter under discussion in these editions and may be found in the corresponding note; where numeration differs from Liebermann's (see the headnote to the laws of Alfred for a fuller explanation), the chapter numbers of his edition are given in square brackets after those assigned in our edition (e.g., "L56"). Liebermann's chapter numbers may be assumed to be the same as those of Turk, Schmid, and Thorpe.

Abbreviations and Short Titles

Æthelberht	In Oliver 2002: 60–81
Hlophere and Eadric	In Oliver 2002: 126–133
Lex Alamannorum [*LexAla*]	In Eckhardt 1934b: II, 1–71
Lex Baiuvariorum [*LexBav*]	In Eckhardt 1934b: II, 73–187
Lex Chamavorum	In Eckhardt 1934c: 50–59
Lex Frisionum [*LexFris*]	In Eckhardt 1934c: 61–167
Lex Ribuaria [*LexRib*]	In Eckhardt 1934a: 1–135
Lex Salica	In Eckhardt 1934a: 1–135
Lex Saxonum [*LexSax*]	In Eckhardt 1934c: 1–33
Mircna Laga	In Liebermann 1903–1916: I, 462–465
Ordal	In Liebermann 1903–1916: I, 386–387
Pactus Legis Alamannorum [*PactLexAla*]	Eckhardt 1954
Pactus Legis Salicae	Eckhardt 1955

[*PactLexSal*]

Rectitudines Singularum Personarum	In Liebermann 1903–1916: 444–453; Thom Gobbit, Early English Laws Project [web resource]
Swerian	In Liebermann 1903–1916: 1, 396–399
Toronto *DOE. Dictionary of Old English, A to I* (online) 2018	Angus Cameron, Ashley Crandell Amos, Antonette diPaolo Healey *et al.*
Wifmannes Beweddung	In Liebermann 1903–1916: 1, 442–443
Wihtred	In Oliver 2002: 60–81

6

Rubrics: Edition and Translation

All manuscripts of Alfred's *domboc*, excluding the fragmentary **Bu**, include a series of rubrics purporting to give the contents of the laws. Though it had been commonplace for Frankish legislation also to commence with a list of rubrics analogous to what appears in the *domboc*, Alfred's was (and would remain) the only pre-Conquest book of laws to do so. Given their near-ubiquity in manuscript witnesses, the rubrics of the *domboc* seem to have been added at an early phase of its transmission: perhaps early enough that they may be understood to reflect the will of Alfred's "immediate political and intellectual heirs."[1] But there is every indication that the work of the rubricator, in spite of its Alfredian or immediately post-Alfredian context, took place at some remove from whatever circumstances first occasioned the *domboc*. Liebermann found the list "too full of error [...] and incomplete to be able to count as authentic"; Keynes and Lapidge point out that the division "is often effected with apparent disregard for content."[2] In spite of these shortcomings, the rubrics represent an early attempt to organize the sprawling contents of the *domboc* into some sort of logical form and are thus important

---

[1] Wormald 1999a: 269 n. 17. Wormald does not rule out the (remote) possibility that the rubrics may even reflect the intentions of the king himself.
[2] "zu fehlerhaft [...] und unvollständig, um als authentisch gelten zu können." Liebermann 1903–1916: III, 40; Keynes and Lapidge 1983: 304 n. 1.

witnesses to its early reception.[3] In the view of Wormald, who concedes their deficiency,

> the manuscript authority for the rubrics is as good as for Ine's code, or the Mosaic preface for that matter. And if there was little logic in laws on different issues within the same chapter, there was not much in an Ine that contradicted Alfred, or even laws of Moses whose scale matched Alfred's own.[4]

That the rubrics are essentially the same in all manuscripts that contain them further suggests that they constitute a very early accretion.[5] Although the organization of quires shows that the rubric list was envisaged from inception as part of the Parker manuscript, three features of the text as written indicate that the rubric numbers were inserted after copying had been completed:

- The very first rubric number is written in the left margin.
- All other numbers are inserted at the conclusion of the preceding paragraph rather than at the beginning of their own, which makes sense if the text were already written flush to the left margin leaving available free space only at the end of paragraphs.
- The numeral LXXXVIIII is forced into a space too cramped for it at the end of its paragraph, and LXXXVIII cannot even be completely fit in. Both seem to be afterthoughts.

Thematic requirements may have driven the numeration of the rubrics. The section of the *domboc* following the rubrics consists of Alfred's version of the laws of Moses. This paradigmatic lawgiver died at the age of 120; the number has further relevance in that Bede in his *Expositio actuum apostolorum* assumes this figure determined the number of electors who chose a replacement for Judas in the first chapter of Acts.[6] It may well be more than coincidence, then, that

---

3   Wormald notes that "the wording of Edward's supposed citation of Ine's law ('ðe flieman feormige') was actually closer to that of the rubric than to that of Ine's text" (1999a: 269).
4   Wormald 1999a: 269.
5   Manuscripts with separate rubrics are **E, G, Ot,** and **H; B** interleaves them into text. See discussion in Richards 2014b: 297–299.
6   Laistner 1939: 11, "It was fitting that the mystery exhibited by the Lawgiver [Moses] in his years [of life] should by their number be designated by the preachers of the new grace" (*Oportebat enim ut sacramentum quod legislator in annis exhibuit hoc novae gratiae praedicatores suo numero designarent*). Cf. also Wormald, 1999a: 417.

following the exposition of Mosaic law (and a heavily adapted rendering of Acts 15) are 120 numbered paragraphs dealing with West-Saxon law, a tradition depicted in the Prologue as traceable through the judgments of many "synods" ultimately to the laws given on Mt. Sinai.

The handling of Alfred's laws on injuries suggests that much was sacrificed to maintain this scheme. Material contained under individual rubric headings seems to expand and contract like an accordion. Whatever the rationale behind the composition of the rubrics may have been, the need for clarity of exposition was apparently not primary. Specific problems are addressed in footnotes to the individual rubrics, but even the following brief list of discrepancies demonstrates their consistent inadequacy:

- The first rubric is inserted between Alfred's paraphrase of the "Council of Jerusalem" and his brief discussion of the Golden Rule. The next (II) follows Alfred's discussion of prior English legislative sources allegedly made use of in the *domboc*. Ine's prologue, conversely, is assigned its own number (XLIIII), even though it is not itself a legislative enactment.
- In Alfred's personal injury section, individual rubrics are assigned for a head-wound, a wound near the hairline, and a blow to the ear (XL–XLII). The following rubric (XLIII) subsumes all other wounds from the eye down to the toe and back to the spinal cord (thirty-one separate clauses in this edition).
- Similarly, CII "Concerning an ox's horn" sets the value for the horn; the following rubric (CIII) sets the value for a cow's horn, ox's or cow's tail, ox's or cow's eye (three subclauses in this edition), and then adds the completely unrelated regulation on payment of "barley rent," which should be a separate clause.
- Regulations according to rank are inconsistently either grouped together or separated by rubric: CVIII concerns one who has twenty hides of land; CVIIII ten hides; CX three hides. Conversely, CXIIII claims to be "Concerning a [man whose] *wer* [is] two-hundred"; this clause includes reckonings for men whose wergild is 200, 600,

and 1,200. Furthermore, the paragraph ends with a ruling setting the yearly amount of food render, which should be its own clause.

- The rubrics are often misleading: for example, IX "Concerning having intercourse with a nun" regulates the case of a nun who is abducted from her monastery but goes on to live with her abductor; XLVI "Concerning children" actually deals with the period within which infants must be baptized.

- The rubric numeration often doesn't follow connective meanings: LXXXVII "Concerning burning of wood" has two regulations, one on burning another's tree and one on felling another's tree; LXXXVIII "Concerning taking wood without permission" relates to the second ruling in the previous clause. Either all three should be considered together, or the first should stand alone with the last two joined under one heading. The rubricator has chosen the only grouping that makes no contextual sense.

In the (arguably) post-Conquest manuscript CCCC 383 (**B**),[7] the rubrics (here given without numerals) are inserted into the text above the clauses they head.[8] This proximity seems to have compelled this scribe to recognize the frequent discrepancies between heading and content, leading him to make occasional corrections.[9] For this reason we include in this edition the rubrics from CCCC 383 rather than reduce them to variants in the critical apparatus. While editors as late as the nineteenth century followed the Parker manuscript as a guide to clause numeration, the scribe of CCCC 383 had already (at least in part) perceived the error in this approach.

Finally it should be noted that, here and in subsequent sections of the *domboc*, we leave untranslated the word *wer* ("wergild") even though it was virtually interchangeable with Old English wergild. If

---

[7] Liebermann and Wormald both date this manuscript to a period some decades after the Norman Conquest. But Ker 1957 suggests the end of the eleventh or beginning of the twelfth century, and Powell 2010 accepts this date while offering more evidence seemingly in its favor.

[8] All other manuscripts that contain rubrics list them in a separate table.

[9] Much of the original rubric list is retained in **B**, however. Just a few examples of shared discrepancies include: Rub LXXIII which has *þeow* "slave" where the text reads *esne* (hired worker) (in the later Anglo-Saxon period *esne* was often translated as *servus* (see Pelteret 1995: 273)); the inconsistency in numbering between LXXXVII and LXXXVIII and also between CII and CIII discussed above. Furthermore, **B** sometimes omits rubrics altogether, such as for XLV, XLVI, and XLVII.

maintaining the distinction between the two terms seemed worth the trouble to the scribe, it stands to reason that the translation should reflect his intentions (however inscrutable), particularly given the light shed by the use of this term on the development of the pre-Conquest legal lexicon generally.

/33r/ I Be ðon þæt mon ne scyle oþrum deman buton swa he wille,
þæt him mon deme.

    II **Be** aþum ⁊ be weddum
    III **Be** circena socnum[10]
    IIII **Be** borgbryce
    V **Be** hlafordsearwe
        Be cynincges swicdome[11]
    VI **Be** circena friðe
        Be ciricene friðe

Rubr. I ðon] þæm H   scyle] scule H   buton] butan GH   him mon deme] man him deme GH
Rubr. III circena] cyricena G
Rubr. V searwe] *Hand of the twelfth century writes* swice *above* H
Rubr. VI circena] cyricena G

[10] The word **socnum** appears nowhere in the clause itself. Compare XLVIIII.
[11] This is the first rubric in Cambridge, Corpus Christi College 383 (**B**). Numeration of folios is not given for **B** as these appear above each clause in the manuscript.

I Concerning that one should not judge another except as he wishes that he shall be judged[12]

    II Concerning oaths and concerning vows

    III Concerning churches' asylum

    IIII Concerning breach of security

    V Concerning treason to one's lord

        Concerning treachery to the king

    VI Concerning churches' peace

        Concerning church peace

---

[12] The first Roman numeral referring to the rubric list is placed in the margin before *MP* §49.6. The *O* that begins the paragraph is large and ornate, which may have drawn the rubricator's eye to it. The clause (in translation) reads: "From this one judgment one may reason in such a way that he judge each man rightly; he requires no other book of laws. Let him think that he judge no man in a manner that he would not be judged by him, if he sought judgment over him." The inclusion of this paraphrase of the Golden Rule in the rubrics is somewhat odd. The text continues to describe the early spread of Christianity in and beyond England. This brief historical sketch is then followed by Alfred's "second" prologue, in which he describes his method in selecting the laws to be included. This paragraph similarly begins with a large (somewhat) ornate *I*. The rubricator later assigns Ine's prologue its own number (XLIIII) but does not do the same for Alfred, where logic might dictate that the first rubric should appear. One could be tempted to interpret this placement as a mistake on the part of the rubricator of the Parker manuscript, but since the rubrics are common to both received lines of Alfred's laws, this hypothesis is untenable. At best one might propose that the common exemplar had decorated initials similar to those in Parker, and that the original rubricator was misled in his placement of his first rubric. Conversely, one might simply argue that this first and greatest of the laws was always meant to be assigned the first rubric.

VII **Be** circan stale[13]
 Be ðam ðe steleð on ciricean
VIII **Be** ðon þe mon on cynges healle feohte.
 Be ðam þæt man feohteð on kyninges healle
IX **Be** nunnan hæmede[14]
 Be ðam þe nunnan of mynstre ut alædeð
X **Be** bearneacnum[15] wife ofslægenum
 Be ðam ðæt man ofslea wif mid cilde
XI **Be** twelfhyndes monnes wife forlegenum[16]
 Be hæmedðingum
XII **Be** cirliscre fæmnan onfenge
 Eft

Rubr. VII circan] cyricena G; circean H
Rubr. VIII ðon] þam H cynges] cyninges GOt; kyninges H feohte] \ge/feohte H
Rubr. X ofslægenum] ofslegenum Ot; ofslagenum GH
Rubr. XI monnes] mannes GH
Rubr. XII cirliscre] cierliscre H onfenge] anfenge G

[13] The word **stale** appears nowhere in the clause itself.
[14] The word **hæmede** appears nowhere in the clause itself.
[15] The word **bearneacnum** appears nowhere in the clause itself. (Neither does the **cilde** of B's substitution.)
[16] The word **forlegenum** appears nowhere in the clause itself.

VII Concerning theft from a church
    Concerning one who steals in a church
VIII Concerning that someone fights in the king's hall
    Concerning that someone fights in the king's hall
IX Concerning having intercourse with a nun[17]
    Concerning one who leads a nun out of a minster
X Concerning the killing of a pregnant woman[18]
    Concerning that one slays a woman with child
XI Concerning lying with the wife of a 1,200 man[19]
    Concerning carnal intercourse
XII Concerning seizing a *ceorl*-rank woman[20]
    Further

[17] This rubric is a bit misleading, as the clause deals with a nun who is abducted from a monastery but goes on to live with her abductor. **B** makes this clearer.
[18] Also under this rubric are rulings as to how the amount of *any* fine (*wite*) should be calculated; furthermore the paragraph contains a clause equating fines for gold-thieves, stud-thieves and bee-thieves. These stipulations should be separate entries.
[19] That is, a man whose wergild is 1,200 shillings. This clause also addresses the fines for lying with the wife of a man whose wergild is 600 shillings or of a *ceorl*. **B**'s emendation provides a more appropriate general heading.
[20] This rubric also covers clauses addressing various types of rape; the final clause sets fines for the same offenses against more high-born women. **B**'s emendation ties it to the previous clause.

XIII Be wudu bærnette

    Be wudebernete, ⁊ gif man afylled bið on gemænum weorce

XIIII Be dumbera monna dǽdum

    Be dumbra manna dædum

XV Be þam monnum þe beforan biscopum feohtað

    Be ðam þæt man toforan bisceope feohteð

    Be ðam gif man of myran folan adrifþ oððe cucealf

    Ðe oðrum his unmagum ætfæsteð[21]

XVI Be nunnena onfenge

    Be nunnena andfencgum

XVII Be ðam monnum þe heora wæpen to monslyhte lænað

    Be þam þe heore wepna lænað to manslihte

XVIII Be ðam þe munecum heora feoh butan leafe befæstað[22]

    Be þam þe munecan heore feoh befæstað

Rubr. XIII wudu bærnette] [ ]dubærnete Ot; wuda bærnette H
Rubr. XIIII dumbera] dumbra GOt; dumb\r/a H   monna] manna GH
Rubr. XV þam] ðan G   monnum] mannum GH
Rubr. XVI onfenge] anfengum H   monnum] mannum G   heora] \hi/ora Ot; hyra G
wæpen] wæpn G; wæpna H   monslyhte] manslihte G; manslyhte H
Rubr. XVIII munecum] *Hand of the twelfth century writes* þe man *over* munecum H
befæstað] befestað G

---

[21] The text uses the (quite different) verb *oðfæste*.
[22] Text uses *oðfæstan* rather than **befæstan**.

XIII Concerning burning wood[23]

> Concerning burning wood, and if a person is killed during shared work

XIIII Concerning the deeds of dumb men[24]

> Concerning the deeds of dumb men

XV Concerning men who fight in the presence of bishops[25]

> Concerning that a man fights before a bishop
>
> Concerning if a man causes abortion of a foal from a mare or a cow-calf
>
> He who afflicts the child of another

XVI Concerning seizing nuns[26]

> Concerning seizings of nuns

XVII Concerning men who lend their weapons for killing a man

> Concerning those who lend their weapons for killing a man

XVIII Concerning someone who entrusts monks with their property without permission.

> Concerning someone who entrusts monks with their property[27]

---

[23] Also under this rubric is a clause concerning a person who is killed during shared work felling trees, which should probably be a separate entry. **B** includes both topics in the ruling.

[24] The clause concerns both deaf and dumb.

[25] The clause begins with those who fight in the presence of an archbishop and moves to those who fight in the presence of bishops or ealdormen. This rubric also covers a clause on stealing pregnant livestock and causing the dam to foal, and another concerning a guardian who allows a child entrusted to him to die. Both these later stipulations should be separate entries. **B** assigns them their own rubrics.

[26] The clause on seizing a nun is followed by three concerning restitution by different ranks should a contractually betrothed woman fornicate with one who is not her intended husband. This second group should constitute a separate entry.

[27] A rare instance in which **B** is less specific than **E**.

XIX **B**e preosta gefeohte
    Be preosta gefeohte
XX **B**e eofetes andetlan[28]
    Be cynincges gerefan ðyfðe
XXI **B**e hundes slite
    Be hundes slite
XXII **B**e nietena misdædum
    Be nytena misdædum
XXIII **B**e ceorles mennenes niedhæmede
    Be ceorles mennenes nydhemede
XXIIII **B**e twyhundum men æt hloþslyhte
    Be twyhyndum men æt hloðslihte

Rubr. XX eofetes andetlan] ðeofes andettan H
Rubr. XXI slite] slyte Ot
Rubr. XXII nietena] nytena GH
Rubr. XXIII *om.* H   niedhæmede] niedhæmde G
Rubr. XXIIII hloþslyhte] hloþslihte GH

[28] andetlan is a *hapax legomenon*. It does not appear in the text itself.

XVIIII Concerning fighting of priests[29]
    Concerning fighting of priests
XX Concerning the admission of an offense
    Concerning theft by a king's reeve[30]
XXI Concerning a dog's bite
    Concerning a dog's bite
XXII Concerning the misdeeds of cattle[31]
    Concerning the misdeeds of cattle
XXIII Concerning the rape of a *ceorl*'s female slave
    Concerning the rape of a *ceorl*'s female slave
XXIIII Concerning a two-hundred [wergild] man slain by a band
    Concerning a two-hundred [wergild] man slain by a band

---

[29] This clause actually concerns a priest who slays another man.

[30] This clause seems to have caused problems for both scribes, although Parker is closer than **B**. The ruling concerns someone who reveals an offense to the king's reeve in the public assembly and then tries to withdraw the accusation (see discussion in edition). The Parker rubric – matching all other manuscripts except **B** – changes *geyppe* ("should reveal") in the text to *andetlan* ("admission"), with the resultant implication that the defendant is admitting his own offense. **B** changes the uncommon word *eofot* ("offense") to the more specific *þeofðe* ("theft"), then interprets *cyninges gerefan* ("king's reeve") as a genitive modifying the theft rather than a dative indicating the person to whom the revelation is made. The result presents a very different case, in which the plaintiff reveals in public assembly the theft of (by) the king's reeve. See also the variant in **H**, which comes close to what is found in **B**.

[31] The clause specifically addresses the case in which a cow/ox wounds a person.

/33v/ xxv **Be** six hyndum men
    Be sixhyndu*m men*
xxvi **Be** .XII. hyndum men
    Be twylfhendu*m men*
xxvii **Be** ungewintredes wifmonnes nedhæmde
    Be ungewintredes wifmannes slæge
xxviii **Be** swa gerades monnes slege
xxviiii **Be** folcleasunge gewyrhtum
xxx **Be** godborgum
    Be godborhgum
xxxi **Be** ciepemonnum
    Be cypmannum

Rubr. xxvii wifmonnes] wifmannes G; H *misunderstands, giving* be tyngewintredes mannes nydhæmede "Concerning forcible violation by (of?) a ten-year-old man"; *confusion perhaps caused by language of following rubric*; H *gives* Be ungewintr[ ]des monnes wif nedhæmd[ ]   nedhæmde] niedhæmde G
Rubr. xxviii monnes] mannes GH   slege] sleges G; slæge H; slegi (?) Ot
Rubr. xxviii folcleasunge] folcleasunga G
Rubr. xxxi ciepe monnum] cype mannum G; cyp mannum H

/33v/ xxv Concerning a six-hundred [wergild] man[32]

Concerning a six-hundred [wergild] man

xxvi Concerning a 12-hundred man[33]

Concerning a 12-hundred man

xxvii Concerning the rape of an underage girl[34]

Concerning the slaying of an underage girl[35]

xxviii Concerning the killing of a man in this condition[36]

xxviiii Concerning making false statements detrimental to the public good

xxx Concerning pledges confirmed by invocation of God

Concerning pledges confirmed by invocation of God

xxxi Concerning merchants

Concerning merchants

---

[32] According to his usual practice, the rubricator should have included this and the following clause under the previous rubric.

[33] See previous note.

[34] This clause is followed by two rulings on how the responsibility for payment of wergild should be divided if a man without paternal or maternal kin slays another. These stipulations should represent a new entry, and should be linked to the text of the next rubric. (See, for example, xxxvi.)

[35] Curiously, **B** changes **nedhæmde** ("rape") to **slæge** ("slaying") although the text addresses only rape. But *slæge* sometimes refers to non-lethal acts of violence.

[36] See previous note. The rubric as it stands makes no sense as the condition referred to is the (partial) kinlessness mentioned in the previous clauses but falsely included under the heading of raping an underage girl. Here the culpability of the previous clause is reversed, and the kinless man becomes victim rather than slayer.

XXXII **Be** cierlisces monnes byndellan

Be ceorlisces mannes bindelan

XXXIII **Be** speres gemeleasnesse[37]

Be speres gymeleaste

XXXIIII **Be** boldgetale

Be boldgetale

XXXV **Be** ðon ðe mon beforan ealdormen on gemote gefeohte[38]

Be ðam ðe beforan aldormen on gemote feohte

XXXVI **Be** cierlisces monnes flet gefeohte

Eft

Be cyrlisces monnes flettegefeohte

Rubr. XXXII cierlisces monnes] cyrlisces mannes G; cyrlisc[ ] Ot
Rubr. XXXIII gemeleasnesse] gymeleasnesse GH
Rubr. XXXV ðon] ðam GH   ealdormen] ealdermen H
Rubr. XXXVI cierlisces] cyrlisces G   monnes] mannes GH   flet] flett H

[37] Neither **gemeleasnesse** nor **gymeleaste** appears in the clause itself.
[38] The word **feohte** is written on right side of line above with separation mark as the scribe ran out of space.

XXXII Concerning the binding of a *ceorl*-rank man[39]

Concerning the binding of a *ceorl*-rank man

XXXIII Concerning carelessness with a spear

Concerning carelessness with a spear

XXXIIII About a district[40]

About a district

XXXV Concerning that someone fights in the assembly in the presence of the king's *ealdorman*[41]

Concerning he who fights in the assembly in the presence of the king's *ealdorman*

XXXVI Concerning fighting in a *ceorl*'s house[42]

Following[43]

Concerning fighting in a *ceorl*'s house

---

[39] This paragraph also includes several stipulations on shearing hair or beard.

[40] The rubric is somewhat misleading: the clause actually concerns a person wanting to relocate from one district to another.

[41] This also contains a ruling about fighting in the presence of the ealdorman's substitute or the king's priest (the *Eft* of B's rubric).

[42] Here the rubricator follows his usual practice of discussing restitution to other ranks of men in the same clause, as opposed to XXIV, XXV, and XXVI. The text then contains two clauses that should each constitute a separate entry. The first concerns breaking and entering, ranging from offenses against the king to those against a *ceorl*. The second addresses someone who sets aside the obligations of Lent.

[43] This insertion correctly links the following clause to the previous one. However, the paragraph as a whole suffers from the same problems as described in the previous footnote.

Rubr. XXXVII boclondum] boclandum GH
Rubr. XXXVIII fæhðe] fæhðum GH
Rubr. XXXVIIII freolse] freolsum H
Rubr. XLII earslege] earslæge H
Rubr. XLIII eagwunde] eag\ena/wunde H oðerra] oðra G; oðre H missenlicra]
mislicra G; mis\t/licra H lima] *om.* G

XXXVII Concerning book-lands[44]
    Concerning book-land
XXXVIII Concerning an act of violence[45]
XXXVIIII Concerning freedom [from work] on mass-days
XL Concerning a head-wound
    Concerning a headwound and [wounds to] another limb
XLI Concerning a hair-wound[46]
XLII Concerning a blow to the ear
XLIII Concerning a person's eye-wound and other various limbs[47]
XLIIII Concerning Ine's judgments[48]
    Concerning Ine's law

---

[44] That is, land deeded by charter. The rubric is somewhat uninformative: the clause concerns limits on the right to sell land under entail.

[45] Again, the rubric is vague. The paragraph addresses prohibitions against attacking an enemy before attempting to settle in court. These stipulations are followed by rulings about when a man may fight without incurring wergild, which would be better entered under a separate rubric. The translation here is in keeping with the analysis of *fæhðe* in Niles 2015.

[46] This rubric does not, of course, refer to wounding the hair, but rather to different assessments according to whether or not a wound is above the hairline and thus not visible.

[47] Here the rubricator simply lumps together the remainder of the personal injury clauses: thirty-one in this edition and a good two-and-a-half pages in the manuscript! There is no room within the written text in which rubrics could have been inserted. **B** more logically sets a single rubric for all personal injury rulings.

[48] This is Ine's prologue, not actually a legal ruling. As discussed above, the rubricator does not include a rubric for Alfred's Prologue.

XLV **Be** Godes ðeowa regole
XLVI **Be** cildum
XLVII **Be** sunnan dæges weorcum
XLVIII **Be** ciricsceattum
     Be ciricsceatte
XLVIIII **Be** ciricsócnum⁴⁹
     Be ciricsocnum
L **Be** gefeohtum
     Be gefeohtum
/34r/ LI **Be** stale
     Be stale
LII **Be** ryhtes bene⁵⁰
     Be rihtes bene
LIII **Be** ðam wrecendan, ær \ʰᵉ/ him ryhtes bidde
     Be þam wrecendan
LIIII **Be** reaflace
     Be reaflace

Rubr. XLV regole] regule H
Rubr. XLVII weorcum] wyrcum G
Rubr. XLVIII ciricsceattum] cyricsceatum G
Rubr. LIII ær \he/ him] ær man G; ær hine man H (*end of rubrics in* Ot)

⁴⁹ The word **socnum** appears nowhere in the clause itself. Compare III.
⁵⁰ The word **bene** appears nowhere in the clause itself.

XLV Concerning the rule for God's servants

XLVI Concerning children[51]

XLVII Concerning working on Sunday

XLVIII Concerning church taxes

Concerning church tax

XLVIIII Concerning church asylums

Concerning church asylums

L Concerning fighting

Concerning fighting

/34r/ LI Concerning stealing[52]

Concerning stealing

LII Concerning petition for justice

Concerning petition for justice

LIII Concerning he who exacts redress before he petitions him for[53] justice

Concerning he who exacts redress

LIIII Concerning robbery

Concerning robbery

---

[51] The ruling has to do with the time limit within which one must baptize a child.

[52] This clause actually deals with the complicity of the household if the head of the house commits theft.

[53] The perpetrator of the avenged offense.

LV Be ðam monnu*m* þe hiora gelondan bebycggað⁵⁴

    Be landbygene

LVI Be gefongenum ðeofum

    Be gefangenu*m* ðeofu*m*

LVII Be ðam ðe hiora gewitnessa beforan bisc*epe* áleogað

    Be þa*m* þe heore gewitnesse geleogað

LVIII Be hloðe

    hloðe

LVIIII Be herige

    Be herge

LX Be ðeofslege

    Be ðeofslæge

LXI Be forstolenum flæsce

    Be forstolenu*m* flæsce

Rubr. LV ðam] þan G   monnum] mannum GH   hiora] hira G; he\o/ra H   gelondan] gelandan G; \ge/landan H

Rubr. LVI gefongenum] gefangenum GH

Rubr. LVII ðam] þan G   hiora] hyra G; he\or/a H   gewitnessa] gewitnesse GH

Rubr. LVIII herige] herge G; her\e/ge H

---

⁵⁴ Text uses *geleod* rather than **gelondan**; a later hand corrects *land* in B's rubric to *leodan*.

LV Concerning those who sell their countrymen

  Concerning selling land[55]

LVI Concerning captured thieves

  Concerning captured thieves

LVII Concerning those who deny their testimony in the presence of the bishop[56]

  Concerning those who deny their testimony in the presence of the bishop

LVIII Concerning a band

  a band[57]

LVIIII Concerning a troop[58]

  Concerning a troop

LX Concerning killing a thief

  Concerning killing a thief

LXI Concerning stolen meat

  Concerning stolen meat

---

[55] B seems to have misinterpreted the meaning of *gelondan* in his source.

[56] Following the ruling on denying one's testimony or oath in the presence of the bishop are definitions for a band of thieves and a troop of thieves; this sentence should have a separate entry and subsume the next two clauses (i.e., LVIII and LVIIII).

[57] This noun is in the dative case, indicating that a preposition – in this case undoubtedly *Be* "Concerning" – has been omitted.

[58] See footnote 56. However, this paragraph ends with a ruling concerning the inability of a thief to exculpate himself once in the king's confinement, which should constitute a separate entry.

LXII **Be** cirliscum ðeofe gefongenum
  Be ceorliscum ðeofum gefangenum

LXIII **Be** cyninges geneate
  Be cinges geneate

LXIIII **Be** feorran cumenum men butan wege gemetton
  Be feorran cumenan men

LXV **Be** swa ofslegenes monnes were
  Be swa ofslagenes mannes were

LXVI **Be** ðon ðe monnes geneat stalige
  Be ðam þe mannes geneat stalige

LXVII **Be** elðeodies[59] monnes slege
  Be ælðeodiges mannes slæge

LXVIII **Be** witeðeowes monnes slege

LXVIIII **Be** ciepemonna fore uppe on londe
  Be cypmanna fare uppe land

LXX **Be** fundenes cildes foster
  Be fundenes cildes fostre

LXXI **Be** þon þe mon dearnenga bearn gestriene
  Be ðam þe dearnunge bearn stryneð

Rubr. LXII gefongenum] gefangenum GH
Rubr. LXIII cyninges] kyninges H
Rubr. LXIIII gemetton] \ge/mettum H
Rubr. LXV ofslegenes] ofsla\e/nes   monnes] mannes GH
Rubr. LXVI ðon] þan G; þam H   monnes] mannes GH   geneat] *om.* G
Rubr. LXVII elðeodies] ælþeodiges GH   monnes] mannes GH
Rubr. LXVIII monnes] mannes GH
Rubr. LXVIIII ciepemonna] cypmanna G; cypemanna H   fore] fare H   uppe] up G;
upp H   londe] land G; land stryne H ("taken mistakenly from end of LXXI"
[Liebermann])
Rubr. LXXI þon] ðan G; þam H   mon] man GH   dearnenga] dearnunga
GH   gestriene] gestrune G; gestri_ne H

[59] Note that the *g* usual in forms of *elþeodig* is missing; *g* is no longer actually pronounced (except perhaps as an offglide of the previous *i*).

LXII Concerning the capture of a *ceorl*-rank thief
Concerning the capture of *ceorl*-rank thieves
LXIII Concerning a man in the king's service
Concerning a man in the king's service
LXIIII Concerning meeting a man come from far away off the
road
Concerning a man come from far away
LXV Concerning the *wer* of such a man who is slain[60]
Concerning the *wer* of such a man who is slain
LXVI Concerning theft by someone in a man's service
Concerning theft by someone in a man's service
LXVII Concerning the slaying of a foreigner[61]
Concerning the slaying of a foreigner
LXVIII Concerning the slaying of a penal slave
LXVIIII Concerning merchants' traveling in the countryside
Concerning merchants' traveling in the countryside
LXX Concerning the fostering of a foundling
Concerning the fostering of a foundling
LXXI Concerning a child conceived secretly
Concerning he who conceives a child secretly

---

[60] This should be subsumed under the previous rubric.
[61] Appended to the rulings on killing a foreigner are assessments of wergild for Welsh taxpayers. These clauses should constitute a separate entry, since as taxpayers the Welsh discussed here probably are not considered foreigners.

LXXII **Be** ðeofes onfenge æt ðiefðe

Be ðeowes mannes onfenge æt ðyfðe

LXXIII **Be** ðon þe mon sweordes onlæne oðres ðeowe[62]

Be ðam þe his sweord alæne oðres ðeowan

LXXIIII **Be** ðon þe cierlisc mon flieman feormige

Be þam þe cyrlis man feormige flyman

LXXV **Be** ðon þe mon wíf bycgge, ⁊ þonne sio gift tostande.

Be þam þe man wif bycge, ⁊ seo gift wiðstande

LXXVI **Be** Wilisces monnes londhæfene

Be Wylisces mannes landhæfene

/34v/ LXXVII **Be** cyninges horsweale

Be cinincges horswale

LXXVIII **Be** monslihte

Be manslihte

LXXVIIII **Be** þeofslihte, þæt he mote aðe gecyðan

Be ðeof slihte

LXXX **Be** ðeofes onfenge, ⁊ hine ðonne forlæte

Be ðeofes andfenge, ⁊ hine swa forlæte

Rubr. LXXII ðeofes] þeowes\mannes/ H (cf. rubric in B)   ðiefðe] ðeofe G; þyfþe H
Rubr. LXXIII ðon] þan G; þam H   mon] man GH   sweordes] \his/ sweord H   on
læne] a læne H   ðeowe] ðeowa\n/ H
Rubr. LXXIIII ðon] þan G; þam H   cierlisc] cyrlisc G   mon] man GH   flieman] fly-
man GH
Rubr. LXXV ðon] þan G; \þam/ H   mon] man H; *abbrev.* G   bycgge] bicge G; bycge
H   sio] seo GH
Rubr. LXXVI wilisces] wylysces G   monnes] mannes G; man\nes/ H   londhæfene]
landhæfene G; landhæwene H
Rubr. LXXVII cyninges] kyninges H
Rubr. LXXVIII monslihte] manslihte G; man\n/slyhte H
Rubr. LXXVIIII þeofslihte] þeofslyhte H   mote aðe gecyðan] he þæt mote aðe G; mott
\þæt/ mid aþe H
Rubr. LXXX hine ðonne] hine ðænne G; hine man ðonne H

[62] The text here reads *esne* in place of þeowe.

---

[63] B's *ðeow* ("slave") occurs also in **H** (see apparatus); both share a misinterpretation of the clause as a reference to the misdeeds of slaves.

[64] The concern of the clause is far more specific than the rubric indicates: this involves killing a man when out raiding with a troop.

[65] The rubric incompletely describes the content of the clause, which finishes: "he slew him for a thief as he was running away."

LXXXI **Be** cirlisces monnes ontygnesse æt ðiefðe
　　Be ceorlisces monnes betogenesse
LXXXII **Be** þon ðe ryhtgesamhiwan bearn hæbben, ⁊ þon*n*e se wer
　　gewite[66]
　　Be ða*m* ðe rihtgesamhiwan bearn habban
LXXXIII **Be** unalefedu*m* fære from his hlaforde
　　Be unalyfedum fare fra*m* his laforde
LXXXIIII **Be** ceorles weorðige
　　Be ceorles worðige
LXXXV **Be** borges ondsæce
LXXXVI **Be** ceorles gærstune
　　Be ða*m* þ*æt* ceorlas habbað land gemæne ⁊ gærstunas
LXXXVII **Be** wuda bærnette
　　Be wude bærnete

Rubr. LXXXI cirlisces] cyrlisces G; cierlisces H　monnes] mannes GH　ontygnesse æt
ðiefðe] ontygnesse æt ðyfðe G; æt þyfðe betogenisse H
Rubr. LXXXII þon] þan G; ðam H　ryhtgesamhiwan] rih\t/gesamhiwon G; rihtgesam-
hiwan H　hæbben] habben G; habban H
Rubr. LXXXIII unalefedum] unalyfedum G; unagelyfedum H　from] fram GH
Rubr. LXXXIIII ceorles] ciorles H　weorðige] w\e/orðige H
Rubr. LXXXV ondsæce] andsæce GH
Rubr. LXXXVII wuda] wudu H

---

[66] **gewite** is written on the right side of the line above with a separation mark as the
scribe ran out of space. The word **ryhtgesamhiwan** appears nowhere in the clause
itself; nor does the word **wer** occur elsewhere in the *domboc* with the meaning of
husband/man.

---

[67] *ceorl* logically should be in the plural as it is in the text since a single person cannot hold a common meadow. **B** makes this emendation.

[68] This paragraph has two clauses: one concerning the burning of trees and one the felling of trees. The subsequent rubric introduces an assessment based on the size of the tree felled. All three of these rulings could be subsumed under the same rubric; conversely, the first could stand alone and the second two together. The distribution arrived at by the rubricator – that is, the first two together and the third alone – makes no sense.

LXXXVIII Be wuda onfenga butan leafe
    Be wude andfenge
LXXXVIIII Be burgbryce
    Be burhbryce
XC Be stæltyhtlan
    Be staltihlan
XCI Be ðon þe mon forstolenne ceap befehð
XCII Be witeþeowum men
    Be witeðeowum mannum
XCIII Be unaliefedes mæstennes onfenge[69]
    Be unalefedum mæstenum andfencge
XCIIII Be gesiðcundes monnes geþinge
    Be gesiðcundes mannes geðinge
XCV Be ðon ðe gesiðcund mon fierd forsitte
    Be þam þe gesiðcund man fyrde forsitte

Rubr. LXXXVIII onfenge] anfenge H
Rubr. LXXXVIIII burgbryce] burhbrece G; burhbryce H
Rubr. XC stæltyhtlan] staltihlan G; staltyhtlan H
Rubr. XCI ðon] ðam H   mon] man GH   ceap befehð] befehþ ceap H
Rubr. XCII men] mannum H
Rubr. XCIII unaliefedes] unalyfedes GH   mæstennes] mæstenes GH
Rubr. XCIIII monnes] mannes GH
Rubr. XCV ðon] þan G; þam H   gesiðcundmon] gesiðcundman GH   fierd] fyrd G; fyrd\e/ H

[69] The text uses the verb *gemette* "should encounter" rather than **gefenge** "should catch."

LXXXVIII Concerning taking wood without permission[70]
    Concerning taking wood
LXXXVIIII Concerning breaking into a fortified dwelling
    Concerning breaking into a fortified dwelling
XC Concerning accusation of theft[71]
    Concerning accusation of theft
XCI Concerning the finding of stolen livestock
XCII Concerning a penal slave
    Concerning a penal slave
XCIII Concerning the capture of swine eating mast without permission[72]
    Concerning the capture of swine eating mast without permission
XCIIII Concerning a nobly born man's legal settlement
    Concerning a nobly born man's legal settlement
XCV Concerning a nobly born man neglecting his *fyrd*-duty[73]
    Concerning a nobly born man neglecting his *fyrd*-duty

[70] See previous note. To further muddle the rubrication, another clause is added to the stipulation about cutting down a particularly large tree that each household should pay (presumably yearly, although that is not stated) an assessment in cloth.

[71] Appended to the rulings on accusation of theft is a clause stating that any man may deny a charge of instigating wrongdoing or killing, which should have its own entry.

[72] Appended to this paragraph is a clause about how to pay for pasturage for pigs. Although the rulings all concern swine, the last is not directly related to the first two in the paragraph, and should have its own entry.

[73] This clause also addresses the penalty for a man of *ceorl*-rank who neglects his *fyrd*-duty.

XCVI **Be** diernum geðinge

Be ðyrnum geþincðe

XCVII **Be** forstolenes monnes forefonge

Be forstolenes mannes forfenge

XCVIII **Be** werfæhðe tyhtlan

Be werfæhðe tyhlan

XCVIIII **Be** ewes weorðe

Be eowe wyrðe

C **Be** gehwelces ceapes angelde[74]

Be gehwylces ceapes wyrðe

CI **Be** cierlisces monnes stale

Be cyrlisces mannes stale

CII **Be** oxan horne

/35r/ CIII **Be** cuus horne

Rubr. XCVI diernum] dyrnum GH
Rubr. XCVII monnes] mannes GH   forefonge] forefenge G; forfenge H
Rubr. XCVIII werfæhðe] werfæhte G   tyhtlan] tihtlan GH
Rubr. XCVIIII ewes] eowes GH
Rubr. C gehwelces] gehwylces GH
Rubr. CI cierlisces] cyrlisces G; cirlisces H   monnes] mannes GH   stale] tale G

---

[74] The word **angelde** appears nowhere in the clause itself.

---

[75] The ruling is more specific than the rubric indicates. The situation involves a man in possession of a slave who claims that the slave was sold to him by a man now dead, and the text describes the legal procedure by which he can exculpate himself from a charge of theft.

[76] Appended to this clause is one containing regulations on when a penal slave may be lashed; it should have a separate entry.

[77] The paragraph also addresses when the man's wife shares culpability.

[78] See following note.

[79] This paragraph includes assessments on the value of a cow's horn, the value of an ox's or cow's tail, and the value of an ox's or cow's eye. Clearly these rulings should be linked to the previous rubric. However, the paragraph ends with the assessment of tax in "barley rent" for each worker, which should have its own entry.

CIIII **Be** hýrgeohte
    Be hyroxan[80]

CV **Be** ciricsceatte
    Be ciricsceatte

CVI **Be** þon þe mon to ceape fordræfe
    Be þam þe man to ceace fordræfe

CVII **Be** gesiðcundes monnes fære
    Be gesiðcundes mannes fare

C\V/III **Be** þon þe hæfð .xx. hida londes
    Be ðam þe hafð xx hida

CVIIII **Be** .x. hidum
    Be tyn hidum

CX **Be** .iii. hidum
    Be ðreom hidum

Rubr. CIII cuus] cu GH
Rubr. CV ciricsceatte] cyricsceatum G; ciricsceattum H
Rubr. CVI þon] ðan G; ðam H   mon] man GH   ceape] ceace GH
Rubr. CVII monnes] mannes GH
Rubr. CVIII þon] ðan G; þam H   londes] landes GH

[80] In the text **B** similarly changes **geoht** ("yoke") to **oxan** ("oxen").

CIIII Concerning rent of a yoke
  Concerning rent of oxen
CV Concerning church tax
  Concerning church tax
CVI Concerning when a man is driven *to ceape*[81]
  Concerning when a man is driven *to ceace*
CVII Concerning the departure of a nobly born man
  Concerning the departure of a nobly born man
CVIII Concerning one who has twenty hides of land[82]
  Concerning one who has twenty hides of land
CVIIII Concerning ten hides[83]
  Concerning ten hides
CX Concerning three hides
  Concerning three hides

---

[81] The interpretation of the phrase **to ceape/to ceace** is difficult: see notes to §66 in Ine and discussion in Chapter 3. **G** is the earliest witness to contain the reading **ceace,** though only in the rubric (no version of **G**'s Ine survives).

[82] Both this and the next two clauses prohibit a man who wants to move from leaving an excessive amount of his land uncultivated. All three clauses should be subsumed under the previous rubric.

[83] See previous note.

CXI **Be** gyrde londes
    Be gyrde
CXII **Be** gesiðcundes monnes dræfe óf londe
    Be gesiðcundes mannes drafe of lande
CXIII **Be** sceapes gonge mid his fliese
    Be sceapes gange
CXIIII **Be** twyhundum were
    Be twyhindu*m* were
CXV **Be** wertyhtlan
    Be wertyhlan
CXVI **Be** wergeldðeofes forefonge[84]
    Be wergildðeofes forfenge
CXVII **Be** anre nihtes ðiefðe
    Be anre nihte ðyfte

Rubr. CXI gyrdelondes] gyrdelandes G; girdelandes H
Rubr. CXII monnes] mannes GH
Rubr. CXIII sceapes] sce\a/pes   fliese] flese G; flyse H
Rubr. CXV wertyhtlan] wertihlan G; wertihtlan H
Rubr. CXVI wergeldðeofes] wergildþeofes GH   forefonge] forefenge GH
Rubr. CXVII ðiefðe] ðyfðe GH

[84] Text has *gefangen* rather than **forefangen**.

CXI Concerning a yard of land [=1/4 hide][85]
    Concerning a yard
CXII Concerning the driving of a nobly born man from the land
    Concerning the driving of a nobly born man from the land
CXIII Concerning a sheep going with his fleece
    Concerning a sheep going
CXIIII Concerning a [man whose] *wer* [is] 200[86]
    Concerning a [man whose] *wer* [is] 200
CXV Concerning accusation of an act for which wergild must be paid
    Concerning accusation of an act for which wergild must be paid
CXVI Concerning capture of a thief who owes wergild for his offense
    Concerning capture of a thief who owes wergild for his offense
CXVII Concerning theft that is one night old[87]
    Concerning theft that is one night old

---

[85] The clause deals with the case of a lord changing the rental requirements for a quarter-hide of land; the crucial element in the ruling is not so much the amount of land as the choices the renter has in accepting the change of contract.

[86] This rubric is somewhat misleading: this clause sets the *manbot* (that is, the price due to a lord for the killing of his subordinate) for men whose *wer* is respectively 200, 600, and 1,200 shillings. Furthermore, added to the paragraph is another defining the yearly amount of food render to the lord, which should have its own entry.

[87] The narrative of this clause puts a specific condition on the ruling that precedes it; the stipulation should be included under the same rubric.

CXVIII **Be** ðon ðe ðeowwealh frione mon ófslea
    Be þam þe ðeowwalh frigne man ofslea

CXVIIII **Be** forstolenes ceapes forefonge
    Be forstolene ceape

CXX **Be** þon gif mon oðres godsunu slea oððe his godfæder.
    Be godfæderes oððe godsunes slæhte

Rubr. CXVIII ðon] þan G; \ðam/ H   þeowwealh] þeofwealh G   frione] freonne G;
frigne H   mon] man H; *abbrev.* G
Rubr. CXVIIII forefonge] forefenge G; forfenge H
Rubr. CXX þon] þan ðe G; þam H   mon] man GH   slea] ofslea H

---

[88] The two rulings to which this rubric applies are followed by a clause releasing a free man from responsibility to compensate for the misdeeds of a kinsman who is a slave; this passage should have its own entry.

7

Alfred's Prologue

The text of the Vulgate given below the Old English in our edition is
that of *Biblia sacra iuxta latinam vulgatam versionem, vol. II:
Exodus-Leviticus*, ed. Henri Quentin (1929) and, for the brief selection from Acts with which the Prologue concludes, *Nouum testamentum latine secundum editionem Sancti Hieronymi*, eds. John
Wordsworth and Henry White (1920 [repr. 1950]). These are standard critical editions of the Vulgate and *may* represent what was
available to Alfred and his circle as they composed the *domboc*.[1] We
supply these texts for the convenience of the reader alone and with
two caveats. First, it should be understood that multiple versions of
the Vulgate (and indeed of the Latin Bible itself) circulated in
Alfred's lifetime. Alfred's reign was preceded by a major effort on the
part of Carolingian court theologians such as Theodulf of Orléans
and Alcuin of York to produce more authoritative recensions of the

[1] See Marsden 2004: 79. The hazards of speculating about what text Alfred and his
circle had before them are greater than many seem to realize: the Vulgate "is not,
and never was, a uniform revision of the Old and New Testaments but a collection
of generally approved translations varying widely in character and origin and
brought together during the fifth and sixth centuries. [...] [T]o the discomfiture of
scholars of the medieval period, there was not yet anything like a universal text.
No papal decree had identified and prescribed such a text. There were huge variations between the volumes of scripture circulating, in respect of the nature and
quality of their texts. The major problem was continuing contamination by the Old
Latin texts" (72). It should be noted that we have added modern punctuation to
Quentin's text of Exodus.

Vulgate.[2] Thus one may not say with strict certainty which version of the Vulgate is likely to have been employed by Alfred and his circle, nor may it be assumed that their work was unaffected by Old Latin readings.[3] Second, the possibility may not be ruled out that Alfred's rendering of Exodus drew upon legal treatises known to have circulated in his own lifetime even if the evidence for his having done so is uncertain (see above, 61–65). Our giving the Vulgate text – a salutary practice initiated by Turk's edition, and an accident of Liebermann's given its reproduction of *Quadripartitus* in a parallel column – is meant only to facilitate comparison, and readers will want to compare carefully any divergent readings with other early medieval texts containing the legal clauses of Exodus made use of by Alfred. Square brackets enclose substantial text of the Vulgate comprising more than a phrase omitted from Alfred's rendering.

Though the assumptions guiding our editorial approach were earlier enumerated, the peculiarities of the Prologue require that a bit more be said here. Given what has been pointed out in prior chapters, the reader will understand why it cannot be taken for granted that Alfred's aim was to present his readers with a faithful rendering of legal clauses in Exodus. In short, we hold that Alfred and his circle were not motivated by any particular veneration of Mosaic law as a model to be followed by royal legislation, nor was their aim simply to furnish contemporaries with Mosaic ordinances in the vernacular for ease of reference.[4] It is probably significant, though too little noted in studies of Alfred's laws, that the Prologue closes with the Council of Jerusalem, which cut drastically the number of Mosaic ordinances Gentile Christians were bound to observe and sealed the defeat of the Judaizing party in the Apostolic era. The introduction of such a theme points to the principal aim of the Prologue: tracing the descent of written legal tradition from Mount Sinai to the end of the ninth century.

---

[2] See Power 1924; Marsden 2004: 72–73.

[3] As late as the eleventh century, Old Latin variants were finding their way into manuscripts of the Vulgate in Anglo-Saxon England and elsewhere. The influence of Old Latin versions on the Old English *Heptateuch* is demonstrated in Marsden 1994.

[4] The complexities of eighth- and ninth-century attitudes toward biblical law are described in Heydemann 2020; on possible attitudes in England, see (in the present volume) Chapter 2 n. 50.

Our views of Alfred's likely purposes account for some differences between our rendering and those of Thorpe and Liebermann (for example, in *MP* §12). The foregoing should also establish why, where the language of the Prologue seems even faintly ambiguous, no recourse to the language of the Vulgate (whatever this may have been) is had as a way of restoring the sense of the Old English. However common are descriptions of Alfred's Prologue as a partial "translation" of Exodus, the term is misleading when not used with qualification.

A Note on the Translation

In just two of the critical editions so far published does a translation into Modern English accompany the *domboc*. The Prologue is translated without omissions in only one of these – Thorpe's edition of 1840. Prior editors' work thus furnished few useful models as we sought to arrive at a style conveying the sense as well as the connotations of Alfred's language. For the most part, we have preferred accuracy to elegance. While the several instances in which Alfred's rendering shows itself inferior to the Vulgate (cf. *MP* §2) may not be pleasing to the ear, allowing the *domboc* to keep all its repetitions and clumsy phrasing permits us to see West-Saxon prose much as it was – and, perhaps, to spot shades of meaning otherwise hidden (as in *MP* §48).

Though we have sought not to conceal the literary defects of the *domboc*, our pursuit of this aim does not extend as far as emulating its syntax where doing so results in unidiomatic Modern English. (Thorpe's translation was guided by no such scruples.) Thus, in our translation of the Prologue and subsequent laws of Alfred and Ine, most subjunctives occurring in subordinate clauses are rendered indicative. Imperatives in the negative (*ne dem ðu,* etc.) are rendered in the periphrastic future tense, and with the second-person plural pronoun ("You will not judge") in order to avoid the fustiness of "Judge thou not" and like expressions. To do otherwise would be misleading since there are few indications that Alfred aims in the Prologue for a consistently elevated register; indeed, most translations of the Bible into English prior to the Authorized ("King

James") Version (1611) strove for immediacy and informality.⁵ The Victorian habit of translating as much as possible with obscure archaisms (e.g., Thorpe's "Shun thou ever leasings" [*MP* §44]) is likewise avoided.⁶ Having said all this, we make no claim that the rules just enumerated have been adhered to with perfect regularity. Moreover, there have been more than a few instances in which the renderings of Thorpe and of subsequent translators, both in the Prologue and in the legislative sections of the *domboc*, could not realistically be improved upon, in spite of our differences with them on some matters of substance. Occasional echoes of the phrasing of prior translations in our own have thus been unavoidable, though in general our practice is to employ, where possible, Modern English equivalents to Old English words to a greater extent than, e.g., Attenborough, and to retain rather than disguise the ambiguities of the original text where these appear insuperable.

⁵ See Brook 1965: 102–103.
⁶ The model in this instance was probably the usage of the Coverdale Psalter.

/36r/ Leges Aluredi[7]

Prologue[8] [D]RYHTEN WÆS SPRECENde ðas word to Moyse
⁊ þus cwæð: Ic eóm Dryhten ðin God. Ic ðe utgelædde of
Egipta londe ⁊ of hiora ðeowdome.

MP 1[9] Ne lufa ðu oþre fremde godas ofer me.

- - - - - - - - - - - - - - - -

Exodus xx ¹Locutusque est Dominus cunctos sermones hos: ²⁰:²Ego sum Dominus
Deus tuus qui eduxi te de terra Aegypti de domo servitutis. ²⁰:³Non habebis deos
alienos coram me. [²⁰:⁴Non facies tibi sculptile, neque omnem similitudinem quae est
in caelo desuper et quae in terra deorsum, nec eorum quae sunt in aquis sub terra.
²⁰:⁵Non adorabis ea neque coles. Ego sum Dominus Deus tuus fortis zelotes, visitans
iniquitatem patrum in filiis, in tertiam et quartam generationem eorum qui oderunt
me, ²⁰:⁶et faciens misericordiam in milia his qui diligunt me et custodiunt praecepta
mea.]

Prol. Dryhten] Drihten G   ⁊ éom drihten] eam dryhten H   útgelædde of Egipta
londe] útgelædde of Egypta lande G; uttgelæde of Egypta lande H   hiora ðeowdome]
hyra þeowdome G; heora þeowdome H

---

⁷   Later addition to top of page.
⁸   In both CCCC 173 (**E**) and Cotton Nero A.i (**G**), a large space intended for the initial in **dryhten** is left blank.
⁹   The manuscript of the *MP* is written continuously with no numeration until –I–
appears in the margin before the clause here labeled §49.6. We have followed
Liebermann's numeration of the clauses until §49.9, which we have moved from
the Prologue to the laws proper.

The lord was speaking these words to Moses and said as follows: I am the Lord your God. I led you out from the land of the Egyptians and from slavery to them.[10]

> MP 1 You will not love other strange gods in place of me.[11]

---

[10] The overall structure of the Prologue may be owing to the conventions observed in some patristic homilies, which commence "with a combination of the Ten Commandments and the two commandments from the New Testament"; examples are given in Bethurum (1957: 323). In the Prologue, however, the Decalogue and Christ's summary of the law (here reduced to the Golden Rule) are separated by legal clauses from Exodus not held to be binding on Christians and, presumably for that reason, adapted to prevent confusion on this point.

[11] The interpretation of *non facies tibi sculptile* was a disputed matter in Francia prior to Alfred's accession, with differences over the Second Council of Nicaea (787), which overthrew the iconoclasts of the Byzantine church and reestablished the veneration of images, provoking Theodulf of Orléans to author the *Libri Carolini*, now more often referred to as the *Opus Caroli regis contra synodum* (Freeman 1998; see also Noble 2009: 158–206). Agobard of Lyons likewise favored a highly restricted use of images within places of worship (Noble 2009: 314–316). Whether Carolingian thought had any effect on Alfred's is unclear. Yet Liebermann's view that Alfred, in omitting Exodus 20:4, was under the sway of "the Catholic belief of his time" (see Chapter 5, 162–163) seems, given the texts just mentioned, to mischaracterize the varieties of Catholic thought on images in the eighth and ninth centuries. The Council of Elvira (§36; Dale 1882: 326) asserted that "There ought not to be pictures in a church, lest that which is worshiped and adored be painted on walls" (*Placuit picturas in ecclesia esse non debere, ne quod colitur et adoratur in parietibus depingatur*). Though evidence for subsequent citations of this fourth-century synod is lacking (Noble 2009: 12), the text of the council as a whole was copied throughout the early and later Middle Ages (Dale 1882: 313–314; Reichert 1990: 28); its use by Halitgar of Cambrai in the first half of the ninth century attests to its currency in Francia (Jurasinski 2010b: 39). In any case, Alfred's omission of this clause is paralleled in some Old English homilies and probably has more to do with the standard numeration of the Decalogue in the West, which made the prohibition on the manufacture of images effectively subordinate to the condemnation of idolatry (MacCullough 2005: 145–146). The rationale ultimately derives not from the relaxation of attitudes toward images evinced by II Nicaea but from Augustine's *Quaestiones in Heptateuchum Libri* VII (Fraipoint and De Bruyne 1958: 103 [*Quaest. Exodi* LXXI.2]: "To what does it pertain: *do not make for yourselves an idol nor any image ... unless to what was said* [prior]: *For you there will not be any gods before me?*" (*Quo enim pertinet: "non facies tibi idolum neque ullum simulacrum" ... nisi ad id quod dictum est: "non erunt tibi dii alii praeter me"?*) Cf. also Kleist 2002; Bicknell 1955: 288.

MP 2 Ne minne noman ne cig ðu on idelnesse; forðon þe ðu ne bist unscyldig wið me, gif ðu on idelnesse cigst minne noman.

MP 3 Gemyne þæt ðu gehalgige þone ræstedæg; wyrceað eow VI dagas ⁊ on þam siofoðan restað eow: forðam on VI dagum Crist geworhte heofonas ⁊ eorðan, sæs ⁊ ealle gesceafta þe on him sint, ⁊ hine gereste on þone siofoðan dæg, ⁊ forðon Dryhten hine gehalgode.

- - - - - - - - - - - - - - - -

20:7Non adsumes nomen Domini Dei tui in vanum, nec enim habebit insontem Dominus eum qui adsumpserit nomen Domini Dei sui frustra. [Cf. Leviticus 19:12.] 20:8Memento ut diem sabbati sanctifices. 20:9Sex diebus operaberis et facies omnia opera tua; 20:10septimo autem die sabbati Domini Dei tui; non facies omne opus tu et filius tuus et filia tua, servus tuus et ancilla tua, iumentum tuum et advena qui est intra portas tuas. 20:11Sex enim diebus fecit Dominus caelum et terram et mare et omnia quae in eis sunt, et requievit in die septimo. Idcirco benedixit Dominus diei sabbati et sanctificavit eum.

MP §2 noman] naman GH   ðu on idelnesse] þu on ydelnesse H   forðon þe] forðam H   bist] byst GH   cigst] \ge/cygst H   noman] naman GH
MP §3 Gemyne] Gemune G; Gemun H   gehalgige] gehalgie GH   ræstedæg] restedæg G; restendæg H   wyrceað] wyrcað GH   þam siofoðan] ðone seofoðan G   forðam] forðan G   VI] syx H   sæs] sæ GH   him sint] hym sindon G; heom sindon H   siofoðan] seofoðan GH   forðon] forðan G; forðam H

MP 2 You will not invoke my name idly: for you will not be guilt-less with me, if you take my name idly.

MP 3 Remember to keep holy the day of rest; you will work six days and on the seventh you shall rest; because Christ[12] made the heavens and the earth in six days, the seas and all the creatures that are in them, and he rested on the seventh day, and therefore the Lord made it holy.[13]

---

[12] Liebermann suggested (1903–1916: III, 43) that Alfred derived this from the Fourth Gospel (John 1:3) and noted also a Cynewulfian parallel in *Christ* III, ll. 1379–1380: "Lo, I made thee, man, first, with my hands" (*Hwæt ic þec, mon, hondum minum ærest geworhte*) (Cook 1900: 52; the point had earlier been made in Turk 1893: 35). But the theme occurs in other sources, such as the Compline hymn *Iesu, redemptor seculi* in which Christ is addressed as "maker of all" (*tu fabricator omnium*; see Milfull 1996: 425) and Alcuin's *Versus de patribus regibus et sanctis Euboricensis ecclesiae* (Godman 1982: 2): "Christ divine, strength and wisdom of the Father Almighty / life, salvation, creator, redeemer, and lover of mankind […]" (*Christe deus, summi virtus sapientia patris / vita, salus, hominum factor, renovator, amator*). To isolate a source for Alfred's language is probably not necessary, however, as conflation of the first and second persons of the Trinity is a commonplace of the early and late Middle Ages that saw special emphasis in the Carolingian era (Fichtenau 1957: 48). It originates in responses to the Arian heresy (the view that Christ was "made" by the Father rather than eternally begotten, on which see Williams 2001: 59, 97); Treschow has, perhaps accordingly, read it as "[a] modifi-cation of the text toward Trinitarian theology" (Treschow 1994: 91). The theme may be invoked here to forestall any lapses into nontrinitarian readings of Exodus, a concern more plainly evident in Ælfric's homily for Mid-Lent Sunday: "The sec-ond commandment is: Do not take the Lord's name in vain; that is, do not believe that Christ your Lord was created, but believe that he is like his Father, eternally begotten of him" (*Þæt oðer bebod is; Ne underfoh ðu ðines drihtnes naman on ydelnesse. þæt is ne gelyf ðu ðæt crist þin drihten sy gesceaft. ac gelyf þæt hé is gelic his fæder. æfre of him gecenned*) (Godden 1979: 117). Ælfric is certainly more careful than Alfred to follow the language of Scripture, which does not attribute the work of creation to the second person of the Trinity outright even as it allows for such an understanding; cf. Hebrews 1:2 and Colossians 1:16, whence the word-ing of the Nicene Creed, "through whom all things were made" (*per quem omnia facta sunt*).

[13] Omission of the Vulgate's list of those obliged to observe the Sabbath occurs as well in Ælfric's version of the Decalogue in his sermon for Mid-Lent Sunday (Godden 1979: 118); one or both instances may be attributable to the uncertain (and disputed) nature of Sunday observance in pre-Conquest England (on which see Haines 2010; also Chapter 4, 134–136).

MP 4 Ara ðinum fæder ⁊ þinre medder, ða þe Dryhten sealde, þæt ðu sie þy leng libbende on eorþan.

MP 5 Ne sleah ðu.

MP 6 Ne lige ðu dearnenga.

MP 7 Ne stala ðu.

20:12Honora patrem tuum et matrem tuam ut sis longevus super terram quam Dominus Deus tuus dabit tibi.

20:13Non occides.

20:14Non moechaberis.

20:15Non furtum facies.

MP §4 medder] meder GH   Drihten] Drihten GH   þy] þe H
MP §6 deanenga] dearnunga GH   gewitnesse] gewitnessea G

MP 4 Honor your father and mother, they whom the Lord gave you, so that you may live long on the earth.[14]

MP 5 Do not kill.

MP 6 Do not fornicate.[15]

MP 7 Do not steal.

[14] The *Old English Heptateuch* has simply "Honor your father and mother" (*Arwurða fæder and modor*) (Marsden 2008: 116), which omits the relative clause over which Alfred seems to have stumbled. A similar omission occurs in Ælfric's Mid-Lent Sunday sermon (Godden 1979: 119).

[15] The sense here is certainly "do not commit adultery," conveyed with an idiom that occurs in §27 of Ine's laws. But given the rendering of the Council of Jerusalem later in the Prologue (*MP* §49.5), it may not be ruled out that the phrase was here understood to denote "fornication". The phrase certainly has this meaning in other texts (see, e.g., the materials discussed in Clayton 2013: 80), all fornication in this era being necessarily "secret" as it involved relations with married women or women under their fathers' or guardians' authority. Liebermann (1912: 27) read the clause as forbidding all "illegitimate intercourse" that perhaps reveals "the chaste mind of this moral prince, even when dealing with the Bible." Other translations into Old English seem to reflect uncertainty over *non moechaberis*, lit. "Do not commit adultery." The rendering in the *Old English Heptateuch* (Marsden 2008: 116) could not be more vague (*Ne synga þu*, "Do not sin"), while Ælfric in his Mid-Lent Sunday sermon seems to understand the sin in question as adultery while adding qualifying language: "The fifth commandment is: Do not engage in fornication. Each man who has relations without legitimate marriage, he does so wrongfully; and he who has relations outside of his marriage, he is an adulterer" (*Þæt fifte bebod is; Ne únrihthǽm ðu; Ælc ðæra manna þe hæmð buton rihtre æwe. he hæmð unrihtlice; And se ðe ofer his æwe hæmð. he is forlír*) (Godden 1979: 119). Doubt over the interpretation of *non moechaberis* was present in the patristic era as well; see especially the extensive discussion in Augustine's *Quaestionum in heptateuchum* (Fraipont and De Bruyne, 1958: 104–105 [*Quaest. Exodi* LXXI.4]). The problem, as Augustine notes here, is that the verb in question is a loanword from Greek referring solely to adultery (cf. the LXX, οὐ μοιχεύσεις; Rahlfs 1952: 120), with the unsettling result that fornication is nowhere explicitly condemned in the Decalogue. (In earlier Greek law, μοιχεία had referred to "clandestine sexual intercourse with a free, respectable woman against the will of her *kýrios*": see Thür 2006.) Augustine nonetheless understands the prohibition to apply as well to the behavior of the unmarried on exegetical grounds. Concerns about the interpretation of Alfred's language here are also evident in Matthew Parker's *Testimonie of Antiquitie*: see Chapter 5, 163–164.

MP 8 Ne sæge ðu lease gewitnesse.

MP 9 Ne wilna ðu þines nehstan ierfes mid unryhte.

MP 10 Ne wyrc ðe gyldne godas oððe sylfrene.

- - - - - - - - - - - - - - - -

20:16Non loqueris contra proximum tuum falsum testimonium.

20:17Non concupisces domum proximi tui, nec desiderabis uxorem eius, non servum, non ancillam, non bovem, non asinum, nec omnia quae illius sunt.

20:23Non facietis mecum deos argenteos nec deos aureos facietis vobis.

MP §9 wilna] gewylna H   nehstan] niehstan G; nyhstan H   ierfes] yrfes H   unryhte] unrihte G
MP §10 wyrc] wyrce   ðe] ðu ðe H   gyldne] gyldene GH

MP 8 Do not give deceitful testimony.[16]

MP 9 Do not wrongfully covet the possessions of your neighbor.[17]

MP 10 Do not make for yourself gods of gold or silver.[18]

---

[16] Alfred omits "against your neighbor" (*contra proximum tuum*), as does Ælfric from his Mid-Lent Sunday sermon: "The eighth commandment is: Do not be a deceitful witness; this commandment forbids lying" (*þæt eahteoðe bebod is; Ne beo ðu leas gewita; þis bebod wiðcweð leasunge*) (Godden 1979: 119). The phrase is retained in the *Old English Heptateuch*. As with MP §1, the omissions may be traced to Augustine's view (*Quaest. Exodi* LXXI.6) that the commandment prohibits all lying (Fraipoint and De Bruyne 1958: 105). The phrase in question is also omitted in Christ's summary of the Decalogue in Matthew 19:18.

[17] Alfred omits the reference to desiring another's wife, perhaps because this was understood in MP §6, but more likely due to the influence of patristic tradition, wherein it was suggested that the commandments on coveting a neighbor's wife (*non concupisces uxorem proximi tui*) and property (*non concupisces domum proximi tui* in the Old Latin text) ought to be considered a single ordinance: see Augustine, *Quaest. Exodi* LXXI.1 (Fraipoint and De Bruyne 1958: 102). Cf. also Ælfric's Decalogue: "The tenth commandment is: Do not covet another's possessions. This commandment forbids evil desire and worldly avarice" (*þæt teoðe bebod is; Ne gewilna ðu oðres mannes æhta; Ðis bebod wiðcweð unrihtwisre gewilnunge. and woruldlice gitsunge*) (Godden 1979: 119). Use of a word meaning "possessions, property" to denote persons in servitude was commonplace, as in Werferth's translation of Gregory's *Dialogi* (Hecht 1900: 80): ⁊ *hi genamon þær of þæs biscopes æhte twe3en lytle cnihtas* ("and they took there from the bishop's property two little boys"). See also Pelteret 1995: 261–262.

[18] Liebermann views this as an attempt to compensate for the earlier omission of *Non facies tibi sculptile* perhaps also directed at the pagan population of the north (1: 37 [§32]).

MP 11 Þis sint ða domas þe ðu him settan scealt: Gif hwa gebycgge cristenne þeow, VI gear ðeowige he; ðy siofoðan beo he
frioh órceapunga; mid swelce hrægle he ineode, mid swelce
gange he ut. Gif he wíf self hæbbe, gange hio ut mid him. Gif
se hlaford him þonne wif sealde, sie hio ⁊ hire bearn þæs hlafordes. Gif se þeowa þonne /36v/ cweðe: "Nelle ic from minum
hlaforde ne from minum wife ne from minum bearne ne from
minum ierfe," brenge hine þonne his hlaford to ðære dura þæs
temples ⁊ þurhþyrlige his eare mid æle, to tácne þæt he sie
æfre siððan þeow.

- - - - - - - - - - - - - - - -

XXI ¹Haec sunt iudicia quae propones eis: ²¹:²Si emeris servum hebraeum, sex annis
serviet tibi. In septimo egredietur liber gratis. ²¹:³Cum quali veste intraverit cum tali
exeat: si habens uxorem et uxor egredietur simul. ²¹:⁴Sin autem dominus dederit illi
uxorem et peperit filios et filias, mulier et liberi eius erunt domini sui; ipse vero exibit
cum vestitu suo. ²¹:⁵Quod si dixerit servus, "Diligo dominum meum et uxorem ac
liberos, non egrediar liber," ²¹:⁶offeret eum dominus diis, et adplicabitur ad ostium et
postes perforabitque aurem eius subula et erit ei servus in saeculum.

MP §11 sint] sindon G; synt H   him] heom H   gebycgge] gebicge G; gebycge
H   cristenne] cristene H   VI] syx H   ðeowige] þeowie H   ðy siofoðan] ði seofoðan
G; ⁊ on þam seofoðan H   frioh] freoh G; freo H   órceapunga] órceapunge G; on
ceapunge H   hrægle] reafe H   ineode] inn eode H   swelce] swilce G; swylce
H   gange he út] ga he út G; gange utt H   wíf self hæbbe] wif hæbbe sylf G; wif silf
hæbbe H   hio] heo GH   him ðonne wif sealde] þonne him wif sealde H   sie hio] si
héo G; sy heo H   þæs] ðas G   cweþe] cwæþe H   from] fram GH   ierfe] yrfe
GH   brenge] brynge G; bringe H   to ðære dura þæs temples] at ðas temples dura
G   þurhþyrlige] ðurhðirlige G; þurhþyrlie H   æle] ále G; ane æle H   sie] sy
H   siððan] syððan G

MP 11 These are the judgments you shall set before them: If someone purchases a Christian slave,[19] let him serve for six years; on the seventh, let him go free without payment; with such clothing[20] as he entered, let him depart with such. If he has a wife, let her go out with him. But if it was the lord who gave him his wife, let her and her children be the lord's. If, however, the slave should say: "I will not [depart] from my lord nor from my wife nor from my child nor from my possessions,"[21] then his lord shall bring him to the door of the temple[22] and pierce through his ear with an awl, as a token that he shall be thenceforth and forever a slave.

[19] Liebermann asserts that this clause does not implicitly oppose Christian and heathen slaves, as Danes captured in battle, presumably the only non-Christian slaves to be found in Wessex at this time, were "soon brought forcibly (*gezwungen*) by their lords to the baptismal font" (1903–1916: III, 43).

[20] *Textus Roffensis* modernizes to *reafe*, a word favored as well by the *Old English Heptateuch* (Marsden 2008: 116).

[21] This addition has been taken as proof that slaves in Anglo-Saxon England were permitted some amount of moveable property (and perhaps their own dwellings as well), on which see Pelteret 1995: 83. Liebermann suggests the influence of Deuteronomy 15:16, where the servant's refusal to depart implies that he has prospered under his master's hand: *sin autem dixerit nolo egredi eo quod diligat te et domum tuam et bene sibi apud te esse sentiat.* The simplest explanation, however, would seem to be that Alfred is here projecting onto the situation of the slave in Exodus conditions obtaining in Anglo-Saxon England.

[22] Both Alfred and the *Old English Heptateuch* opt for this cautious rendering of *offerat diis* (translated as "bring him to the Gods" in the Douay version and in William Tyndale's 1530 translation of the Pentateuch) even though the parallel clause in Deuteronomy (15:17) permits no such translation: see also *MP* §37. The line as rendered in the Vulgate follows the Hebrew more closely than do many contemporary translations, most of which smooth over what may be a frozen expression referring to "a domestic deity" or deities, perhaps the "household gods" of Genesis 31:19, who were located at the sacred doorpost (Noth 1962: 178) but is more likely an idiom for judges, as is more explicitly the case in *MP* §28 = Exod. 22:9, where the statement that a dispute may proceed *ad deos* is again avoided in the Old English. Alfred's rendering may reflect contemporary circumstances, as both purchases and manumissions took place before the doors of a church (Pelteret 1995: 142).

MP 12 Ðeah hwa gebycgge his dohtor on þeowenne, ne sie hio
ealles swa ðeowu swa oðru mennenu: nage he hie út on elðeodig folc to bebycgganne. Ac gif he hire ne recce, se ðe hie
bohte, læte hie freo on elðeodig folc. Gif he ðon*n*e alefe his
suna mid to hæmanne, do hiere gyfta: locige þæt hio hæbbe
hrægl; ⁊ þæt weorð sie hiere mægðhades, þæt is se weotuma,²³
agife he hire þone. Gif he hire þara nan ne do, þon*n*e sie hio
frioh.

----

²¹˸⁷Si quis vendiderit filiam suam in famulam, non egredietur sicut ancillae exire consueverunt.
²¹˸⁸Si displicuerit oculis domini sui cui tradita fuerit, dimittet eam. Populo autem
alieno vendendi non habet potestatem si spreverit eam. ²¹˸⁹Sin autem filio suo despon-
derit eam, iuxta morem filiarum faciet illi. [²¹˸¹⁰Quod si alteram ei acceperit,]
providebit puellae nuptias et vestimenta et pretium pudicitiae non negabit. ²¹˸¹¹Si tria
ista non fecerit egredietur gratis absque pecunia.

MP §12 gebycgge] gebicge GH   on þeowenne] to þeowte H   ne sie hio] ne sie he G;
ne beo heo H   ðeowu] þeow H   oðru mennenu] oðre mennenu G; oðer þeowwifman H   hie] hi G; hy H   út] ut G; utt H   elðeodig] ælðeodig GH   bebycgganne]
bebycganne G; syllanne H   hire] hyre GH   hie] hy H   læte hie freo on elðeodig
folc] læte hie faran freo on ælðeodig folc G; læte hy frige on ælþeodig folc H   alefe]
alyfe GH   suna] sunea G; sune H   hiere] hyre GH   locige] locie G; ⁊ locie H   hio]
heo GH   weorð sie hiere mægðhad] weorð sie hyre mægðhades G; sy wurð hire
mægþhades H   þæt is se weotuma] þæt is sie wituma G; þæt his se wituma H   agife
he hire ðone] agyfe he hyre ðone G; agyfe hire þene H   þara] þare H   hio frioh] heo
freoh GH

²³ This word appears only here and in §29.

MP 12 Though someone should buy[24] his [the Christian slave's] daughter in servitude, let her not be entirely as much a slave as other maidservants: he has not the power to sell her to a strange people.

But if he does not like her, whom he bought, he shall let her go free among a strange folk.[25] However, if he allows his son to have her, let him [the son] give her [marriage-]gifts: let him look that she have clothing; and the worth of her maidenhood, that is the bride-price, let him give her that. If he does none of these things for her, then let her be free.

[24] Though it is the form attested in all of the Old English manuscripts, Liebermann, following Wilkins and Thorpe, assumes **gebyccge** to be an error for *bebycgge* and translates the term as *verkauf[en]* "sell." But if, as Pelteret observes, Alfred has "so heavily abbreviated Exodus 21:7–11 that it has completely changed the meaning of the biblical text" (Pelteret 1995: 83), there seem few reasons to assume that fidelity to his source was suddenly felt important as the translator's hand approached the Vulgate's *uendiderit*. MP §12 probably represents a wholly new clause whose idiosyncrasies are not likely to be explained by reference to the biblical source alone. If the Old English is left unemended, the clause deals not with a free man's sale of his daughter into slavery, but rather with how the children of the "Christian slave" who has agreed to permanent service in his lord's household are to be treated upon being purchased. (For another possible instance of Alfred having the conditions of one clause bleed into the next where they do not in the original, see MP §30 and n.) Such an interpretation agrees with Alfred's substitution at the outset of this clause of Ðeah for the expected *gif* (Vulgate *si*). Moreover, it may shed light on what is meant by Alfred's **ne sie hie ealles swa ðeowu swa oðru mennenu**, a total departure from the Vulgate for which Pelteret saw no clear solution (1995: 83). Liebermann's text of E places a colon between this clause and **nage he hie út on elðeodig folc to bebycgganne**, the implication being presumably that the latter specifies the privilege distinguishing this slave from other *mennenu*: she is not to be resold. Though the point should not be pressed too far, *mennen* seems to have connoted slavery of a specifically sexual nature in some Old English texts (see Girsch 1994: 48–49), and it is perhaps relevant that early law placed stringent prohibitions upon the subsequent sale of female slaves married to free men, of which the most forceful are found in the *Excerpta de libris Romanorum et Francorum* (Bieler 1975: 148): "If anyone who has power in his own affairs is resolved to have his slave woman in marriage, if he afterwards does not want to have her, it is not allowed; but if he is resolved to sell her, we command that he shall be sold (*eum uenundari iubemus*), and we make that slave woman the ward of a priest" (*in sacerdotis ponimus potestatem*). Cf. Wulfstan's *Sermo ad Anglos* (Bethurum 1957: 270).

[25] Alfred's changes here purify Exodus of its allowance for a slave girl to be purchased for the purposes of concubinage (*si alteram ei acceperit*). The fate of the woman sold after her marriage is treated in the *Excerpta* as well (quoted earlier), which requires that the woman in question not be returned to servitude but instead be placed under the protection of a priest. Whether **on elðeodig folc** refers specifically to her being sold (or, in the latter case, released) to a "foreign people," the assumption of all prior commentators, seems uncertain. The *Old English Penitential* translates *alienam* "another's [woman]" with *elðeodigum* (Raith 1933: 21), a word that typically means "foreign" but cannot in this instance.

MP 13 Se mon se ðe his gewealdes monnan ófslea, swelte se
deaðe. Se ðe hine þonne nedes ofsloge²⁶ oððe unwillum oððe
ungewealdes, swelce hine God swa sende on his honda, ⁊ he
hine ne ymbsyrede,²⁷ sie he feores wyrðe ⁊ folcryhtre bote, gif
he friðstowe gesece.²⁸ Gif hwa ðonne of giernesse ⁊ gewealdes
ófslea his þone nehstan þurh searwa, aluc ðu hine from minum
weofode, to þam þæt he deaðe swelte.

- - - - - - - - - - - - - - - -

²¹ᐟ¹²Qui percusserit hominem volens occidere morte moriatur. ²¹ᐟ¹³Qui autem non est
insidiatus, sed deus illum tradidit in manus eius, constituam tibi locum quo fugere
debeat. ²¹ᐟ¹⁴Si quis de industria occiderit proximum suum et per insidias, ab altari meo
evelles eum ut moriatur.

MP §13 monnan] man GH   ymbsyrede] ymbe ne syrede G; ne syrwde ymbe H   fol-
cryhtre] folcrihtre G; folcrihtere H   friðstowe] fryðstowa G   giernesse] geornesse
GH   nehstan] nyehstan G; nyhstan H   searwa] syrwunge H   minum] minan G

²⁶ On erasure.
²⁷ *Hapax legomenon.*
²⁸ Compare *Ine* §5.

MP 13 The man who intentionally slays someone – let him die the death. However, he who slew him out of necessity or unwillingly or accidentally,[29] as God sent to his hands, and he did not lie in wait [for his victim]: let him be worthy of life and of the remedy permitted by folk-law,[30] if he should seek a place of refuge. But if someone with deliberation and intent[31] slays his neighbor through guile, take him away from my altar, that he may die the death.

---

[29] For Liebermann, "Alfred lays emphasis on [the importance of] evil intent in wrong-doing, in contrast to ancient Germanic law" (1903–1916: III, 44 n. 4; our translation). On the historiography from which Liebermann drew such views, see Jurasinski 2014a. The circumstances here enumerated as entitling homicides to asylum are closely paralleled in penitential canons: see, e.g., *Poenitentiale Theodori* I, iv, 3–7. On *friðstowe*, see Plummer 1902: 153.

[30] The idiom is paralleled in *Ine* §5, which shows Alfred to have read this portion of Exodus in light of the sanctuary norms of his own day, though in Ine's ordinance the offender is spared and entitled to compensate for his wrongs by virtue of his having approached a church alone. For Alfred, it is the inward disposition of the offender that is crucial, an attribute of his thinking that perhaps accounts for some of the potentially innovative clauses within the code proper: cf. MP §16; *Alfred* §5.3 and §44.1 [L 42.1].

[31] Alfred's translation of *per insidias* is tautological and perhaps, for that reason, was an existing legal expression (as in "without let or hindrance").

*MP*14 Se ðe slea his fæder oððe his modor, se sceal deaðe sweltan.

*MP*15 Se ðe frione forstele ⁊ he hine bebycgge, ⁊ hit onbestæled³² sie, þæt he hine bereccan ne mæge, swelte se deaðe. Se ðe werge his fæder oððe his modor, swelte se deaðe.

*MP*16 Gif hwa slea /37r/ his ðone nehstan mid stane oððe mid fyste, ⁊ he þeah utgongan mæge bi stafe, begite him læce ⁊ wyrce his weorc ða hwile þe he self ne mæge.

- - - - - - - - - - - - - - - -

²¹:¹⁵Qui percusserit patrem suum et matrem morte moriatur. ²¹:¹⁶Qui furatus fuerit hominem et vendiderit eum, convictus noxae morte moriatur. ²¹:¹⁷Qui maledixerit patri suo et matri morte moriatur. ²¹:¹⁸Si rixati fuerint viri et purcusserit alter proximum suum lapide vel pugno, et ille mortuus non fuerit sed iacuerit in lectulo, ²¹:¹⁹si surrexerit et ambulaverit foris super baculum suum, innocens erit qui percussit; ita tamen ut operas eius et inpensas in medicos restituat.

MP § 14 sweltan] swyltan G; swelte se deaþe H

MP § 15 frione] freonne GH   forstele] forsteleþ H   he hine bebycgge] hine bebycge G   ⁊ hit] ⁊ hit hym G   bereccean] bereccan GH   werge] wyrge G; wyrie H

MP § 16 nehstan] nyhstan   utgangan] -gen *corrected to* -gan *by Joscelyn?*   mæge] mage G   begite] begyte GH   self] sylf GH

³² *Hapax legomenon.*

MP 14 He who strikes his father or his mother, he shall die [the] death.

MP 15 He who steals a free[33] person and sells him, and it should be proved, so that he may not expurgate himself, let him die the death. He who curses his father or his mother, let him die the death.

MP 16 If someone should strike his neighbor with a stone or a fist, and he may nonetheless go out with a staff, let him obtain for him a physician and perform his work in the time that he himself may not.[34]

---

33 The theft of slaves was classified according to Liebermann as an offense involving chattel in Anglo-Saxon law, which is the rationale for Alfred's addition of a requirement that the person stolen be free in order for the punishment of death to apply.

34 On sick-maintenance, see Oliver 2008 and Jurasinski 2014b; also Chapter 2, 67–69. The biblical clause was early adapted to the tradition of Latin penitentials and possibly played some role in shaping provisions of Irish secular law as well. In neither, however, is an offender obliged to perform the work of the man he has injured, an idiosyncrasy of Alfred's translation that appears as well in the *Scriftboc*, a compilation of penitential canons in English that may, in the view of Vogel (1978: 73) and Cubitt (2006: 53), have appeared as early as the reign of Alfred. The influence of the penitential tradition is palpable in Alfred's omission of *innocens* (see also MP §17), which is paralleled by the Latin penitentials that draw upon this clause of Exodus, as in the compilation attributed to Cummean (Bieler 1975: 120–121): "He who by a blow in a quarrel renders a man incapacitated or maimed shall meet (the injured man's) medical expenses and shall make good the damages for the deformity and shall do his work until he is healed and do penance for half a year" (*Qui per rixam ictu debilem uel deformem hominem reddit, inpensa in medicos curat et maculae pretium et opus eius donec sanetur restituat et dimidium anni peniteat*). As above, MP §13, Alfred is concerned with the inward state of the offender. No one, according to the pastoral theology of the penitentials, who struck his neighbor could be without the spiritual guilt that his action made manifest. The requirement that the offender do the work of his victim is perhaps intended as well to remedy the spiritual condition of the offender in a way that compensation would not have done.

MP 17 Se ðe slea his agene þeowne esne³⁵ oððe his mennen, ⁊ he
ne sie idæges³⁶ dead, ðeah he libbe twa niht oððe ðreo, ne bið
he ealles swa scyldig, forþon þe hit wæs his agen fioh. Gif he
ðonne sie idæges dead, ðonne sitte sio scyld on him.

- - - - - - - - - - - - - - - -

²¹:²⁰Qui percusserit servum suum vel ancillam virga et mortui fuerint in manibus eius,
criminis reus erit. ²¹:²¹Sin autem uno die supervixerint vel duobus, non subiacebit poe-
nae quia pecunia illius est.

MP §17 þeowne esne oððe his mennen] slea þeowne esne oððe his wifman H   sie] sy
GH   libbe] lybbe G   niht] nyht H   bið] byþ H   scyldig] scyldyg G   forðon þe]
forðan ðe G; forðam *om.* ðe H   his] hys G   fioh] feoh G; þeow H   Gif he ðonne]
Gyf ðonne he G   sie idæges dead] idæges sie dead G; byð idæges dead H   sio] seo
GH

³⁵ Liebermann, following *Quadripartitus* ("He who strikes with a rod his male or
   female slave" (*Qui percusserit seruum uel ancillam suam uirga*)), translates the subordinate clause as follows: *Wer seinen eigenen Sklavenknecht oder seine Sklavin
   schlägt* [...] ("whoever strikes his own male or female slave [...]).") The phrase
   þeowne esne ("unfree servant") also occurs in *Wihtred* §18 [L23]; the modifier was
   necessary as an *esne* was not necessarily unfree.
³⁶ *Hapax legomenon.*

MP 17 He who strikes his own slave or maidservant, and he [or she] is not dead on that same day, though [the servant] should live for two days or three, the master will not be entirely so guilty, because it was his own loss.[37] If the servant, however, should die on the same day, then let the guilt rest on him [i.e., the master].[38]

---

[37] The *Textus Roffensis* scribe substitutes *ðeow* ("slave") for *fioh* ("property") (*ne byþ he ealles swa scyldig, forðam hit wæs his agen þeow*), thus refusing to repeat Alfred's equation of slaves with personal wealth, and along with it, his assertion that the death of the slave constitutes a de facto monetary loss to the master requiring no further penalties. His doing so may reflect the improved fortunes of slaves in the aftermath of the Norman Conquest. A reaction against the rather dehumanizing terms with which Old English prose writers referred to laborers in bondage is evident in the language with which the bishops convened at Westminster in 1102 by Anselm of Canterbury condemned the institution as "that abominable trade, in which until now it was customary to sell men in England as if they were brute beasts" (*illud nefarium negotium, quo hactenus homines in Anglia solebant uelut bruta animalia uenundari*) (Winterbottom 2007: 192; see also Pelteret 1995: 78).

[38] For a detailed discussion of this and related clauses, see Jurasinski 2010b. Liebermann's judgment that here Alfred departs from the Vulgate "only seemingly" (*nur scheinbar*) (1903–1916: III, 45), his changes amounting to little more than reversing the order of the first and second provisions, is surely mistaken. Alfred begins by widening the range of situations to which this clause is applicable and extending the period in which the death of the slave after a beating may be culpable (ðeah he libbe twa niht oððe ðreo). The three-day period was perhaps meant to bring the text into conformity with §5 of the Council of Elvira, which saw wide circulation in subsequent collections of canon law in the years prior to Alfred's reign. Whereas Exodus had concerned itself with male and female slaves subjected to punitive beatings, Alfred includes the *esne*, a person who occupied an uncertain zone between bondage and freedom. The *virga*, understood in the Vulgate to be the instrument of punishment, is absent, since for Alfred, whose thinking here seems to have been influenced by pastoral writings, any violence visited upon any servant by his or her master is a potential matter of concern. But Alfred does not retain the assertion of the Vulgate that the master is in such a case *criminis reus*, as there was in Alfred's day no imposition of secular punishments on masters who took the lives of their servants. Alfred's concern, as above, is with the wrath that brought about the beating, and thus the king replaces the Vulgate's provision for specific penalties with an assertion that the master is scyld[ig]. The peculiar idiom employed – ðonne sitte sio scyld on him – is used elsewhere specifically to designate spiritual guilt, as in *Guthlac A* l. 478: *On eow scyld siteð* (Roberts 1979: 97).

MP 18 Gif hwa on cease eácniende wif gewerde,[39] bete þone
æwerdlan, swa him domeras gereccen. Gif hio dead sie, selle
sawle wið sawle.

MP 19 Gif hwa oðrum his eage oðdo, selle his agen fore: toð fore
teð, honda wið honda, fet fore fet, bærning[40] for bærninge,
wund wið wunde, læl wið læle.

MP 20 Gif hwa áslea his ðeowe oððe his ðeowenne þæt eage ut ⁊
he þonne hie gedo ánigge, gefreoge hie for þon. Gif he þonne
ðone toð ófaslea, do þæt ilce.

- - - - - - - - - - - - - - - -

²¹:²²Si rixati fuerint viri et percusserit quis mulierem praegnantem et abortivum qui-
dem fecerit sed ipsa vixerit, subiacebit damno quantum expetierit maritus mulieris et
arbitri iudicarint. ²¹:²³Sin autem mors eius fuerit subsecuta, reddet animam pro anima,
²¹:²⁴oculum pro oculo, dentem pro dente, manum pro manu, pedem pro pede,
²¹:²⁵adiustonem pro adiustone, vulnus pro vulnere, livorem pro livore. ²¹:²⁶Si percusserit quispiam oculum servi sui aut ancillae et luscos eos fecerit, dimittet liberos pro
oculo quem eruit. ²¹:²⁷Dentem quoque si excusserit servo vel ancillae suae, similiter
dimittet eos liberos.

MP §18 cease] ceaste GH   gewerde] gewyrde G   bete] gebete G   æwerdlan]
ǽwyrdlan G; æwyrdlan H   gereccen] getæcan G; gereccan H   hio] heo GH   sie] sy
GH   selle] sylle GH

MP §19 his] hys GH   oðdo] ofdo H   selle] sylle GH   fore] for GH   teð] toð G; toþ
H   honda wið honda] handa for handa G; handa wiþ handa H   fet fore fét] fet for
fet G; fett for fett H   bærning] bærninge G   læl] læle G

MP §20 áslea] aslea G; ofslea H   ðeowe] þeowan H   ðeowenne] þeowene   ut]
utt H   hie] hy H   ánigge] áneage G; anegede H   hie] hí G; heo H   ðon] ðan G   ilce]
sylfe G

[39] This word appears only here and in §26.
[40] Corrected by scribe from *berning*.

MP 18 If someone in the course of a quarrel should injure a pregnant woman, let him compensate for the damage as the judges may counsel for him. If she should die, give soul for soul.[41]

MP 19 If someone should put out another's eye, let him give his own for it: tooth for tooth, hand for hand, feet for feet, burning for burning, wound for wound, bruise for bruise.

MP 20 If someone should strike out the eye of his male or female slave and thereby make them one-eyed, let him free them for that. If, however, he should strike out a tooth, let him do the same.

---

[41] Omission of the Vulgate's *abortivum* is held by Liebermann to be evidence of Alfred's squeamishness: "Abortion in the Vulgate perhaps seemed indecent to Alfred" (*Der Abortus in der Vulgata schien Ælfred wohl unanständig*) (1903–1916: III, 45 n. 3). We may not rule out, however, that Alfred is avoiding altogether a legal conundrum posed by the norms of his own day. Penitential manuals such as those of Theodore (I, xiv, 27; Finsterwalder 1929: 310) assert plainly the then-conventional view that it is a graver offense to deliberately kill an *infantem* forty days after conception (*ut homicida peniteat*) than before (*I annum peniteat*). Alfred's apparent resistance to this notion may have been shared, for the *Old English Canons of Theodore* (§A 29) render it in such a way as to invite confusion: "Women who discard their infants, they are judged in the same respect as [those who do this] before the child was quickened" (Þa wif þe doð awegaworpenessa heora bearna, þi ylcan gemete syn hi gedemde ær þan þa bearn cwice syn) (Fulk and Jurasinski 2012: 6). The *Scriftboc* (§xvi, 19.1) also requires a woman to do penance *swa se myrðra* "as a murderess" should her *geeacnung* ("conception") be destroyed "before it was ensouled" (*ær-ðon hit gesawlad wære*) (Spindler 1934: 184). That no such distinction is apparent in Exodus, which appears to regard such incidents as matters to be dealt with by arbitration, may well have induced Alfred to omit the clause entirely and accept the consequent ambiguity. Liebermann's speculation that the husband is absent because Alfred wished "to protect unmarried pregnant women" (*unvermählte Schwangere zu schützen*) seems reasonable enough given the informality even of child-bearing unions at this time – though as such observations accumulate in Liebermann's commentary, they seem to work against his broader argument that the Prologue can have had no legislative force.

MP 21 Gif oxa ofhnite wer oððe wíf, þæt hie dead sien, sie he mid
stanum ofworpod, ⁊ ne sie his flæsc eten; se hlaford bið unscyldig. Gif se oxa hnitol wære twam dagum ær oððe ðrim, ⁊ se
hlaford hit wisse ⁊ hine inne betynan nolde, ⁊ he ðonne wer
oððe wíf ofsloge, sie he mid stanum ofworpod, ⁊ sie se hlaford
ófslegen oððe forgolden, swa ðæt witan to ryhte finden. Sunu
oþþe dohtor gif he ofstinge, ðæs ilcan domes sie he wyrðe. Gif
he ðonne ðeow oððe ðeowmennen ofstinge, geselle þam hlaforde xxx scill /37v/ seolfres, ⁊ se oxa mid stanum ofworpod.

MP 22 Gif hwa adelfe wæterpyt oððe betynedne ontyne ⁊ hine
eft ne betyne, gelde swelc neat swelc ðær on befealle, ⁊ hæbbe
him ðæt deade.

- - - - - - - - - - - - - - - -

²¹:²⁸Si bos cornu petierit virum aut mulierem et mortui fuerint, lapidibus obruetur et
non comedentur carnes eius; dominusque bovis innocens erit. ²¹:²⁹Quod si bos cor-
nipta fuerit ab heri et nudiustertius, et contestati sunt dominum eius nec reclusit eum,
occideritque virum aut mulierem, et bos lapidibus obruetur et dominum illius occi-
dent. ²¹:³⁰Quod si pretium ei fuerit impositum, dabit pro anima sua quicquid fuerit
postulatus. ²¹:³¹Filium quoque et filiam si cornu percusserit simili sententiae subiacebit. ²¹:³²Si servum ancillamque invaserit, triginta siclos argenti dabit domino, bos vero
lapidibus opprimetur. ²¹:³³Si quis aperuerit cisternam et foderit et non operuerit eam,
ceciderítque bos vel asinus in eam, ²¹:³⁴dominus cisternae reddet pretium iumentorum;
quod autem mortuum est ipsius erit.

MP §21 hie dead sien] hy deade syn H   sie] sy H   ofworpod] oftorfod H   eten] éten
G; geeten H   bið] byð H   twam dagum ær oððe ðrim] twam dagum oððe þrim æ r
G; twam dagum ær oððe þrym H   ⁊ se hlaford hit wisse] Gif he hit ðonne wiste G; ⁊
se hlaford hit wiste H   ⁊ hine inne] ⁊ he hine *om.* inne G; ⁊ hine innan H   sie] sy
H   ofworpod] ofworpen H   sie] sy H   ófslegen] ofslagen G   oððe forgolden] oððe
se man forgolden H   ryhte] rihte GH   witan] wytan H   finden] findan G; fyndaþ
H   gyf] gif G   ofstinge] stynge H   þæs ilcan domes sie he wyrðe] sy he þæs ilcan
domes wyrðe G; þæs ilcan domes sy he wyrðe H   þeow] þeowan H   ðeowmennen]
ðeowne G; þeowene H   ófstinge] ofstinge G; ofstynge H   geselle] gesylle GH   xxx]
þryttig H   ⁊ se oxa mid stanum ofworpod] ⁊ se oxa sie mid stanum ofworpad G; ⁊
sy se oxa mid stanum ofworpen H
MP §22 adelfe] delfe G   wæterpyt] wæterpitt H   ontyne] untyne H   swelc neat
swelc] swylc neat swylc G; swylc neat swa H

MP 21 If an ox should gore a man or woman, so that they die, let it be slain by stoning, and let its flesh not be eaten; the lord will be guiltless. If the ox was given to pushing with its horns two or three days before, and the lord knew of it and did not wish to enclose him, and it then killed a man or woman, let it be slain by stoning, and let the lord be slain or paid for, as the assembly may deem right.[42] If it gore a son or daughter, let him be worthy of the same judgment. If, however, it should gore a male or female slave, let the lord give thirty silver shillings and the ox be killed by stoning.

MP 22 If anyone digs a water pit or opens an enclosed one and afterwards does not close it, let him pay for whatever animal that may fall therein, and let him keep the carcass.

---

[42] Whereas Exodus places the choice between compensation and vengeance in the hands of the decedent's kin, Alfred appears to leave both the type of penalty and the amount of the judgment up to a separate body of arbitrators. Presumably this addition was meant to align Exodus with contemporaneous law, but the possibility may not be ruled out that, both here and in §24, Alfred's aim was to urge the pursuit of pecuniary judgments.

MP 23 Gif oxa oðres monnes oxan gewundige, ⁊ he þon*n*e dead
sie, bebycggen þone oxan ⁊ hæbben him þæt weorð gemæne ⁊
eac ðæt flǽsc swa ðæs deadan. Gif se hlaford þon*n*e wisse, þæt
se oxa hnitol wære, ⁊ hine healdan nolde, selle him oðerne
oxan fore ⁊ hæbbe him eall ðæt flæsc.

MP 24 Gif hwa forstele oðres oxan ⁊ hine ofslea oððe bebycgge,
selle twegen wið ⁊ feower sceap wið anu*m*. Gif he næbbe
hwæt he selle, sie he self beboht wið ðam fio. [Exod. 22.1 +
22.3 b]

----

²¹ᐟ³⁵Si bos alienus bovem alterius vulneravit et ille mortuus fuerit, vendent bovem
vivum et dividunt pretium; cadaver autem mortui inter se dispertient. ²¹ᐟ³⁶Sin autem
sciebat quod bos cornipeta esset ab heri et nudiustertius et non custodivit eum dominus suus, reddet bovem pro bove et cadaver integrum accipiet.
xxii.¹Si quis furatus fuerit bovem aut ovem et occiderit vel vendiderit, quinque boves
pro uno bove restituet et quattuor oves pro una ove. <²²ᐟ³ᵇSi non habuerit quod pro
furto reddat venundabitur>.⁴³

MP §23 monnes] mannes GH   gewundige] gewundie H   sie] sy GH   bebycggen]
bebicgan GH   hæbben] habbon G; habben H   him] heom H   wisse] wiste GH   ⁊
hine healdan nolde] ⁊ he hyne healdan nolde G   selle] sylle GH   eall] eal H
MP §24 bebycgge] bebycge G; bebicge H   selle] sylle   wið] *om.* G   feower] IIII
G   selle] sylle GH   sie he self] sy he sylf GH   ðam] þan H   fio] feo GH

⁴³ Cf. *Liber ex lege Moysi* (Meeder 2009: 196): *Si quis furatus fuerit bouem aut ouem*
et occiderit uel uenderit: v boues pro uno boue restituet et IIII oues pro una oue
restituet si non habuerit quod pro furto redat uenundabitur. See commentary for
discussion of differences between this version and what appears in the Vulgate.

MP 23 If an ox wounds another's ox, and the latter then dies, let them sell the [living] ox and share the payment and also the flesh of the dead one. If, however, the lord knew that the ox was given to pushing with its horns and he would not restrain it, let him give the ox [to the owner of the dead ox] and let him have all the flesh [as well].

MP 24 If someone should steal another's ox and slay him or sell him, let him give two for it and four [sheep] for one. If he does not have what he should give, let him be sold himself in exchange for the livestock.[44]

---

[44] Alfred's version of this clause would seem to offer sure evidence of borrowing from the *Liber ex lege Moysi*, which likewise appends to the ordinance quoted above the latter part of Exod. 22:3. Alfred does not, however, follow the *Liber* in subsequently adding the entirety of 22:4, his appropriation of the latter being evident only in his substitution of twofold restitution for the fourfold penalty recommended in 22:1 (though this could be a principle Alfred adduced from the text as a whole, given its occurrence at 22:7). Alfred makes this addition at the expense of coherence, here applying to the grave offense of having slain or sold another's livestock a penalty meant only for cases in which the animal has been recovered alive. Though the similarity of treatment is noteworthy, it is possible to make too much of the parallelism here between the *Liber* and the *domboc*, given that Alfred's presumptive borrowing from the *Liber* does not extend to other features of the text. Both the *Liber* and the *domboc* present a version of the laws of Exodus meant to have some bearing on the legislation of their own day, and we may assume that doing so in both cases involved a certain amount of corrective emendation. The expedient preferred by the compiler of the *Liber* is meant solely to ensure coherence: 22:3b and 22:4 clearly belong with 22:1 (presumably oxen were not even in ancient Israel kept in one's own dwelling, though they might be very close by). For this very reason the verses were so placed many centuries later by the editors of the New Revised Standard Version. Given the several cases in which Alfred's language agrees with the Vulgate over readings in the *Liber*, it cannot be ruled out that Alfred's own corrections were arrived at independently; certainly they are in keeping with tendencies manifest throughout his translation. At all events, the twofold restitution may reflect the influence of Augustine's *Quaestiones in Heptateuchum*, where the soundness of the fivefold restitution is questioned (Fraipoint and De Bruyne 1958: 112 [*Quaest. Exodi* LXXXIII]).

MP 25 Gif ðeof brece mannes hús nihtes ⁊ he weorðe þær ofsle-
gen, ne sie he na mansleges scyldig. Gif he siððan æfter sunnan
upgonge þis deð, he bið mansleges scyldig ⁊ he ðonne self
swelte, buton he nieddæda⁴⁵ wære.⁴⁶ Gif mid him cwicum sie
funden þæt he ær stæl, be twyfealdum forgielde hit.

MP 26 Gif hwa gewerde oðres monnes wingeard oððe his æcras
oððe his landes awuht, gebete swa hit mon geeahtige.

MP 27 Gif fyr sie ontended rýt⁴⁷ to bærnanne, gebete þone
æfwerdelsan⁴⁸ se ðæt fýr ontent.

- - - - - - - - - - - - - - - -

²²:²Si effringens fur domum sive suffodiens fuerit inventus, et accepto vulnere mortuus
fuerit, percussor non erit reus sanguinis. ²²:³Quod si orto sole hoc fecerit, homicidium
perpetravit et ipse morietur. [Si non habuerit quod pro furto reddat, venundabitur.]
²²:⁴Si inventum fuerit apud eum quod furatus est vivens sive bos sive asinus sive ovis,
duplum restituet. ²²:⁵Si laeserit quispiam agrum vel vineam et dimiserit iumentum
suum ut depascatur aliena, quicquid optimum habuerit in agro suo vel in vinea pro
damni aestimatione restituet. ²²:⁶Si egressus ignis invenerit spinas et comprehenderit
acervos frugum, sive stantes segetes in agris, reddet damnum qui ignem succenderit.

MP §25 weorðe] wurðe H   ofslegen] ofslagen G   na] *om.* G; *later addition to*
H?   upgonge] úpgange G; uppgange H   self swelte] sylf swelte G; swylte H (*om.*
self)   buton] butan GH   nieddæda] -de (*later corrected to* -da *by Joscelyn?*);
nyddæde H   sie] sy H   forgielde hit] forgylde he hit G; forgylde hit H
MP §26 gewerde] gewyrde G; awyrde H   monnes] mannes GH   wingeard] wynge-
ard H   æcras] æceras GH   awuht] awiht G; awyht H   mon] man GH   geeahtige]
geæhtie H
MP §27 fyr] fir H   sie] sy H   rýt] rit *amended to* rýt *by Joscelyn* G; ryht H   bær-
nanne] bærnenne H   æfwerdelsan] æwyrdlan GH   fýr] *om.* H   ontent] ontende G;
ontendeþ H

⁴⁵ *Hapax legomenon.*
⁴⁶ Cf. *Collatio Legum Mosaicarum et Romanarum* (Frakes 2011: 175, 217): "Just as
the Twelve Tables order a thief in the night to be killed in any case [, or a thief in
the daytime] if he dares to defend himself with a weapon, know oh Jurists, that
Moses ordained this earlier, just as a close reading shows. Moses says: 'If a thief is
found digging through a wall by night and someone strikes him and he dies, he
who struck him is not a murderer. 2. If, however, the sun rises on him, he who
struck is responsible for the death; and he himself will die.'" (*Quod si duodecim
tabularum nocturnum furem[, quoquo modo, diurnum] autem se audeat telo
defendere, interfici iubent, scitote, iuris consulti, quia Moyses prius hoc statuit,
sicut lectio manifestat. Moyses dicit: Si perfodiens nocte parietem inventus fuerit
fur et percusserit eum alius et mortuus fuerit hic, non est homicida is qui percusserit eum. 2. si autem sol ortus fuerit super eum, reus est mortis percussor: et ipse
morietur.*)
⁴⁷ *Hapax legomenon.*
⁴⁸ *Hapax legomenon.*

MP 25 If a thief should break into a man's house at night[49] and be slain there, let him [the slayer] not [be deemed] culpable for the homicide. If he does this after sunrise, he will be culpable for the homicide; and let him suffer death himself, unless he were constrained by necessity [in killing the thief]. If, while he [the thief] lives, that which he has stolen is found, let him pay twice its value.

MP 26 If someone should damage another man's vineyard or his fields or his land in any respect, let him pay restitution as it is determined.

MP 27 If a fire is set in order to burn ears of corn, let him who set the fire compensate for the damage.[50]

---

[49] According to Wormald (1999a: 419–420), Alfred's **nihtes** is some of the chief evidence for influence from the *Collatio*, which quotes from an Old Latin version of Exodus having *nocte* (the Vulgate does not). The *Collatio* also begins with a reference to the "thief in the night" (*nocturnum furem*) of the Twelve Tables. The possibility of influence from Old Latin readings – perhaps the simpler explanation – may not be ruled out.

[50] Interpretative problems surround Alfred's word rýt, a *hapax legomenon* left untranslated in Thorpe's edition (Liebermann renders it as "uprooted brushwood" [*ausgerissenes Gestrüpp*]). The difficulties posed by this word are by no means resolved by consideration of the Vulgate given the divergent readings of earlier manuscripts: while the exemplar seems to have contained *spinas*, "thorns," many versions available in the early Middle Ages have instead *spicas* "ears of corn" (as is evidenced here by *Quadripartitus*). The latter implies deliberate burning of another's harvest, a possibility not envisaged by Alfred according to Liebermann (which would, as he notes, have required a much harsher penalty).

MP 28 Gif hwa oðfæste his friend fioh, gif he hit self stæle, forgylde be twyfealdu*m*. Gif he nyte, hwa hit stæle, geladige hine
selfne, þæt he ðær nán facn ne gefremede. Gif hit ðonne /38r/
cucu feoh wære, ⁊ he secgge, þæt hit here name oððe hit self
ácwæle, ⁊ gewitnesse hæbbe, ne þearf he þæt geldan. Gif he
ðonne gewitnesse næbbe, ⁊ he him ne getriewe, swerige he
þon*ne*.

----

²²:⁷Si quis commendaverit amico pecuniam aut vas in custodiam, et ab eo qui suscep-
erat furto ablata fuerint, si invenitur fur duplum reddet. ²²:⁸Si latet dominus domus
adplicabitur ad deos, et iurabit quod non extenderit manum in rem proximi sui ²²:⁹ad
perpetrandam fraudem, tam in bove quam in asino et ove ac vestimento. Et quicquid
damnum inferre potest ad deos utriusque causa perveniet et si illi iudicaverint duplum
restituet proximo suo. [²²:¹⁰Si quis commendaverit proximo suo asinum bovem ovem
et omne iumentum ad custodiam et mortuum fuerit aut debilitatum vel captum ab
hostibus nullusque hoc viderit, ²²:¹¹iusiurandum erit in medio quod non extenderit
manum ad rem proximi sui suscipietque dominus iuramentum et ille reddere non
cogetur. ²²:¹²Quod si furto ablatum fuerit restituet damnum domino. ²²:¹³Si comestum
a bestia deferet ad eum quod occisum est et non restituet. ²²:¹⁴Qui a proximo suo
quicquam horum mutuo postularit et debilitatum aut mortuum fuerit domino non
praesente reddere conpelletur. ²²:¹⁵Quod si inpraesentiarum fuit dominus non restituet
maxime si conductum venerat pro mercede operis sui.]

MP §28 his] hys G   friend] frynd G; freond H   fioh] feoh GH   hit] hyt G   self] sylf
H   stæle] stele H   gif] gyf G   nyte] nite GH   hit] hyt G; hitt H   stæle] stele
H   geladie] gá ladige G; geladie H   selfne] sylfne H   facn ne gefremede] facen ón ne
gefremede G; fanc on ne fremede H   cucu] cwicu G   secgge] secge G; sæcge H   hit
self] hyt sylf G; þæt hit sylf H   ⁊ gewitnesse] ⁊ he gewitnesse GH   geldan] gyldan
GH   gif] gyf G   getriewe] getrywe G; getreowe ne sy H   swerige he þonne] swerge
he ðænne G; swerie he þonne H

MP 28 Should someone entrust property to his friend: if he [the recipient] steals it himself, let him pay twofold restitution.[51] If he does not know who stole it, let him submit to proof that he did no wrong.[52] If, however, it was living property, and he should say that a troop[53] took it or that it died on its own, and he has a witness, he need not pay for it. If, however, he does not have a witness, and he [the owner] does not believe him, let him swear.[54]

---

[51] As the clause is understood by Liebermann, Alfred's version envisages a case different from that of the Vulgate, perhaps from a misunderstanding of *invenitur fur* as "found to be a thief" and *ab* as "by" rather than "from."

[52] Alfred's **geladie hine selfne** is perhaps another cautious omission of "the gods" (see also *MP* §§11, 39), though as an equivalent for the sense of the Vulgate the simple reference to the oath is perfectly adequate. *Quadripartitus* (MS Hk) here inserts *id est iudices* out of similar concern. The verb indicates an oath unambiguously at *Alfred* §13.4.

[53] As Liebermann would have it, a possible allusion to the Danes, though a likelier source of inspiration is the *captum ab hostibus* of the omitted text. Cf. *Ine* §14, where a group in excess of thirty-five men is designated a *here* ("troop"). While it is not certain that Alfred here employs the term in the specific sense established by Ine, the evidence from Ine's laws suffices to show that not every use of *here* must refer to the Danes.

[54] Liebermann observes that the very different version in Alfred's text handles a situation not otherwise dealt with in English secular law, and it is perhaps for this reason that the Alfredian rendering had been assumed by Laughlin (1876: 199) to offer genuine insights into Anglo-Saxon legal procedures. 22:12–15 are, according to Liebermann, perhaps omitted because of their excessive intricacy and irrelevance to agricultural practice in Alfred's day.

MP 29 Gif hwa fæmnan beswice unbeweddode ⁊ hire midslæpe,⁵⁵ forgielde hie ⁊ hæbbe hi siððan him to wife. Gif ðære fæmnan fæder hie ðonne sellan nelle, agife he ðæt feoh æfter þam weotuman.⁵⁶

MP 30 Ða fæmnan þe gewuniað onfón gealdorcræftigan ⁊ scinlæcan ⁊ wiccan, ne læt þu ða libban.

----

²²:¹⁶Si seduxerit quis virginem necdum desponsatam et dormierit cum ea, dotabit eam et habebit uxorem. ²²:¹⁷Si pater virginis dare noluerit, reddet pecuniam iuxta modum dotis quam virgines accipere consueverunt. ²²:¹⁸Maleficos non patieris vivere.

MP §29 beswice] beswyce GH   unbeweddode] unbeweddude G   hire] hyre G   midslæpe] midslepe G   forgielde] forgylde GH   hie] heo H   hi] hie G; hy H   hie] hi G; heo H   sellan] syllan GH   þam] ðæm G   weotuman] *preceded by* witoman *in* G; *crossed out by later, probably c. sixteenth-century, hand*
MP §30 gewuniað] gewilniað H   onfon] ánfón G   gealdorcræftigan] galdorcræft G; galdercræftigan   scinlæcan] scinlacan H   ða] hi H

⁵⁵ *Hapax legomenon.*
⁵⁶ This word occurs only here and in *MP* §12.

MP 29 If someone deceives a virgin not yet betrothed[57] and sleeps with her, let him compensate her[58] and have her as a wife. If, however, her father will not give her [to him], let him give [her money] equivalent to the bride-price.[59]

MP 30 Those women who are accustomed to receive enchanters and magicians and witches – do not permit them to live.[60]

[57] Here (according to Liebermann) **unbeweddode** must mean "not yet engaged" rather than "unmarried," the former indeed being the sense of *necdum desponsatam*. Cf. *Alfred* §21, where it is established that a betrothed woman who fornicates with someone other than her intended husband is obligated to compensate the guarantor of the marriage. The line between betrothal and marriage was probably less certain in Alfred's day than in our own if conditions in ninth-century Wessex resembled those elsewhere in Europe, on which see Reynolds 2001: 316.

[58] Liebermann insists that the payment here made is the bride-price, "which differs from the Vulgate" (*anders als Vulg[ata]*).

[59] Here *æfter* presumably renders *iuxta modum;* **weotuma** is earlier used (see above, MP §12) to render *pretium pudicitiae*. That Alfred does not change the requirement of the source that payment be made to the woman rather than her father is perhaps noteworthy given that this was not to be expected in the earlier law of marriage (as some have understood it). Cf. *Alfred* §13, the language of which suggests that the woman herself was the recipient of compensation in cases of molestation or assault.

[60] The remarkable expansion of this clause is explained only in part by Turk's conjecture (accepted by Liebermann) that Alfred's **gewuniað onfon** derives from the previous chapter's *quam virgines accipere consuerunt* (Turk 1893: 37). A similar instance of perhaps unconscious repetition may be found in other clauses of the Prologue (see MP §12). However clumsy, however, this borrowing may have been suggested by sources not apparent to Liebermann or Turk. According to Meaney (2006: 133), one may discern a parallel between Alfred's language here and the *Poenitentiale Theodori* (1, xv, 4; McNeill and Gamer 1938: 198):

> If a woman performs diabolical incantations or divinations, she shall do penance for one year or the three forty-day periods, or forty days, according to the nature of the offense. Of this matter it is said in the canon: He who celebrates auguries, omens from birds, or dreams, or any divinations according to the custom of the heathen, or introduces such people into his houses, in seeking out any trick of the magicians – when these become penitents, if they belong to the clergy they shall be cast out; but if they are secular persons they shall do penance for five years.

The "canon" quoted in this clause is §24 of the Council of Ankara (314), portions of which may have circulated independent of Theodore's penitential at this time.

MP 31 ⁊ Se ðe hæme mid netene, swelte he deaðe.

MP 32 ⁊ Se ðe godgeldum ónsecge ofer God anne, swelte se deaðe.

MP 33 Utan cumene ⁊ elðeodige ne geswenc ðu no, forðon ðe ge wæron giu elðeodige on Egipta londe.

MP 34 Þa wuduwan ⁊ þa stiopcild ne sceððað ge, ne hie nawer deriað. Gif ge þonne elles doð, hie cleopiað to me, ⁊ ic gehiere hie ⁊ ic eow þonne slea mid minum sweorde ⁊ ic gedó, þæt eowru wíf beoð wydewan ⁊ eowru bearn beoð steopcild.

MP 35 Gif ðu fioh to borge selle þinum geferan, þe mid þe eardian wille, ne niede ðu hine swa swa niedling⁶¹ ⁊ ne gehene þu hine mid ðy eacan.

MP 36 Gif mon næbbe buton anfeald hrægl hine mid to wreonne ⁊ to werianne, ⁊ he hit to wedde selle, ær sunnan setlgonge sie hit agifen. Gif ðu swa ne dest, þonne cleopað he to me, ⁊ ic hine gehiere, forðon ðe ic eom swiðe mildheort.

- - - - - - - - - - - - - - - - -

²²:¹⁹Qui coierit cum iumento morte moriatur. ²²:²⁰Qui immolat diis occidetur praeter Domino soli. ²²:²¹Advenam non contristabis neque adfliges eum; advenae enim et ipsi fuistis in terra Aegypti. ²²:²²Viduae et pupillo non nocebitis. ²²:²³Si laeseritis eos, vociferabuntur ad me et ego audiam clamorem eorum ²²:²⁴et indignabitur furor meus: percutiamque vos gladio et erunt uxores vestrae viduae et filii vestri pupilli. ²²:²⁵Si pecuniam mutuam dederis populo meo pauperi qui habitat tecum, non urguebis eum quasi exactor nec usuris opprimes. ²²:²⁶Si pignus a proximo tuo acceperis vestimentum, ante solis occasum redde ei, ²²:²⁷ipsum enim est solum qui operitur indumentum carnis eius, nec habet aliud in quo dormiat. Si clamaverit ad me exaudiam eum quia misericors sum.

MP §31 mid] *in right margin of* G   netene] nietene G; nytene H   he] se
MP §32 godgeldum] godgyldum GH   ónsecge] onsæcge H   ofer] of G   anne] ænne H
MP §33 elðeodige] ælðeodige G; ælþeodige H   geswenc] geswænc H   no] þá G; ðone H   forðon] forþam   giu] iú G; *om.* H   elðeodige] ælðeodige G; ælþeodige H   londe] lande GH
MP §34 wuduwan] wydwan G; wydewan H   stiopcild] steopcild G; steopcyld H   sceððað] sceaððan G; scyþþað H   ne] *om.* G; ⁊ ne H   hie] hy H   nawer] nahwer G; nawer H   deriað] né nederiað (né *crossed out by later hand*) G   hie] hy H   cleopiað] clipiað H   gehiere] gehyre G; gehire H   hie] hy H   ic gedó] ic eow gedó H   eowru] eowre GH   wydewan] wudewan H   eowru] eowre GH   beoð] *om.* H   steopcild] steopcyld H
MP §35 fioh] feoh GH   selle] gesylle G; sylle H   wille] wylle H   niede] nyd H   swa swa needling] swa niedling G; swa nydling H   ⁊] *om.* G   gehene] gehyne G; gehyn H
MP §36 ⁊] oððe GH   selle] sylle G; syˡyˡlle H   setlgonge] setlgange GH   sie] sy GH   agifen] agyfen G   cleopað] clypiað H   he] hy H   gehiere] gehyre H   forðon] forðam H   eom] eam H   swiðe] swyþe H

⁶¹ **niede** [...] **swa niedling** constitutes a *figura etymologica*. The term *niedling* is a *hapax legomenon* in this form. The translation of Orosius contains the only other attestations: *niedlingas* (2x) and *niedlingum* (1x).

MP 31 He who lies with cattle, let him die [the] death.

MP 32 He who sacrifices to idols rather than to God alone, let him die the death.

MP 33 Do not oppress those come from afar and foreigners, because you were once foreigners in the land of Egypt.

MP 34 Widows and orphans you will not harm, nor will you ever hurt them. If you do otherwise, they will cry out to me, and I will hear them and I will then strike you with my sword; and I will arrange that your wives will be widows and your children will be orphans.

MP 35 If you give property to be borrowed by your fellow, who will dwell with you, do not oppress him like a slave and do not abuse him with interest.

MP 36 If someone has but one article with which to cover and clothe himself,[62] and he gives it to you in pledge, let it be returned to him before the setting of the sun. If you do not do so, then he will cry out to me, and I will hear him, because I am greatly merciful.

---

[62] Another tautology (cf. *MP* §13), perhaps legal in origin.

MP 37 Ne tæl ðu /38v/ ðinne Dryhten, ne ðone hlaford þæs folces
ne werge þu.

MP 38 Þine teoðan sceattas ⁊ þine frumripan⁶³ gongendes ⁊
weaxendes agif þu Gode.

MP 39 Eal ðæt flæsc þæt wildeor læfen ne eten ge þæt, ac sellað
hit hundum.

MP 40 Leases monnes word ne rec ðu no þæs to geherianne, ne
his domas ne geðafa ðu, ne nane gewitnesse æfter him ne saga
ðu.

- - - - - - - - - - - - - - - -

²²:²⁸Diis non detrahes et principi populi tui non maledices. ²²:²⁹Decimas tuas et primi-
tias non tardabis offerre. [Primogenitum filiorum tuorum dabis mihi. ²²:³⁰De bubus
quoque et ovibus similiter facies. Septem diebus sit cum matre sua; die octavo reddes
illum mihi.] ²²:³¹[Viri sancti eritis mihi.] Carnem quae a bestiis fuerit praegustata non
comeditis sed proicietis canibus. xxiii¹Non suscipies vocem mendacii, nec iunges
manum tuam ut pro impio dicas falsum testimonium.

MP §37 Dryhten] Drihten H   werge] wyrg G; werig H
MP §38 sceattas] sceat\tas/ H   gongendes] gangendes GH   agif] agyf G
MP §39 Eal] Eall H   wildeor] \wyld/deor H   læfen] læfan H   sellað] syllað GH
MP §40 monnes] mannes GH   rec] rece G; recce H   no] na G;   *om.* H   þæs] *om.* G;
in margin of H.   gehieranne] gehyranne G; gehiranne H   saga] sege G

⁶³ *Hapax legomenon.*

MP 37 Do not blaspheme your Lord, nor may you curse the lord of the people.[64]

MP 38 The tenth part of your money and your first fruits of animals and crops you will give to God.[65]

MP 39 All the flesh that wild animals have left – do not eat it, but give it to dogs.[66]

MP 40 You will not consider obeying the word of a dishonest man, nor will you consent to his judgments, nor will you repeat any of his testimony.

---

[64] A substantial departure from the source, perhaps reavealing something of Alfredian political thought (as may be the case with MP §41, whose difficulties are even greater) as well as further unease with "the gods." See also Augustine, *Quaestiones in Heptateuchum* (Fraipoint and De Bruyne 1958: 113 [*Quaest. Exodi* LXXXVI]), where the persons so referred to are designated *principes qui iudicant populum* whose authority is not to be questioned but who are not entitled either to sacrifices or worship. According to Liebermann, the conjecture of Lambarde and Wilkins that by *dryhten* Alfred here means an earthly potentate may be dismissed on the ground that *tælan* occurs frequently enough with *dryhten* as an epithet for God the Father, as in Ælfric's version of Num. 14:11 (Marsden 2008: 145): *God cwæð: hu lange tælð þis folc me?* As it occurs here, *hlaford* should be taken to mean "king."

[65] Though the reference here is to the "sanctification and redemption of the firstborn" (cf. Num. 18: 14–16), "You will give me the first-born of your sons" (*Primogenitum filiorum tuorum dabis mihi*) probably presented too many potential pitfalls for an unlearned audience to be reproduced in Alfred's Prologue. Representing as it did to Alfred and his circle of clerics an ordinance anticipating and ultimately superseded by the New Law, it was probably considered preferable to omit the clause lest it provoke needless confusion.

[66] Liebermann (1903–1916: III, 47) conjectures that the first sentence (*Viri sancti eritis mihi*) is omitted because it threatened to bring the laity too close to the condition of the clergy (*Laien zu sehr dem Klerus anzunähern*). The prohibition bears some relation to those in penitential canons attributed to Archbishop Theodore (e.g., I, vii, 6) and perhaps is reproduced here in anticipation of the norms to be observed by gentiles established at the Council of Jerusalem. The clause in question (*viri sancti eritis mihi*) may have been omitted so that the *domboc* would not appear to require observance of dietary rules enumerated in the Torah as a condition of one's salvation (even the Theodorean clause had made exceptions to the rule enumerated here in cases of necessity).

MP 41 Ne wend ðu ðe no on þæs folces unræd ⁊ unryht gewill
on hiora spræce ⁊ geclysp ofer ðin ryht, ⁊ ðæs unwisestan lare
ne him ne geðafa.

MP 42 Gif ðe becume oðres mannes giemeleás fioh on hond, þeah
hit sie ðin feond, gecyðe hit him.

MP 43 Dem ðu swiðe emne. Ne dem ðu oðerne dóm þam wele-
gan, oðerne ðam earman; ne oðerne þam liofran ⁊ oðerne þam
laðran ne dem ðu.

MP 44 Ónscuna ðu á leasunga.

MP 45 Soðfæstne man ⁊ unscyldigne ne ácwele ðu þone næfre.

----

²³:²Non sequeris turbam ad faciendum malum, nec in iudicio plurimorum adquiesces
sententiae ut a vero devies. ²³:⁴Si occurreris bovi inimici tui aut asino erranti reduc ad
eum. ²³:⁶Non declinabis in iudicio pauperis. ²³:⁷Mendacium fugies. Insontem et iustum
non occides, [quia aversor impium.]

MP §41 wend] \ge/wend H   no] ná G; na H   unryht] unriht G; on unriht H   hiora]
hyra G; hi\o/ra H   spræce] spæce G   geclysp] geclæsp G; geclebs H   ryht] riht
G   unwisestan] \un/wisestan   ⁊ ðæs] ⁊ on þæs G   ne him ne geðafa] þu ne geþafa H
MP §42 becume] becyme G   monnes] mannes GH   giemeleás] gymeleas GH   fioh]
feoh G   hond] handa G   hit] hyt G   sie] sy H   feond] fiond H   gecyðe] gecyþ H
MP §43 emne] rihte ⁊ swiðe emne G; rihtne dom H (*om.* emne)   ðam] ðæm G   liof-
ran] leofran G; leofan H   laðran] laðan H   dem] dæm H
MP §44 Ónscuna ðu á leasunga] Onscuna ða leosunga H
MP §45 man] mann G   ácwele] ácwelle G; acwel H   þone] ðæne G

MP 41 Do not turn to the folly and unjust desire of the people, in their words and their clamor, against that which is lawful for you, nor agree to their most unwise counsel.

MP 42 If another's stray cattle should come into your possession, though it may belong to your foe, announce[67] it to him.

MP 43 Judge very evenly. Do not give one judgment to the rich man and another to the poor; nor one for a friend and another for an enemy.[68]

MP 44 Always shun lies.

MP 45 A truthful and guiltless man – never slay him.

[67] It has been implied that the substitution of **gecyðe hit him** for "lead it back to him" (*reduc ad eum*) was a concession to "Germanic" habits of mind regarding enmity; this is the seeming implication of Turk (1893: 36): "We are reminded here of the difficulties caused the *Heliand* poet not long before Æ[lfred]'s day by many Christian conceptions and conjunctions." But the change might just as easily have been meant to keep safe the person discovering the errant cattle should charges of theft be subsequently pursued.

[68] Cf. Legatine Capitulary §13 (Dümmler 1895: 24), where the language of Exodus made use of by Alfred in this and subsequent clauses on judging is likewise paraphrased.

MP 46 Ne onfoh ðu næfre médsceattum, forðon hie ablendað ful óft wisra monna geðoht ⁊ hiora word onwendað.

MP 47 Þam elðeodegan ⁊ utan cumenan ne læt ðu no uncuðlice wið hine, ne mid nanu*m* unryhtu*m* þu hine ne drece.

MP 48 Ne swergen ge næfre under hæðne godas, ne on nanum ðingum ne cleopien ge to him.

--- --- --- --- --- --- --- ---

23:8Nec accipias munera quae excaecant etiam prudentes et subvertunt verba iustorum. 23:9Peregrino molestus non eris; [scitis enim advenarum animas, quia et ipsi peregrini fuistis in terra Aegypti.] 23:13[Omnia quae dixi vobis custodite.] Et per nomen externorum deorum non iurabitis neque audietur ex ore vestro.

MP §46 ðu] \þu/ H   médsceattum] metsceattum H   forðon hie] forðon hí G; forðon ðe hy H   ablendað] ablændað H   monna] manna GH   hiora] hyra G; heora H   onwendað] awendaþ H
MP §47 elðeodegan] ælþeodegan G; \ælþeodi/gan H   cumenan] cymenan G   no] na GH   unryhtum] unrihtum G
MP §48 swergen] sweren G; swer\i/gen H   hæðne] hæð\e/ne H   nanum] nænegum G   cleopien] clypigen G; clipien H   him] hym G; heom H

MP 46 Never receive bribes, for they often blind the thoughts of wise men and misdirect their words.

MP 47 The foreigner and he who has come from afar – do not deal unkindly with him, nor may you afflict him with wrongs.[69]

MP 48 Never swear by heathen gods, nor shall you invoke them in any respect [in the course of litigation?].[70]

---

[69] Chapters 10–12, concerning observance of the Sabbath rest, are omitted. *Ine* §20 deals with "a person who has come from far off or a stranger" who is to be regarded as a thief if he strays off the road and doesn't blow a horn.

[70] Alfred's **ne on nanum ðingum,** which implies (only to condemn it) some distinction between major and trivial invocations of other gods, may faintly echo of *Poenitentiale Theodori* I, xv, 1, with its contrast of "major" and "minor" sacrifices (McNeill and Gamer 1938: 198; Finsterwalder 1929: 310): "He who sacrifices to demons in trivial matters shall do penance for one year; but he who [does so] in serious matters shall do penance for ten years" (*Qui immolant demonibus in minimis I annum peniteant. Qui vero in magnis X annos peniteant*). Above all, however, use of *ðingum* refers to the oaths that were the mainstay of judicial proof at this time; the unintended result is a requirement less strict than the Vulgate's.

MP 49 Þis sindan ða domas þe se ælmihtega God self sprecende wæs to Moyse ⁊ him bebead to healdanne; ⁊ siððan se áncenneda Dryhtnes sunu, ure God, þæt is hælend Crist, on middangeard cwom, he cwæð /39r/ ðæt he ne come no ðas bebodu to brecanne ne to forbeodanne, ac mid eallum godum to ecanne; ⁊ mildheortnesse ⁊ eaðmodnesse he lærde.

MP §49 sindan] sindon H ælmihtega] ælmihtiga H self] sylf GH healdanne] healdende G; healdenne H áncenneda] acenneda GH Dryhtnes] godes H ure God] *om.* H is] ys G hælend Crist] hælende crist GH middangeard] woruld H com G; becom H no] na H bebodu] word H (bebodu *added above*) ecanne] icanne G; geecenne H eaðmodnesse] eadmodnesse H

MP 49 These are the judgments that almighty God was speaking himself to Moses and bade him keep; and after the only begotten son of the Lord our God, that is the savior Christ, came into the world, he declared, that he did not come in any way to break or forbid these commandments, but rather to increase them with all good [laws];[71] and he taught mercy and humility.

[71] While Turk held **godum** to be an adjective modifying **bebodu** ("good laws"), Liebermann took it to be a substantive referring to no specific ordinances though semantically linked with **mildheortnesse 7 eaðmodnesse.** Liebermann's interpretation underlies Wormald's rendering: "[H]e said that he came not to break these commandments nor to countermand them, but to extend them with everything good, and he taught mercy and humility" (Wormald 1999a: 421). We should note that *eacan* (here in the inflected form of the infinitive) is no sound rendering of *adimplere*, which earlier and later translators of this scriptural passage into Old English render with some form of the verb *fyllan* (the Gothic cognate of which – *usfulljan* – is likewise employed in Wulfila's fourth-century translation of the Bible: see Streitberg 1965: 3, where it renders πληρῶσαι ("bring to completion")). So Alfred very likely means something by his substitution of *eacan*, a word that, as Wormald's translation captures, typically means "extend, expand upon." The choice is unremarked by Liebermann, but it seems to pose some difficulties for his assumption that Alfred cannot have meant *Gesetze*: laws can only be expanded upon with other laws. And indeed, this is the understanding of this passage likely to have been current in Alfred's day. In the commentary of Jerome that no doubt furnished some of the dominant views of this period, we are told that "those things which, because of the weakness of those who heard them, were rude and unfinished, he brought to completion with his preaching, revoking [allowances] for anger and the exchange of retaliation, prohibiting also lust hidden in the mind" (*ea, quae ante, propter infirmitatem audientium, rudia et inperfecta fuerant, sua predicatione compleuerit, iram tollens et uicem talionis, excludens et occultam in mente concupiscentiam*) (Hurst and Adrien 1969: 26–27). Cf. also Augustine, *De Sermone Domini in Monte* (§9.21), where entry into the kingdom of heaven is held contingent on fulfilling not only the precepts of the Mosaic law but of those "added" (*a me addantur* in Augustine's paraphrase) by Christ (Mutzenbecher 1967: 22). For Alfred, as for his contemporaries, Christ's fulfillment of the law is accomplished by adding some new laws that were implicit in the Torah. Such an understanding of the New Covenant is evident from a subsequent statement (§49.1) in the Prologue that the apostles went *Cristes æ to læranne*, "to teach Christ's law."

Why would this notion have appealed to an Anglo-Saxon lawmaker? Some sense is available from comparison of this text with legislative prologues. In attributing to Christ the intention to supplement (*to ecanne*) the Torah, Alfred makes use of an idiom earlier employed by *Hloðhere and Eadric, Wihtred,* and *Ine* in the prologues to their respective codes, which employ this ambiguous verb to describe the manner in which their ordinances (*domas*) add to the ancestral laws (*æ*) of the Kentish or West-Saxon people. But whereas the earlier codes rely upon both traditional, unwritten laws and royal judgments, speaking of both in such a way as to make distinctions difficult, Alfred locates the origins of law solely in written sources (the Torah, unnamed ecclesiastical synods) and thereby sidesteps the problems of oral law that seem to have been faced by the earliest English-speaking kings to make use of written legislation. See also Chapter 2, 57–59.

MP 49.1 Ða æfter his ðrowunge, ærþam þe his apostolas tofarene wæron geond ealle eorðan to læranne, 7 þa giet ða hie ætgædere wærón, monega hæðena ðeoda hie to Gode gecerdon. Þa hie ealle ætsomne wæron, hie sendan ærendwrecan to Antiohhia 7 to Syrie, Cristes æ to læranne.

MP 49.1 Then after his passion, before his apostles went through all the world to teach, and were still together, they turned many heathen peoples to God. When they all were assembled, they sent messengers to Antioch and to Syria, to teach the law of Christ.[72]

---

[72] The narrative surrounding the apostolic letter to the Gentile Christians of Antioch, Syria, and Cilicia in Acts 15 is compressed beyond recognition. The purpose of use of the written medium in Acts is to clarify for these communities their moral and ritual obligations – matters over which the "Pharisees" among the early Christians had sown confusion with their insistence that these converts observe the laws of Moses as did Jews. Alfred instead presents the letter as a response to the earlier failure of spoken admonitions. The change is senseless – unless we bear in mind the effort throughout the Prologue to diminish the importance of the oral over the written in matters of law. Note that *æ* is now nearly indistinguishable from *dom* in Alfred's text, as was not the case in prior Kentish legislation. (Cf. Wormald 1999a: 95, n. 330.)

MP 49.2 Þa hie ða ongeaton, þæt him ne speow, ða sendon hie ærendgewrit to him. Þis is ðonne þæt ærendgewrit þe ða apostolas sendon ealle to Antiohhia ⁊ to Syria ⁊ to Cilicia, ða sint nu of hæðenum ðeodum to Criste gecirde:

MP 49.3 "Ða apostolas ⁊ þa eldran broðor hælo eow wyscað; ⁊ we eów cyðað, þæt we geascodon, þæt ure geferan sume mid urum wordum to eow comon ⁊ eow hefigran to healdanne þonne we him budon, ⁊ eow to swiðe gedwealdon mid ðam manigfealdum gebodum, ⁊ eowra sawla ma forhwerfdon þonne hie geryhton. Ða gesomnodon we us ymb þæt, ⁊ ús eallum gelicode ða, þæt we sendon Paulus ⁊ Barnaban; ða men wilniað hiora sawla sellan for Dryhtnes naman.

Acts xv ²²Tunc placuit Apostolis et senioribus cum omni ecclesia, eligere uiros ex eis, et mittere Antiocham cum Paulo et Barnaba: Iudam qui cognominatur Barsabbas, et Silam, uiros primos in fratribus: scribentes per manus eorum: ¹⁵:²³Apostoli et seniores fratres, his qui sunt Antiochae, et Syriae, et Ciliciae fratribus ex gentibus, salutem. ¹⁵:²⁴Quoniam audiuimus quia quidam ex nobis exeuntes, turbauerunt uos uerbis, euertentes animas uestras, quibus non mandauimus: ¹⁵:²⁵placuit nobis collectis in unum, eligere uiros et mittere ad uos, cum carissimis nostris Barnaba et Paulo, ¹⁵:²⁶hominibus qui tradiderunt animas suas pro nomine Domini nostri Iesu Christi.

MP §49.2 hie ða ongeaton] hy onge\a/ton H   hie] hy H   ærendgewrit] ærend gewritt H   to him. Þis is ðonne þæt ærendgewrit] *om.* H (*in left margin, a scribe has added* "[æ]rend gewrit to him" *and, in the line immediately below,* "is is ðone þæt")   Antiohhia] antiochia GH   Syria] siria G   Cilicia] cilitia H   sint] sind GH   hæðenum] hæð\e/num H   gecirde] gecyrred G; gecyrrede H

MP §49.3 eldran] ieldran G; yldran H   broðor] broðra H   geascodon] geahsodon G; geaxodon H   comon] coman H   hefigran] hefigran wisan budan GH   healdanne] healdonne H   him] hym G   to swiðe gedwealdon] eow swyðe gedweldon H   manigfealdum] monigfealdum G   forhwerfdon] forhwyrfdon G; for\h/wyr\f/don H   hie geryhton] hie rihton G; heo gerihton H   gesomnodon] gisamnodan G; gesamnoden H   eallum gelicode ða] eallum ða gelicode \þa/ H   sendon] sendan G   ða men wilniað] ða men willað G; ða gewilinað H   hiora] hyra G; hira H   sellan] \to/ syllanne H   him] hym G

MP 49.2 When they perceived that they had no success, then they sent a written message[73] to them. This is the document that the apostles sent together to Antioch and to Syria and to Cilicia, which were then newly turned from heathen observances to Christ:

MP 49.3 "The apostles and the elder brothers wish you health; and we declare to you that we learned, that some of our fellowship came to you with our words and [imposed] on you a heavier burden than we asked, and too greatly led you astray with manifold ordinances, and have ensnared your souls more than they have righted them. Then we assembled ourselves concerning that, and it pleased all of us, that we should send Paul and Barnabas: those men wish to give their souls for the name of the Lord.

---

[73] The same term is used to describe royal writs, and Harmer (1952: 11) notes some of the parallels between Alfred's translation of the letter in Acts 15 and the formulaic elements of these documents.

MP 49.4 Mid him we sendon Iudam ⁊ Silam, þæt eow þæt ilce secggen.

MP 49.5 Þæm halgan Gaste wæs geðuht ⁊ ús, þæt we nane byrðenne on eow settan noldon ofer þæt ðe eow nedðearf wæs to healdanne: þæt [is] ðon*ne*, þæt ge forberen, þæt ge deofol-geld ne weorðien, ne blod ne ðicggen ne asmorod, ⁊ from dier-num geligerum; ⁊ þæt⁷⁴ ge willen, þæt oðre men eów ne don, ne doð ge ðæt oþrum monnum.

MP 49.6 ⁷⁵ Of ðissum anu*m* dome mon mæg geðencean, þæt he æghwelcne on ryht gedemeð; ne ðearf he nanra domboca oþerra. Geðence he, þæt he nanum men ne deme þæt he nolde ðæt he him demde, gif he ðone dóm ofer hine sohte.

- - - - - - - - - - - - - - - -

¹⁵:²⁷Misimus ergo Iudam et Silam, qui et ipsi uobis uerbis referent eadem. ¹⁵:²⁸Uisum est enim Spiritui sancto et nobis, nihil ultra inponere uobis oneris quam haec necessa-rio: ¹⁵:²⁹ut abstineatis uos ab immolatis simulacrorum, et sanguine [suffocato], et for-nicatione: a quibus custodientes uos, bene agetis. Ualete.

MP §49.4 sendon] sendað G; send\on/ H   þæt eow þæt ilce secggen] *þæt eow þæt ilce secgað* G; ðæt \hy/ eow ðæt icle secgan H
MP §49.5 Ðæm] þam G   halgan] halgam G   noldon] noldan G   nedðearf] niedðearf G; nydðearf H   healdanne] healdenne G; heade_ne H   ðæt [is] ðonne] "is" *given in* GH   forberen] forberan GH   deofolgeld] deofolgyld G; diofolgyld H   weorðien] weorðian G; wurðian H   ðicggen] ðicgan GH   from] fram GH   dier-num] dyrnum GH; G *ends with* doþ ge ðæt   willen] willan H   doð] do H
MP §49.6 ðissum] ðy\s/sum H   mon] man H   geðencean] geþencan H   æghwelcne] æghwylcne \dom/ H   gedemeð] \ge/deme H   nanra] nanre H   oþera] oþera \cepan/ H   Geðence] Geðænce H   nolde ðæt he him demde] nolde ðæt man him demde H   sohte] ahte H (E's sohte *in a latter hand, over erasure*)

⁷⁴ Changed from *þet* by scribe.
⁷⁵ Scribe later added -I- in margin to mark first paragraph of the laws proper. This is surely misplaced.

MP 49.4 With them we sent Judas and Silas, that they might say the same to you.

MP 49.5 It seemed to the Holy Ghost and to us, that we did not wish to impose on you any burden beyond what was needful to hold: that is, then, that you abandon the worship of devils, that you taste neither blood nor strangled [animals], and [that you keep] from [engagement in] fornication;[76] and what you wish that other men not do to you, do not to other men."[77]

MP 49.6 From this one judgment one may reason in such a way that he judge each man rightly; he requires no other book of laws. Let him think that he judge no man in a manner that he would not be judged by him, if he sought judgment over him.

---

[76] For the most part, a faithful rendering, with the exception of **þæt ge deofolgeld ne weorðien**. Though this does not disagree with the prohibition announced in the Vulgate, it is somewhat more sweeping. The worship of pagan deities remained a temptation for the newly converted in this era. Notable evidence for the durability of pre-Christian belief is the settlement negotiated in Iceland in the year 1000, which made baptism compulsory but did not forbid worship of other gods so long as this was done privately. See Miller 1991: 2085. On **diernum geligerum** and its ambiguities, see MP §6 and n.

[77] It has often been noted (Hodgkin 1906: 300; Plummer 1902: 124) that this negative statement of the Golden Rule appended by Alfred to the text of the "council" may show his dependence upon a quite early manuscript of the Vulgate. This may be so; yet Liebermann suggests (III: 48) that such speculations are unnecessary, for close enough parallels may be found, for example, in Tobit 4:16: *Quod ab alio odis fieri tibi vide ne alteri tu aliquando facias*. Inexact renderings of this saying occur as well in Ælfric's explication of the Lord's Prayer ("Feria III De Dominica Oratione"; Clemoes 1997: 327) and in the work of Wulfstan (Napier 1883: 29 [III], 73 [X], 112 [XXII]); cf. also *Grið* §12. The version in Alfred is, in Liebermann's view, simply the proverbial form.

MP 49.7 Siððan ðæt þa gelamp, þæt monega ðeoda Cristes geleafan onfengon, þa wurdon monega seonoðas geond ealne middangeard gegaderode, ⁊ eac swa geond Angelcyn, siððan hie
Cristes geleafan onfengon, halegra biscepa ⁊ eác oðerra geðun-
genra witena; hie ða gesetton, for ðære mildheortnesse þe Crist
lærde, æt mæstra hwelcre misdæde þætte ða weoruldhlafor-
das[78] moston mid hiora leafan buton synne æt þam forman
gylte þære fiohbote ónfon, þe hie ða gesettan; buton æt hlafordsearwe hie nane mildheortnesse ne dorston gecweðan,
forþam ðe God ælmihtig þam nane ne gedemde þe hine ofer-
hogdon, ne Crist Godes sunu þam nane ne gedemde þe hine to
deaðe sealde, ⁊ he bebead þone hlaford lufian swa hine.

MP §49.7 Siððan] Syþþan H   monega] manega H   onfengon] underfengon
H   monega] manega H   seonoðas] synoðas H   middangeard] middan eard H   swa
geond] swylce on H   angelcyn] angelcynne H   siððan hie] syððan hy H   geleafan]
\ge/leafan H   halegra biscepa] haligra biscopa H   hie] hy H   mildheortnesse] mild-
heornnesse H   hwelcre] gehwylcere H   ðætte] ðæt H   weoruldhlafordas] woruldhla-
fordas H   hiora] he\o/ra H   fiohbote] fohbota H   þe hie ða gesettan] *om.* H   buton
æt hlafordsearwe] butan \æt hlafordsearwe/ H   hie] ðe hy ða ?gesetton H (*water
damage*)   þam nanege demde] ðam nane \mildheortnesse/ ne gedemde H   oferhog-
don] oferhogodon H   sealed] gesealde H   hine] hine selfne H

[78] *Hapax legomenon.*

MP 49.7 After it happened that many peoples received the faith of Christ, then many synods were gathered through all the world, and also among the English, after they received the faith of Christ, of holy bishops and also of other distinguished counselors; they then established, because of the mercy that Christ taught, that worldly lords might with their leave [and] without sin receive the monetary payment that they [the bishops] established at the first offense for most of those misdeeds; but for betrayal of one's lord they dared not proclaim any mercy, for God almighty judged none for those who despised him, nor did Christ, God's son, grant any [mercy] to those who gave him to death,[80] and he laid down [that one should] love one's lord just as oneself.[81]

---

[80] The familiar passage to which Alfred's description of the Passion seems expressly contrary ("And then Jesus said, 'Father, forgive them; for they know not what they do'") occurs only in the gospel of St. Luke (23:34). Identical sentiments are given utterance by St. Peter (Acts 3:17) and by St. Stephen on the verge of his martyrdom (Acts 7:60), but for audiences with limited access to biblical texts, Christ's petition was, perhaps, a detail easily missed. Its isolation in narratives of the Passion to Luke's gospel, along with (perhaps) the Germanic literary tradition of depicting Christ as a warrior, may have contributed to its omission where we might expect it in *The Dream of the Rood*. This line of reasoning should not be pressed too far, however, as Luke 23:34 seems to have captured the imagination of whoever composed the *Hêliand*, where it receives an expansive translation (ll. 5539–5542): "He did not wish, however, for that deed to be avenged on the wrathful Jews, but he bade mighty God, the father, that he not be wrathful to that company of men, to that nation, 'because they do not know what they do'" (*huand sia ni uuitun, huat sia duot*) (Behagel 1882 (rev. 1984: 195)). Alfred's text probably alludes here to the text of Psalm 68 [69], whose details were conventionally read as anticipating the Passion (68:22 "And they gave me gall for food, and in my thirst, they gave me vinegar to drink"), and whose imprecations (68:25 "Pour out thy indignation upon them, and let the heat of thy wrath take hold of them") are quoted by Peter (Acts 1:20) in reference to Judas. As an interpretative statement, this clause of the Prologue is not, strictly speaking, in error. Cf. also the laws of Alfred (n. 32), where Chapter 12 of the Legatine Capitulary (quoted in full) illustrates the extent to which Alfred's thinking is in this instance perfectly conventional.

[81] A theme repeated at MP §37. On this passage, Wormald has suggested that Alfred's "loyalty obsession" (manifest in laws such as §45 of the code proper, "the sole law to this effect in all the early medieval West") may account for "how [Alfred's] preface came to make the unique and bizarre claim that Christ ordered that one love one's lord as oneself" (Wormald 1999a: 283). A solemn duty to fight and die for one's lord is indeed, as Wormald notes here, a preoccupation running through not only texts attributed to Alfred but texts composed at his instigation or on his behalf. See also *Alfred* §§1.1, 4.2.

MP 49.8 Hie ða on monegum senoðum monegra menniscra misdæda bote gesetton, 7 on monega senoðbéc⁷⁹ hie writan, hwær
anne dom hwær oþerne.

MP §49.8 Hie] Hy H   monegum senoðum] manigum \synoþ*um*/ H   monegra] manegra H   gesetton] gesettan H   monega] manegra H   senoðbec] synoþbec H   hie] hy
H   writan] writon H   anne] ænne

---

⁷⁹ *Hapax legomenon.*

MP 49.8 Then they established in many synods the remedies for the various misdeeds of men, and they wrote in many books of synodal decrees, in one place one judgment and in one place another.

8

The Laws of Alfred

The text of Alfred's laws given here differs in numeration from all modern editions beginning with Schmid's. The divergence begins with §5 (headed by the Roman numeral VI due to the assignment of the first rubric number to a concluding section of the Prologue). Contained under this heading according to the prior numeration are the main clause and first four subclauses dealing with sanctuary, but also a fifth subclause stipulating that theft on certain holy days and during Lent should be fined double. Without the influence of the rubrication (the incoherence of which is established at 183–184), this final clause would almost surely have been made independent by previous editors. The illogic of the received numeration is likewise shown in, e.g. §§10–11 (Liebermann's §§9–9.2) and §42 (Liebermann's 40.2). But to avoid confusion, we have also included (where clause numbers differ) the standard edition numbers in square brackets preceded by an L (for Liebermann). As Liebermann's numeration follows that of his modern predecessors, the clause numbers given in square brackets may be expected to be the same for Schmid's and Thorpe's editions. Thus our §6 designates Liebermann's (and others') §5.5.

The extent to which Alfred relied, as he claims at the outset of his laws, on other texts is one of the major questions facing an editor of the *domboc*. A full account of this problem is given in Chapter 2, but a brief recapitulation seems appropriate here. With the exception of the personal injury tariffs written in evident mimicry of Æthelberht's (but without directly reproducing them), the structure of Alfred's laws does not help elucidate whence the borrowings issued, though their apparent formlessness may itself be in observance of prior legislative convention. As Wormald points out, it is not an "accident that the only 'barbarian' code as disorganized as Alfred's was Ine's," the latter perhaps having served as a kind of "model" for the former.[1] Even the influence from Æthelberht's laws seems to have taken the form of inspiration rather than outright borrowing. While the list of injury tariffs with which *Alfred* concludes follows (at least at first) the head-to-toe layout of *Æthelberht* (and indeed, of all the "barbarian" laws), the monetary penalties assigned in *Alfred* differ pronouncedly from those in *Æthelberht*. A second list of tariffs includes rulings paralleled in *Æthelberht* that are omitted from the initial schedule but also departs from *Æthelberht* by adding new clauses; these may rely on an earlier, perhaps orally transmitted tradition given parallels with Frisian laws (see Oliver 2015).

The second source named by Alfred is included in his own appendix: the laws of his West-Saxon ancestor, Ine. Both texts constituted for their earliest readers a somewhat disorderly whole of more-or-less uniform normative force in spite of Alfred's assertion that he meant for Ine's laws to be held "in another way." The rubricator's numeration of Ine's laws as coextensive with Alfred's made it inevitable that distinctions between the two texts would blur in the minds of subsequent legislators. That they were so joined probably owed as much to the rubricator's numerological scheme as the content of the respective "codes." *Ine* contains twenty clauses on theft, while *Alfred* has a mere two. With respect to theft, then, we could assume that at least some of Ine's edicts were still viable, a conclusion seemingly borne out by an allusion to Ine's laws in the legislation of Edward the Elder.[2] Yet some of Ine's rulings must have been only historical at the time of Alfred's compilation. While Ine's kingdom was concerned with devising regulations for Welsh subjects under West-Saxon rule, this differentiation was probably less relevant centuries later.

The relationship of Ine's to Alfred's laws as originally envisaged by the latter (as opposed to the place *Ine* was assumed to have in the

---

[1] Wormald 1999a: 270.
[2] *II Edward* §5.2.

domboc immediately after Alfred's death) is further suggested by the several instances in which clauses of *Ine* are emended in *Alfred*. These emendations have the effect of strengthening the position of a central authority and are thus in keeping with Alfredian preoccupations exhibited elsewhere in the *domboc* (e.g., MP §§37, 49.7). For example, *Ine* §44 stipulates that a man must pay 30 shillings for each of the first three trees (belonging to another) that he fells. *Alfred* §14 requires only a 5-shilling payment for each large tree, but adds a 30-shilling fine payable to the fisc. *Ine* §25 requires a merchant engaging in business "out in the countryside" to do so in the presence of witnesses. *Alfred* §35 stipulates that these witnesses must be pre-approved by the king's reeve. (Centralization can also be the motive for *Alfred* §11, which corrects discrepant fines.) *Ine* §45 sets the fine for breaking into the fortified dwelling of a king or bishop at 120 shillings. *Alfred* §41 emends this: the fine remains 120 for the king's dwelling, but is only 90 for an archbishop's and a scant 60 for a bishop's. The recompense for an ealdorman drops from 80 to 60, and for a king's thegn from 60 to 30. A single aim seems to underlie these disparate rulings.

The last of the sources mentioned by Alfred are the laws of the Mercian king Offa. Any vernacular record of these is no longer extant, but Wormald was certain (Wormald 1999a: 106–107) that by the "laws" of Offa Alfred meant the Legatine Capitulary. This work of ecclesiastical legislation was composed at the urging of Pope Hadrian by George and Theophylact, bishops of Ostia and Todi respectively. The history of this document is perhaps best given in its own words:[3]

We were first received by Jænberht, archbishop of the holy church of *Dorovernia* [Canterbury], which is called by another name, Kent, where St. Augustine rests in the body, and residing there we advised him of those things which were necessary. Journeying from there, we arrived at the court of Offa, king of the Mercians. And he received both us and the sacred letters sent from the highest see with immense joy and honour on account of his reverence for the blessed Peter and your apostolate. Then Offa, king of the Mercians, and Cynewulf, king of the West Saxons, met together in a council; and to him also we delivered your holy writings; and they promised

---

[3] Dümmler 1895: 20–21; Whitelock 1955: 770–771.

forthwith that they would reform these vices. Then, when counsel had been taken with the aforesaid kings, bishops and elders of the land, we, considering that the corner of the world extends far and wide, allowed Theophylact, the venerable bishop, to visit the king of the Mercians and the parts of Britain.

Myself, however, taking with me a helper, [...] I went on into the region of the Northumbrians, to King Ælfwold and Eanbald, archbishop of the holy church of the city of York. [...] [The king] forthwith with all joy fixed a day for a council, at which assembled all the chief men of the region, both ecclesiastical and secular. But it was related in our hearing that there were other, no less serious vices requiring correction there; for, as you know, since the time of the holy pontiff, Augustine, no Roman priest has been sent there except ourselves. We wrote a capitulary concerning the various matters and produced them in their hearing, treating all of them in order.

Keynes and Lapidge (1983: 305 n. 5) note that "the capitulary was later read out, both in Latin and in the vernacular, in a Mercian council convened by Offa."

Though the Legatine Capitulary deserves more attention than it has received from historians of English law, and while Alfred and his circle may well have been aware of it, evidence for use of the document as a source during the preparation of the *domboc* seems ambiguous: the connections are few and mostly fairly general (but see §9 and n). Furthermore, while some clauses from the capitulary have loose parallels in the laws of Ine, no one has ever suggested a relationship of any kind between these two texts (§2 of the capitulary addresses the carrying out of baptism; §17 concerns tithing: both, as we have seen, are prominent concerns in *Ine*). The same applies to the laws of Wihtred (§15 of the capitulary prohibits unjust and incestuous marriages; cf. *Wihtred* §§3–5 [L3–6]; §19 of the capitulary urges casting out pagan customs and obstinate pagans; cf. *Wihtred* §§9–10 [L12–13]). Sometimes the evils condemned by the capitulary are described in such broad terms that it would be surprising if more legislation of the period did not furnish parallels to its language, as in its condemnation at §14 of "deception, violence and robbery" ([*f*]*raus, violentia et rapina*). If the clauses just mentioned suggest anything, it is that early medieval legislators sometimes spoke in similar ways merely because they brought to similar problems a shared view of the world. If any reverberations of the

Legatine Capitulary are indeed discernible in Alfred's laws, this may owe more to Alfred's relationship with the remnants of the Mercian clerical elite than direct consultation of the text. Alfred lists the Mercian bishop Wærferth as one of his closest counselors. We know that Wærferth was responsible for the translations of the *Dialogues of Gregory the Great* into Old English, and a Mercian element in the vocabulary of Alfredian prose (evident to Wormald in the term *boldgetæl*, which occurs as well in the *Dialogues*) has long been noted.[4] But if Wærferth or others in Alfred's circle were familiar with the Legatine Capitulary, even this would not require us to believe that, when referring to Offa's laws, Alfred really had in mind this particular document, which (as will be seen) Alfred's resemble in only the most general way.

In all likelihood, Alfred claimed to derive his laws from those of Kent and Mercia so as to soothe the feelings of new subjects amid the expanded sway of Wessex over neighboring kingdoms. The legal traditions of Kent and Mercia were thenceforth subsumed into those of the new West-Saxon hegemony, laying the groundwork for a greater kingdom of the English, a notion already foreshadowed in the ethnic nomenclature employed by Ine's laws.

A summary account ought to be given here as well of the seeming "innovations" of Alfred's laws, a term used with the concession that such clauses may give only the appearance of novelty amid the near-silence of the legislative record in England at this time. His text begins by mentioning the importance of keeping one's oath and pledge. Whether or not this refers to an oath of loyalty to the king has been debated, though the hypothesis may be strengthened by the fact that this section is immediately followed by the first Anglo-Saxon laws against treason. Yet a review of these clauses in the present study (Chapter 3, 102–111) suggests that they were devised with different purposes in mind; some bear signs of influence from Alfred's clerical advisors. The famous clause about a man impaling himself on the spear of another is among the first English ordinances to address overtly what later periods would call the question of *mens rea* (also dealt with in *MP* §13). Lastly, although Alfred is not the first to address assault (such rulings date back to the laws of

---

4   Wormald 1999a: 274.

Æthelberht), his text contains a much greater number and percentage of such clauses than that of any other legislator, even excluding the personal injury tariffs. Where Ine focuses on offenses concerning property, Alfred's concern is to a great extent with offenses concerning persons.

Some discrepancies between the valuation of currency during the reigns of Ine and Alfred are worth noting here. In the time of Ine, the West-Saxon shilling contained four pennies; by the time of Alfred it was valued at five pennies (see n. 30 to §4.1 and n. 168 to §50 for calculations of the ratio in *Alfred*). All interpretations of fines should take this difference into account.[5]

---

[5] We are grateful to Rory Naismith for helping us with these calculations. For an overview of coinage in early Wessex, see Blackburn 2003.

[{ɪ}]⁶

Prologue [L49.9]⁷ Ic ða Ælfred cyning þás togædere gegaderode ⁊ awritan het, monege þara þe ure foregengan heoldon, ða ðe me licodon; ⁊ manege þara þe me ne licodon ic áwearp /40r/ mid minra witena geðeahte, ⁊ on oðre wisan bebead to healdanne.

Af Prol. awritan] awriten H   monege] manige H   þa ðe] \þara/ ðe H   licodon] licedan H   manege] monige H   licodon] lycodon H   awearp] awe\a/rp H   minra] minre H   on oðre] \on/ oðre H   healdanne] healdenne H

---

⁶ The first Roman numeral referring to the rubric list is placed in the margin before *MP* §49.6. The rubric heading reads: *Beðon þæt mon ne scyle oþrum deman butan swa he wille þæt him mon deme* ("Concerning that one should not judge another except as he wishes that he shall be judged"). The next Roman numeral does not appear until the first clause of Alfred's code proper, following a long paragraph on Alfred's method in selecting the rulings to be included.
⁷ In the margin in a secretary hand is written: *hae leges referant ad Ina in fodere legum saxonum* ("These laws refer to Ine in the compact of the laws of the Saxons").

Prologue [L49.9] Then I, Alfred the king, gathered these[8] [rulings] together and commanded to be written many of them which our ancestors held – those that pleased me. And many of them that did not please me I discarded with the consent of my counselors,[9] and directed them to be held in a different manner.

[8] Wormald (1999a: 279) claims "the 'þas' of Alfred's opening sentence could as well look back to 'synod-books' from all over the world, England included, as forward to the predecessors he was about to name. [...] This passage was thus saying two different things: on the one hand, he made (some) selections from the accepted legislation of Christendom; on the other, he gathered up some of his English predecessor's decrees and *left the rest alone*." But see Chapter 2, 69–75.

[9] Oliver 2015 discusses the expertise of these counselors. Among them was Grimbald of Saint-Bertin, who could well have brought knowledge of canon law of the sort exhibited in the Prologue. Pratt (2007: 161) maintains that parallels between the *MP* and the writings of Archbishop Fulk of Reims can be linked through Grimbald. Two clauses, both in the personal injury tariffs (§47 and §71), demonstrate unambiguous knowledge of the laws of Æthelberht, although these do not seem to have served as the basis for any rulings outside the schedule of compensations for personal injury. There are also several overlaps in rare vocabulary, among them: *ceas* ("strife"), *ciricfrið* ("church peace"), *edorbrecþ* ("hedge break") *fæderenmæg* ("paternal kin.") Furthermore, the personal injury tariffs share many rulings with the *Lex Frisionum* to the exclusion of other barbarian legal compilations, although this probably indicates shared practice rather than actual familiarity with the Carolingian text. Wormald (1999a: 277) points out that Alfred's words here repeat a *topos* of legislative modesty found as early as the seventh Novella of Justinian and conventional in Frankish, Lombard, and Carolingian compilations.

Forðam ic ne dorste geðristlæcan þara minra awuht fela on gewrit settan, forðam me wæs uncuð, hwæt þæs ðam lician wolde ðe æfter ús wæren. Ac ða ðe ic gemette awðer oððe on Ines dæge, mines mæges, oððe on Offan Mercna cyninges, oððe on Æþelbryhtes þe ærest fulluhte onfeng on Angelcynne, þa ðe me ryhtoste ðuhton, ic þa heron gegaderode, ⁊ þa oðre forlét.

[L49.10] Ic ða Ælfred Westseaxna cyning eallum minum witum þas geeowde, ⁊ hie ða cwædon, þæt him þæt licode eallum to healdanne.

---

forðam] forðon H   wæren] wæron H   ða ðe] þa þa H   awðer] aþær H   mercna] myrc\e/na H   æþelbryhtes] æþelberhte H   fulluhte] fulluht H   rihtoste] rihtest H   forlet] forlett H   west seaxna] west seaxena H   cyning] cyng H   geeowde] geowde H   hie] hy H   him] heom H   to healdanne] wel to healdene H

Thus I did not dare presume to set many of mine in writing, because it was not known to me, what would please those who came after us. But those that I found either from the time of Ine, my kinsman,[10] or of Offa, king of the Mercians,[11] or of Æthelberht who first in England received baptism,[12] those which seemed most just to me, I gathered herein, and left out the others.[13]

[L49.10] I, Alfred, king of the West Saxons, then presented these [rulings] to all my counselors, and they then said, that it pleased them all to hold [them].

---

[10] Alfred's ancestor Ingield was Ine's brother.

[11] Offa was king of the Mercians 757 to 796.

[12] Æthelberht acceded to the Kentish throne sometime between 587 and 590, and ruled until 616x618. His laws were probably promulgated after 597, which saw the arrival of Augustine's mission in Kent, and before the death of Augustine sometime between 604 and 610.

[13] Wormald points out that "Alfred was [here] professing a greater respect for precedent than he actually practised" (Wormald 1999a: 279). He makes no reference to Kentish laws that followed Æthelberht's – those promulgated by Hloþhere and Eadric between 679 and 686 and Wihtred in 695, nor does he mention the laws of the Kentish king Eorconberht (known only through remarks in Bede, *Historia Ecclesiastica* iii.8). Yet Alfred's laws manifest in the Prologue (see Chapter 2, 57–59) some awareness of Hloþhere and Eadric's laws and perhaps of Wihtred's.

{11}

1 Æt ærestan we lærað, þæt mæst ðearf ís, þæt æghwelc mon his að 7 his wed wærlice healde.

1.1 Gif hwa to hwæðrum þissa genied sie on woh, oððe to hlafordsearwe oððe to ængum unryhtum fultume, þæt is þonne ryhtre to áleoganne þonne to gelæstanne.

Af §1 æghwelc mon] æghwilc man H   wed] wedd H   hwæðrum þissa] hwæðerum þisra H   genied] genyd H   sie] sy H   ængum] ænigum H   unryhtum] unrihtum H   is] *om.* H   ryhtre] rihtre H   aleoganne] aleogenne H

1   First we instruct, that it is most needful, that each man should prudently keep his oath and his vow.[14]

1.1 If someone is wrongfully forced to either of these things – either to treason against one's lord or to any unlawful assistance – then it is better to repudiate [the oath] than to perform it.[15]

---

[14] Keynes and Lapidge (1983: 306 n. 6) point out that:

This law would presumably cover all oaths and pledges made in the normal course of affairs, on which order in Anglo-Saxon society depended; but Alfred may have had uppermost in his mind an oath of loyalty sworn to him by his subjects [...] It may have been Alfred, consciously following Carolingian example [...], who first introduced a general oath of loyalty to the king; later Anglo-Saxon kings themselves followed suit.

Thomas (2014: 102–103) holds that "the Alfredian law marks a turning point in the history of early medieval law in that it for the first time equates criminal activity – particularly theft or connivance in theft – with a breach of fidelity." Both Wormald and Pratt argue similarly (see Pratt 2007: 232–238 and citations therein). A Carolingian model could have been provided by the oath of 802, "required from all freemen over the age of 12, which equated fidelity with a whole range of obligations in respect of God, ruler and justice" (Pratt 2007: 234). Little evidence exists for such an oath in Alfred's England apart from Charter S 362, dated to 901, which discusses the forfeiture of the estates of Ealdormann Wulfhere (see Pratt 2007: 239). Cf. also Legatine Capitulary §18 (Dümmler 1895: 26): "The eighteenth chapter: Of the vows of Christians, and that they be fulfilled. For through this the ancient patriarchs and prophets pleased God" (*Decimum octavum caput. De voto christianorum, ut impleant illud. Antiqui namque patriarchae et prophetae per hoc placuerunt Domino*). For further discussion of this section, see Chapter 3, 107–109.

[15] Keynes and Lapidge (1983: 306, n. 7) indicate that "Alfred is here reiterating a principle previously enunciated by Bede (and before him, by Origen) that it is better to leave an oath unfulfilled if the performance of it will entail a worse crime than the act of oath-breaking itself." Fruscione (2014: 46) points out that "Alfred is the first king in England to be influenced by the Roman concept of *laesae maiestatis* (*hlafordsearo*), brought to England through the Church. The prohibition of treachery is part of a group of laws pertaining to kingship which together aimed to protect the king and his power."

1.2 [Gif he þonne þæs weddie þe hym riht sy to gelæstanne]¹⁶ ꝺ
þæt aleoge, selle mid eaðmedum his wæpn ꝺ his æhta his freondum
to gehealdanne ꝺ beo feowertig nihta on carcerne on cyninges tune;
ðrowige ðær swa biscep him scrife, ꝺ his mægas hine feden, gif he
self mete næbbe.

Af §1.2 selle] sylle H   eaðmedum] eadmedum H   his] hys H   gehealdanne] gehecal-
denne H   feowertig] .XL. H   on] æt H   ðrowige] þrowie H   biscep] biscop
H   feden] fedan H   self] sylf H

¹⁶ From *Textus Roffensis* (H). The variant also occurs in Liebermann's *Ld* and *So*
(with different orthography) and may derive in these sixteenth-century texts either
from H or (somewhat less likely) a witness no longer extant.

1.2 [If he should, however, pledge himself to that which it is right for him to perform] and [subsequently] repudiate it, let him humbly give his weapons and his possessions to his friend-group[17] to hold, and let him be in the prison[18] on an estate of the king for forty nights, and there undergo [penance?] in accordance with what the bishop prescribes,[19] and let his kinsman feed him, if he himself has no food.

---

[17] Alexander Murray plausibly suggests that the "friend-group" should be seen as "not a strict kin-group at all, but as a kindred-based group composed of interested relatives, friends and dependents" (Murray 1983: 136. See Oliver 2002: 75, fn. e for further discussion.)

[18] In his translation of Augustine's *Soliloquies*, Alfred describes "the estates of every king (*ælces cynges hama*): some men are in the chamber, some in the hall, some on the threshing floor, some in prison (*on carcerne*)"; he further refers to "men who in this life, are brought to a king's prison (*kincges carcerne gebrohte*)" (Keynes and Lapidge 1983: 144 and 151 respectively; Carnicelli 1969: 77 and 96). *Alfred* §1.2 is the first reference to imprisonment in Anglo-Saxon law. Thomas (2014: 105) claims that "the closest parallel for the *domboc*'s association of penitence and incarceration are to be found" in "the relatively extensive documention of the Frankish church. [...] [I]ncarceration is also prescribed for members of the secular clergy in the writings of Chrodegang of Metz and Theodulf of Orléans, both of whom also attest the penitential function of the prison." Thomas goes on (110–112) to claim, however, that the use of prisons was very rare: "[T]his was an innovative use of a largely unfamiliar judicial punishment," and "the ideological motivation behind this innovation was not sufficiently strongly felt to leave a lasting mark upon judicial practice in late Anglo-Saxon England."

[19] Liebermann claims that the referent is not penance in the strict sense, while Oakley (1923: 145 n. 3) sees this as the first mention of penance in West-Saxon law. The latter position seems eminently reasonable. That the church should hold jurisdiction over the offense of perjury is to be expected: oaths were sworn at the altar or involved other sacred objects (Oakley 1923: 187–188). Thomas (2014: 104–105) shows just how thoroughly this provision of Alfred's laws is suffused with ecclesiastical discipline:

> The verb *scrifan* used here is part of a well-developed Old English vocabulary relating to penance. Moreover, both the specification that the penance is to be appointed by a bishop and the stipulation that the offender relinquish his weapons [...] mirror the prescriptions associated with the performance of public penance – reserved for the expiation of serious faults – in contemporary Continental documentation. Similarly, the sentence of forty nights' imprisonment in the Alfredian code recalls both the common use of the forty-day period in the prescriptions of penitential handbooks, and the Lenten period during which those undertaking public penance were excluded from the church.

For discussion of the connection between oath-breaking and penance in the Fonthill letter, see Roach 2012: 347–348.

1.3 Gif he mægas næbbe oððe þone mete næbbe, fede cyninges gerefa hine.

1.4 Gif hine mon togenedan scyle, ⁊ he elles nylle, gif hine mon gebinde, þolige his wæpna ⁊ his ierfes.²⁰

1.5 Gif hine mon ófslea, licgge he orgilde.²¹

1.6 Gif he út oðfleo ær þam fierste, ⁊ hine mon gefó, sie he feowertig nihta /40v/ on carcerne, swa he ær sceolde.

1.7 Gif he losige, sie he afliemed ⁊ sie ámænsumod óf eallum Cristes ciricum.

1.8 Gif þær ðonne oþer mennisc borg sie, bete þone borgbryce swa him ryht wisie, ⁊ ðone wedbryce swa him his scrift scrife.

Af §1.3 næbbe² *om.* H
Af §1.4 togenedan] togenydan H þolige] þolie H ierfes] yrfes H
Af §1.5 mon] man H licgge] lecge H orgilde] orgylde H
Af §1.6 ærþam] ærþan H fierste] fyrste H mon] man H sie] sy H feowertig] .XL. H sceolde] sc\e/olde H
Af §1.7 Gif he losige] Gif he þonne losie H sie] sy H afliemed] aflymed H sie] sy H ámænsumod] amansemod H ciricum] cyricum H
Af §1.8 borg] borh H sie] sy H borgbryce] borhbrice H wedbryce] wedbrice H

²⁰ This generally means "inheritance," but see *MP* §11 and *Ine* §6 for parallel uses as "possessions."
²¹ *Hapax legomenon*, but cf. *ægild*.

1.3 If he has no kinsmen or has no food, let the king's reeve feed him.

1.4 If he has to be forced thither, and he resists, if he needs to be bound, let him forfeit his weapons and his property.[22]

1.5 If he is killed [while resisting], let him lie without wergild.[23]

1.6 If he escapes before the due time, and he is caught, let him be forty nights in prison, as he should have been before.

1.7 If he escapes, let him be banished and excommunicated from all churches of Christ.

1.8 If other(s) stand(s) surety for him, let him pay for his breach of surety as law indicates, and for the breach of faith as his confessor prescribes.

---

[22] We concur with Liebermann's assessment that this refers to personal property, not estates that would belong to the family.

[23] Liebermann says the responsibility for binding him and bringing him to justice belongs to the accusers; it is also they who are released from the obligation to pay wergild if he is killed in the act of resisting justice.

{III}

2 Gif hwa þara mynsterhama hwelcne for hwelcere scylde gesece, þe cyninges feorm to belimpe, oððe oðerne frione hiered þe árwyrðe sie, age he þreora nihta fierst him to gebeorganne, buton he ðingian wille.

2.1 Gif hine mon on ðam fierste geyflige mid slege oððe mid bende oððe þurh wunde, bete þara æghwelc mid ryhte ðeodscipe, ge mid were ge mid wite, ⁊ þam hiwum hundtwelftig scill ciricfriðes²⁴ to bote ⁊ næbbe his agne forfongen.

Af §2 þara] þæra H   hwelcne for hwelcere scylde gesece] hwylcne gesece for hwylcere scylde H   frione hiered] freonne hyred H   sie] sy H   fierst] fyrst H
Af §2.1 mon] man H   fierste] fyrste H   geyflige] geyflie H   slege] slæge H   þara æghwelc] þæra æghwylc H   hundtwelftig] .CXX.   to] *om.* H   næbbe] hæbbe H   agne forfongen] agen forfangen H

²⁴ This compound appears elsewhere only in the laws of Æthelberht (§6) and Wulfstan's *Institutes of Polity*; it lends some support to Alfred's claim that he drew on Æthelberht's laws.

2 If someone for whatever offense should seek out some sanctuary that is supported by the king's render[25] or another free and honorable [religious] househould, let him have a three-night time period to protect himself [therein],[26] unless he wishes to settle.

2.1 If he is harmed during that time period with a blow or by binding or through a wound, let each of them compensate according to lawful regulations both with wergild and with fine, and to the household [of the minster] 120 shillings as compensation for [breach of] church peace, and he [who harmed him] shall not receive his own [compensation otherwise due him].

[25] For render see *Ine* §72 and n. Asser §102 mentions "the two monasteries which he [Alfred] himself had instituted (*quae ipse fieri imperaverat*)" (Keynes and Lapidge 1983: 107; Stevenson 1959: 88). These were Athelney and Shaftesbury; he had planned a monastery and convent (later Nunnaminster), but these were not completed until after his death. (See also Pratt 2007: 45–48.)

[26] Schmid clarifies the clause thus: a minster that does not belong to the king's property (hence they must pay render) or a free religious brotherhood are both granted a limited entitlement to offer sanctuary. (If the minster were under direct protection of the king, the fine for breach of sanctuary would be 5 pounds, as in §3.) Thorpe suggests that the **frio hired** might be "a monastery of private foundation, but free from the bishop's jurisdiction, having the right of electing their own head, the free disposal of their temporalities, and enjoying the privilege of *jus asyli*." Dyer (1980: 14–19) describes for the area around Worcester "the creation of a number of well-endowed minster churches (*monasterii*) in the seventh and eighth centuries [...] The charters show that these early minsters were family property and were inherited, sometimes through a number of generations." *Alfred* §5 stipulates that the church would allow a seven-day asylum period; this clause reduces the period to three days for the monastic household.

{IIII}

3 Gif hwa cyninges borg abrece, gebete þone tyht swa him ryht wisie, 7 þæs borges bryce, mid v pundum mærra pæninga. Ærcebiscepes borges bryce oððe his mundbyrd gebete mid ðrim pundum. Oðres biscepes oððe ealdormonnes borges bryce oððe mundbyrd gebete mid twam pundum.

{v}

4 Gif hwa ymb cyninges feorh sierwe, ðurh hine oððe ðurh wreccena feormunge oððe his manna, sie he his feores scyldig 7 ealles þæs ðe he age.

 4.1 Gif he hine selfne triowan wille, do þæt be cyninges wergelde.
/41r/

Af §3 borg] borh H tyht] tihtlan H pæninga] peninga H ærcebiscepes] Ercebiscopes H ðrim] .III. H biscepes] bisceopes B (B's *version commences at* "Oþres bisceopes"); biscopes H ealdormonnes] ealdormannes B; ealdermannes H bryce] brice H twam] .II. B
Af §4 sierwe] syrwie BH wreccena] \eard/wreccena B; wrecena H feormunge] feormung B sie] sy BH
Af §4.1 selfne] sylfne BH triowan] treowsian B; treowan H wergelde] wergylde BH

3 If someone breaches the king's security,[27] let him compensate for that offense as law indicates, and for the breach of that security with 5 pounds of greater pennies.[28] Let him compensate breaching an archbishop's security or violation of his *mund* with three pounds. Let him compensate breaching the security of a bishop [of other rank] or an ealdorman, or the violation of [their] *mund* with two pounds.

4 If someone plots against the king's life, either by his own actions, or by the harboring of those who have been banished or of his men,[29] let him be liable for his life and all that he owns.

4.1 If he wishes to exculpate himself, let him do so by [an oath in the amount of] the king's wergild.[30]

---

[27] Cf. *Æthelberht* §5.

[28] "Greater pennies" are both heavier and cast of pure silver. (See DuCange 1883–1887: s.v. *denarii meri et bene pesantes*.)

[29] The referent of "his" in **his manna** is hopelessly ambiguous.

[30] The *Anglo-Saxon Chronicle* s.a. 694 states that "This year the people of Kent settled with Ine, and gave him 30,000 in friendship, because they had burned his brother Mul"; see also Chapter 1, 21–24. *Mircna Laga* §2 gives the same figure for a king's wergild: *Ðonne bið cynges anfeald wergild syx þegna wer be Myrcna laga, þæt is xxx þusend sceatta ⁊ þæt bið ealles cxx punda* ("Then the king's single wergild is the *wer* of six thanes according to the law of the Mercians, that is 30 thousand *sceattas* and that is in all 120 pounds.") As Attenborough points out, the wergilds for kings were thus the same in Mercia and Wessex. If the Wessex shilling contained 5 pence, then the king's wergild was 6,000 shillings. The accused must thus gather oath-helpers whose combined wergild equaled at least 6,000 shillings.

4.2 Swa we éac settað be eallum hadum, ge ceorle ge eorle: se ðe ymb his hlafordes fiorh sierwe, sie he wið ðone his feores scyldig ⁊ ealles ðæs ðe he age, oððe be his hlafordes were hine getriowe.

Af §4.2 fiorh] feorh BH   sierwe] syrwie B; syrw\i/e H   sie] sy BH   getriowe] getre-owie BH

4.2 Thus we also establish for all ranks, either *ceorl* or *eorl*:[31] he who plots against his lord's life, let him be liable for his life and all that he owns, or exculpate himself by [an oath in the amount of] his lord's wergild.[32]

---

[31] **ge ceorle ge eorle** is perhaps a frozen formulaic expression here meaning "all free men."

[32] Cf. §12 of the Legatine Capitulary (Dümmler 1895: 24; Whitelock 1955: 771):

> Let no one dare to conspire to kill a king (*in necem regis nemo communicare audeat*), for he is the Lord's anointed (*christus Domini*), and if anyone take part in such a crime, if he be a bishop or anyone of the priestly order, let him be expelled from it and cast out from the holy heritage, just as Judas was ejected from the apostolic order; and everyone who has consented to such sacrilege shall perish in the eternal fetters of anathema (*aeterno anathematis vinculo interibit*), and, associated with Judas the betrayer, be burnt in the eternal fires; as it is written: "*Not only they that do such things, but they also that consent to them who do them*" [Rom. 1: 32] escape not the judgment of God.

The context in the Legatine Capitulary is rather different from what is found in Alfred; the emphasis in the former is upon the status of the king as the "Lord's anointed." Accordingly, it seems appropriate to question whether the clause from the Legatine Capitulary has any bearing on Alfred's view of lordship. Although Wormald (1991: 215) adduces this as a possible source for this clause, he himself points out that "Treason legislation [...] was widespread in 'barbarian' codes and capitularies by the end of the ninth century; unless Alfred were as insular as many of his subsequent admirers he need not have found the requisite 'predecessor' in 786." Treason against one's lord is regulated in *Lex Alamannorum* with the penalty of loss of life or a redemption determined by the lord or the nobles of the land. (See *LexAla* §24; a similar stipulation can be found in *LexBav* §2.1.) Unsurprisingly, given the hostile relations between Saxons and Franks, treachery against the king is regulated in the *Capitulare de partibus Saxoniae* §11 (see *LexSax*) and repeated in *LexSax* §24. (See also Fruscione 2014: 40–42.) Compare *MP* §49.7 and note, where sentiments to this effect are attributed to the unnamed "synods" out of which Alfred's laws were composed.

{VI}

5 Eac we settað æghwelcere cirican, ðe biscep gehalgode, ðis frið:[33] gif hie fahmon geierne oððe geærne, þæt hine seofan nihtum nan mon út ne teo. Gif hit þonne hwa dó, ðonne sie he scyldig cyninges mundbyrde ⁊ þære cirican friðes (mare, gif he ðær mare ófgefo), gif he for hungre libban mæge, buton he self útfeohte.[34]

5.1 Gif hiwan hiora cirican maran þearfe hæbben, healde hine mon on oðrum ærne, ⁊ ðæt næbbe ðon ma dura þonne sio cirice.

5.2 Gewite ðære cirican ealdor, þæt him mon on þam fierste mete ne selle.

Af §5 æghwelcere] æghwylcere B; æghwylc\e/re H   cirican] cyricean B   biscep] bis-ceop B; biscop H   hie] *om.* H   fahmon] ge fahmon \ciricgan/ B; fagman H   geierne] geyrne BH   ut] ut\t/ H   ðonne] ðo\ne/ on B   sie] sy BH   gif] gyf B   mæge] mæg\e/ B   self] sylf BH   útfeohte] ut\t/feohte H
Af §5.1 hiora] heora B; he\o/ra H   ærne] huse B   ðon] ðon\ne/ H   sio cirice] seo cyrice B; \seo/ circe H
Af §5.2 cirican] ciricean B; ciric_an H   ðam] *om.* B   mete] \mete/ H   selle] sylle BH

---

[33] This constitutes one of only a handful of instances in which the simplex is used to mean "sanctuary" (cf. *Christ* 1001). Compounds with *friþ-* as a first element repre-sent the more common terms for sanctuary in Old English, both in pre- and post-Christian formulations. (See Fruscione 2003: 162–180.)

[34] *Hapax legomenon.*

5 Likewise we establish for any church, which the bishop has consecrated, this sanctuary: if [someone's] enemy reaches it by running on foot or on horseback, that he should not be dragged out for seven nights, if he can survive his hunger, unless he fights his way out [of the boundaries of the sanctuary].[35] If someone should [drag him out], then he is liable for the king's *mundbyrd* and the [payment for violation of] the church peace (and more, if he seizes more [people] there).[36]

5.1 If a household has greater need of their church, let him be kept in another building, and let that have no more doors than the church.

5.2 Let the head of the church make sure that he is not given food during that period.[37]

---

[35] We follow Attenborough in moving these two conditional clauses to the end of the first sentence in our translation: "The words *gif hit ... ofgefo* form a parenthesis which can hardly be rendered in modern English, without transposition of the sentences" (Attenborough 1922: 194).
Liebermann claims that this does not refer to the sanctuary-seeker fighting his way out but defending the door (presumably outside) in such a way that blood is drawn. Thorpe suggests that he fights outside the boundaries of his sanctuary, where it would be permissible to seize him; this interpretation is not incompatible with the sense that he is fighting his way out to escape. Fruscione (2003: 150) points out that, contrary to Continental laws, bringing weapons inside the church does not constitute a breach of asylum; sanctuary is violated only when the offender tries to fight his way out.

[36] Cf. *Ine* §5.

[37] The *Historia Regum* (1129) recounts the story of Offa, son of Aldfrith, who sought asylum in the church at Lindesfarne in 750 during conflict over the Northumbrian succession. He was besieged for a while there by King Eadberht, and was near death from starvation when he was finally brought out (*pœne defunctus fame de ecclesia sine armis abstractus est*). Arnold 1885: II, 40 (§41); see also Fruscione 2003: 155 and 159.

5.3 Gif he self his wæpno his gefan utræcan wille, gehealden hi hine xxx nihta ⁊ hie hine his mægum gebodien.

5.4 Eac cirican frið: gif hwelc mon cirican gesece for ðara gylta hwylcum, þara ðe ær geypped nære, ⁊ hine ðær on Godes naman geandette, sie hit healf forgifen.

6 [L5.5] Se ðe stalað on Sunnanniht oððe on Gehhol oððe on Eastron oððe on ðone halgan Þunresdæg on Gangdagas: ðara gehwelc we willað sie twybote, swa on Lenctenfæsten.

Af §5.3 Gif] Gyf B   self] sylf BH   wæpno] wæpna H   wille] \wylle/ B   gehealden] gehealdan BH   xxx] ðrittig B   hie] hi BH   mægum] magum BH   gebodien] gebeoden B; gebodie H
Af §5.4 cirican] cyricean B; cyric_an H   gif] \is/ gyf B; g\y/f H   cirican] ciricean B; cyric_an H   ðara] ðæra H   þara] þæra B; \þæra/ H   sie] sy BH   forgifen] forgyfen B
Af §6 gehhol] geol BH   gehwelc] gehwylc B; æghwylc H   sie] sy BH   swa] \al/swa B

5.3 If he himself is willing to hand over his weapons to his foes, let them hold him for 30 nights and let them announce this to his kinsmen.[38]

5.4 Likewise church sanctuary: if some man seeks out the church for whatever offense that had not previously been discovered, and he there confesses himself in God's name, let it be forgiven by half.

6 [L.5.5] He who steals on Sunday (night)[39] or on Christmas or on Easter or on Holy Thursday [or][40] during Rogation Days: each of those [offenses] we wish to count two-fold, as in the Lenten fast.

[38] The total period, then, would be thirty-seven days. In his *Libellus de exordio atque procursu* [...] *Dunhelmensis ecclesie*, Symeon of Durham relates a vision of the Saint Cuthbert that appeared to Abbot Edred in 883; the latter was commanded to petition King Guthred that Cuthbert's church be established "as a safe place of refuge for fugitives (*locum refugii*), so that whoever flees to [his] body for whatever cause may have thirty-seven days peace (*pacem*) which may not on any pretext ever be broken" (Rollason 2000: 124–125 (§ii.13); see also Fruscione 2003: 156–157).

[39] Attenborough points out that two citations of **Sunnanniht** "Sunday night" in Bosworth/Toller "clearly indicate the night between Saturday and Sunday." But the time period seems to be Sunday reckoned as the Sabbath in Jewish law, which is common practice at this time; see McReavy 1935: 320, also *Wihtred* §8 [L9].

[40] The scribe of **B** inserts ⁊ (which can stand for "and" or "or") here. Rogation days were April 25 (the "Major Rogation") and the three days before the feast of the Ascension (the "Minor Rogation"). Since Holy Thursday is not included in the Rogation, the emendation in **B** seems reasonable. (Liebermann suggests, conversely, that **on Gangdagas** was included to differentiate Holy [or Maundy] Thursday from the Thursday in the Minor Rogation.) The "Major Rogation" (from Latin *rogare*, "ask") "was a Christianized version of the pagan observance of the 'Robigalia', which took the form of processions through the cornfields to pray for the preservation of the crops from mildew. [...] In England [Rogation days] were adopted by the Council of Clovesho [can. 16]" (Cross and Livingstone 1983: 1193).

{VII}

7 [L6] Gif hwa on cirican hwæt geðeofige, forgylde þæt angylde, ⁊
ðæt wite swa to ðam angylde belimpan wille, ⁊ slea mon þa hond óf
ðe he hit mid gedyde.

    7.1 [L6.1] Gif he /41v/ ða hand lesan wille, ⁊ him mon ðæt geða-
fian wille, gelde swa to his were belimpe.

{VIII}

8 [L7] Gif hwa in cyninges healle gefeohte oððe his wæpn gebrede, ⁊
hine mon gefó, sie ðæt on cyninges dome, swa deað swa lif, swa he
him forgifan wille.

    8.1 [L7.1] Gif he losige, ⁊ hine mon eft gefó, forgielde he hine self
á be his weregilde, ⁊ ðone gylt gebete, swa wer swa wite, swa he
gewyrht age.

Af §7 cirican] cyricean B; ciric_an H   hond] hand BH   gedyde] \stæl/ dyde H
Af §7.1 lesan] lysan B; \a/lysan H   wille] wylle B   geðafian] geðafyan   wille] wylle
B   gelde] gylde BH
Af §8 in] on BH   cyninges] kyninges BH   healle] halle B   gefeohte] \ge/feohte
H   wæpn] wæpne B; wæpen H   sie] sy BH
Af §8.1 mon] man H   gefó] \eft/ gefó H   forgielde] forgylde BH   self] sylf B; sylf\ne/
H   weregilde] wergylde B   gewyhrt] gewyhrt\e/ B

7 [L6] If someone steals something from a church, let him pay for it single-fold, and the fine such as is appropriate to the single-payment, and let the hand be struck off with which he did it.[41]

7.1 [L6.1] If he wishes to redeem the hand, and it is permitted him, let him pay in accordance with his wergild.[42]

8 [L7] If someone fights in the king's hall or draws his weapon, and he is caught, let it be according to the king's judgment: either death or life, whichever the king wishes to grant him.[43]

8.1 [L7.1] If he escapes and is caught afterwards, let him always pay for himself with his wergild, and recompense for that offense – either [with] wergild or fine – which he has committed.[44]

---

[41] Compare *Ine* §18 and §38, which similarly require the amputation of the offending hand.

[42] §75 sets the fine for striking off a hand at 66 shillings 6 and 1/3 pennies (a seeming miscalculation for 66 shillings, 3 1/3 pennies, which would represent 1/3 of a freeman's wergild). Presumably the ratio would remain the same but the amount would vary according to the individual's wergild.

[43] Compare to *Ine* §6, which requires in addition that the aggressor lose all that he owns. Attenborough suggests an alternate translation of "on such terms as the king is willing (to forgive him)." The two interpretations represent the same reality: the king will always be able to dictate the terms upon which the transgressor's life is spared.

[44] The first wergild (contra Attenborough) is the escapee's own, and is paid to the lord as a fine; the second wergild is his victim's (if there was one), and is paid to the victim or his kin.

{VIIII}

9 [L8] **Gif** hwa nunnan of mynstere ut alæde butan kyninges lef-nesse[45] oððe bisc*epes*, geselle hundtwelftig scill, healf cyninge, healf biscepe 7 þære cirican hlaforde, ðe ðone munuc[46] age.

9.1 [L8.1] Gif hio leng libbe ðonne se ðe hie utlædde, nage hio his ierfes owiht.

9.2 [L8.2] Gif hio bearn gestriene, næbbe ðæt ðæs ierfes ðon mare ðe seo modor.

Af §9 mynstere] mynstre BH kyninges] cyninges BH lefnesse] leafe BH geselle] gesylle BH hundtwelftig] hundtwentig B; cxx H biscepe] bisceope B 7] *om.* B þære] *om.* H ðone munuc] þa nunnan BH
Af §9.1 hio (3x)] heo BH se ðe] s_e \þe/ H ierfes] yrfes BH owiht] nawiht B; awuht H
Af §9.2 hio] heo B gestriene] gestryne B; gestri_ne H næbbe] nage H ðæs] \þes/ (*in left margin*) H ierfes] yrfes B; irfes H ðon mare] na mare B; ðe mare H ðe] þonne B seo] seo BH modor] moder B

---

45 This term appears elsewhere only in the Old English translation of Bede's *Historia*, "another work with signs of Mercian provenance and a considerable Mercian vocabulary" and in §24 (Dammery 1990: 239, n. 92). Dammery suggests its occurence here might imply that this clause was drawn from the laws of Offa.
46 Note that **B** and **H** both give *nunnan* ("nun") in place of *munuc* ("monk.")

9 [L8] If someone leads a nun from a minster without the permission of the king or bishop,[47] let him pay one hundred and twenty shillings, half to the king and half to the bishop or[48] the lord of the church that owns the [nun].[49]

9.1 [8.1] If she outlives the man who took her out, she does not own any of his inheritance.

9.2 [L8.2] If she produces a child, it does not have the inheritance any more than the mother.[50]

---

[47] The abduction of a nun is addressed more thoroughly in *LexBav* §11: "If someone takes a nun, that is one who is dedicted to God, from a cloister and takes her as wife against the law of the Church, let the bishop of that place with agreement of the king or the lord demand her back. [...] We know, that he is guilty of an offense who robs one betrothed to another: how much more is a man guilty of an offense, who has taken possession of a woman betrothed to Christ."

[48] The 7 in the manuscript can be read as "and" or "or." If one takes it as "and," the interpretation must be that the bishop and head of the "church that owns the nun" split the fine. Expanding the 7 as "or" – admittedly, a less common expansion of the abbreviation – gives a more plausible reading of the clause. The *hlaford* of a nun would most commonly be an abbess.

[49] Liebermann translates **munuc** as "monastic person," while admitting that no other such use exists. The masculine reading is, however, supported by the demonstrative ðone in all manuscript witnesses. Liebermann's translation then is more strictly literal than the one given here.

[50] §§15 and 16 of the Legatine Capitulary of 786 (Dümmler 1895: 25) prohibit marriages to vowed virgins (*ancillis Dei*) and assert that children born to nuns are as illegitimate as those issuing from adulterous unions (*Adulterinos namque filios ac sanctimonialium auctoritate apostolica spurios et adulteros iudicamus*); a vowed virgin is truly the spouse of Christ (*sponsam Christi vocitare non dubitamus*). Wormald argues that "the crucial point is that in this respect the provisions of 786 and of Alfred's code stand not only together but also alone" (Wormald 1991: 216). That is, both address in sequence the illegal coupling and the repudiation of the child.

9.3 [L8.3] Gif hire bearn mon ofslea, gi\ᵉ/ļde⁵¹ cyninge þara medrenmæga dæl; fædrenmægum⁵² hiora dæl mon agife.

{x}

10 [L9] Gif mon wíf mid bearne ófslea, þon*n*e þæt bearn in hire sie, forgielde ðone wifman fullan gielde, ⁊ þæt bearn be ðæs fædrencnosles were healfan gelde.⁵³

11 [L9.1] Á sie þæt wite LX scill, oððæt angylde árise to XXX scill; siððan hit to ðam árise þæt angylde, siððan sie þæt wite CXX scill.

   11.1 [L9.2] Geo wæs goldðeofe⁵⁴ ⁊ stódðeofe⁵⁵ ⁊ beoðeofe,⁵⁶ ⁊ manig witu maran ðon*n*e oþru; nu sint eal gelic buton manðeofe: CXX scill.

Af §9.3 hire bearn mon] man hire bearn B; hire bearn man H   gi\e/lde] gylde BH   cyninge] \þam/ cyninge H   þara] þæra B   medrenmæga] medra maga B; med\d/ren mæga H   hiora] heora B; hi\o/ra H   mon agife] man agyfe B

Af §10 mon] man B; hwa wif of slea mid bearne H   sie] sy BH (*added later in* H)   forgielde] forgylde B; forgilde H   ðone wifman] heo H   gielde] gylde B   healfan] halfan B   gelde] gylde BH

Af §11 sie] sy BH   LX] syxti B   XXX] ðrittig B   ðam] ðæm   sie] sy BH   CXX] hund twelftig B

Af §11.1 Geo] hwilon B   manig] manegu H   sint] synd B   eal gelic] eall\e/   gelic] gelice B; gelic\e/ H   buton] butan BH   CXX] hund twelftig B

⁵¹ Scribe later added e above line; insertion point marked by dot under l.
⁵² This rare compound appears as *fædringmagas* in the laws of Æthelberht; it supports Alfred's claim that he drew on Æthelberht's laws.
⁵³ Compare *MP* §18.
⁵⁴ *Hapax legomenon.*
⁵⁵ *Hapax legomenon.*
⁵⁶ *Hapax legomenon.*

9.3 [L8.3] If her child is killed, let the mother's portion [of the wergild] be given to the king;[57] let the father's kin be given their portion.

10 [L9] If a woman bearing a child is slain when the child is in her, let [the slayer] pay full recompense for the woman, and compensate for the child by half the wergild [appropriate to] the father's kin.[58]

11 [L9.1] The fine shall always be 60 shillings until the single-recompense reaches 30 shillings; after the single-recompense reaches this amount or higher, then the fine shall be 120 shillings.

11.1 [L9.2] Earlier the fines for a gold-thief and a stud-thief and a bee-thief[59] and many fines were greater than others; now all are alike except theft of a person:[60] 120 shillings.

---

[57] The mother's portion is 1/3 of the wergild. *LexRip* §37.2 allots a widow 50 *solidi* as dower and 1/3 of all they have attained as a couple.

[58] *PactLexSal* §41.19 and *LexRip* §36.10 similarly require half a wergild (100 *solidi*) for the killing of a fœtus or a child before he has a name. *LexRip* stipulates that killing both mother and unborn/newly born child, however, draws a fine of 700 *solidi*. *PactLexSal* §65e contradicts the earlier clause in requiring a payment of 600 *solidi* for killing a fœtus if it can be determined that the fœtus was male. The possibility of compensation for the slain woman does not exist in §18 of the *MP*.

[59] *PactLexSal* §8 concerns fines for stealing bees and hives; in *LexSax* §30 the theft of a hive from within someone else's enclosure is punishable by death.

[60] I.e., slave. This clause pertains to Alfred's aim, announced in the Prologue, to harmonize discrepant laws.

{XI}

12 [L10] **Gif** mon hæme mid twelfhyndes monnes wife, hund/42r/ twelftig scill gebete ðam were; syxhyndum men hundteontig scill gebete; cierliscum men feowertig scill gebete.

{XII}

13 [L11] **Gif** mon on cirliscre fæmnan breost gefó, mid v scill hire gebete.

13.1 [L11.1] Gif he hie oferweorpe ⁊ mid ne gehæme, mid x scill gebete.

13.2 [L11.2] Gif he mid gehæme, mid LX scill gebete.

13.3 [L11.3] Gif oðer mon mid hire læge ær, sie be healfum ðæm þonne sio bot.

Af §12 mon] man BH   twelfhyndes] .xx.hyndes H   monnes] mannes BH   hundt-welftig] cxx H   ðam] man BH (*added later in* H)   syxhyndum] syxhundum B   hund-teontig] hundteontigon B; C H   cierliscum] ceorliscum B; cyrliscum H   feowertig] feowertigum B

Af §13 mon] man BH   cirliscre] ceorliscre B; cyrliscne \fæmnan/ H   V] fif B   hire] \hire/ B (B *adds at end of clause* gyf he mid gehæmede tyn scill gebete)

Af §13.1 hie] hig B; Gif he ofer weorpe \hy/ H   mid] *om.* B   x] tyn B

Af §13.2 LX] syxti B   gebete] hit gebete H

Af §13.3 mon] man BH   læge] \ge/læge H   sie] sy BH   ðæm þonne] *om.* B; ðæm \ðonne/ H   sio] seo BH

12 [L10] If a person has intercourse with the wife of a 1,200-man, let him pay 120 shillings to the husband; for a 600-man let him pay 100 shillings; for a man of *ceorl* rank let him pay 40 shillings.

13 [L11] If a man seizes a *ceorl*-woman on the breast, let him recompense her[61] with 5 shillings.[62]

 13.1 [L11.1] If he throws her down but does not have intercourse with her, let him recompense with 10 shillings.

 13.2 [L11.2] If he has intercourse with her, let him recompense with 60 shillings.[63]

 13.3 [L11.3] If another man lay with her before, let the recompense be half.[64]

---

[61] Usually the fine for such an offense would go to the man under whose protection she lives. (Hough 2014b: 179.) Carole Hough, adducing §29 (in which a man who rapes a female slave must pay 5 shillings restitution plus the 60 shilling fine required by §11), suggests – surely correctly – that the fine would also be assessed in this case.

[62] Following §20, this occurs "without her permission"; the penalty is there doubled if the woman is a nun. Compare *PactLexSal* §20 where the fine is 45 *solidi* (roughly 9x the fine in Alfred!), also *LexFris* §22.88. The vernacular term for touching a woman with lustful intention preserved in *LexBav* §8.3 is *horcrift*, roughly "whore-grip."

[63] This contradicts the 40-shilling fine established in §12. The difference is presumably owing to the fact that one is a married woman and one a virgin. Continental laws often demand higher fines for raping a virgin than a married woman. (See Oliver 2011: 182–184.) Another possibility is that the difference is due to the violence of the act; see Hough 1993. See also Hough 1997.

[64] It is not clear whether the prior intercourse was consensual or not (though §13.4 suggests the former). *LexFris* §9.3–7 paints a grisly picture of penalties incurred by gang rape: the first man paid 4 shillings; the second, 3; the third, 2; the fourth, 1; and the fifth and any subsequent, 1/3 shilling each.

13.4 [L11.4] Gif hie mon teo, geladie (ge)hie⁶⁵ be sixtegum hida, oððe ðolige be healfre þære bote.

13.5 [L11.5] Gif borenran wifmen ðis gelimpe, weaxe sio bót be ðam were.

{XIII}

14 [L12] Gif mon oðres wudu bærneð, oððe heaweð unaliefedne, forgielde ælc great treow mid v scill, ⁊ siððan æghwylc, sie swa fela swa hiora sie, mid v pæningum; ⁊ xxx scill to wite.

15 [L13] Gif mon oðerne æt gemænan weorce óffelle ungewealdes, agife mon þam mægum þæt treow, ⁊ hi hit hæbben ær xxx nihta of þam lande, oððe him fó se to se ðe ðone wudu age.

Af §13.4 hie] hi B; Gif man teo hy H   mon] man B   geladie] gehladige B; geladige
H   (ge)hie] hi B; hy H   sixtegum hida] sixtigum hidum B; lx hida H   ðolige] þolie
BH   healfre] healfere B   þære] *om.* B
Af §13.5 borenran] \æðel/borenran B; Gif þis \bett/ borenran H   weaxe] wexe
B   sio] seo BH
Af §14 mon] man BH   unaliefedne] unalyfedne BH   forgielde] forgylde BH   v ... v]
fif B   sie ... sie] sy BH   æghwylc, sie swa feola swa hiora sy] ælc swa monig swa þær
sy H   fela] feola BH   hiora] heora BH   pæningum] penegum B; peningum H   xxx]
þrittig \half pund/ B
Af §15 mon] man BH   óffelle] off\æ/ealle B; \weorce/ offealle H   ungewealdes] unge-
waldes B   agife mon] agyfe man B; agife man H   mægum] magon B; magum
H   xxx] þrittig B   þam] ðæm BH   lande] lande don H   fó se to se ðe] fo to se ðe B;
fo to se \þe/ H

⁶⁵ Thorpe and Schmid silently emend the manuscript reading of *geladie gehie* to *geladie hi*. Liebermann, followed by Attenborough, prints *geladiege hie*. But *geladiege*
does not represent a possible Old English form: the options for the verb are *geladie*
or *geladige* (both pronounced identically due to palatalization of *g*). A likely
scenario is that the exemplar read *geladige*, but the scribe automatically wrote the
geladie of his own orthographic practice; he then copied the word-ending -*ge* at the
beginning of the following pronoun. The term *geladian* only appears in legal texts;
cf. *MP* §28.

13.4 [L11.4] If she is accused [of having lain with another man], let her clear herself by [an oath in the value of] sixty hides,[66] or forfeit half the compensation.[67]

13.5 [L11.5] If this happens to a [nobly] born[68] woman, let the compensation increase according to the *wer*.

14 [L12] If a someone burns another's wood or cuts it down without permission, let him compensate for each large tree with 5 shillings,[69] and afterwards each [smaller tree], however many there may be, with 5 pennies; and 30 shillings as fine.[70]

15 [L13] If someone kills another accidentally [by felling a tree on him] while working together, let the tree be given to the kin [of the slain man], and they must take it from the land before 30 nights, or let the owner take it.[71]

---

[66] This is the only instance in *Alfred* in which an oath is sworn in hides. The practice is otherwise limited to the laws of Ine and mentioned as well in the *Dialogue of Ecgbert* (Haddan and Stubbs: III, 404; see also Liebermann 1910), where it is asserted that various clerical grades may swear *secundum numerum* [...] *trubutariorum* (Haddan and Stubbs 1871: 404). The value in *Alfred* is roughly one shilling per hide. (See *Ine* §14 and n.)

[67] Cf. *Alfred* §21.

[68] Cf. *Ine* §34 *deorborenran* "nobly born."

[69] *Ine* §44.1 requires the first three trees felled to be recompensed with 30 shillings each, but requires no extra compensation for further trees. But this means a poacher in Alfred's time pays only 1/6 the fine for each large tree as he would have in Ine's day. Perhaps this represents another instance of the Alfredian "mercy" announced in the Prologue (evident also in Alfred's not retaining the twelvefold restitution for theft of ecclesiastical property maintained in Ine's laws: see *Ine* §4 and n).

[70] Contrast with *Ine* §44 where different fines are established for felling or burning another's wood. These clauses suggest that Ine's laws were to be understood as superseded by Alfred's.

[71] The tree here serves as a kind of compensation for the family of the victim, who was presumably either servile or of low rank. Its value is suggested by the entitlement of the lord (and employer) to appropriate it for his own use should it not be delivered within thirty days. As the incident was an accident during shared work, no wergild or fine are due from the survivor. Compare *LexRib* §70.1; also §36 of the Council of Tribur (895), which urges that the survivor be judged *innocens de morte defuncti* should he have warned of the danger while felling the tree (Boretius and Krause 1897: 234).

{XIIII}

16 [L14] Gif mon sie dumb oððe déaf geboren, þæt he ne mæge
synna onsecggan ne geandettan, bete se fæder his misdæda.

{XV}

17 [L15] Gif mon beforan ærcebiscepe gefeohte oððe wæpne
gebregde, mid L scill ꝸ hundteontegu*m* gebete; gif beforan oðru*m*
biscepe oððe ealdormen ðis gelimpe, mid hundteontegu*m* scill
gebete.

18 [L16] Gif mon cu oððe /42v/ stodmyran forstele ꝸ folan oððe
cealf ófadrife, forgelde mid scill⁷² ꝸ þa moder be hiora weorðe.

19 [L17] Gif hwa oðrum his unmagan oðfæste, ꝸ he hine on ðære
fæstinge forferie,⁷³ getriowe hine facnes se ðe hine fede, gif hine hwa
hwelces teo.

{XVI}

20 [L18] Gif hwa nunnan mid hæmeðþinge oððe on hire hrægl oððe
on hire breost butan hire leafe gefó, sie hit twybete swa we ær be
læwdum men fundon.

Af §16 mon sie] man sy BH   mæge synna] mæge his synna B; mæge synne
H   onsecggan ne geandettan] geandettan ne ætsacan B; onsægan ne andettan H
Af §17 mon] man BH   ærcebiscepe] erce bisceope B; ærcebiscope H   gebregde]
gebrede B; gebre_de H   L] fiftigum B   hundteontegum] hund teontigum B; *om.*
H   biscepe] bisceope B; biscope H   ealdormen] ealdormenn H   hundteontegu*m*]
hundteontigum B; C H
Af §18 mon] man BH   stodmyran] stod mære B   folan oððe cealf ófadrife] folan
\oððe/ cealf of adrifeð H   forgelde] forgylde B; forgilde H   mid scill] mid sixtig
\feowertigum/ scill B   moder] modor B   hiora] heora BH   weorðe] wyrðe B
Af §19 ꝸ he] ꝸ \he/ H   getriowe] getreowige B; getreowsie H   facnes] facnesse B   se
ðe] \se/ ðe B   hwelces] hwylces BH
Af §20 hæmeðþinge] hæmedðinge BH   on¹] *om.* B   sie] sy BH   twybete] twibote B;
twybote H   swa we ær] swa we ær anfandlice H   læwdum men] læwedu*m* men B;
læwedum mannum H

⁷² Variants in **B** suggest the penalty of a shilling was felt to be an error.
⁷³ *Hapax legomenon.*

16 [L14] If a person is born dumb or deaf, so that he cannot deny nor confess his offenses, let the father compensate for his misdeeds.[74]

17 [L15] If someone fights in the presence of an archbishop or draws a weapon, let him compensate with 150 shillings; if this happens before another bishop or an ealdorman, let him compensate with 100 shillings.[75]

18 [L16] If a person steals a cow or stud-mare and drives away a foal or calf, let him compensate with a shilling and for the mothers according to their worth.

19 [L17] If someone entrusts his dependent [child][76] to another, and [the guardian] allows it to die while in that care, let [the guardian] who supported him clear himself of wrongdoing, if someone accuses him of something.[77]

20 [L18] If someone seizes a nun with carnal intent either on her clothing or on her breast without her permission, let the compensation be twice what we earlier set for lay[wo]men.[78]

---

[74] Wormald (1999a: 282) points out that this clause has no equivalent in Continental laws and suggests that this type of legislation was "law-making in response to contingency such as typified Roman imperial edicts and several sub-Roman *leges* (and *Ine*); the primary (legal) meaning of the very word *dom* was 'judgement.'"

[75] Compare §39 and *Ine* §6.1.

[76] The term *unmag* literally means "without power" and thus the referent is probably a young child (although Attenborough allows for the possibility of any defenseless dependent).

[77] *MP* §28 discusses the responsibility of a person who has had any property entrusted to him; he must likewise swear his innocence if it goes missing.

[78] §13 sets the fine for touching a laywoman's breast at 5 shillings.

21 [L18.1] Gif beweddodu fæmne hie forlicgge, gif hio sie cirlisc, mid LX scill gebete þam byrgean, ⁊ þæt sie on cwicæhtum⁷⁹ feogodum,⁸⁰ ⁊ mon nænigne mon on ðæt ne selle.

21.1 [L18.2] Gif hio sie syxhyndu, hundteontig scill geselle þam byrgean.

21.2 [L18.3] Gif hio sie twelfhyndu, cxx scill gebete þam byrgean.

{XVII}

22 [L19] Gif hwa his wæpnes oðrum onlæne, þæt he mon mid ófslea, hie moton hie gesomnian, gif hie willað, to þam were.

22.1 [L19.1] Gif hi hie ne gesamnien, gielde se ðæs wæpnes onlah þæs weres ðriddan dæl ⁊ þæs wites ðriddan dæl.

22.2 [L19.2] Gif he hine triewan wille, þæt he to ðære læne facn ne wiste, þæt he mot.

Af §21 beweddodu] beweddo B; beweddod H   hie] heo B; hy H   hie ... hio] heo ... heo BH   forlicgge] forlicge BH   sie ... sie] sy BH   cirlisc] ceorlisc B   mid] *om.* B   LX] syxtig B   þam byrgean] ðam ðe hit gebyrige B; ðam þe hit geby\rie/ H   mon nænigne mon] man næningne man B; man nænigne man H   selle] sylle BH

Af §21.1 Gif hio sie syxhyndu] Gyf heo sy six hynde BH   geselle] gesylle B; gebete H   þam byrgean] ðam \ðe hit/ to gebyrian B; ðam þe hit gebyrie H

Af §21.2 hio sie] heo sy B; hio sy H   twelfhyndu] twelfhynde B; .xx.hynde H   cxx] hundtwelftig B   þam byrgean] ðam ðe to \hit/ gebyrige B; ðam þe hit gebyrie H

Af §22 wæpnes] wæpne B; wæpn H   onlæne] læne BH   mon mid] mid man B; man mid H   hie (2x)] hi B; hy H   gesomnian] gesamnian B; gesa\o/mn_an H   gif hie willað] gyf hi willað BH   þam] þæm BH

Af §22.1 Gif hi hie ne gesamnien] gyf heo hi ne gesamnian B; Gif hy heo gesa\o/mn_ an nellen H   gielde] gylde B; gilde H   onlah] onlænde B; \þæs/ onlan H   ðriddan dæl] ðridda dæll B

Af §22.2 triewan] triwian B; trywan H   to ðære læne] to ðære fore ⁊ to ðære læne H   facn] facne B   ne wiste] nyste BH

---

⁷⁹ *Hapax legomenon.*
⁸⁰ *Hapax legomenon.*

21 [L18.1] If a contractually betrothed woman fornicates [with someone other than her intended husband], if she is of *ceorl* rank, let her compensate the guarantor[81] [to the marriage] with 60 shillings, and that must be in livestock,[82] and no person [in servitude] can be given for that.[83]

21.1 [L18.2] If she is [of] 600 [rank], let her compensate the guarantor with 100 shillings.

21.2 [L18.3] If she is [of] twelve-hundred rank, let her compensate the guarantor with 120 shillings.

22 [L19] If someone loans his weapon to another so that he can kill a man, they may combine to pay the *wer* if they want to.

22.1 [L19.1] If they do not want to, let him who loaned the weapon pay a third of the *wer* and a third of the fine.[84]

22.2 [L19.2] If he wishes to clear himself [by oath] that he knew of no malice when he made the loan, he may do so.

---

[81] Namely, the one who gave surety for the completion of the marriage contract. See *Wifmannes Beweddung* §6.

[82] Both **cwicæhtum** and **feogodum** are *hapax legomena*. The first, literally "with live possessions" clearly refers to "livestock." Interpretation of the second hinges on one's reading of the ambiguous first element of the compound, *feo*, which can mean "property" or "cattle" (and the two are, of course, not mutually exclusive). Possibly the payment can be made in "livestock and/or other property"; this assumes a missing conjunction. The reading of "livestock" alone implies that the second term serves as a gloss to the first.

[83] *Ine* §57.1 allows a slave to be given as part of a wergild payment. Pelteret (1995: 84–85) proposes that this clause "provides the first evidence in the laws of slaves as more than mere chattels ... [The fact that the woman could pay in cattle but not slaves] implies that slaves were regarded by some members of society as property just like cattle, but the very promulgation of this provision suggests that this view of them was becoming unacceptable."

[84] *Æthelberht* §23.2 [L20] requires that the man who loaned the weapon pay 20 shillings.

23 [L19.3] Gif sweordhwita oðres monnes wæpn to feormunge onfó, oððe smið monnes andweorc, hie hit gesund begen agifan, swa hit hwæðer hiora ǽr onfenge, buton hiora hwæðer ǽr þingode, þæt he hit angylde healdan ne ðorfte.

{XVIII}

24 [L20] Gif mon oðres monnes munuce feoh oðfæste butan ðæs munuces hlafordes lefnesse,[85] ⁊ hit him losige, þolige his se ðe hit ǽr ahte.

Af §23 monnes (2x)] mannes BH   wæpn] wepn B   onfó] underfo B   hie] hi B; hy H   agifan] agyfen B; agifen H   hiora (2x)] heora B; he\o/ra H   onfenge] underfenge B   hwæðer] hweðer B

Af §24 mon oðres monnes] man oþres \mannes/ H   munuce] muneke B; munuke H   feoh oðfæste] feoh befæste B (*om. here in* H)   munuces hlafordes] munekes \aldres/ B; \his/ hlafordes H   lefnesse] hleafe B; leafe feoh befæste H   losige] losie H   þolige] þolie B

---

[85] This term appears elsewhere only in the Mercian-influenced Old English translation of Bede and §9; Dammery suggests this might indicate that this clause was drawn from the laws of Offa.

23 [L19.3] If a sword-polisher takes another person's weapon to [re]furbish, or a smith someone's tool, they must both give it back unhurt just as they received it earlier, unless the two of them earlier agreed, that he [the craftsman] might not be held [liable] for compensation for it.[86]

24 [L20] If someone entrusts property to another man's monk without the permission of the monk's lord, and it is lost from him, let him who owned it before forfeit it.[87]

---

[86] This language of this clause is difficult to untangle, but the meaning seems to be that if a weapon or tool has been committed to a craftsman, he is liable for its use while it is in his possession unless he and the owner earlier agreed that he would not have responsibility for any misuse of the weapon during this time. *Grágás* states unambiguously that "Whatever object of value belonging to someone else a man has on loan, the man who has the use of it is responsible for it" (Dennis, Foote, and Perkins 2000: 86). Another possibility suggested by Thorpe is that the smith should not be liable for loss or damage while in his custody.

[87] Old English *feoh* can mean "property," but could also be translated as "livestock." The clause is one of several in Ine's and Alfred's laws urging that transfers of property to others' use or possession be witnessed to.

{XVIIII}

25 [L21] /43r/ Gif preost oðerne mon ófslea, weorpe mon to handa
⁊ eall ðæt he him hames bohte, ⁊ hine biscep onhadige, þonne hine
mon of ðam mynstre agife, buton se hlaford þone wer forðingian
wille.

Af §25 mon] man BH   mon to handa] man to \him/ hande B   eall] eal H   him
hames bohte] he him mid hames brohte B; he mid him hames brohte H   biscep] bis-
ceop B; biscop H   onhadige] unhadie B   agife] agyfe B   forðingian] fore ðingian
B   wille] wylle B

25 [L21] If a priest slays another man, he shall be turned in as well as all that he bought for his home [in the church community],[88] and the bishop shall defrock him when he is expelled from the minster, unless the lord is willing to negotiate payment of the *wer* [of the slain man].[89]

[88] The interpretation of the phrase **eall ðæt he him hames bohte** (literally "all that he bought himself of home") has long been in doubt. Attenborough translates it "all the share of the monastic property which he has bought for himself." Both the **H** and **B** replace *bohte* "bought" with *brohte* "brought," indicating that the meaning was even then difficult to decipher. Whitelock suggests that "the intention is to give the man his property for him to use it towards paying the wergild"; she finds support for this view in the *Dialogues of Egbert* §14 (Haddan and Stubbs 1871: 410), which states that a man in precisely this situation should be given things he offered the church "that he may have something to redeem him[self] with" (*ut habeat unde se redimat*). A somewhat simpler solution is suggested by charter S244, a grant from Ine to *fratri* Begano of a single hide of land plus a fishery. "Beaga was presumably a monk of Muchelney, and the grant indicates that individual members of a religious community in early Wessex could and did own private property" (Edwards 1988: 200–203). The charter shows also that the property of individual members of the regular clergy might be augmented during their lifetimes in spite of the austere ideals of the Rule of St. Benedict.

[89] Otherwise the wergild for the slain man will be the responsibility of the ex-priest and his kin-group.

{xx}

26 [L22] Gif mon on folces gemote cyninges gerefan geyppe eofot, ⁊
his eft geswican wille, gestæle on ryhtran hand, gif he mæge; gif he
ne mæge, ðolie his angyldes.

{xxi}

27 [L23] Gif hund mon toslite oððe abite, æt forman misdæde
geselle VI scill; gif he him mete selle, æt æfteran cerre XII scill; æt
ðriddan XXX scill.

    27.1 [L23.1] Gif æt ðissa misdæda hwelcere se hund losige, ga
ðeos bót hwæðre forð.

    27.2 [L23.2] Gif se hund ma misdæda gewyrce, ⁊ he hine hæbbe,
bete be fullan were swa dolgbote swa he wyrce.

Af §26 folces] folc\es/ H   eofot] þeofðe B; geeofot yppe H   ryhtran] rihtran
B   mæge] mage H   ðolie] ðolige BH

Af §27 mon] man BH   geselle] gesylle BH   selle] sylle BH   æt æfteran cerre] æt ðam
oðran cyrre B; æt æfteran ci_rre H   æt ðriddan] æt þriddan ci_rre H

Af §27.1 ðissa] ðisra B   hwelcere] hwylcere B; hwylc\e/re H   hwæðre] ðeah
hwæðere B; hweþ\e/re H

Af §27.2 were] we\re/ H   dolgbote] dolhbote BH   swa he wyrce] \oððe/ swa \hwætt/
he ge wyrce B; swa he gewyrce H

26 [L22] If a person should reveal an offense[90] to the king's reeve in the folk assembly, and he afterwards wishes to withdraw [the accusation], let him accuse the correct party if he can; if he cannot, let him forfeit the single-payment [due him for the offense].[91]

27 [L23] If a dog gashes or bites[92] someone, at the first misdeed let him pay 6 shillings. If he [continues to] offer it food, at the second offense 12 shillings, at the third 30 shillings.

   27.1 [L23.1] If at any of these misdeeds the dog escapes, the compensation is nevertheless applicable.

   27.2 [L23.2] If the dog commits more misdeeds, and he keeps it, let [the owner] pay according to the full *wer* for any wound [the dog] inflicts.

---

[90] The phrase **geyppe eofot** means "reveal an offense." The grammatical structure does not indicate whose offense is being revealed. The rubricator heads this paragraph *Be eofetes andetlan* ("Concerning the admission of an offense") crucially changing *geyppe* ("reveal") to *andetlan* ("admission"). Though the grammar may be ambiguous, the meaning is not. Clearly a person will not admit an offense in the public assembly and then later attempt to withdraw the admission; the declaration must rather be an accusation against another.

[91] B adds *ond fo to ðam wite* ("and let [the reeve] take the fine.") *Ine* §55 prohibits the resolution of disputes outside the processes established by the king and his representatives; this clause may be intended to discourage an accuser from trying to make an advantageous settlement with the defendant out of court.

[92] Liebermann claims **abitan** means "bite a man to death," but the possibility that a dog that had killed three people would be allowed to live makes no sense. Even less plausible is the concept that an owner might only have to pay *wer* after his dog has killed four times. Indeed, the Toronto *DOE* defines the verb as follows: "1. to bite, rend, tear with the teeth (someone / something); mainly of the action of (wild) animals."

{XXII}

28 [L24] Gif neat mon gewundige, weorpe ðæt neat to honda oððe foreðingie.

{XXIII}

29 [L25] Gif mon ceorles mennen to nedhæmde geðreatað, mid v scill gebete þam ceorle; 7 LX scill to wite.

29.1 [L25.1] Gif ðeowmon þeowne to nedhæmde genede, bete mid his eowende.[93]

Af §28 mon] man B; mannes neat man H   honda] handa BH   foreðingie] fore\ge/þingie H

Af §29 mon] man B; *om.* H (*clause occurs in* H *after* §§30–30.3)   nedhæmde] nydhæmede BH   geðreatað] man geþreatað H   v] fif B   ceorle] ciorle H   LX] syhtig B

Af §29.1 ðeowmon] ðeow man BH   nedhæmede genede] nydhæmede genyde B; to nydhæmede genide H   eowende] hyde H

[93] *Hapax legomenon.*

28 [L24] If a beast should wound someone, let [the owner] turn that beast over [to the wounded person] or let him settle [with the wounded person].[94]

29 [L25] If someone rapes a *ceorl*'s slave, let him recompense the *ceorl* with 5 shillings, and 60 shillings as fine.

    29.1 [L25.1] If a slave rapes a slave, let him compensate with his ?testicles.[95]

---

[94] This may mean that the wounded person has the option of accepting the livestock as part of the *wer* payment. Older views that the animal was handed over for vengeance are perhaps not appropriate given the value both of livestock and of dogs (see Jurasinski 2014a). In *MP* §31 (derived from Exodus and thus of perhaps limited relevance) an ox who kills someone is slain by stoning, and the meat is not eaten. The owner is not liable unless the ox had a tendency to push with his horns, in which case the owner bears responsibility and is either put to death or redeemed. Only the fines for very minor wounds would be worth less than the price of a cow/bull. Although no specific price is set in *Alfred* (or *Ine*), an ox – the most valuable animal after the horse – was worth 6 shillings in Æthelstan's reign, a cow 4, a pig 2, and a sheep 1. (See Banham and Faith 2014: 86 with translation from pence to shillings at 5:1).

[95] **eowende** is a *hapax legomenon* of uncertain etymology; the form is present participle but the root has thus far evaded satisfactory analysis. The London manuscript of the *Quadripartitus* translates the phrase as *testiculos perdat* "let him lose his testicles," all others as *castretur* "let him be castrated." *Textus Roffensis* changes *mid his eowende* to *mid his hyde* "with his hide"; i.e. the punishment is flogging rather than castration, which reflects a tendency of this and other twelfth-century manuscripts to eliminate severe bodily penalties for slaves (see Jurasinski 2015: 98).
    The temptation to attach this *hapax* to PIE **ie-* "go" only attested in Old English in the suppletive *eode* "he went" falters both on the vocalic grade of the root (which we would expect in the present to be e rather than o) and on the fact that none of the numerous reflexes of this root in other languages demonstrates a similar specialization of meaning. Krogmann 1936: 35–38, noting the number of PIE reflexes beginning with **ue-* with the semantics of "dampness, flowing" suggests an origin in PIE **aue-* (or perhaps **eue-*) "to dampen, sprinkle, flow" (see Pokorny 1959: s.v. 9. au(e)-). Although this root appears both in other Germanic languages (Hartmann von *Aue*) and other insular languages (Stratford on *Avon*), it appears elsewhere in Old English only with the *−d−* extension which gives us "water," "otter," etc. (see Watkins 2000: s.v. wed-[1]). The root vowel alternates almost exclusively between *a* and zero; furthermore, once again none of the abundantly attested reflexes in other languages demonstrates a similar specialization of meaning. The Toronto *DOE* (s.v. *eowend*) describes the term as a "noun of uncertain etymology" and refers the reader with a ? to *eowan* "to display, show."

{XXIIII}

30 [L29] **Gif** mon twyhyndne mon unsynnigne mid hloðe ofslea, gielde se ðæs sleges andetta sie wer ⁊ wite; ⁊ æghwelc mon ðe on siðe wære geselle xxx scill to hloðbote.

{XXV}

30.1 [L30] Gif hit sie syxhynde mon, ælc mon to hloðbote[96] LX scill, ⁊ se slaga wer ⁊ fulwite.

{XXVI}

30.2 [L31] Gif he sie twelfhynde, ælc hiora hundtwelftig scill, /43v/ se slaga wer ⁊ wite.

30.3 [L31.1] Gif hloð ðis gedó ⁊ eft oðswerian wille, tio hie ealle; ⁊ þonne ealle forgielden þone wer gemænum hondum ⁊ ealle án wite, swa to ðam were belimpe.

{XXVII}

31 [L26] **Gif** mon ungewintrædne wifmon to niedhæmde geðreatige, sie ðæt swa ðæs gewintredan monnes bot.

Af §30 Gif mon twyhyndne mon] Gyf man twyhynde man BH   mid hloðe ofslea] ofslea mid hloþe H   gielde] gylde B; gilde H   se] se \ðe/ H   sie] sy BH   æghwelc] ælc H; æghwylc H   mon] *om.* H   siðe] syþe B   geselle] ge sylle B   xxx] ðritag B   hloðbote] loðbote B

Af §30.1 sie] sy BH   syxhyndne mon] syx hynde man BH   mon] *om.* B; man H   LX] feowertig \scill/ B   fulwite] fu\l/wite H

Af §30.2 sie] sy BH   twelfhynde] .xii.hynde H   hiora] heora B; he\o/ra H   hundtwelftig] .cxx. H   se slaga] \⁊/ se slaga B

Af §30.3 oðswerian wille] ætswerian wylle B   tio hie] teo hi B; teo \man/ hy H   forgielden] forgylden B; forgilden H   wer] wær H   gemænum hondum] *gemæne* handum B; gemæn*um* handum H   were belimpe] were \to/ belimpe B

Af §31 ungewintrædne wifmon] ungewintredne wifman B; ungewintredne \wif/man H   niedhæmde] nydhæmede BH   sie] sy B   gewintredan monnes] gewintredes mannes B; gewintredan mannes H

[96] The term is unattested in the corpus of Old English outside of this clause and the clause immediately prior.

30 [L29] If someone in a band[97] slays an innocent 200-[wergild] man,[98] let him who admits the slaying pay *wer* and fine; and let each man who was on the expedition add 30 shillings as compensation for taking part in the band.[99]

30.1 [L30] If it is a 600-[wergild] man, let each man give 60 shillings as compensation for taking part in the band, and the slayer *wer* and full fine.

30.2 [L31] If he should be [a] 1,200-[wergild man], each of [the members of the band] 120 shillings, the slayer *wer* and fine.

30.3 [L31.1]. If the band should do this, and afterwards wish to deny it,[100] let them all be accused; and then let all pay the *wer* communally and all a single fine, such as is appropriate to the *wer*.[101]

31 [L26] If someone rapes an underage girl,[102] let the compensation be the same as for a mature person.[103]

---

[97] Between seven and thirty-five men, according to *Ine* §14. Liebermann's chapter numbers here appear in the order of his edition, where they are rearranged so as to reconcile a discrepancy in Lambarde's edition with the numeration of Schmid and Thorpe. Attenborough's numeration does not follow Liebermann's for these clauses.

[98] That is, a *ceorl*.

[99] *Ine* §34 sets the higher fine of 50 shillings.

[100] Whitelock: "i.e., each wishes to deny being the actual slayer."

[101] Either the members of the band genuinely do not know who was responsible for a slaying that no one admits or they are concealing their knowledge of who the perpetrator was. In either case, the band must share the payment of recompense. *LexFris* §14 leaves the judgment as to the perpetrator up to ordeal by lot.

[102] Grave goods in some Anglo-Saxon cemeteries suggest that this may indicate a girl younger than twelve (Crawford 1999: 26–27).

[103] Old English *gewintred* can mean either "of age" or "elderly." Hough 1997 adduces clauses from other barbarian laws in which a contrast for purposes of compensating homicide is established between women of child-bearing age and those that are not, either because they are too young or too old. (See also Oliver 2011: 194–1990.) Hough thus interprets this clause as ruling that compensation for a young girl is the same as for a woman past child-bearing age. The other, more common, interpretation, is that compensation for an underage girl is the same as that for a woman (of any age). Two reasons exist for preferring this interpretation. First, the clauses that Hough is bringing as parallels address homicide, not rape. Penalties for rape in barbarian law are contingent upon virginity or lack thereof; the rape of a woman past child-bearing age is never explicitly considered (see Oliver 2011: 182–184). Second, the term *gewintred* occurs in only one other place in West Saxon law: *Ine* §39 requires that the relatives of a child whose father has died maintain the homestead *oððæt hit gewintred sie* ("until the child has reached maturity"). No possible connotation of "old age" can be applicable here.

32 [L27] Gif fædrenmæga mægleas mon gefeohte ⁊ mon ófslea, ⁊ þon*n*e gif medrenmægas hæbbe, gielden ða þæs weres ðriddan dæl [ðriddan dæl þa gegyldan, for ðriddan dæl]¹⁰⁴ he fleo.

32.1 [L27.1] Gif he medrenmægas nage, gielden þa gegildan healfne, for healfne he fleo.

{XXVIII}

32.2 [L28] Gif mon swa geradne mon ofslea, gif he mægas nage, gielde mon healfne cyninge, healfne þa*m* gegildan.

{XXVIIII}

33 [L32] Gif mon folcleasunge¹⁰⁵ gewyrce, ⁊ hio on hine geresp¹⁰⁶ weorðe, mid nanum leohtran ðinge gebete þon*n*e him mon aceorfe þa tungon óf, þæt hie mon na undeorran weorðe moste lesan, ðonne hie mon be þam were geeahtige.

Af §32 fædrenmæga mægleas] fædren ma\æ/ga mæigleas B; fæd\d/ren mæga H   mon²] man H   medrenmægas] meddren magas B; me\d/dren mægas H   gielden] gylden B; gilden H   dæl ... fleo] dæl for ðriddan dæl he fleo B; ðriddan dæl ða gegyldan . for ðriddan dæl he fleo H
Af §32.1 Gif he medrenmægas nage] gyf \he/ medren magas næbbe B; Gif he medren magas nage H   gielden] gylden B; gilden H   gegildan] gegyldan B   for] and for H
Af §32.2 mon (2x)] man BH   mægas] magas BH   gielde] gylde B; gilde H   mon] man BH   healfne cyninge] healfe kyninge B; healfne \were þam/ cyninge H   gegildan] gegyldan B
Af §33 mon] man H (*first two occurrences only*)   hio] heo BH   geresp weorðe] geræf weorðe B; weorðe geræf H   gebete] \ne/ gebete B   tungon] tungan BH   hie] heo B; hy H   lesan] alysan H   hie] heo B; hy H   hie] heo B; *om.* H   geeahtige] ge ehtige B

¹⁰⁴ This phrase, necessary to the meaning, is lacking in Parker (E) and has been inserted here from *Textus Roffensis*.
¹⁰⁵ *Hapax legomenon*.
¹⁰⁶ *Hapax legomenon*. Possible etymologies are murky, but the meaning is clear in context.

32 [L27] If someone who has no paternal kin fights and kills someone, and if he nonetheless has maternal kin, let them pay a third portion of the *wer*, and his associates a third portion, and for the third portion let him flee.[107]

32.1 [L27.1] If he has no maternal kin, let the associates pay half, for half let him flee.

32.2 [L28] If someone kills a man in this condition – that is, he has no kin – let him pay half to the king and half to the associates.[108]

33 [L32] If someone engages in public slander, and he is convicted of it, let him pay with no lighter settlement than that one should cut out his tongue, nor shall it be redeemed for a lesser worth than is reckoned according to his *wer*.[109]

---

[107] he fleo ("let him flee") is unclear. *Ine* §75 states that if a Welsh slave kills an English man, his lord has the option to free him rather than pay restitution. If the slave has free kin, they must then pay the *wer*. If not, *heden his þa gefan* ("his enemies may take possession of him"). Perhaps this is what the guilty party here is fleeing. Whitelock suggests that "the payment of their proper share frees the kinsmen from the dangers of a vendetta, even if the whole wergild is not paid. The slayer himself remains exposed if his own third is unpaid." Thorpe reads the phase straightforwardly as banishment, citing the Old Danish *Eric's Zealand Law* II §3 *ok han sly siælf frithlös* ("and let him flee frithless").

[108] O'Brien (1996: 348) indicates that the division of wergild between king and associates "implies an assumption by both artificial kin groups and the king of some or all of the kin's obligations to protect or avenge."

[109] Wormald notes that the penalty "happens to be that of the Theodosian Code, hence of the 'Breviary of Alaric,' and its topicality in the ninth century is shown by its appearance both in a forged decretal and in the writings of Hincmar" (1999a: 282). The tongue would be redeemed at 1/3 of the value of the wergild; c.f. §56. In the same fashion, *Ine* §18 and §38 and *Alfred* §7 require amputation of the hand for theft.

{xxx}

34 [L33] Gif hwa oðerne godborges[110] oncunne ⁊ tion wille, þæt he
hwelcne ne gelæste ðara ðe he him gesealde, agife þone foreað on
feower ciricum, ⁊ se oðer, gif he hine treowan wille, in XII ciricum dó
he ðæt.

{xxxi}

35 [L34] Eác is ciepemonnum gereht: ða men ðe hie up mid him
læden, gebrengen beforan kyninges gerefan on folcgemote, ⁊ gerecce
hu manige þara sien; ⁊ hie nimen þa men mid him þe hie mægen eft
to folcgemote to ryhte brengan; ⁊ þonne him ðearf sie ma manna úp
mid him to habbanne on hiora fore, gecyðe symle, swa óft swa him
ðearf sie, /44r/ in gemotes gewitnesse cyninges gerefan.

Af §34 tion wille] teon wylle B; teon wille H   hwelcne] hwylcne BH   foreað] for aþ
H   treowan wille] treowian wylle B   in] innan B   XII ciricum] twelf cyricum B; .XII.
ciric   dó he ðæt] do þæt (*added later in right margin*) H
Af §35 ciepemonnum] cype monnum B; cypemannum H   hie] hi B; hy H   him]
heom BH   læden] lædað B; lædan H   gebrengen] gebringan B; gebringe H   ger-
ecce] gerecca B   manige] monie B; monige H   þara sien] þæra syn BH   hie] hi B; hy
H   him] heom B; up mid him H   hie mægen] hig magon B; hy magon H   to folcge-
mote] to folc\gemote/ H   to ryhte] *om.* B; \to/ ryhte H   brengan] bringan B   þonne
him] þonon heom B   sie] sy B   ma manna] *om.* B   hiora] heora B; to he\o/ra
H   symle] symble B; simle H   him⁵] *om.* B   gewitnesse] gewitnysse B

[110] *Hapax legomenon.*

34 [L33] If someone charges another [with having given] a pledge [confirmed by invocation] of God[111] and wishes to accuse him, that he did not perform one of those things that he promised him, let [the accuser] give a preliminary oath[112] in four churches, and the other, if he wishes to exculpate himself, let him [swear the necessary oath] in twelve churches.[113]

35 [L34] Also this is the law for merchants: they shall bring before the king's reeve in the folk assembly those men that they are taking up [country] with them, and count how many of them there are; and they shall take with them [only] the men that they might afterwards bring to justice at the folk assembly.[114] And if there is again need for them to take more men up with them to have on their journey, let them declare [this] likewise, as often as there is need, to the king's reeve with the witness of the assembly.[115]

---

[111] Compare *mennisc borg* (paraphrastically: "other(s) stand(s) surety") in §1.8, where the authority invoked is human and not divine. See also Chapter 3, 109–111.

[112] Attenborough defines the *fore-að* as "often … merely an oath of integrity; a declaration that the party bringing the suit entered it not out of malice, etc., but solely to procure the rights to which he was entitled by law."

[113] As Attenborough points out, the repetitions of the oath by accuser and defendant "would involve one or other of the parties in manifold perjury, and contempt of the saints and the church."

[114] Compare to *Ine* §25, which requires a merchant doing trade out in the countryside (as opposed to the town markets) to do so in front of witnesses.

[115] The men accompanying the merchant will be able to swear to the legitimacy of the transactions performed. However, the confirmation must be renewed each time the merchant travels, whether or not the accompanying group is the same or different. Liebermann says this refers to foreign and not native helpers as the latter would not need to be brought before the assembly. But this clause seems to guarantee that those the merchant said he would take with him actually accompanied him: he cannot falsely introduce another witness to the purchase who wasn't along on the trip. Keynes and Lapidge (1983: 308 n. 19) add the possibility that "the purpose of this clause was probably to ensure that all traffic within and across the two frontiers of the kingdom was carefully regulated: there was always the danger that men up to no good might masquerade as traders." The two interpretations are not necessarily contradictory.

{XXXII}

36 [L35] Gif mon cierliscne mon gebinde unsynnigne, gebete mid x scill.

36.1 [L35.1] Gif hine mon beswinge, mid xx scill gebete.

36.2 [L35.2] Gif he hine on hengenne alecgge, mid xxx scill gebete.

36.3 [L35.3] Gif he hine on bismor to homolan[116] bescire, mid x scill gebete.

Af §36 mon (2x)] man H   cierliscne] ceorliscne B   unsynnigne] unscyldigne B   x] tyn B
Af §36.1 mon] man BH   xx] twentig B
Af §36.2 hengenne alecgge] hengene ge bringe BH   xxx] ðritag B
Af §36.3 on bismor] \on bysmer/ H   homolan bescyre] homelan bescyre B; homelan bescire H

[116] *Hapax legomenon.*

36 [L35] If someone binds an innocent *ceorl*, let [the man who bound him] compensate with 10 shillings.[117]

36.1 [L35.1] If someone flogs [an innocent *ceorl*], let him pay with 20 shillings.

36.2 [L35.2] If he puts him in confinement, let him pay with 30 shillings.[118]

36.3 [L35.3] If he shears his hair to the point of mutilation to shame him, let him pay with 10 shillings.[119]

---

[117] *Æthelberht* §25 [L24] stipulates a fine of 20 shilllings for binding a free man; this represents 20 percent of a freeman's wergild, while Alfred's fine is only 5 percent.

[118] The meaning of *on hengenne alecgge* is somewhat opaque. Schmid (followed by Attenborough) suggests that, lacking a prison, a man could be tied to the stocks. The purport is clearly that the accused is somehow restrained by a method other than binding, as that was already covered in §36.

[119] The term **homelan** is a *hapax legomenon*. Given that the related verb *hamelian* means "to mutilate," one might interpret this as a partial scalping, in which some of the scalp is removed along with the hair. (Scalping is prescribed for particularly grave offenses in Visigothic law; see Oliver 2011: 176.) The argument against this interpretation is that the fine seems much too low for a permanently visible injury. Liebermann interprets the action as shaving the head to resemble a fool or madman. Grimm 1899: 702–703 provides several legislative comparanda concerning forcible haircuts. Thorpe claims that "it formed part of an ignominious punishment inflicted upon slaves and offenders of the worst class," but evidence for this in early medieval England is uncertain; David Pelteret knows of none (p.c.).

36.4 [L35.4] Gif he hine to preoste bescire unbundenne, mid xxx scill gebete.

36.5 [L35.5] Gif he ðone beard ófascire, mid xx scill gebete.

36.6 [L35.6] Gif he hine gebinde ⁊ þon*ne* to preoste bescire, mid LX scill gebete.

Af §36.4 bescire] bescyre BH
Af §36.5 *Given in right margin, in a later hand*: Gif he þone beard of ascere mid xx scill gebet B
Af §36.6 to] \to/ B
LX] syxtig (feowertig *written above, in later hand*) B

36.4 [L35.4] If he shears him unbound as a priest,[120] let him pay with 30 shillings.

36.5 [L35.5] If he shears off his beard, let him pay with 20 shillings.

36.6 [L35.6] If he binds him, and then shears him as a priest, let him pay with 60 shillings.[121]

[120] The stigma of slavery may to some extent account for the prohibition against shearing a man "as a priest": "[A]mong the Greeks and Romans such a custom was a badge of slavery. On this very account, the shaving of the head was adopted by the monks. Towards the end of the fifth, or beginning of the sixth, century, the custom passed over to the secular clergy" (Fanning 1912: 779). That such associations should have persisted into the late ninth century seems remarkable given the more conventional view that the tonsure represented the crown of thorns: see Ceolfrith's letter in Bede, *Historia ecclesiastica*, v.21 (Colgrave and Mynors 1969: 548–549); also Æthelwulf, *De abbatibus* (Campbell 1967: 8–9) ll. 67–68: "[H]e rejoiced to carry on his head the crown which Christ formerly bore on his precious head" (*gaudebatque suo capiti portare coronam / uertice quam Christus quondam portabat opimo*). But the treatment of Childeric III upon the accession of Pippin in 750 as narrated in the *Annales regni Francorum* (Rau 1987: 14) was doubtless intended on one level as a form of humiliation: "Childeric however, who was falsely called a king, was tonsured and put in a monastery" (*Hildericus vero, qui false rex vocabatur, tonsoratus est et in monasterium missus*); cf. also Einhard, *Vita Karoli* §1. *Wihtred* §6 [L7] urges a wary attitude toward tonsured men not known to be bound by a rule.

[121] Liebermann emends this to 40 following B, reasoning that this would be the sum of the fines stipulated in §36 and §36.4.

{XXXIII}

37 [L36] Eac is funden: gif mon hafað spere ofer eaxle, ⁊ hine mon
on asnaseð,¹²² gielde þone wer, butan wite.

  37.1 [L36.1] Gif beforan eagum asnase, gielde þone wer.

Af §37 funden] \ge/funden H   mon] man H   hafað] hæfð B   mon] man
BH   asnaseð gielde] onsnæseþ gylde B; \on/asnæseð gilde H
Af §37.1 *Given in margin, in a later hand:* Gif beforan eagum gylde þone wer
B   asnase] asnæse H   gielde] gilde H

¹²² The two instances of this verb in this paragraph are *hapax legomena*.

37 [L36] Likewise it is determined: if someone has a spear on [his] shoulder,[123] and someone impales himself on it, let him pay the *wer*, without a fine.[124]

37.1 [L36.1] If he should impale himself before the eyes [of the spear-carrier], let him pay the *wer*.

---

[123] The point of the spear is behind the shoulder; §37.1 deals with the case where the spear is reversed.

[124] As Fruscione (2014: 44) points out, the relevance of intent or its absence is foreshadowed in *MP* §13; the topicality of such concerns is likewise evidenced by, e.g., §36 of the Council of Tribur. Wormald (1999a: 282) earlier proposed that this is an example of case law. But the possibility should not be discounted that this provision owes something to customs shared beyond England. A similar clause in *LexFris Add.* III §11, the judgment of Saxmund, reads:

If any man holds a weapon in his hand and this strikes another by whatever cause, against the will of the man who holds it in his hand, he need only compensate it according to the type of wound.

(*Si homo quislibet telum manus tenet, et ipsum casu quolibet inciderit super alium, extra voluntatem eius qui illud manu tenet, in simplo iuxta qualitatem vulneris componat.*)

When Frisian law is written in the vernacular several centuries later, the stipulation reappears (Buma and Ebel 1963: 50):

Riüstring §IV.12: [...] or if a serious injury is done behind the back with a weapon carried backwards, but without intention [...].

([...] *ieftha ther werth en ergere dede urbek eden mith bekwardiga wepne and bi unwille*) [...].

Though the correspondence is not very close between the Frisian laws mentioned here and *Alfred*, the latter cannot have been known in Frisia in either the early or later Middle Ages, and so this group of clauses attests in all likelihood to the survival of an oral tradition in Wessex whose most visible traces are Frisian.

37.2 Gif hine mon tio gewealdes on ðære dæde, getriowe hine be þam wite ⁊ mid ðy þæt wite afelle [L36.2] gif se ord sie ufor þonne hindeweard sceaft.

37.3 Gif hie sien bu gelic, ord ⁊ hindeweard sceaft, þæt sie butan pleo.

{XXXIIII}

38 [L37] **Gif** mon wille of boldgetale in oðer boldgetæl hlaford secan, do ðæt mid ðæs ealdormonnes gewitnesse, þe he ær \in/[125] his scire folgode.

Af §37.2 mon] man BH   tio] teo BH   getriowe] getriowsie B; getrywe H   ðy] ðam BH   afelle] afylle BH   gif] \⁊ þis beo/ gyf B; *colored initial in* H *suggests that scribe considered it new clause*   sie] \si/ B; sy H   ufor] þreo fingre ufor H
Af §37.3 Gif hie sien] \Ac/ gyf hi syn B; Gif hy syn H   bu] buta B   gelic] gelice B   sie] sy BH
Af §38 mon] man H   wille of boldgetale] wylle of boldgetæl B; of bold getale wi\l/le H   ealdormonnes] ealdormannes BH   gewitnesse] gewitnysse B   \in/ his scire] on his scire H

[125] Added later by scribe above line.

37.2 If he is accused of violent intention in the deed, let him clear himself by [an oath equal to] the fine, and with that the fine is dismissed, [L36.2] if the point is higher than the shaft in the back.[126]

37.3 If they are equal in height, the point and the shaft in the back, that shall not be considered danger[ous intention].

38 [L37] If someone wishes [to leave] from his district[127] to seek a lord in another district, let him do so with the knowledge of the ealdorman, to whom he was subject before in his shire.[128]

---

[126] *Textus Roffensis* stipulates that the point must be three fingers higher than the back.

[127] Old English *boldgetal* is literally "a number of houses." Whitelock points out that Wærferth uses it to translate *provincia*: only three other occurances appear in the corpus, all in the Old English *Dialogues of Gregory*. These and other possible Mercianisms in the laws of Alfred may survive as traces of Offa's laws; yet Dammery (1990: 239) holds that these "cannot, however, be construed as conclusive evidence of borrowing from Offa's law, since Alfred had several Mercian advisors at his court who could have been actively involved in the preparation of his law-code" (1990: 249–240). Cf. Asser (Stevenson 1959: 62 (§77)), which describes the recruitment to Alfred's court of Wærferth (Bishop of Worcester), Plegmund (Archbishop of Canterbury), and the priests Æthelstan and Werwulf, "which four King Alfred called to himself from Mercia" (*Quos quattuor Ælfred rex de Mercia ad se advocaverat*).

[128] Nicholas Brooks (2003: 154) suggests the possibility that "the structure of shires run by ealdormen dates from the reign of King Ine (685–725); in that case the references in Ine's laws to *scirmen* and to ealdormen and their *scirs*, could be accepted as referring to this same system. [See *Ine* §§8, 37.1, 40.] Otherwise we must regard them either as a later updating (perhaps when the code had been appended to Alfred's lawbook) or as referring not to the shires familiar to us in later times but rather to an older system of smaller units of lordship." Pratt (2007: 98) postulates that this clause may indicate "a problem of peasant vagrancy. Many West Saxons had accepted Danish rule in 878." Further, Pratt mentions charter S362 in which Wulfhere, ealdorman of Wiltshire and his wife have to forfeit their estate when the former deserts in violation of an oath earlier sworn to the king (Pratt 2007: 239). Compare *Ine* §40. See also §1 and n. 14.

38.1 [L37.1] Gif he hit butan his gewitnesse do, geselle se þe hine to men feormie cxx scill to wite: dæle he hwæðre ðæt, _____¹²⁹healf cyninge in ða scire ðe he ǽr folgode, healf in þa ðe he oncymð.

38.2 [L37.2] Gif he hwæt yfla gedon hæbbe ðær he ær wæs, bete ðæt se ðe hine ðonne to men onfo, ⁊ cy_____¹³⁰ninge cxx scill to wite.

{xxxv}

39 [L38] /44v/ Gif mon beforan cyninges ealdormen on gemote gefeohte, bete wer ⁊ wite, swa hit ryht sie, ⁊ beforan þam cxx scill ðam ealdormen to wite.

39.1 [L38.1] Gif he folcgemot mid wæpnes bryde árǽre, ðam ealdormen hundtwelftig scill to wite.

Af §38.1 butan] buton B   gewitnesse] *ge*witnysse B   geselle se þe] gesylle \se ðe/ B; gesylle se þe H   hine] hyne H   feormie] feormige H   cxx] hund twelftig B   dæle he hwæðre ðæt] dæle he hwæðere *þæt* B; dæle he þæt hweð\e/re H   cyninge] \þam/ cyninge BH (*later addition in both*)   folgode] folgade \⁊/ H   in þa ðe he oncymð] onða ðe he \þonne/ on cymð H
Af §38.2 yfla] to yfele BH   hæbbe] hæfð BH   ðonne] ðonnon B; bete ðæt þonne se ðe hine H   onfo] underfo B; \under/onfó H   cxx] hund twelftig B
Af §39 gefeohte] feohtæþ B   ryht sie] riht sy BH   cxx] hund twelftig   ealdormen to wite] ealdor*man* ⁊ hund twelftig scill to wite B; ealder men H
Af §39.1 *om.* B (*see end of previous clause*)   folcgemot] folces gemot H   ealdormen] ealdermen H

¹²⁹ Gap in line.
¹³⁰ Gap in line.

38.1 [37.1] If he does it without his knowledge, let him who took him on as his man pay 120 shillings as fine: however, he should divide that, half to the [lord][131] in the shire he belonged to before and half to [the lord] in that [shire] where he has arrived.[132]

38.2 [L37.2] If he has commited some offense where he was before, let him who took him on as his man compensate for that, and 120 shillings to the king as fine.[133]

39 [L38] If someone fights in the assembly in the presence of the king's ealdorman, let him compensate with *wer* [of the person he injured] and fine, according to the law, and furthermore let him pay 120 shillings to the *ealdorman* as fine.[134]

39.1 [L38.1] If he disrupts the folk meeting by drawing his weapon, 120 shillings to the *ealdorman* as fine.[135]

---

[131] Text reads (erroneously) "king."
[132] *Ine* §40 requires that the man himself, not the lord, pay the fine: 60 shillings to his first lord.
[133] The fine to the king is thus doubled.
[134] He pays the *wer* for any injury he has caused, the fine to the king, and a further fine to the ealdorman who was present at the altercation. *Æthelberht* §7 requires double compensation for disturbance of *mæthlfrith* ("assembly peace") *LexBav* §2.10 requires of one who starts a fight in the house of the lord "due to arrogance or drunkenness" that he pay for whatever damage has been caused and 40 shillings to the fisc *propter stultitiam suam in publico* ("due to his stupidity in public").
[135] These two clauses seem to allow the huge fine of 240 shillings for someone who draws his weapon in the king's assembly. Each action individually is fined at 120 shillings. *Alfred* §40.1 states that drawing a weapon in a *ceorl*'s house but not using it to fight draws half the fine of a fight.

39.2 [L38.2] Gif ðises hwæt beforan cyninges ealdormonnes gingran gelimpe oððe cyninges preoste, xxx scill to wite.

{XXXVI}

40 [L39] **Gif** hwa on cierlisces monnes flette gefeohte, mid syx scill gebete ðam ceorle.

40.1. [L39.1] Gif he wæpne gebrede ꝛ no feohte, sie be healfum ðam.

40.2. [L39.2] Gif syxhyndum þissa hwæðer gelimpe, ðriefealdlice [arise be ðære cierliscan bote, twelfhyndum men twyfealdlice][136] be þæs syxhyndan bote.

41 [L40] Cyninges burgbryce bið cxx scill, ærcebiscepes hundnigontig scill, oðres biscepes ꝛ ealdormonnes LX scill, twelfhyndes monnes xxx scill, syxhyndes monnes xv scill; ceorles edorbryce[137] v scill.

41.1 [L40.1] Gif ðisses hwæt gelimpe, ðenden fyrd ute sie, oððe in lenctenfæsten, hit sie twybote.

42 [L40.2] Gif mon in lenctenne halig ryht in folce butan leafe alecgge, gebete mid cxx scill.

Af §39.2 ðises] ðisses B   ealdormonnes] ealdormannes B; ealder mannes H   gingran] gi_ngran H   xxx] ðrittig B
Af §40 cierlisces monnes] ceorlisces mannes B; ciorlisces monnes H   mid syx scill gebete] mid vi scill gebete B; gebete mid .vi. scll   ceorle] ciorle H
Af §40.1 gebrede] gebre_de H   no] ne BH   sie] sy BH
Af §40.2 Gif syxhyndum] Gyf \on/ vi hundu*m* B   þissa] \ðissa/ H   hwæðer] hweðer B   ðriefealdlice ... be] ðryfealdlice arise bæ ðære cyrliscan bote twelf hyndu*m* *men* twifealdlice B; ðri f\e/aldlice arise be ðære cierliscan bote H   syxhyndan] syxhyndu*m* B
Af §41 burgbryce] burh bryce B; burhbrice H Ot *commences with this chapter at* hun\d/nigontig f. 5ov   cxx] hundtwelftig   ærcebiscepes] erce *bisceopes* B; Ercebiscopes H   biscepes] bisceopes B; biscopes H   ealdormonnes] ealdormannes B; ealdermannes H   xv] syxtig B   twelfhyndes] twelf hyndes B; .Xii. hyndes H   monnes (2x)] mannes BH   xxx] ðrittig B   ceorles ... scill] *Given in margin, in later hand:* ceorles eoder bryce fif scill B; ceorles edorbrice.v.scll H
Af §41.1 ðenden] ðonne BH   sie] sy BH   lenctenfæsten] lenctene B   hit sie twybote] *in right margin, in a later hand:* si hit twibote B; hit sy twy bote H
Af §42 Gif mon in lenctenne] *Given in margin, in a later hand:* Gif man on lencten B; Gif man on lengten H   on folce] in folce BH   butan leafe] buton leafe B; butan \leafe/ H   alecgge] alecge B; ale\c/ge H   cxx] hundtwelftigu*m* BH   scill] scillingu*m* B

---

[136] This necessary phrase is missing from Parker but appears in **B** and **H** (added here from **H**).

[137] This compound appears elsewhere only in the laws of Æthelberht.

39.2 [L38.2] If something of this nature should occur before the subordinate[138] of a king's ealdorman or the king's priest, 30 shillings as fine.

40 [L39] If someone fights in a *ceorl*'s house, let him recompense the *ceorl* with six shillings.[139]

40.1 [L39.1] If he draws a weapon but does not fight, let it be half that.

40.2 [L39.2] If, however, this happens to a [man whose wergild is] 600, three-fold [the compensation of a *ceorl*]; for a [man whose wergild is] 1,200, twice the compensation of [a man whose wergild is] 600.

41 [L40] [The fine for] breaking into the king's fortified dwelling is 120 shillings; an archbishop's 90; another [lesser] bishop's or an ealdorman's 60 shillings; a man [whose *wer* is] 1,200 [shillings], 30 shillings; a man [whose *wer* is] 600 [shillings], 15 shillings; breaking into a *ceorl*'s enclosure 5 shillings.[140]

40.1 [L40.1] If something of this nature occurs while the army is out [on duty], or in the Lenten fast, it is double compensation.

42 [L40.2] If someone in the folk sets aside holy law without dispensation during Lent,[141] let him compensate with 120 shillings.

---

138 Likely, a junior officiating on the part of the ealdorman.

139 This must be in addition to whatever *wer* is appropriate to injury and the fine to the king. Compare rulings against fighting in public in *Hlophere and Eadric* §7 to §9 [L11–13] and *Ine* §6.

140 Note that the *ceorl*'s dwelling is not fortified, but rather surrounded by an *edor* (originally "hedge"). For the archaeological evidence on enclosed settlements, see Hamerow 2012: 109–119. For earlier rulings on breaking and entering, see *Æthelberht* §22 [L17], §28 [L27], §29 and *Ine* §46.

141 The prohibition is against transgression of ecclesiastical regulations (*halig ryht*) such as eating meat, transacting business, exacting lawful revenge, etc., during Lent.

{XXXVII}

43 [L41] Se mon se ðe bocland hæbbe, ⁊ him his mægas læfden,
þon*ne* setton we, þæt he hit ne moste sellan of his mægburge, gif þær
bið gewrit oððe gewitnes, ðæt hit ðara manna forbod wære þe hit on
fruman gestríndon ⁊ þara þe hit him sealdon, þæt he swa ne mote; ⁊
þæt þon*ne* on cyninges ⁊ on biscopes gewitnesse gerecce beforan his
mægum.

Af §43 *om.* B   mon] man H   him his] him \þonne/ his H   mægas læfden] yldran
læfdan H   moste sellan] mot syllan H   gewrit oððe gewitnes] gewritt oððe gewitnes
\se/ H   forbod] fod bod H   gestríndon] gestri_ndon H   mægum] magum H(Ot?)

43 [L41] [In the case of] the man who has bookland[142] which his kin left to him: we thus determine that he may not sell it out of his kindred if there is writing or testimony that it was forbidden by those who first acquired it or[143] by those who gave it to him, that he thus might not [remove it from the family possession]. And let him [who is contesting the sale] declare this in the presence of his kin with the knowledge of the king and of the bishop.[144]

[142] **bocland** is land deeded by charter; unlike *folcland*, it can be alienated from family property. Keynes and Lapidge (1983: 309 n. 24) state that:

> Although bookland could normally be bequeathed to anyone of the owner's choosing, the original grant of (the king) or the owner might on occasion stipulate that it could not in fact be alienated outside the kindred. For during the eighth century bookland was increasingly created not so much to enable a layman to endow a church, as to entitle him to hold his land free from the public burdens (with the exception of bridge-work, etc.) and in such cases it might be advisable to protect the long-term interests of the kindred by explicitly restricting the owner's powers of alienation. [...] This practice may well have originated in eighth-century Mercia, suggesting the possibility that it was an analogous clause in Offa's code that gave rise to the present clause in Alfred's.

For an alternative interpretation, see Dammery 1990: 240 (here summarizing an earlier version of Wormald 1991).

[143] The manuscript has ⁊, which can mean "and" or "or." Liebermann assumes the first, but witness of constraint on sale, whether initial or later, remains constraint.

[144] Whether the person making the sale or those wishing to block the sale must bring the justification is unclear. But it seems more likely to be the person who has brought the charge of illegal breaking of the entail; the seller, conversely, would have to establish that there were no such constraints, but that would seem to require an oath rather than a declaration. Keynes and Lapidge (1983: 309 n. 25) suggest a third option: "It may be that it is the owner of the bookland who is required to announce in public the existence of the special restrictions on his powers of alienation, so as to prevent him from disregarding them at the expense of his kindred."

{XXXVIII}

44 [L42] Eac we beodað: se mon se ðe his gefán hamsittendne wite, þæt /45r/ he ne feohte, ærðam he him ryhtes bidde.

44.1 [L42.1] Gif he mægnes hæbbe, þæt he his gefán beride 7 inne besitte, gehealde hine VII niht inne 7 hine ón ne feohte, gif he inne geðólian wille; 7 þonne ymb VII niht, gif he wille on hand gan 7 wæpenu sellan, gehealde hine XXX nihta gesundne 7 hine his mægum gebodie 7 his friondum.

44.2 [L42.2] Gif he ðonne cirican geierne, sie ðonne be ðære cirican are, swa we ær bufan cwædon.

44.3 [L42.3] Gif he ðonne þæs mægenes ne hæbbe, þæt he hine inne besitte, ride to þam ealdormen, bidde hine fultumes; gif he him fultuman ne wille, ride to cyninge, ær he feohte.

Af §44 *om.* B   mon] man H   ærðam] ær ðam ðe H
Af §44.1 *om.* B   inne besitte] hine \inne/ besitte H *(presumably added in accordance with* §44.3)   VII (2x)] seofan   feohte] fe\o/hte H   ymb] ymbe H   7 wæpenu sellan] and \his/ wæpnu syllan H   his mægum gebodie 7 his friondum] his freondum \7 his magum/ bebeode H; magum Ot
Af §44.2 *om.* B   cirican geierne, sie] cir\i/cean geyrne sy H; [ ]ne geierne s\i/e Ot   cirican] cir\i/cean H
Af §44.3 *om.* B   mægenes] mægnes H   fultuman ne wille] fultom\i/an nelle H

44 [L42] Likewise we command: for the man who knows that his enemy is sitting at home, that he not fight him before he offers to settle according to law.

44.1 [L42.1] If he has sufficient force [of numbers] that he may surround his enemy and besiege him inside, let him hold him seven nights therein and not attack him, if he is willing to endure it inside; and after seven nights, if he wishes to turn himself in[145] and give up his weapons, let him hold him unharmed for thirty nights, and summon for him his kin and his friend-group.[146]

44.2 [L42.2] If he however makes it to a church [for sanctuary], let it be according to church privilege, as we spoke of before above.[147]

44.3 [L42.3] If he however does not have [sufficient] force that he may besiege him inside, let him ride to the ealdorman and ask him for support; if he is not willing to give him support, let him ride to the king before he attacks.

---

[145] The phrase *on hand gan* denotes formal submission to another's authority; the offender is entrusting himself to the mercy of his foe – in Germanic terms, placing himself under the *mund* of his enemy. The gesture upon which mercy is contingent here is likewise close to the legal ritual referred to as *deditio* in Continental sources, on which see Roach 2012.

[146] That the party is obliged to summon the kin and allies of the besieged man indicates that he is not to be slain even after 30 days have elapsed – for their presence at his dwelling would surely preclude this.

[147] See *Alfred* §2.

44.4 [L42.4] Eac swelce, gif mon becume on his gefán, 7 he hine ǽr hamfæstne ne wite, gif he wille his wæpen sellan, hine mon gehealde xxx nihta 7 hine his freondum gecyðe; gif he ne wille his wæpenu sellan, þonne mot he feohtan on hine. Gif he wille on hond gan 7 his wæpenu sellan, 7 hwa ofer ðæt on him feohte, gielde swa wer swa wunde swa he gewyrce, 7 wite, 7 hæbbe his mæg forworht.

45 [L42.5] Eac we cweðað, þæt mon mote mid his hlaforde feohtan orwige, gif mon on ðone hlaford fiohte; swa mót se hlaford mid þy men feohtan.

Af §44.4 om. B   swelce] swylce H   mon becume] man becyme H   hamfæstne] þam-fæstne H   sellan] syllan H   mon] man H   ne wille] nelle H   wæpenu] wæpen H   hond] hand H   wæpenu] wæpen H   7 hwa] 7 gif hwa H   on him] on hine H   gielde] gylde H   wunde] wundwite H   swa he gewyrce] swa ðær he gew-yrce H   7 wite ... forworht] 7 wite ðæt he hæbbe his mæg forworht H (scribe misun-derstands clause, taking wite to be a form of the verb witan)
Af §45 om. B   mon] man H   þy] þam H

The Laws of Alfred

44.4 [L42.4] Similarly, if a man comes upon his enemy, and he did not know before that he was in his house, if he [the enemy] wishes to give up his weapons, let him be held for thirty nights and let his friend-group be notified. If he is not willing to give up his weapons then [the accuser] may attack him. If he [the enemy] wishes to turn himself in and give up his weapons, and someone attacks him despite that, let [the attacker] pay such *wer* as is due for wounding [he has caused], and a fine, and he has forfeited his kin-compensation.[148]

45 [L42.5] Likewise we declare, that one may fight at the side of his lord without incurring liability if someone fights against his lord; the lord may similarly fight at the side of [his] man.[149]

[148] As discussed in n. 198 to *Ine* §76, we accept Liebermann's hypothesis that this phrase includes a shift in meaning for **mæg** from "kin" to "restitution due kin for injury/manslaughter" similar to the shift of *wer* from "man" to "wergild" (although the latter represents more of an abbreviation than an actual semantic shift). Ine's clause reads: *Ne þearf se frige mid þam þeowan mæg gieldan, buton he him wille fæhðe ofaceapian* ("A free man need not pay kin-compensation for a slave, unless he wishes to protect him from violent retribution"). Although these are the only two such uses adduced by Liebermann, the interpretation seems to fit well in both cases. Keynes and Lapidge (following Whitelock) translate this portion of the clause as "he has forfeited his right to avenge his kin[sman]." Schmid interprets this phrase as the attacker having forfeited the right to the support of his kin-group, and Attenborough similarly as "his kinsman shall forfeit his claim to protection as a result of his action."

[149] That is, any killing done while fighting on behalf of one's lord is not legally open to retribution by the kin of the slain man. This and the following clause represent "the sole law to this effect in all the early medieval West" (Wormald, 1999a: 283). The *Poenitentiale Theodori* (i.iv.1) stipulates that, while a slaying to avenge a relative entails a penance of seven to ten years (halved if one pays compensation), a killing ordered by one's lord obliges one to "keep away from the church for forty days" (McNeill and Gamer 1938: 187).

45.1 [L42.6] Æfter þære ilcan wisan mon mot feohtan mid his geborene mæge, gif hine mon on woh onfeohteð, buton wið his hlaforde: þæt we ne liefað.

45.2 [L42.7] ⁊ mon mot feohtan órwige, gif he gemeteð oþerne æt his æwum wife, betynedum durum oððe under anre reón,¹⁵⁰ oððe æt his dehter æwumborenre¹⁵¹ \oððe æt his swistær borenre/¹⁵² oððe æt his medder ðe wære to æwum wife forgifen his fæder.

Af §45.1 *om.* B   geborene] geborenum H   buton] butan H   liefað] lyfað H
Af §45.2 *om.* B   gemeteð oþerne] oðerne gemeteð H   æt (3x)] mid H   betynedum]
betynede H   oððe æt his swistær borenre] \oððe mid his swister æwumborenre/ H
(*later addition in right margin*)

¹⁵⁰ *Hapax legomenon.*
¹⁵¹ *Hapax legomenon.*
¹⁵² Added later by scribe above line. That the added text occurs as well in *Textus Roffensis* and appears to occur in **Ot** makes its authenticity quite likely.

45.1 [L42.6] In the same manner a man may fight at the side of his born kin, if they are attacked wrongfully, except against his lord: that we do not allow.[153]

45.2 [L42.7] And a man may fight without incurring liability if he finds another with his lawful wife, behind doors or under a single blanket or with his lawfully born daughter,[154] or with his born sister, or with his mother who was given as lawful wife to his father.[155]

---

[153] Cf. the episode of Cynewulf and Cyneheard in the *Anglo-Saxon Chronicle* s.a. 755 (=757), which pointedly asserts that fidelity to one's lord outweighs obligations to one's kin.

[154] For the overlap of the meanings "marriage" and "law" in the Old English term æ, see Fischer 1986: 84–95.

[155] These are the women whose *mund* belongs to the head of the household. *LexBav* §8.1 similarly allows a husband to kill a man found in bed with his wife without incurring wergild obligations.

{XXXVIII[I]}[156]

46 [L43] /45v/ Eallum frioum monnum ðas dagas sien forgifene,
butan þeowum monnum ⁊ esnewyrhtan: XII dagas on gehhol ⁊ ðone
dæg þe Crist ðone deofol oferswiðde ⁊ sanctus Gregorius gemynd-
dæg ⁊ VII dagas to eastron ⁊ VII ofer ⁊ an dæg æt sancte Petres tide
⁊ sancte Paules ⁊ on hærfeste ða fullan wican ǽr sancta Marian
mæssan ⁊ æt eallra haligra weorðunge anne dæg; ⁊ IIII
Wodnesdagas on IIII ymbrenwicum[157] ðeowum monnum eallum sien
forgifen, þam þe him leofost sie to sellanne æghwæt ðæs ðe him
ænig mon for Godes noman geselle oððe hie on ænegum hiora hwil-
sticcum[158] geearnian mægen.

Af §46 frioum monnum] freo_mannum H   monnum] mannum H   esnewyrhtan]
esne wyrhtum H   sien forgifene] syn forgifen\n/e H   gehhol] gehhel H (geol *written
above*)   ðone deofol oferswiðde] oferswiðde ðone deofol H; [ ]eofol oferswiþ\d/e
Ot   VII] seofon H   B *resumes at* dagas to eastron (eastrum H)   VII] seofen B; .VII.
H   æt] to H   hærfeste] herfeste BH   wican] wucan BH   Marian] maria B (*end
Ot*)   anne] an B   IIII (2x)] feower B   ymbrenwicum] ymbrenwucum B; ymbrenwu-
can H   monnum] mannum H   sien] synd B; syn H   forgifen] forgyfen B; forgifen
H   leofost sie] leofest sy B; leofast sy H   sellanne] syllanne BH   ænig] *om*. B   mon]
man BH   noman geselle] naman gesylle BH   hie] heo BH   ænegum] ænigum
BH   hiora] heora B; he\o/ra H   hwilsticcum] hwil styccum BH   geearnian mægen]
gearnian magan B; geearni_an magen H

[156] Some wear exists at the bottom of the page where the number is, but no trace of
the missing I can be discerned under normal lighting.
[157] *Hapax legomenon*, but variations on *ymbrendagas* ("ember days") are common.
[158] This term appears elsewhere only in glosses and the Old English *Dialogues of
Gregory*.

46 [L43] To all free men these days are given [off from work] except for slaves and *esnas*: twelve days at Christmas, and the day that Christ overcame the devil,[159] and the commemoration day of St Gregory,[160] and seven days before Easter and seven after, and one day at the feastday of St. Peter and St. Paul,[161] and in the harvest the full week before St. Mary's mass,[162] and at the honoring of All Saints[163] one day. And four Wednesdays on the four weeks in which Ember days fall[164] shall be given to all slaves, so that they can give to whoever is most dear to them a portion of whatever any man gives them in God's name or that they may earn in their fragments of time [in which they work on their own].[165]

---

[159] February 15.

[160] March 12. Gregory the Great enjoyed a special status in the Anglo-Saxon church as "Apostle of the English"; See Hayward 2004: 26–28.

[161] June 29.

[162] August 15.

[163] November 1.

[164] "Ember days (corruption from Lat. *Quatuor Tempora*, four times) are the days at the beginning of the seasons ordered by the Church as days of fast and abstinence. [...] The purpose of their introduction, besides the general one intended by all prayer and fasting, was to thank God for the gifts of nature, to teach men to make use of them in moderation, and to assist the needy" (Mershman 1909: 399). By the eleventh century, the Ember days fell on the Wednesday, Friday, and Saturday following: the feast of St. Lucia (December 13), Ash Wednesday (late February–early March), Whitsunday/Pentecost (fifty days after the Resurrection of Christ: mid-June), and the feast of the Exaltation of the Cross (September 14).

[165] One of a handful of passages in Old English prescriptive texts indicating that unfree status was no impediment to owning property; cf. also *Old English Canons of Theodore* §A24 (Fulk and Jurasinski 2012: 5 and n.)

{XL}

47 [L44] Heafodwunde to bote, gif ða ban beoð butu ðyrel, xxx scill geselle him mon.

47.1 [L44.1] Gif ðæt uterre ban bið þyrel, geselle xv scill to bote.

{XLI}

48 [L45] Gif in feaxe bið wund inces lang, geselle anne scill to bote.

48.1 [L45.1] Gif beforan feaxe bið wund inces lang, twegen scill to bote.

{XLII}

49 [L46] Gif him mon áslea oþer eare of, geselle xxx scill to bote.

49.1 [L46.1] Gif se hlyst oðstande, þæt he ne mæge gehieran, geselle LX scill to bote.

{XLIII}

50 [L47] Gif mon men eage ofáslea, geselle him mon LX scill 7 VI scill 7 VI pæningas 7 ðriddan dæl pæninges to bote.

Af §47 beoð butu ðyrel] beoð butu þyrle B; butu beoð ðyrl\e/ H   geselle] gesylle BH
Af §47.1 uterre] uttre B; utre H   þyrel] ðyrl BH   geselle] gesylle BH   xv] fihtyne B
Af §48 inces] ynces BH   geselle] gesylle BH
Af §48.1 Gif] gyf he B   inces] ynces BH
Af §49 mon] man BH (H *gives* Gif man him of aslea)   oþer eare] þæt oðer eare B   of] *om.* B (H *see above*)   geselle] *g*esylle BH   xxx] ðrittig B
Af §49.1 hlyst] lyst B   oðstande] ætstande B   mæge gehieran] mæg gehyran B; mæge gehiran H   geselle] gesylle BH   LX] syxti B   to bote] him to bote B (H *gives* .LX. scll to bote gesylle)
Af §50 mon men eage] man men his eage H   geselle] gesylle BH   LX] syxti B   VI] syx B   pæningas] penegas B; peningas H   pæninges] peniges B; peni_ges H

47^{166} [L44] As compensation for a headwound, if both bones are pierced, let him be paid 30 shillings.

47.1 [L44.1] If the outer bone [alone] is pierced, let him pay 15 shillings as compensation.^{167}

48 [L45] If a wound is an inch long above the hairline, let him pay one shilling as compensation.

48.1 [L45.1] If a wound is an inch long below the hairline, two shillings as compensation.

49 [L46] If someone strikes off either ear, let him pay 30 shillings as compensation.

49.1 [L46.1] If his hearing ceases to function, so that he can no longer hear, let him pay 60 shillings as compensation.

50 [L47] If someone strikes the eye from a man, he shall be given 60 shillings and 6 shillings and 6 pennies and a third of a penny as compensation.^{168}

---

[166] The remaining clauses all concern personal injury and seem to have been prepared with an awareness of similar provisions in Æthelberht, though the latter are not here reproduced (in spite of suggestions to the contrary in *Alfred*'s prefatory remarks).

[167] These bones refer to the tabula of the skull. The skull formation is composed of an outer and inner bone (tabulum) separated by a tissue called the diploe. The Anglo-Saxon laws are the only ones to regulate skull wounds according to the damage to the tabula; on the Continent the rulings are based on the size of bone slivers that are separated from the skull. This concordance provides solid evidence that Alfred did, in fact, know the laws of Æthelberht. (See Oliver 2010, and compare *Æthelberht* §36.)

[168] At 5 pennies to the shilling, 2/3 of a wergild should be 66 shillings, 3 1/3 pennies. But the same sum occurs in §75. No coin was ever struck in the amount of 1/3 penny, nor do we have any such extant fragment of a cast penny. As Rory Naismith points out, "[I]n the absence of any surviving third-penny pieces, [this fraction] must indicate a penny by weight or goods to the value of one third of a penny. The question of the general applicability of the law codes may be a moot point, as their relation to actual suits is notoriously obscure, and so how fines were paid in practice cannot be known. But if nothing else the laws must be used with some caution as evidence for coin-use" (Naismith 2012: 267). Barbarian laws generally assess the striking off of a hand, foot, or eye at 50 percent of the wergild; this holds true for Æthelberht. *Alfred*'s fine is thus considerably below the norm.

50.1 [L47.1] Gif hit in ðam heafde sie, ⁊ he noht geseon ne mæge mid, stande ðriddan dæl þære bote inne.

51 [L48] Gif mon oðrum þæt neb ófaslea, gebete him mid LX scill.

52 [L49] Gif mon oðrum ðone toð onforan heafde ófaslea, gebete þæt mid VIII scill.

52.1 [L49.1] Gif hit sie se wongtoð, geselle IIII scill to bote.

52.2 [L49.2] Monnes tux bið XV scill weorð.

53 [L50] Gif monnes \ᶜ/eacan¹⁶⁹ mon forslihð, þæt hie beoð forode, gebete mid XV scill.

54 [L50.1] Monnes cinban, gif hit bið toclofen, geselle mon XII scill to bote.

55 [L51] Gif monnes ðrotbolla bið þyrel, gebete mid XII scill.

Af §50.1 in] on H   sie] sy H   ðam] ðan B   sie] sy BH   ne mæge] \ne/ mæge H   stande ðriddan] stande \se/ þriddan H
Af §51 *Given in left margin, in a later hand:* Gif man oþru*m* þ*æt* nebb ofaslea gebete hit mid feowertig scill B; Gif man oðrum ðæt nebb of aslea gebete him mid .lx. scll H
Af §52 mon] man BH   onforan heafde ófaslea] ofslea onforan heafde H   gebete] gebetað B; \ge/bete H   VIII] eahta B
Af §52.1 sie se] sie ðe B; sy \þe/ H   wongtoð] wang toþ H   IIII] feower B
Af §52.2 Monnes] mannes H   xv] syxtyne B
Af §53 Gif monnes \ᶜ/eacan mon forslihð] Gyf man mannes ceacan forslea B; Gif mannes ceacan man for slyhð H   hie beoð forode] heo beon forede B; hy beon fored\e/ H   gebete þæt mid VIII] fiftyne scill gebete B; gebete mid .xv. scll H
Af §54 Monnes cinban] mannes cin\n/bán H   geselle] gesylle BH   xii] twelf B
Af §55 monnes] mannes BH   þyrel] ðyrl B   gebete mid] gebete ðæt mid H   XII] twelf B

¹⁶⁹ Scribe later added *c* above line.

50.1 [L47.1] If it remains in the head, but he may not see any-thing with it, let a third part of the compensation be withheld.

51 [L48] If someone strikes the nose[170] off another, let him compensate him with 60 shillings.

52 [L49] If someone strikes out from another the tooth in the front of the head, let him compensate that with 8 shillings.

52.1 [L49.1] If it is the molar, let him pay 4 shillings as compensation.

52.2 [L49.2] A person's canine tooth is worth 15 shillings.

53 [L50] If someone strikes a man's jaws, so that they are both broken [namely, upper and lower jawbones], let him pay with 15 shillings.

54 [L50.1] A person's chinbone, if it is shattered, let him be paid 12 shillings as compensation.

55 [L51] If a man's Adam's apple is pierced, let him be paid 12 shillings.

---

[170] The term "neb" originally meant "beak." "At least by the time of Alfred's laws (871x901), the sense of beak had been metaphorically extended from fowl to human" (Oliver 2011: 99). Liebermann says that in this usage *neb* might include the mouth, which is otherwise omitted from *Alfred*'s personal injury tariffs; *Æthelberht* here has both nose and mouth (§§43–44 [L44–45]).

56 [L52] Gif monnes tunge bið of heafde oþres monnes dædum dón, þæt biþ gelic 7 eagan[171] bot.

57 [L53] Gif mon bið on eaxle wund, *þæt* þæt liðseaw útflowe, gebete mid xxx scill.

58 [L54] Gif se earm bið forad bufan elmbogan, þær sculon xv scill to bote.

58.1 [L55] Gif ða earmscancan[172] beoð begen forade, sio bot bið xxx scill.

59 [L56] Gif se ðuma bið ófaslægen, þam sceal xxx scill to bote.

59.1 [L56.1] Gif se nægl bið ófaslegen, ðam sculon v scill to bote.

60 [L57] Gif se scytefinger bið ófaslegen, sio bót bið xv scill; his nægles bið iii scill.

Af §56 monnes (2x)] mannes BH   dædum] dedum   dón] *gedon* B; \ge/dón H   7] *om.* H   eagan] eagon B
Af §57 Gif mon bið on eaxle wund] Gyf mon on eaxle bið gewunded B; Gif man bið on ða eaxle \ge/wund\ed/ H   xxx] ðrittig B
Af §58 forad] forod H   bufan elmbogan] bufan ðam elbogan B; bufan \þæm/ el_ bogan H   xv] fiftyne B
Af §58.1 sio] seo BH   xxx] ðrittig B
Af §59 Gif se] Gyf ðe B   ófaslægen] ofaslagen B   ðam sceal] ðæm sceall B; þæm sc\e/ al H   xxx] ðrittig B
Af §59.1 nægl] nægel B   ófaslegen] ofaslagen B; ofaslægen H   ðam sculon v scill to bote] seo bot bið fift[   ] scill B
Af §60 ófaslegen] ofaslagen B; of aslægen H   sio] seo BH   7] *om.* H   bot] *om.* H   xv] fiftyne B   iii] iiii B

[171] The scribe has wrongly used the Tironian note 7 to represent *an*; the expansion would give *and eagan* ("and eye") rather than *an eagen* ("an eye").
[172] *Hapax legomenon.*

56 [L52] If someone's tongue is struck from the head by another man's deed, the compensation is equal to that for an eye.

57 [L53] If a man is wounded on the shoulder, so that synovia flows out, let him compensate with 30 shillings.[173]

58 [L54] If the arm is broken above the elbow, 15 shillings are due as compensation.

 58.1 [L55] If the armbones both are broken, the compensation is 30 shillings.[174]

59 [L56] If the thumb is struck off, for that 30 shillings shall be the compensation.

 59.1 [L56.1] If the nail is struck off, for that 5 shillings shall be the compensation.

60 [L57] If the "shooting finger" is struck off, the compensation is 15 shillings; its nail is 3 shillings.

---

[173] Compare §72 and §77.
[174] "Both" probably refers to upper and lower arm rather than radius and ulna: these two are likely subsumed under breaking of the lower arm.

61 [L58] Gif se midlesta finger sie ófaslegen, sio bot bið xɪɪ scill; ⁊ his nægles bot bið ɪɪ scill.

62 [L59] Gif se goldfinger sie ofaslegen, to þam sculon xvɪɪ scill to bote; ⁊ his nægles ɪɪɪɪ scill to bote.

63 [L60] Gif se lytla finger bið ófaslegen, ðam sceal to bote vɪɪɪɪ scill, ⁊ an scill his nægles, gif se sie ófaslegen.

64 [L61] Gif mon bið on hrif wund, geselle him mon xxx scill to bote.

64.1 [L61.1] Gif he ðurhwund bið, æt gehweðerum muðe xx scill.

65 [L62] Gif monnes ðeoh bið þyrel, geselle him mon xxx scill to bote.

65.1 [L62.1] Gif hit forad sie, sio bot eac bið xxx scill.

66 [L63] Gif se sconca bið þyrel beneoðan cneowe, ðær sculon xɪɪ scill to bote.

66.1 [L63.1] Gif he forad sie beneoðan cneowe, geselle him xxx scill to bote.

Af §61 medlesta] midleste B; midlæsta H   sie] sy B; bið H   ófaslegen] ofaslagen B; of aslægen H   sio] seo BH   bot bið *om.* B

Af §62 sie] sy B; bið H   ófaslegen] ofaslægen BH   þam] ðæm H   xvɪɪ] feofentyne B   to bote] *om.* B

Af §63 lytla] lytle B   bið] sy B   ófaslegen (2x)] ofaslagen B; of aslægen H   ðam sceal] ðæm sce\a/l H   vɪɪɪɪ] nigon B; .ix. H   se sie] he sy B; se bið H

Af §64 mon bið on hrif wund] mon \on/ rif\e/ \ge/wund\ed/ bið B; man bið on hrife wund H   geselle] gesylle BH   mon] man H   xxx] ðrittig B   to bote] *om.* B   Af §64.1 gehweðerum] ægðran B; ægðrum H   xx] twentig B

Af §65 monnes] mannes H   þyrel] þurl (*later corrected to* þyrl) B   geselle] gesylle BH   mon] man BH   xxx] ðrittig B

Af §65.1 sie] sy BH   sio] seo BH   eac] *om.* B

Af §66 sconca] scanca BH   þyrel] ðurl (*later corrected to* ðyrl) B   xɪɪ] twelf B   to bote] *om.* B

Af §66.1 sie] sy B; bið H   geselle] gesylle BH   him] him man H   xxx] ðritti B

61 [L58] If the middle finger is struck off, the compensation is 12 shillings; and the compensation for its nail is 2 shillings.

62 [L59] If the ring finger[175] is struck off, for that 17 shillings shall be compensation; and for its nail 4 shillings as compensation.

63 [L60] If the little finger is struck off, for that 9 shillings shall be compensation, and one shilling for its nail, if it is struck off.

64 [L61] If someone is wounded in the abdomen, let him be paid 30 shillings as compensation.

    64.1 [L61.1] If the wound goes through it, at each opening[176] 20 shillings.

65 [L62] If a man's thigh is pierced, let him be paid 30 shillings as compensation.

    65.1 [L62.1] If it is broken, the compensation is likewise 30 shillings.

66 [L63] If the lower leg is pierced below the knee, 12 shillings shall be the compensation.

    66.1 [L63.1] If it is broken below the knee, let him give 30 shillings as compensation.

---

[175] **goldfinger** refers to the finger that bears the gold ring (our "ring finger").
[176] Literally, "mouth."

67 [L64] Gif sio micle ta við ófaslegen, geselle him xx scill to bote.

67.1 [L64.1] Gif hit sie sio æfterre ta, xv scill to bote geselle him mon.

67.2 [L64.2] Gif seo midleste ta /46v/ sie ófaslegen, þær sculon viiii scill to bote.

67.3 [L64.3] Gif hit við sio feorþe ta, ðær sculon vi scill to bote.

67.4 [L64.4] Gif sio lytle ta sie ófaslegen, geselle him v scill.

68 [L65] Gif mon sie on þa herðan¹⁷⁷ to ðam swiðe wund, þæt he ne mæge bearn [gestrienan],¹⁷⁸ gebete him ðæt mid lxxx scill.

69 [L66] Gif men sie se earm mid honda mid ealle ofácorfen beforan elmbogan, gebete ðæt mid lxxx scill.

70 [L66.1] Æghwelcere wunde beforan feaxe ⁊ beforan sliefan ⁊ beneoðan cneowe sio bot við twysceatte mare.

Af §67 sio] *om.* B; seo H   micle] mycle B; mi\c/cle H   ófaslegen] ofaslagen B; of aslægen H   geselle him] gesylle him mon B; gesylle him man H   xx] twentig B
Af §67.1 Gif hit sie sio æfterre ta] Gyf hit seo æftere ta sy B; Gif seo æftere tá sy of aslægen H   xv] fiftene B   geselle him mon] *om.* B (*gives only* to bote *after compensation amount*); gesylle him man .xv. scll to bote H
Af §67.2 Gif seo medleste] Gyf seo midlæste B; Gif seo midlæste H   sie] sy BH   ófaslegen] ofaslagen B; of aslægen H   sculon] scylan B   viiii] nigon B; .ix. H
Af §67.3 sio] seo BH   vi] syx B
Af §67.4 sio] seo BH   sie ófaslegen] sy ofaslagen B; við of aslægen H   geselle] gesylle BH   him v] him mon fif B
Af §68 mon] man H   sie] sy BH   herðan] hærðan B   ðam] ðan   wund] gewundad B; \ge/wund\ed/ H
gestrienan (*supplied from* H; *scribe of* E *likely skipped this word in his exemplar*)] begytan B   lxxx] hund eahtatig B
Af §69 sie] sy BH   mid honda mid ealle] *om.* B   ofácorfen] ofacoruen B   elmbogan] el_bogan H   gebete ðæt] gebete \ðæt/ H   lxxx] hund eahtatig B
Af §70 Æghwelcere] æghwylcere B; Æghwylcre H   sliefan] slefan B; slyfan H   sio] seo BH   twysceatte] twyggylde B

---

¹⁷⁷ This term appears elsewhere in the Brussels glossary, where it renders *testiculi*. (Wright and Wülcker 1884: I, 292).
¹⁷⁸ We follow Schmid/Liebermann in adding *gestrienan*, though the word occurs only in H.

67 [L64] If the big toe is struck off, let him give him 20 shillings as compensation.

67.1 [L64.1] If it is the next toe, let him be given 15 shillings as compensation.

67.2 [L64.2] If the middle toe is struck off, 9 shillings shall be the compensation.

67.3 [L64.3] If it is the fourth toe, then 6 shillings are due as compensation.

67.4 [L64.4] If the little toe be struck off, let him pay him 5 shillings.[179]

68 [L65] If someone is wounded in the testicles so severely, that he may not conceive children, let him compensate him for that with 80 shillings.[180]

69 [L66] If a man's arm including his hand is cut off below the elbow, let him compensate that with 80 shillings.

70 [L66.1] Any wound below the hairline, and below the sleeve, and beneath the knee is two-fold more.[181]

---

[179] This completes a typical personal injury schedule moving from head to toe as seen in almost all barbarian laws (see Oliver 2011). The clauses that follow have no distinguishable organization, although many of them parallel rulings found in *Lex Frisionum*. (See discussion in Oliver 2015.)

[180] This is considerably less than the three wergilds required as compensation for a similar injury in *Æthelberht*. See discussion in Oliver (in press).

[181] *Æthelberht* §61 [L57] similarly fines a bruise that is visible more highly than one which is covered by clothing. Concern with the degree to which a wound is apparent runs throughout barbarian laws (see Oliver 2011: Chapter 6).

71 [L67] Gif sio lendenbræde bið forslegen, þær sceal LX scill to bote.

71.1 [L67.1] Gif hio bið onbestungen, geselle XV scill to bote.

71.2 [L67.2] Gif hio bið ðurhðyrel, ðonne sceal ðær XXX scill to bote.

72 [L68] Gif mon bið in eaxle wund, gebete mid LXXX scill, gif se mon cwic sie.

73 [L69] Gif mon oðrum ða hond utan forslea, geselle him XX scill to bote, gif hine mon gelacnian mæge.

73.1 [L69.1] Gif hio healf onweg fleoge, þonne sceal XL scill to bote.

74 [L70] Gif mon oþrum rib forslea binnan gehaldre hyde, geselle X scill to bote.

74.1 [L70.1] Gif sio hyd sie tobrocen, 7 mon ban ófádo, geselle XV scill to bote.

Af §71 sio] seo BH   lendenbræde] lendenbreda B   forslegen] forslægen BH   LX]
syxtig B
Af §71.1 hio] heo BH   geselle] *om*. B; gesylle H   XV] fiftene   to bote] *om*. B
Af §71.2 hio] heo BH   ðurhðyrel] ðurh ðurl (*later corrected to* ðyrl) B   sceal] sce\a/l
H   ðær] *om*. B; *added later in* H
Af §72 mon] man H   wund] gewundad B; \ge/wund\od/ H   LXXX] hund eahtat\ti/
B   mon] man H   sie] sy BH
Af §73 Gif mon] Gyf man on B; Gif man H   hond] hand BH   uton] utan
BH   geselle] gesylle BH   gif] Gyf (*seems to interpret as new provision*) B   mon]
man BH
Af §73.1 hio] he B; heo H
XL] syxtag (*in right margin, a later hand corrects to* feowertig) B
Alf §74 mon] man BH   rib] ribb B; rib\b/ H   gehaldre] gehalre BH   geselle] gesylle
BH   x] tyn B
Alf §74.1 sio] seo BH   sie] sy BH   mon] man BH   geselle] gesylle BH   XV] fiftyne
B   to bote] *om*. B

71 [L67] If the scrotum is struck off, 60 shillings shall be compensation for that.[182]

71.1 [L67.1] If it is pierced into, let him pay 15 shillings as compensation.

71.2 [L67.2] If it is pierced through, then 30 shillings shall be compensation for that.[183]

72 [L68] If someone is wounded on the shoulder, let him pay with 80 shillings, if the man is alive.[184]

73 [L69] If a man strikes the outside of another's hand, let him pay him 20 shillings as compensation, if he can be healed.[185]

73.1 [L69.1] If it is half struck-off, then 40 shillings shall be the compensation.

74 [L70] If one breaks another man's rib without breaking the skin, let him pay 10 shillings as compensation.

74.1 [L70.1] If the skin is broken, and a bone [fragment] is removed, let him pay 15 shillings as compensation.

---

[182] lendenbræde must refer to the scrotum. Bruce O'Brien describes the difficulties faced by the twelfth-century translator of the *Instituta Cnuti* when confronted with this obscure term: "The translator of the *Institutes* turned to a glossary like Ælfric's and introduced a flaw into his text. The word he wanted to translate was *lendenbræde* 'loins,' in King Alfred's list of fines to different parts of the body. The translator rendered this word as *assatura renum* 'roast kidneys,' transforming a wounding of the body between the hip and lowest rib into something rather different. He had found *bræde* in the glossary with *assatura* as its gloss and had borrowed it, assuming *bræde* and *(lande)bræde* were the same thing. He must have noticed the oddity, but probably felt that the authority of his dictionary, and his moderate ability in English, forced him to translate as he did" (O'Brien 2011: 163–164)

[183] The subclauses refer to piercing into and piercing through the scrotum. It is difficult to imagine an enemy managing to pierce into but not though the penis or the testicles with available weaponry. As did §68, these rulings echo Æthelberht §64, and are unparalled in any near-contemporary Frankish laws, providing further evidence that Alfred in fact knew the laws of Æthelberht.

[184] Cf. §57; also §77, which requires 20 shillings for injuring the shoulder and another 15 if a bone is removed. The wound envisaged here is obviously more serious, although the text does not elaborate.

[185] There is no permanent damage to bone or muscle.

75 [L71] Gif monnes eage him mon ófaslea, oððe his hand oððe his fot, ðær gæð gelic bot to eallum: VI pæningas ⁊ VI scill ⁊ LX scill ⁊ ðriddan dæl pæninges.

76 [L72] Gif monnes sconca bið ófaslegen wið ðæt cneou, ðær sceal LXXX scill to bote.

77 [L73] Gif mon oðrum ða sculdru forslea, geselle him mon XX scill to bote.

77.1 [L74] Gif hie mon inbeslea ⁊ mon ban ófado, geselle mon ðæs to bote XV scill.

78 [L75] Gif mon ða greatan sinwe forslea, gif hie mon gelacnian mæge, þæt hio hal sie, geselle XII scill to bote.

78.1. [L75.1] Gif se mon healt sie for þære sinwe wunde, ⁊ hine mon gelacnian ne mæge, geselle XXX scill to bote.

79 [L76] Gif ða /47r/ smalan sinwe mon forslea, geselle him mon VI scill to bote.

80 [L77] Gif mon oðrum ða geweald forslea uppe on þam sweoran ⁊ forwundie to þam swiðe, þæt he nage þære geweald, ⁊ hwæðre lifie swa gescended, geselle him mon C scill to bote, buton him witan ryhtre ⁊ mare gereccan.

Alf §75 monnes eage him mon ófaslea] om. B (gives instead Gif mon him slea oþþe his hand); H identical except for mannes ... man   fot] fott B   VI pæningas] syx penegas B; .vi. peningas H   VI] syx B   LX] syxtig B   pæninges] penegas B; peni_ges H
Alf §76 monnes sconca] mannes sceanca B; mannes scanca H   ófaslegen] ofaslagen B; of aslægen H   cneou] cneow BH   sceal] sce\a/l H   LXXX] hund eahtati B
Alf §77 mon] man BH   geselle] gesylle BH   mon] man H
Alf 77.1 Gif hie] Gyf hine B; Gif hi\n/e H   mon] man H   mon] man BH   geselle mon] gesylle mon BH   XV] fiftyne B
Alf §78 mon] man H   sinwe] synewe B   hie] hine B; hi_ne H   mon] man B   hio] he B; heo H   sie] sy BH   geselle] gesylle BH   XII] twelf
Alf §78.1 se mon] \se/ man H   sie] sy BH   sinwe] synewe B   XXX] xx (a later hand corrects in right margin to XXX scill) B
Alf §79 sinwe] synewan B   mon (2x)] man BH   geselle] gesylle BH   VI] syx B
Alf §80 mon] man BH   uppe] up\pe/ H   sweoran] sweore B   forwundie] forwundige H   þære] þær B; ðæra H   hwæðre] ðeahhwæðere B; hwæð\e/re H   lifie] lifige B; libbe H   gescended] gescend B; gescynded H   geselle] gesylle BH   mon] om. H   C] hund B   ryhtre] rihtre B; mare H gereccan] gereccan ⁊ ryhtre H

75 [L71] If someone strikes a man's eye from him, or his hand or his foot, an equal compensation applies to all: 6 pennies and 6 shillings and 60 shillings and a third of a penny.[186]

76 [L72] If a person's lower leg is struck off up to the knee, 80 shillings shall be the compensation.[187]

77 [L73] If someone injures another in the shoulder, let him be paid 20 shillings as compensation.

77.1 [L74] If one strikes into it and removes a bone [fragment], let him be paid for that 15 shillings as compensation.[188]

78 [L75] If someone injures the greater sinew, if he can be healed so that it is sound, let him pay 12 shillings as compensation.

78.1 [L75.1] If the man is lame due to the wound to the sinew, and he cannot be healed, let him pay 30 shillings as compensation.

79 [L76] If someone injures the smaller sinew, let him be paid 6 shillings as compensation.

80 [L77] If someone injures the power up on the neck, and wounds it so greatly, that he does not have power, and nonetheless lives thus afflicted,[189] let him be paid 100 shillings as compensation, unless the *witan* adjudge more by law.

---

[186] See n. 168 to §50.

[187] Compare §69 discussing cutting off the lower arm *up to* the elbow; *wið* here has the same meaning.

[188] Presumably in addition to the fine for striking the shoulder; compare §§57, 72.

[189] The meaning of **geweald** ("power, force") is uncertain here. Thorpe likens it to OHG *waltowahso* and OFr *walde-waxe* ("*nervus (colli)*"): that is, the nerves at the top of the spinal cord. Liebermann concurs with this interpretation.

9

The Laws of Ine

We have seen that, after the Elizabethan re-discovery of Old English, the laws of Alfred were restored to something resembling the place of prominence they enjoyed during the latter part of the Anglo-Saxon period, with the king himself being regarded in later centuries (most famously by Blackstone) as a kind of English Theodosius. This was, in some respects, a favorable development given the importance long assigned to the spurious *Leges Edwardi Confessoris*. Yet Ine's laws have rather unfairly been compelled to exist in the shadow of Alfred's in spite of their being the longest and most revealing legislative statement to survive in Old English from the seventh century. That Ine's laws share material with the slightly later laws of Wihtred, king of Kent, likewise demonstrates the immediate importance of Ine's undertaking even outside the territorial boundaries of Wessex.

The circumstances in which Ine's laws survive, however, preclude any complacent use of this text as evidence for seventh-century conditions. As Alfred claims to have selected his judgments from those of his predecessors and evidently intended for Ine's to serve more than merely historical purposes within the *domboc,* it is not certain that Alfred's version of Ine's laws gives the text in its entirety.[1] Nor

---

[1] Dammery doubts this, however: "Even if Alfred was responsible for appending the Ine code to his own, it seems most unlikely that he altered it. His claim that he used the laws of his predecessors selectively can be explained by reference to his use of Ine's code in the composition of his own law" (Dammery 1990: 1, 267). Wormald's assessment is more pointed: "It [...] beggars belief that Alfred excised some Ine laws (for example on idolatry), to which he could have had no objection, yet left in place those that he had modified" (Wormald 1999a: 278).

do Ine's laws have even the structure we find in *Æthelberht*. Some clauses are repeated (such as §18 and §38 requiring a thief to have his hand cut off) and some appear to add qualifications to judgments earlier given (such as §37 in which a person letting a thief escape must pay the thief's wergild and §74.1 in which the fine for the same offense must be negotiated with the king and his reeve). Clauses evidently displaced from their original order over the course of the text's transmission (e.g., §42) further suggest incremental growth over a long period while throwing into doubt the possibility that *Ine* ever existed in anything like a single "archetypal" form. In the final analysis, "Ine's laws" may well represent an accumulated heap of judgments rendered throughout – and even *after* – Ine's reign:

[S]ome laws transmitted by Alfred under Ine's name could be laws of his successors. West-Saxon kings could have gone on having their *domas* recorded well into the eighth century. […] The more important conclusion is that West-Saxon law-makers are regularly found responding to problems laid before them. Law-making in writing had gone "live". *Domas* had become part of the king's job.[2]

Whatever the origins of this compilation, it remains convenient to refer to it as "Ine's laws," and as Alfred and his circle are evidently the only ones to have seen it as it appeared before it became part of the *domboc*, the term may be safely used on their authority.

The ambit of Ine's laws, vast when compared with that of his ancestors, gives an impression of innovation that may be deceptive given the silence surrounding this text. Many terms are here attested for the first time, and with them new approaches towards law itself (or at least – and this is more likely – the first codification of such approaches). No laws prior to Ine's issue ordinances regulating *borh* ("surety") or prescribe judicial mutilation. Animal husbandry and agriculture are a concern in Ine as they are not in the Kentish laws, yielding laws concerning the *cu* ("cow") with his *cuuhorn* ("cow-horn)," *sceap* ("sheep") with his *flys* ("fleece"), and *swin* ("swine") munching acorns under a shade tree, as well as the water-dwelling *æl* ("eel") and *leax* ("salmon"). We are introduced to the *gebur* ("peasant farmer") who works his *æcer* ("acre") in the *gedalland* ("land

---

[2] Wormald 1999a: 104–105.

farmed in common"), along with the administrative terms *scir* ("shire") and *scírmann* ("[?offical] man of the shire")[3] and *gerefa* ("prefect, steward, reeve"). Ine's laws are also the first to address the duties of the *fyrd* ("army"), as well as the concomitant *fyrdwite* ("fine for avoiding military service"). Much of the institutional structure of Wessex must have been in place well in advance of Alfred's accession if Ine's laws are to be trusted.

Should *Ine*'s prologue be a reliable guide to dating the text – an assumption that, as we have seen, may be untenable – the (?initial) laws must have been established between the accession of Ine in 688 and the death of Bishop Eorconwald in 693. Barbara Yorke points out that "perhaps one of [the code's] most interesting aspects is the way it legislates for all Ine's subjects – the British [*Wilisc*, 'Welsh'] as well as the Anglo-Saxon." She continues that the laws "indicate that although the West Saxons were nominally Christian, many Christian practices such as infant baptism [*fulwiht*] and church tithes [*cyric-sceat*] had yet to become widely practiced. [...] The topic is also relevant to the question of integration of the British subjects, for the Britons of the west country were Christians long before the conversion of the West Saxons [in 635]."[4] Concern with ecclesiastical affairs is also evident in *Ine*'s being the first to issue regulations concerning a *mynster* ("monastery, minster") ruled over by an *abbod* ("abbot") or *abbodesse* ("abbess").[5] It is also the first to require tithing to the church, to establish the right of sanctuary (earlier hinted at in *Æthelberht* §6), and (if the standard relative chronology of *Ine* and *Wihtred* is to be accepted) to include a prohibition against working on *Sunnandæg*.

Often attributed to *Ine* §38 and §66 is the establishment of the judicial ordeal in Anglo-Saxon England. This is a procedure in which a defendant submerges his hand in boiling water and the hand is then bandaged. After three days the wrappings are removed, and guilt or innocence is determined according to whether the burn is festering or not. However (as discussed in n. 172 to §66 and Chapter 3, 81–101), this view is based on variants confined to **B**, **H**, and **G**,

---

3 See n. 128 to *Alfred* §38.
4 York 1990: 138–139. But see Chapter 1, 19–20.
5 Ine's sister Cuthburh founded a double monastery at Wimbourne.

all very late manuscripts; it does not seem to be supported by the reading in **E**.

In spite of their chaotic and probably compromised state, the laws of Ine offer a remarkably ample sense of the daily lives of ordinary people in seventh-century England. Woodsmen cut down trees, heifers roam the countryside breaking hedges, offenders seek sanctuary and elsewhere fugitives are illegally given shelter, roving bands or troops of thieves terrorize the countryside (or at least are warned against doing so), foundlings are fostered, children are conceived out of wedlock, and the king stands as guardian for foreigners and the kinless. No other legislative text of this period paints such a vivid picture of the people for whom it was intended.

Whether the term *Englisc* (§§24, 47.1, 58, 75) is merely a shorthand for "not British" or suggests that English-speakers were beginning to sense the possibility of a shared political destiny, it is notable that portions of Ine's laws are recast or alluded to in the subsequent compilations by Edward, Æthelstan, Eadmund, Edgar, Æthelred, and Cnut and seem in particular to have held the interest of Wulfstan.[6] (Subsequent use of the contemporaneous laws of Kent is, in comparison, somewhat limited.)[7] While it is unlikely that Ine's laws would have remained a part of the legislative tradition for so long had they not been attached to Alfred's (and had the rubrics given in **E** not treated them as continuous with Alfred's legislation), subsequent use of this text suggests that it enjoyed an importance throughout the Anglo-Saxon period somewhat out of proportion to the attention it has received from modern historians.

---

[6] Likely references include II *Edward* §5.2 (*Ine* §30), II *Edgar* §3 (*Ine* §4), §5 (*Ine* §3), II *Æthelstan* §1.1 (*Ine* §37), II *Eadmund* §6 (*Ine* §6), II *Cnut* §59 (*Ine* §6) §76–76.1 (*Ine* §61), *Norðleoda laga* §§7 (*Ine* §32), *Grið* §7 (*Ine* §32). See also Liebermann 1903–1916: III, 67 (§26) and Rabin 2015. The language of Ine's laws typically undergoes severe alteration in subsequent royal legislation if it is indeed employed at all. The language of II *Edgar* §§3 and 5, which attributes recycled provisions to "the *domboc*," suggests that later legislators (as Liebermann notes) "read Alfred and Ine in unison" (*lasen Af-Ine vereint*), regarding the text as a *Doppelwerk* (1903–1916: III, 67). (The list of clauses employing *Ine* just given was assembled in part with the help of an unpublished work on the sourcing of Old English legislation by Patrick Wormald furnished by Charles D. Wright and Frederick Biggs; it should be pointed out that full scope of subsequent use of Ine's laws remains unclear.)

[7] See Rabin 2019.

It has been necessary in this edition as well to depart from the received numeration of clauses given problems evident early in the text (L13.1 is clearly not a subclause of L13, whereas L15 does elaborate on a previous clause) that become more pervasive as it proceeds (L35.1 is a new clause unrelated to the prior one; L44 is in fact a subclause; L49.3 is not a subclause of the preceding; L64–66 are manifestly subclauses). Finally, it should be noted that the shilling at the time of Ine seems to have contained four pennies. It is difficult to account for the valuation of an ox eye at 5 pennies and a cow's at a shilling in §62.3 if both equal the same amount. By the time of Alfred, the shilling was worth 5 pennies.[8]

---

[8]   Once again, we thank Rory Naismith for helping us with these reckonings.

{XLIIII}[9]

Prologue. Ic, Ine, mid Godes gife Wesseaxna kyning, mid geðeahte ⁊ mid lare Cenredes mines fæder ⁊ Heddes mines biscepes ⁊ Eorcenwoldes mines biscepes, mid eallum minum ealdormonnum ⁊ þæm ieldstan witum minre ðeode ⁊ eác micelre gesomnunge Godes ðeowa, wæs smeagende be ðære hælo urra sawla ⁊ be ðam staþole ures rices, þætte ryht æw ⁊ ryhte cynedomas ðurh ure folc gefæstnode ⁊ getrymede wæron, þætte nænig ealdormonna ne us undergeðeodedra æfter þam wære awendende ðas ure domas.

{XLV}

1 Ærest we bebeodað þætte Godes ðeowas hiora ryhtregol on ryht healdan.

1.1 Æfter þam we bebeodað þætte ealles folces æw ⁊ domas ðus sien gehealdene.

Ine Prol. gife] gyfe B   Wesseaxna] WES SEXENA B; west seax\e/na H   kyning] cyning BH   Cenredes] cænredes H   eorcenwoldes] erconwoldes B; eorcenwaldes H   ealdormonnū] ealdormannum B; ealder mannum H   ðæm] ðam BH   ieldstan] yldestan BH   witum] witan B   gesomnunge] somnunge B; gesamnunge H   ðeowa] ðeowena B   hælo] hæle BH   urra] ure B; u_re H   þætte] þæt\te/ B; ðæt\te/ H   æw] æwe B; æw\e/ H   getrymede] getrymmede B   þætte] þæt B; ðæt\te/ H   ealdormonna] ealdormanna B; ealder manna H   undergeðeodedra] under geðeodendra B; under geðeode\n/dra H   þam] ðem B
Ine §1 godes] godas B   hiora] heora B; he\o/ra H   on ryht healdan] gyman ⁊ on riht healdon B; on riht healden HBu
Ine §1.1 þam] þæm Bu   bebeodað] beodað BH   þætte] þæt B; þæt\te/ H   æw] ǽ B   sien] syn BH   gehealdene] gehealdenne Bu

9   The clause number is inserted here by the rubricator. This marks it as a continuation of (or appendix to) Alfred, but the paragraph is not itself a legal ruling.

Prologue I, Ine, by God's gift king of the West Saxons, with the advice and instruction of Cenred my father and Hædde my bishop and Eorconwald my bishop,[10] with all my ealdormen and the senior counselors of my people and also a great gathering of God's servants,[11] have been considering the well-being of our souls and the foundation of our kingdom, so that just law and just royal judgments[12] should be established and made strong throughout our folk, so that after this time no ealdorman nor any other subject to us should depart from these our judgments.

1 First we command[13] that God's servants hold their proper rule according to law.

1.1 Next we command that the law and judgments regarding all the folk be held as follows.

---

[10] Hædde was Bishop of Winchester, the see of the kingdom of Wessex, from 676 until his death in 705. Eorconwald was Bishop of London, the see of the East Saxons, from ?675–693; he was chosen by Theodore of Tarsus, the great early Archbishop of Canterbury. Ine's rule had expanded beyond Wessex proper. But the specifically West-Saxon nature of this promulgation is demonstrated by the absence of the Archbishop of Canterbury. To Liebermann, the linkage of Cenred to the two named bishops suggests that he had abdicated the kingship to become a monk (Liebermann 1903–1916: III, 68). Fruscione (2003: 138) points out that the presence of the two bishops as well as the large gathering of "God's servants" demonstrates both the religious concerns of Ine's laws as well as Ine's personal piety, which would eventually lead him to abdicate in order to undertake pilgrimage to Rome. Yet Ine's self-assertion in his brief prologue is in marked contrast to Wihtred's presence at the outset of his laws, who is overshadowed by the bishops present at its assembly.

[11] Liebermann takes these to be abbots and priests. See also Chapter 2, 46–49.

[12] This doublet maintains the distinction between *æw* (traditional or established law) and *domas* (specific rulings or judgments) found also in the prologues to the Kentish laws of Hloþhere and Eadric and Wihtred, and later echoed in Alfred. Ine's use of the term **cynedomas** is unique: elsewhere it means "kingdom" or "royal rank." Wormald (1999a: 104) indicates that "it highlights the hardening adhesive between kingship and law-making. Ine went beyond Kentish kings in actually demanding that his officials and subjects obey his decrees."

[13] Not the royal "we," but king and *witan*.

{XLVI}

2 Cild binnan ðritegum nihta sie gefulwad; gif hit swa ne sie, xxx sciłł gebete.

2.1 Gif hit ðonne sie dead butan fulwihte, gebete he hit mid eallum ðam ðe he age.

{XLVII}

3 Gif ðeowmon wyrce on Sunnandæg be his hlafordes hæse, sie he frioh, ⁊ se hlaford geselle xxx sciłł to wite.[14]

3.1 Gif þonne se ðeowa butan his gewitnesse wyrce, þolie his hyde.

3.2 Gif ðonne se frigea ðy dæge wyrce butan his hlafordes hæse, ðolie his freotes.

Ine §2 ðritegum] .xxx. BBu nihta] nihtum HBu sie (2x)] sy BH gefulwad] gefullad B; gefullod HBu

Ine §2.1 sie] sy BH fulwihte] fulluhte BH ðam] þæm Bu

Ine §3 ðeowmon] ðeow man H wyrce] werce Bu sie] sy BH frioh] freo B; freoh H, Bu geselle] gesylle BH

Ine §3.1 gewitnesse] gewitnysse B

þolie his hyde] B *adds* oððe hydgyldes; H *adds in right margin* oððe hyd gyld

Ine §3.2 butan his hlafordes hæse] buton hlafordes hæse Bu ðolie his freotes] B *adds* oððe sixtig scill ⁊ preost twy scyldi; H *(right margin) gives* oððe .lx. scll ⁊ preost twy scildig

---

[14] Compare to *Wihtred* §8 [L9, 10, 11].

2 A child must be baptized within thirty nights; if it is not, let him pay 30 shillings.[15]

2.1 If it should die, however, without baptism, let him compensate for that with all that he owns.

3 If a slave works on Sunday at his lord's command,[16] let him be free, and the lord must pay 30 shillings as fine.[17]

3.1 If, however, the slave works without his [lord's] knowledge, let [the slave] pay with his hide.[18]

3.2 If, however, a freeman works on that day without his lord's command, let him pay with his freedom.[19]

---

[15] Whether the fine is assessed against the guardian or the priest is uncertain. The latter interpretation is supported by the *Pœnitentiale Theodori* (I, xiv, 28): "If an infant that is weak and is a pagan has been recommended to a presbyter [for baptism] and dies [unbaptized], the presbyter shall be deposed" (McNeill and Gamer 1938: 197). *Wihtred* §5 [L6] similarly punishes a priest for neglecting baptism. It is perhaps relevant that Ine's predecessor Cædwalla was not baptized until just before his death. But delayed or "clinical" baptism was the practice of emperors in late antiquity, and its attestation here may reveal little about lay piety in this period. That Ine urges the prompt baptism of infants likewise need not be taken to indicate a still-pervasive paganism, as such exhortations occur in a homily attributed to Wulfstan (Napier xxiv; see Jurasinski 2019: 38).

[16] *Wihtred* §8 [L9, 10, 11] similarly prohibits working on Sunday. The paragraph begins with an *esne* (hired labourer) performing slave work; *Ine* instead applies this to persons of unambiguously servile status.

[17] As Fruscione (2014: 36) points out, **wite** (throughout this edition translated as "fine") "has a common etymology with Latin *videre* and Gothic *witan* 'observe'; its meaning advanced from 'observe,' 'perceive,' or 'notice,' to 'punish.' The word came to imply the existence of a controlling power with the authority to punish."

[18] *Wihtred* §8.1 [L10] allows a payment to the *esne*'s master of 6 shillings to avoid being whipped. The post-Conquest scribes of **B** and **H** add "or a fine to avoid flogging."

[19] **B** and **H** add *oððe sixtig scill; 7 preost twyscildi* (**B**'s orthography) "or let him pay 60 shillings and a priest the double fine." Schmid holds this to be a corruption of the text; all other previous editors include it parenthetically. Liebermann presumes the reference in these later manuscripts is to a village/country priest who works as a farmer. Working on Sunday is prohibited in many barbarian laws: see *LexAla* §38; *LexBav* §7.3a; *LexFris* §18.

{XLVIII}

4 /47v/ Ciricsceattas sin agifene be s*anc*te Martines mæssan; gif hwa
ðæt ne gelæste, sie he scyldig LX sciłł ⁊ be XIIfealdum agife þone ciricsceat.

{XLVIIII}

5 Gif hwa sie deaðes scyldig ⁊ he cirican geierne, hæbbe his feorh ⁊
bete, swa him ryht wisige.

    5.1 Gyf hwa his hyde forwyrce ⁊ cyricean geierne, sy him sio
swingelle forgifen.

{L}

6 Gif hwa gefeohte on cyninges huse, sie he scyldig ealles his ierfes,²⁰
⁊ sie on cyninges dome, hwæðer he lif age þe nage.

    6.1 Gif hwa on mynster gefeohte, CXX sciłł gebete.

    6.2 Gif hwa on ealdormonnes huse gefeohte oððe on oðres
geðungenes witan, LX sciłł gebete he ⁊ oþer LX geselle to wite.

    6.3 Gif ðonne on gafolgeldan huse oððe on gebures gefeohte, CXX
sciłł to wite geselle ⁊ þæm gebure VI sciłł.

Ine §4 sin] sien Bu   agifene] ageuene B   sie] sy BH   lx] feortig B   ciricsceat] ciric-
sceatt H
Ine §5 he] *om.* H, Bu   cirican] cyrican B; ciric_an H   geierne] geyrne B; geyrne H;
geærne Bu   wisige] wisie B, Bu; wisi_e H
Ine §5.1 forwyrce] forwerce Bu   cirican] cyrican B; cir\i/cean H   geierne] geyrne B;
ge irne H   hæbbe] habbe Bu   sie] sy BH   sio] seo BH   swingelle] swingle BH
Ine §6 gefeohte on cyninges huse] on cyninges huse gefeohte H   sie] sy BH   his ier-
fes] his yrfes B; \his/ yrfes H   sie] sy BH   age þe nage] lif hæbbe [ ] Bu
Ine §6.1. mynster] mynstre BH   CXX] hundtwelftig B
Ine §6.2 on] in B   ealdormonnes huse gefeohte oððe on oðres geðungenes witan] ealdor mannes huse feohte oððe on oðres geðungenes witan B; ealder mannes huse oððe
on oþres witan geþungenan gefeohte H   LX (*both occurrences*)] syxtig B   geselle]
gesylle he B; *om.* H
Ine §6.3 Gif ðonne] Gif mon Bu   gafolgeldan] gafolgylden B; gafold gildan H; [ ]
gildan Bu   CXX] hundtwelftig B   geselle] gesylle BH   gebure VI] gebures syx B

---

²⁰ This generally means "inheritance," but see *MP* §11 and *Alfred* §1.4 for parallel
uses as "possessions."

4 Church dues are to be given by St. Martin's Mass; [21] if someone neglects this, let him be liable for [a fine of] 60 shillings and let him render the church dues twelve-fold. [22]

5 If someone has commited an offense for which he owes his life and he flees into a church, let him keep his life and make restitution according to how [judgment of] law directs him. [23]

    5.1 If someone has committed an offense for which the penalty is whipping and he flees into a church, let him be spared the whipping. [24]

6 If someone fights in the king's house, let him be liable for all he owns, and let it be up to the king's judgment whether he should keep his life or not. [25]

    6.1 If someone fights in the minster, let him pay 120 shillings. [26]

    6.2 If someone fights in an ealdorman's house or that of another eminent councilor, let him pay [the householder] 60 shillings and 60 additionally as fine.

    6.3 If he should fight in the house of a renter or a farmer, let him pay 120[27] shillings as a fine and 6 shillings to the farmer.

---

[21] November 11; this remained the date to pay church dues throughout the Anglo-Saxon period. This same date is stipulated in the Icelandic *Grágás* for payment to the needy. See also §65.

[22] The fine is a secular penalty due to the king, while the multiplied payment goes to the church. The latter payment matches the twelve-fold restitution for theft from a church established in *Æthelberht* §1.

[23] Compare *MP* §13 and *Alfred* §5.

[24] The subclause refers to those in servitude for whom whipping rather than payment of fine would be applicable.

[25] Compare to *Æthelberht* §9 [L3]; also *Hloþhere and Eadric* §7 [L11] and §9 [L13].

[26] As demonstrated in §6.2, the fine for fighting is 120 shillings. If the fight takes place in a religious establishment, the king allows the minster the full fine. The next clause stipulates that if the fight takes place in a nobleman's dwelling, the fine is split between the king and the noble homesteader.

[27] *Quadripartitus* emends this to 30 shillings. In all likelihood, the scribe concluded that an error had been made in ascribing a greater total for this offense than for fighting in the church or an ealdorman's house. Schmid and Thorpe concur. Liebermann suggests that the original fine may have been xxx shillings, emended by the scribe of the Parker manuscript to cxx to bring the fine into line with others for insubordination to the king. Note that §6.5 set a fine of 30 shillings for an altercation in words rather than blows, as implied in the earlier clauses.

6.4 ⁊ þeah hit sie on middum felda gefohten, cxx sciⱦ to wite sie agifen.²⁸

6.5 Gif ðonne on gebeorscipe hie geciden, ⁊ oðer hiora mid geðylde hit forbere, geselle se oðer xxx sciⱦ to wite.

{LI}

7 Gif hwa stalie, swa his wíf nyte ⁊ his bearn, geselle LX sciⱦ to wite.

7.1 Gif he ðonne stalie on gewitnesse ealles his hiredes, gongen hie ealle on ðeowot.

7.2 X wintre cniht mæg bion ðiefðe gewita.

{LII}

8 Gif hwa him ryhtes bidde beforan hwelcum scirmen oððe oþrum deman ⁊ ábiddan ne mæge, ⁊ him wedd sellan nelle, gebete xxx sciⱦ ⁊ binnan VII nihton gedó hine ryhtes wierðne.

{LIII}

9 Gif hwa wrace dó, ærðon he him ryhtes bidde, þæt he him on/48r/ nime agife ⁊ forgielde ⁊ gebete mid xxx sciⱦ.

{LIIII}

10 Gif hwa binnan þam gemærum ures rices reaflác ⁊ niednæme²⁹ dó, agife he ðone reaflac ⁊ geselle LX sciⱦ to wite.

Ine §6.4 þeah hit sie on middum felda gefohten] ðeah hit sy on middan felda ge fohtan B; þeah hit sy gef\e/ohten on middan felda H   cxx] hundtwelftig B   sie] sy BH
Ine §6.5 Gif ðonne on] [ ]onne bið on Bu   hie] hi B; hy H   hiora] heora B; he\o/ra H   geselle] gesylle BH   scill to wite] to wite scll H
Ine §7 stalie] stalige BH   wíf nyte] wif \hit/ nyte H   geselle] gesylle BH   lx] syxti B
Ine §7.1 stalie] stalige H   gewitnesse] gewitnysse B   gongen] gangen B; gán (*with word-length space after*) H   hie] heo B; hy H   ðeowot] ðeowet BH; ðeowut Bu
Ine §7.2 .x.] tyn B   bion] beon B, Bu; \beon/ H   ðiefðe] þyfðe BH; þeofðe Bu   gewita] gewytte Bu
Ine §8 hwa him] hwa hine Bu   hwelcum] hwylcum B; hwylcum H   oþrum] *om.* H   ábiddan ne mæge] him ryht abiddan ne mæge H   wedd] wed B, Bu; wed\d/ H   sellan] syllan BH   nelle] nylle B   gebete] \gebete/ H; gebete mid Bu   .vii.] seofen B   nihton] niht B; nihtum H, Bu   wierðne] wyrðe BH; weorðe Bu
Ine §9 wrace] wræce Bu   ærðon] ær H   forgielde] forgylde B, Bu   gebete] bete B   mid] *om.* B
Ine §10 niedname] nydnæme B; reaflac ⁊ nydnæme binnan þam gemærum ures rices H   dó] ge do H   geselle] gesylle BH   .lx.] syxti B

---

²⁸ See previous note.
²⁹ The term occurs in later legislation (as *nydnæme*) only in VI *Æthelred* §39 and II *Cnut* §§52–52.1.

6.4 And even if the fight takes place in an open field, 120[30] shillings shall be paid as fine.

6.5 If, however, they quarrel at drinking, and one person bears it with patience, let the other [who resorted to violence] pay 30 shillings as fine.[31]

7 If someone steals, but his wife and his child(ren) do not know it, let him pay 60 shillings as a fine.[32]

7.1 If, however, he steals with the knowledge of all his household, let them all go into servitude.

7.2 A ten-year old child may be accesory to theft.[33]

8 If someone demands justice before a certain shireman or another judge and he cannot obtain it, nor will [the accused] give him surety, let [the accused] pay 30 shillings and within 7 nights do for him such justice as he is entitled to.[34]

9 If someone exacts redress, before he asks [the perpetrator] for justice, he shall return what he took from him and compensate [him] and pay 30 shillings [as a fine].[35]

10 If someone within the boundaries of our kingdom commits robbery and forceful plunder, let him return the plunder and give 60 shillings as a fine.[36]

---

[30] See note above.

[31] **geciden** means to have a verbal altercation. Compare *Hloþhere and Eadric* §7 [L11].

[32] For another instance of the separate culpability of husband and wife see *Wihtred* §9 [L12].

[33] **gewita** could also mean "witness." In early Kent and Wessex the child reaches legal maturity at the age of 10. Compare *Hloþhere and Eadric* §4 [L6].

[34] Compare *Hloþhere and Eadric* §6 [L8]. Liebermann says the fine is not for failing to appear, but for refusing to answer or accept the pronounced judgment. *PactLexSal* §LVI addressed both options.

[35] The compensation is presumably for damage to person or property.

[36] *Ine*, as do the laws of the Continent, distinguishes between simple theft and robbery involving force. Compare *Æthelberht* §23.1 [L19].

{LV}

11 Gif hwa his agenne geleod bebycgge, ðeowne oððe frigne, ðeah he scyldig sie, ofer sæ, forgielde hine his were.

{LVI}

12 Gif ðeof sie gefongen, swelte he deaðe, oððe his lif be his were man aliese.

{LVII}

13 Gif hwa beforan biscepe his gewitnesse ⁊ his wed aleoge, gebete mid cxx sciℓℓ.

Ine §11 geleod] leodan B; \leod/ H   bebycgge] gebycge H; bebycge Bu   frigne] frige B   sie] sy BH   ofer sæ] *a later hand adds* sende B   forgielde] forgylde B; forgilde H   his were] be his were B (*a later hand adds in left margin* ⁊ wið godd deoplice bete); be his were H

Ine §12 sie] sy BH   gefongen] gefangen H   swelte] swylte BH   man] mon B; *om.* H; monn Bu   aliese] alyse BH

Ine §13 biscepe] bisceope B; biscope H, Bu   his] \his/ H   gewitnesse] gewitnysse B   wed] wedd H   .cxx.] hundtwelftig B; hundtwelftigum Bu

11 If someone sells over the sea his own countryman, slave or free, even though he is guilty [of an offense],[37] let him compensate by payment of his [own] *wer*.[38]

12 If a thief is caught, let him suffer death, or his life can be redeemed by [payment of] his wergild.[39]

13 If someone gives false witness or denies his pledge before the bishop,[40] let him compensate with 120 shillings.

[37] Liebermann says this is a penal slave sold for profit. Note that *Wihtred* §21 [L26] allows the sale of a thief overseas. In *Æthelred* v, §2 (echoed in vi, §9), Wulfstan states that "Christian men who are innocent of crime shall not be sold out of the land, least of all to the heathen" (Roberston 1925). This is quite different from what Ine says: he requires that anyone who sells a man out of the land, even if the person sold is "guilty (of an offense)," expiate the deed by payment of his own wergild. Wulfstan is implying that selling a "guilty" person is somehow not as grave an offense.

[38] A slave has no wergild, so it appears that the wergild paid to the king as fine must be that of the seller. *PactLexAla* §39.2 contains the same grammatical ambiguity found in *Ine*; however, *LexAla* §46 states that in the case of a freeman the seller must pay his kin the wergild of the unlawfully sold freeman; if the sold man has no kin a fine of 200 shillings is due the fisc. This fine is doubled for a free woman.

[39] *Wihtred* §21 [L26] allows three options: death, redemption by monetary payment, and sale over the sea. But *Ine* §11 prohibits the last for the kingdom of the West Saxons. The phrasing may rely upon the biblical idiom *morte moriatur*; Heydemann (2020: 108) notes its occurrence in Carolingian legislation.

[40] The offense is of less magnitude than a false oath as it concerns a *wedd* ("promise, pledge").

14 [L13.1] Ðeofas we hatað oð VII men; from VII hloð oð xxxv; siððan bið here.

{LVIII}

14.1 [L14] Se ðe hloþe betygen sie, geswicne⁴¹ se hine be cxx hida oððe swa bete.

{LVIIII}

14.2 [L15] Se ðe here____teama⁴² betygen sie, he hine be his wergilde áliese oððe be his were geswicne.

14.3 [L15.1] Se að sceal bion healf be huslgengum.⁴³

15 [L15.2] Þeof, siððan he bið on cyninges bende, nah he þa swicne.

Ine §14 (B *follows E in indicating no chapter break between this clause and the preceding; the clause begins in both with ð/þ, subsequently changed to Ð in B*) .vii.] seofen B (both occurrences); from seofon mannum hloð H .xxxv.] fíf and ðrittig bið here] \7 syððan/ here B
Ine §14.1 betygen sie] betogen sy BH geswicne] geclensie B; geswicne he hine Bu .cxx.] hundtwelftigum B swa bete] swa gebete B; bete swa H
Ine §14.2 betygen sie] betogen sy BH; betigen sie Bu wergilde] weregilde H áliese] alyse BH were] *om.* B geswicne] geclænsie B
Ine §14.3 bion] beon BH; byon Bu
Ine §15 cyninges] kininges Bu bende] bendum B swicne] geswicne B; \ge/swicne H

---

⁴¹ A rare term.
⁴² Gap.
⁴³ This word appears only here and in (slightly later) Kentish laws of Wihtred, which share other commonalities with *Ine*.

14 [L13.1] [A group of] up to seven men we call thieves; from seven to thirty-five a band; more is a troop.

14.1 [L14] He who is accused of taking part in a raid by a band [of thieves], let him clear himself by [an oath of] 120 hides or pay equivalent compensation.[44]

14.2 [L15] He who is accused of taking part in a raid by a troop [of thieves], let him redeem himself with his wergild or clear himself by [an oath equal to] his wergild.[45]

14.3 [L15.1] The oath shall be half for a communicant.[46]

15 [L15.2] A thief, once he is in the king's confinement, does not have the right to clear himself by an oath.

[44] Swearing oaths in hides occurs only in *Ine*, *Alfred* §11 and perhaps obliquely in the Northumbrian *Dialogue of Archbishop Egbert*, *c.*750; Seebohm (1902: 378–381) postulates that Egbert knew the laws of Ine. There is generally a one-to-one correspondence between the number of hides necessary for the oath and the number of shillings involved in the fine or compensation. The fine here would thus be 120 shillings. Although other instances have the value of the oath expressed in money (see, for example, *Alfred* §4 and §36), later laws refer far more commonly to the number of oath-swearers required. See discussion in Chadwick 1905: 134–139; also Liebermann 1910.

[45] In all these cases, damages owed would be required in addition to the fine paid the king.

[46] The term **huslgenga** also appears in §19, as well as in *Wihtred* §18 [L23], which suggests the existence in Kent of legal privileges for a known communicant comparable to those attested here. The relevant clauses in *Ine* are commonly understood as offering incentives to receive the Eucharist and an indication that some were still resistant to the new faith altogether (see §2 and note). But for a king of this period to require the newly converted to approach the altar seems improbable given the awe in which the Sacrament was held and the infrequency of lay communion. The association between the Eucharist and the oath, and the status of the Eucharist as a kind of ordeal in itself, should not be overlooked (see Lea 1892: 344–351; Jurasinski 2019). Liebermann claims the plural **huslgengum** indicates that *all* the oath-helpers must also be communicants, but *Ine*'s language requires no such conclusion.

{LX}

16 [L16] Se ðe ðeof ofslihð, se mot gecyðan mid aðe, þæt he hine synnigne ofsloge; nalles ða gegildan.

{LXI}

17 [L17] Se ðe forstolen flæsc findeð ⁊ gedyrneð, gif he dear, he mot mid aðe gecyðan þæt he hit age; se ðe hit ofspyreð,⁴⁷ he ah ðæt meldfeoh.⁴⁸

{LˆXII}⁴⁹

18 [L18] Cierlisc mon gif he óft betygen wære: gif he æt siðestan sie gefongen, slea mon hond [of]⁵⁰ oððe fot.

{LXIII}

19 [L19] Cyninges geneat, gif his wer bið twelfhund sciŀŀ, he mot swerian for syxtig hida, gif he bið huslgengea.

Ine §16 gecyðan] geceþan Bu   mid aðe] mid his aðe H   sinnigne] scyldig B   gegildan] gyldan B; gegildanum Bu
Ine §17 gedyrneð] gederneð Bu   ofspyreð] ofspyrað B; ofspereð Bu
Ine §18 Cierlisc] cyrlisc B; ciorlisc H; Cirlisc Bu   betygen] betogen BH; betwygen Bu   siðestan] si þestan B; sið\m/estan H   sie] sy BH   gefongen] gefangen BH   mon] man BH   fot] fot of B
Ine §19 swerian] swerigan H; swerigen Bu   syxtig] sixti B; lx H   huslgengea] huslgenga BH

⁴⁷ *Hapax legomenon.*
⁴⁸ *Hapax legomenon.*
⁴⁹ Scribe omitted x, added later in raised position with insertion mark.
⁵⁰ Clause is ungrammatical as it stands; *of* inserted on the model of §38.

16 [L16] He who kills a thief may declare with an oath that he killed him because he was [found] guilty [in the act]; this does not apply to his associates.[51]

17 [L17] He who finds stolen meat and hides it, if he dare, may declare with an oath that he owns it; the one who traces it gets the reward due an informant.[52]

18 [L18] A man of *ceorl* rank who has often been accused: if he is finally caught [in the act], let his hand or foot be struck off.[53]

19 [L19] A member of the king's household, if his *wer* is 1,200 shillings,[54] may swear [an oath in the value of] sixty hides, if he is a communicant.[55]

[51] See *Swerian* §4, MP §25. Thorpe suggests this stipulation is to prevent killing a thief with the principal goal of claiming a reward. Liebermann says the associates of the thief may not act as witnesses against the killer. Exactly who these associates are is unclear: they may be his fellow thieves, or they may be those who constitute the group that would stand with him in oath-statements or payment of wergild. Compare §20.1 and §35. Nowell translates it as "so escape without paying ought," which approaches but does not match the Old English.

[52] *Swerian* §3 provides a sample oath. The reward may well be equivalent to the 10 shillings for a person who turns in a thief described in §28.

[53] This ruling is the first in English law to require judicial mutilation. Reiterated in §38.

[54] Not all the king's men had the same wergild; that would depend on service and rank. The term *geneat* generally refers to a high-ranking subordinate. The *Anglo-Saxon Chronicle* (Bately 1986: 60) records that among those who died in 896 was *Æðelferð cyninges geneat* ("Eðelferð, the king's *geneat*"); on the basis of this and other evidence Hough concludes (2014: 84–85) that the *geneat* referred to here must have been a high-ranking member of the nobility rather than a mere servant or retainer. But see §21 for evidence that the term can also apply to those of lower rank.

[55] See *Ine* §14.3. While it is possible that the exclusion would apply to those who might be still unconverted pagans (recall that the previous king of Wessex was only baptized on his deathbed) or foreign counselors not attached to a local minster, the sacramental theology of this period should be borne in mind.

{LXIIII}

20 [L20] /48v/ Gif feorcund mon oððe fremde butan wege geond wudu gonge 7 ne hrieme ne horn blawe, for ðeof he bið to profi-anne: oððe to sleanne oððe to áliesanne.

{LXV}

20.1 [L21] Gif mon ðonne þæs ófslægenan weres bidde, he mot gecyþan, þæt he hine for ðeof ofsloge, nalles þæs ofslegenan gegildan ne his hlaford.[56]

20.2 [L21.1] Gif he hit ðonne dierneð, 7 weorðeð ymb long yppe, ðonne rymeð he ðam deadan to ðam aðe, þæt hine moton his mægas unsyngian.[57]

Ine §20 feorcund mon] feor cuman man B; feorcund man H   geond] ge on B   gonge] gonde (*corrected by a later hand to* gonge) B   hrieme] ryme B; hryme H; hrime Bu   aliesanne] alysenne B; \a/lysanne H; lesanne Bu
Ine §20.1 mon] man BH   ófslægenan] ofslæg\e/nan H   ðeof] ðeofðe (?) Bu   nalles] nalæs BH   ofslegenan] ofslægenan BH   gegildan] gyldan B; gegildanne H
Ine §20.2 dierneð] dyrneð B; dirneð H, Bu   weorðeð] wurð H   ymb] emb B; ymb\e/ H   rymeð] remeð Bu (Kentish?)   his mægas] \his/ magos (*corrected to* magas *by a later hand*) B; his magas H; his mæges Bu   unsyngian] unscyldigne gedon H

[56] Compare to §34.
[57] *Hapax legomenon.*

20 [L20] If [either] a person who has come from far off or a stranger travels off the road through the woods and does not shout out or blow a horn, he is to be taken for a thief: either to be slain or to be redeemed [by ransom].[58]

20.1 [L21] If [some]one then claims the *wer* of the slain man, [the killer] must declare that he slew him assuming he was a thief; neither the slain man's associates nor his lord [have a further claim] in this regard.[59]

20.2 [L21.1] If, however, he conceals [the killing], but it is revealed after a while, then he clears the way to the oath [being sworn] for the dead man, so that his kinsmen may prove him innocent.[60]

---

[58] This clause is paralleled in *Wihtred* §23 [L28]. Liebermann assumes that the captor receives a reward, while right to condemn the man or the fine paid to avoid the death penalty belongs to the king. Compare §28, which allows a 10-shilling reward to one who captures a thief. *MP* §47 suggests that the problem was the stealthy approach and not simply mistrust of outsiders: "the foreigner and he who has come from afar – do not deal unkindly with him, nor may you afflict him with wrongs." On the uncertain descent of this clause, see Chapter 2, 49–51.

[59] For **gegildan** "associates" compare §16; for lack of culpability in slaying a thief compare §35.

[60] See also §35 and note on concealed killing.

{LXVI}

21 [L22] Gif ðin geneat stalie ⁊ losie ðe, gif ðu hæbbe byrgean,
mana þone þæs angyldes. Gif he næbbe, gyld ðu þæt angylde, ⁊ ne
sie him no ðy ðingodre.

Ine §21 losie] losige BH   hæbbe] habbe Bu   byrgean] borgas B; byrg\e/an H; bergan
Bu   mana] manna Bu   angyldes] angyldas B; angeldes Bu   ne sie him no ðy ðin-
godre] ne sy him na ðe geðingodre B; ne sy him na ðe geðingrode H

21 [L22] If a member of your household⁶¹ steals and runs away,⁶² if you have [one who stands] surety [for him], claim from him the single value [of the stolen goods]. If [the thief] does not have [one who stands surety], you pay the single value, but [the thief] is not thus released from culpability.⁶³

---

⁶¹ The **geneat** of this clause appears to be of lower standing than the king's *geneat* of §19. This figure may be more akin to the *geneat* described in §2 of *Rectitudines Singularum Personarum*, composed perhaps around 1025:

> *Geneatriht is mistlic be ðam ðe on lande stænt: on sumon he sceal landgafol syllan 7 gærsswyn on geare 7 ridan 7 auerian 7 lade lædan, wyrcan 7 hlaford feormian, ripan 7 mawan, deorhege heawan 7 sæte haldan, bytlian 7 burh hegegian, nigefaran to tune feccan, cyricsceat syllan 7 almesfeoh, heafodwearde healdan 7 horswearde, ærendian fyr swa nyr, swa hwyder swa him mon to tæcð.*

> (The duty of the tenant [*geneat*] is diverse, according to [the customs] that stand on the estate. In some he must pay land tax and a pasturage pig each year, and ride and provide horses for team work and carry loads, labor, provide food for the lord, reap and mow, cut the animal-hedge, and maintain snares, build and fence the dwellings within an enclosure, and lead newcomers to the enclosure, pay church tribute and alms money, hold head-guard (duties) and guard horses, go on errands, either further or nearer or to wherever he is sent.)

⁶² Use of second-person address occurs only here in *Ine*.

⁶³ Liebermann takes this to mean for damages done and the fine thus incurred. The lord has responsibility for replacing the goods stolen by the man in his service.

{LXVII}

22 [L23] Gif mon elðeodigne ófslea, se cyning ah twædne dǽl weres, þriddan dæl sunu oðð e mægas.

22.1 [L23.1] Gif he ðonne mægleas sie, healf kyninge, healf se gesið.

22.2 [L23.2] Gif hit ðonne abbod sie oðð e abbodesse, dælen on þa ilcan wisan wið þone kyning.

Ine §22 elðeodigne] ælðeodigne mon B; ælðeodigne H   cyning] cyng B; kining Bu   twædne dǽl weres] twegen dælas þæs weres B; twegen dæl\as þæs/ weres H   mægas] magas BH; mæges Bu (*end* Bu)
Ine §22.1 sie] sy BH   healf (2x)] half B
Ine §22.2 abbod] abbud BH   sie] sy BH   abbodesse] abbudisse BH   dælen] dælon BH   kyning] cyning B

22 [L23] If a foreigner is killed, the king gets two parts of the *wer*, the third goes to the son[s][64] or kinsmen.

22.1 [L23.1] If he is without kinsmen, half to the king and half to the nobleman [under whose protection he has been residing].[65]

22.2 [L23.2] If, however, [his previous host] is an abbot or abbess, let the division be the same as for the king.

---

[64] This could be plural if a nasal extension stroke was missing.

[65] Hough (1997: 166) points out that the nominative **se gesið** should be in the dative, parallel to **kyninge**, and also discusses the curiosity that the king receives less recompense if the slain person is kinless rather than more (as might be expected). The anomaly is attributed to corruption.

23 [L23.3] Wealh gafolgelda cxx sci~~ll~~, his sunu c, ðeowne lx, somhwelcne fiftegum. Weales hyd twelfum.

23.1 [L24.2] Wealh, gif he hafað v hida, he bið syxhynde.[66]

{LXVIII}[67]

24 [L24] Gif witeðeow Engliscmon hine forstalie,[68] hó hine mon ⁊
ne gylde his hlaforde.

24.1 [L24.1] Gif hine mon ofsléa, ne gylde hine mon his mægum,
gif hie hine on xii monðum ne áliesden.

Ine §23 gafolgelda] gafolgylda BH   cxx] hund twelftig B   c] hund\red/ B   ðeowne]
ðeow\ne/ B   lx] sextig B   somhwelcne fiftegum] somhwylcne mid fiftig BH   twel-
fum] mid twelf*u*m B; mid twelfum H
Ine §23.1 hafað] hæfð BH   v] fif BH
Ine §24 Engliscmon] ænglisc man H
Ine §24.1 mon (2x)] man H   mægum] magu*m* B; magum H   hie] hy BH   xii] twelf
BH   áliesden] alysdon BH

---

[66] This clause follows §24 in the manuscript; it has clearly been misplaced by scribal
error (and is so misplaced in B and H as well). Compare §32.
[67] Due to the misplacement of §23.1, this number follows the *twelfum* of §23 in the
manuscript.
[68] This term used only here and in vi *Æthelstan* §6.3.

23 [L23.3] A Welsh[69] tax-payer [has a wergild of] 120 shillings, his son 100, a slave [a worth of] 60, some fifty.[70] A Welshman [can redeem his] skin [from a beating with] twelve [shillings].[71]

[72]23.1 [L24.2] A Welshman, if he has five hides, is [due a wergild of] 600.[73]

24 [L24] If an English penal slave escapes ["steals himself"], he should be hanged and no payment is due his lord.

24.1 [L24.1] If he is killed, one need not recompense his kin, if they have not ransomed him within twelve months.

---

[69] Here and throughout these laws the term "Welsh" is used for Celtic-speaking inhabitants of Wessex, not those resident in Wales, who would be subject to Welsh law.

[70] In *Æthelberht* §16 [L10–11] different ranks of slaves have different worths. *Ine* §3 discusses the penalty when a slave works on Sunday; the parallel in *Wihtred* §8 [L9] concerns an *esne* ("hired labourer") who performs servile work. Perhaps the 60 shillings in *Ine* §23 is actually the price of a hired laborer and 50 the price of a slave. §32 sets the wergild of a Welshman who owns no property – that is, a hired worker – at 60 shillings. It is true that §75 requires the owner of a Welsh slave who has killed an Englishman to pay 60 shillings to redeem him from execution. But the immensity of his offense may well require an augmented compensation.

[71] In the laws of Hwyll Dda, differentiation is by position rather than land-holding:
[T]he worth of the steward and the chief of kindred is nine kine and nine score kine; of a noble and every person who has an office from a lord, six kine and six score kine; every man of the bodyguard without office, four kine and four score kine; every innate Welshman and foreigner dependent on the king, three kine and three score kine; every foreigner dependent on a nobleman, half that of the king's foreigner. (See Jenkins 1986: 155.)

[72] This clause was probably meant to follow §24.1.

[73] Compare §32.

{LXVIIII}[74]

25 [L25] Gif ciepemon uppe on folce ceapie, do þæt beforan gewit-
nessum.

25.1 [L25.1] Gif ðiefefioh[75] mon æt ciepan befo, ⁊ he hit næbbe
beforan godum weotum geceapod, gecyðe hit be wite, þæt he ne
gewita ne gestala[76] nære, oððe gielde to wite VI ⁊ XXX sciłł/49r/.

{LXX}

26 [L26] To fundes cildes fostre: ðy forman geare geselle VI sciłł, ðy
æfterran XII, ðy ðriddan XXX, siððan be his wlite.

{LXXI}

27 [L27] Se ðe dearnenga bearn gestrieneð ⁊ gehileð, nah se his
deaðes wer, ac his hlaford ⁊ se cyning.[77]

Ine §25 ciepemon uppe] cepe man uppe B; ceap_man \uppe/ H   ceapie] ceapige BH
beforan gewitnessum] beforan gewitnysse B; be\foran ge/witnesse H
Ine §25.1 Gif ðiefefioh mon æt ciepan] Gyf mon feoh (*a later hand adds* forstolen *in
the margin*) æt cyp\men/ B; Gif man forstolen feoh æt ce\eapmon/ H   weotum]
witu*m* B; witum H   ne gewita] newita B; nage wita H   gielde] gylde B; gilde H   VI]
syx B
Ine §26 fundes] fundenes BH   geselle] gesylle BH   VI] syx B   ðy] ðu B; ⁊ ðy
H   æfterran] æftran B; æfteran geare H   XII] twelf   ðy] ðu B; ⁊ þy H   siððan] ⁊
siððan H
Ine §27 dearnenga] dearnunga BH   gestrieneð] gestreonað B; gestryn_ð H   gehileð]
geheleð BH   cyning] cyng B

[74] Due to the misplacement of §23.1, this text follows the *syxhynde* of that clause.
[75] *Hapax legomenon.*
[76] Compare to *Swerian* §3 (*ne gewita ne gewyrhta*).
[77] MP §7 renders the prohibition against adultery as *Ne lige þu dearnunga*, and it is
therefore uncertain whether *Alfred* refers here to adultery or (as here) to fornication.

25 [L25] If a merchant does trade out in the countryside,[78] let him do it in the presence of witnesses.

25.1 [L25.1] If stolen property is found in the merchant's possession, and he has not bought it in the presence of good witnesses, let him declare [with an oath] in the amount of the fine that he was neither accessory nor thief, or let him give as fine 6 and 30 shillings.[79]

26 [L26] For the fostering of a foundling:[80] for the first year give 6 shillings; for the next, 12; for the third, 30; and afterwards according to his appearance.[81]

27 [L27] He who conceives a child out of wedlock and hides it – he will not have its *wer* upon its death, but [it goes to] his lord and the king.[82]

---

[78] Thus not in the markets or the ports.

[79] He thus needs thirty-six oath supporters. Cf. *Hlophere and Eadric* §11–11.3 [L16–16.3].

[80] The foster-care is paid by the king, to whom the wergild for the foundling would be due. Liebermann suggests this could also include illegitimate children not openly recognized. This would then tie it to the following clause.

[81] The meaning of this is unclear. Liebermann translates it *Körperbeschaffenheit* ("physique, constitution"), which seems to imply that the amount is related to how much the child might eat according to his size. Attenborough suggests that perhaps "more should be paid for a child which appears to be of aristocratic origin."

[82] The clause implies that recognition even of a child born out of wedlock entitles the father to compensation upon its (violent) death. Liebermann suggests that the last tironian note (7) should be translated as "or" rather than "and," with the meaning that the *wer* goes to the king only when the child has no other lord, but compare §22.1.

{LXXII}

28 [L28] Se ðeof gefehð, ah x sciłł, ⁊ se cyning ðone ðeof; ⁊ þa mægas him swerian aðas unfæhða.⁸³

28.1 [L28.1] Gif he ðonne oðierne⁸⁴ ⁊ orige⁸⁵ weorðe, þon*n*e bið he⁸⁶ wites scyldig.

28.2 [L28.2] Gif he onsacan wille, do he ðæt be ðam féo ⁊ be ðam wite.

{LXXIII}

29 [L29] **Gif** mon sweordes onlæne oðres esne ⁊ he losie, gielde he hine⁸⁷ ðriddan dæle; gif mon spere selle, healfne; gif he horses onlæne, ealne he hine gylde.

Ine §28 Se] se ðe B; Se \þe/ H   ah] he ah BH   x] tyn B   mægas] magas BH   unfæhða] unfæðða B; unfehþa H

Ine §28.1 Gif] \⁊/ gif H   oðierne] oðerna \do/ B; oþyrne H   ⁊] *om.* B

Ine §28.2 onsacan] æt sacan B   be ðam féo] be þam \were/ H

Ine §29 oðres] oðru*m* B   he losie] hit losige B; he losige H   gielde he hine ðriddan dæle] be ðriddan dæle he hit gylde B; gilde he hine ðriddan dæle H   selle] sylle BH   healfne] healfne \dæl/ H   gif he horses] gyf mon hors B; Gif man hor_ses H   onlæne] læne H

⁸³ *Hapax legomenon.* Cf. §12. The phrase **aðas unfæhða** is equivalent to the *unceases áð* of §35.

⁸⁴ *Hapax legomenon.*

⁸⁵ *Hapax legomenon.* Cf. Old High German *urouge* ("invisible").

⁸⁶ **he** in this clause and the next refers to the captor, who pays a fine for his delict.

⁸⁷ **hine** is ambiguous; the context indicates that the person who loaned the weapon/horse must pay the master of the **esne** for abetting the escape.

28 [L28] He who catches a thief receives 10 shillings,[88] and the king the thief; and his kinsmen swear oaths to renounce feuding.[89]

28.1 [L28.1] If, however, he escapes and cannot be found, then [the captor] is liable for a fine.[90]

28.2 [L28.2] If he wishes to deny [his culpability], let him do so [by swearing an oath in the amount of] the [stolen] property and the fine.[91]

29 [L29] If someone lends a sword to another's *esne*[92] and he escapes, let [the lender] pay [the lord] one third [of the *esne*'s value]; if he gives a spear, half; if he lends a horse, he compensates [the lord] for all [the value of the *esne*].

[88] Likely the *meldfeoh* ("reward due an informant") discussed in §17; this may also apply to the person who catches a stranger lurking off the beaten path, as described in §20.

[89] Niles 2015 cautions against the translation **fæhð** as "feud" on (in part) etymological grounds, but given the role assumed here for the captured thief's kin, use of the term seems warranted. Compare *Wihtred* §21–21.1 [L26–26.1]. Liebermann assumes the legal power of the Kentish king may have been less than that of the West Saxon.

[90] Compare §37. Liebermann says the fine could be the same amount as would be due were the thief to have appeared before a judge and been found guilty; nothing in the text substantiates or refutes this hypothesis. The Old English **he** is ambiguous as to whether it refers to thief or captor, but the clause implies that the thief has disappeared for good. (However, compare §74.)

[91] That is, he swears an oath equal to the sum value of the stolen property and the fine. Maurer thought this refers to the thief (see Liebermann 1903–1916: III, 73), but we concur with Liebermann's reading as the captor. According to §28, the thief is long gone.

[92] The rubric has here *þeow* ("slave").

{LXXIIII}

30 [L30] Gif mon cierliscne monnan fliemanfeorme⁹³ teo, be his
agnum were geladige⁹⁴ he hine; gif he ne mæge, gielde hine his agne
were; ⁊ se gesiðmon swa be his were.

{LXXV}

31 [L31] Gif mon wíf gebyccge, ⁊ sio gyft forð ne cume, agife þæt
feoh ⁊ forgielde ⁊ gebete þam byrgean swa his borgbryce sie.

Ine §30 mon cierliscne monnan] man cyrliscne mannan B; man cierliscne man H   fie-
manfeorme] flyman feormienne B; flyman formie H   teo] *om.* H   agnum] agenon B;
agenum H   geladige] geladie H   gielde hine] gylde he hine B; gilde \he/ hine H   his
agne] be his agenum B; \be/ his agena\n/ H   swa] eac swa B; \eac/ swa H
Ine §31 gebyccge] bycge BH   sio] seo BH   forgielde] forgylde B; forgilde
H   byrgean] *corrected to* borgean *from* byrgean B; byrgean H   borgbryce sie] borh
bryce sy BH

---

⁹³ *Hapax legomenon.*
⁹⁴ This term only appears in legal texts.

30 [L30] If a *ceorl* is accused of harboring a fugitive, let him clear himself with [an oath equal to] his own *wer*; if he cannot, let him compensate with his own *wer*; and a nobleman likewise according to his [own] *wer*.[95]

31 [L31] If a man makes a contract for a wife, but the marriage does not take place,[96] let [the bride's guardian] return the bride-gift and compensate [the groom], and pay the guarantor [the price] for the breaking of his surety.[97]

---

[95] Cited in II *Edward* §5.2.

[96] This clause neatly demonstrates "the two parts to an Anglo-Saxon marriage: the engagement, when the terms were agreed upon, and the wedding, when the bride was given to the bridegroom with feasting and ceremony" (Fischer 1986: 25). In the second clause, the Old English literally reads "and the gift is not forthcoming." The term **gift** is the most common noun used for the wedding ceremony itself (Fischer 1986: 36–44). A survival is found in the language of the Rite for the Solemnization of Matrimony in the *Book of Common Prayer*: "Who gives this woman to be married to this man?" Parallels are suggested by Hough (2007: 64): "The *Theodore Penitential* II, 12.34 states that if a girl refused to live with the man to whom she is betrothed, his money is to be repaid plus a third, although if he backs out of the agreement, he simply loses his money; while under seventh-century Lombard law, Rothair's edict 192 states that if the relatives of a betrothed girl connive at her marrying someone else, her original fiancé is entitled to payment of double the marriage portion." Schmid reverses the direction of the penalties by interpreting **sio gyft** as the brideprice. An English rendering of his translation reads: "If someone has bought a wife and the bride-price is not paid, let him pay the money and give compensation and recompense the guarantors according to the degree of the breaking of the surety." A difficulty for Schmid's rendering is that the bride-price is first referred to as **gyft** ("gift") and immediately thereafter as **feoh** ("property").

[97] Compare *Æthelberht* §76 [L77–81]. *Wifmann's Beweddung* provides further insight into later practice.

{LXXVI}

32 [L32] Gif Wiliscmon hæbbe hide londes, his wer bið CXX sciłł; gif
he þon*n*e healfes hæbbe, LXXX sciłł; gif he nænig hæbbe, LX scillin-
ga.⁹⁸

{LXXVII}

33 [L33] Cyninges horswealh⁹⁹ se ðe him mæge geærendian: ðæs
wergield bið CC sciłł.

Ine §32 Wiliscmon] wylisc man B; wil\i/sc man H   londes] landes B; land\es/ H   CXX]
hund twelftig B   healfes hæbbe] healfe hæbbe B; hæbbe healfes H   LXXX] hund
eahtati B   nænig hæbbe] næbbe nan land B; nænig næbbe H   LX] sixti B
Ine §33 geærendian] geerendian B; geærndi_an H   ðæs] ðes H   wergield] wer gyld
B; wer\e gild/ H   CC] twa hund B   bið] is H

⁹⁸ Compare to §23.1.
⁹⁹ *Hapax legomenon.*

32 [L32] If a Welshman has a hide of land, his *wer* is 120 shillings; if he, however, has half, 80 shillings; if he has none,[100] 60 shillings.

33 [L33] A Welsh horseman in the king's service who can act as his courier: his wergild is 200 shillings.[101]

---

[100] Cf. *Norðleoda Laga* (§8) which Liebermann dates 920–954. The later text adds here *and þeah freo sie* "and nonetheless is free." *Ine* here refers to a free worker who seems to be the equivalent of an Anglo-Saxon *esne* (a hired labourer). Both *esnas* and slaves are assigned worth rather than wergild (see *Æthelberht* §80). Cf. *Ine* §23 and note.

[101] What exactly is meant by **horswealh** is uncertain. The first element of the compound is obviously "horse." The second is less clear. The term "Welsh" originally meant "foreign"; in *PactLexSal* §41.9 the wergild for a Roman (i.e., not Frankish) property owner is referred to as *walaleodi*. The word came to be applied specifically to the Britons, and this compound might represent an early example of this usage. The meaning of "slave, servant" arose later from a common position of the Welsh in Anglo-Saxon territories. Perhaps the wergild of a Welshman in service to the king is doubled to match that of an English-speaker. (In the laws of Hwyll Dda, a freeman's *sarhaed* [roughly *mund*] and worth [wergild] is doubled for a person in the king's or queen's service: see Jenkins 1986: 8–39.) Whatever the ethnicity of the king's horseman, this clause assigns the servant an English *ceorl*'s wergild. The duties require one who is comfortable traveling on horseback: **geærendian** can mean to transact business, ride on errands, and/or serve as messenger. Whitelock (1955: 402) associates this with the *laadrincmann* of *Æthelberht* §13 [L7]; Oliver 2002: 87–88 questions this connection. The *Anglo-Saxon Chronicle* reports that among the king's men who died of disease in 897 was *Ecgulf cynges horsþegn*; the chronicler goes on to say that of the dead *ic þa geðungnestan nemde* ("I named the most distinguished") (Bately 1986: 60). Attenborough is probably right in assuming that this is a higher status person than indicated in these laws; the year the *Chronicle* refers to postdates *Ine* by about two centuries.

{LXXVIII}

34 [L34] Se ðe on ðære fore wære þæt mon monnan ofsloge, getriewe hine ðæs sleges ⁊ ða fore gebete be ðæs ofslegenan wergielde.

34.1 [L34.1] Gif his wergield sie CC sciłł, gebete mid L sciłł, ⁊ ðy ilcan /49v/ ryhte do man be ðam deorborenran.

{LXXVIIII}

35 [L35] Se ðe ðeof slihð, he mot aðe gecyðan, þæt he hine fleondne for ðeof sloge, ⁊ þæs deadan mægas him swerian unceases¹⁰² áð. Gif he hit þonne dierne ⁊ sie eft yppe, þonne forgielde he hine.¹⁰³

Ine §34 ðære] ðere B   ðæt] ðær B   mon monnan] mon mon\n/ B *(scribe later changes vowel in second word to* a); man man H   getriewe] getrywie B; getriwe H   ⁊ ða] oððe B   *ofslegenan wergielde] ofslægenan wer gyrde B; of slægnan were H   wergield sie] wergyld sy B; wergild sy H   CC] twa hund B   L] fiftig B   ðy] ða BH   mon] man BH
Ine §35 slihð] sluhþ H   aðe] mid aðe H   fleondne] fleonde H   ðæs] ðes B   mægas] magas BH   unceases] unceastes H   dierne] dyrne BH   sie] sy BH   forgielde] for gylde B; for gilde H

¹⁰² *Hapax legomenon.* The phrase **unceases áð** is equivalent to the *aðas unfæhða* of §28.
¹⁰³ Compare to §21.

34 [L34] He who was on a raid in which a man was killed,[104] let him clear himself [by oath] of culpability for the death and compensate for his part in the raid according to the slain man's wergild.

34.1 [L34.1] If his wergild is 200 shillings, let him compensate with 50 shillings and the same law applies to someone nobly born.

35 [L35] He who kills a thief may declare on oath that he slew him for a thief as he was running away, and the kin of the dead man must swear him an oath not to engage in hostilities against him.[105] If he, however, conceals [the slaying] and it afterwards becomes known, then he must make restitution for him.[106]

---

[104] Whitelock takes **sloge** as subjunctive "to indicate purpose rather than result," and translates this clause: "Whoever was present on the expedition made for the purpose of killing a man [...]"; she thus adds an intentionality to the clause not necessarily present in the original.

[105] For **ceas** ("strife"), compare *Æthelberht* §13. This term is a variant of *aðas unfæhða* in §28.

[106] Compare to §16 and §20.1. This clause and *Ine* §20.2 are the earliest Anglo-Saxon ordinances differentiating between a killing which is open and one which is concealed. But the result is not what we might expect. Frankish law considered homicide followed by concealment as "murder," and the distinction also exists in the north (Jurasinski 2002: 22). All of this would seem to suggest that the classification of concealed homicide as an especially heinous offense requiring unusual penalties was of common Germanic inheritance. Yet here and elsewhere in Ine's laws, concealed homicide is remedied by payment alone.

36 [L35.1] Gif mon to þam men feoh geteme ðe his ær oðswaren
hæfde, ⁊ eft oðswerian wille, oðswerige be ðam wite ⁊ be ðæs feos
weorðe; gif he oðswerian nylle, gebete þone mænan að twybote.

{LXXX}

37 [L36] Se ðe ðeof gefehð, oððe him mon gefongenne agifð, ⁊ he
hine þon*ne* álæte oððe þa ðiefðe gedierne, forgielde þone þeof his
were.¹⁰⁷

37.1 [L36.1] Gif he ealdormon sie, ðolie his scire, buton him kyning arian wille.

Ine §36 mon] man H   þam] þæm H   ær oðswaren] ætsworen B; oþsworen
H   oðswerian (*both occurrences*)] ætswerian B   oðswerige] swerig*e* B; oþswerie
H   weorðe] wyrðe BH   twybote] twyg bote B
Ine §37 gefehð] fehð H   gefongenne agifð] gefonge ne agyfð B; gefangenne agifð
H   ðiefðe gedierne] þyfþe gedyrne B; þyfðe gedirne H   forgielde] forgylde B; forgilde
H   his were] be his were BH
Ine §37.1 ealdormon sie] ealdorman sy B; ealder man sy H   ðolie] þolige H   kyning]
cyning B; se cyning H

¹⁰⁷ Compare to §28.

36 [L35.1] If a man is vouched to warranty for property which he earlier has denied on oath [was illegally obtained], and he wishes to deny it on oath again, let him deny it by [an oath in the amount of] the fine and by [an oath in the amount of] the property. If he does not wish to deny it [the second time], let him pay for the false oath two-fold.[108]

37 [L36] He who catches a thief, or to whom [a thief] is entrusted as a prisoner, and then lets him go or conceals the theft, let him compensate by the *wer* of the thief.

    37.1 [L36.1] If he is an *ealdorman*, let him forfeit his shire, unless the king is willing to show him mercy.

---

[108] Ambiguous as to whether it is the fine or the property restitution that is doubled. Schmid believes the former, Liebermann the latter. The first denial on oath was specifically linked to the amount of the fine; it thus seems logical that a false oath would require a double fine.

{LXXXI}

38 [L37] Se cirlisca mon se ðe oft betygen wære ðiefðe, ⁊ þon*ne* æt
siðestan synnigne gefó in ceape oððe elles æt openre scylde: slea him
mon hond óf oððe fót.[109]

{LXXXII}

39 [L38] Gif ceorl ⁊ his wif bearn hæbben gemæne, ⁊ fere se ceorl
forð, hæbbe sio modor hire bearn ⁊ fede. Agife hire mon VI sciʬ to
fostre, cu on sumera, oxan on wintra. Healden þa mægas þone
fr[um]stol,[110] oððæt hit gewintred sie.

[{LXXXIII}][111]

40 [L39] Gif hwa fare unáliefed fram his hlaforde oððe on oðre scire
hine bestele, ⁊ hine mon geahsige, fare þær he ær wæs ⁊ geselle his
hlaforde LX sciʬ.

Ine §38 cirlisca mon] ceorlisce man B; ciorlisca man H   betygen] betogen BH   wære]
were B   ðiefðe] ðyfðe B; þifðe H   synnigne] syn ninge B   gefó] man gefo H   ceape]
ceace BH   elles æt openre scylde] æt openre scylde elles H   hond] handa B; hand
H   óf] *om.* H
Ine §39 fere se ceorl forð] fære se ceorl forð B; se ciorl forð fære H   sio] seo BH   ⁊
fede] an\d/ fede . ⁊ H   hire mon] man hire H   VI] syx B   wintra] wintran
B   Healden] healdan B   mægas] magas BH   gewintred sie] ge wintrod sy B; gewintred sy H
Ine §40 unáliefed] unalyfede B; un alyfed H   hlaforde (*both occurrences*)] laforde
B   mon] man H   geahsige] geacsige B; geaxie H   fare þær he ær wæs] fare þær he
wæs ær H   geselle] gylde B; gesylle H   LX] syxtig B

[109] A reiteration of §18.
[110] Manuscript has a hole here.
[111] Paragraph number omitted by scribe. A cramped addition in the margin is barely
     legible under normal lighting: it appears to be a small LXXX. A waterstain on this
     part of the page increases the difficulty of legibility.

38 [L37] A man of the rank of *ceorl*, who has often been accused of theft, and finally, then, is openly caught either with the goods or in the unlawful act: let his hand or foot be struck off.[112]

39 [L38] If a *ceorl* and his wife have a child together, and the *ceorl* dies, the mother shall keep and support her child. She should be given 6 shillings for the foster, a cow in summer, an ox in winter. Let the kin maintain the homestead until the child has reached maturity.[113]

40 [L39] If someone moves away from his lord without permission or steals away into another shire, and he is found, let him return to where he was before and let him pay his lord 60 shillings.[114]

---

[112] The mutilation requirement is a reiteration of §18. Liebermann suggests that the inclusion of both these clauses presents the possibility that the scribe may have used two different exemplars. Although the Parker manuscript reads **ceape**, all translators except Schmid and Thorpe follow **H** and **B**'s reading of *ceace* ("cauldron"), a presumptive reference to the ordeal. (Note that §66 has a similar use of *ceap*, and see footnote to that clause.) If we accept this reading – one isolated to the very latest manuscripts – the situation would be that the thief was found guilty in the ordeal. (Compare VI *Æthelstan* §1.4.) This emendation does not, however, seem necessary. Schmid, using the text as it stands, translates the clause: "and he is finally caught culpable with the livestock or otherwise in open guilt" (*und man ihn endlich fehlbar fängt mit dem Vieh oder sonst in offener Schuld*). Schmid's translation aligns this clause with *Wihtred* §21 [L26], which uses the phrase *æt hæbbendre handa* ("with the goods in hand"). Compare further §43 and §47, where *ceape* is livestock.

[113] §7.2 implies that the child comes of age at 10; cf. *Æthelberht* §76.2 [L78] and *Hlophere and Eadric* §4 [L6]; also *Wifmannes Beweddung*.

[114] *Alfred* §38 doubles the fine.

{LXXXIIII}

41 [L40] Ceorles worðig sceal beon wintres ⁊ sumeres betyned. Gif he bið untyneð, ⁊ recð his neahgebures ceap in on his agen geat, nah he æt þam ceape nanwuht: adrife hine ut /5or/ ⁊ ðolie æfwerdlan.

{LXXXV}

42 [L41] Borges mon mót oðsacan, gif he wát, *þæt* he ryht deð.

{LXXXVI}

43 [L42] Gif ceorlas gærstun hæbben gemænne oððe oþer gedálland to tynanne, ⁊ hæbben sume getyned hiora dæl sume næbben, ⁊ etten hiora gemænan æceras oððe gærs, gán þa þon*ne* þe ðæt geat agan ⁊ gebete þam oðrum þe hiora dǽl getynedne hæbben þone æwerdlan þe ðær gedon sie. Abidden him æt þam ceape swylc ryht swylce hit kyn sie.

43.1 [L42.1] Gif þon*ne* hryðera hwelc sie þe hegas brece ⁊ ga in gehwær, ⁊ se hit nolde gehealdan se hit age oððe ne mæge, nime se hit on his æcere mete ⁊ ófslea; ⁊ nime se agenfrigea his fél ⁊ flæsc ⁊ þolie þæs oðres.

Ine §41 Ceorles] Ciorles H   worðig] worði B; wurðig H   untyneð] untyned BH   recð] receþ H   neahgebures] neh hebures B   geat] geat in H   þam ceape] þam \ceape/ H   nanwuht] nan wiht B   æfwerdlan] æfwyrlan B; þone æfwyrdlan H
Ine §42 Borges mon] \B/orges mon B; B orges man H   oðsacan] ætsacan BH
Ine §43 ceorles] ciorlas H   gærstun hæbben] habban gærstun B   gemænne] gemæne B; gemæ_ne H   gedálland] *om.* H, *but alias* ge dal land *added later above the line*   hiora (all occurrences)] heora BH   næbben] nabben H   agan] agon BH   gebete] gebeten BH   þam] ðæm B   getynedne] betyned H   æwerdlan] æfwyrdlan BH   sie] sy BH   Abidden him] abiddon heom; abidden he\o/m H   kyn sie] cyn sy B; cynn sy H
Ine §43.1 hryðera] hrið\e/ra H   hwelc] hwylc B; gehwilc H   sie] sy BH   in gehwær] gehwær in H   gehealden] \ge/healden H   se hit (2x)] se \þe/ hit H   mete] gemete BH   agenfrigea] agenfriga BH   fél ⁊] *om.* BH   þolie] ðolige H

41 [L40] A *ceorl*'s pasturage shall be fenced winter and summer. If it is not fenced, and his neighbor's livestock strays in through his own opening, he has no claim on the livestock: let him drive it out and suffer the damage [that the livestock did].

42 [L41] A person may deny surety [that he has promised for another] if he knows that he does it justly.[115]

43 [L42] If *ceorls* have to fence a common meadow or otherwise shared land,[116] and some have fenced their part and some have not, [and livestock get in and] eat their shared crops or grass, let those who are responsible for the gap go then and pay the others who have fenced their part for the damages that were done there. Let [those who fenced their land] demand from them for [damage done by] the cattle such lawful recompense as is proper.[117]

43.1 [L42.1] If, however, it should be one of those heifers that breaks hedges and gets in everywhere, and [the owner] does not wish to or is not able to contain it, let him who finds it on his crop-field take it and kill it; and let the owner take its hide and meat, and forfeit the rest.[118]

---

[115] Liebermann holds that this clause has almost surely been misplaced from the original order. §41 and §43 make a natural sequence.

[116] The Anglo-Saxon plough requires a team of oxen ranging in size from two to eight, depending on – among other factors – the size and type of plough. Pictorial evidence displays oxen always working in pairs, making communal farming almost a necessity (Banham and Faith 2014: 50–57).

[117] Attenborough asserts that "round the arable land lay the common meadows and pasture lands, enclosed by a strip of forest which provided mast pasture for the swine and served as a means of defense. The fencing of the arable land was obviously a necessary precaution."

[118] The owner loses the value of the animal as work-beast, milk-supplier, or breeder.

{LXXXVII}

44 [L43] Ðonne mon beam on wuda forbærne, ⁊ weorðe yppe on þone ðe hit dyde, gielde he fulwite: geselle LX sciłł forþamþe fyr bið þeof.

44.1 [L43.1] Gif mon afelle on wuda wel monega treowa ⁊ wyrð eft undierne, forgielde III treowu ælc mid XXX sciłł. Ne ðearf he hiora má geldan, wære hiora swa fela swa hiora wære, forþon sio æsc¹¹⁹ bið melda, nalles ðeof.

{LXXXVIII}

44.2 [L44] Gif mon þonne aceorfe an treow, þæt mæge XXX swina undergestandan¹²⁰ ⁊ wyrð undierne, geselle LX sciłł.

45 [L44.1] Gafolhwitel¹²¹ sceal bion æt hiwisce VI pæninga weorð.

Ine §44 weorðe] wyrðe BH   gielde] gylde B; gilde H   fulwite] ful\l/wite BH   geselle] gesylle B; ⁊ gesylle H   LX] syxtig B
Ine §44.1 afelle] afylle B; afylle\þ/ H   wel] well (*added by later hand?*) B   monega] manega B; manige H   wyrð] wurð þæt B   undierne] undyrne BH   forgielde] forgylde B; forgilde H   III] ðreo B   treowu] treowa B   xxx] ðrittig B   hiora má geldan] nan má gildan H; heora magyldan H   hiora (2x)] heora B; he\o/ra H   fela] feola B; fe\o/la H   forþon] forðan B   sio] seo BH   æsc] eax B; æx H   nalles] nalæs BH
Ine §44.2 xxx] ðrittig B   undergestandan] understandan B   wyrð] wurð B   undierne] undyrne B; undirne H   geselle] gesylle BH   LX] syxtig B
Ine §45 sceal bion æt hiwisce] æt hiwisce sceal beon B; sce\a/l beon æt hiwisce H   VI pæninga weorð] syx penega wurð B; .vi. peninga wyrð H

¹¹⁹ Metathesis of *æcs* ("axe") to *æsc* ("ash").
¹²⁰ *Hapax legomenon.*
¹²¹ *Hapax legomenon.* See fn. to translation of this clause.

44 [L43] When someone burns a tree in the forest, and it becomes known who did it, let him pay a full fine; let him pay 60 shillings because "fire is a thief."[122]

44.1 [L43.1] If a man fells many trees in the forest, and it afterwards is revealed, let him make restitution for three trees each with 30 shillings. He need not make restitution for more no matter how many there were, because the axe is an informant but not a thief.[123]

44.2 [L44] If, however, a man cuts down a tree under which thirty swine may stand[124] and it becomes known, let him pay 60 shillings.

45 [L44.1] An assessment paid in cloth[125] shall be worth 6 pennies for each household.[126]

---

[122] A legal proverb embedded in legislation: fire "steals" wood by consuming it.

[123] As opposed to fire, the axe, although it serves as evidence or perhaps informer through the sound of chopping (Grimm 1899: 47 provides parallels), leaves the fallen wood available to the rightful owner. (A different hand adds to Nowell's translation in RP 9865: *the axe maketh a noyse and is not a pyric theefe.*) Contrast with *Alfred* §14, which sets an equal fine for felling or burning another's wood. The tree feller presumably intended to remove the trunk for sale.

[124] Schmid interprets the clause as referring to a fruit-producing tree capable of nourishing thirty swine. An alternative interprets the value of the tree as a shade-provider. The two interpretations are not mutually exclusive. That the tree is of extraordinary size is demonstrated by the fine, which is double the normal fine for a large tree.

[125] Literally "tax-whittle."

[126] Grimm (1899: 378–380) provides parallels of taxes paid in cloth or clothing. Vinogradoff 1911: 329 suggests that a higher status freeman might pay *gafol* while a bound tenant was required to provide service. Liebermann considers this assessment too high to be demanded from each individual household and assumes it must refer rather to a community payment. Note that §59 values a ewe with her lamb at a shilling (=5 pence). But this does not seem out-of-line with the food-render required by §70. Nowell (RP 9865) omits this clause from his edition and translation.

{LXXXVIIII}

46 [L45] Burgbryce mon sceal betan cxx sciłł kyninges 7 biscepes, þær his rice bið; ealdormonnes lxxx sciłł; cyninges ðegnes lx sciłł; gesiðcundes monnes landhæbbendes xxxv; 7 bi ðon ansacan.

{xc}

47 [L46] Ðonne mon monnan betyhð *þæt* he ceap forstele oððe for/5ov/stolenne gefeormie, þon*ne* sceal he be lx hida onsacan þære þiefðe, gif he aðwyrðe bið.

47.1 [L46.1] Gif ðonne Englisc onstal[127] ga forð, onsace þon*ne* be twyfealdum. Gif hit ðon*ne* bið Wilisc onstal, ne bið se að na ðy mara.

48 [L46.2] Ælc mon mot onsacan frymþe 7 werfæhðe,[128] gif he mæg oððe déar.

Ine §46 Burgbryce mon] burhbryce man BH   sceal] sce\a/l H   cxx] hund twelftig B   biscepes] bisceopes B; biscopes H   ealdormonnes] ealdormannes B; Ealdermannes H   lxxx] hundeahtatig B   ðegnes] ðegnas B   lx] syxti B   monnes] mannes BH   xxxv] fif 7 xxx B   7 bi ðon ansacan] 7 bið\am/ ofsacan B; 7 byþ on ansacan H
Ine §47 mon monnan] mon mon\an/ B; man mon H   forstele] forstæle BH   forstolenne] forstolene B   gefeormie] gefeormige H   sceal] sce\a/l H   lx] syxti B   onsacan] ætsacan B   þiefðe] ðeofðe B; ðyfðe H   aðwyrðe] andwyrðe B
Ine §47.1 Englisc] englisc mon B   onstal] stalað B   onsace] æt sace B   þonne] *om.* B   bið Wilisc onstal] *om.* B   na ðy mara] na ðe mare B; mare (*om.* na ðy) H
Ine §48 mon] man BH   onsacan] ætsacan B   frymþe] fyrmðe BH   mæg] mæge B; mæg\g/ H   déar] dear\r/ B; dearr H

[127] A rare word.
[128] This word is used only here and in §57.

46 [L45] Breaking into a fortified dwelling¹²⁹ shall be recompensed [at the rate of] 120 shillings for king or bishop within his realm;¹³⁰ 80 shillings for an ealdorman; 60 shillings for a king's thegn;¹³¹ 35 shillings for a landowner of noble rank; and these same amounts serve [as the value of] the oath of denial.

47 [L46] If a man is accused of the theft of livestock or of supplying stolen [livestock] with fodder, then he must deny the theft by [an oath of] sixty hides, if he is oathworthy.¹³²

47.1 [L46.1] If an Englishman pursues the accusation, let him deny it by two-fold [oath]. If, however, a Welshman pursues the accusation, the oath is no greater [than 60].¹³³

48 [L46.2] Every person may clear himself of instigating [wrongdoing] or an act of violence requiring payment of wergild, if he is able or dares to.¹³⁴

---

¹²⁹ This need not necessarily mean the house, but simply the stockade surrounding it. Compare *Æthelberht* §28 [L27–28], which states: "If a freeman breaks into an enclosure, let him pay with 6 shillings. [28.1] If a person takes property therein, let that man pay 3[-fold] as compensation." The lower fine represents the fact that this clause refers to breaking into a freeman's – as opposed to a noble's – enclosed property.

¹³⁰ That is, within Ine's jurisdiction. The ruling does not (necessarily) apply to bishops outside Wessex. *Alfred* §41 maintains the fine for breaking into a king's dwelling, but halves that for a bishop's.

¹³¹ *Alfred* §41 requires a 30-shilling fine in the case of a person of 1,200-shilling wergild, and 15 for a person of 600-shilling wergild; the reduction in fine may signify that breaking and entering were less common in the later kingdom.

¹³² The oath is only allowed to free people. In various later laws oathworthiness is forfeited in cases of perjury, failure in the ordeal, or other misconduct showing a person to be untrustworthy. (See Liebermann 1903–1916: II, 376.)

¹³³ Schmid rightly refers to this clause as *dies dunkle Gesetz* ("this opaque law"). Perhaps *onstal* (whose precise meaning is unclear) refers to a particular type of charge? Schmid compares it to Frisian *onbring*, which is an accusation amplified by oath, thus requiring an amplified oath of exculpation.

¹³⁴ Most translators follow Thorpe's suggestion that **frymþ** is equivalent to the later term *flymene-fyrmþe* ("harboring a fugitive"). The emendation is not strictly necessary and we have thus retained the reading of the text itself.

{XCI}

49 [L47] **Gif** mon forstolenne ceap befehð, ne mot hine mon tieman to ðeowum men.

{XCII}

50 [L48] **Gif** hwelc mon bið witeðeow niwan geðeowad, 7 hine mon betyhð, þæt he hæbbe ær geðiefed ær hine mon geðeowode, þonne ah se teond ane swingellan æt him. Bedrife hine to swingum be his ceape.

{XCII[I][135]}

51 [L49] **Gif** mon on his mæstenne unaliefed swín gemete, genime þonne VI sciłł weorð wed.

51.1 [L49.1] **Gif** hie þonne þær næren oftor þonne æne, geselle sciłł se agenfrigea 7 gecyðe, þæt hie þær oftor ne comen, be þæs ceapes weorðe.

51.2 [L49.2] **Gif** hi ðær tuwa wæren, geselle twegen sciłł.

52 [L49.3] **Gif** mon nime æfesne on swynum: æt þryfingrum þæt ðridde, æt twyfingrum[136] þæt feorðe, æt þymelum þæt fifte.

Ine §49 forstolenne] forstolene B   tieman] tyman BH   ðeowum] ðeowan BH   men] menn H

Ine §50 hwelc] hwylc B; \hwylc/ H   mon] man H   betyhð] betyh B   geðiefed] geðeofad BH   mon] man H   geðeowode] geðeowade BH   swingellan] swingelan B; swinge_lan H   swingum] swing\l/um H

Ine §51 mon] man H   mæstenne] mæstene BH   unaliefed] unalufed B; unalyfed H   VI] syx B   weorð wed] wurð wed B; weorð wedd H

Ine §51.1 hie] hi BH   næren] næron BH   geselle] gesylle BH   scill] \ænne/ scilling   agenfrigea] agenfriga BH   hie] hi B; hy B   ne comen] ne comon B; næron H   weorðe] wyrðe BH

Ine §51.2 tuwa] twiga H   wæren] wæron BH   geselle] gesylle BH   twegen] .ii. H

Ine §52 æfesne] æbesne BH   þæt] \spic/ þæt B

---

[135] Scribe omitted last I.
[136] *Hapax legomenon.*

49 [L47] If someone captures stolen livestock, a slave cannot be vouched to warranty for it.

50 [L48] If someone has been newly reduced to the position of penal slave,[137] and he is accused of having committed theft before he was made a slave, then the accuser has [the right] to flog him once. He shall compel him to lashings by [an oath in] the amount of his [stolen] property.

51 [L49] If someone finds swine on his pasture without permission, let him then take a pledge-payment of 6 shillings.[138]

    51.1 [L49.1] If they were not there more than once, however, let the owner give a shilling and declare that they had not come more often, by [an oath equal to] the price of the livestock.

    51.2 [L49.2] If they were there twice, let him give two shillings.

52 [L49.3] If [rent] for pasturage is paid in pigs: [if the bacon is] three-fingers thick, [let it be] every third [pig], at two-fingers, every fourth, at [the width of] a thumb, every fifth.[139]

---

[137] In general, a "penal slave" is a person who enters into servitude to work off a fine he or she did not have the wherewithal to pay in money or goods. But Pelteret (1995: s.v. *witeþeow*) shows that penal slavery was also imposed for a range of grave offenses.

[138] Exactly what this payment of security is for remains unclear; perhaps it is to ensure that the landowner will be restituted for what the pigs have eaten on his property. Six shillings represents a substantial sum, however. If our interpretation is correct, the swine-owner would almost surely receive some of his money back once the damages have been assessed.

[139] The payment for pasturage of pigs is determined by the thickness of the (not explicitly named) bacon: better feeding produces thicker bacon.

{XCIIII}

53 [L50] Gif gesiðcund mon þingað wið cyning oððe wið kyninges ealdormonnan for his inhiwan¹⁴⁰ oððe wið his hlaford for ðeowe oððe for frige, nah he þær nane witerædenne, se gesið, forðon he him nolde ær yfles gestieran æt ham.

{XCV}

54 [L51] Gif gesiðcund mon landagende forsitte fierd, geselle CXX sciłł ꝛ ðolie his landes; unlandagende¹⁴¹ LX sciłł; cierlisc XXX sciłł to fierdwite.

{XCVI}

55 [L52] Se ðe diernum geðingum betygen sie, geswicne hine be CXX /51r/ hida þara geðingea oððe CXX sciłł geselle.

Ine §53 gesiðcund mon] gesiðcund man BH　cyning] cyng B　kyninges] cynges B　ealdormonnan] ealdormannum B; ealder man H　inhiwan] inn hiwum H　þær] ðar B　witerædenne] witeræddene B; wite rædene H　he him nolde ær] he nolde him ær B　yfles] yfeles B; yf\e/les H　gestieran] gestyran BH

Ine §54 gesiðcund mon] se sið cunde man B; gesicund man\n/ H　forsitte fierd] fyrde forsitte BH　geselle] gesylle BH　CXX] hundtwelftig B　ðolie] þolige H　unlandagende] Land agende H　LX] syxti B　cierlisc] ceorlisc B; Ce\o/rlisc H　XXX] ðrittig B　fierdwite] \ferd/wite B; fyrd wite H

Ine §55 diernum] dyrnum BH　betogen sie] betygen sy B; betogen sy H　geswicne hine] geclænsie he hine B; geladie hine H　CXX] hundtwelftigum B　geðingea] ðinga B　CXX] hundtwelftig B　geþingea] ðinga B; geþinga H　geselle] gesylle BH

¹⁴⁰ *Hapax legomenon.*
¹⁴¹ *Hapax legomenon.*

53 [L50] If a nobly born man settles with the king or with the king's ealdorman on behalf of [a member of] his household, or with his lord on behalf of a slave or a free man, the nobleman does not receive any portion of the fine, because he was unable earlier to restrain him at home from wrongdoing.[142]

54 [L51] If a nobly born man who owns property neglects [his duty to serve] in the army, let him pay 120 shillings and forfeit his land; [a noble] who does not own property, 60 shillings; a man of *ceorl*-rank, 30 shillings as *fyrd*-fine.[143]

55 [L52] He who is accused of [making] secret compacts,[144] let him clear himself of [the accusation of making] those compacts by [an oath of the value of] 120 hides, or let him pay 120 shillings.[145]

---

[142] As Whitelock points out, this implies that a man of **gesið** rank could have a lord other than a king. *LexBav* §II.5 and §VII.2 similarly fines the owner of a slave for not keeping him under control; *LexFris* §IX.17 requires an owner to pay for offenses commited by his slave. (See Wilda 1842: 1.653–165.) §43.1 discusses penalties for an owner who cannot control his heifer.

[143] The increase in fine for higher ranks reflects not only their status, but also the importance of their respective duties within the *fyrd*. The standing *fyrd* was established later by Alfred, so this clause must refer to a man who neglects the call from his lord to join a military expedition.

[144] Liebermann takes this as an evasion of the formal legal process in order to avoid paying a fine. According to Thorpe, "secret compositions are forbidden by nearly every early code of Europe; for by such a proceeding both the judge and the crown lost their profits." Often mentioned in connection with this principle (under varied titles) as one of its earliest attestations is the *Pactus pro tenore pacis domnorum Childeberti et Chlotharii regum* §3 (Boretius 1883: 5), which asserts that a person who wishes to conceal a theft and receive compensation for the wrong without the knowledge of a judge (*occulte sine iudice*) is himself a kind of thief (*latroni similis est*). (This sort of language would go on to be commonplace in later legislation: see, e.g., *LexBav* §XVII.)

[145] The clause establishes the one-to-one ratio of hides to shillings.

{XCVII}

56 [L53] Gif mon forstolenne man befo æt oþrum, ⁊ sie sio hand oðcwolen¹⁴⁶ sio hine sealde þam men þe hine mon ætbefeng, tieme þonne þone mon to þæs deadan byrgelse, swa oðer fioh swa hit sie, ⁊ cyðe on þam aðe be LX hida, þæt sio deade hond hine him sealde. Þonne hæfð he þæt wite afylled mid þy aðe, agife þam agendfrio þone monnan.

56.1 [L53.1] Gif he þonne wite hwa ðæs deadan ierfe hæbbe, tieme þonne to þam ierfe ⁊ bidde ða hond þe þæt ierfe hafað, þæt he him gedó þone ceap unbeceasne¹⁴⁷ oþþe gecyðe, þæt se deada næfre þæt ierfe ahte.

Ine §56 mon¹] man BH   sie sio] sy seo BH   oðcwolen] acwolon B   sio] ðe BH   sealde] s\e/ealde H   mon] *abbrev.* m *(with macron) in* B; *om.* H   tieme] tyme BH   þonne þone mon] ðonne \þone man/ H   þæs deadan byrgelse] ðæs deadan byrgenne B; þære gyrgenne ðæs deadan mannes H   fioh] feoh BH   swa hit sie] swa hweðer swa hit sy BH (sy *added later in* H)   ðam] ðem B   LX] feortig B   sio] seo BH   hond] hand BH   þy] ði B   agife] \⁊/ agife H   agendfrio] agendfreo B   monnan] man BH
Ine §56.1 þonne] þanne *(changed from earlier* þonne?) H   ierfe (4x)] yrfe BH   tieme] tyme BH   hond] hand H   hafað] hafeþ H   unbeceasne] unbesacene BH

¹⁴⁶ *Hapax legomenon.*
¹⁴⁷ *Hapax legomenon.*

56 [L53] If one catches a stolen person [=slave] in another's possession, and if the man [*hand*] is dead who sold him to that man in whose possession he was caught, then let [the man who currently has the slave] be vouched to warranty at the dead man's grave[148] – and likewise for whatever other property it might be – and let him declare with an oath [in the value] of sixty hides, that the dead man [*hand*] sold it to him. When he has avoided the fine [by means of] the oath, let the owner be given that man.

56.1 [L53.1] If he, however, knows who owns the dead man's inheritance, let him then vouch the estate to warranty and request of the man [*hand*] that has the inheritance, that he grant him the property uncontested or declare that the dead man never owned [that property as part of] the inheritance.

---

[148] This assumes he does not know who the heirs are; the subclause deals with the case in which he does know the heirs. Thorpe says that "This practice of citing the dead to warranty is common to the laws of Germany and Scandanavia," and gives parallels. (Hence the vouching at the gravesite). The practice described in this clause remained a feature of English law as late as "the middle of the thirteenth century" (Poole 1955: 73).

{XCVIII}

57 [L54] Se þe bið werfæhðe¹⁴⁹ betogen ⁊ he onsacan wille þæs sleges mid aðe, þonne sceal bion on þære hyndenne an kyningæde¹⁵⁰ be xxx hida, swa be gesiðcundum men swa be cierliscum, swa hwæþer swa hit sie.

57.1 [L54.1] Gif hine mon gilt, þonne mot he gesellan on þara hyndenna gehwelcere monnan ⁊ byrnan ⁊ sweord on þæt wergild, gif he ðyrfe.

58 [L54.2] Witeðeowne monnan wyliscne mon sceal bedrifan be xII hidum swa ðeowne to swingum, Engliscne be feower ⁊ xxx hida.

Ine 57 onsacan] ætsacan B   bion] beon BH   hyndenne] hyndene B   kyningæde] cyningæðe BH   xxx] ðrittig B   sie] sy BH
Ine §57.1 mon gylt] \man/ gylt H   gesellan] gesyllan BH   þara] ðæra B; þa\e/ra H   hyndenna] hynden\n/a H   gehwelcere] gehwylcre B; gehwylc\e/re H   monnan] monna H   ðyrfe] ðurfe BH
Ine §58 monnan] man H   mon] man H   xII] twelf B   hidum] hyndum B   feower ⁊ xxx] fowær ⁊ ðrittig B; xxxiiii. hida H

¹⁴⁹ This word is used only here and in §48.
¹⁵⁰ *Hapax legomenon.*

57 [L54] He who is accused of an act of violence requiring payment of wergild,[151] and he wishes to deny the slaying under oath, then there shall be in the hundred one [who can swear] the king's oath [to the value of] thirty hides,[152] both in the case of a nobly born man and for a man of *ceorl* rank, whichever it be.[153]

57.1 [L54.1] If recompense is made for [the slain man], then he may include in each hundred [shillings] a man [=slave] and a byrnie and a sword towards the wergild, if he needs to.[154]

58 [L54.2] A Welshman in the position of penal slave shall be forced to be lashed like a slave [by an oath of] twelve hides; an Englishman by [an oath of] thirty-four hides.[155]

---

[151] The violence referred to here may not necessarily constitute "feuding" as conventionally understood and the translation is thus mindful of points made in Niles 2015.

[152] A plea against a charge of homicide requires a higher-than-usual standard of oath-helper. For every hundred hides demanded by the oath, at least one oath-helper must be a king's man who can swear in the value of thirty hides. This is half the level of oath assigned in §19 to a 1,200-shilling-[wergild] man who is a communicant, which implies at least one person must be a 600-shilling, or lower-ranked, nobleman.

[153] Ambiguous as to whether this refers to the slayer or the slain man, although the former seems more likely.

[154] Either each 100 shillings of wergild can be replaced (at least in part) by a slave, a byrnie and a sword, or each may contain as partial payment one (or perhaps two) of these. (The symbol 7 usually stands for "and," but can also mean "or"). The value of a Welsh slave was 50 shillings (see §32 and note), which would leave only 50 for the armor. Although this intuitively seems low, *LexRib* §36.11 allows the following substitutions in partial payment for wergild:
    12 shillings: a healthy, seeing stallion; a good byrnie; a moulted falcon
    7 shillings: a sword with sheath
    6 shillings: a decorated helmet; good leg-protectors; a falcon that can kill cranes
    3 shillings: a healthy, seeing mare; a sword without sheath; an untrained falcon
    2 shillings: a healthy, seeing ox; a shield and spear
    1 shilling: a horned, healthy, seeing cow
This adds up to 31 shillings out of a wergild of 200. *Alfred* §21 requires a fine paid in livestock, but specifically prohibits the substitution of a slave.

[155] Schmid and Thorpe, comparing the usual ratio of fines for English vs. Welsh, both suggest (probably correctly, although contrary to all manuscript readings) emending this to twenty-four.

{XCVIIII}

59 [L55] Ewo bið mid hire giunge sceape sciłł weorð oþþæt XII niht ofer eastran.

{C}

60 [L56] Gif mon hwelcne ceap gebygð ⁊ he ðon*ne* onfinde him hwelce unhælo on binnan XXX nihta, þon*ne* weorpe þone ceap to honda; oððe swerie, þæt he him nan facn on nyste, þa he hine him sealde.

{CI}

61 [L57] /51v/ Gif ceorl ceap forstilð ⁊ bireð into his ærne, ⁊ befehð þærinne mon, þon*ne* bið se his dǽl synnig; butan þa*m* wife anu*m*, forðon hio sceal hire ealdore hieran. Gif hio dear mid aðe gecyðan, þ*æt* hio þæs forstolenan ne onbite, nime hire ðriddan sceat.

Ine §59 Ewo] Eowu (*a scribe has later written an* e *over the* u) BH mid hire] \mid/ hire B giunge] geonge B; geongan H XII] feowertyne B; xiiii H eastran] east\r/on B

Ine §60 hwelcne] hwylcne H gebygð] gebygeð BH onfinde] afinde B hwelce] hwylcne B; on hwylce H (*see below*) unhælo] unhæle B on binnan] binnon (*om.* on) H XXX] ðrittig B weorpe þone ceap] weorpe he ðone \ceap/ H to honda] to handa (*a later hand adds* þam syllend) B; to handa H swerie] swerige H

Ine §61 ceorl] ciorl H forstilð] forsteleþ H bireð] bereð B; byrð H ærne] huse (*scribe later writes* ærne *over this word*) H befehð þærinne mon] \mann/ befehþ \hitt/ ðær in B; hit man ðærinne befehð H þonne bið se his dǽl synnig] ðonne \biþ/ his dæl synnig (*a later hand writes above* scyldig) B; þonne biþ his dæl scyldig H forðon hio] for ðan heo B; forðon heo H ealdore hieran] ealdre hyran B; hlaforde hyran H hio (2x)] heo BH ðriddan sceat] ðæne ðriddan dæl ðære æhta B; ðriddan gescead H

59 [L55] A ewe with her young sheep is worth a shilling until the twelfth night after Easter.[156]

60 [L56] If someone buys any property and within thirty days he finds some flaw in it, then he should return the property to the hands [of the seller]; or [the seller] must swear that he knew of no defect when he sold it to him.[157]

61 [L57] If a *ceorl* steals property and takes it into his house, and it is caught therein, then he is liable for his portion [of the household goods]; only his wife is exempted, because she must obey her superior. If she dare declare on oath, that she did not partake of the stolen goods, let her take her third portion [of the household goods].[158]

---

[156] H changes this to fourteen.

[157] Compare to *Hlophere and Eadric* §11 [L16]; see also *Swerian* §7 and §9. *Æthelberht* §76 [L77–81] similarly invokes the principle of unblemished goods in the case of the bridal contract.

[158] For a somewhat different interpretation of the wife's liability, compare §7. That the wife is owed or responsible for one-third of the household is also demonstrated, for example, in *Grágás*: for a destitute couple who have to give up their offspring "the children are to be divided between the families, two-thirds to the father's family and one-third to the mother's family" (Dennis, Foote, and Perkins 2000: 31).

{CII}

62 [L58] Oxan horn bið x pæninga weorð.

{CIII}

62.1 [L59] Cuuhorn \ᵇⁱᵈ/¹⁵⁹ twegea pæninga;

62.2 oxan tægl bið sciłł weorð, cus bið fifa; ¹⁶⁰

62.3 oxan eage bið v *pæninga* weorð, cus bið sciłł weorþ.

63 [L59.1] Mon sceal simle to beregafole¹⁶¹ agifan æt anu*m* wyrhtan
VI wæga.¹⁶²

{CIIII}

64 [L60] Se ceorl se ðe hæfð oðres geoht¹⁶³ ahyrod, gif he hæbbe
ealle on foðre to agifanne, gesceawige mon, agife ealle. Gif he
næbbe, agife healf on fodre, healfe on oþru*m* ceape.

{CV}

65 [L61] Ciricsceat mon sceal agifan to þa*m* healme 7 to þam heo-
rðe þe se mon on bið to middum wintra.

Ine §62 x] feowertyne B; teon H   pæninga] peninga H   weorð] wurð B
Ine §62.1 bið twegea pæninga] twegea peniga wurð B; bið .v. peninga weorð H
Ine §62.2 oxan tægl bið scill weorð, cus bið fifa] Oxan tægl bið .iiii. peonega wurð .
cu tægl bið fif penega wurð B; Oxan tægl bið scill weorð. Cu bið .v. peninga H (*out of
order in* H)
Ine §62.3 v] fif B   weorð] wurð B   cus] Cu \eage/ B; Cu H   scill weorþ] scillinges
(*om.* weorþ) H
Ine §63 simle] symble B   agifan] agyfen H   VI wæga] vi. pund wæga H
Ine §64 ceorl se ðe] ciorl þe H   hæfð] hæfu (u *subsequently corrected to* ð) B; hæbbe
H   geoht] oxan B; g\e/oht H   ahyrod] ahyred BH   agife ealle] *om.* H   fodre] foðre
H
Ine §65 mon sceal agifan] man \sceal/ agyfan B; man sceal agyfan H   healme] halme
B   middum] middan B; midde H

¹⁵⁹ Scribe adds this later above line.
¹⁶⁰ All other manuscripts add some version of *pæningas* ("pennies").
¹⁶¹ *Hapax legomenon*. The compound is inverted to create another *hapax legomenon*
in charter S359 (*gauolbærer* ("barley-rent")).
¹⁶² The *Quadripartitus* compiler omitted this clause; Liebermann postulates he found
it untranslatable.
¹⁶³ Term is attested only twice in the Old English corpus.

62 [L58] An ox horn is worth 10 pennies.

62.1 [L59] A cow horn is worth 2 pennies.

62.2 An ox tail is worth a shilling, a cow's is 5.[164]

62.3 An ox eye is worth 5 shillings, a cow's is worth a shilling.

63 [L59.1] One should always give as "barley rent" 6 weys[165] for each worker.[166]

64 [L60] A *ceorl* who has hired another's yoke, if he is able to pay it all in fodder, make sure he gives all. If he cannot, let him pay half in fodder and half in other goods.

65 [L61] Church tax shall be paid from that farmstead[167] and that hearth where the man is dwelling in mid-winter.[168]

---

[164] Although the higher valuation for a cow's tail contradicts (as Liebermann observes) other rulings, in which an ox is worth five times a cow and an ox's eye outranks a cow's by the same ratio, the loss of the tail might well be more drastic for a cow than for an ox. Without a tail, she cannot keep away flies and would be forced to keep on the move in an attempt to avoid them, thus taking in less nourishment. While this might cause decreased musculature for an ox, the result for a cow would be less milk production and also possible damage (or at least weakening) of a calf in utero. (M. E. Takabi, p.c.; also American Veterinary Medical Association, "Literature Review on the Welfare Implications of Tail Docking of Cattle" [2014]). The foregoing analysis considers only tail-docking, in which the lower switch is cut off. However, the upper portion of the tail protects the anus on both cow and ox, but crucially also the vulva of the cow. Thus if the entire tail is cut off from the cow, the result will leave the vulva open to potential bacterial infection.

[165] Unit of measure. Harmer (1914: 73) states that "the earliest evidence as to the weight of the Anglo-Saxon *wæg* is supplied by the *Historia Monasterii de Abingdon* [...] which states that in the tenth century the *pondus*, or wey, contained twenty-two stone. The fact that this amount is called the *pondus Abbendunense* suggests that other standards may have been in use."

[166] Thorpe suggests aligning **wyrhta** linguistically with the *factus* family of the Capitularies, meaning a certain measure of (?worked) land. Nowell (RP 9865) omits this clause from his edition and translation.

[167] **healm** literally means straw. This appears to be a conjunct *pars pro toto*: from the stalk and from the hearth – that is, from the farmstead and the house. For archeological evidence as to the existence of hearths in Anglo-Saxon buildings, see Hamerow 2012: 43–45.

[168] §4 states that the tax is to be paid on St. Martin's Day: November 11.

{CVI}

66 [L62] Þon*n*e mon bið tyhtlan betygen, ⁊ hine mon bedrifeð to ceape,[169] nah þon*n*e self nane wiht to gesellanne beforan ceape:[170] Þon*n*e gæð oðer mon seleð his ceap fore, swa he þon*n*e geþingian mæge, on ða rædenne, þe he him ga to honda, oððæt he his ceap him geinnian mæge. Þon*n*e betyhð hine mon eft oþre siðe ⁊ bedrifð to ceape:[171] Gif hine forð nele forstandan se ðe him ær ceap fore sealde, ⁊ he hine þon*n*e forfehð, þolige þon*n*e his ceapes se ðe he him ær fore sealde.

Ine §66 mon] man H   betygen] betogen BH   ceape (*first two occurrences*)] ceace BH   self] sylf B   gesellanne] syllanne B; gesyllanne H (*clause added later in left margin*)   rædenne] ræden_ne H   honda] handa BH   hine mon] hine \mon/ H   ceape (*fifth occurrence*)] ceace BH   forð nele] \forð/ nylle B   se ðe] se \þe/ H   hine þonne] hine \þonne/ H   þolige þonne] ðolie ðonne B; þolige \þonne/ H   he him] \he/ him H

[169] Following H and B, Liebermann emends to *ceace*; see footnote to translation.
[170] See following.
[171] See following.

66 [L62] When someone is accused of an offense, and he is required to compensate in goods and he does not have property to give for such compensation: if another man goes and gives his property for him – in whichever way he may settle [with the accuser] – [let it be] on the condition that [the accused] goes into his hands [in servitude] until he can restore to him [the value of] his property. If he is later accused a second time and required to compensate in goods: if the person who earlier gave the property for him does not wish again to stand up for him, and [the second accuser] captures him, then the man who earlier stood surety for him forfeits his property.[172]

---

[172] See Chapter 3, 81–101. The clause allows for various interpretations depending on the translation of (some uses of) *ceap* as illustrated in the following more literal rendering:

> When someone is accused of an offense, and he is driven to **ceape**, but he himself has nothing to give in place of **ceape**: then another man goes [and] gives his *ceap* for [him] – however he then may settle – on the condition, that he goes to his hands, until he can restore his *ceap* to him. When he is accused again another time and driven to **ceape**: If he who earlier gave the *ceap* for him does not wish to stand up for him, and he [the second accuser] captures him, let him forfeit his *ceapes* who gave it for him before.

Two different meanings of *ceap* are used in this paragraph. One, indicated here in ***bold italics***, clearly has the common Old English meaning of "goods" or "property." The other, indicated here in **bold**, is considerably less certain. Thorpe relates this *ceap* to *cippos*, defined by Du Cange as *instrumentum quo reorum pedes constringuntur* ("instrument by which the feet of malefactors are constricted": namely, stocks) (Du Cange 1883–1887: s.v.). The problem with Thorpe's analysis is that the term cannot be an Old English cognate of the Latin *cippus* (as the root would then look something like *hiff-*) and nowhere else in the laws do we find borrowings from Latin (a possible exception being *Ine* §12). Liebermann's solution is to emend these uses of *ceap* to *ceac* ("cauldron") (such as would be used in the hot-water ordeal), as this is the term used in **H**, **B**, and **G** (rubric only). He thus claims that these clauses in *Ine* (this and §38) represent the first reference to judicial ordeal in Anglo-Saxon law. (Contra the first see §38 and note.) However, the only time *ceac* is seemingly used in connection with the ordeal is in these late manuscripts. (The tract known as *Ordal* assumes that the procedure requires the use of an *alfæt* ("fire-cauldron") – itself a very rare term.) Schmid ingeniously interprets both uses of *ceap* as referring to property, and renders the clause: "If a charge is raised against someone and he is required to give security, but himself has nothing which he can pledge for security [...]" (*Wenn gegen Jemand eine Klage erhoben wird und man ihn zur Pfandbestellung anhält, er aber selbst nichts hat, was er als Pfand geben kann* [...]). Beginning with *Æthelstan* II, we find the term *ceapgyld* "compensation in goods"; the translation above is based on this parallel and Schmid's analysis, translating the bold-faced **ceap** as "compensate in goods" and the bold italic *ceap* as "property." Nowell (RP 9865) emends the *ceace* of **B** back to *ceape* in its second appearance, and translates both as "driven to pledge." It is safe to say that the earliest secure evidence for the ordeal in Anglo-Saxon England

{CVII}

67 [L63] Gif gesiðcund mon fare, þonne mot he habban his gerefan mid him 7 his smið 7 his cildfestran[173].

{CVIII}

67.1 [L64] Se ðe hæfð xx hida, se sceal tæcnan xII hida gesettes landes, þonne he faran wille.

{CVIIII}

67.2 [L65] /52r/ Se ðe hæfð x hida, se sceal tæcnan vI hida gesettes landes.

{CX}

67.3 [L66] Se ðe hæbbe þreora hida, tæcne oþres healfes.

Ine §67 mon] man BH
Ine §67.1 xx] twentig B   tæcnan] tæcan B; tæc\n/an H   xII] twelf B
Ine §67.2 x] tyn B   tæcnan] tæcan B; tæc\n/an H   vI] syx B
Ine §67.3 þreora] ðreo B; .iii. H; Ot *resumes here*   tæcne] tæce B; tæc\n/e H   oþres healfes] oðres healfes hides gesettes H

is 1 *Edward* §3, not the clauses of Ine's laws conventionally adduced in connection with it; cf. also *Æþelstan* vI §1.4, compiled sometime between 930 and 940. Cf. the requirement of §50 that someone who accuses a penal slave of theft has the right *bedrif[an] hine to swingum be his ceape* ("to compel him to lashings by [an oath in] the amount of his [stolen] property"). This strongly parallels the phrase **hine mon bedrifeð to ceape** "he is driven to *ceape*" given in the literal translation above.

173 *Hapax legomenon.*

67 [L63] If a noble man moves [to a different district], he may take with him his reeve and his smith[174] and his children's nurse.[175]

67.1 [L64] He who has twenty hides must show that he has cultivated twelve hides, if he wishes to move.[176]

67.2 [L65] He who has ten hides must show six cultivated hides.

67.3 [L66] He who has three hides must show one and a half.

[174] That the smith is an important figure in barbarian law is unsurprising in a culture in which weapons were highly valued and either passed on as heirlooms or returned to the donor at the death of the warrior. The somewhat elevated status of the smith in early medieval western Europe left traces of itself in Germanic legend, as attested by the figure Vǫlundr in the Old Norse *Poetic Edda*; Beowulf wears chain mail made by Wēland (the Old English cognate of the name). In *Æthelberht* §13 [L7] the king's smith is awarded "an ordinary person-price" of 100 shillings. *LexAla* §80 sets the fine for killing a smith (an unfree member of the household) equal to a swineherd who watches over forty swine with a trained dog and an apprentice, a shepherd with a flock of eighty, a seneschal, a groom with twelve horses in his care, a cook with an apprentice, and a baker.

[175] Thorpe comments that the importance of this position is demonstrated by the fact "that so late as the time of Edw. I it was considered treason against the lord, for his tenant to debauch the nurse of his children."

[176] Charles-Edwards (1976: 185) holds these several chapters (L63–67) to constitute a somewhat unified whole. One of the underlying principles seemingly enumerated here is that a re-settler cannot leave a wasteland behind. Liebermann takes this to ensure that the ground will remain arable; Attenborough to provide for the king's food-render. The two interpretations are not incompatible. *Grágás* requires more globally that "no man shall let his farm become waste" (Dennis, Foote, and Perkins 2000: 112).

{CXI}

68 [L67] Gif mon geþingað gyrde landes oþþe mare to rædegafole[177]
7 geereð: gif se hlaford him wile þæt land aræran to weorce 7 to
gafole, ne þearf he him onfon gif he him nan botl ne selð; 7 þolie
þara æcra.

{CXII}

69 [L68] Gif mon gesiðcundne monnan adrife, fordrife þy botle, næs
þære setene.

{CXIII}

70 [L69] Sceap sceal gongan mid his fliese oð midne sumor; oððe
gilde þæt flies mid twam pæningum.

Ine §68 geþingað gyrde landes] gyrde landes geþingeð H; [ ]ugað gyrde londes
Ot   geereð] ereð (*with space left for ge-prefix*) H   selð] sylþ B; slihð H   þolie] þol-
ige H   þara] his H   æcra] acera B; æcera H
Ine §69 monnan] man\n/ H
Ine §70 fliese] flyse BH   flies] fleos B; flys H   pæningum] penegum B; penegum H

[177] *Hapax legomenon.*

68 [L67] If someone takes on a fourth part of a hide[178] or more at fixed rent and ploughs it: if the lord [later] wishes to raise the land [in terms of value] in regard to work and to rent, he need not accept this if he [the lord] does not give him a dwelling, and he must forfeit the crops.[179]

69 [L68] If a nobleman is driven away, let him be driven from his dwelling, but not from his cultivated land.[180]

70 [L69] A sheep must go with its fleece until mid-summer, or the fleece must be recompensed with two pennies.[181]

---

[178] **gyrd** (literally "yard") is defined in the Toronto *DOE* as "an area of land of varying extent according to the locality, most frequently 30 acres, a fourth part of a hide." Wormald (1999a: 104) states that this paragraph is so syntactically intertwined that "[t]he impression is that Ine is reacting to a particular case. [...] All the circumstances get into writing now that scribes feel, rightly or wrongly, competent to itemize everything bearing on a decision reached."

[179] Is the subject of þolie "let him forfeit" the *he* of the main clause ("he [the renter] need not accept this") or of the subordinate clause ("if he [the lord] does not give him a dwelling")? Schmid and Thorpe both assume that the renter keeps the crops; he does not suffer for not fulfilling the additional demands imposed by the landlord. Thorpe adds that, "It is still a principle of our law, that if the landlord of a tenant at will determine the tenancy by ejecting the tenant, the latter shall have the crop without paying any rent." Liebermann, Attenborough, and Eckhardt assume that the renter forfeits the crops. The former reading accords better with the Old English: although the Tironian note 7 can have a meaning of "and" or "or," it only rarely indicates "but," which would be required for the interpretation of Liebermann *et al.* Whitelock, probably rightly, assumes "that the situation considered is when the original agreement has expired, and the lord will not renew it on the old terms." Charles-Edwards (1976: 186) holds the clause to disclose "the root of medieval English villeinage."

[180] The translation above is a literal rendering of this opaque clause; Schmid suggests persuasively that one might augment it as "[fruits of] the cultivated land." Attenborough proposes that one might equate **seten** with *landseten* ("land in occupation"), and thus the evicted man retains control over his tenants and their property although not over his house. Schmid's reading seems preferable.

[181] Attenborough suggests that two pennies would be deducted from the price of a sheep shorn before that date. This makes sense: the full complement of wool would count in the overall value.

{CXIIII}

71 [L70] Æt twyhyndum¹⁸² were mon sceal sellan to monbote xxx
sciłł, æt vi hyndum lxxx sciłł, æt xii hyndum cxx sciłł.

72 [L70.1] Æt x hidum to fostre x fata hunies, ccc hlafa, xii ambra
wilisc ealað, xxx hluttres, tu eald hriðeru oððe x weðeras, x gees, xx
henna, x cesas, amber fulne buteran, v leaxas, xx pundwæga¹⁸³
foðres ⁊ hundteontig æla.

{CXV}

73 [L71] **G**if mon sie wertyhtlan¹⁸⁴ betogen ⁊ he hit þonne geondette
beforan aðe ⁊ onsace ǽr, bide mon mid þære witerædenne oððæt se
wer gegolden sie.

Ine §71 mon] man BH   sellan] syllan BH   monbote] manbote H   vi] syx
BH   lxxx] hund eahtatig B   xii] twelf   cxx] hund twelftig B
Ine §72 x (2x)] tyn B   hunies] huniges H   ccc] ðreo hund B   hlafa] hla\fa/ H   xii]
twelf B   ambra] ambre\s/ H   wilisc] wylisces B; wilisc\es/ H   ealað] ealoð BH   xxx]
ðrittig B   hluttres] hlut\t/res H   tu eald hriðeru] twa ealda ryðeru B; .ii. eald\e/
hryðeru H   x] tyn   x gees, xx henna, x cesas] *om.* B, *but added in right margin by a*
later hand;.x. gés \⁊/ xx. henna .x. cysas H   v] fif B   xx] twentig B   xx pundwæga]
⁊ .xx. \pund/ wæga H   foðres] fodres H   hundteontig] c. H
Ine §73 sie (2x)] sy BH   wertyhtlan] wer tyhlan B   geondette] geandette BH   bide]
abide BH   mon] man H   witerædenne] wite ræde_ne H

---

¹⁸² Attested only in *Ine* and *Alfred*.
¹⁸³ *Hapax legomenon*.
¹⁸⁴ *Hapax legomenon*.

71 [L70] For a person whose *wer* is 200 [the slayer] must give 30 shillings as man-price [to the lord of the slain man]; for [a person of] 600, 80 shillings, for [a person of] 1,200, 120 shillings.[185]

72 [L70.1] For 10 hides, food render [to the lord][186] should be 10 vats of honey,[187] 300 loaves, 12 pails of Welsh ale, 30 of clear ale, two full-grown cows or 10 wethers, 10 geese, 20 hens, 10 cheeses, a full pail of butter, 5 salmon, 20 pound-weights of fodder and 100 eels.

73 [L71] If a person is accused of an act for which wergild[188] must be paid and then confesses on oath but has denied it previously, one should wait to collect the fine until the *wer* has been paid.

[185] Attenborough relates the **manbot** "price paid to a lord for injury to one of his men" to the *drihtinbeag* (*hapax legomenon*; literally "lord-ring") of 50 shillings due the king in *Æthelberht* §12 [L6]. Compare also §78.

[186] Liebermann assumes the food-render is owed by a village, not an individual household; probably to the lord of the village, who then would have his own responsibility for food render for the king. See *Æthelberht* §17 [L12]; also Oliver 1998. Similar lists can be found in, among many, charters S146, 1188 (Harmer #1), 1197 (Harmer #4), 1482 (Harmer #2); the last two indicate that the goods are collected once a year. S146, a grant by Offa to the Church of Worcester in 793x796 provides "the only surviving statement of the amount the king could draw from an estate as his farm" (Whitelock 1955: 467). This lists "two tuns full of pure ale and a coomb full of mild ale, and a coomb full of Welsh ale, and seven oxen and six wethers and 40 cheeses and six long *peru* and 30 'ambers' of unground corn and four 'ambers' of meal" (Whitelock 1955: 467). **Cumb** is a vessel of unknown size; two of its four appearances in the corpus are here. **Amber** appears frequently and glosses Latin words for vessels of many different sizes ranging from from *lagena* ("flask, flagon") (MkGl) to *cadus* ("barrel") (see *DOE*, s.v.); we have translated it above as "pail."

[187] Charter S1188, in which Ealdormann Oswulf makes a donation to Canterbury in 805x810, allows a render option of one liquid measure of honey or two of wine: honey thus had twice the value of wine.

[188] It is ambiguous (and perhaps deliberately so) whether the offense involves a victim to whom wergild is due, or is of such a nature that the perpetrator must pay his own wergild.

{CXVI}

74 [L72] **Gif** mon wergildðeof gefehð, ⁊ he losige ðy dæge þam
monnum ðe hine gefoð, þeah hine mon gefo ymb niht, nah him mon
mare æt ðon*ne* fulwite.[189]

{CXVII}

74.1 [L73] **Gif** hit bið niht eald þiefð, gebeten þa þone gylt þe hine
gefengon swa hie geþingian mægen wið cyning ⁊ his gerefan.

Ine §74 losige] losie B; losi_e H   ðy] ði B   monnum] mannu*m* B   mon (2x)] man
BH   ymb] ymbe B   ðonne] ðonon B
Ine §74.1 þiefð] ðyfð BH   hie] hig B; hy H   mægen] magon BH   cyning] cyninḡ B

[189] Compare to §28.

74 [L72] If a thief is caught who owes wergild for his offense,[190] and he escapes on the day that he was caught from the men who caught him, but he is caught again before night, [the captors] need pay no more than the full fine.[191]

74.1 [L73] If the theft is a night old, then let those who caught him [and allowed him to escape] pay whatever debt [for their careless-ness] that they may arrange with the king and his reeve.[192]

---

[190] At least three interpretations are possible for this *hapax* compound: 1 a man who owes his own wergild for an assessed fine; 2 one who refuses to pay another's wer-gild for damage inflicted on him (thus conjoining it with the previous clause); 3 a thief who has forfeited his right to wergild by his illegal act (following Schmid). In the early laws of Wessex, a wergild other than the victim's can be assessed as:
- Payment of the perpetrator's wergild to release/redeem him from corporal punishment (*Ine* §12; *Alfred* §6.1).
- Payment of another's wergild for aiding and abetting an offense (*Ine* §36).

The compound occurs nowhere else, and the context is not detailed enough to choose between these options, if the term was indeed not deliberately coined to allow for various possibilities.

[191] Compare to §28 and §37. According to §28, a person who captures a thief is due a reward of 10 shillings; according to §37, those who let him go are subject to a fine. If he is recaptured within one night this fine is limited to the *ful wite* of 60 shil-lings.

[192] Thorpe suggests that the increased penalty for not re-capturing the thief within a short period of time was a "safeguard against collusion." A further day might allow the thief to summon "unexceptional compurgators and thus assure his acquittal [...] materially lessening the chances of redress to the prosecutor and [...] defeating the ends of justice."

{CXVIII}

75 [L74] **Gif** ðeowwealh¹⁹³ Engliscne monnan ofslihð, þon*ne* sceal se ðe hine ah weorpan hine to honda hlaforde ⁊ mægum /52v/ oððe LX sciłł gesellan wið his feore.

75.1 [L74.1] Gif he þon*ne* þone ceap nelle fore gesellan, þon*ne* mot hine se hlaford gefreogean. Gielden siððan his mægas þone wer, gif he mægburg hæbbe freo. Gif he næbbe, heden his þa gefan.

76 [L74.2] Ne þearf se frige mid þam þeowan mæg gieldan, buton he him wille fæhðe ofaceapian,¹⁹⁴ ne se þeowa mid þy frigean.

Ine §75 monnan] man BH　se ðe] se \þe/ H　weorpan hine] weorpan \hine/ H　mægum] magu*m* BH　LX] syxtig B　gesellan] gesyllan BH
Ine §75.1 nelle] nylle H　gesellan] syllan B; gesyllan H　Gielden] gyldan B; gildon H　mægas] magas BH　mægburg] mægborh B; mægburh H　his þa gefan] his ðonne ða gefan H
Ine §76 frige] frigea H　mæg] men B　gieldan] gyldan BH　ofaceapian] of\a/ceapian H　þy] þam BH

¹⁹³ *Hapax legomenon.*
¹⁹⁴ *Hapax legomenon.*

75 [L74] If a Welsh[195] slave kills an English man, then the owner shall turn him over to the [slain man's] lord and kin or pay 60 shillings for his life.[196]

75.1 [L74.1] If, however, he does not wish to pay this amount for him, then the lord may free him. His kinsmen must afterwards pay the *wer* [for the slain man], if he has free kin. If he does not, then his enemies may take possession of him.[197]

76 [L74.2] A free man need not pay kin-compensation for a [penal] slave, unless he wishes to protect him from violent retribution, nor need the slave do so for a freeman.[198]

---

[195] Could also mean "foreign."

[196] §23 sets the value of a Welsh slave at "50 shillings, some 60." No matter what the value of the slave, he must be redeemed for top shilling if he kills an Englishman. Liebermann postulates that the killing of a Welsh freeman by a Welsh slave is handled under Welsh law.

[197] They have the legal right to kill him, but they can also enslave him.

[198] Liebermann proposes that we see here a shift of **mæg** from "kin" to "restitution due kin for manslaughter" similar to the shift of *wer* from "man" to "wergild" (although the latter represents an abbreviation rather than an actual semantic alteration). Such a meaning would be extremely rare: the only other example that Liebermann adduces is *Alfred* §44.4 in which a person attacking an enemy who is trying to turn himself in must pay *wer* and fine and *hæbbe his mæg forworht*, which we (following Liebermann's hypothesis) render as "has forfeited his kin-compensation." In other words, he himself can no longer collect wergild. Both instances support Liebermann's reading. Furthermore, this interpretation accounts for the accusative singular of **mæg** in this clause.

The compound *mægbot* occurs in 1 *Cnut* in respect to violating church peace, for which the offender has to pay his own *wer* (§2.4), the full fine for breaking the king's *mund*, and *ægþer ge mægbote ge manbote* ("both restitution to kin and *manbot*").

{CXVIIII}

77 [L75] **Gif** mon ceap befehþ forstolenne, ⁊ sio hond tiemð þonne
sio hine mon ætbefehþ to oþrum men: gif se mon hine þonne onfon
ne wille ⁊ sægþ þæt he him næfre þæt ne sealde ac sealde oþer,
þonne mot se gecyðan, se ðe hit tiemþ to þære honda, þæt he him
nan oðer ne sealde buton þæt ilce.[199]

{CXX}

78 [L76] **Gif** hwa oðres godsunu slea oððe his godfæder, sie sio
mægbot ⁊ sio manbot gelic; weaxe sio bot be ðam were, swa ilce
swa sio manbot deð þe ðam hlaforde sceal.

    78.1 [L76.1] Gif hit þonne kyninges godsunu sie, bete be his were
þam cynnige swa ilce swa þære mægþe.

    78.2 [L76.2] Gif he þonne on þone geonbyrde þe hine slog, ðonne
ætfealle sio bot þam godfæder, swa ilce swa þæt wite ðam hlaforde
deð.

    78.3 [L76.3] Gif hit bisceopsunu sie, \sie/[200] be healfum þam.

Ine §77 sio hond tiemð] seo hand tymð BH sio] seo BH ætbefehþ] ætbefehð ðe
B þonne] *om.* B ne wille] nylle \þæs ceapes/ H þonne mot se gecyðan] ðonne
\mot/ sege \cyþan/ (*both additions in later hand*) B tiemð] tymð BH ðære] ðara
B honda] handa BH
Ine §78 sie] sy BH sio (4x)] seo BH
Ine §78.1 hit þonne] hit \þonne/ H sie] sy B; sy cyninges godsunu H cynnige] cinge
B; cyninge H swa ilce] swa \same/ B (*later hand fills space left blank in manuscript*);
swa same (*second word added to blank space later?*) H
Ine §78.2 slog] sloh BH sio] seo BH swa ilce] swa \same/ B (*later hand fills space
left blank in manuscript*); swa same (*cramped writing of* same *suggested later addition
to blank space*) H; *end* Ot
Ine §78.3 bisceopsunu] biscopsunu H sie (2x)] sy BH þam] ðem B; þam seo bote H

[199] Compare to §35.
[200] Added later by scribe above line.

77 [L75] If stolen goods are seized, and then the man [*hand*] in whose possession the goods were seized vouches a second man to warranty: if the second man will not accept it and says that he never sold him that [property in question] but sold him something else, then he who vouches [him] to warranty must declare, that he sold him none other than that same [property].[201]

78 [L76] If someone slays another person's godson or his godfather, let the man-price [paid] to the [religious] kinsman be equal [to that paid] to the lord;[202] the price [paid the kinsman] shall increase according to the *wer*, just as does the man-price owed to the lord.[203]

   78.1 [L76.1] If, however, it is the king's godson, let him pay his *wer* to the king as well as to the kin.

   78.2 [L76.2] If [the decedent], however, was resisting in a fight the one who slew him, the compensation to the godfather is nullified, just as is the fine due to the lord.[204]

   78.3 [L76.3] If [the slain person] is a bishop's [god]son,[205] let [the compensation] be half [that for a king's godson].

---

[201] Liebermann believes this clause may contain traces of oath formulae. Compare to *Hlophere and Eadric* §11 [L16].

[202] Ine's laws end as they began with regulations concerning the ecclesiastical estates. Liebermann believes this may be a later addition. In the narrative of Cynewulf and Cyneheard related in the *Anglo-Saxon Chronicle* s.a. 755, the sole survivor of the defeated force was left alive because he was the godson of the ealdorman who fought with the victors (*alle butan anum, se wæs þæs aldormonnes godsunu, 7 he his feorh generede 7 þeah he wæs oft gewundad*). Bately 1986: 37.

[203] For the amount of *manbot*, see §71.

[204] The fine is waived if the killing happened in the course of an altercation.

[205] In spite of the omitted modifier, the reference must be to spiritual kinship, as in prior clauses.

Appendix: Handlist of Prior Editions

Prior Scholarly Editions of the *Domboc*[1]

1568   John Day, a notable London publisher of Protestant tracts including John Foxe's *Actes and Monuments* ("Book of Martyrs") and the anonymous *Testimonie of Antiquitie*, prints William Lambarde's Αρχαιονομια, *sive de priscis anglorum legibus libri, sermone Anglico, vetustate antiquissimo, aliquot ab hinc seculis conscripti, atque nunc demum, magno iurisperitorum, & amantium antiquitatis omnium commodo, è tenebris in lucem vocati.* Lambarde was called to the bar one year prior to its publication after a long residence at Lincoln's Inn (Dunkel 1965: 33). The *domboc* takes up pages 1–44 and is edited to commence with Ine's laws in spite of the order of the manuscripts. These and all other works of legislation Lambarde translates into Latin. The texts are based upon transcripts prepared years earlier by Laurence Nowell.

1644   Roger Daniel reprints in Cambridge Abraham Wheelocke's revised edition of Lambarde's Αρχαιονομια. The *domboc* is given on pages 1–35, with Ine's laws again preceding Alfred's. Wheelocke's changes amount

---

[1]   The many partial editions and translations of the *domboc*'s contents are here excluded from consideration.

for the most part to emending the orthography and style of Lambarde's translation.

1761   David Wilkins, a canon of Canterbury Cathedral and immigrant from Prussia (his name was Anglicized from Wilke: see Oliver 2002: 252), publishes *Leges Anglo-Saxonicæ Eccesiasticæ & Civiles* (London). Wilkins reprints the prefaces by Wheelocke (xviii–xxii) and Lambarde (xxiii–xxiv). Some elements of the latter's commentary also abide in Wilkins's edition, though this portion of the work expands significantly beyond the occasional remarks made in the prior editions of Αρχαιονομια. Wilkins's own preface is among the first scholarly documents to note the similarities between the laws of Anglo-Saxon England and those of their contemporaries elsewhere in Germanic-speaking Europe. His edition will be widely used for decades to come. But assessments of his scholarship in the century that followed would prove harsh: "[I]t must, though reluctantly, be acknowledged by everyone competent to judge, that, as a translator of Anglo-Saxon, he not unfrequently betrays an ignorance even of its first principles, that, although not unparalleled, is perfectly astounding" (Thorpe 1840: ix). Ine's laws are given at 14–27, Alfred's at 28–46.

1832   Rheinhold Schmid, then Professor of Law at the University of Jena, publishes *Die Gesetze der Angelsachsen* (Leipzig). His Introduction describes at length his own process of learning Old English grammar through the work of Jakob Grimm and Rasmus Rask and his desire, unfulfilled through circumstances outside his control (viii), to examine in person the relevant manuscripts. In his view, the need for a new edition amid what was then a widespread and growing interest in Germanic antiquities necessitated foregoing this crucial step. Reliance on Lambarde's and Wilkins's editions, corrected according to the editor's philological acumen, renders Schmid's text in this first attempt at an edition fatally compromised. Nonetheless, Schmid here establishes (for good or ill) the Anglo-Saxon laws within the preserve of comparative philology. Significantly, it is the first edition in which translations and commentary are in a language other than Latin and the first in which they are assigned chapter numbers whose use persists into the present. (*Ine* 14–31, *Alfred* 32–57.)

1840   Benjamin Thorpe's *Ancient Laws and Institutes of England* (London: Eyre and Spottiswoode), published simultaneously in two- and one-volume versions (each with different pagination), is the first in which an editor consistently examines the available manuscripts (though not all of them) and the first in which translations and commentary are given in English. (The apparatus omits to include variants from **Ot** and **Bu** but is otherwise comprehensive.) The order of Ine's and Alfred's laws for the first time follows the manuscripts, with Alfred's laws occupying pages 20–44 and Ine's 45–65. Thorpe inherited the project from Richard Price upon the latter's death, and several of the notes in Thorpe's expansive commentary are Price's.

1858   Rheinhold Schmid, now Professor of Law at the University of Bern, issues the second edition of his *Gesetze der Angelsachsen* (Leipzig) in place of a planned supplementary volume. This time the text is based (like Thorpe's) on a collation of **E** with **B**, **G**, and **H**, and places to the right of Schmid's German translation readings from *Quadripartitus* (referred to by Schmid as *die alte lateinische Uebersetzung* [xi]). The commentary is more incisive than Thorpe's and retains its value into the present; as a running concordance to other legislative works, its worth is undiminished. But Ine's laws (pages 20–57) are restored to their position before Alfred's (pages 58–105). The edition concludes with an *antiquarisches Glossar* that is a stunning monument to Schmid's learning. Turk (1893: 5) judged it "the best edition of the A.-S. Laws" yet published.

1903–1916 Liebermann's *Gesetze der Angelsachsen* builds on the foundations established by Schmid and Thorpe (as well as those of Turk's fine 1893 edition of Alfred's laws, which gives for the first time readings from **Ot** and **Bu** as well as those of **E, B, G,** and **H**) to create a monumental work of scholarship published incrementally in three volumes.[2] Volume 1, dedicated to Konrad von Maurer ("dem altmeister der germanischen Rechtsgeschichte"), is the first edition in any language to print all relevant legislative texts of the pre-Conquest era, with readings of the extant manuscripts supplied in parallel columns. Liebermann's edition also includes *Quadripartitus* and other translations of the post-Conquest era. (Variants from Αρχαιονομια are given in the apparatus under the assumption, devastatingly critiqued in the years prior to Liebermann's death, that Lambarde had access to now-lost witnesses.) The description of manuscripts with which the volume begins is richly detailed and authoritative.

---

[2] Whether Turk's edition deserves its own place in this list is uncertain. In its organization and layout, it represents an excellent specimen of the philological editions that were then a mainstay of academic publishing in English literary studies, a field still anxious in those years to demonstrate its worth and rigor as an academic subject. It says much for the merits of a work of scholarship this old that consultation of Turk's edition still offers many rewards. Yet Turk's emphasis on the philological aspects of editing the *domboc* caused him to confine the ambit of his work within arbitrary constraints that limited its ultimate usefulness. The *domboc*, we are told at the outset, will be considered primarily as a product of the Alfredian literary revival: "[I]ts [the *domboc*'s] chief claim to special consideration rests upon its author's great significance in Anglo-Saxon literature" (1893: v). To consider even the sources of Alfred's laws would be an undertaking "legal, rather than literary, in character" and therefore beyond Turk's purposes (1893: 40). Turk's edition also suffered from being prepared in the knowledge that Liebermann's *Gesetze der Angelsachsen* was soon to appear. It lacks a translation or even a glossary and offers no commentary on the clauses of the laws. Yet its discussion of prior work, its attention to the manuscript evidence, and its insights into the contents of the laws lend it lasting value as a supplement to the more ambitious works described here. Richard Dammery's 1990 doctoral dissertation, regrettably never revised for publication, likewise merits acknowledgement here as the most important scholarly treatment of the *domboc* between Liebermann's *Gesetze* and the later work of Patrick Wormald.

Alfred's and Ine's laws are restored to their order in the manuscripts (*Alfred* pages 16–88, *Ine* pages 89–123). The second volume appears in two sections in 1906 and 1912, constituting (respectively) a *Wörterbuch* and *Rechts- und Sachglossar*; to this day they are the most detailed reference works of their kind. Volume III, dedicated to Heinrich Brunner and Friedrich William Maitland (with an unfortunate apology for the position of Germany in World War I), gives the introductions and commentaries to the editions of Volume I. Liebermann's symphonic treatment of these texts, unparalleled before or since, was immediately deemed a work of overwhelming magnitude. His transcriptions of the manuscripts are of astounding accuracy. This and other features of the edition give it permanent value. Frederic Levi Attenborough's edition of 1922, which regrettably omits to print the *Mosaic Prologue*, "makes of course no attempt to compete with Liebermann's edition" (v) and is by the author's own description intended for the use of Anglophone students intimidated by Liebermann's *Gesetze*.

Bibliography

Abrams, Lesley. 1991. "A Single-Sheet Facsimile of a Diploma of King Ine for Glastonbury." In Lesley Abrams and James P. Carley, eds., *The Archaeology and History of Glastonbury Abbey. Essays in Honour of the Ninetieth Birthday of C. A. Ralegh Radford*. Woodbridge: Boydell, 97–134.

Ackerman, Gretchen P. 1982. "J. M. Kemble and Sir Frederic Madden: 'Conceit and Too Much Germanism?'" In Carl Berkhout and Milton McC. Gatch, eds., *Anglo-Saxon Scholarship: The First Three Centuries*. Boston: G. K. Hall, 167–182.

Adams, Henry, *et al.* 1876. *Essays in Anglo-Saxon Law*. Boston: Little, Brown & Co.

Alexander, Louis M. 1995. "The Legal Status of the Native Britons in Late Seventh-Century Wessex as Reflected by the Law Code of Ine." *Haskins Society Journal* 7: 31–38.

Andersson, Theodore M. 1974. "The Caedmon Fiction in the *Heliand* Preface." *PMLA* 89: 278–284.

Arngart, O., ed. 1955. *The Proverbs of Alfred*. 2 vols. Lund: C. W. K. Gleerup.

Arnold, Thomas, ed. 1885 [repr. 2012]. *Symeonis Monachi Opera Omnia*, vol. II: *Historia Regum*. Cambridge: Cambridge University Press.

Attenborough, Frederick Levi, ed. 1922 [repr. 1963]. *The Laws of the Earliest English Kings*. Cambridge: Cambridge University Press.

Bakhuizen van den Brink, Jan Nicolaas, ed. 1954. *Ratramnus: De corpore et sanguine Domini*. Amsterdam: North-Holland Publishing Company.

Banham, Debby and Rosamond Faith. 2014. *Anglo-Saxon Farms and Farming*. Oxford: Oxford University Press.

Barney, Stephen A., *et al.*, transl. 2006. *The Etymologies of Isidore of Seville*. Cambridge: Cambridge University Press.

Bartlett, Robert. 1986. *Trial by Fire and Water: The Medieval Judicial Ordeal*. Oxford: Clarendon.

Bassett, Steven. 1992. "Church and Diocese in the West Midlands: The Transition from British to Anglo-Saxon Control." In John Blair and Richard Sharpe, eds., *Pastoral Care Before the Parish*. Leicester: Leicester University Press, 13–40.

Bately, Janet, ed. 1986. *The Anglo-Saxon Chronicle, A Collaborative Edition*, vol. III: *MS A*. Woodbridge: D. S. Brewer.

    2009. "Did Alfred Actually Translate Anything? The Integrity of the Alfredian Canon Revisited." *Medium Ævum* 78: 189–215.

Baxter, Stephen, *et al*., eds. 2009. *Early Medieval Studies in Memory of Patrick Wormald*. Aldershot: Ashgate.

Behagel, Otto, ed. 1882 [rev. 1984]. *Heliand und Genesis*. Altdeutsche Textbibliothek 4. 9th ed. rev. Burkhard Taeger. Tübingen: Max Niemeyer.

Berkhofer, Robert H. 2016. "Forgery and Pope Alexender III's Decretal on *Scripta authentica*." In *Texts and Contexts in Legal History: Essays in Honor of Charles Donahue*. Berkeley, CA: Robbins Collection, 95–111.

Berkhout, Carl and Milton McC. Gatch, eds. 1982. *Anglo-Saxon Scholarship: The First Three Centuries*. Boston: G. K. Hall.

Bethurum, Dorothy. 1932. "Stylistic Features of the Old English Laws." *Modern Language Review* 27: 263–279.

    ed. 1957. *The Homilies of Wulfstan*. Oxford: Clarendon.

Bettenson, Henry, transl. 1984. *St. Augustine: Concerning the City of God against the Pagans*. London: Penguin.

Biddle, Martin and D. J. Keene. 1976. "Winchester in the Eleventh and Twelfth Centuries." In Martin Biddle, ed., *Winchester in the Early Middle Ages*. Oxford: Clarendon.

Bicknell, E. J. 1955. *A Theological Introduction to the Thirty-Nine Articles of the Church of England*. 3rd edn. rev. H. J. Carpenter. London: Longmans, Green & Co.

Bieler, Ludwig, ed. and transl. 1975. *The Irish Penitentials*. Scriptores Latini Hiberniae V. Dublin: Institute for Advanced Studies.

Binchy, D. A. 1972. "Celtic Suretyship, A Fossilized Indo-European Institution?" *Irish Jurist* 7, 360–372.

Bischoff, Bernhard and Michael Lapidge. 1994. *Biblical Commentaries from the Canterbury School of Theodore and Hadrian*. Cambridge Studies in Anglo-Saxon England 10. Cambridge: Cambridge University Press.

Blackburn, Mark. 2003. "Alfred's Coinage Reforms in Context." In Timothy Reuter, ed., *Alfred the Great: Papers from the Eleventh-Centenary Conferences*. Aldershot: Ashgate.

Blackstone, William. 1765 (vol. I); 1769 (vol. IV) [repr. 1979]. *Commentaries on the Laws of England*. 4 vols. Chicago: University of Chicago Press.

Blair, John. 2005. *The Church in Anglo-Saxon Society*. Oxford: Oxford University Press.

    and Richard Sharpe. 1992. *Pastoral Care Before the Parish*. Leicester: Leicester University Press.

Blunt, Christopher and Michael Dolley. 2012. "The Anglo-Saxon and Later Coins." Rev. Martin Allen and Mark Blackburn. In Martin Biddle, ed. *The Winchester Mint and Coins and Related Finds from the Excavations of 1961–71.* Oxford: Clarendon: 611–634.

Bonner, Gerald. 1973. "Bede and Medieval Civilization." *Anglo-Saxon England* II: 71–90.

Boretius, Alfred, ed. 1883. *Capitularia regum Francorum I.* Hanover: Hahnsche Buchhandlung

  and Victor Krause, eds. 1887. *Capitularia Regum Francorum II.* Hanover: Hahnsche Buchhandlung.

Bosworth, Joseph and T. Northcote Toller. 1898. *An Anglo-Saxon Dictionary.* Oxford: Oxford University Press.

Bothe, Lukas, Stefan Esders, and Han Nijdam, eds., *Wergild, Compensation and Penance: The Monetary Logic of Early Medieval Conflict Resolution.* Leiden: Brill.

Bowker, Alfred. 1902. *The King Alfred Millenary. A Record of the Proceedings of the National Commemoration.* London: MacMillan.

Brasington, Bruce. 2016. *Order in the Court: Medieval Procedural Treatises in Translation.* Leiden: Brill.

Breen, Q. 1944–1945. "The Twelfth-Century Revival of the Roman Law." *Oregon Law Review* 24: 244–287 [repr. in Nelson Peter Ross, ed., *Christianity and Humanism: Studies in the History of Ideas* (Grand Rapids: Eerdmans, 1968), 131–182].

Brommer, Peter, ed. 1984. *Capitula episcoporum,* I. (Monumenta Germaniae Historica.) Hanover: Hahnsche Buchhandlung.

Brook, Stella. 1965. *The Language of the Book of Common Prayer.* London: Andre Deutsch.

Brooks, Nicholas. 1984. *The Early History of the Church at Canterbury: Christ Church from 597 to 1066.* Leicester: Leicester University Press.

  2003. "English Identity from Bede to the Millennium." *Haskins Society Journal* 14: 33–51.

  2009. "The Fonthill Letter, Ealdorman Ordlaf and Anglo-Saxon Law in Practice." In Baxter *et al.,* eds., *Early Medieval Studies in Memory of Patrick Wormald.* Aldershot: Ashgate, 301–318.

  and S. E. Kelly, eds. 2013. *Charters of Christ Church Canterbury.* 2 vols. Oxford: Oxford University Press [for the British Academy].

  2015. "The Laws of King Æthelberht of Kent: Preservation, Content, and Composition." In Bruce R. O'Brien and Barbara Bombi, eds. *Textus Roffensis: Law, Language, and Libraries in Early Medieval England.* Turnhout: Brepols, 105–136.

Brunner, Heinrich. 1890. "Über absichtslose Missethat im altdeutschen Strafrechte." *Sitzungsberichte der Berliner Akademie,* 817–842 [repr. in Heinrich Brunner, *Forschungen zur Geschichte des Deutschen und Französischen Rechtes.* Stuttgart: J. G. Cotta, 487–523].

1887–1892. *Deutsche Rechtsgeschichte.* 2 vols. Leipzig: Duncker & Humblot.

Buma, Wybren Jan and Wilhelm Ebel, eds. 1963. *Das Rüstringer Recht.* Göttingen: Musterschmidt.

Cameron, Angus. 1974. "Middle English in Old English Manuscripts." In Beryl Rowland, ed., *Chaucer and Middle English Studies in Honour of Rossell Hope Robbins.* Kent, OH: Kent State University Press.

and Ashley Crandell Amos, Antonette diPaolo Healey, *et al.,* eds. 2018. *Dictionary of Old English: A to I.* [Online resource.] Toronto: Dictionary of Old English Project.

Campbell, Alistair. 1959. *Old English Grammar.* Oxford: Clarendon.

1967. Æthelwulf: De Abbatibus. Oxford: Clarendon.

Campbell, James. 2000. *The Anglo-Saxon State.* London: Hambledon.

2001. "What is Not Known about the Reign of Edward the Elder." In N. J. Higham and D. H. Hill, eds., *Edward the Elder: 899–924.* London: Routledge, 12–24.

2003 [repr. 2016]. "Placing King Alfred." In Timothy Reuter, ed. *Alfred the Great: Papers from the Eleventh-Centenary Conferences.* London: Routledge, 3–26.

Carella, B. 2005. "The Source of the Prologue to the Laws of Alfred." *Peritia* 19, 91–118.

2011. "Evidence for Hiberno-Latin Thought in the Prologue to the Laws of Alfred." *Studies in Philology* 108, 1–26.

Carnicelli, Thomas, ed. 1969. *King Alfred's Version of St. Augustine's "Soliloquies."* Cambridge, MA: Harvard University Press.

Carroll, Christopher. 2001. "The Last Great Carolingian Church Council: The Tribur Synod of 895." *Annuarium historiae conciliorum* 33: 9–25.

Chadwick, H. Munro. 1905. *Studies on Anglo-Saxon Institutions.* Cambridge: Cambridge University Press.

Chadwick, Nora K., Kathleen Hughes, Christopher Brooke, and Kenneth Jackson. 1958. *Studies in the Early British Church.* Cambridge: Cambridge University Press.

Chapman, Mark. 2012. *Anglican Theology.* London: Continuum.

Charles-Edwards, Thomas. 1976. "The Distinction between Land and Moveable Wealth in Anglo-Saxon England." In P. H. Sawyer, ed., *Medieval Settlement: Continuity and Change* London: Edward Arnold, 180–190.

1997. "Anglo-Saxon Kinship Revisited." In *The Anglo-Saxons from the Migration Period to the Eighth Century. An Ethnographic Perspective.* Woodbridge: Boydell, 171–204.

2013. *Wales and the Britons 350–1064.* Oxford: Oxford University Press.

Clayton, Mary, ed. and transl. 2013. *Two Ælfric Texts: The Twelve Abuses and The Vices and Virtues.* Woodbridge: D. S. Brewer.

Clemoes, Peter, ed. 1997. *Ælfric's Catholic Homilies. The First Series*. EETS No. S.S. 17. Oxford: Oxford University Press.

Colbourn, H. Trevor. 1965 [repr. 1974]. *The Lamp of Experience: Whig History and the Intellectual Origins of the American Revolution*. New York: W. W. Norton.

Colgrave, Bertram and R. A. B. Mynors, eds. and transl. 1969. *Bede's Ecclesiastical History of the English People*. Oxford: Clarendon.

Collingwood, Robin George and John Nowell Linton Myres. 1937. *Roman Britain and the English Settlements*. Oxford: Clarendon.

Contreni, John J. 1995. "The Pursuit of Knowledge in Carolingian Europe." In Richard E. Sullivan, ed. *"The Gentle Voices of Teachers": Aspects of Learning in the Carolingian Age*. Columbus: Ohio State University Press, 106–141.

Coogan, Michael, ed. 2001. *The New Oxford Annotated Bible*. Oxford: Oxford University Press.

Cook, Albert Stanburrough, ed. 1900 [repr. 1964]. *The Christ of Cynewulf*. Hamden: Archon.

1924. "Aldhelm's Legal Studies." *Journal of English and Germanic Philology* 23, 105–113.

Corrêa, Alicia, ed. 1992. *The Durham Collectar*. London: Boydell.

Crawford, Sally. 1999. *Childhood in Anglo-Saxon England*. Stroud: Sutton Publishing, Ltd.

Crick, Julia. 2015. "Historical Literacy in the Archive: Post-Conquest Imitative Copies of Pre-Conquest Charters and Some French Comparanda." In Martin Brett and David A. Woodman, eds., *The Long Twelfth-Century View of the Anglo-Saxon Past*. Aldershot: Ashgate, 159–190.

Cross, F. L. and E. A. Livingstone. 1983. *The Oxford Dictionary of the Christian Church*. Oxford: Oxford University Press.

Cubitt, Catherine. 1995. *Anglo-Saxon Church Councils, c.650–c.850*. Leicester: Leicester University Press.

2006. "Bishops, Priests and Penance in Late Saxon England." *Early Medieval Europe* 14: 41–63.

Cummings, Brian, ed. 2011. *The Book of Common Prayer: The Texts of 1549, 1559, and 1662*. Oxford: Oxford University Press.

Dale, Alfred William Winterslow. 1882. *The Synod of Elvira and Christian Life in the Fourth Century*. London: MacMillan & Co.

Dammery, Richard J. E. 1990. *The Law Code of King Alfred the Great*. Unpublished PhD dissertation, 2 vols., Cambridge University (16684).

Day, David. 1999. "Hands Across the Hall: The Legalities of Beowulf's Fight with Grendel." *JEGP* 98: 313–324.

Davis, R. H. C. 1971. "Alfred the Great: Propaganda and Truth." *History* 56: 169–182 [repr. in R. H. C. Davis, *From Alfred the Great to Stephen*. London: Hambledon, 1991, 33–46].

De Jong, Mayke. 1997. "What Was *Public* about Public Penance? *Paenitentia Publica* and Justice in the Carolingian World." In *La giustizia nell'alto medioevo (secolo ix–xi)*. Settimane di studio del Centro Italiano di studi sull'alto Medioevo XLIV. Spoleto: Centro italiano di studi sull'alto Medioevo, 863–904.

Delage, Marie-José, ed. and transl. 1971. *Césaire d'Arles: Sermons au Peuple*, vol. I. Paris: Éditions du Cerf.

Dennis, Andrew, Peter Foote, and Richard Perkins, trans. 2000. *Laws of Early Iceland: Grágás*. Manitoba: University of Manitoba Press.

Dickens, A. G. 1959. *Thomas Cromwell and the English Reformation*. New York: Harper & Row.

Discenza, Nicole Guenther. 2005. *The King's English: Strategies of Translation in the Old English "Boethius."* Albany: SUNY Press.

Dobbie, Elliot Van Kirk, ed. 1942. *The Anglo-Saxon Minor Poems*. ASPR 6. New York: Columbia University Press.

Dombart, B. and A. Kalb, eds. 1955. *Sancti Aurelii Augustini De civitate Dei libri xi-xxii*. Corpus Christianorum Series Latina XLVIII. Turnhout: Brepols.

Douglas, David C. 1964. *William the Conqueror: The Norman Impact upon England*. Berkeley: University of California Press.

Downer, L. J., ed. 1972. *Leges Henrici Primi*. Oxford: Clarendon.

Drew, Katherine Fisher. 1991. *The Laws of the Salian Franks*. Philadelphia: University of Pennsylvania Press.

Du Cange, Domino [Charles du Fresne], *et al.*, eds. 1883–1887. *Glossarium mediæ et infimæ latinitatis*. Niort: L. Favre.

Dümmler, Ernst, ed. 1895. *Epistolae Karolini aevi 2*. MGH Epistolae IV. Berlin: Weidmann.

ed. 1899. *Epistolae Karolini aevi 3*. MGH Epistolae V. Berlin: Weidmann.

Dumville, David. 1992. *Wessex and England from Alfred to Edgar*. Woodbridge: Boydell.

Dunkel, Wilbur. 1965. *William Lambarde, Elizabethan Jurist: 1536–1601*. New Brunswick: Rutgers University Press.

Dyer, Christopher. *Lords and Peasants in a Changing Society: The Estates of the Bishopric of Worcester, 680–1540*. Cambridge: Cambridge University Press, 1980.

Ebel, Friedrich and Georg Thielmann. 2003. *Rechtsgeschichte. Von der Römischen Antike bis zur Neuzeit*. Heidelberg: C. F. Müller.

Eckhardt, Karl August, ed. 1934a. *Die Gesetze des Karolingerreiches 714–911. I: Salische und Ribuarische Franken*. Weimar: Hermann Böhlhaus Nachfolger.

ed. 1934b. *Die Gesetze des Karolingerreiches 714–911. II: Alemannen und Bayern*. Weimar: Hermann Böhlhaus Nachfolger.

ed. 1934c. *Die Gesetze des Karolingerreiches 714–911. III: Sachsen, Thüringer, Chamaven und Friesen*. Weimar: Hermann Böhlhaus Nachfolger.

ed. 1954. *Die Gesetze des Merowingerreiches 481–714*. II: *Pactus Legis Alamannorum: Recensio Chlothariana*. Göttingen: Musterschmidt Verlag.

ed. 1955. *Die Gesetze des Merowingerreiches 481–714*. I: *Pactus Legis Salicae: Recensio Merovingicae*. Göttingen: Musterschmidt Verlag.

Edwards, Heather. *The Charters of the Early West Saxon Kingdom*. Oxford: B. A. R. (British Series 198), 1988.

Fanning, William H. W. 1912. "Tonsure." *Catholic Encyclopedia*, vol. XIV. New York: Robert Appleton: 779

Fichtenau, Heinrich. 1957. *The Carolingian Empire*. Transl. Peter Munz. Oxford: Blackwell [repr. Harper & Row, 1964].

Finsterwalder, Paul Willem, ed. 1929. *Die Canones Theodori Cantuarensis und ihre Überlieferungsformen*. Weimar: Hermann Böhlau.

Firey, Abigail. 2009. *A Contrite Heart: Persecution and Redemption in the Carolingian Empire*. Leiden: Brill.

Fischer, Andreas. 1986. *Engagement, Wedding, and Marriage in Old English*. Heidelberg: Carl Winter Verlag.

Flechner, Roy. 2009. "An Insular Tradition of Ecclesiastical Law: Fifth to Eighth Century." In James Graham-Campbell and Michael Ryan, eds. *Anglo-Saxon/Irish Relations Before the Vikings*, Proceedings of the British Academy 157. Oxford: Oxford University Press, 23–46.

Flower, Robin and Hugh Smith, eds. 1941 [repr. 1973]. *The Parker Chronicle and the Laws*. EETS o.s. 208. Oxford: Oxford University Press.

Förster, Max. 1894. "Über die Quellen von Ælfrics exegetischen Homiliae Catholicae." *Anglia* 16 (n.f. 4): 1–61.

Fournier, Paul. 1909. "Le *liber ex lege Moysi* et les tendances bibliques du droit canonique irlandais." *Revue Celtique* 30: 221–234.

Fraipoint, I. and D. De Bruyne, eds. 1958. *Sancti Aurelii Augustini quaestionum in heptateuchum libri vii*. CCSL XXXIII. Turnhout: Brepols.

Frakes, Robert M., ed. and transl. 2011. *Compiling the* Collatio Legum Mosaicarum et Romanarum *in Late Antiquity*. Oxford: Oxford University Press.

Franklin, Michael. 1992. "The Cathedral as Parish Church: The Case of Southern England." In David Abulafia, Michael Franklin, and Miri Rubin, eds. *Church and City 1000–1500: Essays in Honour of Christopher Brooke*. Cambridge: Cambridge University Press, 173–198.

Frantzen, Allen. 1983. *The Literature of Penance in Anglo-Saxon England*. New Brunswick: Rutgers University Press.

1986. *King Alfred*. Boston: Twayne.

Franzen, Christine. 1991. *The Tremulous Hand of Worcester: A Study of Old English in the Thirteenth Century*. Oxford: Oxford University Press.

Freeman, Ann, ed. 1998. *Opus Caroli regis contra synodum (Libri Carolini)*. With Paul Meyvaert. Hanover: Hahnsche Buchhandlung.

Freeman, E. A. 1872. "King Ine (Part I)." *Proceedings of the Somerset Archaeological and Natural History Society* 18: 1–59.

1874. "King Ine (Part II)." *Proceedings of the Somerset Archaeological and Natural History Society* 20: 1–57.

Fruscione, Daniela. 2003. *Das Asyl bei den germanischen Stämmen im frühen Mittelalter.* Cologne: Böhlau.

2014. "Beginnings and Legitimation of Punishment in Early Anglo-Saxon Legislation from the Seventh to the Ninth Century." In Nicole Marafioti and Jay Paul Gates, eds., *Capital and Corporal Punishment in Anglo-Saxon England.* Rochester, NY: Boydell and Brewer: 34–47.

Fry, Timothy, ed. and transl. 1981. *The Rule of St. Benedict.* Collegeville: Liturgical Press.

Fulk, R. D. 1992. *A History of Old English Meter.* Philadelphia: University of Pennsylvania Press.

, Robert E. Bjork, and John D. Niles, eds. 2008. *Klaeber's Beowulf.* Toronto: University of Toronto Press.

and Stefan Jurasinski, eds. 2012. *The Old English Canons of Theodore.* Early English Text Society SS. 25. Oxford: Oxford University Press.

Gaddis, Michael. 2005. *There Is No Crime for Those Who Have Christ: Religious Violence in the Christian Roman Empire.* Berkeley: University of California Press.

Gates, Jay Paul and Nicole Marafioti, eds. 2014. *Capital and Corporal Punishment in Anglo-Saxon England.* Rochester, NY: Boydell, 2014.

Gautier, Alban. 2006. "Manger et boire à la mode étrangère: adoption, adaptation et rejet des pratiques festives continentales dans la Grande-Bretagne du VIIe siècle." *Médiévales* 51: 37–52.

Geary, Patrick. 2008. "Judicial Violence and Torture in the Carolingian Empire." In Ruth Mazo Karras, Joel Kaye, and E. Ann Matter, eds., *Law and the Illicit in Medieval Europe.* Philadelphia: University of Pennsylvania Press.

Gibbon, Edward. 1781. *The History of the Decline and Fall of the Roman Empire,* vol. III. London: W. Strahan.

Girsch, Elizabeth Stevens. 1994. "Metaphorical Usage, Sexual Exploitation, and Divergence in the Old English Terminology for Male and Female Slaves." In Allen J. Frantzen and Douglas Moffat, eds. *The Work of Work: Servitude, Slavery and Labor in Medieval England.* Glasgow: Cruithne Press, 30–54.

Gittings, Robert, ed. 2002. *John Keats. Selected Letters.* Oxford: Oxford University Press.

Gittos, Helen. 2013 [repr. 2015]. *Liturgy, Architecture, and Sacred Places in Anglo-Saxon England.* Oxford: Oxford University Press.

Godden, Malcolm, ed. 1979. *Ælfric's Catholic Homilies: The Second Series.* EETS ss. 5. Oxford: Oxford University Press.

2000. *Ælfric's Catholic Homilies: Introduction, Commentary and Glossary.* Oxford: Oxford University Press.

2007. "Did King Alfred Write Anything?" *Medium Ævum* 76: 1–23.

2009. "Ælfric and the Alfredian Precedents." In Hugh Magennis and Mary Swan, eds., *A Companion to Ælfric*. Brill's Companions to the Christian Tradition XVIII. Leiden: Brill.

Godman, Peter, ed. and transl. 1982. *Alcuin: The Bishops, Saints, and Kings of York*. Oxford: Oxford University Press.

Goffart, Walter. 1997. "The First Venture into 'Medieval Geography': Lambarde's Map of the Saxon Heptarchy (1568)." In Jane Roberts and Janet L. Nelson, eds., *Alfred the Wise: Studies in Honour of Janet Bately on the Occasion of her Sixty-fifth Birthday*. Cambridge: D. S. Brewer, 53–60.

Grant, Raymond J. S. 1974. "Laurence Nowell's transcript of BM Cotton Otho B. xi." *Anglo-Saxon England* III: 111–124.

1996. *Lawrence Nowell, William Lambarde, and the Laws of the Anglo-Saxons*. Amsterdam: Rodopi.

Green, D. H. 1994. *Medieval Listening and Reading: The Primary Reception of German Literature 800–1300*. Cambridge: Cambridge University Press.

Green, Eugene A. 1989. "Ælfric the Catechist." In Thomas L. Amos, Eugene A. Green, and Beverly Mayne Kienzle, eds., *De Ore Domini: Preacher and Word in the Middle Ages*. Kalamazoo: Medieval Institute Publications, 61–74.

Green, Richard Firth. 1999 [repr. 2002]. *A Crisis of Truth. Literature and Law in Ricardian England*. Philadelphia: University of Pennsylvania Press.

Greenberg, Janelle. 2001. *The Radical Face of the Ancient Constitution: St. Edward's "Laws" in Early Modern Political Thought*. Cambridge: Cambridge University Press.

2010. "'St. Edward's Ghost': The Cult of St. Edward and His Laws in English History." In Stefan Jurasinski, Lisi Oliver, and Andrew Rabin, eds., *English Law Before Magna Carta: Felix Liebermann and Die Gesetze der Angelsachsen*. Leiden: Brill, 273–300.

Gretsch, Mechthild. 1994. "The Language of the 'Fonthill Letter.'" *Anglo-Saxon England* 23: 57–102.

Grierson, Philip. 1940. "Grimbald of St. Bertin's." *The English Historical Review* 55: 529–561.

Grimm, Jacob. 1899 [1828]. *Deutsche Rechtsalterthümer*, eds. Andreas Heusler and Rudolf Hübner. 4th ed. Leipzig: Dieterich'sche Verlagsbuchhandlung.

Haddan, Arthur West and William Stubbs (eds.) 1871. *Councils and Ecclesiastical Documents Relating to Great Britain and Ireland*, vol. III. Oxford: Clarendon.

Haines, Dorothy. 2010. *Sunday Observance and the Sunday Letter in Anglo-Saxon England*. Cambridge: D. S. Brewer.Halleck, Reuben Post. 1900. *History of English Literature*. New York: American Book Company.

Hamerow, Helena. 2012. *Rural Settlements and Society in Anglo-Saxon England*. Oxford: Oxford University Press.

Harmer, Florence E., ed. 1914. *Select English Historical Documents of the Ninth and Tenth Centuries.* Cambridge: Cambridge University Press.
1952. *Anglo-Saxon Writs.* Manchester: Manchester University Press.

Hayward, Paul. 2004. "Gregory the Great as 'Apostle of the English' in Post-Conquest Canterbury." *Journal of Ecclesiastical History* 55: 19–57.

Hazeltine, Harold Dexter. 1938. "Felix Liebermann 1851–1925." *Proceedings of the British Academy* 25: 319–360 [repr. Oxford University Press (with new pagination)].

Hecht, Hans, ed. 1900. *Bischofs Wærferth von Worcester Übersetzung der Dialoge Gregors den Grossen.* Bibliothek der angelsächsischen Prosa 5. Leipzig: Georg Wigand.

Hess, Hamilton. 2002. *The Early Development of Canon Law and the Council of Serdica.* Oxford: Oxford University Press.

Heydemann, Gerda. 2020. "The People of God and the Law: Biblical Models in Carolingian Legislation." *Speculum* 95: 89–131.

Hibbard, Laura A. 1921. *Athelston,* a Westminster Legend. *PMLA* 36: 223–244.

Hodgkin, Thomas. 1906. *The History of England. From the Earliest Times to the Norman Conquest.* London: Longmans, Green & Co.

Houard, David. 1776. *Traités sur les coutumes Anglo-Normandes.* Paris: Dubuc.

Hough, Carole A. 1993. "A Reappraisal of Æthelberht 84." *Nottingham Medieval Studies* 37: 1–6.
1997. "A Reconsideration of Ine, Ch. 23: With a Note on *Juliana,* Line 242a." *Neuphilologische Mitteilungen* 98: 43–51.
2000. "Penitential Literature and Secular Law in Anglo-Saxon England." *Anglo-Saxon Studies in Archaeology and History* 11: 133–141.
2001. "Palaeographical Evidence for the Compilation of *Textus Roffensis.*" *Scriptorium* 55: 57–79.
2007. "Women and the Law in Seventh-Century England." *Nottingham Medieval Studies* 51: 207–230.
2014a. "Legal and Documentary Writings." In Carole A. Hough, *"An Ald Reht": Essays in Anglo-Saxon Law.* Cambridge: Cambridge Scholars Press, 2–25.
2014b. "Alfred's *Domboc* and the Language of Rape: A Reconsideration of Alfred ch. 11." In Carole A. Hough, *"An Ald Reht": Essays in Anglo-Saxon Law.* Cambridge: Cambridge Scholars Press, 169–202.
2015. "The Earliest English Texts? The Language of the Kentish Laws Reconsidered." In Bruce R. O'Brien and Barbara Bombi, eds. 2015. *Textus Roffensis: Law, Language, and Libraries in Early Medieval England.* Turnhout: Brepols, 137–156.
2018. "Biblical Analogues for Early Anglo-Saxon Law." In Matthew W. McHaffie, Jenny Benham and Helle Vogt, eds. *Law and Language in the Middle Ages.* Leiden: Brill, 287–301.

Hurst, D. and M. Adrien, eds. 1969. *S. Hieronymi presbyteri commentariorum in Matheum libri iv.* CCSL LXXVII [1, 7]. Turnhout: Brepols.

Hyams, Paul. 1981. "Trial by Ordeal: The Key to Proof in the Early Common Law." In Morris S. Arnold, Thomas A. Green, Sally A. Scully, and Stephen D. White, eds. *On the Laws and Customs of England. Essays in Honor of Samuel E. Thorne*. Chapel Hill: University of North Carolina Press, 90–126.

Ibbetson, David. 1999. *A Historical Introduction to the Law of Obligations*. Oxford: Oxford University Press.

Idzerda, Stanley. 1954. "Iconoclasm during the French Revolution." *American Historical Review* 60: 13–26.

Ivarsen, Ingrid. In press. "King Ine (688–726) and the Writing English Law in Latin." *English Historical Review*.

Jenkins, Dafydd, ed. 1986. *Hywel Dda: The Law*. Llandysul, Dyfed: Gomer Press.

John, Eric. 1996. *Reassessing Anglo-Saxon England*. Manchester: Manchester University Press.

Jolly, Karen Louise. 2013. "Dismembering and Reconstructing MS Durham, Cathedral Library, A.IV.19." In Jonathan Wilcox, ed., *Scraped, Stroked, and Bound: Materially Engaged Readings of Medieval Manuscripts*. Turnhout: Brepols, 177–200.

Jones, Allen E. 2009. *Social Mobility in Late Antique Gaul*. Cambridge: Cambridge University Press.

Jurasinski, Stefan. 2002. "*Reddatur Parentibus:* The Vengeance of the Family in Cnut's Homicide Legislation." *Law and History Review* 20: 157–180.

2006. "Andrew Horn, Alfredian Apocrypha, and the Anglo-Saxon Names of the *Mirror of Justices*." *The Journal of English and Germanic Philology* 105: 540–563.

2010a. "Sanctuary, House-Peace, and the Traditionalism of Alfred's Laws." *Journal of Legal History* 31: 129–148.

2010b. "Violence, Penance and Secular Law in Alfred's Mosaic Prologue." *Haskins Society Journal* 22: 25–42.

2012. "Slavery, Learning and the Law of Marriage in Alfred's Mosaic Prologue." In László Sándor Chardonnens and Bryan Carella, eds. *Secular Learning in Anglo-Saxon England: Exploring the Vernacular*, Amsterdam: Rodopi, 45–64.

2014a. "Noxal Surrender, the Deodand, and the Laws of King Alfred." *Studies in Philology* 111, 195–224.

2014b. "'Sick-Maintenance' and Earlier English Law." In Jay Paul Gates and Nicole Marafioti, eds., *Capital and Corporal Punishment in Anglo-Saxon England*. Rochester, NY: Boydell, 2014, 74–91.

2015a. *The Old English Penitentials and Anglo-Saxon Law*. Cambridge: Cambridge University Press, 2015.

2015b. "Scribal Malpractice and the Study of Anglo-Saxon Law in the Twelfth Century." In Bruce R. O'Brien and Barbara Bombi, eds., *Textus Roffensis: Law, Language, and Libraries in Early Medieval England*. Turnhout: Brepols, 83–101.

2019. "Royal Law in Wessex and Kent at the Close of the Seventh Century." In Stefan Jurasinski and Andrew Rabin, eds., *Languages of the Law in Early Medieval England: Essays in Memory of Lisi Oliver*. Leuven: Peeters, 25–44.

, Lisi Oliver, and Andrew Rabin, eds., 2010. *English Law Before Magna Carta: Felix Liebermann and Die Gesetze der Angelsachsen*. Leiden: Brill.

and Andrew Rabin, eds. 2019. *Languages of the Law in Early Medieval England: Essays in Memory of Lisi Oliver*. Leuven: Peeters.

Karn, Nicholas. 2015. "*Textus Roffensis* and Its Uses." In Bruce R. O'Brien and Barbara Bombi, eds., *Textus Roffensis: Law, Language, and Libraries in Early Medieval England*. Turnhout: Brepols, 49–68.

Kelly, S. E., ed. 2015. *Charters of Chertsey Abbey*. Anglo-Saxon Charters 19. Oxford: Oxford University Press.

Ker, Neil Ripley. 1957. *A Catalogue of Manuscripts Containing Anglo-Saxon*. Oxford: Clarendon.

Keynes, Simon 1992. "The Fonthill Letter." In Michael Korhammer, ed., *Words, Texts, and Manuscripts: Studies in Anglo-Saxon Culture Presented to Helmut Gneuss on the Occasion of his Sixty-fifth Birthday*. Cambridge: D. S. Brewer, 53–97.

1993. *The Councils of Clofesho*. Eleventh Brixworth Lecture; Vaughan Papers in Adult Education no. 38. Leicester: University of Leicester/Friends of All Saints' Church, Brixworth.

1999. "The Cult of King Alfred the Great." *Anglo-Saxon England* 28: 225–356.

and Michael Lapidge, eds. and trans. 1983. *Alfred the Great. Asser's Life of King Alfred and Other Contemporary Sources*. London: Penguin.

Kirby, D. P. 1991. *The Earliest English Kings*. London: Unwin Hyman.

Kleist, Aaron. 2002. "The Division of the Ten Commandments in Anglo-Saxon England." *Neuphilologische Mitteilungen* 103: 227–240.

Klingshirn, William E. 1994. *Caesarius of Arles. The Making of Christian Community in Late Antique Gaul*. Cambridge: Cambridge University Press.

Krogmann, Willy. 1936. "Zwei ae. Wortdeutungen." *Anglia* 60: 33–38.

Krusch, Bruno, ed. 1885. *Fortunati presbyteri italici opera pedestria*. MGH AA 4,2. Berlin: Weidmannsche Buchhandlung.

and Wilhelm Levison, eds. 1937–1951. *Gregorii episcopi Turonensis libri historiarum x*. MGH SS rer. Merov. 1, 1. Hanover: Hahnsche Buchhandlung.

Krutzler, Gerald. 2011. *Kult und Tabu: Wahrnehmungen der Germania bei Bonifatius*. Berlin: LIT Verlag.

L'Huillier, Peter. 1997. "The Making of Written Law in the Church." *Studia Canonica* 31: 117–146.

Laistner, M. L. W., ed. 1939 [repr. 1970]. *Bedae venerabilis exposition actuum apostolorum et retractatio*. Cambridge, MA: The Medieval Academy of America.

Lambarde, William. 1568. Αρχαιονομια, *sive de priscis anglorum legibus libri, sermone Anglico, vetustate antiquissimo* [...]. London: John Day.

Lambert, Tom. 2017. *Law and Order in Anglo-Saxon England*. Oxford: Oxford University Press.

Lapidge, Michael. 1981. "Some Latin Poems as Evidence for the Reign of Athelstan." *Anglo-Saxon England* 9: 61–98.

1996. "Latin Learning in Ninth-Century England." In *Anglo-Latin Literature, 600–899*. London: Hambledon, 1996, 409–454. 2006. *The Anglo-Saxon Library*. Oxford: Oxford University Press.

Laughlin, J. Laurence. 1876. "The Anglo-Saxon Legal Procedure." In *Essays in Anglo-Saxon Law*. Boston: Little, Brown, and Co.

Lea, Henry Charles. 1892. *Superstition and Force*. 4th ed. Philadelphia: Lea Brothers & Co.

Leinbaugh, Theodore. 1982. "Ælfric's *Sermo de Sacrificio in Die Pascae*: Anglican Polemic in the Sixteenth and Seventeenth Centuries." In Carl Berkhout and Milton McC Gatch, eds., *Anglo-Saxon Scholarship: The First Three Centuries*. Boston: G. K. Hall, 51–68.

Levison, Wilhelm, ed. 1905. *Vitae Sancti Bonifatii*. Hanover: Hahnsche Buchhandlung.

Levy, Ernst. 1942. "Reflections on the First 'Reception' of Roman Law in the Germanic States." *American Historical Review*: 48.20-29.

Lewis, Suzanne. 1995. "Henry III and the Gothic Rebuilding of Westminster Abbey: The Problematics of Context." *Traditio* 50: 129–172.

Liebermann, Felix. 1896. "Kesselfang bei den Westsachsen im siebenten Jahrhundert." *Sitzungsberichte der königlich preussischen Akademie der Wissenschaften zu Berlin*, 829–838.

ed. 1903–1916. *Die Gesetze der Angelsachsen*. 3 vols. Halle: Niemeyer.

1910. "Die Eideshufen bei den Angelsachsen." In *Historische Aufsätze Karl Zeumer zum sechsigsten Geburtstag als Festgabe dargebracht von Freunden und Schülern*. Weimar: Hermann Böhlaus Nachfolger, 1–8.

1912. "King Alfred and Mosaic Law." *Transactions of the Jewish Historical Society* 6: 21–31.

1913. *The National Assembly in the Anglo-Saxon Period*. Halle a.S. [repr. New York: Burt Franklin].

Lindsay, W. M., ed. 1911 [repr. 2008]. *Isidori Hispalensis episcopi etymologiarum sive originum libri xx*. 2 vols. Oxford: Oxford University Press.

Lowe, Kathryn. 1993. "'As Fre as Thowt'?: Some Medieval Copies and Translations of Old English Wills." *English Manuscript Studies, 1100–1700*: 4, 1–23.

Loyn, Henry, ed. 1971. *A Wulfstan Manuscript Containing Institutes, Laws and Homilies*. Early English Manuscripts in Facsimile 17. Copenhagen: Rosenkilde & Bagger.

Lucas, Peter J. 2000. "Scribal Imitation of Earlier Handwriting: 'Bastard Saxon' and its Impact." In Marie-Clotilde Hubert, Emmanuel Poulle and Marc H. Smith, eds. *Le statut du scripteur au moyen age*. Paris: École des Chartes, 151–160.

Lynch, Joseph. 1998. *Christianizing Kingship: Ritual Sponsorship in Anglo-Saxon England*. Ithaca, NY: Cornell University Press.

MacCulloch, Diarmaid. 2005. *The Reformation: A History*. London: Penguin.

Machan, Tim William. 2003. *English in the Middle Ages*. Oxford: Oxford University Press.

Maine, Henry Sumner. 1884 [repr. 1963]. *Ancient Law*. Boston: Beacon Press.

Maitland, Frederic William. 1897 [repr. 1996]. *Domesday Book and Beyond: Three Essays in the Early History of England*. Cambridge: Cambridge University Press.

　　1898. *Roman Canon Law in the Church of England*. London: Methuen & Co.

Marafioti, Nicole. 2014. *The King's Body. Burial and Succession in Late Anglo-Saxon England*. Toronto: University of Toronto Press.

　　2015. "Seeking Alfred's Body: Royal Tomb as Political Object in the Reign of Edward the Elder." *Early Medieval Europe* 23: 202–228.

Marsden, Richard. 1994. "Old Latin Interventions in the Old English *Heptateuch*." *Anglo-Saxon England* 23: 229–264.

　　1995. *The Text of the Old Testament in Anglo-Saxon England*. Cambridge: Cambridge University Press.

　　2000. "Translation by Committee? The 'Anonymous' Text of the Old English Hexateuch." In Rebecca Barnhouse and Benjamin C. Withers, eds., *The Old English Hexateuch: Aspects and Approaches*. Kalamazoo: Medieval Institute Publications, 41–90.

　　2004. "Wrestling with the Bible: Textual Problems for the Scholar and Student." In Paul Cavill, ed., *The Christian Tradition in Anglo-Saxon England: Approaches to Current Scholarship and Teaching*. Cambridge: D. S. Brewer, 70–90.

　　ed. 2008. *The Old English Heptateuch and Ælfric's Libellus de Veteri Testamento et Novo*. EETS no. 330. Oxford: Oxford University Press.

McAuley, Finbarr. 2006. "Canon Law and the End of the Ordeal." *Oxford Journal of Legal Studies* 26: 473–513.

McCracken, George E. and Allen Cabaniss. 1957. *Early Medieval Theology*. Philadelphia: The Westminster Press.

McKitterick, Rosamond. 2004. *History and Memory in the Carolingian World*. Cambridge: Cambridge University Press.

　　2008. *Charlemagne: The Formation of a European Identity*. Cambridge: Cambridge University Press.

McNeill, John T. and Helena M. Gamer, transl. 1938. *Medieval Handbooks of Penance*. New York: Columbia University Press.

McReavy, L. L. 1935. "The Sunday Repose from Labour: An Historico-Theological Examination of the Notion of Servile Work." *Ephemerides Theologicae Lovanienses* 12, 291–323.

Meaney, Audrey. 1986. "St. Neot's, Æthelweard, and the *Anglo-Saxon Chronicle: A Survey*." in Paul E. Szarmach, ed. *Studies in Earlier Old English Prose*. Albany: SUNY Press, 193–244.

2006. "Old English Legal and Penitential Penalties for Heathenism." In Simon Keynes and Alfred P. Smyth, eds., *Anglo-Saxons: Studies Presented to Cyril Roy Hart*. Dublin: Four Courts, 127–158.

Meeder, Sven, ed. 2009. "The *Liber ex lege Moysi*: Notes and Text." *Journal of Medieval Latin* 19: 173–218.

Mershman, Francis. 1909. "Ember-days." *The Catholic Encyclopedia*, vol. v. New York: Robert Appleton: 399.

Migne, J-P., ed. 1864. *Sancti Aurelii Augustini, Hipponensis episcopi, opera omnia*. Patrologia Latina 35. Paris: Garnier.

Milfull, Inge B. 1996. *The Hymns of the Anglo-Saxon Church*. Cambridge Studies in Anglo-Saxon England 17. Cambridge: Cambridge University Press.

Miller, William Ian. 1991. "Of Outlaws, Christians, Horsemeat, and Writing: Uniform Laws and Saga Iceland." *Michigan Law Review* 89: 2081–2095.

Molyneaux, George. 2014. "Did the English Really Think They Were God's Elect in the Anglo-Saxon Period?" *Journal of Ecclesiastical History* 65: 721–737.

Momma, Haruko. 2013. *From Philology to English Studies: Language and Culture in the Nineteenth Century*. Cambridge: Cambridge University Press.

Mordek, Hubert, Klaus Zechiel-Eckes, and Michael Glatthaar, eds. and transl. 2013. *Die Admonitio generalis Karls des Großen*. MGH Fontes 16. Wiesbaden: Harrassowitz Verlag.

Morrish, Jennifer. 1986. "King Alfred's Letter as a Source on Learning in England in the Ninth Century." In Paul Szarmach, ed., *Studies in Earlier Old English Prose*. Albany: SUNY Press.

Munro, Dana Carleton, ed. and transl. 1900. *Translations and Reprints from the Original Sources of European History: Selections from the Laws of Charles the Great*. Philadelphia: Department of History of the University of Philadelphia.

Murdoch, Brian. 1983. *Old High German Literature*. Boston: G. K. Hall.

1998. "Authority and Authenticity: Comments on the Prologues to the Old Frisian Laws." In Rolf Bremmer Jr., Thomas S. B. Johnston, and Oebele Vries, eds., *Approaches to Old Frisian Philology*. Amsterdamer Beiträge zur älteren Germanistik 49. Amsterdam: Rodopi, 215–243.

Murphy, Michael. 1982. "Antiquary to Academic: The Progress of Anglo-Saxon Scholarship." In Carl Berkhout and Milton McC. Gatch, eds. 1982. *Anglo-Saxon Scholarship: The First Three Centuries.* Boston: G. K. Hall, 1–18.

Murray, Alexander C. 1983. *Germanic Kinship Structure: Studies in Law and Society in Antiquity and the Early Middle Ages.* Toronto: Pontifical Institute of Mediaeval Studies.

Mutzenbecher, Almut, ed. 1967. *Sancti Aurelii Augustini de sermone Domini in monte libros duos.* CCSL XXXV [VII, 2]. Turnhout: Brepols.

Mynors, R. A. B., R. M. Thomson, and M. Winterbottom, eds. 1998. William of Malmesbury: *Gesta Regum Anglorum*, vol. 1. Oxford: Clarendon.

Naismith, Rory. 2012. *Money and Power in Anglo-Saxon England.* Cambridge: Cambridge University Press.

Napier, Arthur, ed. 1883. *Wulfstan. Sammlung der ihm zugeschriebenen Homilien nebst Untersuchungen über ihre Echtheit.* Berlin: Weidmannsche Buchhandlung.

Niles, John D. 2009. "Trial by Ordeal in Anglo-Saxon England: What's the Problem with Barley?" In Baxter *et al.*, eds., *Early Medieval Studies in Memory of Patrick Wormald.* Aldershot: Ashgate, 36–82.

   2015. "The Myth of the Feud in Anglo-Saxon England." *JEGP* 114: 163–200.

Noble, Thomas F. X. 2009. *Images, Iconoclasm, and the Carolingians.* Philadelphia: University of Pennsylvania Press.

Noth, Martin. 1962. *Exodus: A Commentary.* Philadelphia: Westminster Press.

Nottarp, Hermann. 1956. *Gottesurteilstudien.* Munich: Kösel.

O'Brien, Bruce R. 1996. "From *Morðor* to *Murdrum:* The Preconquest Origin and Norman Revival of the Murder Fine." *Speculum* 71: 321–357.

   1999. *God's Peace and King's Peace: The Laws of Edward the Confessor.* Philadelphia: University of Pennsylvania Press.

   2011. *Reversing Babel: Translation among the English during an Age of Conquests, c. 800 to c. 1200.* Newark: University of Delaware Press.

   , and Barbara Bombi, eds. 2015. *Textus Roffensis: Law, Language, and Libraries in Early Medieval England.* Turnhout: Brepols.

O'Neill, Patrick P., ed., *King Alfred's Old English Prose Translation of the First Fifty Psalms* (Cambridge, MA: Medieval Academy of America, 2001).

Oakley, Thomas Pollock. 1923. *English Penitential Discipline and Anglo-Saxon Law in their Joint Influence.* New York: Longmans, Green & Co.

Oliver, Lisi. 1998. "Towards Freeing a Slave in Germanic Law.". In Jay Jasanoff, H. Craig Melchert, and Lisi Oliver, eds. *Mír Curad: Studies in Honor of Calvert Watkins.* Innsbruck: Innsbrucker Beiträge zur Sprachwissenschaft, 549–560.

   2002. *The Beginnings of English Law.* Toronto: University of Toronto Press, 2002.

2008. "Sick-Maintenance in Anglo-Saxon Law." *JEGP* 107: 303–326.

2010. "Æthelberht's and Alfred's Two Skulls." *Heroic Age* 14. *[Unpaginated: digital publication.]*

2011. *The Body Legal in Barbarian Law.* Toronto: University of Toronto Press.

2014. "Genital Mutilation in Germanic Law." In Jay Paul Gates and Nicole Marafioti, eds. *Capital and Corporal Punishment in Anglo-Saxon England.* Rochester, NY: Boydell, 2014, 48–73.

2015. "Who Wrote Alfred's Laws?" In Bruce R. O'Brien and and Barbara Bombi, eds. *Textus Roffensis: Law, Language, and Libraries in Early Medieval England.* Turnhout: Brepols, 231–254.

In press. "*Wergild* and *wite* in Anglo-Saxon Law." In Lukas Bothe, Stefan Esders, and Han Nijdam, eds., *Wergild, Compensation and Penance: The Monetary Logic of Early Medieval Conflict Resolution.* Leiden: Brill.

Orme, Nicholas. 2007. *Cornwall and the Cross: Christianity 500–1560.* Oving: Phillimore.

Parker, Matthew [and John Joscelyn?]. 1566 [?]. *A Testimonie of Antiquitie, Shewing the Auncient Fayth in the Church of England Touching the Sacrament of the Body and Bloude of the Lord* [...]. London: John Day.

Parker, William Riley. 1967. "Where Do English Departments Come From?" *College English* 28: 339–351.

Parkes, Malcolm. 1976. "The Palaeography of the Parker Manuscript of the *Chronicle,* Laws and Sedulius, and Historiography at Winchester in the Late Ninth and Tenth centuries." *Anglo-Saxon England* 5: 149–172.

Pelteret, David A. E. 1995. *Slavery in Early Mediaeval England.* Woodbridge: Boydell.

Plumer, Eric, ed. 2003. *Augustine's Commentary on Galatians.* Oxford: Oxford University Press.

Plummer, Charles and John Earle, eds. 1892 (vol. I); 1899 (vol. II) [repr. 1952]. *Two of the Saxon Chronicles Parallel, with Supplementary Extracts from the Others.* 2 vols. Oxford: Oxford University Press.

1902 [repr. 1970]. *The Life and Times of Alfred the Great. Being the Ford Lectures for 1901.* Oxford: Clarendon.

Pollock, Frederick and Fredric William Maitland. 1898 [repr. with supplements 1968]. *The History of English Law.* 2 vols. Cambridge: Cambridge University Press.

Pokorny, Julius. 1959. *Indogermanisches Etymologisches Wörterbuch.* Bern/Stuttgart: Francke Verlag.

Poole, A.L. 1955. *Domesday Book to Magna Carta, 1087–1216.* Oxford: Oxford University Press.

Powell, Kathryn. 2010. "The 'Scipmen' Scribe and Cambridge, Corpus Christi College 383." *Heroic Age* 14. [Unpaginated: digital publication.]

Powell, Timothy. 1994. "The 'Three Orders' of Society in Anglo-Saxon England." *Anglo-Saxon England* 23: 103–132.

Power, Edmund. 1924. "Corrections from the Hebrew in the Theodulfian MSS. of the Vulgate." *Biblica* 5: 233–258.

Pratt, David. 2007. *The Political Thought of King Alfred the Great*. Cambridge: Cambridge University Press.

Preston, Todd. 2012. *King Alfred's Book of Laws. A Study of the* Domboc *and its Influence on English Identity, with a Complete Translation*. Jefferson, NC: McFarland.

Pryce, Huw. 1992. "Pastoral Care in Early Medieval Wales." In John Blair and Richard Sharpe, eds. *Pastoral Care Before the Parish*. Leicester: Leicester University Press, 41–62.

Pulsiano, Phillip. 1998. "Benjamin Thorpe (1782–1870)." In Helen Damico, ed., *Medieval Scholarship: Biographical Studies on the Formation of a Discipline*, vol. II: Literature and Philology. New York: Garland, 75–92.

Quentin, Henri, ed. 1929. *Biblia Sacra iuxta vulgatam versionem: Libros Exodi et Levitici ex interpretatione Sancti Hieronymi*. Rome: Typis Polyglottis Vaticanis.

Rabin, Andrew. 2010. "Felix Liebermann and *Die Gesetze der Angelsachsen*." In Stefan Jurasinski, Lisi Oliver, and Andrew Rabin, eds., *English Law Before Magna Carta: Felix Liebermann and Die Gesetze der Angelsachsen*. Leiden: Brill 1–8.

, ed. and trans. 2015. *The Political Writings of Archbishop Wulfstan*. Manchester: Manchester University Press.

2019. "The Reception of Kentish Law in the Eleventh Century: Archbishop Wulfstan as Legal Historian." In Stefan Jurasinski and Andrew Rabin, eds. *Languages of the Law in Early Medieval England: Essays in Memory of Lisi Oliver*. Leuven: Peeters 225–240.

Rahlfs, Alfred, ed. 1952. *Septuaginta. Id est vetus testamentum Graece iuxta* LXX *interpretes*. 4th ed. Stuttgart: Privileg. Württ. Bibelanstalt.

Raith, Josef, ed. 1933 [repr. 1964]. *Die altenglische Version des Halitgar'schen Bussbuches*. Hamburg: Henri Grand.

Rau, Rheinhold, ed. 1987. *Quellen zur Karolingischen Reichsgeschichte. Erster Teil*. Berlin: Rütten and Loening.

Reichert, Eckhard. 1990. *Die Canones der Synode von Elvira. Einleitung und Kommentar*. Unpublished doctoral dissertation, University of Hamburg.

Reynolds, Philip Lyndon. 2001. *Marriage in the Western Church*. Leiden: Brill.

Richards, Mary. 1988. *Texts and Their Traditions in the Medieval Library of Rochester Cathedral Priory*. Transactions of the American Philosophical Society 78. Philadelphia: American Philosophical Society.

2010. "I–II Cnut: Wulfstan's *Summa*?" In Stefan Jurasinski, Lisi Oliver, and Andrew Rabin, eds., *English Law Before Magna Carta: Felix Liebermann and Die Gesetze der Angelsachsen*. Leiden: Brill, 137–156.

ed. 2014a. *The Old English Poem "Seasons for Fasting": A Critical Edition*. Morgantown: West Virginia University Press.

2014b. "The Laws of Alfred and Ine." In Nicole Guenther Discenza and Paul E. Szarmach, eds., *A Companion to Alfred the Great*. Leiden: Brill, 282–309.

2015. "The *Textus Roffensis:* Keystone of the Medieval Library at Rochester." In Bruce R. O'Brien and Barbara Bombi, eds., *Textus Roffensis: Law, Language, and Libraries in Early Medieval England*. Turnhout: Brepols, 19–48.

Richardson, H. G. and G. O. Sayles. 1966. *Law and Legislation from Æthelberht to Magna Carta*. Edinburgh: Edinburgh University Press.

Rio, Alice, ed. 2011. *Law, Custom, and Justice in Late Antiquity and the Early Middle Ages: proceedings of the 2008 Byzantine Colloquim*. London: King's College London/Centre for Hellenic Studies.

Roach, Levi. 2012. "Penance, Submission and *Deditio:* Religious Influences on Dispute Settlement in Anglo-Saxon England (871–1066)." *Anglo-Saxon England* 41, 343–371.

2013. "Law Codes and Legal Norms in Later Anglo-Saxon England." *Historical Research* 86, 465–486.

Roberts, Jane, ed. 1979. *The Guthlac Poems of the Exeter Book*. Oxford: Clarendon.

and Janet L. Nelson, eds. 1997. *Alfred the Wise: Studies in Honour of Janet Bately on the Occasion of her Sixty-Fifth Birthday*. Cambridge: D. S. Brewer.

Robertson, Agnes Jane, ed. 1925. *The Laws of the Kings of England from Edmund to Henry I*. Cambridge: Cambridge University Press.

ed. 1956 [repr. 2009]. *Anglo-Saxon Charters*. Cambridge: Cambridge University Press.

Rodwell, Warwick. 1982. "From Mausoleum to Minster: The Early Development of Wells Cathedral." In Susan M. Pearce, ed. *The Early Church in Western Britain and Ireland*. Oxford: B.A.R. (British Series 102).

Rollason, David, ed. and transl. 2000. Simeon of Durham: *Libellus de Exordio atque Procursu Istius, hoc est Dunhelmensis, Ecclesie*. Oxford: Clarendon.

Rusche, Philip. 2002. "St. Augustine's Abbey and the Tradition of Penance in Early Tenth-Century England." *Anglia* 120: 159–183.

Sanders, Willy. 1972. "Die Buchstaben des Königs Chilperich." *Zeitschrift für deutsches Alterum und deutsche Literatur* 101: 54–84.

Sauer, Hans, ed. 1978. *Theodulf Capitula in England*. Munich: Wilhelm Fink.

Schmid, Rheinhold. 1858. *Die Gesetze der Angelsachsen*. Leipzig: Brockhaus.

Schmidt-Wiegand, Ruth. 1989. "Die Malbergischen Glossen, eine frühe Überlieferung germanischer Rechtssprache." In Heinrich Beck, ed. *Germanische Rest- und Trümmersprachen*. Berlin: Walter de Gruyter, 157–174.

Scholz, Bernhard W. 1966. "Eadmer's Life of Bregwine, Archbishop of Canterbury, 761–764." *Traditio* 22, 127–148.

Schreiber, Carolin, ed. 2002. *King Alfred's Old English Translation of Pope Gregory the Great's* Regula Pastoralis *and its Cultural Context.* Frankfurt: Peter Lang.

Schreyer-Mühlpfordt, Brigitta. 1956. "Sprachliche Einigungstendenzen in deutschen Schrifttum des Frühmittelalters." *Wissenschaftliche Annalen* 5: 295–303.

Schröer, Arnold, ed. 1885. *Die angelsächsischen Prosabearbeitungen der Benedictinerregel.* Bibliothek der angesächsischen Prosa 2. Kassel: Georg H. Wigand.

Schuster, Louis A., *et al.,* eds. 1973. *The Complete Works of St. Thomas More,* vol. VIII [The Confutation of Tyndale's Answer]. New Haven: Yale University Press.

Seebohm, Frederic. 1902. *Tribal Custom in Anglo-Saxon Law.* London: Longman, Green and Co.

Sisam, Kenneth. 1923–1925 [repr. 1953]. "The Authenticity of Certain Texts in Lambard's *Archaionomia* 1568." In Kenneth Sisam, *Studies in the History of Old English Literature.* Oxford: Clarendon.

Sheppard, Steve, ed. 2003. *The Selected Writings and Speeches of Sir Edward Coke,* vol. I. Indianapolis: Liberty Fund.

Short, Ian, ed. 2009. *Geffrei Gaimar: Estoire des Engleis / History of the English.* Oxford: Oxford University Press.

Simpson, John and Edmund Weiner, eds. 2017. *The Oxford English Dictionary.* Oxford: Clarendon. [Online resource.]

Skeat, Walter W., ed. and transl. 1890–1900. *Ælfric's Lives of the Saints.* 4 vols. EETS 76, 82, 94, 114 [repr. in 2 vols. 1966]. London: Oxford University Press.

Smith, A. H., ed. 1935 [repr. 1966]. *The Parker Chronicle (832–900).* New York: Appleton-Century-Crofts.

Smith, David Chan. 2014. *Sir Edward Coke and the Reformation of the Laws: Religion, Politics and Jurisprudence, 1578–1616.* Cambridge: Cambridge University Press.

Snook, Ben. 2015. *The Anglo-Saxon Chancery. The History, Language and Production of Anglo-Saxon Charters from Alfred to Edgar.* Woodbridge: Boydell.

Somerville, Robert and Bruce Brasington, ed. and trans. 1998. *Prefaces to Canon Law Books in Latin Christianity.* New Haven: Yale University Press.

Sonderegger, Stefan. 1964. "Die althochdeutsche Lex Salica-Übersetzung." In Richard Laufner, ed. *Festgabe für Wolfgang Jungandreas zum 70. Geburtstag am 9. Dezember 1964.* Trier: Trier Arbeitsgemeinschaft für Landesgeschichte und Volkskunde [...], 113–122.

Spindler, Robert, ed. 1934. *Das altenglische Bussbuch.* Leipzig: Bernhard Tauchnitz.

Stacey, Robin Chapman. 2007. *Dark Speech: The Performance of Law in Early Ireland.* Philadelphia: University of Pennsylvania Press.

Stancliffe, Clare. 1983. "Kings Who Opted Out." In Patrick Wormald, ed. *Ideal and Reality in Frankish and Anglo-Saxon Society*. Oxford: Blackwell, 154–176.

Stanley, Eric Gerald. 2000. *Imagining the Anglo-Saxon Past: The Search for Anglo-Saxon Paganism and Anglo-Saxon Trial By Jury*. Woodbridge: D. S. Brewer.

Stenton, F. M. 1947. *Anglo-Saxon England*. 2nd ed. Oxford: Clarendon.

Streitberg, Wilhelm, ed. 1965. *Die Gotische Bibel*. Heidelberg: Carl Winter.

Stevenson, William Henry, ed. 1959. *Asser's Life of King Alfred*. Oxford: Clarendon.

Sweet, Henry, ed. 1871. *King Alfred's West-Saxon Version of Gregory's Pastoral Care*. EETS o.s. 45. London: Oxford University Press.

Szarmach, Paul E., ed. 1985. *Studies in Earlier Old English Prose*. Albany: SUNY Press.

Tardif, Joseph. 1895. "Un abrégé juridique des Étymologies d'Isidore de Séville." In *Mélanges Julien Havet*. Paris: Ernest Leroux, 659–681.

Taylor, Alice. 2016. *The Shape of the State in Medieval Scotland, 1124–1290*. Oxford: Oxford University Press.

Thijs, Christine. 2005. "Levels of Learning in Anglo-Saxon Worcester: The Evidence Reassessed." *Leeds Studies in English* 36: 105–131

Thomas, Daniel. 2014. "Incarceration as Judicial Punishment in Anglo-Saxon England." In Jay Paul Gates and Nicole Marafioti, eds. 2014. *Capital and Corporal Punishment in Anglo-Saxon England*. Rochester, NY: Boydell, 2014, 92–112.

Thompson, A. Hamilton and U. Lindelöf, eds. 1927. *Rituale Ecclesiae Dunelmensis. The Durham Collectar*. London: Bernard Quaritch.

Thorpe, Benjamin, ed. 1840. *Ancient Laws and Institutes of England*. London: Eyre and Spottiswoode.

   ed. and transl. 1844. *The Homilies of the Anglo-Saxon Church*, vol. 1. London: Ælfric Society.

Thorpe, Lewis, transl. 1974. *Gregory of Tours. The History of the Franks*. London: Penguin.

Thür, Gerhard. 2006. "Moicheia." In Hubert Cancik and Helmuth Schneider, eds. *Brill's New Pauly*. Leiden: Brill. [Unpaginated: digital publication.]

Tiersma, Peter. 1999. *Legal Language*. Chicago: University of Chicago Press.

Torkar, Roland. 1981. *Eine altenglische Übersetzung von Alcuins* De virtute et vitiis, *kap.* 20. Munich: Wilhelm Fink.

Toswell, M. J. 2014. *The Anglo-Saxon Psalter*. Turnhout: Brepols.

Treadgold, Warren. 1997. *A History of the Byzantine State and Society*. Stanford: Stanford University Press.

Treharne, Elaine M. 1999. "Romanticizing the Past in the Middle English *Athelston*." *The Review of English Studies* 50 (197): 1–21.

Treschow, Michael. 1994. "The Prologue to Alfred's Law Code: Instruction in the Spirit of Mercy." *Florilegium* 13, 79–110.

Turk, Milton Haight, ed. 1893. *The Legal Code of Alfred the Great.* Halle: Max Niemeyer.

Ubl, Karl. 2014. *Die Karolinger: Herrscher und Reich.* Munich: C. H. Beck.

Vinogradoff, Paul. 1911. *The Growth of the Manor.* London: George Allen and Co.

Vogel, Cyrille. 1978. *Les "Libri Paenitentiales."* Turnhout: Brepols.

Von Schwind, Ernst, ed. 1926. *Lex Baiwariorum.* MGH LL. Nat. Germ. 5.2. Hanover: Hahnsche Buchhandlung.

Wallace-Hadrill, J. M. 1950. "The Franks and the English in the Ninth Century: Some Common Historical Interests." *History* 35: 202–218.

    1962 [repr. 1982]. *The Long-Haired Kings.* London: Methuen [repr. University of Toronto Press].

    1988. *Bede's "Ecclesiastical History of the English People": A Historical Commentary.* Oxford: Clarendon.

Waitz, G., *et al.* (eds). 1911. *Einhardi vita Karoli Magni.* SS rer. Germ. 25. Hanover: Hahnsche Buchhandlung.

Washington, H. A., ed. 1854. *The Writings of Thomas Jefferson*, vol. VI, Washington, D. C.: Taylor and Maury.

Watkins, Calvert. 2000. *American Heritage Dictionary of Indo-European Roots.* 2nd ed. Boston: Houghton-Mifflin.

Watson, Alan, ed. and transl. 1985. *The Digest of Justinian.* [Latin text ed. Th. Mommsen.] 4 vols. Philadelphia: University Of Pennsylvania Press.

Wenisch, Franz. 1979. *Spezifisch anglisches Wortgut in den nordhumbrischen Interlinearglossierungen des Lukasevangeliums.* Heidelberg: C. Winter.

Whitelock, Dorothy. 1955. *English Historical Documents* I: *c.500–1042.* New York: Oxford University Press.

    1969. "William of Malmesbury on the Works of King Alfred." In D. A. Pearsall and R. A. Waldron, eds. *Literature and Civilization: Studies in Memory of G. N. Garmonsway.* London: Athlone [Bloomsbury], 78–93.

    1976. "Bede and His Teachers and Friends." In Gerald Bonner, ed., *Famulus Christi. Essays in Commemoration of the Thirteenth Centenary of the Birth of the Venerable Bede.* London: SPCK, 19–39.

    , M. Brett, and C. N. L. Brooke, eds. 1981. *Councils and Synods, with Other Documents Relating to the English Church:* I, A.D. *871–1204.* Oxford: Clarendon.

Whittaker, William Joseph, ed. 1895. *The Mirror of Justices.* Publications of the Selden Society VII. London: Bernard Quaritch.

Wieacker, F. 1944. *"Ratio Scripta.* Das römische Recht und die abendländische Rechtswissenschaft." In F. Wieacker, *Vom Römischen Recht.* Leipzig: Koehler & Amelang, 195–284.

Wilda, Wilhelm. 1842. *Geschichte des Deutschen Strafrechts.* Halle: C. A. Schwetschke und Sohn.

Wilkins, David, ed. 1721. *Leges Anglo-Saxonicæ Ecclesiasticæ & Civiles.* London: Bowyer and Gosling.

Williams, Rowan. 2001. *Arius: Heresy and Tradition.* Grand Rapids: Eerdmans.

Winkler, John Frederick. 1992. "Roman Law in Anglo-Saxon England." *Journal of Legal History* 13, 101–107.

Winterbottom, Michael, ed. 2007. William of Malmesbury: *Gesta Pontificum Anglorum,* vol. 1: Text and Translation. Oxford: Clarendon.

Withers, Benjamin C. 1999. "A 'Secret and Feverish Genesis': The Prefaces of the Old English Hexateuch." *The Art Bulletin* 81: 53–71.

Wittig, Joseph. 1983. "King Alfred's *Boethius* and its Latin Sources: A Reconsideration." *Anglo-Saxon England* 11: 157–198.

Wollstonecraft, Mary. 1790. *A Vindication of the Rights of Men.* London: J. Johnson.

Wordsworth, John and Henry White, eds. 1920 [repr. 1950]. *Nouum Testamentum latine secundum editionem Sancti Hieronymi.* Oxford: Clarendon.

Wormald, Patrick. 1977. "*Lex Scripta* and *Verbum Regis:* Legislation and Germanic Kingship from Euric to Cnut." P. H. Sawyer and I. N. Wood, eds. *Early Medieval Kingship.* Leeds, 1977, 105–138 [repr. 1999b: 1–43].

1986. "Charters, Law and the Settlement of Disputes in Anglo-Saxon England." In Wendy Davies and Paul Fouracre, eds., *The Settlement of Disputes in Early Medieval Europe.* Cambridge: Cambridge University Press, 149–168.

1991. "In Search of King Offa's 'Law-Code.'" First published in *People and Places in Northern Europe, 500-1600: Studies Presented to P. H. Sawyer.* Woodbridge: Boydell Press, 1991, 25–45 [repr. 1999b, 201–224].

1994. '*Engla Lond:* The Making of an Allegiance.' *Journal of Historical Sociology* 7: 1–24.

1997a. "The Lambarde Problem: Eighty Years On." First published in Jane Roberts and Janet Nelson, eds., *Alfred the Wise: Studies in Honour of Janet Bately on the Occasion of her Sixty-Fifth Birthday.* Cambridge: D. S. Brewer, 237–275 [repr. 1999b: 139–176].

1997b. "Giving God and King their Due: Conflict and its Regulation in the Early English State." First published in *Settimane di studio del centro italiano di studi sull'alto medioevo* 44: 549–90 [repr. 1999b: 333–337].

1998. "Frederic William Maitland and the Earliest English Law." *Law and History Review* 16: 1–25.

1999a. *The Making of English Law: King Alfred to the Twelfth Century.* Oxford: Blackwell.

1999b. *Law and Legal Culture in the Early Medieval West.* London and Rio Grande: The Hambledon Press.

2004a. "Living with King Alfred." *Haskins Society Journal* 15: 1–39.

2004b. "Ine." *Oxford Dictionary of National Biography.* Oxford: Oxford University Press. [Unpaginated: digital publication.]

2005. *The First Code of English Law.* Canterbury: Barristers of Becket Chambers.

2009. "Anglo-Saxon and Scots Law." *The Scottish Historical Review* 88, 192–206.

2014. *Papers Preparatory to The Making of English Law: King Alfred to the Twelfth Century Volume* II, *From God's Law to Common Law*. Stephen Baxter and John Hudson, eds. London: University of London/Early English Laws Project.

Wright, Neil, ed. 1988. *The "Historia Regum Brittanie" of Geoffrey of Monmouth.* II. *The First Variant Version: A Critical Edition.* Rochester, NY: D. S. Brewer.

Wright, Thomas and Richard Paul Wülcker, eds. 1884. *Anglo-Saxon and Old English Vocabularies*, vol. I. 2nd ed. London: Trübner.

Wright, William Aldis, ed. 1887. *The Metrical Chronicle of Robert of Gloucester*, vol. I. London: Eyre and Spottiswoode.

Yeager, Stephen M. 2014. *From Lawmen to Plowmen: Anglo-Saxon Legal Tradition and the School of Langland.* Toronto: University of Toronto Press.

Yorke, Barbara. 1990 [repr. 2002]. *Kings and Kingdoms of Early Anglo-Saxon England.* London: Routledge.

1995. *Wessex in the Early Middle Ages.* Leicester: Leicester University Press.

1999. "Ine." In Michael Lapidge *et al.*, eds. *The Blackwell Encyclopaedia of Anglo-Saxon England.* Oxford: Blackwell, 251–252.

2004. "Cædwalla." *Oxford Dictionary of National Biography.* Oxford: Oxford University Press. [Unpaginated: digital publication.]

Zeumer, Karl, ed. 1902. *Leges Visigothorum.* MGH LL Nat. Germ. I. Hanover: Hahnsche Buchhandlung.

Topical Index to the Laws of Alfred and Ine

Entries reflect the prevailing concerns of the *domboc* and Old English terms peculiar to the text that have attracted substantial commentary. Where entries are of great length or cover matters of particular historical interest, they are organized into subsections. Exceptions are made for "accusations," "*bot*," "*ceap*," "oaths," and "theft," given their frequency of occurrence within the text and the unlikelihood that subcategorizations of these occurrences would disclose any meaningful patterns. In spite of its reliance on biblical materials, the language of the *Mosaic Prologue* (*MP*) has shown a capacity in prior scholarship to shed light on aspects of ninth-century Wessex. *MP* is therefore included in the index, though its uncertain relationship to provisions of the *domboc* issued by Alfred (and Ine) should be borne in mind.

Index Nominum et Rerum

For EU product safety concerns, contact us at Calle de José Abascal, 56–1°,
28003 Madrid, Spain or eugpsr@cambridge.org.

www.ingramcontent.com/pod-product-compliance
Ingram Content Group UK Ltd.
Pitfield, Milton Keynes, MK11 3LW, UK
UKHW010248140625
459647UK00013BA/1726